# PLAYFAIR
# CRICKET ANNUAL 2003

## 56th edition

### EDITED BY BILL FRINDALL

*All statistics by the Editor unless otherwise stated*

# PREFACE

With the dust hardly settled on the African World Cup we must prepare for another long season in which two of those hosts will play leading roles. With a bonus three-match international joust against Pakistan, this summer will focus on seven five-day Tests and 13 limited-overs internationals. Again there is upheaval on the domestic front with the Benson & Hedges Cup being replaced by a 20-over competition. Many will question the wisdom of encouraging professional cricketers to engage in an even more frenetic version of the instant game. And how many will brave the rush hours of city traffic to watch it. Get caught in a jam even briefly and you could miss an entire innings. In format the B & H was the best designed of the one-day frolics and it also provided a handy pipe-opener to the season.

The more limited-overs cricket I see, and I watched or scored most of the 52 World Cup games, the more bored I become by its stereotyped format. That tournament enhanced the view that if you remove the draw from the result line you will have very few memorable matches. Fielding restrictions encourage aggressive batting for the first 15 overs. Then comes the middle-distance graveyard shift while singles are pushed and nurdled until the final ten overs and happy hour. It has always seemed a gross imbalance to restrict the bowlers to a certain number of balls but allow a batsman to remain for the entire innings. One solution would be to allow a bowler an extra over for every wicket he takes. Had this option been available to Stephen Fleming when New Zealand had reduced Australia to 84 for 7 at Port Elizabeth, he would have been able to fire Sean Bond (10-2-23-6) for another six overs and perhaps end their neighbour's record run of success. All bowlers will applaud the idea but very few are administrators.

This season will see some new faces on the county stage. Scotland, generously funded by the ICC and ECC, compete in the 45-over league, while Loughborough, frequently the strongest of the UCCE sides, enter the first-class records. In October that university is due to open the new National Cricket Academy to its first intake. Victories in the Frizzell County Championship will be worth 14 points, an increase of two. One element of scoring confusion has been eliminated by awarding a one-run penalty for wides in all competitions.

When modern technology works it really is wonderful. Last year I was able instantly to relay copy and scan proofs from New Zealand. This time we have been able to update the book's many Test match and Limited-Overs career and general records to within a fortnight of its publication. Even Philip Weston's move from Worcestershire to Gloucestershire, revealed in this morning's press, has been seamlessly engineered in the County Register. Once again this magic has mainly been due to the skill and vigour of Chris and Caroline Leggett and their team at Letterpart. Ian Marshall, Headline's Non-fiction Deputy Publishing Director, deserves reward for extending *Playfair*'s press day by a fortnight and condemning Jo Roberts-Miller to a week of late nights as she checked this edition's final proofs.

As usual we are greatly indebted to the county clubs' administrators, scorers and statisticians, to Alan Fordham and Andrew Smith (ECB), to Neville Birch (MCCA) and to many overseas correspondents including Charlie Wat (Australia), Francis Payne (New Zealand), Andrew Samson (South Africa) and Rajesh Kumar (India and World Cup stats). Philip Bailey has again been a fount of data, while Ric Finlay and David Fitzgerald have constantly updated their invaluable Test and LOI programmes. Robin Abrahams (CricInfo), Ron Nuttall, David Mitchell and Debbie Frindall have been valuable contributors. Thank you everyone.

BILL FRINDALL
Urchfont
Wiltshire
27 March 2003

# THE EIGHTH WORLD CUP

Measured purely in cricketing terms the 2003 ICC World Cup was anything but a galloping success. Far too many one-sided games in a protracted 42-match preliminary stage were followed by a so-called Super Six round rendered meaningless by earlier points being carried forward, especially those awarded to Zimbabwe and Kenya for forfeited games. The most enthralling contests were the opening one in which West Indies gained a three-run victory over the hosts on the back of a superb century from Brian Lara, and Australia's nail-biting two-wicket win against England led by the epic batting of Bevan and Bichel. Many of the encounters were eminently forgettable.

The later stages desperately needed the presence of South Africa and either England or West Indies. Hussain's team never recovered from the Harare saga and Hooper's were victims of the lack of reserve days in the opening round. A lethargic South Africa, having lost narrowly to West Indies and New Zealand, were bizarrely eliminated by their inability to read a simple chart, the brainchild of two cunning English statisticians.

The seven-week tournament (the Olympics take 16 days) was designed as a vehicle for television but no one restricted to the terrestrial variety saw a ball in Britain. The excruciatingly long campaign took a heavy toll of its players, encouraging a host of high-profile retirements, while its captaincy turnover rivalled that of kickball managers. Bangladesh, England, Holland, Pakistan and South Africa will all next take the field under a new pyjama leader. Sri Lanka would have joined them if Sanath Jayasuriya had been allowed to fall on his sword.

The opening ceremony was brilliant, a fitting reward for some outstanding choreography and two years of planning and rehearsal. The grounds were excellently appointed, the majority of the pitches ideal for the instant game and the tournament extremely well organised. Nor was it lacking in drama. Unfortunately little of it emanated from the actual cricket. Shane Warne's ridiculous raid on his mum's pill cupboard; that endless three-way battle involving an England team (manoeuvred by a PCA representative), the ECB and the ICC; the exceptional courage of Henry Olonga and Andy Flower in making their declaration against the Mugabe regime; and the ambush marketing plight of the Indians. All contributed to a glut of cricket headlines on the front pages of the world's papers.

On the field the batting of Tendulkar, Lara, Gilchrist, Ponting and the unknown Canadian-born Aussie, John Davison, who savaged the West Indian attack for a record-breaking 67-ball century, plus the unique opening hat-trick salvo of Chaminda Vaas all etched their places in the memory. The Final merely confirmed what all but the most one-eyed non-Australian had predicted for months, namely that Ricky Ponting's team, even bereft of a key player or three, was in a different league from the rest. It was a privilege to watch their cohesion, skills and genuine elation at being part of such a supreme unit. Why, one of them even 'walked'.

# 2003 WORLD CUP RESULTS

The eighth World Cup (the first to be staged in Africa) was played over 43 days in February and March 2003. Its record tally of 54 matches (two unplayed) was divided among 12 venues in South Africa, two in Zimbabwe and one in Kenya. Because of the dew factor only ten of the games were floodlit day/night affairs (†), five apiece at Newlands and Kingsmead.

| Match | Pool | Feb | Venue | Match | Result | |
|---|---|---|---|---|---|---|
| **PRELIMINARY ROUND** | | | | | | |
| 1 | B | Sun 9 | †Cape Town | SA v WI | WI | 3 runs |
| 2 | A | Mon 10 | Harare | Z v N | Z | 86 runs (D/L) |
| 3 | B | Mon 10 | Bloemfontein | NZ v SL | SL | 47 runs |

| Match | Pool | Feb | | Venue | Match | Result | |
|---|---|---|---|---|---|---|---|
| 4 | A | Tue | 11 | Johannesburg | A v P | A | 82 runs |
| 5 | B | Tue | 11 | †Durban | B v C | C | 60 runs |
| 6 | B | Wed | 12 | Potchefstroom | SA v K | SA | 10 wickets |
| 7 | A | Wed | 12 | Paarl | I v H | I | 68 runs |
| 8 | A | Thu | 13 | Harare | Z v E | Z | Forfeited |
| 9 | B | Thu | 13 | Port Elizabeth | WI v NZ | NZ | 20 runs |
| 10 | B | Fri | 14 | Pietermaritzburg | SL v B | SL | 10 wickets |
| 11 | A | Sat | 15 | Pretoria | A v I | A | 9 wickets |
| 12 | B | Sat | 15 | †Cape Town | K v C | K | 4 wickets |
| 13 | A | Sun | 16 | East London | E v H | E | 6 wickets |
| 14 | A | Sun | 16 | Kimberley | P v N | P | 171 runs |
| 15 | B | Sun | 16 | Johannesburg | SA v NZ | NZ | 9 wickets (D/L) |
| 16 | B | Tue | 18 | Benoni | WI v B | – | No Result |
| 17 | A | Wed | 19 | Harare | Z v I | I | 83 runs |
| 18 | B | Wed | 19 | Paarl | SL v C | SL | 9 wickets |
| 19 | A | Wed | 19 | Port Elizabeth | E v N | E | 55 runs |
| 20 | A | Thu | 20 | Potchefstroom | A v H | A | 75 runs (D/L) |
| 21 | B | Fri | 21 | Nairobi | K v NZ | K | Forfeited |
| 22 | B | Sat | 22 | Bloemfontein | SA v B | SA | 10 wickets |
| 23 | A | Sat | 22 | †Cape Town | E v P | E | 112 runs |
| 24 | B | Sun | 23 | Pretoria | WI v C | WI | 7 wickets |
| 25 | A | Sun | 23 | Pietermaritzburg | I v N | I | 181 runs |
| 26 | B | Mon | 24 | Nairobi | K v SL | K | 53 runs |
| 27 | A | Mon | 24 | Bulawayo | A v Z | A | 7 wickets |
| 28 | A | Tue | 25 | Paarl | P v H | P | 97 runs |
| 29 | B | Wed | 26 | Kimberley | NZ v B | NZ | 7 wickets |
| 30 | A | Wed | 26 | †Durban | E v I | I | 82 runs |
| 31 | A | Thu | 27 | Potchefstroom | A v N | A | 256 runs |
| 32 | B | Thu | 27 | East London | SA v C | SA | 118 runs |
| 33 | A | Fri | 28 | Bulawayo | Z v H | Z | 99 runs |
| 34 | B | Fri | 28 | †Cape Town | WI v SL | SL | 6 runs |
| | | Mar | | | | | |
| 35 | B | Sat | 1 | Johannesburg | B v K | K | 32 runs |
| 36 | A | Sat | 1 | Pretoria | I v P | I | 6 wickets |
| 37 | A | Sun | 2 | Port Elizabeth | A v E | A | 2 wickets |
| 38 | B | Mon | 3 | Benoni | NZ v C | NZ | 5 wickets |
| 39 | A | Mon | 3 | Bloemfontein | H v N | H | 64 runs |
| 40 | B | Mon | 3 | †Durban | SA v SL | Tied | (D/L) |
| 41 | A | Tue | 4 | Bulawayo | Z v P | – | No result |
| 42 | B | Tue | 4 | Kimberley | WI v K | WI | 142 runs |
| **SUPER SIX** | | | | | | | |
| 43 | | Fri | Mar 7 | Pretoria | A v SL | A | 96 runs |
| 44 | | Fri | Mar 7 | †Cape Town | I v K | I | 6 wickets |
| 45 | | Sat | Mar 8 | Bloemfontein | NZ v Z | NZ | 6 wickets |
| 46 | | Mon | Mar 10 | Johannesburg | I v SL | I | 183 runs |
| 47 | | Tue | Mar 11 | Port Elizabeth | A v NZ | A | 96 runs |
| 48 | | Wed | Mar 12 | Bloemfontein | Z v K | K | 7 wickets |
| 49 | | Fri | Mar 14 | Pretoria | NZ v I | I | 7 wickets |
| 50 | | Sat | Mar 15 | East London | SL v Z | SL | 74 runs |
| 51 | | Sat | Mar 15 | †Durban | A v K | A | 5 wickets |
| **SEMI-FINALS** | | | | | | | |
| 52 | | Tue | Mar 18 | Port Elizabeth | A v SL | A | 48 runs (D/L) |
| 53 | | Thu | Mar 20 | †Durban | I v K | I | 91 runs |
| **FINAL** | | | | | | | |
| 54 | | Sun | Mar 23 | Johannesburg | A v I | A | 125 runs |

# THE 2003 WORLD CUP FINAL

## AUSTRALIA v INDIA

At The Wanderers, Johannesburg on 23 March.
**Result: AUSTRALIA won by 125 runs.**
Toss: India. Award: R.T.Ponting.

| AUSTRALIA | | Runs | Balls | 4/6 | Fall |
|---|---|---|---|---|---|
| † A.C.Gilchrist | c Sehwag b Harbhajan | 57 | 48 | 8/1 | 1-105 |
| M.L.Hayden | c Dravid b Harbhajan | 37 | 54 | 5 | 2-125 |
| * R.T.Ponting | not out | 140 | 121 | 4/8 | |
| D.R.Martyn | not out | 88 | 84 | 7/1 | |
| D.S.Lehmann | | | | | |
| M.G.Bevan | | | | | |
| A.Symonds | | | | | |
| G.B.Hogg | | | | | |
| A.J.Bichel | | | | | |
| B.Lee | | | | | |
| G.D.McGrath | | | | | |
| Extras | (B 2, LB 12, W 16; NB 7) | 37 | | | |
| **Total** | (50 overs; 2 wickets; 206 minutes) | **359** | | | |

| INDIA | | Runs | Balls | 4/6 | Fall |
|---|---|---|---|---|---|
| S.R.Tendulkar | c and b McGrath | 4 | 5 | 1 | 1- 4 |
| V.Sehwag | run out | 82 | 81 | 10/3 | 4-147 |
| * S.C.Ganguly | c Lehmann b Lee | 24 | 25 | 3/1 | 2- 58 |
| M.Kaif | c Gilchrist b McGrath | 0 | 3 | – | 3- 59 |
| † R.Dravid | b Bichel | 47 | 57 | 2 | 5-187 |
| Yuvraj Singh | c Lee b Hogg | 24 | 34 | 1 | 6-208 |
| D.Mongia | c Martyn b Symonds | 12 | 11 | 2 | 7-209 |
| Harbhajan Singh | c McGrath b Symonds | 7 | 8 | – | 8-223 |
| Z.Khan | c Lehmann b McGrath | 4 | 8 | – | 10-234 |
| J.Srinath | b Lee | 1 | 4 | – | 9-226 |
| A.Nehra | not out | 8 | 4 | 2 | |
| Extras | (B 4, LB 4, W 9, NB 4) | 21 | | | |
| **Total** | (39.2 overs; 180 minutes) | **234** | | | |

| INDIA | O | M | R | W | AUSTRALIA | O | M | R | W |
|---|---|---|---|---|---|---|---|---|---|
| Khan | 7 | 0 | 67 | 0 | McGrath | 8.2 | 0 | 52 | 3 |
| Srinath | 10 | 0 | 87 | 0 | Lee | 7 | 1 | 31 | 2 |
| Nehra | 10 | 0 | 57 | 0 | Hogg | 10 | 0 | 61 | 1 |
| Harbhajan Singh | 8 | 0 | 49 | 2 | Lehmann | 2 | 0 | 18 | 0 |
| Sehwag | 3 | 0 | 14 | 0 | Bichel | 10 | 0 | 57 | 1 |
| Tendulkar | 3 | 0 | 20 | 0 | Symonds | 2 | 0 | 7 | 2 |
| Mongia | 7 | 0 | 39 | 0 | | | | | |
| Yuvraj Singh | 2 | 0 | 12 | 0 | | | | | |

Scores after 15 overs: Australia 107-1; India 88-3.

Umpires: S.A.Bucknor and D.R.Shepherd

# WORLD CUP RECORDS 1975 to 2003

## RESULTS SUMMARY

| | Played | Won | Lost | Tied | No Result | Semi-Finalist | Runner-Up | Winner |
|---|---|---|---|---|---|---|---|---|
| Australia | 58 | 40 | 17 | 1 | – | – | 2 | 3 |
| West Indies | 48 | 31 | 16 | – | 1 | 1 | 1 | 2 |
| England | 50 | 31 | 18 | – | 1 | 2 | 3 | – |
| India | 55 | 31 | 23 | – | 1 | 2 | 1 | 1 |
| Pakistan | 53 | 29 | 22 | – | 2 | 3 | 1 | 1 |
| New Zealand | 52 | 28 | 23 | – | 1 | 4 | – | – |
| South Africa | 30 | 19 | 9 | 2 | – | 2 | – | – |
| Sri Lanka | 46 | 17 | 27 | 1 | 1 | 1 | – | 1 |
| Zimbabwe | 42 | 8 | 31 | – | 3 | – | – | – |
| Kenya | 20 | 5 | 14 | – | 1 | 1 | – | – |
| Bangladesh | 11 | 2 | 8 | – | 1 | – | – | – |
| UAE | 5 | 1 | 4 | – | – | – | – | – |
| Canada | 9 | 1 | 8 | – | – | – | – | – |
| Holland | 11 | 1 | 10 | – | – | – | – | – |
| East Africa | 3 | – | 3 | – | – | – | – | – |
| Scotland | 5 | – | 5 | – | – | – | – | – |
| Namibia | 6 | – | 6 | – | – | – | – | – |

## WORLD CUP FINALS

| | | |
|---|---|---|
| 1975 | WEST INDIES (291-8) beat Australia (274) by 17 runs | Lord's |
| 1979 | WEST INDIES (286-9) beat England (194) by 92 runs | Lord's |
| 1983 | INDIA (183) beat West Indies (140) by 43 runs | Lord's |
| 1987-88 | AUSTRALIA (253-5) beat England (246-8) by 7 runs | Calcutta |
| 1991-92 | PAKISTAN (249-6) beat England (227) by 22 runs | Melbourne |
| 1995-96 | SRI LANKA (245-3) beat Australia (241-7) by 7 wickets | Lahore |
| 1999 | AUSTRALIA (133-2) beat Pakistan (132) by 8 wickets | Lord's |
| 2002-03 | AUSTRALIA (359-2) beat India (234) by 125 runs | Johannesburg |

## TEAM RECORDS
## HIGHEST TOTAL

| 398-5 | Sri Lanka v Kenya | Kandy | 1995-96 |
|---|---|---|---|

## HIGHEST TOTAL – BATTING SECOND

| 313-7 | Sri Lanka v Zimbabwe | New Plymouth | 1991-92 |
|---|---|---|---|

## LOWEST TOTAL

| 36 | Canada v Sri Lanka | Paarl | 2002-03 |
|---|---|---|---|

## HIGHEST MATCH AGGREGATE

| 652-12 | Sri Lanka v Kenya | Kandy | 1995-96 |
|---|---|---|---|

## LARGEST MARGINS OF VICTORY

| 10 wkts | India beat East Africa | Leeds | 1975 |
|---|---|---|---|
| 10 wkts | West Indies beat Zimbabwe | Birmingham | 1983 |
| 10 wkts | West Indies beat Pakistan | Melbourne | 1991-92 |
| 10 wkts | South Africa beat Kenya | Potchefstroom | 2002-03 |
| 10 wkts | Sri Lanka beat Bangladesh | Pietermaritzburg | 2002-03 |
| 10 wkts | South Africa beat Bangladesh | Bloemfontein | 2002-03 |
| 256 runs | Australia beat Namibia | Potchefstroom | 2002-03 |
| 202 runs | England beat India | Lord's | 1975 |

## NARROWEST MARGINS OF VICTORY

| | | | |
|---|---|---|---|
| 1 wkt | West Indies beat Pakistan | Birmingham | 1975 |
| 1 wkt | Pakistan beat West Indies | Lahore | 1987-88 |
| 1 run | Australia beat India | Madras | 1987-88 |
| 1 run | Australia beat India | Brisbane | 1991-92 |

## INDIVIDUAL RECORDS – BATTING
### 900 RUNS IN A CAREER

| | | M | I | NO | HS | Runs | Avge | 100 | 50 |
|---|---|---|---|---|---|---|---|---|---|
| S.R.Tendulkar | I | 33 | 32 | 3 | 152 | 1732 | 59.72 | 4 | 12 |
| Javed Miandad | P | 33 | 30 | 5 | 103 | 1083 | 43.32 | 1 | 8 |
| P.A.de Silva | SL | 35 | 32 | 3 | 145 | 1064 | 36.68 | 2 | 6 |
| I.V.A.Richards | WI | 23 | 21 | 5 | 181 | 1013 | 63.31 | 3 | 5 |
| M.E.Waugh | A | 22 | 22 | 3 | 130 | 1004 | 52.84 | 4 | 4 |
| R.T.Ponting | A | 28 | 27 | 3 | 140* | 998 | 41.58 | 3 | 2 |
| S.R.Waugh | A | 33 | 30 | 10 | 120* | 978 | 48.90 | 1 | 6 |
| A.Ranatunga | SL | 30 | 29 | 8 | 88* | 969 | 46.14 | – | 7 |
| B.C.Lara | WI | 25 | 25 | 3 | 116 | 956 | 43.45 | 2 | 6 |
| Saeed Anwar | P | 21 | 21 | 4 | 116 | 915 | 53.82 | 3 | 3 |

## MOST RUNS IN A TOURNAMENT

| | M | I | NO | HS | Runs | Avge | 100 | 50 |
|---|---|---|---|---|---|---|---|---|
| S.R.Tendulkar (I) 2002-03 | 11 | 11 | – | 152 | 673 | 61.18 | 1 | 6 |

## HIGHEST INDIVIDUAL SCORE

| | | | | |
|---|---|---|---|---|
| 188* | G.Kirsten | South Africa v UAE | Rawalpindi | 1995-96 |

## HUNDRED BEFORE LUNCH

| | | | | |
|---|---|---|---|---|
| 101 | A.Turner | Australia v Sri Lanka | The Oval | 1975 |

## MOST HUNDREDS IN A CAREER

| | |
|---|---|
| 4 | S.R.Tendulkar (India) and M.E.Waugh (Australia) |

## HIGHEST PARTNERSHIP FOR EACH WICKET

| | | | | | |
|---|---|---|---|---|---|
| 1st | 194 | Saeed Anwar/Wajahatullah Wasti | P v NZ | Manchester | 1999 |
| 2nd | 318 | S.C.Ganguly/R.Dravid | I v SL | Taunton | 1999 |
| 3rd | 237* | R.Dravid/S.R.Tendulkar | I v K | Bristol | 1999 |
| 4th | 168 | L.K.Germon/C.Z.Harris | NZ v A | Madras | 1995-96 |
| 5th | 148 | R.G.Twose/C.L.Cairns | NZ v A | Cardiff | 1999 |
| 6th | 161 | M.O.Odumbe/A.V.Vadher | K v SL | Southampton | 1999 |
| 7th | 98 | R.R.Sarwan/R.D.Jacobs | WI v NZ | Port Elizabeth | 2002-03 |
| 8th | 117 | D.L.Houghton/I.P.Butchart | Z v NZ | Hyderabad | 1987-88 |
| 9th | 126* | Kapil Dev/S.M.H.Kirmani | I v Z | Tunbridge Wells | 1983 |
| 10th | 71 | A.M.E.Roberts/J.Garner | WI v I | Manchester | 1983 |

## INDIVIDUAL RECORDS – BOWLING
### 30 WICKETS IN A CAREER

| | | Overs | Runs | Wkts | Avge | Best | 4w | R/Over |
|---|---|---|---|---|---|---|---|---|
| Wasim Akram | P | 324.3 | 1311 | 55 | 23.83 | 5-28 | 3 | 4.04 |
| G.D.McGrath | A | 245.0 | 935 | 45 | 20.77 | 7-15 | 2 | 3.81 |
| J.Srinath | I | 283.2 | 1224 | 44 | 27.81 | 4-30 | 2 | 4.32 |
| A.A.Donald | SA | 218.5 | 913 | 38 | 24.02 | 4-17 | 2 | 4.17 |
| W.P.U.C.J.Vaas | SL | 184.0 | 754 | 36 | 20.94 | 6-25 | 2 | 4.09 |
| Imran Khan | P | 169.3 | 655 | 34 | 19.26 | 4-37 | 2 | 3.86 |
| C.Z.Harris | NZ | 194.2 | 861 | 32 | 26.90 | 4- 7 | 1 | 4.43 |

| | | Overs | Runs | Wkts | Avge | Best | 4w | R/Over |
|---|---|---|---|---|---|---|---|---|
| S.K.Warne | A | 162.5 | 624 | 32 | 19.50 | 4-29 | 4 | 3.83 |
| I.T.Botham | E | 222.0 | 762 | 30 | 25.40 | 4-31 | 1 | 3.43 |
| M.Muralitharan | SL | 187.5 | 693 | 30 | 23.10 | 4-28 | 1 | 3.68 |

## MOST WICKETS IN A TOURNAMENT

| | | Overs | Runs | Wkts | Avge | Best | 4w | R/Over |
|---|---|---|---|---|---|---|---|---|
| W.P.U.C.J.Vaas | SL | 88.0 | 331 | 23 | 14.39 | 6-25 | 2 | 3.76 |

## BEST ANALYSIS

| | | | | |
|---|---|---|---|---|
| 7-15 | G.D.McGrath | Australia v Namibia | Potchefstroom | 2002-03 |

## HAT-TRICKS

| | | | | |
|---|---|---|---|---|
| (All bowled) | C.Sharma | India v New Zealand | Nagpur | 1987-88 |
| | Saqlain Mushtaq | Pakistan v Zimbabwe | The Oval | 1999 |
| (1st balls of match) | W.P.U.C.J.Vaas | Sri Lanka v Bangladesh | Pietermaritzburg | 2002-03 |
| | B.Lee | Australia v Kenya | Durban | 2002-03 |

## MOST ECONOMICAL INNINGS BOWLING

| | | | | |
|---|---|---|---|---|
| 12-8-6-1 | B.S.Bedi | India v East Africa | Leeds | 1975 |

## MOST EXPENSIVE INNINGS BOWLING

| | | | | |
|---|---|---|---|---|
| 12-1-105-2 | M.C.Snedden | New Zealand v England | The Oval | 1983 |

## INDIVIDUAL RECORDS – WICKET-KEEPING
## 30 DISMISSALS IN A CAREER

| | | | | |
|---|---|---|---|---|
| 35 | (33ct, 2st) | A.C.Gilchrist | Australia | 20 matches |
| 30 | (23ct, 7st) | Moin Khan | Pakistan | 20 matches |

## MOST DISMISSALS IN AN INNINGS

| | | | | |
|---|---|---|---|---|
| 6 (6ct) | A.C.Gilchrist | Australia v Namibia | Potchefstroom | 2002-03 |

## INDIVIDUAL RECORDS – FIELDING
## 15 CATCHES IN A CAREER

| | | | |
|---|---|---|---|
| 18 | R.T.Ponting | Australia | 28 matches |
| 16 | C.L.Cairns | New Zealand | 28 matches |
| 15 | S.T.Jayasuriya | Sri Lanka | 27 matches |

## MOST CATCHES IN AN INNINGS

| | | | | |
|---|---|---|---|---|
| 4 | M.Kaif | India v Sri Lanka | Johannesburg | 2002-03 |

## INDIVIDUAL RECORDS – GENERAL
## 30 APPEARANCES

| | | | | | |
|---|---|---|---|---|---|
| 38 | Wasim Akram | Pakistan | 33 | S.R.Waugh | Australia |
| 35 | P.A.de Silva | Sri Lanka | 32 | Inzamam-ul-Haq | Pakistan |
| 34 | J.Srinath | India | 30 | M.Azharuddin | India |
| 33 | Javed Miandad | Pakistan | 30 | A.Flower | Zimbabwe |
| 33 | S.R.Tendulkar | India | 30 | A.Ranatunga | Sri Lanka |

## 20 CAPTAINCY APPEARANCES

| | | | | | |
|---|---|---|---|---|---|
| 23 | M.Azharuddin | India | 22 | Imran Khan | Pakistan |

## 30 UMPIRING APPEARANCES

| | | | | | |
|---|---|---|---|---|---|
| 46 | D.R.Shepherd | England | 34 | S.A.Bucknor | West Indies |

# ENGLAND v ZIMBABWE

# SERIES RECORDS

1996-97 to 2000

## HIGHEST INNINGS TOTALS

| England | in England | 415 | | Lord's | 2000 |
|---|---|---|---|---|---|
| | in Zimbabwe | 406 | | Bulawayo | 1996-97 |
| Zimbabwe | in England | 285-4d | | Nottingham | 2000 |
| | in Zimbabwe | 376 | | Bulawayo | 1996-97 |

## LOWEST INNINGS TOTALS

| England | in England | 147 | | Nottingham | 2000 |
|---|---|---|---|---|---|
| | in Zimbabwe | 156 | | Harare | 1996-97 |
| Zimbabwe | in England | 83 | | Lord's | 2000 |
| | in Zimbabwe | 215 | | Harare | 1996-97 |

**HIGHEST MATCH AGGREGATE**   1220 for 36 wickets   Bulawayo   1996-97
**LOWEST MATCH AGGREGATE**   621 for 30 wickets   Lord's   2000

## HIGHEST INDIVIDUAL INNINGS

| England | in England | 136 | M.A.Atherton | Nottingham | 2000 |
|---|---|---|---|---|---|
| | in Zimbabwe | 113 | N.Hussain | Bulawayo | 1996-97 |
| Zimbabwe | in England | 148* | M.W.Goodwin | Nottingham | 2000 |
| | in Zimbabwe | 112 | A.Flower | Bulawayo | 1996-97 |

## HIGHEST AGGREGATE OF RUNS IN A SERIES

| England | in England | 225 | (av 75.00) | M.A.Atherton | 2000 |
|---|---|---|---|---|---|
| | in Zimbabwe | 241 | (av 80.33) | A.J.Stewart | 1996-97 |
| Zimbabwe | in England | 178 | (av 89.00) | M.W.Goodwin | 2000 |
| | in Zimbabwe | 135 | (av 45.00) | A.D.R.Campbell | 1996-97 |

## RECORD WICKET PARTNERSHIPS – ENGLAND

| 1st | 121 | M.A.Atherton (136)/M.R.Ramprakash (56) | Nottingham | 2000 |
|---|---|---|---|---|
| 2nd | 137 | N.V.Knight (96)/A.J.Stewart (73) | Bulawayo | 1996-97 |
| 3rd | 68 | A.J.Stewart (48)/N.Hussain (113) | Bulawayo | 1996-97 |
| 4th | 149 | G.A.Hick (101)/A.J.Stewart (124*) | Lord's | 2000 |
| 5th | 148 | N.Hussain (113)/J.P.Crawley (112) | Bulawayo | 1996-97 |
| 6th | 43 | M.A.Atherton (136)/A.Flintoff (16) | Nottingham | 2000 |
| 7th | 39 | M.A.Atherton (136)/C.P.Schofield (57) | Nottingham | 2000 |
| 8th | 32 | C.P.Schofield (57)/A.R.Caddick (13) | Nottingham | 2000 |
| 9th | 25 | J.P.Crawley (112)/A.D.Mullally (4) | Bulawayo | 1996-97 |
| 10th | 28 | J.P.Crawley (112)/P.C.R.Tufnell (2*) | Bulawayo | 1996-97 |

## RECORD WICKET PARTNERSHIPS – ZIMBABWE

| 1st | 17 | G.W.Flower (12)/G.J.Whittall (12*) | Nottingham | 2000 |
|---|---|---|---|---|
| 2nd | 127 | G.W.Flower (43)/A.D.R.Campbell (84) | Bulawayo | 1996-97 |
| 3rd | 129 | M.W.Goodwin (148*)/N.C.Johnson (51) | Nottingham | 2000 |
| 4th | 122 | M.W.Goodwin (148*)/A.Flower (42) | Nottingham | 2000 |
| 5th | 29 | A.Flower (112)/A.C.Waller (15) | Bulawayo | 1996-97 |

| 6th | 19 | N.C.Johnson (14)/G.J.Whittall (15) | Lord's | 2000 |
| 7th | 79 | A.Flower (112)/P.A.Strang (38) | Bulawayo | 1996-97 |
| 8th | 41 | A.Flower (112)/H.H.Streak (19) | Bulawayo | 1996-97 |
| 9th | 24 | G.J.Whittall (56)/H.H.Streak (8*) | Bulawayo | 1996-97 |
| 10th | 31 | B.C.Strang (37*)/M.Mbangwa (8) | Lord's | 2000 |

## BEST INNINGS BOWLING ANALYSIS

| England | in England | 5- 15 | E.S.H.Giddins | Lord's | 2000 |
| | in Zimbabwe | 4- 40 | D.Gough | Harare | 1996-97 |
| Zimbabwe | in England | 6- 87 | H.H.Streak | Lord's | 2000 |
| | in Zimbabwe | 5-123 | P.A.Strang | Bulawayo | 1996-97 |

## BEST MATCH BOWLING ANALYSIS

| England | in England | 7- 42 | E.S.H.Giddins | Lord's | 2000 |
| | in Zimbabwe | 6-137 | P.C.R.Tufnell | Bulawayo | 1996-97 |
| Zimbabwe | in England | 6- 87 | H.H.Streak | Lord's | 2000 |
| | in Zimbabwe | 7-186 | P.A.Strang | Bulawayo | 1996-97 |

## HIGHEST AGGREGATE OF WICKETS IN A SERIES

| England | in England | 9 | (av 19.33) | D.Gough | 2000 |
| | in Zimbabwe | 8 | (av 22.25) | R.D.B.Croft | 1996-97 |
| Zimbabwe | in England | 9 | (av 20.22) | H.H.Streak | 2000 |
| | in Zimbabwe | 10 | (av 25.90) | P.A.Strang | 1996-97 |

## RESULTS SUMMARY

### ENGLAND v ZIMBABWE – IN ENGLAND

| | Tests | Series | | | Lord's | | | Nottingham | | |
| --- | --- | --- | --- | --- | --- | --- | --- | --- | --- | --- |
| | | E | Z | D | E | Z | D | E | Z | D |
| 2000 | 2 | 1 | – | 1 | 1 | – | – | – | – | 1 |

### ENGLAND v ZIMBABWE – IN ZIMBABWE

| | Tests | Series | | | Bulawayo | | | Harare | | |
| --- | --- | --- | --- | --- | --- | --- | --- | --- | --- | --- |
| | | E | Z | D | E | Z | D | E | Z | D |
| 1996-97 | 2 | – | – | 2 | – | – | 1 | – | – | 1 |
| Totals | 4 | 1 | – | 3 | | | | | | |

# ENGLAND v SOUTH AFRICA

## SERIES RECORDS

1888-89 to 1999-2000

### HIGHEST INNINGS TOTALS

| | | | | |
|---|---|---|---|---|
| England | in England | 554-8d | Lord's | 1947 |
| | in South Africa | 654-5 | Durban | 1938-39 |
| South Africa | in England | 552-5d | Manchester | 1998 |
| | in South Africa | 572-7 | Durban | 1999-00 |

### LOWEST INNINGS TOTALS

| | | | | |
|---|---|---|---|---|
| England | in England | 76 | Leeds | 1907 |
| | in South Africa | 92 | Cape Town | 1898-99 |
| South Africa | in England | 30 | Birmingham | 1924 |
| | in South Africa | 30 | Port Elizabeth | 1895-96 |

**HIGHEST MATCH AGGREGATE**  1981 for 35 wickets  Durban  1938-39
**LOWEST MATCH AGGREGATE**  378 for 30 wickets  The Oval  1912

### HIGHEST INDIVIDUAL INNINGS

| | | | | | |
|---|---|---|---|---|---|
| England | in England | 211 | J.B.Hobbs | Lord's | 1924 |
| | in South Africa | 243 | E.Paynter | Durban | 1938-39 |
| South Africa | in England | 236 | E.A.B.Rowan | Leeds | 1951 |
| | in South Africa | 275 | G.Kirsten | Durban | 1999-00 |

### HIGHEST AGGREGATE OF RUNS IN A SERIES

| | | | | | |
|---|---|---|---|---|---|
| England | in England | 753 | (av 94.12) | D.C.S.Compton | 1947 |
| | in South Africa | 653 | (av 81.62) | E.Paynter | 1938-39 |
| South Africa | in England | 621 | (av 69.00) | A.D.Nourse | 1947 |
| | in South Africa | 582 | (av 64.66) | H.W.Taylor | 1922-23 |

### RECORD WICKET PARTNERSHIPS – ENGLAND

| | | | | |
|---|---|---|---|---|
| 1st | 359 | L.Hutton (158)/C.Washbrook (195) | Johannesburg | 1948-49 |
| 2nd | 280 | P.A.Gibb (120)/W.J.Edrich (219) | Durban | 1938-39 |
| 3rd | 370 | W.J.Edrich (189)/D.C.S.Compton (208) | Lord's | 1947 |
| 4th | 197 | W.R.Hammond (181)/L.E.G.Ames (115) | Cape Town | 1938-39 |
| 5th | 237 | D.C.S.Compton (163)/N.W.D.Yardley (99) | Nottingham | 1947 |
| 6th | 206* | K.F.Barrington (148*)/J.M.Parks (108*) | Durban | 1964-65 |
| 7th | 115 | J.W.H.T.Douglas (119)/M.C.Bird (61) | Durban | 1913-14 |
| 8th | 154 | C.W.Wright (71)/H.R.Bromley-Davenport (84) | Johannesburg | 1895-96 |
| 9th | 71 | H.Wood (134*)/J.T.Hearne (40) | Cape Town | 1891-92 |
| 10th | 92 | C.A.G.Russell (111)/A.E.R.Gilligan (39*) | Durban | 1922-23 |

### RECORD WICKET PARTNERSHIPS – SOUTH AFRICA

| | | | | |
|---|---|---|---|---|
| 1st | 260 | B.Mitchell (123)/I.J.Siedle (141) | Cape Town | 1930-31 |
| 2nd | 238 | G.Kirsten (210)/J.H.Kallis (132) | Manchester | 1998 |
| 3rd | 319 | A.Melville (189)/A.D.Nourse (149) | Nottingham | 1947 |
| 4th | 214 | H.W.Taylor (121)/H.G.Deane (93) | The Oval | 1929 |
| 5th | 192 | G.Kirsten (275)/M.V.Boucher (108) | Durban | 1999-00 |
| 6th | 171 | J.H.B.Waite (113)/P.L.Winslow (108) | Manchester | 1955 |
| 7th | 123 | H.G.Deane (73)/E.P.Nupen (69) | Durban | 1927-28 |
| 8th | 119 | L.Klusener (174)/M.V.Boucher (42) | Port Elizabeth | 1999-00 |
| 9th | 137 | E.L.Dalton (117)/A.B.C.Langton (73*) | The Oval | 1935 |
| 10th | 103 | H.G.Owen-Smith (129)/A.J.Bell (26*) | Leeds | 1929 |

11

## BEST INNINGS BOWLING ANALYSIS

| | | | | | |
|---|---|---|---|---|---|
| England | in England | 9-57 | D.E.Malcolm | The Oval | 1994 |
| | in South Africa | 9-28 | G.A.Lohmann | Johannesburg | 1895-96 |
| South Africa | in England | 7-65 | S.J.Pegler | Lord's | 1912 |
| | in South Africa | 9-113 | H.J.Tayfield | Johannesburg | 1956-57 |

## BEST MATCH BOWLING ANALYSIS

| | | | | | |
|---|---|---|---|---|---|
| England | in England | 15-99 | C.Blythe | Leeds | 1907 |
| | in South Africa | 17-159 | S.F.Barnes | Johannesburg | 1913-14 |
| South Africa | in England | 10-87 | P.M.Pollock | Nottingham | 1965 |
| | in South Africa | 13-192 | H.J.Tayfield | Johannesburg | 1956-57 |

## HIGHEST AGGREGATE OF WICKETS IN A SERIES

| | | | | | |
|---|---|---|---|---|---|
| England | in England | 34 | (av 8.29) | S.F.Barnes | 1912 |
| | in South Africa | 49 | (av 10.93) | S.F.Barnes | 1913-14 |
| South Africa | in England | 33 | (av 19.78) | A.A.Donald | 1998 |
| | in South Africa | 37 | (av 17.18) | H.J.Tayfield | 1956-57 |

## RESULTS SUMMARY

### ENGLAND v SOUTH AFRICA – IN ENGLAND

| | | Series | | | Lord's | | | Leeds | | | The Oval | | | Birmingham | | | Manchester | | | Nottingham | | |
|---|---|---|---|---|---|---|---|---|---|---|---|---|---|---|---|---|---|---|---|---|---|---|
| | Tests | E | SA | D | E | SA | D | E | SA | D | E | SA | D | E | SA | D | E | SA | D | E | SA | D |
| 1907 | 3 | 1 | – | 2 | – | – | 1 | 1 | – | – | – | – | 1 | | | | | | | | | |
| 1912 | 3 | 3 | – | – | 1 | – | – | 1 | – | – | 1 | – | – | | | | | | | | | |
| 1924 | 5 | 3 | – | 2 | 1 | – | – | 1 | – | – | – | – | 1 | 1 | – | – | – | – | 1 | | | |
| 1929 | 5 | 2 | – | 3 | – | – | 1 | 1 | – | – | – | – | 1 | – | – | 1 | 1 | – | – | | | |
| 1935 | 5 | – | 1 | 4 | – | 1 | – | – | – | 1 | – | – | 1 | | | | – | – | 1 | – | – | 1 |
| 1947 | 5 | 3 | – | 2 | 1 | – | – | 1 | – | – | – | – | 1 | | | | 1 | – | – | – | – | 1 |
| 1951 | 5 | 3 | 1 | 1 | 1 | – | – | – | – | 1 | 1 | – | – | | | | 1 | – | – | – | 1 | – |
| 1955 | 5 | 3 | 2 | – | 1 | – | – | – | 1 | – | 1 | – | – | | | | – | 1 | – | 1 | – | – |
| 1960 | 5 | 3 | – | 2 | 1 | – | – | | | | – | – | 1 | 1 | – | – | – | – | 1 | 1 | – | – |
| 1965 | 3 | – | 1 | 2 | – | – | 1 | | | | – | – | 1 | | | | | | | – | 1 | – |
| 1994 | 3 | 1 | 1 | 1 | – | 1 | – | – | – | 1 | 1 | – | – | | | | | | | | | |
| 1998 | 5 | 2 | 1 | 2 | – | 1 | – | 1 | – | – | | | | – | – | 1 | – | – | 1 | 1 | – | – |
| | 52 | 24 | 7 | 21 | 6 | 3 | 3 | 6 | 1 | 3 | 4 | – | 7 | 2 | – | 2 | 3 | 1 | 4 | 3 | 2 | 2 |

### ENGLAND v SOUTH AFRICA – IN SOUTH AFRICA

| | | Series | | | Port Elizabeth | | | Cape Town | | | Johannesburg | | | Durban | | | Pretoria | | |
|---|---|---|---|---|---|---|---|---|---|---|---|---|---|---|---|---|---|---|---|---|
| | Tests | E | SA | D | E | SA | D | E | SA | D | E | SA | D | E | SA | D | E | SA | D |
| 1888-89 | 2 | 2 | – | – | 1 | – | – | 1 | – | – | | | | | | | | | |
| 1891-92 | 1 | 1 | – | – | | | | 1 | – | – | | | | | | | | | |
| 1895-96 | 3 | 3 | – | – | 1 | – | – | 1 | – | – | 1 | – | – | | | | | | |
| 1898-99 | 2 | 2 | – | – | | | | 1 | – | – | 1 | – | – | | | | | | |
| 1905-06 | 5 | 1 | 4 | – | | | | 1 | 1 | – | – | 3 | – | | | | | | |
| 1909-10 | 5 | 2 | 3 | – | | | | 1 | 1 | – | 1 | 1 | – | – | 1 | – | | | |
| 1913-14 | 5 | 4 | – | 1 | 1 | – | – | | | | 2 | – | – | 1 | – | 1 | | | |
| 1922-23 | 5 | 2 | 1 | 2 | | | | 1 | – | – | – | 1 | 1 | 1 | – | 1 | | | |
| 1927-28 | 5 | 2 | 2 | 1 | | | | 1 | – | – | 1 | 1 | – | – | 1 | 1 | | | |
| 1930-31 | 5 | – | 1 | 4 | | | | – | – | 1 | – | 1 | 1 | – | – | 2 | | | |
| 1938-39 | 5 | 1 | – | 4 | | | | – | – | 1 | – | – | 2 | 1 | – | 1 | | | |
| 1948-49 | 5 | 2 | – | 3 | 1 | – | – | – | – | 1 | – | – | 2 | 1 | – | – | | | |
| 1956-57 | 5 | 2 | 2 | 1 | – | 1 | – | 1 | – | – | 1 | 1 | – | – | – | 1 | | | |
| 1964-65 | 5 | 1 | – | 4 | – | – | 1 | – | – | 1 | – | – | 2 | 1 | – | – | | | |
| 1995-96 | 5 | – | 1 | 4 | – | – | 1 | – | 1 | – | – | – | 1 | – | – | 1 | – | – | 1 |
| 1999-00 | 5 | 1 | 2 | 2 | – | – | 1 | – | 1 | – | – | 1 | – | – | – | 1 | 1 | – | – |
| | 68 | 26 | 16 | 26 | 4 | 1 | 3 | 9 | 4 | 4 | 7 | 9 | 9 | 5 | 2 | 9 | 1 | – | 1 |
| Totals | 120 | 50 | 23 | 47 | | | | | | | | | | | | | | | |

# 2003 TOURIST'S REGISTER

Neither Zimbabwe nor South Africa had selected their 2003 touring teams at the time of going to press. See page 14 for key to abbreviations.

## ZIMBABWE

| Full Names | Birthdate | Birthplace | Team | Type | F-C Debut |
|---|---|---|---|---|---|
| BLIGNAUT, Arnoldus Mauritius ('Andy') | 01.08.78 | Salisbury | Mashonaland | LHB/RMF | 1997-98 |
| BRENT, Gary Bazil | 13.01.76 | Sinoia | Manicaland | RHB/RMF | 1994-95 |
| CAMPBELL, Alistair Douglas Ross | 23.09.72 | Salisbury | Mashonaland | LHB/OB | 1990-91 |
| CARLISLE, Stuart Vance | 10.05.72 | Salisbury | Mashonaland | RHB/RM | 1993-94 |
| EBRAHIM, Dion Digby | 07.08.80 | Bulawayo | Mashonaland | RHB/RM | 1999-00 |
| FLOWER, Grant William | 20.12.70 | Salisbury | Mashonaland | RHB/SLA | 1989-90 |
| FRIEND, Travis John | 07.01.81 | Kwekwe | Midlands | RHB/RFM | 1999-00 |
| GRIPPER, Trevor Raymond | 28.12.75 | Salisbury | Mashonaland | RHB/OB | 1996-97 |
| HONDO, Douglas Tafadzwa | 07.07.79 | Bulawayo | Midlands | RHB/RFM | 2000-01 |
| MAHWIRE, Ngonidzashe Blessing | 31.07.82 | Bikita | Mashonaland | RHB/RM | 2000-01 |
| MARILLIER, Douglas Anthony | 24.04.78 | Salisbury | Midlands | RHB/OB/WK | 1998-99 |
| MASAKADZA, Hamilton | 09.08.83 | Harare | Mashonaland | RHB/LBG | 1999-00 |
| MURPHY, Brian Andrew | 01.12.76 | Salisbury | Mashonaland | RHB/LBG | 1995-96 |
| NKALA, Mluleki Luke | 01.04.81 | Bulawayo | Matabeleland | RHB/RFM | 1999-00 |
| PRICE, Raymond William | 12.06.76 | Salisbury | Midlands | RHB/SLA | 1995-96 |
| STREAK, Heath Hilton | 16.03.74 | Bulawayo | Matabeleland | RHB/RFM | 1992-93 |
| TAIBU, Tatenda | 14.05.83 | Harare | Mashonaland | RHB/WK | 1999-00 |
| VERMEULEN, Mark Andrew | 02.03.79 | Salisbury | Matabeleland | RHB/OB | 1997-98 |
| VILJOEN, Dirk Peter | 11.03.77 | Salisbury | Mashonaland | LHB/SLA | 1994-95 |
| WATAMBWA, Brighton Tonderai | 09.06.77 | Salisbury | Mashonaland | RHB/RFM | 1997-98 |
| WISHART, Craig Brian | 09.01.74 | Salisbury | Midlands | RHB/RM | 1992-93 |

## SOUTH AFRICA

| Full Names | Birthdate | Birthplace | Team | Type | F-C Debut |
|---|---|---|---|---|---|
| ADAMS, Paul Regan | 20.01.77 | Cape Town | W Province | RHB/SLC | 1995-96 |
| BOJE, Nico ('Nicky') | 20.03.73 | Bloemfontein | Free State | LHB/SLA | 1990-91 |
| BOUCHER, Mark Verdon | 03.12.76 | East London | Border | RHB/WK | 1995-96 |
| DAWSON, Alan Charles | 27.11.69 | Cape Town | W Province | RHB/RMF | 1992-93 |
| DIPPENAAR, Hendrik Human ('Boeta') | 14.06.77 | Kimberley | Free State | RHB/OB | 1995-96 |
| GIBBS, Herschelle Herman | 23.02.74 | Cape Town | W Province | RHB/RFM/LB | 1990-91 |
| HALL, Andrew James | 31.07.75 | Johannesburg | Gauteng | RHB/RFM | 1995-96 |
| HENDERSON, Claude William | 14.06.72 | Worcester | W Province | RHB/SLA | 1990-91 |
| KALLIS, Jacques Henry | 16.10.75 | Cape Town | W Province | RHB/RFM | 1993-94 |
| KIRSTEN, Gary | 23.11.67 | Cape Town | W Province | LHB/OB | 1987-88 |
| KLUSENER, Lance | 04.09.71 | Durban | KZ-Natal | LHB/RFM | 1993-94 |
| McKENZIE, Neil Douglas | 24.11.75 | Johannesburg | Northerns | RHB/RM | 1994-95 |
| NTINI, Makhaya | 06.07.77 | Zwelitsha | Border | RHB/RF | 1995-96 |
| ONTONG, Justin Lee | 04.01.80 | Paarl | Boland | RHB/OB-LB | 1997-98 |
| PETERSON, Robin John | 04.08.79 | Port Elizabeth | E Province | LHB/SLA | 1998-99 |
| POLLOCK, Shaun Maclean | 16.07.73 | Port Elizabeth | KZ-Natal | RHB/RFM | 1991-92 |
| PRINCE, Ashwell Gavin | 28.05.77 | Port Elizabeth | W Province | LHB | 1995-96 |
| RUDOLPH, Jacobus Andries ('Jacques') | 04.05.81 | Springs | Northerns | LHB/LBG | 1997-98 |
| SMITH, Graeme Craig | 01.02.81 | Johannesburg | W Province | LHB/RM-OB | 1999-00 |
| TERBRUGGE, David John | 31.01.77 | Ladysmith | Gauteng | RHB/RFM | 1994-95 |
| VAN JAARSVELD, Martin | 18.06.74 | Klerksdorp | Northerns | RHB/RM | 1994-95 |
| WILLOUGHBY, Charl Myles | 03.12.74 | Cape Town | W Province | LHB/LFM | 1994-95 |

# THE FIRST-CLASS COUNTIES REGISTER, RECORDS AND 2002 AVERAGES

Career statistics are to 30 March 2003 and include the Eighth World Cup

## ABBREVIATIONS – General

| | | | |
|---|---|---|---|
| * | not out/unbroken partnership | l-o | limited-overs |
| b | born | LOI | Limited-Overs Internationals |
| BB | Best innings bowling analysis | Tests | Official Test Matches |
| Cap | Awarded 1st XI County Cap | Tours | Overseas tours involving first-class |
| f-c | first-class | | appearances |
| HS | Highest Score | | |

## Awards

| | |
|---|---|
| BHC | Benson and Hedges Cup 'Gold' Award |
| CGT | Gillette Cup, NatWest/Cheltenham & Gloucester Trophy Match Award |
| *Wisden* 2001 | One of *Wisden Cricketers' Almanack's* Five Cricketers of 2001 |
| YC 2002 | Cricket Writers' Club Young Cricketer of 2002 |

## ECB Competitions

| | |
|---|---|
| BHC | Benson & Hedges Cup |
| CC | Frizzell County Championship |
| CGT | Cheltenham & Gloucester Trophy |
| NL | National League |
| NWT | NatWest Trophy (1981-2000) |
| SL | Sunday League (1969-98) |

## Education

| | |
|---|---|
| BHS | Boys' High School |
| C | College |
| CFE | College of Further Education |
| CHE | College of Higher Education |
| CS | Comprehensive School |
| GS | Grammar School |
| HS | High School |
| I | Institute |
| IHE | Institute of Higher Education |
| RGS | Royal Grammar School |
| S | School |
| SFC | Sixth Form College |
| SM | Secondary Modern School |
| SS | Secondary School |
| TC | Technical College |
| T(H)S | Technical (High) School |
| U | University |
| UMIST | University of Manchester Institute of Science and Technology |
| UWIC | University of Wales Institute, Cardiff |

## Playing Categories

| | |
|---|---|
| LBG | Bowls right-arm leg-breaks and googlies |
| LF | Bowls left-arm fast |
| LFM | Bowls left-arm fast-medium |
| LHB | Bats left-handed |
| LM | Bowls left-arm medium pace |
| LMF | Bowls left-arm medium fast |
| OB | Bowls right-arm off-breaks |
| RF | Bowls right-arm fast |
| RFM | Bowls right-arm fast-medium |
| RHB | Bats right-handed |
| RM | Bowls right-arm medium pace |
| RMF | Bowls right-arm medium-fast |
| RSM | Bowls right-arm slow-medium |
| SLA | Bowls left-arm leg-breaks |
| SLC | Bowls left-arm 'Chinamen' |
| WK | Wicket-keeper |

## Teams (see also p 121)

| | |
|---|---|
| ACT | Australian Capital Territory |
| B | Bangladesh |
| CD | Central Districts |
| DHR | D.H.Robins' XI |
| EP | Eastern Province |
| GW | Griqualand West |
| K | Kenya |
| KRL | Khan Research Laboratories |
| NSW | New South Wales |
| NT | Northern Transvaal |
| (O)FS | (Orange) Free State |
| PIA | Pakistan International Airlines |
| Q | Queensland |
| RW | Rest of the World XI |
| SAB | South African Breweries XI |
| SAU | South African Universities |
| V | Victoria |
| WA | Western Australia |
| WP | Western Province |

# DERBYSHIRE

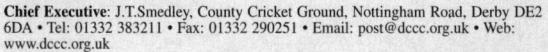

**Formation of Present Club:** 4 November 1870
**Colours:** Chocolate, Amber and Pale Blue
**Badge:** Rose and Crown
**County Champions:** (1) 1936
**Gillette/NatWest/C & G Trophy Winners:** (1) 1981
**Benson and Hedges Cup Winners:** (1) 1993
**National League (Div 1) Winners:** (0); best – 4th (Div 2) 2002
**Sunday League Winners:** (1) 1990
**Match Awards:** CGT 46; BHC 71

**Chief Executive:** J.T.Smedley, County Cricket Ground, Nottingham Road, Derby DE2 6DA • Tel: 01332 383211 • Fax: 01332 290251 • Email: post@dccc.org.uk • Web: www.dccc.org.uk

**First XI Coach:** A.R.K.Pierson. **Captain:** D.G.Cork. **Vice-Captain:** M.J.Di Venuto.
**Overseas Players:** M.J.Di Venuto and Shahid Afridi (*early season*). **2003 Beneficiary:** none. **Scorer:** J.M.Brown. ‡ New registration

**ALI,** Syed **Mohammad** Bukhari, b Bahawalpur, Pakistan 8 Nov 1973. 6'0". Nephew of Taslim Arif (Pakistan 1979-80 to 1980-81). British passport. RHB, LFM. Lahore 1993-94. Railways 1993-94. Islamabad 1994-95. United Bank 1994-95. Rawalpindi 1995-96 to 1998-99. ADBP 1995-96 to 1998-99. Bahawalpur 1998-99. 55 f-c matches in Pakistan before Derbys debut 2002. HS 92 Bahawalpur v Lahore (Rahim Yar Khan) 1998-99. De HS 53 v Durham (Derby) 2002 – on debut. 50 wkts (0+1): 56 (1993-94). De BB 3-48 v Essex (Chelmsford) 2002; 3-48 v Worcs (Worcester) 2002. BB 5-37 Railways v National Bank (Faisalabad) 1993-94. LO HS 19 v Lancs (Manchester) 2002 (CGT). LO BB 4-34 Railways v United Bank (Karachi) 1993-94.

**BASSANO,** Christopher Warwick Godfrey (Grey S, Port Elizabeth; Launceston Church GS; Tasmania U, Hobart), b East London, SA 11 Sep 1975. 6'2". British passport (English mother); son of the late B.S.Bassano (cricket writer, historian and broadcaster). RHB, LB. Debut 2001; cap 2002. First to score 100 in each innings on Championship debut – 186* and 106 v Glos (Derby) 2001. 1000 (1): 1063 (2002). HS 186* (*see above*). LO HS 61 v Glos (Bristol) 2002 (NL).

**CORK,** Dominic Gerald (St Joseph's C, Stoke-on-Trent; Newcastle CFE), b Newcastle-under-Lyme, Staffs 7 Aug 1971. 6'2". RHB, RFM. Debut 1990; cap 1993; captain 1998 to date; benefit 2001. *Wisden* 1995. Staffordshire 1989-90. ECB contract 2001. **Tests:** 37 (1995 to 2002); HS 59 v NZ (Auckland) 1996-97; BB 7-43 v WI (Lord's) 1995 – on debut (record England analysis by Test match debutant); hat-trick v WI (Manchester) 1995 – the first in Test history to occur in the opening over of a day's play. **LOI:** 32 (1992 to 2002-03); HS 31* v NZ (Napier) 1996-97; BB 3-27 v WI (Lord's) 1995. Tours: A 1992-93 (Eng A), 1998-99; SA 1993-94 (Eng A), 1995-96; WI 1991-92 (Eng A); NZ 1996-97; I 1994-95 (Eng A); P 2000-01 (*part*). HS 200* v Durham (Derby) 2000. 50 wkts (6); most – 90 (1995). BB 9-43 (13-93 match) v Northants (Derby) 1995. Took 8-53 before lunch on his 20th birthday v Essex (Derby) 1991. 2 hat-tricks: 1994 and 1995 (*see Tests*). Awards: CGT 4; BHC 4. LO HS 93 v Derbys CB (Derby) 2000 (NWT). LO BB 6-21 v Glam (Chesterfield) 1997 (SL).

**DEAN,** Kevin James (Leek HS; Leek CFE), b Derby 16 Oct 1975. 6'5". LHB, LMF. Debut 1996. Cap 1998. HS 54* v Worcs (Derby) 2002. 50 wkts (2): most – 83 (2002). BB 8-52 v Kent (Canterbury) 2000. 2 hat-tricks (1998, 2000). Award: CGT 1. LO HS 16* v Glam (Cardiff) 1998 (SL) and 16* v Middx (Derby) 2002 (NL). LO BB 5-32 v Glos (Derby) 1996 (SL).

**Di VENUTO,** Michael James (St Virgil's C; Hobart), b Hobart, Australia 12 Dec 1973. 6'0". LHB, RM/LB. Tasmania 1991-92 to date. Sussex 1999; cap 1999. Derbyshire debut/cap 2000. **LOI** (A): 9 (1996-97 to 1997-98); HS 89 v SA (Jo'burg) 1996-97. Tours: Z 1995-96 (Tas); Sc/Ire 1998 (Aus A). 1000 runs (3): most – 1538 (2002). HS 230 v Northants (Derby) 2002. BB (Tas) 1-0. UK BB (Sx) 1-3. De BB 1-16. Awards: CGT 1; BHC 1. LO HS 173* v Derbys CB (Derby) 2000 (NWT). LO BB (Tas) 1-10.

**DUMELOW, Nathan** Robert Charles (Foremark Hall S; Denstone C), b Derby 30 Apr 1981. 5'9". RHB, OB. Debut 2001. HS 61 and CC BB 4-103 v Middx (Southgate) 2001. BB 4-81 v P (Derby) 2001. LO HS 52 v Surrey (Derby) 2002 (NL). LO BB 3-24 v Sussex (Hove) 2002 (NL).

**GAIT, Andrew** Ian (Kearsney C; UNISA), b Bulawayo, Rhodesia 19 Dec 1978. British passport. 6'1". RHB. Free State 1998-99 to 2000-01. Derbyshire debut 2002. HS 175 v Northants (Northampton) 2002. LO HS 138* FS v GW (Bloemfontein) 2000-01 – Free State 1-o record.

**GUNTER, Neil** Edward Lloyd (The Clere S; Newbury C), Basingstoke, Hants 12 May 1981. 6'0". LHB, RFM. Berkshire 2000-01. Derbyshire debut 2002. MCCYC. Awaiting Championship debut. HS 18 and BB 4-14 v WI A (Derby) 2002. LO HS (Berks) 5 (CGT).

**HEWSON, Dominic** Robert (Cheltenham C; West of England U), b Cheltenham, Glos 3 Oct 1974. 5'8". RHB, occ RM. Gloucestershire 1996-2001. Derbyshire debut 2002. HS 168 Gs v Derbys (Bristol) 2001. De HS 102* v Glam (Cardiff) 2002 – on debut. BB (Gs) 1-7. LO HS 64 Gs v SL A (Cheltenham) 1999.

**KERR, Jason** Ian Douglas (Withins HS; Bolton C), b Bolton, Lancs 7 Apr 1974. 6'2". RHB, RMF. Somerset 1993-2001; cap 2001. Derbyshire debut 2002. HS 80 Sm v WI (Taunton) 1995. CC HS 68* Sm v Derbys (Taunton) 1996. De HS 68 v Worcs (Worcester) 2002. BB 7-23 Sm v Leics (Taunton) 1999. De BB 4-32 v Middx (Derby) 2002. Hat-trick 2000. LO HS 65* v Northants (Derby) 2002 (NL). LO BB 4-28 Sm v Hants (Basingstoke) 1997 (SL).

**KHAN, Rawait** Mahmood (Moseley S; Solihull SFC), b Birmingham 5 Mar 1982. Elder brother of Z.M.Khan (Derbyshire 2000). 5'10". RHB, OB. Debut 2001. HS 91 v Indians (Derby) 2002. CC HS 13 v Glos (Bristol) 2001 – on debut. LO HS 29 Derbys CB v Glos CB (Heanor) 2000 (NWT).

**KRIKKEN, Karl** Matthew (Rivington & Blackrod HS & SFC), b Bolton, Lancs 9 Apr 1969. Son of B.E.Krikken (Lancs and Worcs 1966-69). 5'9". RHB, WK. GW 1988-89. Derbyshire debut 1989; cap 1992; benefit 2002. 2nd XI Coach 2003. HS 104 v Lancs (Manchester) 1996. BB 1-54. LO HS 55 v Kent (Derby) 1996 (NWT).

**LUNGLEY, Tom** (St John Houghton SS; SE Derbyshire C), b Derby 25 Jul 1979. 6'1". LHB, RM. Debut 2000. HS 47 v Warwks (Derby) 2001. BB 3-10 (6-41 match) v CU (Cambridge) 2000 – on debut. CC BB 3-43 v Northants (Northampton) 2002. LO HS 45 v Essex (Chelmsford) 2001 (NL). LO BB 4-28 v Essex (Derby) 2001 (NL).

**SELWOOD, Steven** Andrew (Mill Hill S; Albany C, Loughborough U), b Barnet, Herts 24 Nov 1979. Son of T.Selwood (Middlesex and C Districts 1966-73). 6'0". LHB, SLA. Debut 2001. HS 99 v Worcs (Derby) 2002. BB 1-8 (CC). LO HS 93 v Glos (Derby) 2002 (NL). LO BB 1-48 (BHC).

‡**SHAHID** KHAN AFRIDI, Sahibzada Mohammad (Ibrahim Alibhai S and Islamia Science C, Karachi), b Kohat, Pakistan 1 Mar 1980. Younger brother of Tariq Afridi (Karachi). 5'11". RHB, LBG. F-c debut (Combined XI v England A) 1995-96. Karachi 1995-96 to date. Habib Bank 1997-98 to date. Leicestershire 2001; cap 2001. **Tests** (P): 14 (1998-99 to 2001-02); HS 141 v I (Madras) 1998-99; BB 5-52 v A (Karachi) 1998-99 – on debut. **LOI**(P): 176 (1997-98 to 2002-03); HS 109 v I (Toronto) 1998-99; BB 5-40 v E (Lahore) 2000-01. Scored a 37-ball hundred (*LOI record*) which included 11 sixes (*equalled record*) v SL (Nairobi) 1996-97 in his first LOI innings. Tours (P): A 1996-97; WI 1999-00; I 1998-99; B 1998-99. HS 164 Le v Northants (Northampton) 2001. BB 6-101 Habib Bank v KRL (Rawalpindi) 1997-98. Le BB 5-84 Le v Essex (Chelmsford) 2001. Awards: CGT 2. LO HS 112 Pak A v Ind A (Karachi) 1997-98. LO BB 5-36 Habib Bank v Sargodha (Sargodha) 2001-02.

**STUBBINGS, Stephen** David (Frankston HS, Aus; Swinburne U, Aus), b Huddersfield, Yorks 31 Mar 1978. 6'3". LHB, OB. Debut 1997. Cap 2001. 1000 (1): 1047 (2001). HS 135* v Kent (Canterbury) 2000. LO HS 98* v Lancs (Derby) 2002 (NL).

**SUTTON, Luke** David (Millfield S; Durham U), b Keynsham, Somerset 4 Oct 1976. 5'11". RHB, WK. Somerset 1997-98. Derbyshire debut 2000. Cap 2002. HS 140* (carried bat) v Sussex (Derby) 2001. LO HS 60 Brit U v Kent (Oxford) 1998 (BHC).

**WELCH, Graeme** (Hetton CS), b Durham City 21 Mar 1972. 5'11½". RHB, RM. Warwickshire 1994-2000; cap 1997. Derbyshire debut/cap 2001. Tour: SA 1994-95 (Wa). HS 84* Wa v Notts (Birmingham) 1994. De HS 64 v Warwks (Birmingham) 2001 and 64 v Worcs (Derby) 2002. 50 wkts (1): 65 (1997). BB 6-30 v Durham (Chester-le-St) 2001. Award: BHC 1. LO HS 71 Wa v Kent (Maidstone) 1999 (NL). LO BB 6-31 v Middx (Derby) 2002 (NL).

**WHARTON, Lian** James (Ecclesbourne S; Malkworth C), b Holbrook 21 Feb 1977. 5'9". LHB, SLA. Debut 2000. HS 16 v Worcs (Derby) 2002. BB 6-62 v Middx (Lord's) 2002. LO HS 11* v Essex (Chelmsford) 2002 (NL). LO BB 3-23 v Durham (Chester-le-St) 2001 (NL).

## RELEASED/RETIRED
(Having made a first-class County appearance in 2002)

**ALDRED, Paul** (Lady Manner's S, Bakewell), b Chellaston 4 Feb 1969. 5'10". RHB, RM. Derbyshire 1995-2002; cap 1999. Cheshire 1994. HS 83 v Hants (Chesterfield) 1997. 50 wkts (1): 50 (1999). BB 7-101 (13-184 match) v Lancs (Derby) 1999. LO HS 39* v Surrey (Derby) 1999 (NL). LO BB 4-30 v Lincs (Lincoln) 1997 (NWT).

**DOWMAN, Mathew** Peter (St Hugh's CS; Grantham C), b Grantham, Lincs 10 May 1974. 5'10". LHB, RMF. Nottinghamshire 1994-99; cap 1998. Derbyshire 2000-02; cap 2000. Scored 267 for England YC v WI YC (Hove) 1993 – record score in youth 'Tests'. 1000 runs (1): 1091 (1997). HS 149 Nt v Leics (Leicester) 1997. De HS 145* v P (Derby) 2001. BB 4-28 v WI A (Derby) 2002. CC BB 3-16 v Notts (Derby) 2002. Awards: BHC 2. LO HS 92 Nt v Northants (Nottingham) 1997 (BHC). LO BB 3-21 Nt v Worcs (Nottingham) 1996 (BHC).

**PYEMONT, James** Patrick (Tonbridge S; Trinity Hall, Cambridge), b Eastbourne, Sussex 10 Apr 1978. Son of C.P.Pyemont (Cambridge U 1967; cricket and hockey blue). 6'0". RHB, OB. Sussex 1997 – no CC appearances. Cambridge U 1998-99; blue 1998-99. Derbyshire 1999-2002 (dismissed first ball on debut in both innings – first instance by Derbyshire player). Derbyshire 2000-01; captain 2001. HS 124 CU v OU (Lord's) 2000. De HS 43 and De BB 1-37 v I (Derby) 2002. BB 4-101 CU v OU (Cambridge) 2001. LO HS 50 v Hants (Southampton) 2000 (NL).

**WARN, Christopher** James (Chelmer Valley HS; Chelmsford C), b Little Waltham, Essex 22 Aug 1979. RHB, WK. Derbyshire 2002 (one non-CC match). Suffolk 2000-02. HS 1 v Indians (Derby) 2002. Award: CGT 1. LO HS 52* Suffolk v Herefords (Bury St Edmunds) 2001 (CGT).

R.J.Bailey and T.A.Munton left the staff having made no f-c appearances in 2002.

# DERBYSHIRE 2002

## RESULTS SUMMARY

|  | Place | Won | Lost | Tied | Drew | No Result |
|---|---|---|---|---|---|---|
| **County Championship** (2nd Division) | 6th | 7 | 7 |  | 2 |  |
| **All First-Class Matches** |  | 8 | 7 |  | 3 |  |
| **C & G Trophy** | 3rd Round |  |  |  |  |  |
| **Benson & Hedges Cup** | 6th in North Division |  |  |  |  |  |
| **NU National League** (2nd Division) | 4th | 8 | 7 |  |  | 1 |

## COUNTY CHAMPIONSHIP AVERAGES

### BATTING AND FIELDING

| Cap |  | M | I | NO | HS | Runs | Avge | 100 | 50 | Ct/St |
|---|---|---|---|---|---|---|---|---|---|---|
| 2000 | M.J.Di Venuto | 15 | 28 | 3 | 230 | 1538 | 61.52 | 4 | 7 | 29 |
| 2002 | C.W.G.Bassano | 14 | 26 | 1 | 152 | 1063 | 42.52 | 1 | 8 | 13 |
|  | A.I.Gait | 16 | 31 | 1 | 175 | 961 | 32.03 | 1 | 8 | 14 |
| 1993 | D.G.Cork | 8 | 13 | – | 80 | 404 | 31.07 | – | 4 | 11 |
|  | J.I.D.Kerr | 6 | 11 | 1 | 68 | 293 | 29.30 | – | 3 | 2 |
|  | S.A.Selwood | 8 | 16 | – | 99 | 441 | 27.56 | – | 2 | 1 |
| 2001 | G.Welch | 14 | 23 | 5 | 64 | 460 | 25.55 | – | 3 | 8 |
| 2001 | S.D.Stubbings | 9 | 17 | 1 | 128 | 337 | 21.06 | 1 | – | 5 |
| 1998 | K.J.Dean | 16 | 25 | 8 | 54* | 333 | 19.58 | – | 2 | 6 |
| 2002 | L.D.Sutton | 9 | 17 | 1 | 58 | 292 | 18.25 | – | 2 | 29/1 |
| 2000 | M.P.Dowman | 6 | 11 | – | 41 | 194 | 17.63 | – | – | 5 |
|  | D.R.Hewson | 9 | 17 | 1 | 102* | 280 | 17.50 | 1 | – | 6 |
|  | S.M.A.Bukhari | 15 | 24 | 2 | 53 | 333 | 15.13 | – | 1 | 5 |
|  | T.Lungley | 6 | 11 | – | 44 | 145 | 13.18 | – | – | 4 |
| 1992 | K.M.Krikken | 9 | 16 | 1 | 48 | 169 | 11.26 | – | – | 26 |
|  | J.P.Pyemont | 2 | 4 | – | 33 | 37 | 9.25 | – | – | 1 |
|  | L.J.Wharton | 13 | 21 | 11 | 16 | 82 | 8.20 | – | – | 6 |

*Also batted*: N.R.C.Dumelow (1 match) 56, 1.

### BOWLING

|  | O | M | R | W | Avge | Best | 5wI | 10wM |
|---|---|---|---|---|---|---|---|---|
| D.G.Cork | 323.1 | 81 | 951 | 57 | 16.68 | 6-51 | 5 | 1 |
| T.Lungley | 91.4 | 24 | 335 | 14 | 23.92 | 3-43 | – | – |
| K.J.Dean | 578 | 145 | 1922 | 80 | 24.02 | 7-42 | 3 | 2 |
| G.Welch | 486.1 | 157 | 1409 | 55 | 25.61 | 6-60 | 2 | – |
| L.J.Wharton | 192.3 | 40 | 634 | 22 | 28.81 | 6-62 | 2 | – |
| S.M.B.Ali | 405 | 63 | 1708 | 47 | 36.34 | 3-48 | – | – |
| J.I.D.Kerr | 119.2 | 20 | 545 | 13 | 41.92 | 4-32 | – | – |

*Also bowled*: M.P.Dowman 40-12-141-4; N.R.C.Dumelow 6-0-35-0; D.R.Hewson 3-0-16-0; J.P.Pyemont 11-1-33-0; S.A.Selwood 6-1-32-1.

The First-Class Averages (pp 121-135) give the records of Derbyshire players in all first-class county matches (Derbyshire's other opponents being the Indians and West Indies A), with the exception of D.G.Cork and K.J.Dean whose full county figures are as above.

# DERBYSHIRE RECORDS

## FIRST-CLASS CRICKET

| | | | | | | | |
|---|---|---|---|---|---|---|---|
| **Highest Total** | For 645 | | | v | Hampshire | Derby | 1898 |
| | V 662 | | | by | Yorkshire | Chesterfield | 1898 |
| **Lowest Total** | For 16 | | | v | Notts | Nottingham | 1879 |
| | V 23 | | | by | Hampshire | Burton upon T | 1958 |
| **Highest Innings** | For 274 | G.A.Davidson | | v | Lancashire | Manchester | 1896 |
| | V 343* | P.A.Perrin | | for | Essex | Chesterfield | 1904 |

### Highest Partnership for each Wicket

| | | | | | | |
|---|---|---|---|---|---|---|
| 1st | 322 | H.Storer/J.Bowden | v | Essex | Derby | 1929 |
| 2nd | 417 | K.J.Barnett/T.A.Tweats | v | Yorkshire | Derby | 1997 |
| 3rd | 316* | A.S.Rollins/K.J.Barnett | v | Leics | Leicester | 1997 |
| 4th | 328 | P.Vaulkhard/D.Smith | v | Notts | Nottingham | 1946 |
| 5th | 302*† | J.E.Morris/D.G.Cork | v | Glos | Cheltenham | 1993 |
| 6th | 212 | G.M.Lee/T.S.Worthington | v | Essex | Chesterfield | 1932 |
| 7th | 258 | M.P.Dowman/D.G.Cork | v | Durham | Derby | 2000 |
| 8th | 198 | K.M.Krikken/D.G.Cork | v | Lancashire | Manchester | 1996 |
| 9th | 283 | A.Warren/J.Chapman | v | Warwicks | Blackwell | 1910 |
| 10th | 132 | A.Hill/M.Jean-Jacques | v | Yorkshire | Sheffield | 1986 |

† 346 runs were added for this wicket in two separate partnerships

| | | | | | | | |
|---|---|---|---|---|---|---|---|
| **Best Bowling** | For | 10- 40 | W.Bestwick | v | Glamorgan | Cardiff | 1921 |
| **(Innings)** | V | 10- 45 | R.L.Johnson | for | Middlesex | Derby | 1994 |
| **Best Bowling** | For | 17-103 | W.Mycroft | v | Hampshire | Southampton | 1876 |
| **(Match)** | V | 16-101 | G.Giffen | for | Australians | Derby | 1886 |

| | | | | |
|---|---|---|---|---|
| **Most Runs – Season** | 2165 | D.B.Carr | (av 48.11) | 1959 |
| **Most Runs – Career** | 23854 | K.J.Barnett | (av 41.12) | 1979-98 |
| **Most 100s – Season** | 8 | P.N.Kirsten | | 1982 |
| **Most 100s – Career** | 53 | K.J.Barnett | | 1979-98 |
| **Most Wkts – Season** | 168 | T.B.Mitchell | (av 19.55) | 1935 |
| **Most Wkts – Career** | 1670 | H.L.Jackson | (av 17.11) | 1947-63 |
| **Most Career W-K Dismissals** | 1304 | R.W.Taylor | (1157 ct; 147 st) | 1961-84 |
| **Most Career Catches in the Field** | 563 | D.C.Morgan | | 1950-69 |

## LIMITED-OVERS CRICKET

| | | | | | | | |
|---|---|---|---|---|---|---|---|
| **Highest Total** | CGT | 365-3 | | v | Cornwall | Derby | 1986 |
| | BHC | 366-4 | | v | Combined U | Oxford | 1991 |
| | NL | 292-9 | | v | Worcs | Knypersley | 1985 |
| **Lowest Total** | CGT | 79 | | v | Surrey | The Oval | 1967 |
| | BHC | 98 | | v | Worcs | Derby | 1994 |
| | NL | 61 | | v | Hampshire | Portsmouth | 1990 |
| **Highest Innings** | CGT | 173* | M.J.Di Venuto | v | Derbys CB | Derby | 2000 |
| | BHC | 142 | D.M.Jones | v | Minor C | Derby | 1996 |
| | NL | 141* | C.J.Adams | v | Kent | Chesterfield | 1992 |
| **Best Bowling** | CGT | 8-21 | M.A.Holding | v | Sussex | Hove | 1988 |
| | BHC | 6-33 | E.J.Barlow | v | Glos | Bristol | 1978 |
| | NL | 6- 7 | M.Hendrick | v | Notts | Nottingham | 1972 |

# DURHAM

**Formation of Present Club**: 10 May 1882
**Colours**: Navy Blue, Yellow and Maroon
**Badge**: Coat of Arms of the County of Durham
**County Champions**: (0) 8th 1999, 8th (Div 1) 2000
**Gillette/NatWest/C & G Trophy Winners**: (0); best –
quarter-finalist 1992, 2001
**Benson and Hedges Cup Winners**: (0); best – quarter-finalist
1998, 2000, 2001
**National League (Div 1) Winners**: (0); best – 8th (Div 1) 2002
**Sunday League Winners**: (0); best – 7th 1993
**Match Awards**: CGT 23; BHC 20

**Chief Executive**: D.Harker, County Ground, Riverside, Chester-le-Street, Co Durham
DH3 3QR • Tel: 0191 387 1717 • Fax: 0191 387 1616 • Email:
marketing@durham-ccc.org.uk • Web: www.durham-ccc.org.uk

**First XI Coach**: M.D.Moxon. **Captain**: J.J.B.Lewis. **Vice-Captain**: P.D.Collingwood.
**Overseas Players**: M.L.Love, D.Pretorius and (*early season*) J.Srinath. **2003 Beneficiary**:
None. **Scorer**: B.Hunt. ‡ New registration

*Durham initially awarded caps immediately their players joined the staff but revised this
policy in 1998 and now cap players on merit, past 'awards' having been nullified.*

**BRIDGE, Graeme** David (Southmoor S, Sunderland), b Sunderland 4 Sep 1980. 5'8".
RHB, SLA. Debut 1999. HS 49 v Derbys (Darlington) 2002. BB 6-84 v Hants (Chester-le-
St) 2001. Awards: CGT 1; BHC 1. LO HS 50* v Leics (Leicester) 2002 (BHC). LO BB 3-22
v Worcs (Worcester) 2002 (NL).

**‡COETZER, Kyle** James, b Aberdeen, Scotland 14 Apr 1984. RHB, RMF. Scotland U-19.
W Province squad. Durham Academy – awaiting f-c debut.

**COLLINGWOOD, Paul** David (Blackfyne CS; Derwentside C), b Shotley Bridge 26 May
1976. 5'11". RHB, RMF. Debut 1996 v Northants (Chester-le-St) taking wicket of D.J.Capel
with his first ball before scoring 91 and 16; cap 1998. **LOI**: 38 (2001 to 2002-03); HS 100 v
SL (Perth) 2002-03; BB 4-38 v NZ (Napier) 2001-02. 1000 (1): 1108 (2001). HS 190 v SL
(Chester-le-St) 2002. CC HS 153 v Warwks (Birmingham) 2001. BB 4-31 v Derbys (Derby)
2002. Awards: BHC 4. LO HS 118* v Notts (Chester-le-St) 2002 (NL). LO BB 4-31 v Yorks
(Chester-le-St) 2000 (BHC).

**DAVIES, Anthony** Mark (Northfield CS, Billingham), b Stockton-on-Tees 4 Oct 1980. 6'2".
RHB. RM. Debut 2002. HS 33 v Derbys (Darlington) 2002. BB 5-61 v Glam (Chester-le-St)
2002. LO HS 31* v Warwks (Chester-le-St) 2002 (NL). LO BB 4-13 v Sussex (Chester-le-
St) 2001 (NL).

**GOUGH, Michael** Andrew (English Martyrs CS; Hartlepool SFC), b Hartlepool 18 Dec
1979. Son of M.P.Gough (Durham 1974-77). 6'5". RHB, OB. Debut 1998. Tours (Eng A):
NZ 1999-00; B 1999-00. HS 123 v CU (Cambridge) 1998. CC HS 103 v Essex (Colchester)
2002. BB 5-66 v Middx (Chester-le-St) 2001. Award: CGT 1. LO HS 132 v Wales MC
(Cardiff) 2002 (Durham CGT record). LO BB 3-26 v Somerset (Chester-le-St) 2002 (NL).

**HARMISON, Stephen** James (Ashington HS), b Ashington, Northumb 23 Oct 1978. 6'4".
RHB, RF. Debut 1996; cap 1999. Northumberland 1996. **Tests**: 5 (2002 to 2002-03); HS
20* v A (Sydney) 2002-03; BB 3-57 v I (Nottingham) 2002 – on debut. **LOI**: 5 (2002-03);
HS 7; BB 2-39 v SL (Brisbane) 2002-03. Tours: A 2002-03; SA 1998-99 (Eng A); Z
1998-99 (Eng A). HS 36 v Kent (Canterbury) 1998. 50 wkts (2): most – 64 (1999). BB
6-111 v Sussex (Chester-le-St) 2001. LO HS 11* v Glam (Chester-le-St) 2001 (NL). LO BB
4-43 v Glam (Cardiff) 2001 (NL).

**HATCH, Nicholas** Guy (Barnard Castle S; Hull U), b Darlington 21 Apr 1979. 6'7". RHB, RMF. Debut 2001. HS 24 v Sussex (Chester-le-St) 2002. BB 4-61 v Worcs (Chester-le-St) 2002. LO HS 20* v Yorks (Chester-le-St) 2002 (NL). LO BB 3-26 v Glam (Chester-le-St) 2001 (NL).

**HUNTER, Ian** David (Fyndoune Community C, Sacriston; Durham New C), b Durham City 11 Sep 1979. 6'1". RHB, RMF. Debut 2000. HS 65 v Northants (Northampton) 2002. BB 4-55 v Warwks (Birmingham) 2001. LO HS 39 v Leics (Leicester) 2002 (BHC). LO BB 4-29 v Essex (Ilford) 2000 (NL).

**KILLEEN, Neil** (Greencroft CS; Derwentside C; Teesside U), b Shotley Bridge 17 Oct 1975. 6'2". RHB, RFM. Debut 1995; cap 1999. HS 48 v Somerset (Chester-le-St) 1995. 50 wkts (1): 58 (1999). BB 7-85 v Leics (Leicester) 1999. Award: BHC 1. LO HS 32 v Middx (Lord's) 1996 (SL). LO BB 6-31 v Derbys (Derby) 2000 (NL).

**LAW, Danny** Richard (Steyning GS), b Lambeth, London 15 Jul 1975. 6'5". RHB, RFM. Sussex 1993-96; cap 1996. Essex 1997-2000. Durham debut/cap 2001. HS 115 Sx v Young A (Hove) 1995. Du HS 103 v Hants (Chester-le-St) 2001. BB 6-53 v Hants (Southampton) 2001. Hat-trick (Ex) 1998. LO HS 82 Ex v Durham (Chelmsford) 1997 (SL). LO BB 3-26 Ex v Leics (Leicester) 1999 (NL).

**LEWIS, Jonathan** James Benjamin (King Edward VI S, Chelmsford; Roehampton IHE), b Isleworth, Middx 21 May 1970. 5'9½". RHB, RSM. Essex 1990-96; cap 1994; scored 116* on debut v Surrey (Oval). Durham debut 1997; cap 1998; captain 2000 (*part*) to date. 1000 runs (3); most – 1252 (1997). HS 210* v OU (Oxford) 1997 – on Du debut. CC HS 160* v Derbys (Chester-le-St) 1997. BB 1-73. Award: BHC 1. LO HS 102 v Glos (Cheltenham) 1997 (NL).

**LOVE, Martin** Lloyd (Toowoomba GS; Queensland U), b Mundubbera, Queensland, Australia 30 Mar 1974. 6'1". RHB, OB. Queensland 1992-93 to date. Durham debut/cap 2001. **Tests** (A): 2 (2002-03); HS 62* v E (Melbourne) 2002-03 – on debut. Tour: E 1995 (Young A). 1000 (1+2): most – 1364 (2001). HS 251 v Middx (Lord's) 2002. BB 1-5 (Q). LO HS 127* Q v NSW (Brisbane) 2001-02.

**MANN, Christopher** (Boldon CS; South Tyneside C), b South Shields 14 Apr 1981. 6'0". RHB, RM. Former Durham Academy. Staff 2002 – awaiting f-c debut. LO HS (Durham CB) 7 (CGT).

**MUCHALL, Gordon** James (Durham S), b Newcastle upon Tyne, Northumb 2 Nov 1982. 6'1". RHB, RM. Northumberland 1999-2001. England U-19 and former Durham Academy player. Debut 2002. HS 127 v Middx (Lord's) 2002. BB 2-52 v Northants (Chester-le-St) 2002. LO HS 81 v Somerset (Chester-le-St) 2002 (NL).

**MUSTARD, Philip** (Usworth CS), b Sunderland 8 Oct 1982. 5'11". LHB, WK. Former Durham Academy. Debut 2002 – awaiting CC debut. HS 75 v SL (Chester-le-St) 2002 – on debut. LO HS (Durham CB) 8 (NWT).

**PATTISON, Ian** (Seaham CS), b Ryhope, Sunderland 5 May 1982. 5'10". RHB, RM. Debut 2002. HS 27 v Glos (Bristol) 2002. BB 3-41 v Essex (Chester-le-St) 2002. LO HS 48* and LO BB 1-25 Durham CB v Leics CB (Gateshead) 2000 (NWT).

**PENG** GILLENDER, Nicky (Newcastle upon Tyne RGS), b Newcastle upon Tyne, Northumb 18 Sep 1982. 6'2". RHB, OB. Debut 2000. Cap 2001. HS 108 v Derbys (Derby) 2002. Scored 98 v Surrey (Chester-le-St) on debut. Award: CGT 1. LO HS 121 v Worcs (Worcester) 2001 (NL).

**PHILLIPS, Nicholas** Charles (Wm Parker S, Hastings), b Pembury, Kent 10 May 1974. 5'10½". RHB, OB. Sussex 1993-97. Durham debut 1998; cap 2001. HS 53 Sx v Young A (Hove) 1995. CC HS 58* v Essex (Colchester) 2002. BB 6-97 (12-268 match) v Glam (Cardiff) 1999. Took 3-0 v Derbys (Darlington) 2002. Award: CGT 1. LO HS 38* Sx v Essex (Chelmsford) 1996 (SL). LO BB 4-13 v Derbys (Chester-le-St) 1999 (NL).

**PRATT, Andrew** (Willington Parkside CS; Durham New C), b Helmington Row, Crook 4 Mar 1975. Elder brother of G.J.Pratt. 6'0". LHB, WK. Debut 1997. Cap 2001. MCC YC. HS 93 v Glos (Chester-le-St) 2002. LO HS 86 v Derbys (Chester-le-St) 2001 (NL).

**PRATT, Gary** Joseph (Willington Parkside CS), b Bishop Auckland 22 Dec 1981. Younger brother of A.Pratt. 5'11". LHB, OB. Debut 2000. HS 78 v Northants (Northampton) 2002. LO HS 89 v Wales MC (Cardiff) 2002 (CGT).

‡**PRETORIUS, Dewald** (Hoerskool Dr Viljoen), b Pretoria, SA 6 Dec 1977. RHB, RF. Free State 1997-98 to date. **Tests** (SA): 1 (2001-02); HS 5* and BB 1-60 v A (Cape Town) 2001-02. Tour (SA A): Sc/Ire 1999. HS 43 FS v WP (Bloemfontein) 1998-99. BB 6-49 SA A v Ind A (Bloemfontein) 2001-02. LO HS (FS) 7*. LO BB 4-39 FS v GW (Kimberley) 1999-00.

**SCOTT, Gary** Michael (Hetton CS), b Sunderland 21 Jul 1984. 6'0". RHB, OB. Debut 2001 – youngest Durham f-c debutant (17y 19d). No appearances 2002. HS 25 v Derbys (Chester-le-St) 2001 – on debut. LO HS 100 Durham CB v Herefords (Darlington) 2002 (CGT). LO BB 2-32 Durham CB v Bucks (Beaconsfield) 2001 (CGT).

‡**SRINATH, Javagal**, b Mysore, India 31 Aug 1969. 6'3". RHB, RFM. Karnataka 1989-90 to date. Gloucestershire 1995 (cap 1995). Leicestershire 2002; cap 2002. **Tests** (I): 67 (1991-92 to 2002-03); HS 76 v NZ (Hamilton) 1998-99; BB 8-86 (13-132 match) v P (Calcutta) 1998-99. **LOI** (I): 229 (1991-92 to 2002-03; HS 53 v SA (Rajkot) 1996-97; BB 5-23 v B (Dhaka) 1997-98. Tours (I): E 1996; A 1991-92, 1999-00; SA 1992-93, 1996-97, 2001-02; WI 2002; NZ 1993-94, 1998-99; SL 1993-94, 2001; Z 1992-93, 1998-99, 2001; B 2000-01. HS 76 (see Tests). UK HS 52 Le v Yorks (Scarborough) 2002. 50 wkts (1): 87 (1995). BB 9-76 (13-150 match) Gs v Glam (Abergavenny) 1995. Hat-trick Le v Surrey (Oval) 2002. Awards: BHC 2. LO HS 53 (see LOI). LO BB 5-23 (see LOI).

**THORPE, Ashley** Michael (Kent Street Senior HS, Western Australia), b Kiama, NSW, Australia 2 Apr 1975. 5'11". LHB, RM. Qualified by residence. Debut 2002. HS 95 v Essex (Chester-le-St) 2002. LO HS 53 v Notts (Nottingham) 2002 (NL). LO BB 2-49 v Leics (Leicester) 2002 (NL).

‡**WELLS, Vincent** John (Sir William Nottidge S, Whitstable), b Dartford, Kent 6 Aug 1965. 6'0". RHB, RMF. Kent 1988-91. Leicestershire 1992-2002; cap 1994; captain 2000-02; benefit 2001. Durham staff 2003. **LOI**: 9 (1998-99); HS 39 v A (Sydney) 1998-99; BB 3-30 v A (Sydney) 1998-99. Tour (Le): SA 1996-97. 1000 runs (2); most – 1331 (1996). HS 224 Le v Middx (Lord's) 1997. BB 5-18 Le v Notts (Worksop) 1998. Hat-trick 1994. Awards: CGT 4; BHC 1. LO HS 201 Le v Berks (Leicester) 1996 (NWT). LO BB 6-25 Le v Minor C (Leicester) 1998 (BHC).

## RELEASED/RETIRED
(Having made a first-class County appearance in 2002)

**BROWN, Simon** John Emmerson (Boldon CS; S Tyneside Marine & TC), b Cleadon 29 Jun 1969. 6'3". RHB, LFM. Northamptonshire 1987-90. Durham 1992-2002; captain 1996 (part); cap 1998; benefit 2001. **Tests**: 1 (1996); HS 10* and BB 1-60 v P (Lord's) 1996. HS 69 v Leics (Durham) 1994. 50 wkts (7); most – 79 (1996). BB 7-51 v Lancs (Chester-le-St) 2000. Awards: CGT 1; BHC 3. LO HS 18 v Derbys (Derby) 1996 (SL). LO BB 6-30 v Northants (Chester-le-St) 1997 (BHC).

**DALEY, James** Arthur (Hetton CS), b Sunderland 24 Sep 1973. 5'10". RHB, RM. Durham 1992-2002; cap 1999. MCC YC. HS 159* v Hants (Portsmouth) 1994. BB 1-12. LO HS 105 v Surrey (Oval) 2000 (NL).

**HODGE, B.J.** – see LEICESTERSHIRE.

**SYMINGTON, Marc** Joseph (St Michaels S, Billingham; Stockton SFC), b Newcastle upon Tyne, Northumb 10 Jan 1980. 5'8". RHB, RM. Durham 1998-2002. HS 42 v Northants (Northampton) 2002. BB 4-27 v SL (Chester-le-St) 2002. CC BB 3-43 v Worcs (Chester-le-St) 2002. LO HS 34 v Glos (Bristol) 2002 (CGT). LO BB 2-11 v Worcs (Worcester) 2002 (NL).

J.E.Brinkley left the staff having made no f-c appearances in 2002.

# DURHAM 2002

## RESULTS SUMMARY

| | | Place | Won | Lost | Tied | Drew | No Result |
|---|---|---|---|---|---|---|---|
| **County Championship** (2nd Division) | | **9th** | 1 | 11 | | 4 | |
| **All First-Class Matches** | | | 1 | 11 | | 6 | |
| **C & G Trophy** | | 4th Round | | | | | |
| **Benson & Hedges Cup** | | 5th in North Division | | | | | |
| **NU National League** (1st Division) | | **8th** | 5 | 11 | | | |

## COUNTY CHAMPIONSHIP AVERAGES

### BATTING AND FIELDING

| Cap | | M | I | NO | HS | Runs | Avge | 100 | 50 | Ct/St |
|---|---|---|---|---|---|---|---|---|---|---|
| 2001 | M.L.Love | 6 | 8 | 1 | 251 | 576 | 82.28 | 2 | 2 | 3 |
| | M.A.Gough | 8 | 14 | 2 | 103 | 616 | 51.33 | 1 | 3 | 6 |
| 1998 | P.D.Collingwood | 5 | 9 | – | 99 | 371 | 41.22 | – | 3 | 4 |
| | B.J.Hodge | 4 | 8 | – | 73 | 284 | 35.50 | – | 2 | 3 |
| 2001 | D.R.Law | 5 | 8 | 1 | 72* | 227 | 32.42 | – | 2 | 1 |
| | G.J.Pratt | 14 | 24 | – | 78 | 713 | 29.70 | – | 4 | 9 |
| 1999 | J.A.Daley | 2 | 4 | 1 | 59* | 85 | 28.33 | – | 1 | – |
| | G.J.Muchall | 14 | 24 | – | 127 | 544 | 22.66 | 1 | 2 | 12 |
| 2001 | N.Peng | 10 | 18 | – | 108 | 384 | 21.33 | 1 | 1 | 8 |
| 2001 | N.C.Phillips | 9 | 15 | 5 | 58* | 211 | 21.10 | – | 1 | 4 |
| | A.M.Thorpe | 6 | 12 | – | 95 | 242 | 20.16 | – | 2 | 3 |
| 2001 | A.Pratt | 16 | 27 | 1 | 93 | 523 | 20.11 | – | 3 | 40/3 |
| 1998 | J.J.B.Lewis | 9 | 15 | – | 71 | 289 | 19.26 | – | 2 | 2 |
| | I.D.Hunter | 7 | 11 | 1 | 65 | 188 | 18.80 | – | 1 | 2 |
| | M.J.Symington | 9 | 15 | 2 | 42 | 216 | 16.61 | – | – | 6 |
| | G.D.Bridge | 9 | 14 | 2 | 49 | 163 | 13.58 | – | – | 4 |
| | A.M.Davies | 13 | 23 | 7 | 33 | 171 | 10.68 | – | – | 3 |
| | I.Pattison | 3 | 6 | – | 27 | 61 | 10.16 | – | – | – |
| 1999 | N.Killeen | 14 | 21 | 4 | 23 | 151 | 8.88 | – | – | 5 |
| 1999 | S.J.Harmison | 9 | 17 | 3 | 19* | 85 | 6.07 | – | – | 4 |

*Also played*: S.J.E.Brown (1 match – cap 1998) did not bat; N.G.Hatch (3) 1*, 5, 0 (1 ct).

### BOWLING

| | O | M | R | W | Avge | Best | 5wI | 10wM |
|---|---|---|---|---|---|---|---|---|
| A.M.Davies | 336.5 | 95 | 910 | 33 | 27.57 | 5- 61 | 1 | – |
| N.C.Phillips | 169 | 36 | 581 | 20 | 29.05 | 4-103 | – | – |
| N.Killeen | 366.1 | 100 | 1084 | 35 | 30.97 | 4- 26 | – | – |
| S.J.Harmison | 257.4 | 57 | 836 | 26 | 32.15 | 5- 65 | 1 | – |
| G.D.Bridge | 233.5 | 60 | 709 | 19 | 37.31 | 4- 50 | – | – |
| I.D.Hunter | 180 | 37 | 665 | 17 | 39.11 | 3- 62 | – | – |
| M.J.Symington | 124 | 21 | 525 | 13 | 40.38 | 3- 43 | – | – |

*Also bowled*:
P.D.Collingwood 83.4 17 231 8 28.87 4- 31 – –
N.G.Hatch 96 22 318 6 53.00 4- 61 – –
S.J.E.Brown 18.4-3-65-2; M.A.Gough 41-9-132-2; B.J.Hodge 22.4-4-102-1; D.R.Law 66-13-272-4; G.J.Muchall 35.6-158-3; I.Pattison 35-9-159-4; G.J.Pratt 1.3-0-8-0.

The First-Class Averages (pp 121-135) give the records of Durham players in all first-class county matches (Durham's other opponents being the Sri Lankans and Durham UCCE), with the exception of:
 S.J.Harmison 10-17-3-19*-85-6.07-0-0-4ct. 275.2-63-881-28-31.46-5/65-1-0.

# DURHAM RECORDS

## FIRST-CLASS CRICKET

| | | | | | | |
|---|---|---|---|---|---|---|
| **Highest Total** | For 645-6d | | v | Middlesex | Lord's | 2002 |
| | V 810-4d | | by | Warwicks | Birmingham | 1994 |
| **Lowest Total** | For 67 | | v | Middlesex | Lord's | 1996 |
| | V 67 | | by | Durham UCCE | Chester-le-St[2] | 2001 |
| **Highest Innings** | For 251 | M.L.Love | v | Middlesex | Lord's | 2002 |
| | V 501* | B.C.Lara | for | Warwicks | Birmingham | 1994 |

### Highest Partnership for each Wicket

| | | | | | | |
|---|---|---|---|---|---|---|
| 1st | 334* | S.Hutton/M.A.Roseberry | v | Oxford U | Oxford | 1996 |
| 2nd | 258 | J.J.B.Lewis/M.L.Love | v | Notts | Chester-le-St[2] | 2001 |
| 3rd | 205 | G.Fowler/S.Hutton | v | Yorkshire | Leeds | 1993 |
| 4th | 204 | J.J.B.Lewis/J.Boiling | v | Derbyshire | Chester-le-St[2] | 1997 |
| 5th | 185 | P.W.G.Parker/J.A.Daley | v | Warwicks | Darlington | 1993 |
| 6th | 193 | D.C.Boon/P.D.Collingwood | v | Warwicks | Birmingham | 1998 |
| 7th | 127 | D.R.Law/J.E.Brinkley | v | Hampshire | Chester-le-St[2] | 2001 |
| 8th | 134 | A.C.Cummins/D.A.Graveney | v | Warwicks | Birmingham | 1994 |
| 9th | 127 | D.G.C.Ligertwood/S.J.E.Brown | v | Surrey | Stockton | 1996 |
| 10th | 103 | M.M.Betts/D.M.Cox | v | Sussex | Hove | 1996 |

| | | | | | | |
|---|---|---|---|---|---|---|
| **Best Bowling** | For 9- 64 | M.M.Betts | v | Northants | Northampton | 1997 |
| **(Innings)** | V 8- 22 | D.Follett | for | Middlesex | Lord's | 1996 |
| **Best Bowling** | For 14-177 | A.Walker | v | Essex | Chelmsford | 1995 |
| **(Match)** | V 12- 68 | J.N.B.Bovill | for | Hampshire | Stockton | 1995 |

| | | | | |
|---|---|---|---|---|
| **Most Runs – Season** | 1536 | W.Larkins | (av 37.46) | 1992 |
| **Most Runs – Career** | 5670 | J.E.Morris | (av 32.77) | 1994-99 |
| **Most 100s – Season** | 4 | D.M.Jones | | 1992 |
| | 4 | W.Larkins | | 1992 |
| | 4 | J.E.Morris | | 1994 |
| **Most 100s – Career** | 14 | J.E.Morris | | 1994-99 |
| **Most Wkts – Season** | 77 | S.J.E.Brown | (av 25.87) | 1996 |
| **Most Wkts – Career** | 518 | S.J.E.Brown | (av 28.30) | 1992-2002 |
| **Most Career W-K Dismissals** | 195 | M.P.Speight | (190 ct; 5 st) | 1997-2001 |
| **Most Career Catches in the Field** | 92 | P.D.Collingwood | | 1996-2002 |

## LIMITED-OVERS CRICKET

| | | | | | | |
|---|---|---|---|---|---|---|
| **Highest Total** | CGT | 326-4 | v | Herefords | Chester-le-St[2] | 1995 |
| | BHC | 287-5 | v | Leics | Leicester | 1996 |
| | NL | 281-2 | v | Derbyshire | Durham | 1993 |
| **Lowest Total** | CGT | 82 | v | Worcs | Chester-le-St[1] | 1968 |
| | BHC | 133 | v | Glos | Bristol | 2001 |
| | NL | 72 | v | Warwicks | Birmingham | 2002 |
| **Highest Innings** | CGT | 132 M.A.Gough | v | Wales MC | Cardiff | 2002 |
| | BHC | 145 J.E.Morris | v | Leics | Leicester | 1996 |
| | NL | 131* W.Larkins | v | Hampshire | Portsmouth | 1994 |
| **Best Bowling** | CGT | 7-32 S.P.Davis | v | Lancashire | Chester-le-St[1] | 1983 |
| | BHC | 6-30 S.J.E.Brown | v | Northants | Chester-le-St[2] | 1997 |
| | NL | 6-31 N.Killeen | v | Derbyshire | Derby | 2000 |

[1] Chester-le-Street CC (Ropery Lane)  [2] Riverside Ground

# ESSEX

**Formation of Present Club**: 14 January 1876
**Colours**: Blue, Gold and Red
**Badge**: Three Seaxes above Scroll bearing 'Essex'
**County Champions**: (6) 1979, 1983, 1984, 1986, 1991, 1992
**Gillette/NatWest/C & G Trophy Winners**: (2) 1985, 1997
**Benson and Hedges Cup Winners**: (2) 1979, 1998
**National League (Div 1) Winners**: (0); best – 9th 1999
**Sunday League Winners**: (3) 1981, 1984, 1985
**Match Awards**: CGT 51; BHC 91

**Chief Executive**: D.E.East, County Ground, New Writtle Street, Chelmsford CM2 0PG • Tel: 01245 252420 • Fax: 01245 254030 • Email: administration.essex@ecb.co.uk • Web: www.essexcricket.org.uk

**First XI Coach**: G.A.Gooch. **Club Captain**: N.Hussain. **First XI Captain**: R.C.Irani. **Vice-Captain**: A.P.Grayson. **Overseas Players**: S.A.Brant and A.Flower. **2003 Beneficiary**: R.C.Irani. **Scorer**: D.J.Norris. ‡ New registration

**BISHOP, Justin** Edward (Bury St Edmunds County Upper S; John Snow C, Durham U), b Bury St Edmunds, Suffolk 4 Jan 1982. 6'0". LHB, LMF. Debut 1999. HS 23* v Worcs (Southend) 2002. BB 5-148 v Leics (Chelmsford) 2001. LO HS 16* v Hants (Colchester) 2000 (NL). LO BB 3-33 v Worcs (Worcester) 2001 (NL).

**BOPARA, Ravinder** Singh, b Forest Gate 4 May 1985. RHB, RM. Debut 2002. HS 48 v Durham (Colchester) 2002. BB 1-43 (not CC). LO HS (Essex CB) 1 (CGT).

**‡BRANT, Scott** Andrew, b Harare, Zimbabwe 26 Jan 1983. RHB, LFM. Queensland 2001-02 to date. HS 19* and BB 3-23 Q v Victoria (Brisbane) 2001-02. LO HS (Q) 1*. LO BB 3-33 Q v S Aus (Brisbane) 2002-03.

**CLARKE, Andrew** John (St Martin's S, Hutton), b Brentwood 9 Nov 1975. LHB, RM. MCC YC. Debut 2002. HS 31 v Worcs (Southend) 2002. BB 5-54 v Glam (Swansea) 2002 – on debut. LO HS 9 (CGT). LO BB 4-30 v Glos (Gloucester) 2002 (NL).

**COWAN, Ashley** Preston (Framlingham C), b Hitchin, Herts 7 May 1975. 6'4". RHB, RFM. Debut 1995; cap 1997. Cambridgeshire 1993. Tour: WI 1997-98. HS 94 v Leics (Leicester) 1998. 50 wkts (1): 52 (1997). BB 6-47 v Glam (Cardiff) 1999. Hat-trick 1996. Award: BHC 1. LO HS 45 v Middx (Chelmsford) 2001 (BHC). LO BB 5-14 v Middx (Southgate) 2001 (NL). Expected to miss 2003 season following knee surgery.

**DAKIN, Jonathan** Michael (King Edward VII S, Johannesburg) b Hitchin, Herts 28 Feb 1973. 6'4". LHB, RM. Leicestershire 1993-2001; cap 2000. Essex debut 2002. Tour (Le): SA 1996-97. HS 190 Le v Northants (Northampton) 1997. Ex HS 57 v Northants (Northampton) 2002. BB 4-17 v Middx (Chelmsford) 2002. Awards: CGT 1; BHC 1. LO HS 179 Le v Wales MC (Swansea) 2001 (CGT). LO BB 5-30 Le v Kent (Leicester) 1999 (NL).

**‡DENNING, Nicholas** Alexander (Bradfield C; Cheltenham C), b Ascot, Berks 3 Oct 1978. RHB, RFM. Essex staff 2003. Berkshire 1999-2002. MCCYC. Awaiting f-c debut. LO HS (Berks) 1* (CGT). LO BB 3-22 Berks v Ire (Finchampstead) 2002 (CGT)

**FLOWER, Andrew** (Wainona HS, Harare), b Cape Town, SA 28 Apr 1968. 5'10". Elder brother of G.W.Flower (Zimbabwe). LHB, WK, occ RM. Mashonaland 1986-87 to date. MCC 1996-99. *Wisden* 2001. Essex debut/cap 2002. Joins S Australia 2003-04. **Tests** (Z): 63 (1992-93 to 2002-03, 20 as captain); HS 232* v I (Nagpur) 2000-01. **LOI** (Z): 213 (1991-92 to 2002-03, 52 as captain); HS 145 v I (Colombo) 2002-03; scored 115 v SL (New Plymouth) on debut. Tours (Z) (C=captain): E 2000C; SA 1999-00; WI 1999-00C; NZ 1995-96C, 1997-98, 2000-01; I 1992-93, 2000-01, 2001-02; P 1993-94C, 1996-97, 1998-99; SL 1996-97, 1997-98, 2001-02; B 2001-02. 1000 (1): 1151 (2002). HS 232* (*see Tests*). Ex HS 172* v Glam (Chelmsford) 2002. BB 1-1. Awards: BHC 2. LO HS 142* (*see LOI*).

**FOSTER, James** Savin (Forest S, Snaresbrook; Collingwood C, Durham U), b Whipps Cross 15 Apr 1980. 6'0". RHB, WK. British U 2000. Essex debut 2000; cap 2001. Durham UCCE 2001. British U 2001. **ECB Contract 2002. Tests**: 7 (2001-02 to 2002-03); HS 48 v I (Bangalore) 2001-02. **LOI**: 11 (2001-02); HS 13 v I (Bombay) 2001-02. Tours: A 2002-03; WI 2000-01 (Eng A); NZ 2001-02; I 2001-02. HS 103 DU v Worcs (Worcester) 2001. Ex HS 79 v Northants (Northampton) 2001. LO HS 56* v Sussex (Hove) 2001 (NL).

**GRANT, Joseph** Benjamin (Petersvale All-Age S, Jamaica), b White House, Jamaica 17 Dec 1967. 5'11". RHB, RFM. Jamaica 1990-91 to 1995-96. Essex debut 2001. Cambridgeshire 2001. HS 36* Jamaica v Guyana (Albion) 1994-95. Ex HS 30 v I (Chelmsford) 2002. CC HS 15 v Durham (Colchester) 2002. BB 5-38 v CU (Cambridge) 2002. CC BB 4-45 v Derbys (Derby) 2002. LO HS 14 Jamaica v Trinidad (Port-of-Spain) 1991-92. LO BB 3-10 Jamaica v Trinidad (Kingston) 1990-91.

**GRAYSON, Adrian Paul** (Bedale CS), b Ripon, Yorks 31 Mar 1971. 6'1". RHB, SLA. Yorkshire 1990-95. Essex debut/cap 1996. **LOI**: 1 (2001-02); HS 6 and BB 3-40 v Z (Bulawayo) 2001-02. Tour: SA 1991-92 (Y). 1000 runs (4); most – 1275 (1995). HS 189 v Glam (Chelmsford) 2001. BB 5-20 v Yorks (Scarborough) 2001. Award: BHC 1. LO HS 82* v Worcs (Chelmsford) 1997 (NWT). LO BB 4-25 Y v Glam (Cardiff) 1994 (SL).

**HABIB, Aftab** (Millfield S; Taunton S), b Reading, Berkshire 7 Feb 1972. Cousin of Zahid Sadiq (Surrey and Derbys 1988-90). 5'11". RHB, RM. Middlesex 1992 (one match). Leicestershire 1995-2001; cap 1998. Essex debut 2002. **Tests**: 2 (1999); HS 19 v NZ (Lord's) 1999. Tours (Eng A): WI 2000-01 (part); NZ 1999-00; B 1999-00. 1000 runs (2); most – 1055 (1999). HS 215 Le v Worcs (Leicester) 1996. Ex HS 123 v Durham (Chester-le-St) 2002. Award: BHC 1. LO HS 111 Le v Durham (Chester-le-St) 1997 (BHC). LO BB 2-5 Le v Ire (Dublin) 1999.

**HUSSAIN, Nasser** (Forest S, Snaresbrook; Durham U), b Madras, India 28 Mar 1968. Son of J.Hussain (Madras 1966-67); brother of M.Hussain (Worcs 1985). 5'11". RHB, LB. Debut 1987; cap 1989; captain 1999; club captain 2000 to date; benefit 1999. YC 1989. OBE 2002. **ECB contracts 2000, 2001, 2002, 2003. Tests**: 81 (1989-90 to 2002-03, 42 as captain); HS 207 v A (Birmingham) 1997. **LOI**: 88 (1989-90 to 2002-03, 56 as captain – E record); HS 115 v I (Lord's) 2002. Tours (C=captain): A 1998-99, 2002-03C; SA 1999-00C; WI 1989-90, 1991-92 (Eng A), 1993-94, 1997-98; NZ 1996-97, 2001-02C; I 2001-02C; P 1990-91 (Eng A), 1995-96C (Eng A), 2000-01C; SL 1990-91 (Eng A), 2000-01C; Z 1996-97. 1000 runs (5); most – 1854 (1995). HS 207 (*see Tests*). Ex HS 197 v Surrey (Oval) 1990. BB 1-38. Awards: CGT 4; BHC 4. LO HS 136* v Yorks (Chelmsford) 2002 (BHC).

**HYAM, Barry** James (Havering SFC; Westminster C), b Romford 9 Sep 1975. RHB, WK. Debut 1993; cap 1999. MCC YC. HS 63 v Glam (Chelmsford) 2001. LO HS 37 v Leics (Leicester) 1999 (NL).

**IRANI, Ronald Charles** (Smithills CS, Bolton), b Leigh, Lancs 26 Oct 1971. 6'3". RHB, RMF. Lancashire 1990-93. Essex debut/cap 1994; captain 2000 to date; benefit 2003. **Tests**: 3 (1996 to 1999); HS 41 v I (Lord's) 1996; BB 1-22. Took wicket of M.Azharuddin with his fifth ball in Test cricket. **LOI**: 31 (1996 to 2002-03); HS 53 and BB 5-26 v I (Oval) 2002. Tours: NZ 1996-97, 1999-00 (Eng A); P 1995-96 (Eng A); Z 1996-97; B 1999-00 (Eng A). 1000 runs (5); most – 1196 (2000). HS 207* v Northants (Ilford) 2002. 50 wkts (1): 51 (1999). BB 6-71 v Notts (Nottingham) 2002. Awards: CGT 5; BHC 5. LO HS 124 v Durham (Chelmsford) 1996 (NWT). LO BB 5-26 (*see LOI*).

**JEFFERSON, William** Ingleby (Beeston Hall S, Norfolk; Oundle S; St Hild & St Bede C, Durham U), b Derby 25 Oct 1979. Son of R.I.Jefferson (Cambridge U and Surrey 1961-66); grandson of J.Jefferson (Army 1919, Comb Services 1922). 6'9½". RHB, RMF. British U 2000-01. Essex debut 2000; cap 2002. Durham UCCE 2001. Scored 50 and 65 in first two l-o innings. HS 165* v Yorks (Chelmsford) 2002. LO HS 111* v Middx (Lord's) 2002 (NL).

**‡McCOUBREY, Adrian** George Agustus Mathew, b Ballymena, Co Antrim, Ireland 3 Apr 1980. RHB, RFM. Ireland debut 1999. Essex staff 2003. HS 1* and BB 3-38 Ire v Scot (Belfast) 1999 – on debut. LO HS 11 Ire v Berks (Finchampstead) 2002. LO BB 2-20 Ire v Wilts (Salisbury) 2001.

**McGARRY, Andrew** Charles (King Edward VI GS, Chelmsford; SE Essex C of Arts & Technology, Southend), b Basildon 8 Nov 1981. 6'5". RHB, RFM. Debut 1999. HS 11* v CU (Cambridge) 2002. CC HS 5*. BB 3-29 v Worcs (Chelmsford) 2000. LO HS 1 (NL). LO BB 2-20 v Surrey (Colchester) 2000 (NL).

**MIDDLEBROOK, James** Daniel (Pudsey Crawshaw S), b Leeds, Yorks 13 May 1977. 6'1". RHB, OB. Yorkshire 1998-2001. Essex debut 2002. HS 84 Y v Essex (Chelmsford) 2001. Ex HS 67 v Northants (Northampton) 2002. BB 6-82 (10-170 match) Y v Hants (Southampton) 2000 – including 4 wkts in 5 balls. Ex BB 4-38 v Durham (Chester-le-St) 2002. LO HS 19 and LO BB 4-33 v Hants (Southend) 2002 (NL).

**NAPIER, Graham** Richard (The Gilberd S, Colchester), b Colchester 6 Jan 1980. 5'9½". RHB, RM. Debut 1997. HS 104 v CU (Cambridge) 2001. CC HS 56 v Somerset (Chelmsford) 2001. BB 3-47 v Durham (Colchester) 2002. Award: CGT 1. LO HS 79 Essex CB v Lancs CB (Chelmsford) 2000 (NWT). LO BB 6-29 v Worcs (Chelmsford) 2001 (NL).

**PETTINI, Mark** Lewis (Comberton Village C; Hills Road SFC, Cambridge), b Brighton, Sussex 7 Aug 1983. RHB, RM. 5'10". Debut 2001. HS 64 v Durham (Colchester) 2002. LO 75 v Glos (Gloucester) 2002 (NL).

**PHILLIPS, Timothy** James (Felsted S; St Hild & St Bede C, Durham U), b Cambridge 13 Mar 1981. 6'1". LHB, SLA. Debut 1999. Durham UCCE 2001. HS 75 DU v Durham (Chester-le-St) 2002. Ex HS 42 and CC BB 4-102 v Middx (Southgate) 2002. BB 4-42 v SL A (Chelmsford) 1999 – on debut. LO HS 6 (NL). LO BB 2-36 v Middx (Chelmsford) 2002 (NL).

**ROBINSON, Darren** David John (Tabor HS, Braintree; Chelmsford CFE), b Braintree 2 Mar 1973. 5'10½". RHB, RMF. Debut 1993; cap 1997. 1000 (1): 1474 (2002). HS 200 v NZ (Chelmsford) 1999. CC HS 175 v Glos (Gloucester) 2002. Awards: BHC 2. LO HS 137* v Sussex (Hove) 1998 (BHC). LO BB 1-7 (SL).

**SHARIF, Zoheb** Khalid (Warwick S; Chigwell S; Coopers Co & Coborn S), b Leytonstone 22 Feb 1983. LHB, LB. 5'10". Debut 2001. HS 42 v Glos (Gloucester) 2002. BB 4-98 v Northants (Northampton) 2002. No l-o appearances.

**STEPHENSON, John** Patrick (Felsted S; Durham U), b Stebbing 14 Mar 1965. 6'1". RHB, RM. Essex 1985-94 and 2002 (2nd XI captain 2002 to date); cap 1989. Hampshire 1995-2001; cap 1995; captain 1996-97; benefit 2001. Boland 1988-89. **Tests**: 1 (1989); HS 25 v A (Oval) 1989. Tours: WI 1991-92 (Eng A); Z 1989-90 (Eng A). 1000 runs (5); most – 1887 (1990). HS 202* v Somerset (Bath) 1990. BB 7-44 (10-104 match) v Worcs (Worcester) 2002. Awards: CGT 1; BHC 5. LO HS 142 v Warwks (Birmingham) 1991 (BHC). LO BB 6-33 H v Worcs (Southampton) 1997 (SL).

### RELEASED/RETIRED
(Having made a first-class County appearance in 2002)

**CLINTON, Richard** Selvey (Colfes S), b Sidcup, Kent 1 Sep 1981. Son of G.S.Clinton (Kent and Surrey 1974-90). 6'3". LHB, RM. Kent staff 1999-2000 – no f-c appearances. Essex 2001-02. HS 107 v CU (Cambridge) 2002. CC HS 58* v Surrey (Ilford) 2001 – on debut. BB 2-30 v A (Chelmsford) 2001. CC BB – . LO HS 56 v Durham (Ilford) 2001 (NL).

**ILOTT, Mark** Christopher (Francis Combe SMS, Garston), b Watford, Herts 27 Aug 1970. 6'0½". LHB, LFM. Essex 1988-2002; cap 1993; benefit 2002. Hertfordshire 1987-88 (at 16, the youngest to represent that county). **Tests**: 5 (1993 to 1995-96); HS 15 v A (Oval) 1993; BB 3-48 v SA (Durban) 1995-96. Tours: A 1992-93 (Eng A); SA 1993-94 (Eng A), 1995-96; I 1994-95 (Eng A – *part*); SL 1990-91 (Eng A). HS 60 Eng A v Warwks (Birmingham) 1995. Ex HS 54 v Worcs (Worcester) 1996. 50 wkts (6); most – 78 (1995). BB 9-19 (14-105 match; inc hat-trick – all lbw) v Northants (Luton) 1995. Hat-trick 1995. Awards: BHC 2. LO HS 56* v Sussex (Hove) 1995 (SL). LO BB 5-21 v Scot (Forfar) 1993 (BHC).

**RELEASED/RETIRED** continued on p 32

# ESSEX 2002

## RESULTS SUMMARY

| | | Place | Won | Lost | Tied | Drew | No Result |
|---|---|---|---|---|---|---|---|
| County Championship | (2nd Division) | **1st** | 10 | 3 | | 3 | |
| All First-Class Matches | | | 11 | 3 | | 4 | |
| C & G Trophy | | Quarter-Finalist | | | | | |
| Benson & Hedges Cup | | Finalist | | | | | |
| NU National League | (2nd Division) | **3rd** | 10 | 6 | | | |

## COUNTY CHAMPIONSHIP AVERAGES

### BATTING AND FIELDING

| Cap | | M | I | NO | HS | Runs | Avge | 100 | 50 | Ct/St |
|---|---|---|---|---|---|---|---|---|---|---|
| 1994 | R.C.Irani | 10 | 17 | 3 | 207* | 920 | 65.71 | 3 | 1 | – |
| 2002 | A.Flower | 14 | 25 | 5 | 172* | 1048 | 52.40 | 2 | 5 | 32/1 |
| 1997 | D.D.J.Robinson | 16 | 31 | 1 | 175 | 1289 | 42.96 | 4 | 5 | 15 |
| | A.Habib | 14 | 24 | 3 | 123 | 900 | 42.85 | 2 | 7 | 9 |
| 2002 | W.I.Jefferson | 12 | 24 | 4 | 165* | 783 | 39.15 | 2 | 2 | 14 |
| 1989 | J.P.Stephenson | 13 | 24 | 8 | 100* | 562 | 35.12 | 1 | 2 | 7 |
| | M.L.Pettini | 3 | 6 | – | 64 | 157 | 26.16 | – | 2 | 2 |
| 1996 | A.P.Grayson | 6 | 8 | – | 83 | 204 | 25.50 | – | 1 | 5 |
| 1997 | A.P.Cowan | 9 | 13 | 1 | 60* | 293 | 24.41 | – | 2 | 6 |
| | J.M.Dakin | 12 | 16 | 2 | 57 | 300 | 21.42 | – | 1 | 1 |
| 1993 | M.C.Ilott | 5 | 4 | 2 | 28 | 42 | 21.00 | – | – | 4 |
| | T.J.Phillips | 4 | 7 | 2 | 42 | 105 | 21.00 | – | – | 4 |
| | G.R.Napier | 9 | 13 | 2 | 54* | 230 | 20.90 | – | 1 | 6 |
| 2001 | J.S.Foster | 4 | 4 | – | 36 | 80 | 20.00 | – | – | 9/1 |
| | J.D.Middlebrook | 16 | 24 | 4 | 67 | 378 | 18.90 | – | 1 | 7 |
| | R.S.Bopara | 3 | 5 | – | 48 | 89 | 17.80 | – | – | 5 |
| | A.J.Clarke | 2 | 4 | 1 | 31 | 42 | 14.00 | – | – | 1 |
| | R.S.Clinton | 3 | 4 | 1 | 24 | 40 | 13.33 | – | – | 1 |
| | J.E.Bishop | 5 | 8 | 1 | 23* | 52 | 7.42 | – | – | 2 |
| | J.B.Grant | 9 | 11 | 4 | 15 | 34 | 4.85 | – | – | – |

*Also batted:* N.Hussain (1 match – cap 1989) 1, 4; A.C.McGarry (2) 5*, 0, 0 (1 ct); Z.K.Sharif (2) 42; M.E.Waugh (2 – cap 1989) 117, 49, 76 (4 ct).

### BOWLING

| | O | M | R | W | Avge | Best | 5wI | 10wM |
|---|---|---|---|---|---|---|---|---|
| R.C.Irani | 220.5 | 71 | 570 | 26 | 21.92 | 6- 71 | 1 | – |
| J.P.Stephenson | 295.4 | 59 | 1082 | 48 | 22.54 | 7- 44 | 1 | 1 |
| J.M.Dakin | 307.2 | 63 | 1048 | 38 | 27.57 | 4- 17 | – | – |
| A.P.Cowan | 255.1 | 60 | 817 | 29 | 28.17 | 5- 68 | 1 | – |
| G.R.Napier | 172 | 33 | 639 | 20 | 31.95 | 3- 47 | – | – |
| J.B.Grant | 196.1 | 26 | 898 | 25 | 35.92 | 4- 45 | – | – |
| J.E.Bishop | 113 | 16 | 449 | 11 | 40.81 | 3- 59 | – | – |
| M.C.Ilott | 150.5 | 38 | 469 | 11 | 42.63 | 2- 25 | – | – |
| T.J.Phillips | 113.1 | 16 | 472 | 11 | 42.90 | 4-102 | – | – |
| J.D.Middlebrook | 492.2 | 109 | 1463 | 33 | 44.33 | 4- 38 | – | – |
| *Also bowled:* | | | | | | | | |
| A.J.Clarke | 36.3 | 5 | 113 | 7 | 16.14 | 5- 54 | 1 | – |
| A.P.Grayson | 64.1 | 17 | 155 | 5 | 31.00 | 3- 39 | – | – |

R.S.Bopara 2-0-13-0; A.Flower 6-0-19-0; A.C.McGarry 33.5-7-136-0; D.D.J.Robinson 9-1-54-0; Z.K.Sharif 31-0-164-4; M.E.Waugh 4-1-14-0.

The First-Class Averages (pp 121-135) give the records of Essex players in all first-class county matches (Essex's other opponents being the Indians and Cambridge UCCE), with the exception of J.E.Bishop, N.Hussain and W.I.Jefferson whose full county figures are as above, and:

T.J.Phillips 5-8-2-42-113-18.83-0-0-6ct. 146.5-21-604-15-40.26-4/102.

# ESSEX RECORDS

## FIRST-CLASS CRICKET

| | | | | | | |
|---|---|---|---|---|---|---|
| **Highest Total** | For 761-6d | | v | Leics | Chelmsford | 1990 |
| | V 803-4d | | by | Kent | Brentwood | 1934 |
| **Lowest Total** | For 30 | | v | Yorkshire | Leyton | 1901 |
| | V 14 | | by | Surrey | Chelmsford | 1983 |
| **Highest Innings** | For 343* | P.A.Perrin | v | Derbyshire | Chesterfield | 1904 |
| | V 332 | W.H.Ashdown | for | Kent | Brentwood | 1934 |

### Highest Partnership for each Wicket

| | | | | | | |
|---|---|---|---|---|---|---|
| 1st | 316 | G.A.Gooch/P.J.Prichard | v | Kent | Chelmsford | 1994 |
| 2nd | 403 | G.A.Gooch/P.J.Prichard | v | Leics | Chelmsford | 1990 |
| 3rd | 347* | M.E.Waugh/N.Hussain | v | Lancashire | Ilford | 1992 |
| 4th | 314 | Salim Malik/N.Hussain | v | Surrey | The Oval | 1991 |
| 5th | 316 | N.Hussain/M.A.Garnham | v | Leics | Leicester | 1991 |
| 6th | 206 | J.W.H.T.Douglas/J.O'Connor | v | Glos | Cheltenham | 1923 |
| | 206 | B.R.Knight/R.A.G.Luckin | v | Middlesex | Brentwood | 1962 |
| 7th | 261 | J.W.H.T.Douglas/J.Freeman | v | Lancashire | Leyton | 1914 |
| 8th | 263 | D.R.Wilcox/R.M.Taylor | v | Warwicks | Southend | 1946 |
| 9th | 251 | J.W.H.T.Douglas/S.N.Hare | v | Derbyshire | Leyton | 1921 |
| 10th | 218 | F.H.Vigar/T.P.B.Smith | v | Derbyshire | Chesterfield | 1947 |

| | | | | | | |
|---|---|---|---|---|---|---|
| **Best Bowling** | For 10- 32 | H.Pickett | v | Leics | Leyton | 1895 |
| **(Innings)** | V 10- 40 | E.G.Dennett | for | Glos | Bristol | 1906 |
| **Best Bowling** | For 17-119 | W.Mead | v | Hampshire | Southampton | 1895 |
| **(Match)** | V 17- 56 | C.W.L.Parker | for | Glos | Gloucester | 1925 |

| | | | | |
|---|---|---|---|---|
| **Most Runs – Season** | 2559 | G.A.Gooch | (av 67.34) | 1984 |
| **Most Runs – Career** | 30701 | G.A.Gooch | (av 51.77) | 1973-97 |
| **Most 100s – Season** | 9 | J.O'Connor | | 1929, 1934 |
| | 9 | D.J.Insole | | 1955 |
| **Most 100s – Career** | 94 | G.A.Gooch | | 1973-97 |
| **Most Wkts – Season** | 172 | T.P.B.Smith | (av 27.13) | 1947 |
| **Most Wkts – Career** | 1610 | T.P.B.Smith | (av 26.68) | 1929-51 |
| **Most Career W-K Dismissals** | 1231 | B.Taylor | (1040 ct; 191 st) | 1949-73 |
| **Most Career Catches in the Field** | 519 | K.W.R.Fletcher | | 1962-88 |

## LIMITED-OVERS CRICKET

| | | | | | | |
|---|---|---|---|---|---|---|
| **Highest Total** | CGT | 386-5 | | v | Wiltshire | Chelmsford | 1988 |
| | BHC | 388-7 | | v | Scotland | Chelmsford | 1992 |
| | NL | 310-5 | | v | Glamorgan | Southend | 1983 |
| **Lowest Total** | CGT | 57 | | v | Lancashire | Lord's | 1996 |
| | BHC | 61 | | v | Lancashire | Chelmsford | 1992 |
| | NL | 69 | | v | Derbyshire | Chesterfield | 1974 |
| **Highest Innings** | CGT | 144 | G.A.Gooch | v | Hampshire | Chelmsford | 1990 |
| | BHC | 198* | G.A.Gooch | v | Sussex | Hove | 1982 |
| | NL | 176 | G.A.Gooch | v | Glamorgan | Southend | 1983 |
| **Best Bowling** | CGT | 5- 8 | J.K.Lever | v | Middlesex | Westcliff | 1972 |
| | | 5- 8 | G.A.Gooch | v | Cheshire | Chester | 1995 |
| | BHC | 5-13 | J.K.Lever | v | Middlesex | Lord's | 1985 |
| | NL | 8-26 | K.D.Boyce | v | Lancashire | Manchester | 1971 |

# GLAMORGAN

**Formation of Present Club**: 6 July 1888
**Colours**: Blue and Gold
**Badge**: Gold Daffodil
**County Champions**: (3) 1948, 1969, 1997
**Gillette/NatWest/C & G Trophy Winners**: (0); best – finalists 1977
**Benson and Hedges Cup Winners**: (0); best – finalists 2000
**National League (Div 1) Winners**: (1) 2002
**Sunday League Winners**: (1) 1993
**Match Awards**: CGT 43; BHC 56

**Chief Executive**: M.J.Fatkin, Sophia Gardens, Cardiff, CF1 9XR • Tel: 029 2040 9380 • Fax: 029 2040 9390 • Email: glam@ecb.co.uk • Web: www.glamorgancricket.com

**First XI Coach**: J.Derrick. **Captain**: S.P.James. **Vice-Captain**: R.D.B.Croft. **Overseas Player**: M.S.Kasprowicz. **2003 Beneficiary**: None. **Scorer**: G.N.Lewis.

**CHERRY, Daniel** David (Tonbridge S; U of Wales, Swansea), b Newport, Gwent 7 Feb 1980. 5'9". LHB, RM. Debut 1998. No f-c appearances 2000-01. HS 47 v Glos (Cheltenham) 2002.

**COSKER, Dean** Andrew (Millfield S), b Weymouth, Dorset 7 Jan 1978. 5'11". RHB, SLA. Debut 1996; cap 2000. Tours (Eng A): SA 1998-99, SL 1997-98; Z 1998-99, K 1997-98. HS 49 v Sussex (Cardiff) 1999. BB 6-140 v Lancs (Colwyn Bay) 1998. LO HS 27* v Somerset (Taunton) 1999 (NL). LO BB 4-17 v Yorks (Cardiff) 2002.

**CROFT, Robert** Damien Bale (St John Lloyd Catholic CS, Llanelli; Neath Tertiary C; W Glam IHE), b Morriston 25 May 1970. 5'10½". RHB, OB. Debut 1989; cap 1992; benefit 2000. **Tests**: 21 (1996 to 2001); HS 37* v SA (Manchester) 1998; BB 5-95 v NZ (Christchurch) 1996-97. **LOI**: 50 (1996 to 2001); HS 32 v SL (Perth) 1998-99; BB 3-51 v SA (Oval) 1998. Tours: A 1998-99; SA 1993-94 (Eng A), 1995-96 (Gm); WI 1991-92 (Eng A), 1997-98; NZ 1996-97; SL 2000-01; Z 1990-91 (Gm), 1994-95 (Gm), 1996-97. HS 143 v Somerset (Taunton) 1995. 50 wkts (5); most – 76 (1996). BB 8-66 (14-169 match) v Warwks (Swansea) 1992. Awards: CGT 1; BHC 2. LO HS 119 v Surrey (Oval) 2002 (CGT). LO BB 6-20 v Worcs (Cardiff) 1994 (SL).

**DALE, Adrian** (Chepstow CS; Swansea U), b Germiston, SA 24 Oct 1968 (to UK at 6 mths). 5'11½". RHB, RM. Debut 1989; cap 1992; benefit 2002. Tours (Gm): SA 1993-94 (Eng A), 1995-96; Z 1990-91, 1994-95. 1000 runs (4); most – 1472 (1993). HS 214* v Middx (Cardiff) 1993. BB 6-18 v Warwks (Cardiff) 1993. Awards: CGT 2; BHC 3. LO HS 110 v Lincs (Swansea) 1994 (NWT). LO BB 6-22 v Durham (Colwyn Bay) 1993 (SL).

**DAVIES, Andrew** Philip (Dwr-y-Felin CS; Christ C, Brecon), b Neath 7 Nov 1976. 5'11". LHB, RMF. Debut 1995. Wales (MC). No appearances 2000. NW 40 v Essex (Cardiff) 2001. BB 5-79 v Worcs (Cardiff) 2002. LO HS 24 v Sussex (Hove) 2001 (NL). LO BB 5-19 v Lincs (Sleaford) 2002 (CGT).

**HARRISON, David** Stuart (W Monmouth CS; Usk C, Pontypool), b Newport, Gwent 30 Jul 1981. Son of S.C.Harrison (Glamorgan 1971-77). 6'4". RHB, RM. Glamorgan debut 1999. HS 27 v Glos (Bristol) 2000. BB 2-79 v Northants (Cardiff) 2002. LO HS 37* and LO BB 5-26 v Yorks (Leeds) 2002 (NL).

**HEMP, David** Lloyd (Olchfa CS; Millfield S; W Glamorgan C; Birmingham U), b Hamilton, Bermuda 8 Nov 1970. UK resident since 1976. 6'0". LHB, RM. Glamorgan 1991-96; cap 1994. Warwickshire 1997-2001; cap 1997. Wales (MC) 1992-94. Tours: SA 1995-96 (Gm); I 1994-95 (Eng A); Z 1994-95 (Gm). 1000 runs (3); most – 1452 (1994). HS 186* Wa v Worcs (Birmingham) 2001. Gm HS 157 Gm v Glos (Abergavenny) 1995. BB 3-23 v SA A (Cardiff) 1996. CC BB 2-29 Wa v Glos (Birmingham) 2000. Awards: CGT 4; BHC 2. LO HS 121 v Comb U (Cardiff) 1995 (BHC). LO BB 4-32 Wa v Minor C (Lakenham) 1998 (BHC).

**HUGHES, Jonathan** (Coed-y-Land CS, Pontypridd), b Pontypridd 30 Jun 1981. 5'10". RHB, RM. Debut 2001. MCC YC. HS 74 v Worcs (Worcester) 2002. LO HS 9 (NL).

**JAMES, Stephen** Peter (Monmouth S; University C, Swansea; Hughes Hall, Cambridge), b Lydney, Glos 7 Sep 1967. 6'0". RHB. Debut 1985; cap 1992; captain 2001 to date; benefit 2001. Cambridge U 1989-90; blue 1989-90. Mashonaland 1993-94 to 1994-95. **Tests**: 2 (1998); HS 36 v SL (Oval) 1998. Tours: SA 1995-96 (Gm); SL 1997-98; Z 1992-93 (Gm); K 1997-98. 1000 runs (9); most – 1775 (1997). HS 309* v Sussex (Colwyn Bay) 2000. Awards: CGT 3; BHC 2. LO HS 135 v Comb U (Cardiff) 1992 (BHC).

**JONES, Simon** Philip (Coedcae CS; Millfield S), b Swansea 25 Dec 1978. Son of I.J.Jones (Glamorgan and England 1960-68). 6'3½". LHB, RF. Debut 1998. Cap 2002. **Tests**: 2 (2002 to 2002-03); HS 44 and BB 2-61 v I (Lord's) 2002 – on debut. Tour: A 2002-03 (*part*). HS 46 v Yorks (Scarborough) 2001. BB 6-45 v Derbys (Cardiff) 2002. LO HS 12* and BB 1-39 v Notts (Nottingham) 1999 (NL). Expected to miss most of 2003 season following knee surgery.

**KASPROWICZ, Michael** Scott (Brisbane State HS), b South Brisbane, Australia 10 Feb 1972. 6'4". RHB, RF. Queensland 1989-90 to date. Essex 1994; cap 1994. Leicestershire 1999; cap 1999. Glamorgan debut/cap 2002. **Tests** (A): 17 (1996-97 to 2000-01); HS 25 v I (Calcutta) 1997-98; BB 7-36 v E (Oval) 1997. **LOI** (A): 16 (1995-96 to 1998-99); HS 28* v E (Lord's) 1997; BB 3-50 v I (Cochin) 1997-98. Tours (A): E 1995 (Young A), 1997; I 1997-98; P 1998-99. HS 92 Australians v India A (Nagpur) 2000-01. Gm HS 72* v Northants (Northampton) 2002. 50 wkts (3+3); most: 64 (1995-96). BB 7-36 (*see Tests*). Hat-trick (Queensland 1998-99). CC BB 7-83 Ex v Somerset (Weston-s-M) 1994. Gm BB 6-47 (11-105 match) v Durham (Chester-le-St) 2002. LO HS 40 Le v Warwks (Leicester) 1999 (BHC). LO BB 5-60 Ex v Glam (Cardiff) 1994 (NWT).

**MAYNARD, Matthew** Peter (David Hughes S, Anglesey), b Oldham, Lancs 21 Mar 1966. 5'10½". RHB, RM. Debut 1985 v Yorks (Swansea), scoring 102 out of 117 in 87 min, reaching 100 with 3 sixes off successive balls; cap 1987; captain 1996-2000; benefit 1996. *Wisden* 1997. N Districts 1990-91 to 1991-92. Otago 1996-97 to 1997-98. YC 1988. **Tests**: 4 (1988 to 1993-94); HS 35 v WI (Kingston) 1993-94. **LOI**: 14 (1993-94 to 2000); HS 41 v P (Manchester) 1996. Tours: SA 1989-90 (Eng XI), 1995-96 (Gm – captain); WI 1993-94; Z 1994-95 (Gm). 1000 runs (12); most – 1803 (1991). HS 243 v Hants (Southampton) 1991. BB 3-21 v OU (Oxford) 1987. CC BB 1-3. Awards: CGT 4; BHC 9. LO HS 151* v Durham (Darlington) 1991 (NWT) and 151* v Middx (Lord's) 1996 (BHC). LO BB 1-13 (NL).

**PARKIN, Owen** Thomas (Bournemouth GS; Bath U), b Coventry, Warwks 24 Sep 1972. 6'2". RHB, RFM. Dorset 1992. Debut 1994. HS 24* v Essex (Chelmsford) 1998. BB 5-24 v Somerset (Cardiff) 1998. LO HS 14* v Somerset (Cardiff) 2002 (NL). LO BB 5-28 v Sussex (Hove) 1996 (SL).

**POWELL, Michael** John (Crickhowell SS; Pontypool CFE), b Abergavenny 3 Feb 1977. 6'1". RHB, RSM. Debut 1997 scoring 200* v OU (Oxford); cap 2000. 1000 runs (2): most – 1152 (2002). HS 200* (*see above*). CC HS 164 v Notts (Colwyn Bay) 1999. BB 2-39 v OU (Oxford) 1999. CC BB – . LO HS 86 v Middx (Cardiff) 2000 (NL).

**SHAW, Adrian** David (Llangatwg CS; Neath Tertiary C), b Neath 17 Feb 1972. 5'11". RHB, WK. Wales (MC) 1990-92. Debut 1994; cap 1999. No appearances 2002 – 2nd XI captain. HS 140 v OU (Oxford) 1999. CC HS 88* v Glos (Cardiff) 2000. LO HS 48 v Glos (Swansea) 1997 (SL).

**THOMAS, Ian** James (Bedwas CS; Bassaleg CS; UWIC), b Newport, Gwent 9 May 1979. 5'11". LHB, OB. Debut 1998. Wales MC. HS 82 v Essex (Southend) 2000 – on CC debut. BB 1-26 (CC). LO HS 72 v Warwks (Birmingham) 2002 (NL).

**THOMAS, Stuart Darren** (Graig CS, Llanelli; Neath Tertiary C), b Morriston 25 Jan 1975. 6'0". LHB, RFM. Debut v Derbys (Chesterfield) 1992, taking 5-80 when aged 17yr 217d; cap 1997. Tours (Eng A): SA 1995-96 (Gm), 1998-99; NZ 1999-00; Z 1994-95 (Gm), 1998-99. HS 138 v Essex (Chelmsford) 2001. 50 wkts (5; most – 71 (1998). BB 8-50 Eng A v Zim A (Harare) 1998-99 – record Eng A analysis. CC BB 7-33 (10-83 match) v Durham (Cardiff) 2002. Award: BHC 1. LO HS 71* v Surrey (Oval) 2002 (CGT). LO BB 7-16 v Surrey (Swansea) 1998 (SL).

**WALLACE, Mark** Alexander (Crickhowell HS), b Abergavenny, Gwent 19 Nov 1981. 5'9". LHB, WK. Debut 1999. HS 106* v Derbys (Cardiff) 2002. LO HS 39 v Warwks (Cardiff) 2002 (BHC).

**WATKINS, Ryan** Edward (Cross Keys TC), b Abergavenny 9 Jun 1983. LHB, RM. Joined part-time staff 2002 – awaiting f-c debut.

**WHARF, Alexander** George (Buttershaw Upper S; Thomas Danby C), b Bradford, Yorks 4 Jun 1975. 6'5". RHB, RMF. Yorkshire 1994-97. Nottinghamshire 1998-99. Glamorgan debut 2000, scoring 100* v OU (Oxford); cap 2000. HS 101* v Northants (Northampton) 2000. BB 5-63 v Yorks (Swansea) 2001. LO HS 38* Nt v Surrey (Nottingham) 1999 (NL). LO BB 4-29 Y v Notts (Leeds) 1996 (BHC).

## RELEASED/RETIRED

A.W.Evans, T.D.Evison, K.Newell and L.A.Smith left the staff having made no f-c appearances in 2002.

---

## ESSEX RELEASED/RETIRED (continued from p 27)

**WAUGH, Mark** Edward (East Hills HS, Sydney), b Canterbury, Sydney, Australia 2 Jun 1965. Younger twin of S.R.Waugh (NSW, Somerset, Kent and Australia). 6'1". RHB, OB. NSW 1985-86 to date. Essex 1988-90, 1992, 1995 and 2002; cap 1989. *Wisden* 1990. **Tests** (A): 128 (1990-91 to 2002-03); HS 153* v I (Bangalore) 1997-98; BB 5-40 v E (Adelaide) 1994-95. **LOI** (A): 244 (1988-89 to 2001-02); HS 173 v WI (Melbourne) 2000-01; BB 5-24 v WI (Melbourne) 1992-93. Tours (A): E 1993, 1995 (NSW); SA 1993-94, 2001-02; WI 1990-91, 1994-95; NZ 1992-93; P 1994-95; SL 1992-93; Z 1985-86 (Young A), 1987-88 (NSW). 1000 runs (5+1) inc 2000 (1): 2072 (1990). HS 229* NSW v WA (Perth) 1990-91, sharing record 5th wkt stand of 464* with S.R.Waugh. Ex HS 219* v Lancs (Ilford) 1992. BB 6-68 6-68 Aus XI v Board President's XI (Patiala) 1996-97. Ex BB 5-37 v Northants (Chelmsford) 1990. Awards: BHC 2. LO HS 173 (*see LOI*). BB HS 5-24 (*see LOI*).

# GLAMORGAN 2002

## RESULTS SUMMARY

|  | Place | Won | Lost | Tied | Drew | No Result |
|---|---|---|---|---|---|---|
| **County Championship** (2nd Division) | **5th** | 5 | 5 |  | 6 |  |
| **All First-Class Matches** |  | 5 | 5 |  | 7 |  |
| **C & G Trophy** | 4th Round |  |  |  |  |  |
| **Benson & Hedges Cup** | 5th in Midlands/West/Wales Division |  |  |  |  |  |
| **NU National League** (1st Division) | **1st** | 12 | 3 | 1 |  |  |

## COUNTY CHAMPIONSHIP AVERAGES

### BATTING AND FIELDING

| Cap |  | M | I | NO | HS | Runs | Avge | 100 | 50 | Ct/St |
|---|---|---|---|---|---|---|---|---|---|---|
| 1987 | M.P.Maynard | 13 | 20 | 1 | 151 | 1058 | 55.68 | 3 | 6 | 14 |
| 1992 | S.P.James | 13 | 22 | 1 | 249 | 1111 | 52.90 | 4 | 3 | 7 |
| 2000 | M.J.Powell | 15 | 26 | 3 | 135 | 1152 | 50.08 | 3 | 7 | 6 |
| 1992 | A.Dale | 15 | 24 | 1 | 127* | 859 | 37.34 | 2 | 3 | 6 |
| 1992 | R.D.B.Croft | 16 | 24 | 3 | 101* | 747 | 35.57 | 1 | 5 | 8 |
| 2002 | M.S.Kasprowicz | 12 | 19 | 7 | 72* | 352 | 29.33 | – | 1 | 7 |
| 1994 | D.L.Hemp | 11 | 20 | 2 | 108 | 505 | 28.05 | 1 | 2 | 6 |
|  | M.A.Wallace | 16 | 25 | 4 | 106* | 553 | 26.33 | 1 | 2 | 54/3 |
|  | J.Hughes | 6 | 10 | 1 | 74 | 225 | 25.00 | – | 1 | 2 |
|  | I.J.Thomas | 8 | 15 | 1 | 76 | 273 | 19.50 | – | 2 | 2 |
|  | D.D.Cherry | 5 | 8 | – | 47 | 129 | 16.12 | – | – | 4 |
| 2002 | S.P.Jones | 10 | 17 | 6 | 26 | 174 | 15.81 | – | – | 4 |
| 1997 | S.D.Thomas | 15 | 22 | 1 | 47 | 274 | 13.04 | – | – | 4 |
| 2000 | D.A.Cosker | 10 | 13 | 2 | 37 | 115 | 10.45 | – | – | 8 |
|  | A.P.Davies | 5 | 6 | – | 30 | 58 | 9.66 | – | – | – |

*Also batted*: D.S.Harrison (1 match) 0; O.T.Parkin (3) 0, 7, 16 (1 ct); A.G.Wharf (2 – cap 2000) 0, 6.

### BOWLING

|  | O | M | R | W | Avge | Best | 5wI | 10wM |
|---|---|---|---|---|---|---|---|---|
| S.P.Jones | 259.5 | 47 | 870 | 33 | 26.36 | 6- 45 | 2 | – |
| M.S.Kasprowicz | 418.4 | 78 | 1413 | 53 | 26.66 | 6- 47 | 4 | 1 |
| A.P.Davies | 116.2 | 14 | 420 | 15 | 28.00 | 5- 79 | 1 | – |
| S.D.Thomas | 447.1 | 65 | 1535 | 51 | 30.09 | 7- 33 | 3 | 1 |
| R.D.B.Croft | 592 | 127 | 1640 | 39 | 42.05 | 5- 71 | 1 | – |
| D.A.Cosker | 317.5 | 60 | 1012 | 20 | 50.60 | 4-135 | – | – |

*Also bowled*:

| O.T.Parkin | 83.4 | 19 | 247 | 7 | 35.28 | 2- 47 | – | – |
|---|---|---|---|---|---|---|---|---|
| A.Dale | 118 | 22 | 441 | 6 | 73.50 | 1- 15 | – | – |

D.D.Cherry 3-3-0-0; D.S.Harrison 39-6-132-3; M.P.Maynard 1-0-5-0; M.J.Powell 6-0-21-0; I.J.Thomas 6.1-0-30-1; A.G.Wharf 61-7-195-3.

The First-Class Averages (pp 121-135) give the records of Glamorgan players in all first-class county matches (Glamorgan's other opponents being the Sri Lankans), with the exception of: S.P.Jones 11-17-6-26-174-15.81-0-0-4ct. 279.5-48-949-34-27.91-6/45-2-0.

# GLAMORGAN RECORDS

## FIRST-CLASS CRICKET

| | | | | | | |
|---|---|---|---|---|---|---|
| **Highest Total** | For | 718-3d | | v | Sussex | Colwyn Bay | 2000 |
| | V | 712 | | by | Northants | Northampton | 1998 |
| **Lowest Total** | For | 22 | | v | Lancashire | Liverpool | 1924 |
| | V | 33 | | by | Leics | Ebbw Vale | 1965 |
| **Highest Innings** | For | 309* | S.P.James | v | Sussex | Colwyn Bay | 2000 |
| | V | 322* | M.B.Loye | for | Northants | Northampton | 1998 |

### Highest Partnership for each Wicket

| | | | | | | |
|---|---|---|---|---|---|---|
| 1st | 374 | M.T.G.Elliott/S.P.James | v | Sussex | Colwyn Bay | 2000 |
| 2nd | 252 | M.P.Maynard/D.L.Hemp | v | Northants | Cardiff | 2002 |
| 3rd | 313 | D.E.Davies/W.E.Jones | v | Essex | Brentwood | 1948 |
| 4th | 425* | A.Dale/I.V.A.Richards | v | Middlesex | Cardiff | 1993 |
| 5th | 264 | M.Robinson/S.W.Montgomery | v | Hampshire | Bournemouth | 1949 |
| 6th | 230 | W.E.Jones/B.L.Muncer | v | Worcs | Worcester | 1953 |
| 7th | 211 | P.A.Cottey/O.D.Gibson | v | Leics | Swansea | 1996 |
| 8th | 202 | D.Davies/J.J.Hills | v | Sussex | Eastbourne | 1928 |
| 9th | 203* | J.J.Hills/J.C.Clay | v | Worcs | Swansea | 1929 |
| 10th | 143 | T.Davies/S.A.B.Daniels | v | Glos | Swansea | 1982 |

| | | | | | | | |
|---|---|---|---|---|---|---|---|
| **Best Bowling** | For | 10- 51 | J.Mercer | v | Worcs | Worcester | 1936 |
| **(Innings)** | V | 10- 18 | G.Geary | for | Leics | Pontypridd | 1929 |
| **Best Bowling** | For | 17-212 | J.C.Clay | v | Worcs | Swansea | 1937 |
| **(Match)** | V | 16- 96 | G.Geary | for | Leics | Pontypridd | 1929 |

| | | | | |
|---|---|---|---|---|
| **Most Runs – Season** | 2276 | H.Morris | (av 55.51) | 1990 |
| **Most Runs – Career** | 34056 | A.Jones | (av 33.03) | 1957-83 |
| **Most 100s – Season** | 10 | H.Morris | | 1990 |
| **Most 100s – Career** | 52 | A.Jones | | 1957-83 |
| | 52 | H.Morris | | 1981-97 |
| **Most Wkts – Season** | 176 | J.C.Clay | (av 17.34) | 1937 |
| **Most Wkts – Career** | 2174 | D.J.Shepherd | (av 20.95) | 1950-72 |
| **Most Career W-K Dismissals** | 933 | E.W.Jones | (840 ct: 93 st) | 1961-83 |
| **Most Career Catches in the Field** | 656 | P.M.Walker | | 1956-72 |

## LIMITED-OVERS CRICKET

| | | | | | | |
|---|---|---|---|---|---|---|
| **Highest Total** | CGT | 429 | | v | Surrey | The Oval | 2002 |
| | BHC | 318-3 | | v | Combined U | Cardiff | 1995 |
| | NL | 305-6 | | v | Worcs | Cardiff | 2001 |
| **Lowest Total** | CGT | 76 | | v | Northants | Northampton | 1968 |
| | BHC | 68 | | v | Lancashire | Manchester | 1973 |
| | NL | 42 | | v | Derbyshire | Swansea | 1979 |
| **Highest Innings** | CGT | 162* | I.V.A.Richards | v | Oxfordshire | Swansea | 1993 |
| | BHC | 151* | M.P.Maynard | v | Middlesex | Lord's | 1996 |
| | NL | 155* | J.H.Kallis | v | Surrey | Pontypridd | 1999 |
| **Best Bowling** | CGT | 5-13 | R.J.Shastri | v | Scotland | Edinburgh | 1988 |
| | BHC | 6-20 | S.D.Thomas | v | Combined U | Cardiff | 1995 |
| | NL | 7-16 | S.D.Thomas | v | Surrey | Swansea | 1998 |

# GLOUCESTERSHIRE

**Formation of Present Club**: 1871
**Colours**: Blue, Gold, Brown, Silver, Green and Red
**Badge**: Coat of Arms of the City and County of Bristol
**County Champions (since 1890)**: (0); best – 2nd 1930, 1931, 1947, 1959, 1969, 1986
**Gillette/NatWest/C & G Trophy Winners**: (3) 1973, 1999, 2000
**Benson and Hedges Cup Winners**: (3) 1977, 1999, 2000
**National League (Div 1) Winners**: (1) 2000
**Sunday League Winners**: (0); best – 2nd 1988
**Match Awards**: CGT 56; BHC 72

**Chief Executive**: T.E.M.Richardson, County Ground, Nevil Road, Bristol BS7 9EJ • Tel: 0117 910 8000 • Fax: 0117 924 1193 • Email: info@glosccc.co.uk • Web: www.glosccc.co.uk

**Director of Cricket/First XI Coach**: J.G.Bracewell. **Captain**: M.W.Alleyne.
**Vice-Captain**: No appointment. **Overseas Players**: I.J.Harvey and J.N.Rhodes. **2003 Beneficiary**: None. **Scorer**: K.T.Gerrish. ‡ New registration

**ALLEYNE, Mark** Wayne (Harrison C, Barbados; Cardinal Pole S, London E9; Haringey Cricket C), b Tottenham, London 23 May 1968. 5'10". RHB, RM. Debut 1986; cap 1990; captain 1997 to date; benefit 1999. *Wisden* 2000. **LOI**: 10 (1998-99 to 2000-01); HS 53 v SA (E London) 1999-00; BB 3-27 v SL (Sydney) 1998-99. Tours (Eng A) (C=captain): WI 2000-01C; NZ 1999-00C; SL 1986-87 (Gs), 1992-93 (Gs); B 1999-00C. 1000 runs (6); most – 1189 (1998). HS 256 v Northants (Northampton) 1990. 50 wkts (1): 54 (1996). BB 6-49 v Middx (Lord's) 2000. Awards: CGT 3; BHC 3. LO HS 134* v Leics (Bristol) 1992 (SL). LO BB 5-27 v Comb U (Bristol) 1988 (BHC).

**AVERIS, James** Maxwell Michael (Cathedral S, Bristol; Portsmouth U; St Cross C, Oxford), b Bristol 28 May 1974. 5'11". RHB, RMF. Oxford U 1997; blue 1997; rugby blue 1996-97. Gloucestershire debut 1997; cap 2001. HS 43 and BB 5-51 v Notts (Bristol) 2002. Award: BHC 1. LO HS 23* v Lancs (Manchester) 2000 (NL). LO BB 5-20 v Northants (Northampton) 2000 (NL).

**BALL, Martyn** Charles John (King Edmund SS; Bath CFE), b Bristol 26 Apr 1970. 5'8". RHB, OB. Debut 1988; cap 1996; benefit 2002. Tours: I 2001-02; SL 1992-93 (Gs). HS 71 v Notts (Bristol) 1993. BB 8-46 (14-169 match) v Somerset (Taunton) 1993. Award: CGT 1. LO HS 51 v SL A (Cheltenham) 1999. LO BB 5-42 v Yorks (Cheltenham) 1999 (NL).

**BRESSINGTON, Alastair** Nigel (Marling GS, Stroud; UWIC), b Downend, Bristol 28 Nov 1979. 6'1". LHB, RMF. Debut 2000. No f-c appearances 2002. HS 17* v Hants (Cheltenham) 2001. BB 4-36 v Glam (Bristol) 2000 – on debut. LO HS 54 Glos CB v Yorks CB (Cheltenham) 1999 (NWT). LO BB 3-21 Glos CB v Notts CB (Cheltenham) 2000 (NWT).

**FISHER, Ian** Douglas (Beckfoot GS, Bingley; Thomas Danby C, Leeds), b Bradford, Yorks 31 Mar 1976. 5'10½". LHB, SLA. Yorkshire 1995-96 (Y in Zim) to 2001. Gloucestershire debut 2002. Tour: Z 1995-96 (Y). HS 103* v Essex (Gloucester) 2002. BB 5-35 Y v Mashonaland Inv XI (Harare) 1995-96 – on debut. Gs BB 5-73 Y v Essex (Chelmsford) 1999. Gs BB 5-87 v Middx (Southgate) 2002. LO HS 20 and LO BB 3-20 Y v Somerset (Scarborough) 2000 (NL).

**GIDMAN, Alex** Peter Richard (Wycliffe C), b High Wycombe, Bucks 22 Jun 1981. 6'3". RHB, RM. Debut 2002. MCCYC. HS 117 v Northants (Bristol) 2002. BB 3-33 v Middx (Cheltenham) 2002. LO HS 48 v Middx (Southgate) 2002 (NL). LO BB 3-46 v Essex (Gloucester) 2002 (NL).

**HANCOCK, Timothy** Harold Coulter (St Edward's S, Oxford; Henley C), b Reading, Berks 20 Apr 1972. 5'10". RHB, RM. Debut 1991; cap 1998. Oxfordshire 1990. Tour: SL 1992-93 (Gs). 1000 runs (1): 1227 (1998). HS 220* v Notts (Nottingham) 1998. BB 3-5 v Essex (Colchester) 1998. Awards: CGT 3. LO HS 110 v Northants (Bristol) 2000 (NWT). LO BB 6-58 v Scot (Bristol) 1997 (NWT).

**HARDINGES, Mark** Andrew (Malvern C; Bath U), b Gloucester 5 Feb 1978. 6'1". RHB, RMF. Debut 1999. British U 2000. HS 172 v OU (Oxford) 2002. CC HS 22 v Notts (Nottingham) 2001. BB 2-16 v Essex (Bristol) 2000. Award: CGT 1. LO HS 65 v Notts (Nottingham) 2001 (NL). LO BB 4-19 v Salop (Shrewsbury) 2002 (CGT).

**HARVEY, Ian** Joseph (Wonthaggi TC), b Wonthaggi, Victoria, Australia 10 Apr 1972. 5'10". RHB, RMF. Victoria 1993-94 to date. Gloucestershire debut/cap 1999. **LOI** (A): 49 (1997-98 to 2002-03); HS 47* v WI (Sydney) 2000-01; BB 4-28 v Z (Melbourne) 2000-01. Tour: NZ 1994-95 (Aus Academy). HS 136 Vic v S Aus (Melbourne) 1995-96. Gs HS 130* v Middx (Lord's) 2001. BB 7-44 Vic v S Aus (Melbourne) 1996-97. Gs BB 6-19 (10-32 match) v Sussex (Hove) 2000. Hat-trick (Victoria 2001-02). Awards: CGT 1; BHC 4. LO HS 92 v Worcs (Bristol) 2001 (BHC). LO BB 5-19 v Northants (Bristol) 2000 (NL).

**LEWIS, Jonathan** (Churchfields S, Swindon; Swindon C), b Aylesbury, Bucks 26 Aug 1975. 6'2". RHB, RMF. Debut 1995; cap 1998. Wiltshire 1993. Northamptonshire staff 1994. Tour: WI 2000-01 (Eng A). HS 62 v Worcs (Cheltenham) 1999. 50 wkts (3); most – 72 (2000). BB 8-95 v Z (Gloucester) 2000. CC BB 7-56 (10-92 match) v Notts (Bristol) 1999. Hat-trick 2000. Awards: BHC 2. LO HS 33* v Somerset (Bristol) 1998 (BHC). LO BB 4-22 v Surrey (Bristol) 2002 (NL).

**PEARSON, James** Alexander, b Bristol 11 Sep 1983. LHB. Gloucestershire debut 2002. HS 51 v Northants (Bristol) 2002 – on debut. LO HS 7 and BB 1-29 Glos CB v Herefords (Brockhampton) 2001.

**POPE, Stephen** Patrick (Cheltenham Bournside CS), b Cheltenham 25 Jan 1983. 5'8". RHB, WK. Awaiting f-c debut. LO HS (Glos CB) 15 v Herefords (Brockhampton) 2001 (CGT).

‡**RHODES,** Jonathan Neil (*'Jonty'*) (Maritzburg C; Natal U), b Pietermaritzburg, SA 27 Jul 1969. Elder brother of C.B.Rhodes (E Province B and Natal B 1990-91 to 1993-94). 5'8". RHB, RM, outstanding fielder. Natal/KwaZulu-Natal 1988-89 to date scoring 108 v WP (Durban) on debut. *Wisden* 1998. **Tests** (SA): 52 (1992-93 to 2000-01); HS 117 v E (Lord's) 1998. **LOI** (SA): 245 (1991-92 to 2002-03); HS 121 v P (Nairobi) 1996-97; 105 ct – including 5 v WI (Bombay) 1993-94 (*world record*). Tours (I): E 1994, 1998; A 1993-94, 1997-98, 2001-02; WI 1991-92, 2000-01; NZ 1994-95, 1998-99; I 1993-94, 1996-97; P 1994-95, 1997-98; SL 1993-94, 2000; Z 1995-96, 1999-00, 2001-02. HS 172 KZ-Natal v GW (Kimberley) 2001-02. BB 1-13. LO HS 121 (*see LOI*). LO BB 1-2.

**RUSSELL,** Robert Charles (*'Jack'*) (Archway CS; Bristol Poly – "briefly"), b Stroud 15 Aug 1963. 5'8½". LHB, WK, occ OB. Debut 1981 – youngest Glos wicket-keeper (17yr 307d), setting record for most match dismissals on f-c debut – 8 v SL (Bristol) 1981; cap 1985; benefit 1994; captain 1995. Kept throughout world record total without byes – 746-9d by Northants (Bristol) 2002. *Wisden* 1989. **Tests**: 54 (1988 to 1997-98); HS 128* v A (Manchester) 1989; 11 ct v SA (Jo'burg) 1995-96 (Test record); 27 dis 1995-96 series v SA (Eng record). **LOI**: 40 (1987-88 to 1998-99); HS 50 v I (Nottingham) 1990. Tours: A 1990-91, 1992-93 (Eng A); SA 1995-96; WI 1989-90, 1993-94, 1997-98; NZ 1991-92, 1996-97; P 1987-88; SL 1986-87 (Gs). 1000 runs (1): 1049 (1997). HS 129* Eng XI v Boland (Paarl) 1995-96. Gs HS 124 v Notts (Nottingham) 1996. BB 1-4. Awards: CGT 1; BHC 3. LO HS 119* v Brit U (Bristol) 1998 (BHC).

**SILLENCE, Roger** John (Highbury SS; Salisbury Art C), b Salisbury, Wilts 29 Jun 1977. 6'3". RHB, RMF. Debut 2001 taking 5-97 v Sussex (Hove). Wiltshire 1996-2001. HS 101 v Derbys (Bristol) 2002. BB 5-63 v Durham (Bristol) 2002. LO HS (Wilts) 82 v Northants CB (Northampton) 1999 (NWT). LO BB 4-35 v WI A (Cheltenham) 2002.

**SMITH, Andrew Michael** (Queen Elizabeth GS, Wakefield; Exeter U; West of England U), b Dewsbury, Yorks 1 Oct 1967. 5'9". RHB, LMF. Debut 1991; cap 1995; benefit 2001. **Tests**: 1 (1997); HS 4* v A (Leeds) 1997. Tour: P 1995-96 (Eng A – *part*). HS 61 v Yorks (Gloucester) 1998. 50 wkts (5); most – 83 (1997). BB 8-73 (10-118 match) v Middx (Lord's) 1996. Award: BHC 1. LO HS 26* v Kent (Moreton-in-M) 1996 (SL). LO BB 6-39 v Hants (Southampton) 1995 (BHC).

**SPEARMAN, Craig** Murray, b Auckland, NZ 4 Jul 1972. 6'0". RHB. Auckland 1993-94 to 1995-96. Central Districts 1996-97 to date. Gloucestershire debut/cap 2002. **Tests** (NZ): 19 (1995-96 to 2000-01); HS 112 v Z (Auckland) 1995-96. **LOI** (NZ): 51 (1995-96 to 2000-01); HS 86 v Z (Harare) 2000-01. Tours (NZ): SA 2000-01; WI 1995-96; I 1999-00; P 1996-97; SL 1997-98; Z 1997-98, 2000-01. 1000 (1): 1444 (2002). HS 180* (carried bat) v Glam (Cheltenham) 2002. BB 1-37 CD v Wellington (New Plymouth) 1999-00. Awards: CGT 1; BHC 1. LO HS 126 CD v Canterbury (Nelson) 1997-98.

**TAYLOR, Christopher** Glyn (Colston's Collegiate S), b Southmead, Bristol 27 Sep 1976. 5'7". RHB, OB. Debut 2000, scoring 104 v Middx – first to score a hundred at Lord's in a Championship match on his first-class debut. Cap 2001. HS 196 v Notts (Nottingham) 2001. BB 3-126 v Northants (Cheltenham) 2000. Award: BHC 1. LO HS 93 v Warwks (Bristol) 2002 (BHC).

‡**WESTON, William Philip** Christopher (Durham S), b Durham 16 Jun 1973. Son of M.P.Weston (Durham; England RFU); brother of R.M.S.Weston (*see MIDDLESEX*). 6'3". LHB, LM. Worcestershire 1991-2002; cap 1995. Tours (Wo): Z 1993-94, 1996-97. 1000 runs (4); most – 1389 (1996). HS 205 Wo v Northants (Northampton) 1997. BB 2-39 Wo v P (Worcester) 1992. CC BB – . LO HS 134 Wo v Derbys (Derby) 2001 (NL). LO BB (Wo) 1-2 (SL).

**WINDOWS, Matthew** Guy Newman (Clifton C; Durham U), b Bristol 5 Apr 1973. Son of A.R.Windows (Glos and CU 1960-68). 5'7". RHB, LM. Debut 1992; cap 1998. Combined U 1995. Tours (Eng A): SA 1998-99; Z 1998-99. 1000 runs (3); most – 1173 (1998). HS 184 v Warwks (Cheltenham) 1996. BB (Comb U) 1-6. Gs BB – . Awards: CGT 1; BHC 2. LO HS 117 v Northants (Cheltenham) 2001 (NL).

## RELEASED/RETIRED
(Having made a first-class County appearance in 2002)

**BARNETT, Kim** John (Leek HS), b Stoke-on-Trent, Staffs 17 Jul 1960. 6'1". RHB, RM/LB. Derbyshire 1979-98; cap 1982; captain 1983-95; benefit 1992. Boland 1982-83 to 1987-88. Staffordshire 1976. Gloucestershire 1999-2002; cap 1999. *Wisden* 1988. **Tests**: 4 (1988 to 1989); HS 80 v A (Leeds) 1989. **LOI**: 1 (1988); HS 84 v SL (Oval) 1988. Tours: SA 1989-90 (Eng XI); NZ 1979-80 (DHR); SL 1985-86 (Eng B). 1000 runs (16); most – 1734 (1984). HS 239* De v Leics (Leicester) 1988. Gs HS 182* (carried bat) v Middx (Southgate) 2002. BB 6-28 De v Glam (Chesterfield) 1991. Gs BB 2-52 v Worcs (Cheltenham) 1999. Awards: CGT 7; BHC 12. LO HS 136 English XI v SA (Jo'burg) 1989-90. LO BB 6-24 De v Cumb (Kendal) 1984 (NWT).

**GANNON, Benjamin** Ward (Dragon S, Oxford; Abingdon S; Cheltenham & Gloucester CHE), b Oxford 5 Sep 1975. 6'3". RHB, RMF. Gloucestershire 1999-2002. Herefordshire 1996. HS 28 v Essex (Colchester) 2000. BB 6-80 v Glam (Cardiff) 1999 – on debut. LO HS 2. LO BB 2-29 v SL A (Cheltenham) 1999.

**SNAPE, J.N.** – *see LEICESTERSHIRE.*

J.Angel and R.C.J.Williams left the staff having made no f-c appearances in 2002.

# GLOUCESTERSHIRE 2002

## RESULTS SUMMARY

|  | Place | Won | Lost | Tied | Drew | No Result |
|---|---|---|---|---|---|---|
| **County Championship** (2nd Division) | **8th** | 2 | 7 |  | 7 |  |
| **All First-Class Matches** |  | 3 | 7 |  | 7 |  |
| **C & G Trophy** | Quarter-Finalist |  |  |  |  |  |
| **Benson & Hedges Cup** | Quarter-Finalist |  |  |  |  |  |
| **NU National League** (2nd Division) | **1st** | 10 | 4 |  |  | 2 |

## COUNTY CHAMPIONSHIP AVERAGES

### BATTING AND FIELDING

| Cap | | M | I | NO | HS | Runs | Avge | 100 | 50 | Ct/St |
|---|---|---|---|---|---|---|---|---|---|---|
| 2002 | C.M.Spearman | 16 | 32 | 4 | 180* | 1388 | 49.57 | 5 | 6 | 15 |
| 1999 | K.J.Barnett | 7 | 14 | 2 | 182* | 586 | 48.83 | 3 | – | 11 |
| 1999 | I.J.Harvey | 6 | 10 | 1 | 123 | 390 | 43.33 | 1 | 2 | 6 |
| 1985 | R.C.Russell | 16 | 27 | 5 | 119* | 928 | 42.18 | 3 | 4 | 36/2 |
|  | A.P.R.Gidman | 10 | 17 | 1 | 117 | 558 | 34.87 | 1 | 4 | 5 |
| 1998 | M.G.N.Windows | 16 | 30 | 2 | 144 | 917 | 32.75 | 1 | 7 | 6 |
| 1998 | T.H.C.Hancock | 9 | 17 | 3 | 112 | 406 | 29.00 | 1 | 2 | 1 |
|  | I.D.Fisher | 15 | 25 | 1 | 103* | 560 | 25.45 | 1 | 4 | 7 |
| 1990 | M.W.Alleyne | 14 | 25 | 3 | 142* | 555 | 25.22 | 1 | 2 | 12 |
|  | R.J.Sillence | 4 | 7 | – | 101 | 167 | 23.85 | 1 | – | 2 |
| 2001 | C.G.Taylor | 14 | 27 | 1 | 126 | 616 | 23.69 | 1 | 2 | 14 |
|  | J.A.Pearson | 3 | 6 | 1 | 51 | 114 | 22.80 | – | 1 | 2 |
| 1996 | M.C.J.Ball | 6 | 9 | 2 | 63 | 117 | 16.71 | – | 1 | 3 |
| 1999 | J.N.Snape | 4 | 7 | – | 28 | 101 | 14.42 | – | – | 1 |
| 1998 | J.Lewis | 16 | 25 | 6 | 57 | 273 | 14.36 | – | 1 | 6 |
| 1995 | A.M.Smith | 9 | 13 | 6 | 21 | 92 | 13.14 | – | – | 3 |
| 2001 | J.M.M.Averis | 5 | 8 | – | 43 | 83 | 10.37 | – | – | 3 |
|  | B.W.Gannon | 6 | 8 | 4 | 14 | 31 | 7.75 | – | – | 1 |

### BOWLING

|  | O | M | R | W | Avge | Best | 5wI | 10wM |
|---|---|---|---|---|---|---|---|---|
| I.J.Harvey | 152.2 | 29 | 533 | 28 | 19.03 | 6-68 | 3 | 1 |
| A.M.Smith | 270 | 55 | 916 | 31 | 29.54 | 5-69 | 1 | – |
| J.M.M.Averis | 128 | 33 | 432 | 13 | 33.23 | 5-51 | 1 | – |
| R.J.Sillence | 85 | 8 | 397 | 11 | 36.09 | 5-63 | 1 | – |
| J.Lewis | 536.1 | 137 | 1662 | 44 | 37.77 | 6-54 | 2 | 1 |
| A.P.R.Gidman | 99 | 16 | 442 | 10 | 44.20 | 3-33 | – | – |
| B.W.Gannon | 137 | 30 | 521 | 11 | 47.36 | 3-41 | – | – |
| M.W.Alleyne | 266 | 59 | 876 | 17 | 51.52 | 3-76 | – | – |
| I.D.Fisher | 478.1 | 93 | 1643 | 30 | 54.76 | 5-87 | 1 | – |
| M.C.J.Ball | 233 | 45 | 784 | 14 | 56.00 | 3-74 | – | – |

*Also bowled:* K.J.Barnett 12.4-1-67-1; J.N.Snape 26-1-111-2; C.G.Taylor 10-1-36-0; M.G.N.Windows 3.2-0-20-0.

The First-Class Averages (pp 121-135) give the records of Gloucestershire players in all first-class county matches (Gloucestershire's other opponents being the Oxford UCCE).

# GLOUCESTERSHIRE RECORDS

## FIRST-CLASS CRICKET

| | | | | | | |
|---|---|---|---|---|---|---|
| **Highest Total** | For 653-6d | | v | Glamorgan | Bristol | 1928 |
| | V 774-7d | | by | Australians | Bristol | 1948 |
| **Lowest Total** | For 17 | | v | Australians | Cheltenham | 1896 |
| | V 12 | | by | Northants | Gloucester | 1907 |
| **Highest Innings** | For 318* | W.G.Grace | v | Yorkshire | Cheltenham | 1876 |
| | V 310* | M.E.K.Hussey | for | Northants | Bristol | 2002 |

### Highest Partnership for each Wicket

| | | | | | | |
|---|---|---|---|---|---|---|
| 1st | 395 | D.M.Young/R.B.Nicholls | v | Oxford U | Oxford | 1962 |
| 2nd | 256 | C.T.M.Pugh/T.W.Graveney | v | Derbyshire | Chesterfield | 1960 |
| 3rd | 336 | W.R.Hammond/B.H.Lyon | v | Leics | Leicester | 1933 |
| 4th | 321 | W.R.Hammond/W.L.Neale | v | Leics | Gloucester | 1937 |
| 5th | 261 | W.G.Grace/W.O.Moberley | v | Yorkshire | Cheltenham | 1876 |
| 6th | 320 | G.L.Jessop/J.H.Board | v | Sussex | Hove | 1903 |
| 7th | 248 | W.G.Grace/E.L.Thomas | v | Sussex | Hove | 1896 |
| 8th | 239 | W.R.Hammond/A.E.Wilson | v | Lancashire | Bristol | 1938 |
| 9th | 193 | W.G.Grace/S.A.P.Kitcat | v | Sussex | Bristol | 1896 |
| 10th | 131 | W.R.Gouldsworthy/J.G.Bessant | v | Somerset | Bristol | 1923 |

| | | | | | | |
|---|---|---|---|---|---|---|
| **Best Bowling** | For 10-40 | E.G.Dennett | v | Essex | Bristol | 1906 |
| **(Innings)** | V 10-66 | A.A.Mailey | for | Australians | Cheltenham | 1921 |
| | 10-66 | K.Smales | for | Notts | Stroud | 1956 |
| **Best Bowling** | For 17-56 | C.W.L.Parker | v | Essex | Gloucester | 1925 |
| **(Match)** | V 15-87 | A.J.Conway | for | Worcs | Moreton-in-M | 1914 |

| | | | | | |
|---|---|---|---|---|---|
| **Most Runs – Season** | 2860 | W.R.Hammond | (av 69.75) | | 1933 |
| **Most Runs – Career** | 33664 | W.R.Hammond | (av 57.05) | | 1920-51 |
| **Most 100s – Season** | 13 | W.R.Hammond | | | 1938 |
| **Most 100s – Career** | 113 | W.R.Hammond | | | 1920-51 |
| **Most Wkts – Season** | 222 | T.W.J.Goddard | (av 16.80) | | 1937 |
| | 222 | T.W.J.Goddard | (av 16.37) | | 1947 |
| **Most Wkts – Career** | 3170 | C.W.L.Parker | (av 19.43) | | 1903-35 |
| **Most Career W-K Dismissals** | 1016 | J.H.Board | (698 ct; 318 st) | 1891-1914 |
| | 1016 | R.C.Russell | (916 ct; 100 st) | 1981-2002 |
| **Most Career Catches in the Field** | 718 | C.A.Milton | | 1948-74 |

## LIMITED-OVERS CRICKET

| | | | | | | |
|---|---|---|---|---|---|---|
| **Highest Total** | CGT | 351-2 | v | Scotland | Bristol | 1997 |
| | BHC | 308-3 | v | Ireland | Dublin | 1996 |
| | NL | 344-6 | v | Northants | Cheltenham | 2001 |
| **Lowest Total** | CGT | 82 | v | Notts | Bristol | 1987 |
| | BHC | 62 | v | Hampshire | Bristol | 1975 |
| | NL | 49 | v | Middlesex | Bristol | 1978 |
| **Highest Innings** | CGT | 177 A.J.Wright | v | Scotland | Bristol | 1997 |
| | BHC | 154* M.J.Procter | v | Somerset | Taunton | 1972 |
| | NL | 146* S. Young | v | Yorkshire | Leeds | 1997 |
| **Best Bowling** | CGT | 6-21 C.A.Walsh | v | Kent | Bristol | 1990 |
| | | 6-21 C.A.Walsh | v | Cheshire | Bristol | 1992 |
| | BHC | 6-13 M.J.Procter | v | Hampshire | Southampton | 1977 |
| | NL | 6-52 J.N.Shepherd | v | Kent | Bristol | 1983 |

# HAMPSHIRE

**Formation of Present Club**: 12 August 1863
**Colours**: Blue, Gold and White
**Badge**: Tudor Rose and Crown
**County Champions**: (2) 1961, 1973
**Gillette/NatWest/C & G Trophy Winners**: (1) 1991
**Benson and Hedges Cup Winners**: (2) 1988, 1992
**National League (Div 1) Winners**: (0); best – 8th 1999
**Sunday League Winners**: (3) 1975, 1978, 1986
**Match Awards**: CGT 62; BHC 67

**Chief Executive**: G.M.Walker, The Hampshire Rose Bowl, Botley Road, West End, Southampton SO30 3XH • Tel: 023 8047 2002 • Fax: 023 8047 2122 • Email: enquiries.hants@ecb.co.uk • Web: www.hampshire.cricket.org

**First XI Coach**: V.P.Terry. **Captain**: *(tba)*. **Vice-Captain**: W.S.Kendall. **Overseas Players**: S.M.Katich and *(tbc)* Shoaib Akhtar. **2003 Beneficiary**: R.A.Smith (testimonial). **Scorer**: V.H Isaacs. New registration

**ADAMS, James** Henry Kenneth (Sherborne S; University C, London), b Winchester 23 Sep 1980. 6'2". LHB, LM. British U 2002. Hampshire debut 2002. Dorset 1998. HS 48 v Sussex (Hove) 2002 – on Hants debut. BB 2-81 v Surrey (Southampton) 2002. LO HS 17 v Sussex (Hove) 2002 (NL).

**BENHAM, Christopher** Charles (Yately CS; Loughborough U), b Frimley, Surrey 24 Mar 1983. 6'1". RHB, RM/OB. Summer Contract – awaiting f-c debut. LO HS (Hants CB) 0 (CGT).

**BRUNNSCHWEILER, Iain** (King Edward VI S, Southampton), b Southampton 10 Dec 1979. 6'0". RHB, WK. Debut 2000 – awaiting CC debut. No appearances 2002. HS 19 v NZ A (Portsmouth) 2000 – on debut. LO HS 37 Hants CB v Staffs (Winchester) 2002 (CGT).

**CRAWLEY, John** Paul (Manchester GS; Trinity C, Cambridge); b Maldon, Essex 21 Sep 1971. Brother of M.A.Crawley (Oxford U, Lancs and Notts 1987-94) and P.M. (Cambridge U 1992). 6'1". RHB, RM, occ WK. Lancashire 1990-2001; cap 1994; captain 1999-2001. Cambridge U 1991-93; blue 1991-92-93; captain 1992-93. Hampshire debut/cap 2002. YC 1994. **Tests**: 37 (1994 to 2002-03); HS 156* v SL (Oval) 1998. **LOI**: 13 (1994-95 to 1998-99); HS 73 v Z (Harare) 1996-97. Tours: A 1994-95, 1998-99; SA 1993-94 (Eng A), 1995-96; WI 1995-96 (La), 1997-98, 2000-01 (Eng A); NZ 1996-97; Z 1996-97. 1000 runs (8); most – 1851 (1998). HS 286 England A v E Province (Port Elizabeth) 1993-94. CC HS 281* La v Somerset (Southport) 1994. H HS 272 v Kent (Canterbury) 2002 – on Hants debut. BB 1-90. Awards: BHC 2. LO HS 114 La v Notts (Manchester) 1995 (BHC).

**FRANCIS, John** Daniel (King Edward VI S, Southampton; Durham U; Loughborough U), b Bromley, Kent 13 Nov 1980. Younger brother of S.R.G.Francis (*see SOMERSET*). 5'11". LHB, SLA. Debut 2001. Summer Contract. British U 2002. HS 82 v and BB 1-1 Leics (Leicester) 2002. LO HS 103* v Northants (Southampton) 2002 (NL).

**‡GIDDINS, Edward** Simon Hunter (Eastbourne C), b Eastbourne, Sussex 20 Jul 1971. 6'4½". RHB, RFM. Sussex 1991-96; cap 1994. Warwickshire 1998-2000; cap 1998. Surrey 2001-02. Hampshire staff 2003. MCC YC. **Tests**: 4 (1999 to 2000); HS 7 and BB 5-15 v Z (Lord's) 2000. Tour: P 1995-96 (Eng A). HS 34 Sx v Essex (Hove) 1995. 50 wkts (4); most – 84 (1998). BB 6-47 Sx v Yorks (Eastbourne) 1996. Awards: CGT 1; BHC 1. LO HS 13* Sy v Glos (Bristol) 2002 (NL). LO BB 5-20 Sy v Sussex (Oval) 2002 (NL).

**HAMBLIN, James** Rupert Christopher (Charterhouse S; W of England U), b Pembury, Kent 16 Aug 1978. Son of C.B.Hamblin (Oxford U 1971-73). 6'0". RHB, RMF. Debut 2001. HS 50 v Kent (Southampton) 2002. BB 2-44 v Indians (Southampton) 2002. CC BB 1-44. LO HS 61 v Sussex (Hove) 2001 (NL). LO BB 4-29 v Middx (Southgate) 2001 (NL).

‡**KATICH, Simon** Mathew (Trinity C, WA; U of WA), b Middle Swan, Midland, W Australia 21 Aug 1975. 6'0". LHB. SLC. W Australia 1996-97 to 2001-02. NSW 2002-03. Durham 2000; cap 2000. Yorkshire 2002 (one match). **Tests** (A): 1 (2001); HS 15 v E (Leeds) 2001 – on debut. **LOI** (A): 1 (2000-01); dnb v Z (Melbourne) 2000-01. Tours (A): E 2001; SL 1999-00. 1000 (1+2): most – 1632 (1998-99). HS 228* WA v S Aus (Perth) 2000-01. UK HS 168* A v MCC (Arundel) 2001. CC HS 137* Du v Leics (Chester-le-St) 2000. BB 3-21 A v Somerset (Taunton) 2001. CC BB (Du) 1-10. LO HS 118 WA v Vic (Perth) 2001-02. LO BB 3-21 Aus A v SA (Adelaide) 2001-02.

**KENDALL, William** Salwey (Bradfield C; Keble C, Oxford), b Wimbledon, Surrey 18 Dec 1973. 5'10". RHB, RM. Oxford U 1994-96; blue 1995-96. Hampshire debut 1996; cap 1999. 1000 runs (3); most – 1186 (1999). HS 201 v Sussex (Southampton) 1999. BB 3-37 OU v Derbys (Oxford) 1995. H BB 2-46 v Notts (Southampton) 1996. LO HS 110* v Middx (Southampton) 2002 (NL). LO BB 2-48 v Middx (Southampton) 2002 (BHC).

**KENWAY, Derek** Anthony (St George's S, Southampton; Barton Peveril C, Eastleigh), b Fareham 12 Jun 1978. 5'11". RHB, RM, occ WK. Debut 1997; cap 2001. 1000 runs (1): 1055 (1999). HS 166 v Notts (Southampton) 2001. BB 1-5. Award: CGT 1. LO HS 93* v Derbys (Derby) 2001 (NL).

**MASCARENHAS, Adrian Dimitri** (Trinity C, Perth, Australia), b Hammersmith, London 30 Oct 1977. Resident in Australia 1979-96. RHB, RMF. Debut 1996, taking 6-88 v Glamorgan (Southampton); took 16 wickets in first two CC matches; cap 1998. Dorset 1996. HS 104 v Worcs (Southampton) 2001. BB 6-26 v Middx (Southampton) 2001. Awards: CGT 3. LO HS 79 v Worcs (Southampton) 1999 (NL). LO BB 5-27 v Glos (Southampton) 2002 (NL).

**MORRIS, Alexander** Corfield (Holgate S; Barnsley C), b Barnsley, Yorks 4 Oct 1976. Elder brother of Z.C.Morris (Hampshire 1998-99). 6'3". LHB, RMF. Yorkshire 1995-97. Yorks 2nd XI best when 16yr 332d. Hampshire debut 1998; cap 2001. Tour: Z 1995-96 (Y). HS 65 v Sussex (Southampton) 2001. 50 wkts (2): most – 51 (2001). BB 5-39 v Durham (Chester-le-St) 2001. LO HS 48* Y v Durham (Chester-le-St) 1996 (SL). LO BB 5-32 Y v Young A (Leeds) 1995.

**MULLALLY, Alan** David (Cannington HS, Perth, Australia; Wembley & Carlisle TC), b Southend-on-Sea, Essex 12 Jul 1969. 6'5". RHB, LFM. W Australia 1987-88 to 1989-90. Victoria 1990-91. Hampshire 1988 (1 match), 2000 to date; cap 2000. Leicestershire 1990-99; cap 1993. **Tests**: 19 (1996 to 2001); HS 24 v P (Oval) 1996; BB 5-105 v A (Brisbane) 1998-99. **LOI**: 50 (1996 to 2001); HS 20 v Z (Harare) 1996-97; BB 4-18 v A (Brisbane) 1998-99. Tours: A 1998-99; SA 1999-00; NZ 1996-97. HS 75 Le v Middx (Leicester) 1996. H HS 36 v Derbys (Derby) 2001. 50 wkts (5); most – 70 (1996). BB 9-93 (14-188 match) v Derbys (Derby) 2000. Award: CGT 1. LO HS 38 Le v Kent (Leicester) 1994 (SL). LO BB 6-38 Le v NZ (Leicester) 1990.

**POTHAS, Nic** (King Edward VII S; Rand Afrikaans U), b Johannesburg 18 Nov 1973. ECB qualified – EU (Greek) passport. 6'3". RHB, WK. Transvaal 1993-94 to 2000-01. Hampshire debut 2002. **LOI** (SA): 3 (2000-01); HS 24 v P (Singapore) 2000 – on debut. Tours (SA): E 1996 (SA A); WI 2000-01 (SA A); SL 1998-99. HS 165 Gauteng v KZ-Natal (Johannesburg) 1998-99. H HS 99 v Surrey (Southampton) 2002. LO HS 101 Transvaal v EP (Jo'burg) 1995-96.

**PRITTIPAUL, Lawrence** Roland (St John's C, Southsea; Portsmouth C), b Portsmouth 19 Oct 1979. Cousin of S.Chanderpaul (Guyana and West Indies 1991-92 to date). 6'1". RHB, RM. Debut 2000. HS 152 v Derbys (Southampton) 2000. BB 2-43 v Surrey (Oval) 2002. LO HS 61 v Notts (Southampton) 2000 (NL). LO BB 3-33 v Glos (Southampton) 2002 (BHC).

‡(tbc)**SHOAIB AKHTAR** (Elliott HS; Government C, Rawalpindi, b Rawalpindi, Pakistan 13 Aug 1975. 5'11½". RHB, RF. PIA 1994-95 to 1995-96. Rawalpindi 1994-95 to date. ADBP 1996-97 to date. Somerset (one match) 2001. **Tests** (P): 25 (1997-98 to 2002-03); HS 37 and BB 6-11 v NZ (Lahore) 2001-02. **LOI** (P): 81 (1997-98 to 2002-03); HS 43 v E (Cape Town) 2002-03; BB 6-16 v NZ (Karachi) 2002-02. Tours (P): E (Pak A) 1997; A 1999-00; SA 1997-98; I 1998-99; Z 1997-98; B 1998-99, 2001-02. HS 59* KRL v PIA (Lahore) 2001-02. 50 wkts (0+1): 69 (1996-97). BB 6-11 (*see Tests*). LO HS 43 (*see LOI*). LO BB 6-16 (*see LOI*).

**SMITH, Robin** Arnold (Northlands BHS), b Durban, SA 13 Sep 1963. Younger brother of C.L.Smith (Natal, Glam, Hants and England 1977-78 to 1992) and grandson of Dr V.L.Shearer (Natal). 5'11". RHB, LB. Natal 1980-81 to 1984-85. Hampshire debut 1982; cap 1985; benefit 1996; captain 1998-2002; testimonial 2003. *Wisden* 1989. **Tests**: 62 (1988 to 1995-96); HS 175 v WI (St John's) 1993-94. **LOI**: 71 (1988 to 1995-96); HS 167* v A (Birmingham) 1993 – Eng record. Tours: A 1990-91; SA 1995-96; WI 1989-90, 1993-94; NZ 1991-92; I/SL 1992-93. 1000 runs (11); most – 1577 (1989). HS 209* v Essex (Southend) 1987. BB 2-11 v Surrey (Southampton) 1985. Awards: CGT 9; BHC 5. LO HS 167* (*see LOI*). LO BB 2-13 v Berks (Southampton) 1985 (NWT).

**TOMLINSON, James** Andrew (Harrow Way S, Andover; Cardiff U), b Winchester 12 Jun 1982. 6'1". LHB, LFM. Wiltshire 2001. British U 2002. Hampshire debut 2002. HS 23 and BB 2-55 v Indians (Southampton) 2002. CC HS 5. CC BB 2-91 v Surrey (Oval) 2002. LO HS 6 (NL). LO BB 2-15 v Sussex (Southampton) 2002 (NL).

**TREMLETT, Christopher** Timothy (Thornden S, Chandler's Ford; Taunton's C, Southampton), b Southampton 2 Sep 1981. Son of T.M.Tremlett (Hampshire 1976-91); grandson of M.F.Tremlett (Somerset, CD and England 1947-60). 6'7". RHB, RMF. Debut 2000. HS 40* v Kent (Canterbury) 2002. BB 5-57 v Lancs (Manchester) 2002. LO HS 30* v Glam (Southampton) 2000 (NL). LO BB 4-25 v Essex (Southend) 2002 (NL).

**UDAL, Shaun** David (Cove CS), b Cove, Farnborough 18 Mar 1969. Grandson of G.F.U.Udal (Middx 1932 and Leics 1946); great-great-grandson of J.S.Udal (MCC 1871-75). 6'2". RHB, OB. Debut 1989; cap 1992; benefit 2002. **LOI**: 10 (1994 to 1995); HS 11* v Z (Brisbane) 1994-95; BB 2-37 v A (Sydney) 1994-95. Tours: A 1994-95; P 1995-96 (Eng A). HS 117* v Warwks (Southampton) 1997. 50 wkts (7); most – 74 (1993). BB 8-50 v Sussex (Southampton) 1992. Awards: CGT 1; BHC 2. LO HS 78 v Surrey (Guildford) 1997 (SL). LO BB 5-43 v Surrey (Oval) 1998 (SL).

**VAN DER GUCHT, Charles** Graham (Radley C; St Hild & St Bede C, Durham U), b Wimbledon, Surrey 14 Jan 1980. Grandson of P.I.van der Gucht (Gloucestershire 1932-33). 6'0". LHB, LM/SLA. Debut 2000 – awaiting CC debut. Durham UCCE 2001. Summer Contract. Sustained severe leg injuries in road accident 2001 – no appearances 2002. HS 38 DU v Lancs (Durham) 2001. H HS 0* and B 3-75 v Z (Southampton) 2000 – on debut. Award: CGT 1. LO HS 3 and LO BB 3-35 Hants CB v Glam (Southampton) 1999 (NWT).

## RELEASED/RETIRED
(Having made a first-class County appearance in 2002)

**AYMES, Adrian** Nigel (Bellemoor SM, Southampton), b Southampton 4 Jun 1964. 6'0". RHB, WK. Hampshire 1987-2002; cap 1991; benefit 2000. HS 133 v Leics (Leicester) 1998. BB 2-101 v Notts (Nottingham) 2001. Awards: CGT 1; BHC 1. LO HS 73* v Middx (Lord's) 1998 (NWT).

**JOHNSON, Neil** Clarkson (Howick HS, Natal; Port Elizabeth U), b Salisbury, Rhodesia 24 Jan 1970. 6'2". LHB, RFM. EP B 1989-90 to 1991-92. Natal 1992-93 to 1997-98. Leicestershire 1997; cap 1997. Matabeleland 1999-00. WP 2000-01 to date. Hampshire debut/cap 2001. **Tests** (Z): 13 (1998-99 to 2000); HS 107 v P (Peshawar) 1998-99; BB 4-77 v WI (Kingston) 1999-00. **LOI** (Z): 48 (1998-99 to 2000); HS 132* v A (Lord's) 1999; BB 4-42 v K (Taunton) 1999. Tours (Z): E 2000; SA 1999-00; WI 1999-00; P 1998-99; Z 1994-95 (SA A). 1000 (1): 1073 (2001). HS 150 Leics v Lancs (Leicester) 1997. H HS 117 v Kent (Canterbury) 2002. BB 5-79 Natal v Boland (Stellenbosch) 1993-94. H BB 4-20 v Derbys (Southampton) 2001. LO HS 146* Natal v GW (Kimberley) 1996-97 (SBC). LO BB 4-19 Natal v Kenya (Durban) 1996-97 (SBC).

**LANEY, Jason** Scott (Pewsey Vale CS, Marlborough; Leeds Metropolitan U), b Winchester 27 Apr 1973. 5'10". RHB, OB. Hampshire 1995-2002; cap 1996. Matabeleland 1995-96. 1000 runs (1): 1163 (1996). HS 112 v OU (Oxford) 1996. CC HS 105 v Kent (Canterbury) 1996. BB 1-24. Award: CGT 1. LO HS 153 v Norfolk (Southampton) 1996 (NWT).

**SCHOFIELD, James** Edward Knowle (Worcester RGS; Bradford U), b Blackpool, Lancs 1 Jan 1978. 6'0". RHB, RMF. Hampshire 2001-02 taking wicket of M.L.Hayden (Australians) with his first ball. HS 21* v Durham (Chester-le-St) 2001. BB 4-51 v Worcs (Worcester) 2001. LO HS – and BB 1-22 (NL).

**WHITE, Giles** William (Millfield S; Loughborough U), b Barnstaple, Devon 23 Mar 1972. 6'0". RHB, LB. Somerset 1991 (one match). Combined U 1994. Hampshire 1994-2002; cap 1998. Devon 1988-94. 1000 runs (1): 1211 (1998). HS 156 v SL (Southampton) 1998. CC HS 145 v Yorks (Portsmouth) 1997. BB 3-23 v Notts (Nottingham) 1999. LO HS 76 v Glam (Southampton) 1998 (SL). LO BB (Devon) 1-45 (NWT).

I.H.Shah left the staff having made no 1st XI appearances.

# COUNTY CAPS AWARDED IN 2002

| | |
|---|---|
| Derbyshire | C.W.G.Bassano, L.D.Sutton |
| Durham | – |
| Essex | A.Flower, A.Habib, W.I.Jefferson |
| Glamorgan | S.P.Jones, M.S.Kasprowicz |
| Gloucestershire | C.M.Spearman |
| Hampshire | J.P.Crawley |
| Kent | S.R.Waugh |
| Lancashire | D.Byas, M.J.Chilton, S.G.Law, C.P.Schofield, A.J.Swann |
| Leicestershire | M.G.Bevan, G.W.Flower, M.Kaif, J.Srinath, D.I.Stevens |
| Middlesex | Abdul Razzaq, E.C.Joyce, S.G.Koenig |
| Northamptonshire | – |
| Nottinghamshire | S.C.G.MacGill, K.P.Pietersen |
| Somerset | M.P.L.Bulbeck |
| Surrey | M.R.Ramprakash |
| Sussex | M.J.G.Davis |
| Warwickshire | A.Richardson, J.O.Troughton |
| Worcestershire | – |
| Yorkshire | – |

# HAMPSHIRE 2002

## RESULTS SUMMARY

| | Place | Won | Lost | Tied | Drew | No Result |
|---|---|---|---|---|---|---|
| County Championship (1st Division) | 7th | 2 | 5 | | 9 | |
| All First-Class Matches | | 2 | 6 | | 9 | |
| C & G Trophy | 4th Round | | | | | |
| Benson & Hedges Cup | 4th in South Division | | | | | |
| NU National League (2nd Division) | 7th | 6 | 9 | | | 1 |

## COUNTY CHAMPIONSHIP AVERAGES

### BATTING AND FIELDING

| Cap | | M | I | NO | HS | Runs | Avge | 100 | 50 | Ct/St |
|---|---|---|---|---|---|---|---|---|---|---|
| 2002 | J.P.Crawley | 9 | 16 | 2 | 272 | 806 | 57.57 | 1 | 6 | 7 |
| 1985 | R.A.Smith | 14 | 23 | 1 | 104 | 807 | 36.68 | 2 | 3 | 6 |
| 2001 | N.C.Johnson | 16 | 27 | 2 | 117 | 812 | 32.48 | 1 | 6 | 25 |
| 1999 | W.S.Kendall | 16 | 29 | 2 | 88 | 698 | 25.85 | – | 4 | 12 |
| | J.H.K.Adams | 2 | 4 | 1 | 48 | 76 | 25.33 | – | – | 2 |
| 1992 | S.D.Udal | 16 | 24 | 5 | 88 | 480 | 25.26 | – | 1 | 9 |
| 1998 | A.D.Mascarenhas | 15 | 24 | 2 | 94 | 551 | 25.04 | – | 2 | 7 |
| | N.Pothas | 16 | 26 | 1 | 99 | 597 | 23.88 | – | 5 | 30/4 |
| | J.D.Francis | 8 | 14 | – | 82 | 329 | 23.50 | – | 3 | 5 |
| | C.T.Tremlett | 11 | 14 | 6 | 40* | 180 | 22.50 | – | – | 4 |
| 1996 | J.S.Laney | 7 | 13 | – | 89 | 289 | 22.23 | – | 1 | 7 |
| | J.R.C.Hamblin | 4 | 7 | – | 50 | 147 | 21.00 | – | 1 | 2 |
| 1998 | G.W.White | 8 | 14 | 2 | 36 | 234 | 19.50 | – | – | 6 |
| 2001 | D.A.Kenway | 8 | 15 | 2 | 54 | 238 | 18.30 | – | 1 | 15 |
| 1991 | A.N.Aymes | 4 | 5 | 2 | 22* | 32 | 10.66 | – | – | 13/1 |
| 2000 | A.D.Mullally | 13 | 16 | 5 | 23 | 54 | 4.90 | – | – | 1 |
| | L.R.Prittipaul | 2 | 4 | – | 7 | 13 | 3.25 | – | – | – |
| | J.A.Tomlinson | 4 | 7 | 4 | 5 | 9 | 3.00 | – | – | – |

*Also batted*: A.C.Morris (2 matches – 2001) 12, 24; J.E.K.Schofield (1) 0, 18*.

### BOWLING

| | O | M | R | W | Avge | Best | 5wI | 10wM |
|---|---|---|---|---|---|---|---|---|
| A.D.Mullally | 463.2 | 145 | 1156 | 46 | 25.13 | 6-56 | 1 | – |
| C.T.Tremlett | 336 | 83 | 1061 | 36 | 29.47 | 5-57 | 2 | – |
| A.D.Mascarenhas | 407.5 | 137 | 1110 | 36 | 30.83 | 5-87 | 1 | – |
| S.D.Udal | 579.1 | 136 | 1756 | 50 | 35.12 | 5-56 | 3 | – |
| N.C.Johnson | 231.2 | 50 | 769 | 21 | 36.61 | 3-22 | – | – |

*Also bowled*:

| | | | | | | | | |
|---|---|---|---|---|---|---|---|---|
| J.E.K.Schofield | 53 | 14 | 192 | 6 | 32.00 | 3-94 | | |
| J.A.Tomlinson | 131.2 | 12 | 582 | 9 | 64.66 | 2-91 | | |

J.H.K.Adams 21-4-102-2; J.D.Francis 2-1-1-1; J.R.C.Hamblin 61-6-288-3; W.S.Kendall
58.2-12-173-3; D.A.Kenway 1-0-8-0; A.C.Morris 29-5-112-0;
L.R.Prittipaul 28.3-8-74-2; G.W.White 12.1-1-64-1.

The First-Class Averages (pp 121-135) give the records of Hampshire players in all
first-class county matches (Hampshire's other opponents being the Indians), with the
exception of J.H.K.Adams, whose full county figures are as above, and:
   J.P.Crawley 10-17-2-272-821-54.73-1-6-8ct. Did not bowl.
   J.D.Francis 9-16-0-82-358-22.37-0-3-5ct. 2-1-1-1-1.00-1/1.
   J.A.Tomlinson 5-9-5-23-33-8.25-0-0-1ct. 146.3-13-637-11-57.90-2/55.

# HAMPSHIRE RECORDS

## FIRST-CLASS CRICKET

| | | | | | | |
|---|---|---|---|---|---|---|
| **Highest Total** | For | 672-7d | | v | Somerset | Taunton | 1899 |
| | V | 742 | | by | Surrey | The Oval | 1909 |
| **Lowest Total** | For | 15 | | v | Warwicks | Birmingham | 1922 |
| | V | 23 | | by | Yorkshire | Middlesbrough | 1965 |
| **Highest Innings** | For | 316 | R.H.Moore | v | Warwicks | Bournemouth | 1937 |
| | V | 303* | G.A.Hick | for | Worcs | Southampton | 1997 |

## Highest Partnership for each Wicket

| | | | | | | |
|---|---|---|---|---|---|---|
| 1st | 347 | V.P.Terry/C.L.Smith | v | Warwicks | Birmingham | 1987 |
| 2nd | 321 | G.Brown/E.I.M.Barrett | v | Glos | Southampton | 1920 |
| 3rd | 344 | C.P.Mead/G.Brown | v | Yorkshire | Portsmouth | 1927 |
| 4th | 263 | R.E.Marshall/D.A.Livingstone | v | Middlesex | Lord's | 1970 |
| 5th | 235 | G.Hill/D.F.Walker | v | Sussex | Portsmouth | 1937 |
| 6th | 411 | R.M.Poore/E.G.Wynyard | v | Somerset | Taunton | 1899 |
| 7th | 325 | G.Brown/C.H.Abercrombie | v | Essex | Leyton | 1913 |
| 8th | 227 | K.D.James/T.M.Tremlett | v | Somerset | Taunton | 1985 |
| 9th | 230 | D.A.Livingstone/A.T.Castell | v | Surrey | Southampton | 1962 |
| 10th | 192 | H.A.W.Bowell/W.H.Livsey | v | Worcs | Bournemouth | 1921 |

| | | | | | | |
|---|---|---|---|---|---|---|
| **Best Bowling** | For | 9- 25 | R.M.H.Cottam | v | Lancashire | Manchester | 1965 |
| **(Innings)** | V | 10- 46 | W.Hickton | for | Lancashire | Manchester | 1870 |
| **Best Bowling** | For | 16- 88 | J.A.Newman | v | Somerset | Weston-s-Mare | 1927 |
| **(Match)** | V | 17-119 | W.Mead | for | Essex | Southampton | 1895 |

| | | | | |
|---|---|---|---|---|
| **Most Runs – Season** | 2854 | C.P.Mead | (av 79.27) | 1928 |
| **Most Runs – Career** | 48892 | C.P.Mead | (av 48.84) | 1905-36 |
| **Most 100s – Season** | 12 | C.P.Mead | | 1928 |
| **Most 100s – Career** | 138 | C.P.Mead | | 1905-36 |
| **Most Wkts – Season** | 190 | A.S.Kennedy | (av 15.61) | 1922 |
| **Most Wkts – Career** | 2669 | D.Shackleton | (av 18.23) | 1948-69 |
| **Most Career W-K Dismissals** | 700 | R.J.Parks | (630 ct/70 st) | 1980-92 |
| **Most Career Catches in the Field** | 629 | C.P.Mead | | 1905-36 |

## LIMITED-OVERS CRICKET

| | | | | | | |
|---|---|---|---|---|---|---|
| **Highest Total** | CGT | 371-4 | | v | Glamorgan | Southampton | 1975 |
| | BHC | 321-1 | | v | Minor C (S) | Amersham | 1973 |
| | NL | 313-2 | | v | Sussex | Portsmouth | 1993 |
| **Lowest Total** | CGT | 98 | | v | Lancashire | Manchester | 1975 |
| | BHC | 50 | | v | Yorkshire | Leeds | 1991 |
| | NL | 43 | | v | Essex | Basingstoke | 1972 |
| **Highest Innings** | CGT | 177 | C.G.Greenidge | v | Glamorgan | Southampton | 1975 |
| | BHC | 173* | C.G.Greenidge | v | Minor C (S) | Amersham | 1973 |
| | NL | 172 | C.G.Greenidge | v | Surrey | Southampton | 1987 |
| **Best Bowling** | CGT | 7-30 | P.J.Sainsbury | v | Norfolk | Southampton | 1965 |
| | BHC | 6-25 | S.J.Renshaw | v | Surrey | Southampton | 1997 |
| | NL | 6-20 | T.E.Jesty | v | Glamorgan | Cardiff | 1975 |

# KENT

**Formation of Present Club**: 1 March 1859
**Substantial Reorganisation**: 6 December 1870
**Colours**: Maroon and White
**Badge**: White Horse on a Red Ground
**County Champions**: (6) 1906, 1909, 1910, 1913, 1970, 1978
**Joint Champions**: (1) 1977
**Gillette/NatWest/C & G Trophy Winners**: (2) 1967, 1974
**Benson and Hedges Cup Winners**: (3) 1973, 1976, 1978
**National League (Div 1) Winners**: (1) 2001
**Sunday League Winners**: (4) 1972, 1973, 1976, 1995
**Match Awards**: CGT 55; BHC 96

**Chief Executive**: P.E.Millman, St Lawrence Ground, Canterbury, CT1 3NZ • Tel: 01227 456886 • Fax: 01227 762168 • Email: kent@ecb.co.uk • Web: www.kentcountycricket.co.uk

**Director of Coaching/1st XI Coach**: I.J.Brayshaw. **Captain**: D.P.Fulton. **Vice-Captain**: No appointment. **Overseas Player**: A.Symonds. **2003 Beneficiary**: M.A.Ealham. **Scorer**: J.C.Foley. ‡ New registration

**BANES, Matthew** John (Tonbridge S; Collingwood C, Durham U), b Pembury 10 Dec 1979. 5'9". RHB, OB. Kent debut 1999. British U 2000-01. Durham UCCE 2001-02. No Kent appearances 2002. HS 69 DU v Lancs (Durham) 2002. K HS 53 v NZ (Canterbury) 1999 – on debut. CC HS 5. BB 3-65 DU v Lancs (Durham) 2001. LO HS (Kent CB) 82 v Leics CB (Hinckley) 2001 (CGT). LO BB (Kent CB) 1-11 (CGT).

**‡CARBERRY, Michael** Alexander (St John Rigby Catholic C), b Croydon, Surrey 29 Sep 1980. 6'0". LHB, OB. Surrey 2001-02. Kent staff 2003. HS 153* Sy v CU (Cambridge) 2002. CC HS 84 Sy v Glam (Cardiff) 2001. LO HS 20 Sy v Glos (Bristol) 2001 (NL).

**‡DENNINGTON, Matthew**, b Durban, SA 16 Oct 1982. RHB, RMF. Kent staff 2003 – awaiting first-class debut.

**EALHAM, Mark** Alan (Stour Valley SS, Chartham), b Willesborough, Ashford 27 Aug 1969. Son of A.G.E.Ealham (Kent 1966-82). 5'9". RHB, RMF. Debut 1989; cap 1992; benefit 2003. **Tests**: 8 (1996 to 1998); HS 53* v A (Birmingham) 1997; BB 4-21 v I (Nottingham) 1996. **LOI**: 64 (1996 to 2001); HS 45 v WI (Bridgetown) 1997-98; BB 5-15 v Z (Kimberley) 1999-00 – Eng record. Tours: A 1996-97 (Eng A); SA 1999-00 (*part*); SL 1997-98; Z 1992-93 '(K); K 1997-98. 1000 runs (1): 1055 (1997). HS 153* v Northants (Canterbury) 2001. BB 8-36 (10-74 match) v Warwks (Birmingham) 1996. Awards: CGT 2; BHC 6. LO HS 112 v Derbys (Maidstone) 1995 (off 44 balls – SL record). LO BB 6-53 v Hants (Basingstoke) 1993 (SL).

**FERLEY, Robert** Steven (King Edward VII HS; Sutton Valence S; Grey C, Durham U), b Norwich, Norfolk 4 Feb 1982. 5'8". RHB, SLA. Durham UCCE 2001-02. British U 2001-02. Kent summer staff 2001 – awaiting county debut. Norfolk 2001. HS 37* DU v Lancs (Durham) 2002. BB 4-83 DU v Notts (Nottingham) 2002. LO HS (Kent CB) 6 (CGT). LO BB 2-30 Kent CB v Leics CB (Maidstone) 2002 (CGT).

**‡FLANAGAN, Ian** Nicholas (Colne Community S), b Colchester, Essex 5 Jun 1980. 6'0". LHB, OB. Essex 1997-2000. Cambridgeshire 2002. Kent staff 2003. HS 61 Ex v Warwks (Birmingham) 1998. BB (Ex) 1-50 (not CC). LO HS 45 Cambs v Middx CB (Southgate) 2002 (CGT).

**FULTON, David** Paul (The Judd S; Kent U), b Lewisham 15 Nov 1971. 6'2". RHB, SLA, occ WK. Debut 1992; cap 1998; captain 2002 to date. 1000 (2): most – 1892 (2001). HS 208* v Somerset (Canterbury) 2001. Scored 9 hundreds in 2001, including 208*, 104* and 197 in successive innings. BB 1-37 (not CC). LO HS 82 v Yorks (Leeds) 2001 (NL).

**HEWITT, James** Peter (Teddington S; Richmond C; City of Westminster C), b Southwark, London 26 Feb 1976. 6'2½". LHB, RMF. Middlesex 1996-2001; cap 1998. Kent (one match) 2002. HS 75 M v Essex (Chelmsford) 1997. K HS 48* and BB – v Hants (Canterbury) 2002. 50 wkts (1): 60 (1997). BB 6-14 M v Glam (Cardiff) 1997. Took wicket of R.I.Dawson (Glos) with first ball in f-c cricket. LO HS 32* M v Glos (Bristol) 1997 (SL). LO BB 4-24 M v Worcs (Uxbridge) 1998 (SL).

**JONES, Geraint** Owen (Harristown State HS, Toowoomba and MacGregor State HS, Brisbane, Australia), b Kundiawa, Papua New Guinea 14 Jul 1976. Welsh parents. 5'10". RHB, WK. Debut 2001. HS 76* v SL (Canterbury) 2002. CC HS 40 v Leics (Canterbury) 2002. LO HS 39 v Surrey (Oval) 2001 (NL).

**KEY, Robert** William Trevor (Colfe's S), b East Dulwich, London 12 May 1979. 6'1". RHB, RM/OB. Debut 1998; cap 2001. **Tests**: 6 (2002 to 2002-03); HS 52 v A (Melbourne) 2002-03. Tours: A 2002-03; SA 1998-99 (Eng A); Z 1998-99 (Eng A). 1000 (2): most – 1281 (2001). HS 174* England XI v Australia A (Hobart) 2002-03. K HS 160 v Hants (Canterbury) 2002. LO HS 114 v Notts (Nottingham) 2002 (NL).

**KHAN, Amjad** (Skolenpa Duevej, Denmark), b Copenhagen, Denmark 14 Oct 1980. 6'0". RHB, RFM. Debut 2001. Denmark 1998-2000. HS 58 v Sussex (Hove) 2002. 50 wkts (1): 63 (2002). BB 6-52 v Yorks (Canterbury) 2002. LO HS 21 v Warwks (Birmingham) 2002 (NL). LO BB 2-38 Denmark v Kent CB (Maidstone) 1999 (NWT).

**LOUDON, Alexander** Guy Rushworth (Wellesley House; Eton C; Collingwood C, Durham U), b Westminster, London 6 Sep 1980. Younger brother of H.J.H.Loudon (Durham UCCE 2001). 6'3". RHB, OB. Durham UCCE 2001-02. Awaiting County f-c debut. HS 39 DU v Lancs (Durham) 2001. BB 3-86 DU v Worcs (Worcester) 2001. LO HS 53 Kent CB v Leics CB (Hinckley) 2001 (CGT).

**PATEL, Minal** Mahesh (Dartford GS; Erith TC), b Bombay, India 7 Jul 1970. 5'9". RHB, SLA. Debut 1989; cap 1994. **Tests**: 2 (1996); HS 27 and BB 1-101 v I (Nottingham) 1996. Tour: I 1994-95 (Eng A). HS 82 v Leics (Canterbury) 2002. 50 wkts (3); most – 90 (1994). BB 8-96 v Lancs (Canterbury) 1994. LO HS 27* v Somerset (Canterbury) 2001 (CGT). LO BB 3-22 v Essex (Canterbury) 1999 (NL).

**SAGGERS, Martin** John (Springwood HS, King's Lynn; Huddersfield U), b King's Lynn, Norfolk 23 May 1972. 6'2". RHB, RMF. Durham 1996-98. Norfolk 1995-96. Kent debut 1999; cap 2001. HS 61* v Lancs (Canterbury) 2001. 50 wkts (3): most – 83 (2002). BB 7-79 v Durham (Chester-le-St) 2000. Award: BHC 1. LO HS 34* Minor C v Leics (Jesmond) 1996 (BHC). LO BB 5-22 v Glos (Canterbury) 2001 (NL).

‡**SHERIYAR, Alamgir** (George Dixon S; Joseph Chamberlain SFC; Oxford Poly), b Birmingham 15 Nov 1973. 6'1". RHB, LFM. Leicestershire 1994-95. Worcestershire 1996-2002; cap 1997. Kent staff 2003. Tours (Eng A): NZ 1999-00; B 1999-00. HS 21 Wo v Notts (Nottingham) 1997 and 21 Wo v Pak A (Worcester) 1997. 50 wkts (4); most – 92 (1999). BB 7-130 (10-172 match) Wo v Hants (Southampton) 1999. Hat-tricks (2): 1994 (Le), 1999 (Wo). LO HS 19 Wo v Derbys (Chesterfield) 1996 (SL). LO BB 4-18 Wo v Yorks (Leeds) 1997 (SL).

**SMITH, Edward** Thomas (Tonbridge S; Peterhouse, Cambridge), b Pembury 19 Jul 1977. 6'2". RHB, RM. Cambridge U 1996-98, scoring 101 v Glam (Cambridge) on debut; blue 1996-97 (*injured* 1998). Kent debut 1996; cap 2001. British U 1998. 1000 runs (3): most – 1239 (2002). HS 190 CU v Leics (Cambridge) 1997. K HS 175 v Durham (Chester-le-St) 2000. LO HS 87 v WI A (Canterbury) 2002.

**SYMONDS, Andrew** (All Saints Anglican School, Mudgeeraba, Queensland), b Birmingham 9 Jun 1975. 6'1½". RHB, RMF/OB. Emigrated to Australia when 18 months old. Queensland 1994-95 to date. Gloucestershire 1995-96; cap 1996. Kent 1999, 2001; cap 1999. YC 1995. Surrendered England qualification by appearing for Australia A v WI 1996-97. **LOI** (A): 63 (1998-99 to 2002-03); HS 143* v P (Jo'burg) 2002-03; BB 4-11 v I (Sydney) 1999-00. Tours (Aus A): Sc 1998; NZ 1994-95 (Aus Academy). 1000 runs (2); most – 1438 (1995). HS 254* Gs v Glam (Abergavenny) 1995 (including record 16 sixes); hit record 20 sixes in match. K HS 177 v Leics (Canterbury) 1999. BB 6-105 v Sussex (Tunbridge Wells) 2002. Awards: CGT 2; BHC 2. LO HS 143* (*see LOI*). LO BB 6-14 Aus A v Ind A (Los Angeles) 1999.

**TREDWELL, James** Cullum (Southlands Community CS, New Romney), b Ashford 27 Feb 1982. 6'0". LHB, OB. Debut 2001. HS 61 v Yorks (Leeds) 2002. BB 4-103 v Warwks (Birmingham) 2002. LO HS 71 Kent CB v Bucks (Maidstone) 2001 (CGT). LO BB 3-7 v Norfolk (Horsford) 2002 (CGT).

‡**TREGO, Peter** David (Wyvern CS, W-s-M), b Weston-super-Mare, Somerset 12 Jun 1981. 6'0". RHB, RMF. Somerset 2000-02; on Kent staff 2003. HS 140 Sm v WI A (Taunton) 2002. CC HS 62 Sm v Yorks (Taunton) 2000. BB 4-84 Sm v Yorks (Scarborough) 2000. LO HS 24 Sm v Kent (Taunton) 2002 (NL). LO BB 3-14 Sm v Durham (Taunton) 2002 (NL).

**TROTT, Benjamin** James (Court Fields Community S, Wellington; Richard Huish C, Taunton; Plymouth U), b Wellington, Somerset 14 Mar 1975. 6'5". RHB, RMF. Somerset 1997-98. Kent debut 2000. Devon 2000. HS 26 v Sussex (Tunbridge Wells) 2002. BB 6-13 (11-78 match) v Essex (Tunbridge Wells) 2001. Award: CGT 1. LO HS 2* (NL). LO BB 5-18 v Cumb (Barrow) 2001 (CGT).

**WALKER, Matthew** Jonathan (King's S, Rochester), b Gravesend 2 Jan 1974. Grandson of Jack Walker (Kent 1949). 5'8". LHB, RM. Debut 1992-93 (Z tour); UK Debut 1994; cap 2000. Tour: Z 1992-93 (K). HS 275* v Somerset (Canterbury) 1996. BB 1-3 (FCC Select XI). K BB 1-4. Awards: BHC 3. LO HS 117 v Warwks (Canterbury) 1997 (BHC). LO BB 4-24 v Yorks (Leeds) 2001 (NL).

### RELEASED/RETIRED
(Having made a first-class County appearance in 2002)

**FLEMING, Matthew** Valentine (St Aubyns S, Rottingdean; Eton C), b Macclesfield, Cheshire 12 Dec 1964. 5'11½". RHB, RM. Kent 1989-2002; cap 1990; captain 1999-2001 (l-o captain 2002); benefit 2001. Walter Lawrence Trophy 2002. **LOI**: 11 (1997-98 to 1998); HS 33 v WI (Sharjah) 1997-98; BB 4-45 v I (Sharjah) 1997-98 – on debut. Tour: Z 1992-93 (K). HS 138 v Essex (Canterbury) 1997 and 138 v Worcs (Worcester) 1999. BB 5-51 v Notts (Nottingham) 1997. Awards: CGT 3; BHC 7. LO HS 125 v Northants (Canterbury) 2001 (NL). LO BB 5-27 v Hants (Canterbury) 1997 (BHC).

**GOLDING, James** Matthew (Kent C, Canterbury; University C, Worcester), b Canterbury 19 Jul 1977. 6'4". RHB, RMF. Kent 1999-2002. HS 32 v Warwks (Maidstone) 2002. BB 4-76 v SL (Canterbury) 2002. CC BB 3-23 v Somerset (Taunton) 2001. Award: CGT 1. LO HS 47* v Leics (Leicester) 2002 (NL). LO BB 4-42 v Indians (Canterbury) 2002.

**HOCKLEY, James** Bernard (Kelsey Park S, Beckenham), b Beckenham 16 Apr 1979. 6'2". RHB, OB. Kent 1998-2002. HS 74 v Z (Canterbury) 2000. CC HS 46 v Surrey (Canterbury) 2002. BB 1-21. Awards: CGT 1; BHC 1. LO HS 121 v Warwks (Canterbury) 2002 (CGT). LO BB 1-35 (CGT).

**MASTERS, D.D.** – *see LEICESTERSHIRE*.

**NIXON, P.A.** – *see LEICESTERSHIRE*. **RELEASED/RETIRED** continued on p 59

# KENT 2002

## RESULTS SUMMARY

| | Place | Won | Lost | Tied | Drew | No Result |
|---|---|---|---|---|---|---|
| **County Championship** (1st Division) | **3rd** | 7 | 4 | | 5 | |
| **All First-Class Matches** | | 7 | 4 | | 6 | |
| **C & G Trophy** | Semi-Finalist | | | | | |
| **Benson & Hedges Cup** | 3rd in South Division | | | | | |
| **NU National League** (1st Division) | **5th** | 7 | 8 | 1 | | |

## COUNTY CHAMPIONSHIP AVERAGES

### BATTING AND FIELDING

| Cap | | M | I | NO | HS | Runs | Avge | 100 | 50 | Ct/St |
|---|---|---|---|---|---|---|---|---|---|---|
| | J.M.Golding | 3 | 4 | 2 | 32 | 95 | 47.50 | – | – | – |
| 2002 | S.R.Waugh | 4 | 6 | 1 | 146 | 224 | 44.80 | 1 | – | 3 |
| 2001 | R.W.T.Key | 13 | 26 | 1 | 160 | 1090 | 43.60 | 3 | 5 | 10 |
| 2001 | E.T.Smith | 16 | 31 | 2 | 154 | 1233 | 42.51 | 2 | 8 | 4 |
| 1998 | D.P.Fulton | 15 | 30 | 1 | 177 | 1166 | 40.20 | 3 | 4 | 30 |
| 1994 | M.M.Patel | 15 | 20 | 6 | 82 | 561 | 40.07 | – | 5 | 8 |
| 1999 | A.Symonds | 12 | 24 | 2 | 118 | 858 | 39.00 | 2 | 4 | 16 |
| 2000 | P.A.Nixon | 16 | 30 | 7 | 103 | 865 | 37.60 | 1 | 6 | 49/4 |
| 1992 | M.A.Ealham | 14 | 24 | 7 | 83* | 594 | 34.94 | – | 3 | 14 |
| | J.C.Tredwell | 4 | 6 | – | 61 | 161 | 26.83 | – | 2 | 8 |
| 1990 | M.V.Fleming | 4 | 7 | 1 | 42* | 109 | 18.16 | – | – | – |
| 2000 | M.J.Walker | 11 | 22 | 3 | 46 | 342 | 18.00 | – | – | 3 |
| | D.D.Masters | 8 | 7 | – | 68 | 117 | 16.71 | – | 1 | 3 |
| | A.Khan | 16 | 19 | 5 | 58 | 213 | 15.21 | – | 1 | 5 |
| | J.B.Hockley | 4 | 8 | 1 | 46 | 80 | 11.42 | – | – | 1 |
| 2001 | M.J.Saggers | 15 | 19 | 6 | 16* | 73 | 5.61 | – | – | 5 |

*Also batted*: J.P.Hewitt (1 match) 48*; G.O.Jones (3) 40, 28, 18 (2 ct); B.J.Trott (2) 0, 1, 26.

### BOWLING

| | O | M | R | W | Avge | Best | 5wI | 10wM |
|---|---|---|---|---|---|---|---|---|
| M.J.Saggers | 547.3 | 109 | 1702 | 79 | 21.54 | 6- 39 | 6 | – |
| A.Khan | 485 | 75 | 2004 | 63 | 31.80 | 6- 52 | 4 | – |
| M.M.Patel | 522.3 | 152 | 1190 | 36 | 33.05 | 5- 56 | 1 | – |
| M.A.Ealham | 351 | 107 | 954 | 28 | 34.07 | 3- 22 | – | – |
| J.C.Tredwell | 124.2 | 29 | 358 | 10 | 35.80 | 4-103 | – | – |
| D.D.Masters | 243.1 | 46 | 864 | 23 | 37.56 | 4- 36 | – | – |
| A.Symonds | 187.2 | 34 | 602 | 13 | 46.30 | 6-105 | 1 | – |

*Also bowled*:

| | | | | | | | | |
|---|---|---|---|---|---|---|---|---|
| B.J.Trott | 40 | 7 | 151 | 5 | 30.20 | 3- 83 | | |
| M.V.Fleming | 87 | 18 | 251 | 6 | 41.83 | 4- 68 | | |

J.M.Golding 38.1-6-119-2; J.P.Hewitt 26-5-92-0; P.A.Nixon 0.3-0-8-0; M.J.Walker 15.3-4-57-0; S.R.Waugh 3-0-15-0.

The First-Class Averages (pp 121-135) give the records of Kent players in all first-class county matches (Kent's other opponents being the Sri Lankans), with the exception of M.J.Banes, R.S.Ferley and A.G.R.Loudon whose only first-class appearances were in University matches and:

D.P.Fulton 16-31-1-177-1282-42.73-4-4-33ct. Did not bowl.
R.W.T.Key 14-27-1-160-1097-42.19-3-5-10 ct. Did not bowl.

# KENT RECORDS

## FIRST-CLASS CRICKET

| | | | | | | |
|---|---|---|---|---|---|---|
| **Highest Total** | For 803-4d | | v | Essex | Brentwood | 1934 |
| | V 676 | | by | Australians | Canterbury | 1921 |
| **Lowest Total** | For 18 | | v | Sussex | Gravesend | 1867 |
| | V 16 | | by | Warwicks | Tonbridge | 1913 |
| **Highest Innings** | For 332 | W.H.Ashdown | v | Essex | Brentwood | 1934 |
| | V 344 | W.G.Grace | for | MCC | Canterbury | 1876 |

### Highest Partnership for each Wicket

| | | | | | | |
|---|---|---|---|---|---|---|
| 1st | 300 | N.R.Taylor/M.R.Benson | v | Derbyshire | Canterbury | 1991 |
| 2nd | 366 | S.G.Hinks/N.R.Taylor | v | Middlesex | Canterbury | 1990 |
| 3rd | 321* | A.Hearne/J.R.Mason | v | Notts | Nottingham | 1899 |
| 4th | 368 | P.A.de Silva/G.R.Cowdrey | v | Derbyshire | Maidstone | 1995 |
| 5th | 277 | F.E.Woolley/L.E.G.Ames | v | New Zealand | Canterbury | 1931 |
| 6th | 315 | P.A.de Silva/M.A.Ealham | v | Notts | Nottingham | 1995 |
| 7th | 248 | A.P.Day/E.Humphreys | v | Somerset | Taunton | 1908 |
| 8th | 157 | A.L.Hilder/A.C.Wright | v | Essex | Gravesend | 1924 |
| 9th | 171 | M.A.Ealham/P.A.Strang | v | Notts | Nottingham | 1997 |
| 10th | 235 | F.E.Woolley/A.Fielder | v | Worcs | Stourbridge | 1909 |

| | | | | | | |
|---|---|---|---|---|---|---|
| **Best Bowling** | For 10- 30 | C.Blythe | v | Northants | Northampton | 1907 |
| **(Innings)** | V 10- 48 | C.H.G.Bland | for | Sussex | Tonbridge | 1899 |
| **Best Bowling** | For 17- 48 | C.Blythe | v | Northants | Northampton | 1907 |
| **(Match)** | V 17-106 | T.W.J.Goddard | for | Glos | Bristol | 1939 |

| | | | | | |
|---|---|---|---|---|---|
| **Most Runs – Season** | 2894 | F.E.Woolley | (av 59.06) | | 1928 |
| **Most Runs – Career** | 47868 | F.E.Woolley | (av 41.77) | | 1906-38 |
| **Most 100s – Season** | 10 | F.E.Woolley | | | 1928 |
| | 10 | F.E.Woolley | | | 1934 |
| **Most 100s – Career** | 122 | F.E.Woolley | | | 1906-38 |
| **Most Wkts – Season** | 262 | A.P.Freeman | (av 14.74) | | 1933 |
| **Most Wkts – Career** | 3340 | A.P.Freeman | (av 17.64) | | 1914-36 |
| **Most Career W-K Dismissals** | 1253 | F.H.Huish | (901 ct/352 st) | | 1895-1914 |
| **Most Career Catches in the Field** | 773 | F.E.Woolley | | | 1906-38 |

## LIMITED-OVERS CRICKET

| | | | | | | |
|---|---|---|---|---|---|---|
| **Highest Total** | CGT | 384-6 | | v | Berkshire | Finchampstead | 1994 |
| | BHC | 338-6 | | v | Somerset | Maidstone | 1996 |
| | NL | 327-6 | | v | Leics | Canterbury | 1993 |
| **Lowest Total** | CGT | 60 | | v | Somerset | Taunton | 1979 |
| | BHC | 73 | | v | Middlesex | Canterbury | 1979 |
| | NL | 83 | | v | Middlesex | Lord's | 1984 |
| **Highest Innings** | CGT | 136* | C.L.Hooper | v | Berkshire | Finchampstead | 1994 |
| | BHC | 143 | C.J.Tavaré | v | Somerset | Taunton | 1985 |
| | NL | 145 | C.L.Hooper | v | Leics | Leicester | 1996 |
| **Best Bowling** | CGT | 8-31 | D.L.Underwood | v | Scotland | Edinburgh | 1987 |
| | BHC | 6-41 | T.N.Wren | v | Somerset | Canterbury | 1995 |
| | NL | 6- 9 | R.A.Woolmer | v | Derbyshire | Chesterfield | 1979 |

# LANCASHIRE

**Formation of Present Club**: 12 January 1864
**Colours**: Red, Green and Blue
**Badge**: Red Rose
**County Champions (since 1890)**: (7) 1897, 1904, 1926, 1927, 1928, 1930, 1934
**Joint Champions**: (1) 1950
**Gillette/NatWest/C & G Trophy Winners**: (7) 1970, 1971, 1972, 1975, 1990, 1996, 1998
**Benson and Hedges Cup Winners**: (4) 1984, 1990, 1995, 1996
**National League (Div 1) Winners**: (1) 1999.
**Sunday League Winners**: (4) 1969, 1970, 1989, 1998
**Match Awards**: CGT 75; BHC 86

**Chief Executive**: J.Cumbes, Old Trafford, Manchester M16 0PX • Tel: 0161 282 4000 • Fax: 0161 282 4100 • Email: enquiries@lccc.co.uk • Web: www.lccc.co.uk

**Cricket Manager/First XI Coach**: M.Watkinson. **Captain**: W.K.Hegg. **Vice-Captain**: (*tba*). **Overseas Players**: Harbhajan Singh and S.G.Law. **2003 Beneficiary**: Lancashire Academy. **Scorer**: A.West. ‡ New registration

**ANDERSON, James** Michael (St Theodore RC HS and SFC, Burnley), b Burnley 30 Jul 1982. 6'2". LHB, RMF. England U-19. Debut 2002. **LOI**: 14 (2002-03); HS 8; BB 4-25 v Holland (E London) 2002-03. HS 16 v Warwks (Manchester) 2002. 50 wkts (1): 50 (2002). BB 6-23 v Hants (Southampton) 2002. LO HS 8 (*see LOI*). LO BB 4-25 (*see LOI*).

**CHAPPLE, Glen** (West Craven HS; Nelson & Colne C), b Skipton, Yorks 23 Jan 1974. 6'1". RHB, RFM. Debut 1992; cap 1994. Tours (Eng A): A 1996-97; WI 1995-96 (La); I 1994-95. HS 155 v Somerset (Manchester) 2001. Scored 100 off 27 balls in contrived circumstances v Glam (Manchester) 1993. 50 wkts (4); most – 55 (1994). BB 6-30 v Somerset (Blackpool) 2002. Awards: CGT 1; BHC 2. LO HS 81* v Derbys (Manchester) 2002 (CGT). LO BB 6-18 v Essex (Lord's) 1996 (NWT).

**CHILTON, Mark** James (Manchester GS; Durham U), b Sheffield, Yorks 2 Oct 1976. 6'3". RHB, RM. Debut 1997. Cap 2002. British U 1998. HS 107 v DU (Durham) 2002. CC HS 104 v Northants (Northampton) 2001. BB 1-1.CC BB 1-10. Awards: CGT 1; BHC 4. LO HS 102 v Notts (Manchester) 2002 (BHC). LO BB 5-26 Brit U v Sussex (Cambridge) 1997 (BHC).

**‡CROOK, Steven** Paul (Rostever C, S Aus), b Modbury, S Australia 28 May 1983. Younger brother of A.R.Crook (S Australia 1998-99). 5'11". RHB, RFM. British passport. S Australia U-17, U-19. Lancashire staff 2003 – awaiting first-class debut.

**CURRIE, Mark** Robert (Poynton County HS; City of Westminster C), b Manchester 22 Sep 1979. 6'1". RHB, OB. Debut 2002 – awaiting CC debut. Cheshire 1999-2002. MCCYC. HS 48* v WI A (Liverpool) 2002 on debut. LO HS 94 v Cheshire v Lincs (Neston) 2002 (CGT).

**FLINTOFF, Andrew** (Ribbleton Hall HS), b Preston 6 Dec 1977. 6'4". RHB, RM. Debut 1995; cap 1998. YC 1998. **ECB contracts 2000, 2002, 2003. Tests**: 21 (1998 to 2002); HS 137 v NZ (Christchurch) 2001-02; BB 4-50 v I (Bangalore) 2001-02. **LOI**: 52 (1998-99 to 2002-03); HS 84 v P (Karachi) 2000-01; BB 4-17 v NZ (Auckland) 2001-02. Tours (Eng A): SA 1998-99, 1999-00 (Eng); NZ 2001-02; I 2001-02; SL 1997-98; Z 1998-99; K 1997-98. HS 160 v Yorks (Manchester) 1999. BB 5-24 v Hants (Southampton) 1999. Awards: CGT 3; BHC 1. LO HS 143 (off 66 balls) v Essex (Chelmsford) 1999 (NL). LO BB 4-11 v Yorks (Leeds) 2002 (BHC).

‡**HARBHAJAN SINGH**, b Jullundur, India 3 Jul 1980. RHB, OB. Punjab 1997-98 to date. **Tests** (I): 33 (1997-98 to 2002-03); HS 66 v Z (Bulawayo) 2001; BB 8-84 (15-217 match) v A (Madras) 2000-01. Took 28 wickets, including a hat-trick, in 2 Tests v Australia 2000-01. **LOI** (I): 73 (1997-98 to 2002-03); HS 46 v A (Vishakapatnam) 2000-01; BB 5-43 v E (Bombay) 2001-02. Tours (I): E 2002; SA 2001-02; WI 2002; NZ 1998-99, 2002-03; SL 1998-99, 2001; Z 1998-99, 2001. HS 84 Punjab v Haryana (Amritsar) 2000-01. UK HS 54 I v E (Nottingham) 2002. 50 wkts (1): 70 (2000-01). BB 8-84 (15-217 match) (*see Tests*). Hat-trick (India 2000-01). UK BB 7-83 I v Essex (Chelmsford) 2002. LO HS 46 (*see LOI*). LO BB 5-43 (*see LOI*).

**HAYNES, Jamie** Jonathan (St Edmunds C, Canberra; Canberra U), b Bristol 5 Jul 1974. 5'11". RHB, WK. Debut 1996. Represented Australian Capital Territory at cricket and Australian Rules football. HS 80 v SL A (Manchester) 1999. CC HS 57 v Surrey (Oval) 2001. LO HS 59* v Warwks CB (Blackpool) 2001 (CGT).

**HEGG, Warren** Kevin (Unsworth HS, Bury; Stand C, Whitefield), b Whitefield 23 Feb 1968. 5'8". RHB, WK. Debut 1986; cap 1989; benefit 1999; captain 2002 to date. **Tests**: 2 (1998-99); HS 15 v A (Sydney) 1998-99. Tours: A 1996-97 (Eng A), 1998-99; WI 1986-87 (La), 1995-96 (La); NZ 2001-02; SL 1988-89 (La); Z 1988-89 (La). HS 134 v Leics (Manchester) 1996. Held 11 catches (equalling world f-c match record) v Derbys (Chesterfield) 1989. Award: BHC 1. LO HS 81 v Yorks (Manchester) 1996 (BHC).

**HOGG, Kyle** William (Saddleworth HS), b Birmingham 2 Jul 1983. Son of W.Hogg (Lancashire and Warwickshire 1976-83); grandson of S.Ramadhin (Trinidad, Lancashire and West Indies 1949-50 to 1965). 6'4". LHB, RFM. Debut 2001. HS 50 v Somerset (Taunton) 2002. BB 5-48 v Leics (Manchester) 2002. LO HS 24 v Glos (Manchester) 2002 (NL). LO BB 4-20 v Hants (Southampton) 2002 (NL).

**KEEDY, Gary** (Garforth CS), b Wakefield, Yorks 27 Nov 1974. 6'0". LHB, SLA. Yorkshire 1994 (one match). Lancashire debut 1995; cap 2000. Tour: WI 1995-96 (La). HS 57 v Yorks (Leeds) 2002. BB 6-56 (10-155 match) v Durham (Manchester) 2000. LO HS 10* v Essex (Manchester) 2002 (NL). LO BB 5-30 v Sussex (Manchester) 2000 (NL).

**LAW, Stuart** Grant (Craigslea State HS), b Herston, Brisbane, Australia 18 Oct 1968. 6'1". RHB, RM/LB. Queensland 1988-89 to date; captain 1994-95 to 1996-97, 1999-00 to 2001-02. Essex 1996-2001; cap 1996. Lancashire debut/cap 2002. *Wisden* 1997. **Tests** (A): 1 (1995-96); HS 54* v SL (Perth) 1995-96. **LOI** (A): 54 (1994-95 to 1999-00); HS 110 v Z (Hobart) 1994-95; BB 2-22 v P (Sydney) 1996-97. Tours: E 1995 (Young A); Z 1991-92 (Aus B). 1000 runs (6+1); most – 1833 (1999). HS 263 Ex v Somerset (Chelmsford) 1999. La HS 218 v Sussex (Manchester) 2002. BB 5-39 Q v Tasmania (Brisbane) 1995-96. CC BB 3-27 Ex v Worcs (Chelmsford) 1997. La BB 1-24. Awards: CGT 4; BHC 1. LO HS 163 Young A v Surrey (Oval) 1995. LO BB 5-26 Q v SL (Cairns) 1995-96.

‡**LOYE, Malachy** Bernhard (Moulton S), b Northampton 27 Sep 1972. 6'2". RHB, OB. Northamptonshire 1991-2002; cap 1994. Lancashire staff 2003. Tours (Eng A): SA 1993-94, 1998-99; Z 1994-95 (Nh), 1998-99. 1000 runs (3); most – 1198 (1998). HS 322* Nh v Glam (Northampton) 1998 – record Northants score until 2001. Awards: CGT 1; BHC 1. LO HS 124* Nh v Northants CB (Northampton) 2001 (CGT).

**MAHMOOD, Sajid** Iqbal (North C, Bolton), b Bolton 21 Dec 1981. RHB, RMF. Debut 2002. HS 18 v Hants (Manchester) 2002 – on debut. LO HS 11 Lancs CB v Cheshire (Chester) 2001 (CGT).

**MARTIN, Peter** James (Danum S, Doncaster), b Accrington 15 Nov 1968. 6'4". RHB, RFM. Debut 1989; cap 1994; benefit 2002. **Tests**: 8 (1995 to 1997); HS 29 v WI (Lord's) 1995; BB 4-60 v SA (Durban) 1995-96. **LOI**: 20 (1995 to 1998-99); HS 6; BB 4-44 v WI (Oval) 1995 – on debut. Tour: SA 1995-96. HS 133 v Durham (Gateshead) 1992. 50 wkts (4); most – 58 (1997). BB 8-32 (13-79 match) v Middx (Uxbridge) 1997. Awards: CGT 2. LO HS 35* v Worcs (Manchester) 1996 (SL). LO BB 5-16 v Warwks CB (Blackpool) 2001 (CGT).

**REES, Timothy** Martyn (Canon Slade S and SFC, Bolton), b Loughborough, Leics 4 Sep 1984. 6'1". RHB, OB. Debut 2002. HS 16 v Somerset (Taunton) 2002 – on debut. LO HS 7* (NL).

**SCHOFIELD, Christopher** Paul (Wardle HS), b Birch Hill, Rochdale 6 Oct 1978. 6'2". LHB, LB. Debut 1998; cap 2002. **ECB contract 2000. Tests**: 2 (2000); HS 57 v Z (Nottingham) 2000. Tours (Eng A): WI 2000-01; NZ 1999-00; B 1999-00. HS 91 v Warwks (Manchester) 2002. BB 6-120 Eng A v Bangladesh (Chittagong) 1999-00. La BB 5-48 v CU (Cambridge) 2000. CC BB 5-66 v Durham (Manchester) 1999. LO HS 52 v Middx (Shenley) 2002 (NL). LO BB 5-31 v Derbys (Manchester) 2001 (NL).

‡**SUTCLIFFE, Iain** John (Leeds GS; Queen's C, Oxford), b Leeds, Yorks 20 Dec 1974. 6'2". LHB, occ OB. Oxford U 1994-96; blue 1995-96; boxing blue 1993-94. Leicestershire 1995-2002; cap 1997. Lancashire staff 2003. Tour (Le): SA 1996-97. 1000 (2): most – 1088 (2002). HS 203 Le v Glam (Cardiff) 2001. BB 2-21 OU v CU (Lord's) 1996. CC BB (Le) 1-7. Awards: CGT 1; BHC 1. LO HS 105* Le v Notts (Nottingham) 1998 (BHC).

**SWANN, Alec** James (Risade S; Sponne S, Towcester), b Northampton 26 Oct 1976. Son of R.Swann (Northumberland 1969-72; Bedfordshire 1988-95); elder brother of G.P.Swann (see *NORTHAMPTONSHIRE*). 6'1". RHB, RM/OB. Northamptonshire 1996-2001. Lancashire debut/cap 2002. Bedfordshire 1994. 1000 (1): 1073 (2002). HS 154 Nh v Notts (Northampton) 1999. La HS 128 v Yorks (Leeds) 2002. BB 2-30 Nh v Glos (Northampton) 2000. LO HS 83* Nh v Glos (Bristol) 2001 (BHC).

**WOOD, John** (Crofton HS; Wakefield District C; Leeds Poly), b Crofton, Yorks 22 Jul 1970. 6'3". RHB, RFM. GW (LO only) 1990-91. Durham 1992-2000; cap 1998. Lancashire debut 2001. HS 64 v Yorks (Leeds) 2002. 50 wkts (1): 62 (1998). BB 7-58 Du v Yorks (Leeds) 1999. La BB 4-17 v Hants (Southampton) 2002. LO HS 28* Du v Leics (Leicester) 2000 (BHC) and 28* Du v Notts (Nottingham) 2000 (NL). LO BB 5-49 v Glos (Manchester) 2002 (NL).

**YATES, Gary** (Manchester GS), b Ashton-under-Lyne 20 Sep 1967. 6'0". RHB, OB. Debut 1990; cap 1994. Lancashire 2nd XI captain/coach 2002 to date. HS 134* v Northants (Manchester) 1993. BB 6-64 v Kent (Manchester) 1999. LO HS 38 v Essex (Chelmsford) 1996 (SL). LO BB 4-34 v Warwks (Birmingham) 1994 (SL).

## RELEASED/RETIRED
(Having made a first-class County appearance in 2002)

**BYAS, David** (Scarborough C), b Kilham, Yorks 26 Aug 1963. 6'4". LHB, RM. Yorkshire 1986-2001; cap 1991; captain 1996-2001. Lancashire 2002; cap 2002. Tours (Y): SA 1991-92, 1992-93; Z 1995-96. 1000 runs (5); most – 1913 (1995). HS 213 Y v Worcs (Scarborough) 1995. La HS 101 v Warwks (Manchester) 2002. BB 3-55 Y v Derbys (Chesterfield) 1990. Awards: BHC 4. LO HS 116* Y v Surrey (Oval) 1996 (BHC). LO BB 3-19 Y v Notts (Leeds) 1989 (SL).

**DRIVER, Ryan** Craig (Redruth Community C; Durham U), b Truro, Cornwall 30 Apr 1979. 6'3½". LHB, RM. Worcestershire 1998-2000. British U 1999. Lancashire 2001-02. Cornwall 1996-97. HS 64 Wo v Sussex (Worcester) 2000. La HS 56 v Kent (Liverpool) 2002. BB 5-70 v WI A (Liverpool) 2002. CC BB 2-22 v Leics (Leicester) 2002. Award: CGT 1. LO HS 61* Wo v Glos (Worcester) 2000 (NWT). LO BB (Wo) 1-17 (NL).

**FAIRBROTHER, Neil** Harvey (Lymm GS), b Warrington 9 Sep 1963. 5'8". LHB, LM. Lancashire 1982-2002; cap 1985; captain 1992-93; benefit 1995. Transvaal 1994-95. **Tests**: 10 (1987 to 1992-93); HS 83 v I (Madras) 1992-93. **LOI**: 75 (1986-87 to 1999); HS 113 v WI (Lord's) 1991. Tours: NZ 1987-88, 1991-92; I/SL 1992-93; P 1987-88, 1990-91 (Eng A); SL 1990-91 (Eng A). 1000 runs (10); most – 1740 (1990). HS 366 v Surrey (Oval) 1990 (ground record), including 311 in a day and 100 or more in each session. BB 2-91 v Notts (Manchester) 1987. Awards: CGT 6; BHC 10. LO HS 145 v Hants (Manchester) 1990 (BHC). LO BB 1-17 (BHC).

**LLOYD, Graham** David (Hollins County HS), b Accrington 1 Jul 1969. Son of D.Lloyd (Lancs and England 1965-83). 5'9". RHB, RM. Lancashire 1988-2002; cap 1992; benefit 2001. **LOI**: 6 (1996 to 1998-99); HS 22 v A (Oval) 1997. Tours: A 1992-93 (Eng A); WI 1995-96 (La). 1000 runs (5); most – 1389 (1992). HS 241 v Essex (Chelmsford) 1996. BB 1-4. Awards: BHC 2. LO HS 134 v Durham (Manchester) 1997 (SL). LO BB 1-23 (NWT).

**RELEASED/RETIRED** continued on p 75

# LANCASHIRE 2002

## RESULTS SUMMARY

| | Place | Won | Lost | Tied | Drew | No Result |
|---|---|---|---|---|---|---|
| **County Championship** (1st Division) | 4th | 6 | 4 | | 6 | |
| **All First-Class Matches** | | 6 | 4 | | 8 | |
| **C & G Trophy** | 4th Round | | | | | |
| **Benson & Hedges Cup** | Semi-Finalist | | | | | |
| **NU National League** (2nd Division) | 5th | 7 | 7 | | | 2 |

## COUNTY CHAMPIONSHIP AVERAGES

### BATTING AND FIELDING

| Cap | | M | I | NO | HS | Runs | Avge | 100 | 50 | Ct/St |
|---|---|---|---|---|---|---|---|---|---|---|
| 2002 | S.G.Law | 15 | 26 | 3 | 218 | 1216 | 52.86 | 2 | 6 | 21 |
| 2002 | A.J.Swann | 16 | 28 | 2 | 128 | 1006 | 38.69 | 2 | 6 | 12 |
| 1994 | P.J.Martin | 12 | 16 | 5 | 117* | 422 | 38.36 | 1 | 1 | 4 |
| 2002 | C.P.Schofield | 6 | 8 | – | 91 | 262 | 32.75 | – | 2 | 3 |
| 1992 | G.D.Lloyd | 6 | 11 | 1 | 80 | 304 | 30.40 | – | 3 | 4 |
| 2002 | D.Byas | 14 | 23 | 2 | 101 | 634 | 30.19 | 1 | 4 | 15 |
| 2002 | M.J.Chilton | 16 | 28 | 1 | 90 | 654 | 24.22 | – | 4 | 15 |
| 1994 | G.Chapple | 16 | 23 | 1 | 65 | 493 | 22.40 | – | 4 | 6 |
| 1985 | N.H.Fairbrother | 11 | 18 | 1 | 39 | 305 | 17.94 | – | – | 9 |
| 1989 | W.K.Hegg | 15 | 22 | 2 | 43 | 354 | 17.70 | – | – | 43/2 |
| | J.Wood | 7 | 11 | – | 64 | 185 | 16.81 | – | 1 | 2 |
| 2000 | G.Keedy | 14 | 21 | 7 | 57 | 217 | 15.50 | – | 1 | 4 |
| | R.C.Driver | 3 | 5 | – | 56 | 67 | 13.40 | – | 1 | 3 |
| | K.W.Hogg | 6 | 8 | – | 50 | 105 | 13.12 | – | 1 | 3 |
| | J.M.Anderson | 11 | 15 | 8 | 16 | 52 | 7.42 | – | – | 2 |

*Also batted*: A.Flintoff (1 match – cap 1998) 137, 6 (1 ct); S.I.Mahmood (1) 18; J.J.Haynes (1) 4 (1ct); T.M.Rees (1) 16 (1 ct); T.W.Roberts (1) 2 (1 ct); M.P.Smethurst (2) 13, 0*, 6* (1 ct); G.Yates (1 – cap 1994) 3, 14.

### BOWLING

| | O | M | R | W | Avge | Best | 5wI | 10wM |
|---|---|---|---|---|---|---|---|---|
| C.P.Schofield | 99.2 | 18 | 298 | 16 | 18.62 | 4- 35 | – | – |
| J.M.Anderson | 275.4 | 53 | 934 | 46 | 20.30 | 6- 23 | 3 | – |
| P.J.Martin | 452 | 143 | 1126 | 53 | 21.24 | 5- 54 | 1 | – |
| K.W.Hogg | 148 | 37 | 466 | 19 | 24.52 | 5- 48 | 1 | – |
| G.Chapple | 539.3 | 128 | 1594 | 54 | 29.51 | 6- 33 | 3 | 1 |
| J.Wood | 168.5 | 27 | 618 | 17 | 36.35 | 4- 17 | – | – |
| G.Keedy | 382.4 | 87 | 1161 | 31 | 37.45 | 5-122 | 1 | – |

*Also bowled*:
M.P.Smethurst 53.2, 8, 248, 6, 41.33 3- 68 – –
M.J.Chilton 70-17-224-3; R.C.Driver 51-16-157-4; N.H.Fairbrother 6-0-27-0; A.Flintoff 32-8-99-3; S.G.Law 24.4-5-72-1; S.I.Mahmood 2-1-6-0; T.W.Roberts 2-0-6-0; A.J.Swann 8-1-40-0; G.Yates 29-7-76-0.

The First-Class Averages (pp 121-135) give the records of Lancashire players in all first-class county matches (Lancashire's other opponents being West Indies A and Durham UCCE), with the exception of A.Flintoff whose full county figures are as above.

# LANCASHIRE RECORDS

## FIRST-CLASS CRICKET

| | | | | | | |
|---|---|---|---|---|---|---|
| **Highest Total** | For 863 | | v | Surrey | The Oval | 1990 |
| | V 707-9d | | by | Surrey | The Oval | 1990 |
| **Lowest Total** | For 25 | | v | Derbyshire | Manchester | 1871 |
| | V 22 | | by | Glamorgan | Liverpool | 1924 |
| **Highest Innings** | For 424 | A.C.MacLaren | v | Somerset | Taunton | 1895 |
| | V 315* | T.W.Hayward | for | Surrey | The Oval | 1898 |

### Highest Partnership for each Wicket

| | | | | | | |
|---|---|---|---|---|---|---|
| 1st | 368 | A.C.MacLaren/R.H.Spooner | v | Glos | Liverpool | 1903 |
| 2nd | 371 | F.B.Watson/G.E.Tyldesley | v | Surrey | Manchester | 1928 |
| 3rd | 364 | M.A.Atherton/N.H.Fairbrother | v | Surrey | The Oval | 1990 |
| 4th | 358 | S.P.Titchard/G.D.Lloyd | v | Essex | Chelmsford | 1996 |
| 5th | 249 | B.Wood/A.Kennedy | v | Warwicks | Birmingham | 1975 |
| 6th | 278 | J.Iddon/H.R.W.Butterworth | v | Sussex | Manchester | 1932 |
| 7th | 248 | G.D.Lloyd/I.D.Austin | v | Yorkshire | Leeds | 1997 |
| 8th | 158 | J.Lyon/R.M.Ratcliffe | v | Warwicks | Manchester | 1979 |
| 9th | 142 | L.O.S.Poidevin/A.Kermode | v | Sussex | Eastbourne | 1907 |
| 10th | 173 | J.Briggs/R.Pilling | v | Surrey | Liverpool | 1885 |

| | | | | | | |
|---|---|---|---|---|---|---|
| **Best Bowling** | For | 10-46 | W.Hickton | v | Hampshire | Manchester | 1870 |
| **(Innings)** | V | 10-40 | G.O.B.Allen | for | Middlesex | Lord's | 1929 |
| **Best Bowling** | For | 17-91 | H.Dean | v | Yorkshire | Liverpool | 1913 |
| **(Match)** | V | 16-65 | G.Giffen | for | Australians | Manchester | 1886 |

| | | | | | |
|---|---|---|---|---|---|
| **Most Runs – Season** | 2633 | J.T.Tyldesley | (av 56.02) | | 1901 |
| **Most Runs – Career** | 34222 | G.E.Tyldesley | (av 45.20) | | 1909-36 |
| **Most 100s – Season** | 11 | C.Hallows | | | 1928 |
| **Most 100s – Career** | 90 | G.E.Tyldesley | | | 1909-36 |
| **Most Wkts – Season** | 198 | E.A.McDonald | (av 18.55) | | 1925 |
| **Most Wkts – Career** | 1816 | J.B.Statham | (av 15.12) | | 1950-68 |
| **Most Career W-K Dismissals** | 922† | G.Duckworth | (634 ct/288 st) | | 1923-38 |
| **Most Career Catches in the Field** | 556 | K.J.Grieves | | | 1949-64 |

† *W.K.Hegg (1987-2002) has the second-highest aggregate with 797 dismissals (716 ct; 81 st)*

## LIMITED-OVERS CRICKET

| | | | | | | |
|---|---|---|---|---|---|---|
| **Highest Total** | CGT | 381-3 | | v | Herts | Radlett | 1999 |
| | BHC | 353-7 | | v | Notts | Manchester | 1995 |
| | NL | 301-6 | | v | Essex | Chelmsford | 1999 |
| **Lowest Total** | CGT | 59 | | v | Worcs | Worcester | 1963 |
| | BHC | 82 | | v | Yorkshire | Bradford | 1972 |
| | NL | 68 | | v | Yorkshire | Leeds | 2000 |
| | | 68 | | v | Surrey | The Oval | 2002 |
| **Highest Innings** | CGT | 135* | A.Flintoff | v | Surrey | The Oval | 2000 |
| | BHC | 136 | G.Fowler | v | Sussex | Manchester | 1991 |
| | NL | 143 | A.Flintoff | v | Essex | Chelmsford | 1999 |
| **Best Bowling** | CGT | 6-18 | G.Chapple | v | Essex | Lord's | 1996 |
| | BHC | 6-10 | C.E.H.Croft | v | Scotland | Manchester | 1982 |
| | NL | 6-25 | G.Chapple | v | Yorkshire | Leeds | 1998 |

# LEICESTERSHIRE

**Formation of Present Club**: 25 March 1879
**Colours**: Dark Green and Scarlet
**Badge**: Gold Running Fox on Green Ground
**County Champions**: (3) 1975, 1996, 1998
**Gillette/NatWest/C & G Trophy Winners**: (0); best – finalist 1992, 2001
**Benson and Hedges Cup Winners**: (3) 1972, 1975, 1985
**National League (Div 1) Winners**: (0); best – 2nd 2001
**Sunday League Champions**: (2) 1974, 1977
**Match Awards**: CGT 47; BHC 79

**Secretary/General Manager**: K.P.Hill, County Ground, Grace Road, Leicester LE2 8AD
• Tel: 0116 283 2128/1880 • Fax: 0116 244 0363 • Email: leicestershirecc@ukonline.co.uk
• Web: www.leicestershireccc.com

**First XI Coach**: P.Whitticase. **Captain**: P.A.J.DeFreitas. **Vice-Captain**: No appointment.
**Overseas Players**: B.J.Hodge and V.Sehwag. **2003 Beneficiary**: None. **Scorer**: G.A.York.
‡ New registration

**‡AMIN, Rupesh** Mahesh (Riddlesdown HS; John Ruskin C; Croydon C), b Clapham, S London 20 Aug 1977. 6'0". RHB, SLA. Surrey 1997-2002. Leicestershire staff 2003. HS 12 Sy v Leics (Oval) 1998. BB 4-87 Sy v Somerset (Oval) 1999. LO HS (Sy) 0* (NL). LO BB 2-43 Sy v Lancs (Oval) 1997 (SL).

**BRANDY, Damien** Gareth (St John's, Epping; Harlow C), b Highgate, London 14 Sep 1981. 6'1". RHB, RMF. Debut 2002. HS 23 and BB 2-86 v Surrey (Oval) 2002. LO HS 35 v Somerset (Leicester) 2002 (NL).

**BRIGNULL, David** Stephen (Wyggeston & Queen Elizabeth 1 C), b Forest Gate, London 27 Nov 1981. 6'4". RHB, RMF. Staff 2002 – awaiting f-c debut. LO HS (Leics CB) 9* (NWT). BB 2-35 Leics CB v Warwks CB (Coventry) 2001 (CGT).

**CUNLIFFE, Robert** John (Banbury S; Banbury TC), b Oxford 8 Nov 1973. 5'10". RHB, RM. Gloucestershire 1994-2001. Oxfordshire 1991-94. Leicestershire debut 2002. HS 190* v OU (Bristol) 1995. CC HS 108 v Northants (Northampton) 1999. Le HS 30 v Surrey (Oval) 2002. Awards: BHC 3. LO HS 137* v Surrey (Oval) 1996 (BHC).

**DAGNALL, Charles** Edward (Bridgewater HS, Worsley; UMIST), b Bury, Lancs 10 Jul 1976. 6'3". RHB, RMF. Warwickshire 1999-2001. Cumberland 1997-98. Leicestershire debut 2002. HS 16 v Yorks (Leicester) 2002. BB 6-50 Wa v Derbys (Derby) 2001. Le BB 3-55 v Hants (Southampton) 2002. Award: BHC 1. LO HS 28 v Worcs (Worcester) 2002 (NL). LO BB 4-34 Wa v Derbys (Birmingham) 2000 (NL).

**DeFREITAS, Phillip** Anthony Jason (Willesden HS, London), b Scotts Head, Dominica 18 Feb 1966. 6'0". RHB, RFM. UK resident since 1976. Leicestershire 1985-88; cap 1986; captain 2003. Lancashire 1989-93; cap 1989. Boland 1993-94 and 1995-96. Derbyshire 1994-99; cap 1994; captain 1997 (part). *Wisden* 1991. MCC YC. Tests: 44 (1986-87 to 1995-96); HS 88 v A (Adelaide) 1994-95; BB 7-70 v SL (Lord's) 1991. LOI: 103 (1986-87 to 1997); HS 67 v SL (Faisalabad) 1995-96; BB 4-35 v A (Adelaide) 1986-87. Tours: A 1986-87, 1990-91, 1994-95; WI 1989-90; NZ 1987-88, 1991-92; P 1987-88; I 1992-93; Z 1988-89 (La). HS 123* v Lancs (Leicester) 2000. 50 wkts (13); most – 94 (1986). Took his 1000th f-c wicket 1999. BB 7-21 La v Middx (Lord's) 1989. Le BB 7-44 (13-86 match) v Essex (Southend) 1986. Hat-trick 1994. Awards: CGT 5; BHC 4. LO HS 75* La v Hants (Manchester) 1990 (BHC). LO BB 5-13 La v Cumb (Kendal) 1989 (NWT).

**GROVE, Jamie** Oliver (Bury St Edmunds County Upper S), b Bury St Edmunds, Suffolk 3 Jul 1979. 6'1". RHB, RMF. Essex 1998-99. Somerset 2000-01. Leicestershire debut 2002. HS 33 Ex v Surrey (Chelmsford) 1998. Le HS 6. BB 5-90 Sm v Leics (Leicester) 2000 – on Somerset debut. Le BB 1-75. LO HS 13 v Kent (Leicester) 2002 (NL). LO BB 4-36 Sm v Cambs (March) 2001 (CGT).

‡**HODGE, Bradley** John (St Bede's C, Mentone; Deakin U), b Sandringham, Victoria, Australia 29 Dec 1974. 5'8". RHB, OB. Victoria 1993-94 to date. Australia A debut 1999-2000. Durham 2002. Tours (A Academy): Z 1998-99. 1000 (0+1): 1129 (2000-01). HS 140 Vic v S Aus (Adelaide) 2001-02. UK HS 73 and UK BB 1-28 Du v Glos (Bristol) 2002. BB 4-17 Aus A v WI (Hobart) 2000-01. LO HS 118* Vic v ACT (Canberra) 1998-99. LO BB 2-25 Vic v Q (Melbourne) 2000-01.

**MADDY, Darren** Lee (Wreake Valley C), b Leicester 23 May 1974. 5'9". RHB, RM/OB. Debut 1994; cap 1996. **Tests**: 3 (1999 to 1999-00); HS 24 v SA (Durban) 1999-00. **LOI**: 8 (1998 to 1999-00); HS 53 v Z (Harare) 1999-00. Tours (Eng A): SA 1996-97 (Le), 1998-99, 1999-00 (Eng); SL 1997-98; Z 1998-99; K 1997-98. 1000 runs (3); most – 1187 (2002). HS 202 Eng A v Kenya (Nairobi) 1997-98. Le HS 162 v Durham (Darlington) 1998. BB 5-37 v Hants (Southampton) 2002. Awards: CGT 1; BHC 8 (inc 5 in 1998). LO HS 151 v Minor C (Leicester) 1998 (BHC). LO BB 4-16 v Somerset (Taunton) 2000 (NL).

**MALCOLM, Devon** Eugene (St Elizabeth THS; Richmond C, Sheffield; Derby CHE), b Kingston, Jamaica 22 Feb 1963. Qualified for England 1987. 6'2". RHB, RF. Derbyshire 1984-97; cap 1989; benefit 1997. Northamptonshire 1998-2000; cap 1999. Leicestershire debut/cap 2001. *Wisden* 1994. **Tests**: 40 (1989 to 1997); HS 29 v A (Sydney) 1994-95; BB 9-57 v SA (Oval) 1994. **LOI**: 10 (1990 to 1993-94); HS 4; BB 3-40 v I (Gwalior) 1992-93. Tours: A 1990-91, 1994-95; SA 1995-96; WI 1989-90, 1991-92 (Eng A), 1993-94; I 1992-93; SL 1992-93. HS 51 De v Surrey (Derby) 1989. Le HS 50 v Somerset (Taunton) 2001. 50 wkts (9); most – 82 (1996). BB 9-57 (*see Tests*). CC BB 8-63 v Surrey (Leicester) 2001. Awards: CGT 1; BHC 3. LO HS 42 De v Surrey (Oval) 1996 (SL). LO BB 7-35 De v Northants (Derby) 1997 (NWT).

‡**MASTERS, David** Daniel (Fort Luton HS; Mid Kent CHE), b Chatham, Kent 22 Apr 1978. Son of K.D.Masters (Kent 1981-85, Surrey 1986). 6'4". RHB, RMF. Kent 2000-02. Leicestershire staff 2003. HS 68 K v Warwks (Birmingham) 2002. BB 6-27 K v Durham (Tunbridge Wells) 2000. LO HS 12* K v Middx (Canterbury) 2000 (BHC). LO BB 5-20 K v Durham (Maidstone) 2002 (NL).

‡**MAUNDERS, John** Kenneth (Ashford HS; Spelthorne C), b Ashford, Middx 4 Apr 1981. 5'10". LHB, RM. Middlesex 1999 (one non-CC match); 2nd XI debut aged 16y 19d. Leicestershire staff 2003. HS (M) 9. LO HS 49 M v Glam (Cardiff) 2001 (NL).

**NEW, Thomas** James (Quarrydale S), b Sutton in Ashfield, Notts 18 Jan 1985. 5'10". LHB, WK. Leicestershire summer contract since 2001 – awaiting f-c debut. LO HS (Leics CB) 6 (CGT).

**NIXON, Paul** Andrew (Ullswater HS, Penrith), b Carlisle, Cumberland 21 Oct 1970. 6'0". LHB, WK. Leicestershire 1989-99; cap 1994. Kent 2000-02; cap 2000. Cumberland 1987. MCC YC. Tours: SA 1996-97 (Le); I 1994-95 (Eng A); P 2000-01; SL 2000-01 (*no f-c*). 1000 runs (1): 1046 (1994). HS 134* K v Hants (Canterbury) 2000. Le HS 131 v Hants (Leicester) 1994. Awards: BHC 3. LO HS 101 v SL A (Galle) 1998-99.

‡**SADLER, John** Leonard (St Thomas A'Beckett S), b Dewsbury, Yorks 19 Nov 1981. LHB, LM. Leicestershire staff 2003 – awaiting first-class debut. LO HS 19 Y v WI A (Leeds) 2002.

**SEHWAG, Virender**, b Delhi 20 Oct 1978, RHB, OB. Delhi 1997-98 to date. **Tests** (I): 14 (2001-02 to 2002-03); HS 147 v WI (Bombay) 2002-03; BB 1-27. **LOI** (I): 68 (1998-99 to 2002-03); HS 126 v E (Colombo) 2002-3; BB 3-25 v SA (Colombo) 2002-03. Tours (I): E 2002; SA 2001-02; NZ 2002-03. 1000 (1): 1008 (1999-00). HS 274 N Zone v S Zone (Agartala) 1999-2000. UK HS 142 and UK BB 2-52 Indians v Essex (Chelmsford) 2002. BB 4-32 N Zone v S Zone (Bombay) 1998-99. LO HS 126 (*see LOI*). LO BB 4-17 Delhi v Services (Delhi) 1998-99.

‡**SNAPE, Jeremy** Nicholas (Denstone C; Durham U), b Stoke-on-Trent, Staffs 27 Apr 1973. 5'8½". RHB, OB. Northamptonshire 1992-97. Combined U 1994. Gloucestershire 1999-2002; cap 1999. Leicestershire staff 2003. **LOI**: 10 (2001-02 to 2002-03); HS 38 v I (Madras) 2001-02; BB 3-43 v Z (Bulawayo) 2001-02. Tour: Z 1994-95 (Nh). HS 131 Gs v Sussex (Cheltenham) 2001. BB 5-65 Nh v Durham (Nottingham) 1995. Awards: BHC 3. LO HS 104* Gs v Notts (Nottingham) 2001 (NL). LO BB 5-32 Nh v Leics (Northampton) 1997 (BHC).

**STEVENS, Darren** Ian (Hinckley C), b Leicester 30 Apr 1976. 5'11". RHB, RM. Debut 1997; cap 2002. HS 130 v Sussex (Arundel) 1999. BB 1-5. Award: CGT 1. LO HS 133 v Northumb (Jesmond) 2000 (NWT). LO BB 2-26 v Wales CB (Swansea) 2001 (CGT).

**WALKER, George** William (Norwich S), b Norwich, Norfolk 12 May 1984. 5'10". LHB, SLA. Debut 2002. Norfolk 2000-01. HS 37* v Kent (Canterbury) 2002 – on debut.

**WARD, Trevor** Robert (Hextable CS, nr Swanley), b Farningham, Kent 18 Jan 1968. 5'11". RHB, OB. Kent 1986-99; cap 1989; benefit 1999. Leicestershire debut 2001; cap 2001. Tour: Z 1992-93 (K). 1000 runs (6); most – 1648 (1992). HS 235* K v Middx (Canterbury) 1991. Le HS 160* v Northants (Leicester) 2001. BB 2-10 K v Yorks (Canterbury) 1996. Le BB 1-32. Awards: CGT 1; BHC 2. LO HS 131 K v Notts (Nottingham) 1993 (SL). LO BB 3-20 K v Glam (Canterbury) 1989 (SL).

**WHILEY, Matthew** Jeffrey Allen (Harry Carlton CS, East Leake), b Clifton, Nottingham 6 May 1980. 6'5½". RHB, LMF. Nottinghamshire 1998-2000. Leicestershire debut 2001. HS 13* v Warwks (Birmingham) 2002. BB 3-60 v Kent (Leicester) 2002. LO HS 14* v Somerset (Bath) 2002 (NL). LO BB 2-20 v Notts (Leicester) 2002 (BHC).

**WRIGHT, Luke** James, b Grantham, Lincs 7 Mar 1985. Younger brother of A.S.Wright (Leicestershire 2001-02). RHB, RM. Staff 2002 – awaiting f-c debut. LO HS 16 Leics CB v Kent CB (Hinckley) 2001 (CGT).

### RELEASED/RETIRED
(Registered players who made a first-class County appearance in 2002)

**BEVAN, Michael** Gwyl (Western Creek HS, Canberra), b Belconnen, ACT, Australia 8 May 1970. 5'11½". LHB, SLC. S Australia 1989-90. NSW 1990-91 to date. Yorkshire 1995-96; cap 1995. Sussex 1998, 2000; cap 1998. Leicestershire 2002; cap 2002. **Tests** (A): 18 (1994-95 to 1997-98); HS 91 v P (Lahore) 1994-95; BB 6-82 (10-113 match) v WI (Adelaide) 1996-97. **LOI** (A): 205 (1993-94 to 2002-03); HS 108* v E (Oval) 1997; BB 3-36 v P (Melbourne) 1996-97. Tours (A): E 1997, 2001; SA 1996-97; I 1996-97; P 1994-95; Z 1991-92 (Aus B). 1000 runs (3); most – 1598 (1995). HS 203* NSW v WA (Sydney) 1993-94. UK HS 174 Sx v Notts (Hove) 2000. Le HS 146 and UK BB 3-25 v Warwks (Leicester) 2002. BB 6-82 (see Tests). Awards: CGT 2; BHC 7. LO HS 157* Sx v Essex (Chelmsford) 2000 (BHC). LO BB 5-29 Y v Sussex (Eastbourne) 1996 (SL).

**BURNS, Neil** David (Moulsham HS, Chelmsford), b Chelmsford, Essex 19 Sep 1965. 5'10". LHB, WK, occ SLA. W Province B 1985-86. Essex 1986. Somerset 1987-93; cap 1987. Leicestershire 2000-02; cap 2001. Buckinghamshire 1995-99. Conceded no byes as Surrey scored 494 and 492-9d (Oval) 2001 in his final f-c match. HS 166 Sm v Glos (Taunton) 1990. Le HS 111 v Glam (Leicester) 2001. LO HS 90* v Northants (Leicester) 2001 (NL).

**CROWE, Carl** Daniel (Lutterworth GS), b Leicester 25 Nov 1975. 6'0". RHB, OB. Leicestershire 1995-2002. HS 44* v Northants (Northampton) 1999. BB 4-47 v Surrey (Oval) 2001. LO HS 23* v Lancs (Leicester) 2002 (BHC). Award: BHC 1. LO BB 4-30 v Notts (Nottingham) 2001 (NL).

**FLOWER, Grant** William (St George's C), b Salisbury, Rhodesia 20 Dec 1970. 5'10". Younger brother of A Flower (*see Essex*). RHB, SLA. Mashonaland 1989-90. Leicestershire 2002 (one match); cap 2002. **Tests** (Z): 63 (1992-93 to 2002-03); HS 201* v P (Harare) 1994-95 sharing with G.W.Flower in fourth-wicket partnership of 269, the highest stand between brothers in Test cricket. BB 4-41 (8-104 match) v B (Chittagong) 2001-02. **LOI** (Z): 199 (1992-93 to 2002-03); HS 142* v B (Bulawayo) 2000-01; BB 4-32 v K (Dhaka) 1998-99. Tours (Z): E 2000; SA 1999-00; WI 1999-00; NZ 1995-96, 1997-98; I 1992-93, 2000-01, 2001-02; P 1993-94, 1996-97, 1998-99; SL 1996-97, 1997-98, 2001-02; B 2001-02. HS 243* Mashonaland v Matabeleland (Harare) 1996-97. Le HS 75 and Le BB 4-66 v Warwks (Birmingham) 2002 – on debut. BB 7-31 Z v Lahore (Lahore) 1998-99. LO HS 142* (*see LOI*). LO BB 4-32 (*see LOI*).

**KAIF, Mohammad,** b Allahabad, India 1 Dec 1980. RHB, OB. Uttar Pradesh 1997-98 to date. Leicestershire 2002 (one match); cap 2002. **Tests** (I): 4 (1999-00 to 2001); HS 37 v SL (Galle) 2000. **LOI** (I): 48 (2000 to 2002-03); HS 111* v Z (Colombo) 2002-03. Tours (I): E 2002; SA 2001-02 (Ind A); SL 2001. HS 136 India A v SA A (Kimberley) 2001-02. UK HS 77 Indians v WI A (Arundel) 2002. Le HS 43 v Surrey (Leicester) 2002 – on debut. BB 3-4 Uttar Pradesh v Vidarbha (Kanpur) 2001-02. LO HS 120 Uttar Pradesh v Madhya Pradesh (Udaipur) 2001-02. LO BB 4-23 Uttar Pradesh v Rajasthan (Jaipur) 1998-99.

**SRINATH, J.** – *see DURHAM*.

**STEMP, Richard** David (Britannia HS, Rowley Regis), b Erdington, Birmingham 11 Dec 1967. 6'0". RHB, SLA. Worcestershire 1990-92. Yorkshire 1993-98; cap 1996. Nottinghamshire 1999-2001; cap 2000. Leicestershire 2002 (one match). Tours (Eng A): SA 1992-93 (Y); I 1994-95; P 1995-96. Le HS 66 Nt v Hants (Southampton) 2001. Le HS 8*. BB 6-37 Y v Durham (Durham) 1994. Le BB 1-18. Award: BHC 1. LO HS 29* Nt v Somerset (Nottingham) 1999 (NL). LO BB 4-25 Y v Glos (Bristol) 1996 (SL) and Nt v Somerset (Nottingham) 2001 (NL).

**SUTCLIFFE, I.J.** – *see LANCASHIRE*.

**WELLS, V.J.** – *see DURHAM*.

**WRIGHT, Ashley** Spencer (Belvoir HS; King Edward VII S, Melton Mowbray), b Grantham, Lincs 21 Oct 1980. Elder brother of L.J.Wright (Leicestershire). 6'0". RHB, RM. Leicestershire 2001-02. HS 30 v P (Leicester) 2001. CC HS 28 v Kent (Canterbury) 2002. Award: CGT 1. LO HS 112 Leics CB v Durham CB (Gateshead) 2000 (NWT).

S.J.Adshead left the staff having made no f-c appearances in 2002.

---

**KENT RELEASED/RETIRED** (continued from p 48)

**WAUGH, Stephen** Rodger (East Hills HS), b Canterbury, Sydney 2 Jun 1965. Elder twin of M.E.Waugh (NSW, Essex and Australia). 5'11". RHB, RMF. NSW 1984-85 to date. Somerset 1987-88; cap 1988. Ireland 1998. Kent 2002; cap 2002. *Wisden* 1988. **Tests** (A): 156 (1985-86 to 2002-03, 45 as captain); HS 200 v WI (Kingston) 1994-95; BB 5-28 v SA (Cape Town) 1993-94. Holds world record for most nineties in Tests (10). **LOI** (A): 325 (1985-86 to 2001-02, 106 as captain – HS 120* v SA (Leeds) 1999: BB 4-33 v SL (Sydney) 1987-88. Tours (I): E 1989, 1993, 1997, 2001C; SA 1993-94, 1996-97, 2001-02C; WI 1990-91, 1994-95, 1998-99C, 2003C; NZ 1985-86, 1989-90, 1992-93, 1999-00C; I 1986-87, 1996-97, 1997-98, 2000-01C; P 1988-89, 1994-95, 1998-99, 2002-03C (*Sharjah*); SL 1999-00C; Z 1985-86 Young A), 1999-00C. 1000 (2): most – 1314 (1988). HS 216* NSW v WA (Perth) 1990-91, sharing world record 5th wkt stand of 464* with M.E.Waugh. K HS 146 v Yorks (Leeds) 2002. BB 6-51 NSW v Queensland (Sydney) 1988-89. Award: BHC 1. LO HS 140* Somerset v Middx (Lord's) 1988. LO BB 4-32 NSW v Vic (Sydney) 1990-91.

M.J.McCague left the staff (and appeared for Herefordshire) having made no f-c appearances in 2002.

# LEICESTERSHIRE 2002

## RESULTS SUMMARY

| | Place | Won | Lost | Tied | Drew | No Result |
|---|---|---|---|---|---|---|
| **County Championship** (1st Division) | 5th | 5 | 5 | | 6 | |
| **All First-Class Matches** | | 5 | 5 | | 6 | |
| **C & G Trophy** | 4th Round | | | | | |
| **Benson & Hedges Cup** | Quarter-Finalist | | | | | |
| **NU National League** (1st Division) | 6th | 7 | 8 | | | 1 |

## COUNTY CHAMPIONSHIP AVERAGES

### BATTING AND FIELDING

| Cap | | M | I | NO | HS | Runs | Avge | 100 | 50 | Ct/St |
|---|---|---|---|---|---|---|---|---|---|---|
| 2002 | M.G.Bevan | 9 | 14 | 3 | 146 | 697 | 63.36 | 2 | 4 | 4 |
| 1996 | D.L.Maddy | 16 | 29 | 4 | 156 | 1187 | 47.48 | 2 | 8 | 22 |
| 1997 | I.J.Sutcliffe | 16 | 29 | 3 | 125* | 1088 | 41.84 | 2 | 5 | 4 |
| 1994 | V.J.Wells | 11 | 17 | 2 | 150 | 558 | 37.20 | 1 | 3 | 9 |
| 2002 | D.I.Stevens | 16 | 28 | 3 | 125 | 847 | 33.88 | 1 | 6 | 16 |
| 2001 | N.D.Burns | 16 | 24 | 2 | 101 | 720 | 32.72 | 1 | 5 | 61/2 |
| 1986 | P.A.J.DeFreitas | 16 | 23 | 2 | 114 | 609 | 29.00 | 1 | 3 | 10 |
| 2001 | T.R.Ward | 14 | 24 | – | 89 | 554 | 23.08 | – | 4 | 7 |
| | C.D.Crowe | 12 | 16 | 4 | 34 | 172 | 14.33 | – | – | 4 |
| 2002 | J.Srinath | 5 | 7 | – | 52 | 98 | 14.00 | – | 1 | 2 |
| | R.J.Cunliffe | 5 | 10 | 1 | 30 | 121 | 13.44 | – | – | 1 |
| | A.S.Wright | 5 | 8 | 1 | 28 | 94 | 13.42 | – | – | 1 |
| 2001 | D.E.Malcolm | 16 | 22 | 8 | 44 | 138 | 9.85 | – | – | 4 |
| | C.E.Dagnall | 4 | 5 | 1 | 16 | 33 | 8.25 | – | – | 1 |
| | M.J.A.Whiley | 7 | 9 | 2 | 13* | 41 | 5.85 | – | – | 1 |
| | J.O.Grove | 2 | 4 | – | 6 | 13 | 3.25 | – | – | – |

*Also batted*: D.G.Brandy (2 matches) 5, 23, 0 (1 ct); G.W.Flower (1 – cap 2002) 75, 7 (1 ct); M.Kaif (1 – cap 2002) 13, 43; R.D.Stemp (1) 8*, 0; G.W.Walker (1) 7, 37* (1 ct).

### BOWLING

| | O | M | R | W | Avge | Best | 5wI | 10wM |
|---|---|---|---|---|---|---|---|---|
| J.Srinath | 179.2 | 29 | 561 | 30 | 18.70 | 5- 25 | 2 | – |
| V.J.Wells | 155 | 41 | 421 | 19 | 22.15 | 5- 39 | 1 | – |
| D.L.Maddy | 334.3 | 78 | 1025 | 43 | 23.83 | 5- 37 | 2 | – |
| D.E.Malcolm | 477.5 | 79 | 1826 | 60 | 30.43 | 7- 76 | 4 | 1 |
| P.A.J.DeFreitas | 566.4 | 150 | 1594 | 51 | 31.25 | 6-101 | 2 | – |
| C.D.Crowe | 193.2 | 51 | 593 | 16 | 37.06 | 4- 63 | – | – |
| M.J.A.Whiley | 175.4 | 28 | 803 | 16 | 50.18 | 3- 60 | – | – |

*Also bowled*:

| | O | M | R | W | Avge | Best | 5wI | 10wM |
|---|---|---|---|---|---|---|---|---|
| G.W.Flower | 35 | 12 | 98 | 6 | 16.33 | 4- 66 | – | – |
| C.E.Dagnall | 91 | 24 | 270 | 7 | 38.57 | 3- 55 | – | – |

M.G.Bevan 33-1-118-3; D.G.Brandy 17-0-114-2; R.J.Cunliffe 1.1-0-3-0; J.O.Grove 35-6-152-1; M.Kaif 7-0-43-0; R.D.Stemp 17-2-59-1; D.I.Stevens 49-3-201-1; I.J.Sutcliffe 7-0-39-0; G.W.Walker 13-2-50-0; T.R.Ward 11-0-47-1.

Leicestershire played no first-class fixtures outside the County Championship in 2002. The First-Class Averages (pp 121-135) give the records of Leicestershire players in all first-class county matches, with the exception of M.Kaif and D.I.Stevens whose full county figures are as above.

# LEICESTERSHIRE RECORDS

## FIRST-CLASS CRICKET

| | | | | | | |
|---|---|---|---|---|---|---|
| **Highest Total** | For 701-4d | | v | Worcs | Worcester | 1906 |
| | V 761-6d | | by | Essex | Chelmsford | 1990 |
| **Lowest Total** | For 25 | | v | Kent | Leicester | 1912 |
| | V 24 | | by | Glamorgan | Leicester | 1971 |
| | 24 | | by | Oxford U | Oxford | 1985 |
| **Highest Innings** | For 261 | P.V.Simmons | v | Northants | Leicester | 1994 |
| | V 341 | G.H.Hirst | for | Yorkshire | Leicester | 1905 |

### Highest Partnership for each Wicket

| | | | | | | |
|---|---|---|---|---|---|---|
| 1st | 390 | B.Dudleston/J.F.Steele | v | Derbyshire | Leicester | 1979 |
| 2nd | 289* | J.C.Balderstone/D.I.Gower | v | Essex | Leicester | 1981 |
| 3rd | 316* | W.Watson/A.Wharton | v | Somerset | Taunton | 1961 |
| 4th | 290* | P.Willey/T.J.Boon | v | Warwicks | Leicester | 1984 |
| 5th | 322 | B.F.Smith/P.V.Simmons | v | Notts | Worksop | 1998 |
| 6th | 284 | P.V.Simmons/P.A.Nixon | v | Durham | Chester-le-St | 1996 |
| 7th | 219* | J.D.R.Benson/P.Whitticase | v | Hampshire | Bournemouth | 1991 |
| 8th | 172 | P.A.Nixon/D.J.Millns | v | Lancashire | Manchester | 1996 |
| 9th | 160 | W.W.Odell/R.T.Crawford | v | Worcs | Leicester | 1902 |
| 10th | 228 | R.Illingworth/K.Higgs | v | Northants | Leicester | 1977 |

| | | | | | | |
|---|---|---|---|---|---|---|
| **Best Bowling** | For 10- 18 | G.Geary | v | Glamorgan | Pontypridd | 1929 |
| **(Innings)** | V 10- 32 | H.Pickett | for | Essex | Leyton | 1895 |
| **Best Bowling** | For 16- 96 | G.Geary | v | Glamorgan | Pontypridd | 1929 |
| **(Match)** | V 16-102 | C.Blythe | for | Kent | Leicester | 1909 |

| | | | | |
|---|---|---|---|---|
| **Most Runs – Season** | 2446 | L.G.Berry | (av 52.04) | 1937 |
| **Most Runs – Career** | 30143 | L.G.Berry | (av 30.32) | 1924-51 |
| **Most 100s – Season** | 7 | L.G.Berry | | 1937 |
| | 7 | W.Watson | | 1959 |
| | 7 | B.F.Davison | | 1982 |
| **Most 100s – Career** | 45 | L.G.Berry | | 1924-51 |
| **Most Wkts – Season** | 170 | J.E.Walsh | (av 18.96) | 1948 |
| **Most Wkts – Career** | 2130 | W.E.Astill | (av 23.19) | 1906-39 |
| **Most Career W-K Dismissals** | 903 | R.W.Tolchard | (794 ct/109 st) | 1965-83 |
| **Most Career Catches in the Field** | 427 | M.R.Hallam | | 1950-70 |

## LIMITED-OVERS CRICKET

| | | | | | | |
|---|---|---|---|---|---|---|
| **Highest Total** | CGT | 406-5 | v | Berkshire | Leicester | 1996 |
| | BHC | 382-6 | v | Minor C | Leicester | 1998 |
| | NL | 344-4 | v | Durham | Chester-le-St | 1996 |
| **Lowest Total** | CGT | 56 | v | Northants | Leicester | 1964 |
| | BHC | 56 | v | Minor C | Wellington | 1982 |
| | NL | 36 | v | Sussex | Leicester | 1973 |
| **Highest Innings** | CGT | 201 | V.J.Wells | v | Berkshire | Leicester | 1996 |
| | BHC | 158* | B.F.Davison | v | Warwicks | Coventry | 1972 |
| | NL | 152 | B.Dudleston | v | Lancashire | Manchester | 1975 |
| **Best Bowling** | CGT | 6-20 | K.Higgs | v | Staffs | Longton | 1975 |
| | BHC | 6-25 | V.J.Wells | v | Minor C | Leicester | 1998 |
| | NL | 6-17 | K.Higgs | v | Glamorgan | Leicester | 1973 |

# MIDDLESEX

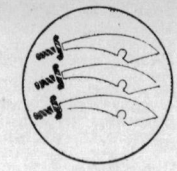

**Formation of Present Club**: 2 February 1864
**Colours**: Blue
**Badge**: Three Seaxes
**County Champions (since 1890)**: (10) 1903, 1920, 1921, 1947, **1976, 1980, 1982, 1985, 1990, 1993**
**Joint Champions**: (2) 1949, 1977
**Gillette/NatWest/C & G Trophy Winners**: (4) 1977, 1980, 1984, 1988
**Benson and Hedges Cup Winners**: (2) 1983, 1986
**National League (Div 1) Winners**: (0); best – 4th (Div 2) 2000
**Sunday League Winners**: (1) 1992
**Match Awards**: CGT 58; BHC 62

**Secretary**: V.J.Codrington, Lord's Cricket Ground, London NW8 8QN • Tel: 020 7289 1300 • Fax: 020 7289 5831 • Email: enquiries.middx@ecb.co.uk • Web: www.middlesexccc.com

**First XI Coach**: J.E.Emburey. **Captain**: A.J.Strauss. **Vice-Captain**: O.A.Shah. **Overseas Players**: Abdul Razzaq, J.H.Dawes (*early season*) and A.A.Noffke. **2003 Beneficiary**: M.A.Roseberry. J.M.J.Smith. ‡ New registration

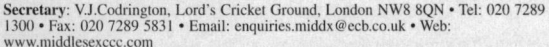

**ABDUL RAZZAQ** (Furqan Model HS, Shahdara, Lahore), b Lahore 2 Dec 1979. 5'11". RHB, RFM. F-c debut (Lahore City) 1996-97. Middlesex debut/cap 2002. **Tests** (P): 24 (1999-00 to 2002-03); HS 134 v B (Dhaka) 2001-02; BB 4-24 v WI (Sharjah) 2001-02. Hat-trick v SL (Galle) 1999-00. **LOI** (P): 124 (1996-97 to 2002-03); HS 112 v SA (Pt Elizabeth) 2002-03; BB 6-35 v B (Dhaka) 2001-02. Tours: E 1997 (Pak A), 2001; A 1999-00; WI 1999-00; SL 1999-00; B 2001-02. HS 203* v Glam (Cardiff) 2002. BB 7-51 Lahore City v Karachi Whites (Thatta) 1996-97 – on debut. M BB 7-133 v Essex (Southgate) 2002. LO HS 112 (*see LOI*).

**ALLEYNE, David** (Enfield GS; Hertford Regional C; City & Islington C), b York 17 Apr 1976. 5'11". RHB, WK. Debut 2001. HS 49* v Derbys (Derby) 2002. LO HS 58 v Notts (Nottingham) 2000 (NL).

**BLOOMFIELD, Timothy** Francis (Halliford S, Shepperton), b Ashford 31 May 1973. 6'2". RHB, RMF. Debut 1997; cap 2001. Berkshire 1996. HS 31* v Northants (Northampton) 2002. 50 wkts (1): 50 (2001). BB 5-36 v Glam (Cardiff) 1999. Award: CGT 1. LO HS 15 v Warwks (Lord's) 1998 (SL). LO BB 4-17 v Somerset (Southgate) 2000 (NWT).

**BROWN, Michael** James (Queen Elizabeth GS, Blackburn; Collingwood C, Durham U), b Burnley, Lancs 9 Feb 1980. 6'0". RHB, OB. Debut 1999. Durham UCCE 2001-02. British U 2001-02. HS 60* DU v Worcs (Worcester) 2001. M HS 24* v CU (Cambridge) 1999 – on debut. CC HS 10 v Warwks (Lord's) 2001. LO HS 18 v Northants (Lord's) 2002 (NL).

**COLEMAN, Alan** James (Longford Community S), b Ashford 13 Dec 1983. 6'2". RHB, RMF. Staff 2002 – awaiting f-c debut. LO HS 14* v Glos (Southgate) 2002 (NL).

**COMPTON, Nicholas** Richard Denis (Harrow S), b Durban, SA 26 Jun 1983. 6'1". Grandson of D.C.S.Compton (Middlesex, England, Holkar, Europeans, Commonwealth and Cavaliers 1936-64); great-nephew of L.H.Compton (Middlesex 1938-56). RHB, OB. Middlesex staff 2002 – awaiting f-c debut. M HS 86* v Lancs (Shenley) 2002 (NL).

**COOK, Simon** James (Matthew Arnold S), b Oxford 15 Jan 1977. 6'4". RHB, RM. Debut 1999. HS 93* v Notts (Lord's) 2001. BB 8-63 v Northants (Northampton) 2002. LO HS 50 v Glam (Cardiff) 2001 (NL). LO BB 3-16 v Glam (Cardiff) 1999 (NL).

‡**DAWES, Joseph** Henry (St Paul's S, Bald Hills; South Bank I, Brisbane), b Herston, Queensland, Australia 29 Aug 1970. 6'2". RHB, RFM. Queensland 1997-98 to date. MCC 2001. HS 26 Q v Tasmania (Brisbane) 2001-02. BB 7-98 Q v S Aus (Adelaide) 2000-01. UK HS 10 and UK BB 4-74 MCC v A (Arundel) 2001 – dismissing Slater, Hayden, Langer and Martyn. LO HS (Q) 1*. LO BB 3-26 Q v Tasmania (Hobart) 2001-02.

**DALRYMPLE, James** William Murray (Radley C; St Peter's C, Oxford), b Nairobi, Kenya 21 Jan 1981. 5'11". RHB, OB. Oxford UCCE 2001-02; captain 2002; blue 2001-02. British U 2001-02. Middlesex debut 2001. HS 148 OU v Glos (Oxford) 2002. M HS 33 v Derbys (Derby) 2002. BB 4-86 OU v CU (Cambridge) 2001. M BB 1-113. M HS 52 v Derbys (Derby) 2002 (NL). LO BB 4-14 v Essex (Southgate) 2001 (NL).

**HOLT, David** Robert (St Benedict's S, Ealing; London U), b Hammersmith, London 29 Dec 1981. RHB, RM. MCC YC 2001. Summer contract 2002 – awaiting 1st XI debut.

**HUNT, Thomas Aaron** *'Thos'* (Acton HS: St Clement Danes S), b Melbourne, Australia 19 Jan 1982. 6'2". Resident in UK since 1985 (English parents). LHB, RMF. Debut 2002 – awaiting CC debut. HS 3. BB 3-43 v CU (Cambridge) 2002 – on debut. LO HS 0 (NL). LO BB 1-24 (NL).

**HUTTON, Benjamin** Leonard (Radley C; Durham U), b Johannesburg, SA 29 Jan 1977. Elder son of R.A.Hutton (Yorkshire, Transvaal & England 1962 to 1975-76); grandson of Sir Leonard (Yorkshire and England 1934-60). 6'2". LHB, RMF. British U 1998-99. Middlesex debut 1999. HS 139 v Derbys (Southgate) 2001. BB 4-37 v SL (Shenley) 2002. CC BB 2-9 v Glam (Southgate) 2000. LO HS 77 v Durham (Chester-le-St) 2001 (NL). LO BB 5-45 v Derbys (Southgate) 2001 (NL).

**JOYCE, Edmund** Christopher (Presentation C, Bray, Co Wicklow; Trinity C, Dublin), b Dublin, Ireland 22 Sep 1978. 5'11". LHB, RM. Ireland 1997 to date. Middlesex debut 1999; cap 2002. 1000 (1): 1267 (2002). HS 129 v Glam (Cardiff) 2002 and 129 v Derbys (Lord's) 2002. BB 1-20 (not CC). LO HS 73 Ire v Warwks (Birmingham) 1998 (NWT).

**KEEGAN, Chad** Blake (Durban HS), b Sandton, near Johannesburg, SA 30 Jul 1979. 6'1". RHB, RF. Debut 2001. MCC YC. HS 30* v Warwks (Birmingham) 2001. BB 4-47 v Worcs (Worcester) 2002. LO HS 24 v Sussex (Lord's) 2002 (BHC). LO BB 5-17 v Hants (Southgate) 2001 (NL).

**KOENIG, Sven** Gaetan (Hilton C; Cape Town U), b Durban, SA 9 Dec 1973. ECB qualified – EU (Italian) passport. 5'10". LHB, OB. Western Province 1993-94 to 1996-97. Transvaal/Gauteng 1997-98 to 2000-01. Middlesex debut/cap 2002. Tour (SA A): E 1996. 1000 (1): 1251 (2002). HS 155 Gauteng v GW (Kimberley) 2000-01. M HS 141* v CU (Cambridge) 2002 – on Middx debut. CC HS 113 v Essex (Southgate) 2002. BB (Gauteng) 1-0. LO HS 116 v Essex (Chelmsford) 2002 (CGT).

**NASH, David** Charles (Sunbury Manor S; Malvern C), b Chertsey, Surrey 19 Jan 1978. 5'8". RHB, occ LB, WK. Debut 1997; cap 2000. Tour: SL 1997-98 (Eng A). HS 114 v Somerset (Lord's) 1998. BB 1-8. LO HS 67 v Sussex (Lord's) 2002 (BHC).

**NOFFKE, Ashley** Allan b Nambour, Queensland, Australia 30 Apr 1977. RHB, RFM. Debut 1998-99 for Australian Academy. Queensland 1999-00 to date. Middlesex debut 2002. Tours (A): E 2001 *(part)*; WI 2003; Z 1998-99 (A Academy). HS 76 v Worcs (Worcester) 2002. BB 8-24 (12-108 match) v Derbys (Derby) 2002. LO HS 58 v Sussex (Lord's) 2002 (BHC). LO BB 4-32 Q v Tasmania (Hobart) 2001-02.

‡**RICHARDS, Mali** Alexander (Cheltenham C), b Taunton, Somerset 2 Sep 1983. LHB. Son of Sir I.V.A.Richards (Leeward Is, Somerset, Queensland, Glamorgan and West Indies 1971-72 to 1993), nephew of D. and M.Richards (Leeward Is). Summer contract 2003. Awaiting f-c debut. LO HS 1 Antigua & Barbuda v Guyana (Gros Inlet, St Lucia) 2002.

**SHAH, Owais** Alam (Isleworth & Syon S), b Karachi, Pakistan 22 Oct 1978. 6'0". RHB, OB. Debut 1996; cap 2000. YC 2001. **LOI**: 15 (2001 to 2002-03); HS 62 v P (Lord's) 2001. Tours (Eng A): A 1996-97; SL 1997-98. 1000 (2); most 1084 (2002). HS 203 v Derbys (Southgate) 2001. BB 3-33 v Glos (Bristol) 1999. Award: BHC 1. LO HS 134 v Sussex (Arundel) 1999 (NL). LO BB 2-2 v Glam (Cardiff) 1998 (BHC).

**STRAUSS, Andrew** John (Radley C; Durham U), b Johannesburg, SA 2 Mar 1977. 5'11". LHB, LM. Debut 1998; cap 2001; captain 2002 (part) to date. Oxfordshire 1996. 1000 (2); most – 1211 (2001). HS 176 v Durham (Lord's) 2001. LO HS 90 v Durham (Chester-le-St) 2000 (NL).

**TUFNELL, Philip** Clive Roderick (Highgate S), b Barnet, Herts 29 Apr 1966. 6'0". RHB, SLA. Debut 1986; cap 1990; benefit 1999. MCC YC. **Tests**: 42 (1990-91 to 2001); HS 22* v I (Madras) 1992-93; BB 7-47 (11-147 match) v NZ (Christchurch) 1991-92, took 11-93 v A (Oval) 1997. **LOI**: 20 (1990-91 to 1996-97); HS 5*; BB 4-22 v NZ (Christchurch) 1996-97. Tours: A 1990-91, 1994-95; SA 1999-00; WI 1993-94, 1997-98; NZ 1991-92, 1996-97; I/SL 1992-93, Z 1996-97. HS 67* v Worcs (Lord's) 1996. 50 wkts (9); most – 88 (1991). BB 8-29 v Glam (Cardiff) 1993. Award: CGT 1. LO HS 18 v Warwks (Lord's) 1991 (BHC). LO BB 5-28 v Leics (Lord's) 1993 (SL).

**WEEKES, Paul** Nicholas (Homerton House SS, Hackney), b Hackney, London 8 Jul 1969. 5'10". LHB, OB. Debut 1990; cap 1993; benefit 2002. Tour: I 1994-95 (Eng A). MCC YC. 1000 runs (1): 1218 (1996). HS 171* v Somerset (Uxbridge) 1996. BB 8-39 v Glam (Lord's) 1996. Awards: CGT 2; BHC 4. LO HS 143* v Cornwall (St Austell) 1995 (NWT). LO BB 4-17 v Kent (Lord's) 2001 (BHC).

**WESTON, Robin** Michael Swann (Durham S; Loughborough U), b Durham 7 Jun 1975. Brother of W.P.C.Weston (see *GLOUCESTERSHIRE*). 5'10". RHB, LB. Durham 1995-97. Derbyshire 1998-99 (scored 72, 129*, 22, 124 and 156 in consecutive CC innings 1999). Middlesex debut 2000; cap 2001. Minor C debut 1991 when aged 15yr 355d (Durham record). HS 156 De v Somerset (Derby) 1999. M HS 135* v Hants (Southgate) 2001. BB (De) 1-15. LO HS 80* v Derbys (Southgate) 2001 (NL).

## RELEASED/RETIRED
(Having made a first-class County appearance in 2002)

**CREESE, Matthew** Leonard (Goffs S; Durham U), b Enfield 13 Feb 1982. 6'3". LHB, SLA. Middlesex 1999 (one match). Durham UCCE 2002. MCCYC. 2nd XI debut when aged 15y 188d. HS 8 DU v Lancs (Durham) 2002. BB 1-37 M v CU (Cambridge) 1999 – on debut. LO HS 34 and LO BB 2-35 Middx CB v Scot (Southgate) 2001 (CGT).

**FRASER, Angus** Robert Charles (Gayton HS, Harrow; Orange Hill HS, Edgware), b Billinge, Lancs 8 Aug 1965. Brother of A.G.J.Fraser (Middx and Essex 1986-92). 6'5". RHB, RMF. Middlesex 1984-2002; cap 1988; benefit 1997; captain 2001 to 2002 (part). MBE 2000. *Wisden* 1995. **Tests**: 46 (1989 to 1998-99); HS 32 v SL (Oval) 1998; BB 8-53 (11-110 match) v WI (P-of-S) 1997-98 – record England innings analysis v WI. **LOI**: 42 (1989-90 to 1999); HS 38* v A (Melbourne) 1990-91; BB 4-22 v A (Melbourne) 1994-95. Tours: A 1990-91, 1994-95 (part), 1998-99; SA 1995-96; WI 1989-90, 1993-94, 1997-98. HS 92 v Surrey (Oval) 1990. 50 wkts (7); most – 92 (1989). BB 8-53 (see *Tests*). M BB 7-40 v Leics (Lord's) 1993. LO HS 38* (see *LOI*). LO BB 5-32 v Derbys (Lord's) 1995 (SL).

**JONES, Ian** (Fyndoune Community C, Sacriston), b Edmonton, Middx 11 Mar 1977. 6'4". RHB, RMF. Somerset 1999. Middlesex 2002 (one match). HS 35 Sm v Durham (Chester-le-St) 1999. BB 3-72 and M HS 29 v Glos (Southgate) 2002. LO HS 6 (twice – CGT and NL). LO BB 3-14 Sm v Surrey (Oval) 2001 (NL).

**LARAMAN, A.** – see *SOMERSET*.

B.Duncan, J.K.Maunders (see *LEICESTERSHIRE*), S.Nikitaras and C.S.Rendell left the staff having made no f-c appearances in 2002.

# MIDDLESEX 2002

## RESULTS SUMMARY

| | Place | Won | Lost | Tied | Drew | No Result |
|---|---|---|---|---|---|---|
| **County Championship** (2nd Division) | **2nd** | 7 | 3 | | 6 | |
| **All First-Class Matches** | | 8 | 3 | | 7 | |
| **C & G Trophy** | 3rd Round | | | | | |
| **Benson & Hedges Cup** | 5th in South Division | | | | | |
| **NU National League** (2nd Division) | **9th** | 4 | 10 | | | 2 |

## COUNTY CHAMPIONSHIP AVERAGES

### BATTING AND FIELDING

| Cap | | M | I | NO | HS | Runs | Avge | 100 | 50 | Ct/St |
|---|---|---|---|---|---|---|---|---|---|---|
| 2002 | Abdul Razzaq | 6 | 9 | 3 | 203* | 364 | 60.66 | 1 | – | 1 |
| 2002 | E.C.Joyce | 16 | 25 | 3 | 129 | 1166 | 53.00 | 4 | 5 | 14 |
| 2000 | D.C.Nash | 14 | 18 | 5 | 100 | 642 | 49.38 | 1 | 4 | 33/1 |
| 1993 | P.N.Weekes | 16 | 23 | 5 | 127* | 887 | 49.27 | 3 | 3 | 22 |
| 2000 | O.A.Shah | 15 | 24 | 3 | 172* | 1019 | 48.52 | 3 | 5 | 4 |
| 2001 | A.J.Strauss | 14 | 23 | 1 | 141 | 985 | 44.77 | 2 | 5 | 12 |
| 2002 | S.G.Koenig | 16 | 27 | 1 | 113 | 1110 | 42.69 | 3 | 7 | 6 |
| | B.L.Hutton | 9 | 17 | 1 | 116 | 512 | 32.00 | 1 | 4 | 18 |
| | A.W.Laraman | 9 | 11 | 2 | 82* | 249 | 27.66 | – | 1 | 3 |
| | A.A.Noffke | 8 | 10 | 1 | 76 | 203 | 22.55 | – | 1 | 3 |
| 2001 | R.M.S.Weston | 7 | 9 | 1 | 72 | 170 | 21.25 | – | 1 | 4 |
| | S.J.Cook | 14 | 17 | 1 | 38* | 224 | 14.00 | – | – | 4 |
| | J.W.M.Dalrymple | 3 | 5 | – | 33 | 66 | 13.20 | – | – | 1 |
| 1990 | P.C.R.Tufnell | 14 | 15 | 8 | 45 | 89 | 12.71 | – | – | 3 |
| | C.B.Keegan | 8 | 10 | – | 24 | 58 | 5.80 | – | – | 1 |

*Also batted*: D.Alleyne (2 matches) 13, 49* (4 ct); T.F.Bloomfield (2 – cap 2001) 31*, 26*; A.R.C.Fraser (2 – cap 1988) 16, 20; I.Jones (1) 29.

### BOWLING

| | O | M | R | W | Avge | Best | 5wI | 10wM |
|---|---|---|---|---|---|---|---|---|
| A.A.Noffke | 305.1 | 57 | 1128 | 45 | 25.06 | 8- 24 | 3 | 1 |
| Abdul Razzaq | 206.3 | 25 | 757 | 26 | 29.11 | 7-133 | 2 | – |
| P.C.R.Tufnell | 514.5 | 104 | 1390 | 45 | 30.88 | 8- 66 | 4 | – |
| S.J.Cook | 344.2 | 65 | 1243 | 39 | 31.87 | 8- 63 | 1 | – |
| A.W.Laraman | 226.4 | 41 | 775 | 20 | 38.75 | 4- 55 | – | – |
| C.B.Keegan | 193.5 | 31 | 806 | 18 | 44.77 | 4- 47 | – | – |
| P.N.Weekes | 367.3 | 52 | 1100 | 18 | 61.11 | 3- 27 | – | – |

*Also bowled*:

| | O | M | R | W | Avge | Best | 5wI | 10wM |
|---|---|---|---|---|---|---|---|---|
| A.R.C.Fraser | 72 | 26 | 190 | 7 | 27.14 | 5- 61 | 1 | – |
| B.L.Hutton | 51 | 9 | 182 | 5 | 36.40 | 2- 17 | – | – |

T.F.Bloomfield 65.1-15-252-4; J.W.M.Dalrymple 12-4-33-0; I.Jones 22.3-3-100-4; E.C.Joyce 14-2-54-0.

The First-Class Averages (pp 121-135) give the records of Middlesex players in all first-class county matches (Middlesex's other opponents being the Sri Lankans and Cambridge UCCE), with the exception of M.J.Brown and M.L.Creese whose only first-class appearances were in University matches, J.W.M.Dalrymple whose full county figures are as above, and:

O.A.Shah 16-25-3-172*-1084-49.27-3-6-5ct. 2-0-15-0.
A.J.Strauss 16-25-1-141-1133-47.20-3-5-16ct. Did not bowl.

# MIDDLESEX RECORDS

## FIRST-CLASS CRICKET

| | | | | | | |
|---|---|---|---|---|---|---|
| **Highest Total** | For 642-3d | | v | Hampshire | Southampton | 1923 |
| | V 665 | | by | W Indians | Lord's | 1939 |
| **Lowest Total** | For 20 | | v | MCC | Lord's | 1864 |
| | V 31 | | by | Glos | Bristol | 1924 |
| **Highest Innings** | For 331* | J.D.B.Robertson | v | Worcs | Worcester | 1949 |
| | V 316* | J.B.Hobbs | for | Surrey | Lord's | 1926 |

### Highest Partnership for each Wicket

| | | | | | | |
|---|---|---|---|---|---|---|
| 1st | 372 | M.W.Gatting/J.L.Langer | v | Essex | Southgate | 1998 |
| 2nd | 380 | F.A.Tarrant/J.W.Hearne | v | Lancashire | Lord's | 1914 |
| 3rd | 424* | W.J.Edrich/D.C.S.Compton | v | Somerset | Lord's | 1948 |
| 4th | 325 | J.W.Hearne/E.H.Hendren | v | Hampshire | Lord's | 1919 |
| 5th | 338 | R.S.Lucas/T.C.O'Brien | v | Sussex | Hove | 1895 |
| 6th | 270 | J.D.Carr/P.N.Weekes | v | Glos | Lord's | 1994 |
| 7th | 271* | E.H.Hendren/F.T.Mann | v | Notts | Nottingham | 1925 |
| 8th | 182* | M.H.C.Doll/H.R.Murrell | v | Notts | Lord's | 1913 |
| 9th | 160* | E.H.Hendren/T.J.Durston | v | Essex | Leyton | 1927 |
| 10th | 230 | R.W.Nicholls/W.Roche | v | Kent | Lord's | 1899 |

| | | | | | | |
|---|---|---|---|---|---|---|
| **Best Bowling** | For 10- 40 | G.O.B.Allen | v | Lancashire | Lord's | 1929 |
| (Innings) | V 9- 38 | R.C.R-Glasgow† | for | Somerset | Lord's | 1924 |
| **Best Bowling** | For 16-114 | G.Burton | v | Yorkshire | Sheffield | 1888 |
| (Match) | 16-114 | J.T.Hearne | v | Lancashire | Manchester | 1898 |
| | V 16-109 | C.W.L.Parker | for | Glos | Cheltenham | 1930 |

| | | | | |
|---|---|---|---|---|
| **Most Runs – Season** | 2669 | E.H.Hendren | (av 83.41) | 1923 |
| **Most Runs – Career** | 40302 | E.H.Hendren | (av 48.81) | 1907-37 |
| **Most 100s – Season** | 13 | D.C.S.Compton | | 1947 |
| **Most 100s – Career** | 119 | E.H.Hendren | | 1907-37 |
| **Most Wkts – Season** | 158 | F.J.Titmus | (av 14.63) | 1955 |
| **Most Wkts – Career** | 2361 | F.J.Titmus | (av 21.27) | 1949-82 |
| **Most Career W-K Dismissals** | 1223 | J.T.Murray | (1024 ct/199 st) | 1952-75 |
| **Most Career Catches in the Field** | 561 | E.H.Hendren | | 1907-37 |

## LIMITED-OVERS CRICKET

| | | | | | | |
|---|---|---|---|---|---|---|
| **Highest Total** | CGT | 304-7 | | v | Surrey | The Oval | 1995 |
| | | 304-8 | | v | Cornwall | St Austell | 1995 |
| | BHC | 325-5 | | v | Leics | Leicester | 1992 |
| | NL | 290-6 | | v | Worcs | Lord's | 1990 |
| **Lowest Total** | CGT | 41 | | v | Essex | Westcliff | 1972 |
| | BHC | 73 | | v | Essex | Lord's | 1985 |
| | NL | 23 | | v | Yorkshire | Leeds | 1974 |
| **Highest Innings** | CGT | 158 | G.D.Barlow | v | Lancashire | Lord's | 1984 |
| | BHC | 143* | M.W.Gatting | v | Sussex | Hove | 1985 |
| | NL | 147* | M.R.Ramprakash | v | Worcs | Lord's | 1990 |
| **Best Bowling** | CGT | 6-15 | W.W.Daniel | v | Sussex | Hove | 1980 |
| | BHC | 7-12 | W.W.Daniel | v | Minor C (E) | Ipswich | 1978 |
| | NL | 6- 6 | R.W.Hooker | v | Surrey | Lord's | 1969 |

† R.C.Robertson-Glasgow

# NORTHAMPTONSHIRE

**Formation of Present Club**: 31 July 1878
**Colours**: Maroon
**Badge**: Tudor Rose
**County Champions**: (0); best – 2nd 1912, 1957, 1965, 1976
**Gillette/NatWest/C & G Trophy Winners**: (2) 1976, 1992
**Benson and Hedges Cup Winners**: (1) 1980
**National League (Div 1) Winners**: (0); best – 3rd 2000
**Sunday League Winners**: (0); best – 3rd 1991
**Match Awards**: CGT 55; BHC 62

**Chief Executive**: S.P.Coverdale, County Ground, Wantage Road, Northampton, NN1 4TJ • Tel: 01604 514455 • Fax: 01604 514488 • Email: post@nccc.co.uk • Web: www.nccc.co.uk

**Director of Cricket/First XI Coach**: K.P.Wessels. **Captain**: M.E.K.Hussey.
**Vice-Captain**: A.L.Penberthy. **Overseas Players**: M.E.K.Hussey and J.Nel. **2003**
**Beneficiary**: None. **Scorer**: A.C.Kingston. ‡ New registration

**ANDERSON, Ricaldo** Sherman Glenroy (Alperton HS; Barnet C; North West London C; London Cricket C), b Hammersmith, London 22 Sep 1976. 5'10". RHB, RFM. Essex 1999-2001. Northamptonshire debut 2002. HS 67* Ex v Sussex (Chelmsford) 2000. Nh HS 51 v Essex (Northampton) 2002. 50 wkts (1): 50 (1999). BB 6-34 (11-111 match) Ex v Northants (Ilford) 2000. NH BB 4-97 v Derbys (Derby) 2002. LO HS 22 Ex v Sussex (Hove) 2001 (NL) and 22 v Derbys (Derby) 2002 (NL). LO BB 3-28 v Glos (Northampton) 2002 (BHC).

**BAILEY, Tobin** Michael Barnaby (Bedford S; Loughborough U), b Kettering 28 Aug 1976. 5'10". RHB, WK. Debut 1996. British U 1998. Bedfordshire 1994-96. HS 96* v Worcs (Worcester) 2000. LO HS 52 Brit U v Glos (Bristol) 1997.

**BAKER, Thomas** Michael (Whitcliffe Mount S; Huddersfield TC), b Dewsbury, Yorks 6 Jul 1981. 6'4". RHB, RFM. Yorkshire staff 2001 – no f-c appearances. Northamptonshire staff 2002 – awaiting f-c debut. LO HS 63 Northants CB v Yorks CB (Northampton) 2002 (CGT). LO BB 2-13 Y v Derbys (Leeds) 2001 (BHC).

**BLAIN, John** Angus Rae (Penicuik HS; Jewel & Esk Valley C), b Edinburgh, Scotland 4 Jan 1979. 6'1". RHB, RMF. Scotland 1996-99. Northamptonshire debut 1997. **LOI** (Scot): 5 (1999); HS 9 and BB 4-37 v B (Edinburgh) 1999. HS 34 v Surrey (Northampton) 2001. BB 6-42 v Kent (Canterbury) 2001. Award: BHC 1. LO HS 11 v Worcs (Kidderminster) 2001 (BHC). LO BB 5-24 v Derbys (Derby) 1997 (SL).

**BROPHY, Gerard** Louis (Welkom BC; Boksburg BC; Witwatersrand TC), b Welkom, SA 26 Nov 1975. ECB qualified – British/EU passport. RHB, WK. Transvaal 1996-97 to 1998-99. Free State 1999-00 to 2000-01. Northamptonshire debut 2002. HS 185 SA Academy v Zim President's XI (Harare) 1998-99. Nh HS 110 v Glam (Cardiff) 2002. LO HS 54 v Essex (Northampton) 2002 (NL).

**BROWN, Jason** Fred (St Margaret Ward HS & SFC), b Newcastle-under-Lyme, Staffs 10 Oct 1974. 6'0". RHB, OB. Debut 1996; cap 2000. Staffordshire 1994-95. Tours: WI 2000-01 (*part*) (Eng A); SL 2000-01 (*no f-c*). HS 35* v Leics (Northampton) 2001. 50 wkts (1): 61 (2000). BB 7-78 (11-131 match) v Sussex (Northampton) 2000. LO HS 16 v Lancs (Manchester) 2002 (NL). LO BB 4-26 v Leics (Northampton) 1997 (SL).

67

**COOK, Jeffrey** William (James Cook HS, Kogarah, NSW), b Sydney, Australia 2 Feb 1972. 6'4". LHB, RM. Resident in UK since 1993 – ECB qualified 2000. Debut 2000. NSW U-19. HS 137 v Glos (Cheltenham) 2000. BB 2-7 v OU (Oxford) 2002. CC BB 2-47 v Middx (Northampton) 2002. Awards: CGT 1; BHC 1. LO HS 130 Northants CB v Wilts (Northampton) 1999 (NWT). LO BB 4-35 v Glos (Bristol) 2002 (NL).

**COUSINS, Darren** Mark (Netherhall CS; Impington Village C), b Cambridge 24 Sep 1971. 6'2". RHB, RMF. Essex 1993-98. Surrey (NL only) 1999. Northamptonshire debut/cap 2000. Cambridgeshire 1990, 1999. HS 29* v Glam (Northampton) 2000. 50 wkts (1): 67 (2000). BB 8-102 v Yorks (Leeds) 2001. LO HS 21 v Sussex (Hove) 2002 (NL). LO BB 5-22 v Middx (Lord's) 2002 (NL).

**GREENIDGE, Carl** Gary (Lodge S and St Michael S, Barbados; Heathcote S, Chingford; W Hatch HS; City of Westminster C), b Basingstoke, Hants 20 Apr 1978. Son of C.Gordon Greenidge (Hampshire, Barbados and West Indies 1970-92). 5'10". RHB, RMF. MCC YC. Surrey 1999-2000. Northamptonshire debut 2002. HS 46 v Derbys (Derby) 2002. 50 wkts (1): 53 (2002). BB 6-40 v Durham (Chester-le-St) 2002. LO HS 20 v Sussex (Northampton) 2002 (NL). LO BB 3-22 v Derbys (Northampton) 2002 (NL).

**HUSSEY, Michael** Edward Killeen (Prindiville Catholic C; Curtin U), b Morley, Perth, Australia 27 May 1975. 5'11". LHB, RM. W Australia 1994-95 to date. Northamptonshire debut/cap 2001; captain 2002 to date. Tour (Aus A): Sc/Ire 1998. HS 329* v Essex (Northampton) 2001 – Northants record. Scored 310 v Glos (Bristol) 2002. 1000 runs (2); most – 2055 (2001). BB 2-21 WA v Q (Perth) 1998-99. Nh BB 1-14. Awards: BHC 3. LO HS 114* v Glam (Cardiff) 2001 (BHC). LO BB 3-52 WA v Vic (Melbourne) 1999-00 (MM).

‡**NEL, Andre** (Dr E.G.Jansen S, Boksburg), b Germiston, SA 15 Jul 1977. RHB, RFM. Easterns 1996-97 to date. **Tests** (SA): 3 (2001-02); HS 7; BB 4-53 v Z (Harare) 2001-02 – on debut. **LOI** (SA): 7 (2000-01 to 2001-02); HS 3*; BB 3-20 v WI (Pt-of-Spain) 2000-01 – on debut. Tours (SA): WI 2000-01; Z 2001-02. HS 44 Easterns v FS (Benoni) 2000-01. BB 6-25 Easterns v Gauteng (Jo'burg) 2001-02. LO HS 17* Easterns v EP (Benoni) 1997-98. LO BB 6-27 Easterns v GW (Benoni) 2000-01.

**PANESAR, Mudhsuden** Singh '*Monty*' (Stopsley HS; Bedford Modern S; Loughborough U), b Luton, Beds 25 Apr 1982. 6'0". LHB, SLA. Bedfordshire 1998-99. Debut 2001. HS 10 and BB 4-11 (8-131 match) v Leics (Northampton) 2001 – on debut. LO HS 16* v Essex (Colchester) 2002 (NL).

**PAYNTER, David** Edward (Clayton Middle S), b Truro, Cornwall 25 Jan 1981. Great-grandson of E.Paynter (Lancashire and England 1926 to 1950-51). RHB, OB. Debut 2002. Debut 2002. HS 20 v Durham (Northampton) 2002 – on debut. LO HS 104 Northants CB v Northants (Northampton) 2001 (CGT). LO BB 1-27 (NL).

**PENBERTHY, Anthony** Leonard (Camborne CS), b Troon, Cornwall 1 Sep 1969. 6'1". LHB, RM. Debut 1989; cap 1994; benefit 2002. Cornwall 1987-89. Tours (Nh): SA 1991-92; Z 1994-95. HS 132* v Glam (Northampton) 2001. BB 5-37 v Glam (Swansea) 1993. Took wicket of M.A.Taylor (A) with his first ball in f-c cricket. Awards: CGT 1; BHC 1. LO HS 81* v Surrey (Northampton) 1997 (SL). LO BB 5-29 v Glos (Bristol) 2000 (NL).

**PHILLIPS, Ben** James (Langley Park S and SFC, Beckenham), b Lewisham, London 30 Sep 1974. 6'6". RHB, RFM. Kent 1996-99. Northamptonshire debut 2002 (one non-CC match). HS 100* K v Lancs (Manchester) 1997. Nh HS 17 and Nh BB 3-28 v OU (Oxford) 2002. BB 5-47 K v Sussex (Horsham) 1997. Award: CGT 1. LO HS K 29 v Glam (Cardiff) 1996 (SL). LO BB 4-25 K v Northants (Canterbury) 2000 (NL).

**POWELL, Mark** John (Campion S, Bugbrooke; Loughborough U), b Northampton 4 Nov 1980. 5'11". RHB, OB. Debut 2000. HS 108* v Glam (Cardiff) 2002. LO HS 64 v Hants (Southampton) 2002 (NL).

**SALES, David** John Grimwood (Caterham S; Cumnor House S), b Carshalton, Surrey 3 Dec 1977. 6'0". RHB, RM. Debut 1996 v Worcs (Kidderminster) scoring 0 and 210* – record Championship score on f-c debut; youngest (18yr 237d) to score 200 in a Championship match; cap 1999. Wellington 2001-02. Tours (Eng A): NZ 1999-00; SL 1997-98; K 1997-98; B 1999-00. Sustained severe knee injury prior to start of England A tour of WI 2000-01 – no f-c appearances 2001. 1000 runs (1): 1291 (1999). HS 303* v Essex (Northampton) 1999 – youngest Englishman (21y 240d) to score a f-c 300. BB 4-25 v SL A (Northampton) 1999. CC BB 2-7 v Yorks (Scarborough) 1999. Award: BHC 1. LO HS 93 v Hants (Southampton) 2002 (NL).

‡**SMETHURST, Michael** Paul (Hulme GS, Oldham; Salford U), b Oldham, Lancs 11 Oct 1976. 6'5". RHB, RM. Lancashire 1999-2002. HS 66 La v Surrey (Manchester) 2000. 50 wkts (1): 56 (2000). BB 7-37 La v NZ A (Liverpool) 2000. CC BB 7-50 La v Durham (Chester-le-St) 2000. Award: CGT 1. LO HS 10* La v Leics (Manchester) 2000 (BHC). LO BB 4-46 La v Hants (Southampton) 1999 (NWT).

**SWANN, Graeme** Peter (Sponne SS, Towcester), b Northampton 24 Mar 1979. Son of R.Swann (Northumberland 1969-72; Bedfordshire 1988-95); younger brother of A.J.Swann (see LANCASHIRE). 6'0". RHB, OB. Debut 1998; cap 1999. Bedfordshire 1996. LOI: 1 (1999-00); dnb v SA (Bloemfontein) 1999-00. Tours (Eng A): SA 1998-99, 1999-00 (Eng); WI 2000-01 (part); Z 1998-99. HS 183 v Glos (Bristol) 2002 – including 114 before lunch on third day. 50 wkts (1): 57 (1999). BB 6-41 (11-126 match) v Leics (Northampton) 1999. LO HS 83 v Leics (Northampton) 2001 (NL). LO BB 5-35 v Durham (Chester-le-St) 1999 (NL).

**WHITE, Robert** Allan (Stowe S; Durham U; Loughborough U), b Chelmsford, Essex 15 Oct 1979. 5'11". RHB, LB. Debut 2000. HS 277 and BB 2-30 v Glos (Northampton) 2002 – highest maiden f-c hundred in UK; included 107 before lunch on first day. LO HS 18 v Lancs (Manchester) 2002 (NL). LO BB 2-18 v Sussex (Northampton) 2002 (NL).

## RELEASED/RETIRED
(Having made a first-class County appearance in 2002)

**CASSAR, Matthew** Edward (Sir Joseph Banks HS, Sydney; Manchester Metropolitan U), b Sydney, Australia 16 Oct 1972. Husband of Jane Cassar (née Smit; England 1991-92 to date). 6'0". RHB, RMF. Derbyshire 1994-2000. ECB qualified/CC debut 1997. Northamptonshire 2001-02. HS 121 De v Sussex (Horsham) 1998. Nh HS 101* v Glos (Northampton) 2002. BB 6-34 (10-134 match) v Glos (Bristol) 2002. Award: CGT 1. LO HS 134 De v Northants (Northampton) 1998 (SL). LO BB 4-29 De v Hants (Southampton) 2000 (NL).

**INNESS, Mathew** William Hunter, b East Melbourne, Australia 13 Jan 1978. RHB, LFM. Victoria 1997-98 to date. Northamptonshire 2002. Nh 27 Vic v NSW (Melbourne) 1997-98 – on debut adding 118 for the 10th wicket with D.S.Berry. Nh HS 25 and Nh BB 7-90 v Glam (Cardiff) 2002. BB 7-19 Vic v NSW (Sydney) 2001-02. Hat-trick (Victoria) 1999-00. LO HS 2* (NL). LO BB 2-28 v Essex (Colchester) 2002 (NL).

**LOYE, M.B.** – see LANCASHIRE.

**ROLLINS, Adrian** Stewart (Little Ilford CS), b Barking, Essex 8 Feb 1972. Brother of R.J.Rollins (Essex 1992-99). 6'5". RHB, occ WK, occ RM. Derbyshire 1993-99; cap 1995. Northamptonshire 2000-02. 1000 runs (3); most – 1142 (1997). HS 210 De v Hants (Chesterfield) 2002. Nh HS 107 v Middx (Northampton) 2002. BB 1-19 (De). LO HS 126* De v Surrey (Derby) 1995 (SL).

**WARREN, R.J.** – see NOTTINGHAMSHIRE.

M.J.Cawdron and L.C.Weekes left the staff having made no f-c appearances in 2002.

# NORTHAMPTONSHIRE 2002

## RESULTS SUMMARY

| | Place | Won | Lost | Tied | Drew | No Result |
|---|---|---|---|---|---|---|
| **County Championship** (2nd Division) | **7th** | 5 | 7 | | 4 | |
| **All First-Class Matches** | | 6 | 7 | | 4 | |
| **C & G Trophy** | 4th Round | | | | | |
| **Benson & Hedges Cup** | 4th in Midlands/West/Wales Division | | | | | |
| **NU National League** (2nd Division) | **6th** | 7 | 8 | | | 1 |

## COUNTY CHAMPIONSHIP AVERAGES

### BATTING AND FIELDING

| Cap | | M | I | NO | HS | Runs | Avge | 100 | 50 | Ct/St |
|---|---|---|---|---|---|---|---|---|---|---|
| | R.A.White | 4 | 7 | 1 | 277 | 556 | 92.66 | 1 | 3 | 1 |
| 2001 | M.E.K.Hussey | 12 | 21 | 2 | 310* | 1379 | 72.57 | 5 | 3 | 14 |
| | M.J.Powell | 3 | 5 | 1 | 108* | 289 | 72.25 | 2 | – | 6 |
| | G.L.Brophy | 4 | 8 | 3 | 110 | 246 | 49.20 | 1 | 1 | 5 |
| | M.E.Cassar | 7 | 9 | 1 | 101* | 343 | 42.87 | 1 | 3 | 4 |
| 1994 | A.L.Penberthy | 16 | 25 | 3 | 130* | 909 | 41.31 | 2 | 5 | 9 |
| | A.S.Rollins | 5 | 10 | – | 107 | 389 | 38.90 | 1 | 2 | 5 |
| 1995 | R.J.Warren | 6 | 11 | 1 | 150* | 369 | 36.90 | 1 | 1 | 1 |
| 1994 | M.B.Loye | 12 | 20 | 1 | 139 | 700 | 36.84 | 4 | – | 6 |
| | J.W.Cook | 14 | 23 | 3 | 90 | 717 | 35.85 | – | 4 | 3 |
| 1999 | G.P.Swann | 10 | 14 | – | 183 | 487 | 34.78 | 2 | 1 | 5 |
| 1999 | D.J.G.Sales | 13 | 21 | – | 179 | 500 | 23.80 | 1 | 2 | 9 |
| | M.W.H.Inness | 4 | 4 | 1 | 25 | 66 | 22.00 | – | – | 5 |
| | T.M.B.Bailey | 16 | 23 | 2 | 68 | 389 | 18.52 | – | 3 | 41/6 |
| | R.S.G.Anderson | 5 | 10 | – | 51 | 166 | 16.60 | – | 1 | – |
| 2000 | D.M.Cousins | 10 | 16 | 7 | 23* | 103 | 11.44 | – | – | 4 |
| 2000 | J.F.Brown | 8 | 11 | 5 | 19 | 64 | 10.66 | – | – | 2 |
| | D.E.Paynter | 2 | 4 | 1 | 20 | 32 | 10.66 | – | – | 2 |
| | C.G.Greenidge | 14 | 18 | 1 | 46 | 147 | 8.64 | – | – | 7 |
| | J.A.R.Blain | 6 | 8 | 2 | 17* | 47 | 7.83 | – | – | 2 |
| | M.S.Panesar | 5 | 5 | 2 | 2* | 4 | 1.33 | – | – | 3 |

### BOWLING

| | O | M | R | W | Avge | Best | 5wI | 10wM |
|---|---|---|---|---|---|---|---|---|
| M.W.H.Inness | 116.4 | 25 | 429 | 15 | 28.60 | 7- 90 | 1 | – |
| M.E.Cassar | 113.3 | 18 | 464 | 16 | 29.00 | 6- 34 | 1 | 1 |
| G.P.Swann | 252.1 | 52 | 854 | 26 | 32.84 | 6-126 | 1 | 1 |
| C.G.Greenidge | 404.1 | 62 | 1613 | 49 | 32.91 | 6- 40 | 3 | – |
| M.S.Panesar | 174.5 | 50 | 502 | 15 | 33.46 | 4- 42 | – | – |
| J.F.Brown | 352.5 | 76 | 1138 | 28 | 40.64 | 4- 88 | – | – |
| A.L.Penberthy | 292 | 76 | 833 | 17 | 49.00 | 3- 21 | – | – |
| D.M.Cousins | 290.2 | 58 | 988 | 20 | 49.40 | 4- 75 | – | – |
| J.A.R.Blain | 173.4 | 17 | 861 | 14 | 61.50 | 4-144 | – | – |

*Also bowled:*

| | | | | | | | | |
|---|---|---|---|---|---|---|---|---|
| R.A.White | 26.4 | 3 | 91 | 5 | 18.20 | 2- 30 | – | – |
| R.S.G.Anderson | 143 | 29 | 550 | 9 | 61.11 | 4- 97 | – | – |
| J.W.Cook | 119 | 24 | 447 | 6 | 74.50 | 2- 47 | – | – |

M.B.Loye 2-1-1-0.

The First-Class Averages (pp 121-135) give the records of Northamptonshire players in all first-class county matches (Northamptonshire's other opponents being Oxford UCCE), with the exception of M.S.Panesar whose full county figures are as above.

# NORTHAMPTONSHIRE RECORDS

## FIRST-CLASS CRICKET

| Highest Total | For 781-7d | | v | Notts | Northampton | 1995 |
|---|---|---|---|---|---|---|
| | V 670-9d | | by | Sussex | Hove | 1921 |
| Lowest Total | For 12 | | v | Glos | Gloucester | 1907 |
| | V 33 | | by | Lancashire | Northampton | 1977 |
| Highest Innings | For 329* | M.E.K.Hussey | v | Essex | Northampton | 2001 |
| | V 333 | K.S.Duleepsinhji | for | Sussex | Hove | 1930 |

### Highest Partnership for each Wicket

| 1st | 375 | R.A.White/M.J.Powell | v | Glos | Northampton | 2002 |
|---|---|---|---|---|---|---|
| 2nd | 344 | G.Cook/R.J.Boyd-Moss | v | Lancashire | Northampton | 1986 |
| 3rd | 393 | A.Fordham/A.J.Lamb | v | Yorkshire | Leeds | 1990 |
| 4th | 370 | R.T.Virgin/P.Willey | v | Somerset | Northampton | 1976 |
| 5th | 401 | M.B.Loye/D.Ripley | v | Glamorgan | Northampton | 1998 |
| 6th | 376 | R.Subba Row/A.Lightfoot | v | Surrey | The Oval | 1958 |
| 7th | 293 | D.J.G.Sales/D.Ripley | v | Essex | Northampton | 1999 |
| 8th | 164 | D.Ripley/N.G.B.Cook | v | Lancashire | Manchester | 1987 |
| 9th | 156 | R.Subba Row/S.Starkie | v | Lancashire | Northampton | 1955 |
| 10th | 148 | B.W.Bellamy/J.V.Murdin | v | Glamorgan | Northampton | 1925 |

| Best Bowling | For 10-127 | V.W.C.Jupp | v | Kent | Tunbridge W | 1932 |
|---|---|---|---|---|---|---|
| (Innings) | V 10- 30 | C.Blythe | for | Kent | Northampton | 1907 |
| Best Bowling | For 15- 31 | G.E.Tribe | v | Yorkshire | Northampton | 1958 |
| (Match) | V 17- 48 | C.Blythe | for | Kent | Northampton | 1907 |

| Most Runs – Season | 2198 | D.Brookes | (av 51.11) | 1952 |
|---|---|---|---|---|
| Most Runs – Career | 28980 | D.Brookes | (av 36.13) | 1934-59 |
| Most 100s – Season | 8 | R.A.Haywood | | 1921 |
| Most 100s – Career | 67 | D.Brookes | | 1934-59 |
| Most Wkts – Season | 175 | G.E.Tribe | (av 18.70) | 1955 |
| Most Wkts – Career | 1097 | E.W.Clark | (av 21.31) | 1922-47 |
| Most Career W-K Dismissals | 810 | K.V.Andrew | (653 ct/157 st) | 1953-66 |
| Most Career Catches in the Field | 469 | D.S.Steele | | 1963-84 |

## LIMITED-OVERS CRICKET

| Highest Total | CGT | 360-2 | | v | Staffs | Northampton | 1990 |
|---|---|---|---|---|---|---|---|
| | BHC | 304-6 | | v | Scotland | Northampton | 1995 |
| | NL | 306-2 | | v | Surrey | Guildford | 1985 |
| Lowest Total | CGT | 62 | | v | Leics | Leicester | 1974 |
| | BHC | 85 | | v | Sussex | Northampton | 1978 |
| | NL | 41 | | v | Middlesex | Northampton | 1972 |
| Highest Innings | CGT | 145 | R.J.Bailey | v | Staffs | Stone | 1991 |
| | BHC | 134 | R.J.Bailey | v | Glos | Northampton | 1987 |
| | NL | 172* | W.Larkins | v | Warwicks | Luton | 1983 |
| Best Bowling | CGT | 7-37 | N.A.Mallender | v | Worcs | Northampton | 1984 |
| | BHC | 5-14 | F.A.Rose | v | Minor C | Luton | 1998 |
| | NL | 7-39 | A.Hodgson | v | Somerset | Northampton | 1976 |

# NOTTINGHAMSHIRE

**Formation of Present Club**: March/April 1841
**Substantial Reorganisation**: 11 December 1866
**Colours**: Green and Gold
**Badge**: Badge of City of Nottingham
**County Champions (since 1890)**: (4) 1907, 1929, 1981, 1987
**Gillette/NatWest/C & G Trophy Winners**: (1) 1987
**Benson and Hedges Cup Winners**: (1) 1989
**National League (Div 1) Winners**: (0); best – 5th 2001
**Sunday League Winners**: (1) 1991
**Match Awards**: CGT 44; BHC 76

**Chief Executive**: D.G.Collier, Trent Bridge, Nottingham NG2 6AG • Tel: 0115 982 3000 • Fax: 0115 945 5730 • Email: administration.notts@ecb.co.uk • Web: www.notts.ccc.co.uk and www.trentbridge.co.uk

**First XI Coach**: M.Newell. **Captain**: J.E.R.Gallian. **Limited-Overs Captain**: C.L.Cairns. **Vice-Captain**: P.J.Franks. **Overseas Players**: C.L.Cairns, S.C.G.MacGill and (*part*) S.Elworthy. **2003 Beneficiary**: W.M.Noon. **Scorer**: G.Stringfellow. ‡ New registration

**AFZAAL, Usman** (Manvers Pierrepont CS; S Notts C), b Rawalpindi, Pakistan 9 Jun 1977. 6'0". LHB, SLA. Debut 1995; cap 2000. Tests: 3 (2001); HS 54 v A (Oval) 2001; BB 1-49. Tours: SA 1996-97 (Nt); WI 2000-01 (Eng A); NZ 2001-02. 1000 runs (3): most – 1275 (2002). HS 151* v Worcs (Nottingham) 2000. BB 4-101 v Glos (Nottingham) 1998. Award: CGT 1. LO HS 95* v Hants (Southampton) 2000 (NL). LO BB 3-8 v Ire (Clontarf) 2002 (CGT).

**ATRI, Vikram** (Fernwood S, Nottingham), b Hull, Yorkshire 9 Mar 1983. RHB, OB. Debut 2002 scoring 98 v WI A (Nottingham) 2002. Awaiting CC debut. Notts 2nd XI debut 1999 when aged 16y 175d. HS 98 (*see above*). LO HS 0 (CGT).

**BICKNELL, Darren** John (Robert Haining County SS; Guildford TC), b Guildford, Surrey 24 Jun 1967. Elder brother of M.P.Bicknell (*see SURREY*). 6'4". LHB, SLA. Surrey 1987-99; cap 1990; benefit 1999. Nottinghamshire debut/cap 2000. Tours (Eng A): WI 1991-92; P 1990-91; SL 1990-91; Z 1989-90. 1000 runs (7); most – 1888 (1991). HS 235* Sy v Notts (Nottingham) 1994. Nt HS 180* v Warwks (Birmingham) 200 – sharing unbroken 1st wkt stand of 406 with G.E.Welton. BB 3-7 Sy v Sussex (Guildford) 1996. Awards: CGT 1; BHC 6. LO HS 135* Sy v Yorks (Oval) 1989 (NWT). LO BB (Sy) 1-11 (SL).

**CAIRNS, Christopher** Lance (Christchurch BHS), b Picton, NZ 13 Jun 1970. Son of B.L.Cairns (CD, Otago, ND and NZ 1971-86). 6'2". RHB, RFM. Nottinghamshire 1988-89, 1992-93 and 1995-96; cap 1993; limited-overs captain 2003. N Districts 1988-89. Canterbury 1990-91 to date (*occasionally*). *Wisden* 1999. Tests (NZ): 55 (1989-90 to 2001-02); HS 126 v I (Hamilton) 1998-99; BB 7-27 v WI (Hamilton) 1999-00. LOI (NZ): 162 (1990-91 to 2002-03, 1 as captain); HS 115 v I (Christchurch) 1998-99; BB 5-42 v A (Napier) 1997-98. Tours (NZ): E 1999; A 1989-90, 1993-94, 1997-98, 2001-02; WI 1995-96 (part); I 1995-96, 1999-00; P 1996-97; SL 1997-98; Z 1997-98, 2000-01. 1000 runs (1): 1171 (1995). HS 126 (*see Tests*). Nt HS 115 v Middx (Lord's) 1995. 50 wkts (3); most – 56 (1992). BB 8-47 (15-83 match) v Sussex (Arundel) 1995. Awards: CGT 2; BHC 1. LO HS 143 Canterbury v Auckland (Christchurch) 1994-95. LO BB 6-37 Canterbury v Wellington (Christchurch) 1996-97.

**CLOUGH, Gareth** David (Pudsey Grangefield S), b Leeds, Yorks 23 May 1978. 6'0". RHB, RM. Yorkshire 1998. Nottinghamshire debut 2001. HS 33 Y v Glam (Cardiff) 1998 – on debut. Nt HS 8. BB 3-69 v Glos (Nottingham) 2001. LO HS 24 v Northants (Northampton) 2001 (NL). LO BB 2-33 v Surrey (Oval) 2001 (NL).

‡**ELWORTHY, Steven** (Chaplin HS, Gwelo; Sandown HS, Jo'burg; Witwatersrand U), b Bulawayo, Rhodesia 23 Feb 1965. 6'4". RHB, RFM. Transvaal B 1987-88. N Transvaal/ Northerns 1988-89 to date. Lancashire 1995-96 to 1996. **Tests** (SA): 3 (1998 to 2002-03); HS 48 v E (Nottingham) 1998 – on debut; BB 4-66 (8-159 match) v NZ (Wellington) 1998-99. **LOI** (SA): 39 (1997-98 to 2002-03); HS 23 v SL (Northampton) 1999; BB 3-17 v I (Sharjah) 1999-00. Tours: E 1998; A 2001-02; WI 1995-96 (La); NZ 1998-99; Z 1994-95 (SA A). HS 89 Northerns v Boland (Pretoria) 1997-98. UK HS 88 La v Worcs (Manchester) 1996 (non CC match). CC HS 45 La v Worcs (Manchester) 1996. 50 wkts (0+1): 52 (2001-02). BB 7-65 NT v Natal (Durban) 1994-95. CC BB 4-80 La v Glos (Manchester) 1996. LO HS 116* N Transvaal v GW (Pretoria) 1994-95. LO BB 4-14 La v Glos (Manchester) 1996 (BHC).

**FRANKS, Paul** John (Southwell Minster CS), b Mansfield 3 Feb 1979. 6'2". LHB, RMF. Debut 1996; cap 1999. YC 2000. **LOI**: 1 (2000); HS 4 v WI (Nottingham) 2000. Tours (Eng A): SA 1998-99; WI 2000-01; NZ 1999-00; B 1999-00. HS 85 v Middx (Lord's) 2001. 50 wkts (2); most – 63 (1999). BB 7-56 v Middx (Lord's) 2000. Hat-trick 1997. Award: CGT 1. LO HS 60 v Kent (Nottingham) 2002 (NL). LO BB 6-27 v Durham (Chester-le-St) 2000 (NL).

**GALLIAN, Jason** Edward Riche (Pittwater House S, Sydney; Keble C, Oxford), b Manly, Sydney, Australia 25 Jun 1971. Qualified for England 1994. 6'0". RHB, RM. Lancashire 1990-97, taking wicket of D.A.Hagan (OU) with his first ball; cap 1994. Oxford U 1992-93; blue 1992-93; captain 1993. Nottinghamshire debut/cap 1998; captain 1998 (part) to date. Captained Australia YC v England YC 1989-90, scoring 158* in 1st 'Test'. **Tests**: 3 (1995 to 1995-96); HS 28 v SA (Pt Elizabeth) 1995-96. Tours: A 1996-97 (Eng A); I 1995-96 (La); SA 1995-96 (part); I 1994-95 (Eng A); P 1995-96 (Eng A). 1000 runs (3); most – 1156 (1996). HS 312 La v Derbys (Manchester) 1996 (record score at Old Trafford). Nt HS 171 v Glam (Colwyn Bay) 2002. BB 6-115 La v Surrey (Southport) 1996. Nt BB 2-28 v Warwks (Nottingham) 1999. Awards: CGT 2; BHC 2. LO HS 134 La v Notts (Manchester) 1995 (BHC). LO BB 5-15 La v Minor C (Leek) 1995 (BHC).

**HARRIS, Andrew** James (Hadfield CS; Glossopdale Community C), b Ashton-under-Lyne, Lancs 26 Jun 1973. 6'1". RHB, RM. Derbyshire 1994-99; cap 1996. Nottinghamshire debut/cap 2000. Tour: A 1996-97 (Eng A). HS 41* v Northants (Northampton) 2002. 50 wkts (2); most – 72 (1996). BB 7-54 (11-122 match) v Northants (Nottingham) 2002. Award: CGT 1. LO HS 16* v Kent (Tunbridge Wells) 2002 (NL). LO BB 5-35 v Hants (Nottingham) 2000 (NL).

**HODGKINSON, Richard** (West Notts C), b Mansfield 9 Dec 1983. RHB, RFM. Nottinghamshire staff 2003 – awaiting first-class debut. LO HS 0 and LO BB 2-43 Notts CB v Oxon (Oxford) 2001.

**LOGAN, Richard** James (Wolverhampton GS), b Stone, Staffs 28 Jan 1980. 6'1". RHB, RMF. Northamptonshire 1999-2000. Nottinghamshire debut 2001. HS 37* v Hants (Nottingham) 2001. BB 6-93 v Derbys (Nottingham) 2001. Award: CGT 1. LO HS 24 v Northants (Northampton) 2001 (NL). LO BB 5-24 v Suffolk (Mildenhall) 2001 (CGT).

**LUCAS, David** Scott (Djanogly CTC, Nottingham), b Nottingham 19 Aug 1978. 6'2". RHB, LMF. Debut 1999. HS 49 v DU (Nottingham) 2002. CC HS 46* v Middx (Nottingham) 2000. BB 5-104 v Essex (Nottingham) 1999. LO HS 19* v Sussex (Hove) 1999 (NL). LO BB 4-27 v Derbys (Derby) 2000 (NL).

**MacGILL, Stuart** Charles Glyndwr (Christ Church GS, Perth), b Mount Lawley, WA 25 Feb 1971. Grandson of C.W.T. (WA 1938-39), son of T.M.D. (WA 1968-76). 6'0". RHB, LBG. W Australia 1993-94. NSW 1996-97 to date. Somerset 1997 (unregistered). Devon 1997 to 1998 (NWT only). Nottinghamshire debut/cap 2002. **Tests**: 19 (1997-98 to 2002-03); HS 43 v E (Melbourne) 1998-99; BB 7-50 (12-107 match) v E (Sydney) 1998-99. **LOI** (A): 3 (1999-00); HS 1 and BB 4-19 v P (Sydney) 1999-00 – on debut. Tours (A): SA 2001-02; WI 1998-99, 2003; P 1998-99. HS 53 NSW v S Aus (Sydney) 2001-02. Nt HS 22 v Worcs (Kidderminster) 2002 – on Notts debut. 50 wkts (0+1): 50 (1997-98). BB 8-111 (14-165 match) v Middx (Nottingham) 2002. LO HS 18 NSW v Vic (Melbourne) 1998-99. LO BB 5-40 NSW v ACT (Canberra) 1998-99.

**McMAHON, Paul** Joseph (Trinity RCS, Nottingham), b Wigan, Lancs 12 Mar 1983. RHB, OB. Debut 2002. HS 15 v v Northants (Northampton) 2002 – on debut. BB 2-22 v WI A (Nottingham) 2002. CC BB – .

**MALIK, Muhammad Nadeem** (Wilford Meadows CS; Bilborough C), b Nottingham 6 Oct 1982. 6'5". RHB, RFM. Debut 2001. 2nd XI debut 1999 when aged 16y 337d. HS 18 v Middx (Lord's) 2002. BB 5-57 v Derbys (Nottingham) 2001. LO HS 11 v Worcs (Nottingham) 2002 (NL). LO BB 2-34 v Yorks (Nottingham) 2001 (NL).

**NOON, Wayne** Michael (Caistor S), b Grimsby, Lincs 5 Feb 1971. 5'9". RHB, WK. Northamptonshire 1989-93. Nottinghamshire debut 1994; cap 1995; benefit 2003. Canterbury 1994-95. Worcs 2nd XI debut when aged 15yr 199d. Tours: SA 1991-92 (Nh), 1996-97 (Nt). HS 83 v Northants (Northampton) 1997. LO HS 46 v Warwks (Birmingham) 1998 (BHC).

**PATEL, Samit** Rohit (Worksop C), b Leicester 30 Nov 1984. RHB, SLA. Debut 2002 – awaiting CC debut. Notts 2nd XI debut 1999 when aged 14yr 274d. HS 35 v WI A (Nottingham) 2002 – on debut. LO HS 18 v Warwks (Birmingham) 2002 (NL). LO BB 2-14 v Yorks (Leeds) 2002 (NL).

**PIETERSEN, Kevin** Peter (Maritzburg C; Natal U), b Pietermaritzburg, SA 27 Jun 1980. ECB qualified – British passport (English mother). 6'4". RHB, OB. Natal/KwaZulu-Natal 1997-98 to 1999-00. Nottinghamshire debut 2001; cap 2002. 1000 (1): 1275 (2001). HS 254* v Middx (Nottingham) 2002. BB 4-141 KZ-Natal v E (Durban) 1999-00. Nt BB 2-46 v Worcs (Nottingham) 2001. LO HS 147 v Somerset (Taunton) 2002 (NL). LO BB 3-39 v Warwks (Nottingham) 2001 (NL).

**RANDALL, Stephen** John (W Bridgford S), b Nottingham 9 Jun 1980. 5'10". RHB, OB. Debut 1999. HS 28 v Glos (Bristol) 2001. BB 2-64 v Derbys (Nottingham) 2001. LO HS 25 v Worcs (Nottingham) 2002 (NL). LO BB 3-44 v Glos (Cheltenham) 2001 (NL).

**READ, Christopher** Mark Wells (Torquay GS; Bath U), b Paignton, Devon 10 Aug 1978. 5'8". RHB, WK. Gloucestershire (L-O) 1997. Nottinghamshire debut 1998; cap 1999. Devon 1995-97. **Tests**: 3 (1999); HS 37 v NZ (Lord's) 1999. **LOI**: 9 (1999-00); HS 26* v SA (Cape Town) 1999-00. Tours (Eng A): SA 1998-99, 1999-00 (Eng); WI 2000-01; SL 1997-98; Z 1998-99; K 1997-98. HS 160 v Warwks (Nottingham) 1999. LO HS 69 v Warwks (Birmingham) 2002 (NL).

**SHAFAYAT, Bilal** Mustapha (Greenwood Dale; Nottingham Bluecoat SFC), b Nottingham 10 Jul 1984. 5'7". RHB, RMF. Debut 2001, scoring 72 and 24 v Middx (Nottingham). Captained Eng U-19 tour of Australia 2002-03. HS 104 v Worcs (Nottingham) 2002. LO HS 66 v Somerset (Taunton) 2002 (NL). LO BB 4-35 v Somerset (Nottingham) 2002 (NL).

**SHRECK, Charles** Edward (Truro S), b Truro, Cornwall 6 Jan 1978. Cornwall 1997 to date. Awaiting f-c debut. Award: CGT 1. LO HS 9 Cornwall v Cumb (Netherfield) 1999 (CGT). LO BB 5-19 Cornwall v Worcs (Truro) 2002 (CGT). Took 5-35 v Worcs (Nottingham) 2002 (NL) – on 1st XI debut.

**SMITH, Gregory** James (Pretoria BHS; Pretoria Technikon), b Pretoria, SA 30 Oct 1971. ECB qualified – British passport. 6'4". RHB, LFM. N Transvaal/Northerns 1993-94 to date. Nottinghamshire debut/cap 2001. Tour (SA A): E 1996. 50 wkts (1): 50 (2001). HS 68 NT v WP (Pretoria) 1995-96. Nt HS 44* v Sussex (Nottingham) 2001. BB 8-53 (11-74 match) v Essex (Nottingham) 2002. Awards: BHC 2. LO HS 16* v Leics (Leicester) 2002 (NL). LO BB 5-11 NT v GW (Kimberley) 1995-96.

**SMITH, Will** Rew (Bedford S), b Luton, Beds 28 Sep 1982. 5'9". RHB, OB. Debut 2002 – awaiting CC debut. Notts 2nd XI debut 1999 when aged 16y 309d. HS 38* v WI A (Nottingham) 2002 – on debut. LO HS 16 v Durham (Nottingham) 2002 (NL).

‡**WARREN, Russell** John (Kingsthorpe Upper S), b Northampton 10 Sep 1971. 6'1". RHB, OB. Northamptonshire 1992-2002; cap 1995. Nottinghamshire staff 2003. 1000 (1): 1303 (2001). HS 201* Nh v Glam (Northampton) 1996. Award: CGT 1. LO HS 100* Nh v Ire (Northampton) 1994 (NWT).

**WELTON, Guy** Edward (Healing CS; Grimsby TC; Nottingham Trent U), b Grimsby, Lincs 4 May 1978. 6'1". RHB, OB. Debut 1997. MCC YC. HS 200* v Warwks (Birmingham) 2000 – sharing unbroken 1st wkt stand of 406 with D.J.Bicknell. Awards: BHC 2. LO HS 104* v Durham (Nottingham) 1999 (NL).

## RELEASED/RETIRED
(Having made a first-class County appearance in 2002)

**BOJE, Nico 'Nicky'** (Grey C, Bloemfontein), b Bloemfontein, SA 20 Mar 1973. Brother of E.H.L.Boje (OFS 1989-1990 to 1990-91). LHB, SLA. (Orange) Free State 1990-91 to date. Nottinghamshire 2002. *Tests*: 21 (1999-00 to 2002-03); HS 85 v 1 (Bangalore) 1999-00; BB 5-62 v SL (Colombo) 2000-01. **LOI** (SA): 88 (1995-96 to 2002-03); HS 129 v NZ (Pretoria) 2000-01; BB 5-21 v A (Cape Town) 2001-02. Tours (SA): E 1996; A 2001-02; WI 2000-01; NZ 1998-99; I 1996-97, 1999-00; SL 1998-99, 2000; Z 1994-95. HS 116 FS v WP (Bloemfontein) 1998-99. Nt HS 84 v Derbys (Nottingham) 2002. BB 6-31 FS v Boland (Bloemfontein) 2002-02. Nt BB 6-128 v Glam (Colwyn Bay) 2002. LO HS 129 (*see LOI*). LO BB 5-21 (*see LOI*).

**JOHNSON, Paul** (Grove CS, Balderton), b Newark 24 Apr 1965. 5'7". RHB, RM. Nottinghamshire 1982-2002; cap 1986; benefit 1995; captain 1996-98. Tours: SA 1996-97 (Nt); WI 1991-92 (Eng A). 1000 runs (9): most – 1518 (1990). HS 187 v Lancs (Manchester) 1993. BB 1-9. CC BB 1-14. Awards: CGT 2; BHC 3. LO HS 167* v Kent (Nottingham) 1993 (SL). LO BB 1-2 (NL).

**KLUSENER, Lance** (Durban HS), b Durban, SA 4 Sep 1971. LHB, RM/OB. Natal/ KwaZulu-Natal 1993-94 to date. Nottinghamshire 2002. *Wisden* 1999. *Tests* (SA): 48 (1996-97 to 2001-02); HS 174 v E (Pt Elizabeth) 1999-00; BB 8-64 v 1 (Calcutta) 1996-97 – on debut. **LOI** (SA): 154 (1995-96 to 2002-03); HS 103* v NZ (Auckland) 1998-99; BB 6-49 v SL (Lahore) 1997-98. Tours (SA): E 1998; A 1997-98, 2001-02; WI 2000-01; NZ 1998-99; I 1996-97, 1999-00; P 1997-98; SL 1998-99, 2000; Z 1999-00, 2001-02. HS 174 (*see Tests*). BB 8-34 Natal v WP (Durban) 1995-96. Nt HS 42 and Nt BB 1-88 v Middx (Lord's) 2002 – on Notts debut. Award: BHC 1. LO HS 142* SA v Northants (Northampton) 1998. LO BB 6-49 (*see LOI*).

**SAVILL, Thomas** Edward (Bilborough C; Homerton C, Cambridge), b Sheffield, Yorks 16 May 1983. 6'6". RHB, RFM. Cambridge UCCE 2002. Nottinghamshire 2002 – no CC appearance. HS 18* CU v Essex (Cambridge) 2002. Nt HS 0. BB 2-42 v WI A (Nottingham) 2002 – on Notts debut. LO HS 35* Notts CB v Oxon (Oxford) 2001 (CGT).

## LANCASHIRE RELEASED/RETIRED (continued from p 53)

**ROBERTS, Timothy** William (Bishop's Stopford S, Kettering; Durham U), b Kettering, Northants 4 Mar 1978. Younger brother of A.R.Roberts (Northants 1987-98). 5'7". RHB, OB. British U 1999. Bedfordshire 2000. Lancashire debut 2001. HS 49 Brit U v NZ (Oxford) 1999 – on debut. La HS 17 v DU (Durham) 2001. CC HS 3. LO HS 55 v Derbys (Derby) 2001 (NL).

**SMETHURST, M.P.** – *see NORTHAMPTONSHIRE*.

G.I.Maiden left the staff having made no f-c appearances in 2002.

# NOTTINGHAMSHIRE 2002

## RESULTS SUMMARY

|  | Place | Won | Lost | Tied | Drew | No Result |
|---|---|---|---|---|---|---|
| **County Championship** (2nd Division) | 3rd | 8 | 5 | | 3 | |
| **All First-Class Matches** | | 9 | 5 | | 4 | |
| **C & G Trophy** | 4th Round | | | | | |
| **Benson & Hedges Cup** | 4th in North Division | | | | | |
| **NU National League** (1st Division) | 9th | 3 | 11 | | | 2 |

## COUNTY CHAMPIONSHIP AVERAGES

### BATTING AND FIELDING

| Cap | | M | I | NO | HS | Runs | Avge | 100 | 50 | Ct/St |
|---|---|---|---|---|---|---|---|---|---|---|
| 2002 | K.P.Pietersen | 10 | 15 | 3 | 254* | 737 | 61.41 | 3 | – | 9 |
| 2000 | U.Afzaal | 16 | 29 | 3 | 134 | 1155 | 44.42 | 4 | 6 | 10 |
| 1998 | J.E.R.Gallian | 15 | 27 | 3 | 171 | 1006 | 41.91 | 4 | 5 | 15 |
| | B.M.Shafayat | 5 | 9 | – | 104 | 332 | 36.88 | 1 | 1 | 4 |
| 1999 | C.M.W.Read | 16 | 25 | 5 | 127 | 694 | 34.70 | 1 | 3 | 60/2 |
| 2000 | D.J.Bicknell | 12 | 21 | – | 112 | 711 | 33.85 | 2 | 5 | 5 |
| | G.E.Welton | 14 | 25 | 1 | 115 | 806 | 33.58 | 1 | 5 | 16 |
| 1986 | P.Johnson | 14 | 25 | 3 | 96 | 662 | 30.09 | – | 5 | 7 |
| | N.Boje | 9 | 16 | 2 | 84 | 409 | 29.21 | – | 2 | 10 |
| 1999 | P.J.Franks | 10 | 14 | 2 | 67 | 301 | 25.08 | – | 3 | 2 |
| 2001 | G.J.Smith | 15 | 20 | 7 | 39* | 243 | 18.69 | – | – | 4 |
| 2000 | A.J.Harris | 13 | 18 | 6 | 41* | 149 | 12.41 | – | – | 5 |
| | R.J.Logan | 12 | 17 | 2 | 32 | 139 | 9.26 | – | – | 4 |
| 2002 | S.C.G.MacGill | 6 | 7 | 1 | 22 | 48 | 8.00 | – | – | 5 |
| | M.N.Malik | 5 | 7 | 1 | 18 | 32 | 5.33 | – | – | – |

*Also batted:* L.Klusener (1 match) 0, 42 (1 ct); P.J.McMahon (1) 15, 0; S.J.Randall (2) 0, 8, 5 (1 ct).

### BOWLING

| | O | M | R | W | Avge | Best | 5wI | 10wM |
|---|---|---|---|---|---|---|---|---|
| A.J.Harris | 392.4 | 84 | 1411 | 63 | 22.39 | 7- 54 | 3 | 2 |
| S.C.G.MacGill | 227.4 | 37 | 930 | 40 | 23.25 | 8-111 | 4 | 1 |
| N.Boje | 238 | 58 | 671 | 27 | 24.85 | 6-128 | 2 | – |
| P.J.Franks | 234.5 | 53 | 813 | 32 | 25.40 | 5- 51 | 1 | – |
| G.J.Smith | 400.1 | 85 | 1275 | 48 | 26.56 | 8- 53 | 1 | 1 |
| M.N.Malik | 112.4 | 25 | 389 | 14 | 27.78 | 4- 55 | – | – |
| R.J.Logan | 302.3 | 64 | 1142 | 35 | 32.62 | 4- 64 | – | – |

*Also bowled:* U.Afzaal 30.3-2-122-0; P.Johnson 1.2-0-12-0; L.Klusener 20-4-88-1; P.J.McMahon 19-2-81-0; K.P.Pietersen 30-3-152-2; S.J.Randall 33-6-140-0; B.M.Shafayat 11-0-40-0.

The First-Class Averages (pp 121-135) give the records of Nottinghamshire players in all first-class county matches (Nottinghamshire's other opponents being West Indies A and Durham UCCE), with the exception of:

  U.Afzaal 17-31-3-134-1164-41.57-4-6-11ct. 63.3-20-180-4-45.00-3/32.

  C.M.W.Read 17-27-5-127-773-35.13-1-4-62ct/2st. Did not bowl.

  T.E.Savill 1-1-0-0-0-0.00-0-0-0ct. 5-1-42-2-21.00-2/42.

# NOTTINGHAMSHIRE RECORDS

## FIRST-CLASS CRICKET

| | | | | | | |
|---|---|---|---|---|---|---|
| **Highest Total** | For | 739-7d | | v | Leics | Nottingham | 1903 |
| | V | 781-7d | | by | Northants | Northampton | 1995 |
| **Lowest Total** | For | 13 | | v | Yorkshire | Nottingham | 1901 |
| | V | 16 | | by | Derbyshire | Nottingham | 1879 |
| | | 16 | | by | Surrey | The Oval | 1880 |
| **Highest Innings** | For | 312* | W.W.Keeton | v | Middlesex | The Oval | 1939 |
| | V | 345 | C.G.Macartney | for | Australians | Nottingham | 1921 |

### Highest Partnership for each Wicket

| | | | | | | |
|---|---|---|---|---|---|---|
| 1st | 406* | D.J.Bicknell/G.E.Welton | v | Warwicks | Birmingham | 2000 |
| 2nd | 398 | A.Shrewsbury/W.Gunn | v | Sussex | Nottingham | 1890 |
| 3rd | 369 | W.Gunn/J.R.Gunn | v | Leics | Nottingham | 1903 |
| 4th | 361 | A.O.Jones/J.R.Gunn | v | Essex | Leyton | 1905 |
| 5th | 266 | A.Shrewsbury/W.Gunn | v | Sussex | Hove | 1884 |
| 6th | 372* | K.P.Pietersen/J.E.Morris | v | Derbyshire | Derby | 2001 |
| 7th | 301 | C.C.Lewis/B.N.French | v | Durham | Chester-le-St | 1993 |
| 8th | 220 | G.F.H.Heane/R.Winrow | v | Somerset | Nottingham | 1935 |
| 9th | 170 | J.C.Adams/K.P.Evans | v | Somerset | Taunton | 1994 |
| 10th | 152 | E.B.Alletson/W.Riley | v | Sussex | Hove | 1911 |
| | 152 | U.Afzaal/A.J.Harris | v | Worcs | Nottingham | 2000 |

| | | | | | | |
|---|---|---|---|---|---|---|
| **Best Bowling** | For | 10-66 | K.Smales | v | Glos | Stroud | 1956 |
| **(Innings)** | V | 10-10 | H.Verity | for | Yorkshire | Leeds | 1932 |
| **Best Bowling** | For | 17-89 | F.C.Matthews | v | Northants | Nottingham | 1923 |
| **(Match)** | V | 17-89 | W.G.Grace | for | Glos | Cheltenham | 1877 |

| | | | | |
|---|---|---|---|---|
| **Most Runs – Season** | 2620 | W.W.Whysall | (av 53.46) | 1929 |
| **Most Runs – Career** | 31592 | G.Gunn | (av 35.69) | 1902-32 |
| **Most 100s – Season** | 9 | W.W.Whysall | | 1928 |
| | 9 | M.J.Harris | | 1971 |
| | 9 | B.C.Broad | | 1990 |
| **Most 100s – Career** | 65 | J.Hardstaff jr | | 1930-55 |
| **Most Wkts – Season** | 181 | B.Dooland | (av 14.96) | 1954 |
| **Most Wkts – Career** | 1653 | T.G.Wass | (av 20.34) | 1896-1920 |
| **Most Career W-K Dismissals** | 957 | T.W.Oates | (733 ct/224 st) | 1897-1925 |
| **Most Career Catches in the Field** | 466 | A.O.Jones | | 1892-1914 |

## LIMITED-OVERS CRICKET

| | | | | | | |
|---|---|---|---|---|---|---|
| **Highest Total** | CGT | 344-6 | | v | Northumb | Jesmond | 1994 |
| | BHC | 296-6 | | v | Kent | Nottingham | 1989 |
| | NL | 329-6 | | v | Derbyshire | Nottingham | 1993 |
| **Lowest Total** | CGT | 123 | | v | Yorkshire | Scarborough | 1969 |
| | BHC | 74 | | v | Leics | Leicester | 1987 |
| | NL | 66 | | v | Yorkshire | Bradford | 1969 |
| **Highest Innings** | CGT | 149* | D.W.Randall | v | Devon | Torquay | 1988 |
| | BHC | 130* | C.E.B.Rice | v | Scotland | Glasgow | 1982 |
| | NL | 167* | P.Johnson | v | Kent | Nottingham | 1993 |
| **Best Bowling** | CGT | 6-10 | K.P.Evans | v | Northumb | Jesmond | 1994 |
| | BHC | 6-22 | M.K.Bore | v | Leics | Leicester | 1980 |
| | | 6-22 | C.E.B.Rice | v | Northants | Northampton | 1981 |
| | NL | 6-12 | R.J.Hadlee | v | Lancashire | Nottingham | 1980 |

# SOMERSET

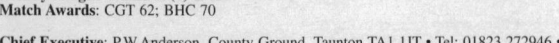

**Formation of Present Club**: 18 August 1875
**Colours**: Black, White and Maroon
**Badge**: Somerset Dragon
**County Champions**: (0); best – 2nd (Div 1) 2001
**Gillette/NatWest/C & G Trophy Winners**: (3) 1979, 1983, 2001
**Benson and Hedges Cup Winners**: (2) 1981, 1982
**National League (Div 1) Winners**: (0); best – 4th 2001
**Sunday League Winners**: (1) 1979
**Match Awards**: CGT 62; BHC 70

**Chief Executive**: P.W.Anderson, County Ground, Taunton TA1 1JT • Tel: 01823 272946 • Fax: 01823 332395 • Email: somerset@ecb.co.uk • Web: None.

**First XI Coach**: K.J.Shine. **Captain**: M.Burns. **Vice-Captain**: M.E.Trescothick. **Overseas Players**: J.Cox and N.A.M.McLean. **2003 Beneficiary**: None. **Scorer**: G.A.Stickley.
‡ New registration

**BLACKWELL, Ian** David (Brookfield Community S), b Chesterfield, Derbys 10 Jun 1978. 6'2". LHB, SLA. Derbyshire 1997-99. Somerset debut 2000; cap 2001. **LOI**: 14 (2002-03); HS 82 v I (Colombo) 2002-03; BB 3-26 v A (Adelaide) 2002-03. HS 122 v Northants (Northampton) 2001. BB 5-49 v Hants (Southampton) 2002. Awards: CGT 1; BHC 1. LO HS 97 De v Glam (Derby) 1999 (NL). LO BB 4-24 v Kent (Taunton) 2002 (NL).

**BOWLER, Peter** Duncan (Scots C, Sydney, Aus; Daramalan C, Canberra, Aus; Nottingham Trent U), b Plymouth, Devon 30 Jul 1963. 6'1". RHB, OB, occ WK. Leicestershire 1986 – first to score hundred on f-c debut for Leics (100* and 62 v Hants). Tasmania 1986-87. Derbyshire 1988-94; cap 1989; scored 155* v CU (Cambridge) on debut – first instance of hundreds on debut for two counties. Somerset debut/cap 1995; captain 1997-98; benefit 2000. 1000 runs (9) inc 2000 (1): 2044 (1992). HS 241* De v Hants (Portsmouth) 1992. Sm HS 207 v Surrey (Taunton) 1996. BB 3-25 v Northants (Taunton) 1998. Awards: BHC 4. LO HS 138* De v Somerset (Derby) 1993 (SL). LO BB 3-31 De v Glos (Cheltenham) 1991 (SL).

**‡BRYANT, James** Douglas Campbell (Maritzburg C; Port Elizabeth U), b Durban 4 Feb 1976. E Province 1996-97 to date. Tour (SA A): WI 2000-01. Somerset staff 2003. HS 149 EP v Northerns (Port Elizabeth) 1999-00. BB (EP) 1-22. LO HS 105* EP v WP (Cape Town) 2000-01.

**BULBECK, Matthew** Paul Leonard (Taunton S; Richard Huish C), b Taunton 8 Nov 1979. 6'3½". LHB, LMF. Debut 1998; cap 2002. HS 76* v Durham (Chester-le-St) 1999. 50 wkts (2); most – 58 (2002). BB 6-93 v Lancs (Taunton) 2002. Award: CGT 1. LO HS 24* v Glam (Cardiff) 2002 (NL). LO BB 5-18 v Somerset CB v Norfolk (Hellesdon) 2001 (CGT).

**BURNS, Michael** (Walney CS), b Barrow-in-Furness, Lancs 6 Feb 1969. 6'0". RHB, RM, WK. Cumberland 1988-90. Warwickshire 1992-96. Somerset debut 1997; cap 1999; captain 2003. Scored earliest hundred in UK f-c matches (160 v OU (Taunton) on 7 Apr 2000). 1000 (1): 1047 (2002). HS 221 v Yorks (Bath) 2001. BB 6-54 v Leics (Taunton) 2001. Awards: CGT 1; BHC 1. LO HS 115* v Middx (Taunton) 1997 (SL). LO BB 4-39 v Glos (Taunton) 1997 (SL).

**CADDICK, Andrew** Richard (Papanui HS), b Christchurch, NZ 21 Nov 1968. Son of English emigrants – qualified for England 1992. 6'5". RHB, RFM. Debut 1991; cap 1992; benefit 1999. Represented NZ in 1987-88 Youth World Cup. *Wisden* 2000. **ECB contracts 2000, 2001, 2002, 2003. Tests**: 62 (1993 to 2002-03); HS 49* v A (Birmingham) 2001; BB 7-46 v SA (Durban) 1999-00. **LOI**: 54 (1993 to 2002-03); HS 36 v A (Oval) 2001; BB 4-19 v SA (Jo'burg) 1999-00. Tours: A 1992-93 (Eng A), 2002-03; SA 1999-00; WI 1993-94, 1997-98; NZ 1996-97, 2001-02; P 2000-01; SL 2000-01; Z 1996-97. HS 92 v Worcs (Worcester) 1995. 50 wkts (8) inc 100 (1): 105 (1998). BB 9-32 (12-120 match) v Lancs (Taunton) 1993. Awards: CGT 2. LO HS 39 v Hants (Taunton) 1996 (SL). LO BB 6-30 v Glos (Taunton) 1992 (NWT).

**COX, Jamie** (Wynyard HS; Deakin U), b Burnie, Tasmania, Australia 15 Oct 1969. 6'0". RHB, OB. Tasmania 1987-88 to date; captain 2000-01 to date. Somerset debut/cap 1999; captain 1999-2001. Tours: Z 1991-92 (Aus B), 1995-96 (Tas). 1000 runs (2+2); most – 1617 (1999). HS 245 Tas v NSW (Hobart) 1999-2000. Sm HS 216 v Hants (Southampton) 1999. BB 3-46 v Middx (Taunton) 1999. Awards: CGT 2. LO HS 114 v Surrey (Taunton) 1999 (NWT). LO BB 3-28 v Durham (Taunton) 1999 (NL).

**DURSTON, Wesley** John (Millfield S), b Taunton 6 Oct 1980. RHB, SLA. Somerset debut 2002 – awaiting CC debut. HS 55 and BB 1-25 v WI A (Taunton) 2002 – on debut. LO HS 50 and 1-32 Somerset CB v Staffs (Walsall) 2000 (CGT).

**DUTCH, Keith** Philip (Nower Hill HS; Weald C), b Harrow, Middlesex 21 Mar 1973. 5'10". RHB, OB. Middlesex 1993-2000. Somerset debut/cap 2001. MCC YC. HS 118 v Essex (Taunton) 2001. BB 6-62 M v Essex (Chelmsford) 2000. Sm BB 4-32 v Essex (Chelmsford) 2001. Award: CGT 1. LO HS 64 v Durham (Chester-le-St) 2002 (NL). LO BB 6-40 v Northants (Northampton) 2001 (NL).

**EDWARDS, Neil** James, b Treliske, Cornwall 14 Oct 1983. LHB, RM. Somerset debut 2002 – awaiting CC debut. HS 31 v WI A (Taunton) 2002 – on debut.

**FRANCIS, Simon** Richard George (Yardley Court, Tonbridge; King Edward VI S, Southampton; Durham U), b Bromley, Kent 15 Aug 1978. Elder brother of J.D.Francis (Hampshire 2001). 6'2". RHB, RMF. Hampshire 1997-2000. British U 1998-99. Somerset debut 2002. HS 30* H v Surrey (Oval) 2000. Sm HS 17 v Le (Leicester) 2002. BB 5-73 v Warwks (Taunton) 2002. LO HS 27 v Kent (Canterbury) 2002 (NL). LO BB 4-60 v Worcs (Worcester) 2002 (NL).

**GAZZARD, Carl** Matthew (Mounts Bay CS, Penzance; Richard Huish C), b Penzance, Cornwall 15 Apr 1982. 6'0". RHB, WK. Somerset debut 2002 – awaiting CC debut. Cornwall 1998 to date. HS 24 v WI A (Taunton) 2002 – on debut. LO HS 16 Cornwall v Cumb (Kendal) 1999 (NWT).

**HOLLOWAY, Piran** Christopher Laity (Millfield S; Taunton S; Loughborough U), b Helston, Cornwall 1 Oct 1970. 5'8". LHB, WK. Warwickshire 1988-93. Somerset debut 1994; cap 1997. Cornwall 2002. Awards: CGT 1; BHC 1. HS 168 v Middx (Uxbridge) 1996. LO HS 117 v Glos (Taunton) 1997 (SL).

**HUNKIN, Christopher** Andrew (Richard Huish C), b St Austell, Cornwall 14 Dec 1980. RHB, RM. Staff 2001 – awaiting f-c debut. Cornwall 2002. LO HS 21* Cornwall v Wales MC (Sully) 2002 (CGT). LO BB 2-43 Cornwall v Cheshire (Toft) 2001 (CGT).

**JOHNSON, Richard** Leonard (Sunbury Manor S; S Pelthorne C), b Chertsey, Surrey 29 Dec 1974. 6'2". RHB, RFM. Middlesex 1992-2000; cap 1995. Somerset debut/cap 2001. Tour: I 1994-95 (Eng A – *part*), 2001-02. HS 69 M v Essex (Chelmsford) 2000. Sm HS 68 v Leics (Taunton) 2001. 50 wkts (4); most – 62 (2001). BB 10-45 M v Derbys (Derby) 1994 (second youngest to take all ten wickets in any f-c match). Sm BB 7-43 (10-75 match) v Hants (Bath) 2002. Award: CGT 1. LO HS 45* M v Durham (Southgate) 1998 (NWT). LO BB 5-50 M v Kent (Lord's) 1997 (NWT).

**JONES, Philip Steffan** (Stradey CS, Llanelli; Neath TC; Loughborough U; Homerton C, Cambridge), b Llanelli, Wales 9 Feb 1974. 6'2". RHB, RMF. Cambridge U 1997; blue 1997. Somerset debut 1997; cap 2001. Wales MC 1992-96. HS 105 v NZ (Taunton) 1999. CC HS 56* v Yorks (Scarborough) 2000. 50 wkts (1): 59 (2001). BB 6-67 CU v OU (Lord's) 1997. Sm BB 6-110 (match 10-156) v Warwks (Birmingham) 2002. LO HS 27 v Northants (Northampton) 2000 (NL). LO BB 5-23 v Warwks (Taunton) 1998 (SL).

‡**LARAMAN, Aaron** William (Enfield GS), b Enfield, Middx 10 Jan 1979. 6'5". RHB, RFM. Middlesex 1998-2002. Somerset staff 2003. HS 82* M v Glos (Southgate) 2002. BB 4-33 M v CU (Cambridge) 2000. CC BB 4-55 M v Northants (Northampton) 2002. LO HS 28 M v Glos (Southgate) 2002 (NL). LO BB 6-42 M v Glam (Cardiff) 2000 (NL).

‡**McLEAN, Nixon** Alexei McNamara (Crapan SS, St Vincent), b Stubbs, St Vincent 20 Jul 1973. 6'4". LHB, RFM. Windward Is 1991-92 to 2000-01. Hampshire 1998-99; cap 1998. KwaZulu-Natal 2001-02 to date. **Tests** (WI): 19 (1997-98 to 2000-01); HS 46 v P (Georgetown) 1999-00; BB 3-53 v SA (Cape Town) 1998-99. **LOI** (WI): 45 (1996-97 to 2002-03); HS 50* v Z (Canterbury) 2000; BB 3-21 v Z (Perth) 2000-01. Tours (WI): E 2000; A 1996-97, 2000-01; SA 1997-98 (WI A), 1998-99. HS 70 H v Surrey (Guildford) 1999. 50 wkts (1): 62 (1998). BB 7-28 WI v FS (Bloemfontein) 1998-99. UK BB 6-110 v Leics (Leicester) 1998. LO HS 50* (*see LOI*). LO BB 5-26 WI Select XI v P (St John's) 1999-00.

**PARSONS, Keith** Alan (The Castle S, Taunton; Richard Huish C), b Taunton 2 May 1973. Identical twin brother of K.J.Parsons (Somerset staff 1992-94). 6'1". RHB, RM. Debut 1992; cap 1999. HS 193* v WI (Taunton) 2000. CC HS 139 v Northants (Taunton) 2001. BB 5-13 v Lancs (Taunton) 2000. Awards: CGT 2. LO HS 121 v Worcs (Taunton) 2002 (CGT). LO BB 4-43 v Surrey (Taunton) 1999 (NWT).

**PARSONS, Michael**, b Taunton 26 Nov 1984. RHB, RMF. Somerset 1st XI debut 2002 – awaiting f-c debut. LO HS 0 and LO BB 3-70 Somerset CB v Cornwall (Camborne) 2002.

**SUPPIAH, Arul** Vivasvan (Exeter U), b Kuala Lumpur, Malaysia 30 Aug 1983. Son of R.Suppiah (Kuala Lumpur). Brother of R.V.Suppiah (Malaysia – vice-captain). 6'0". RHB, SLA. Somerset debut 2002. Malaysia 1999-2001. HS 21 v Lancs (Taunton) 2002. BB 3-46 v WI A (Taunton) 2002. CC BB – . LO HS 70 Somerset CB v Cornwall (Camborne) 2002 (CGT). LO BB 2-36 v Leics (Leicester) 2002 (NL).

**TRESCOTHICK, Marcus** Edward (Sir Bernard Lovell S), b Keynsham 25 Dec 1975. 6'2". LHB, RM. Debut 1993; cap 1999; captain 2002. **ECB contracts 2001, 2002, 2003. Tests**: 31 (2000 to 2002-03); HS 161 v SL (Birmingham) 2002; BB 1-34. **LOI**: 61 (2000 to 2002-03, 1 as captain); HS 137 v P (Lord's) 2001; BB 2-7 v Z (Manchester) 2000. Tours: A 2002-03; NZ 1999-00 (Eng A), 2001-02; I 2001-02; P 2000-01; SL 2000-01; B 1999-00 (Eng A). HS 190 v Middx (Taunton) 1999. BB 4-36 (inc hat-trick) v Young A (Taunton) 1995. CC BB 4-82 v Yorks (Leeds) 1998. Hat-trick 1995. Awards: CGT 3; BHC 3. LO HS 137 (*see LOI*). LO BB 4-50 v Northants (Northampton) 2000 (NL).

**TURNER, Robert** Julian (Millfield S; Magdalene C, Cambridge), b Malvern, Worcs 25 Nov 1967. 6'1½". RHB, WK. Brother of S.J.Turner (Somerset 1984-85). Cambridge U 1988-91; blue 1988-89-90-91; captain 1991. Somerset debut 1991; cap 1994; benefit 2002. Cambridgeshire 1990. Tours (Eng A): NZ 1999-00; B 1999-00. Held 7 catches in an innings v Northants (Taunton) 2001. 1000 runs (2); most – 1217 (1999). HS 144 v Kent (Taunton) 1997. Award: BHC 1. LO HS 70 v Glam (Cardiff) 1996 (BHC).

**WEBLEY, Thomas** (King's C, Taunton), b Bristol 2 Mar 1983. RHB, SLA. Staff 2001 – awaiting f-c debut. 2nd XI debut 1999 when aged 16y 49d. LO HS (Somerset CB) 8 (CGT).

**WOOD, Matthew** James (Exmouth Community C; Exeter U), b Exeter, Devon 30 Sep 1980. 5'11". RHB, OB. Debut 2001. 2nd XI debut 1997 when aged 16y 345d. Devon 1998-2000. HS 196 v Kent (Taunton) 2002. LO HS 88* v Durham (Taunton) 2002 (NL).

## RELEASED/RETIRED
(Registered players who made a first-class County appearance in 2002)

**ROSE, Graham** David (Northumberland Park S, Tottenham), b Tottenham, London 12 Apr 1964. 6'4". RHB, RM. Middlesex 1985-86. Somerset 1987-2002; cap 1988; benefit 1997. 1000 runs (1): 1000 (1990). HS 191 v Sussex (Taunton) 1997. 50 wkts (5); most – 63 (1997). BB 7-47 (13-88 match) v Notts (Taunton) 1996. Awards: BHC 4. LO HS 148 v Glam (Neath) 1990 (SL). LO BB 4-16 v SL (Taunton) 1990.

**TREGO, P.D.** – *see* KENT.

M.N.Lathwell and J.P.Tucker left the staff having made no f-c appearances in 2002. P.W.Jarvis was recalled for two l-o matches.

# SOMERSET 2002

## RESULTS SUMMARY

| | Place | Won | Lost | Tied | Drew | No Result |
|---|---|---|---|---|---|---|
| **County Championship** (1st Division) | 8th | 1 | 7 | | 8 | |
| **All First-Class Matches** | | 1 | 7 | 1 | 8 | |
| **C & G Trophy** | Finalist | | | | | |
| **Benson & Hedges Cup** | 6th in Midlands/West/Wales Division | | | | | |
| **NU National League** (1st Division) | 7th | 5 | 10 | | | 1 |

## COUNTY CHAMPIONSHIP AVERAGES

### BATTING AND FIELDING

| Cap | | M | I | NO | HS | Runs | Avge | 100 | 50 | Ct/St |
|---|---|---|---|---|---|---|---|---|---|---|
| 1999 | M.E.Trescothick | 2 | 4 | – | 134 | 153 | 38.25 | 1 | – | – |
| 2001 | I.D.Blackwell | 14 | 23 | – | 114 | 879 | 38.21 | 3 | 3 | 4 |
| 1999 | M.Burns | 16 | 30 | 2 | 99 | 1047 | 37.39 | – | 9 | 14 |
| | M.J.Wood | 14 | 26 | – | 196 | 908 | 34.92 | 3 | 4 | 5 |
| 1995 | P.D.Bowler | 14 | 25 | 2 | 94 | 766 | 33.30 | – | 7 | 22 |
| 1999 | J.Cox | 13 | 25 | 2 | 176 | 724 | 31.47 | 1 | 3 | 6 |
| 1997 | P.C.L.Holloway | 6 | 11 | – | 77 | 336 | 30.54 | – | 2 | 4 |
| 1994 | R.J.Turner | 16 | 27 | 4 | 83* | 691 | 30.04 | – | 4 | 50/1 |
| 1999 | K.A.Parsons | 14 | 24 | 2 | 68 | 561 | 25.50 | – | 4 | 15 |
| 2001 | R.L.Johnson | 9 | 17 | 4 | 61 | 290 | 22.30 | – | 1 | 2 |
| | P.D.Trego | 3 | 6 | – | 47 | 118 | 19.66 | – | – | 2 |
| 2001 | K.P.Dutch | 15 | 25 | 3 | 74 | 414 | 18.81 | – | 2 | 20 |
| 2002 | M.P.L.Bulbeck | 15 | 25 | 6 | 53* | 344 | 18.10 | – | 1 | 1 |
| 2001 | P.S.Jones | 7 | 8 | 3 | 37* | 76 | 15.20 | – | – | 2 |
| | S.R.G.Francis | 10 | 16 | 8 | 17 | 67 | 8.37 | – | – | – |
| 1992 | A.R.Caddick | 5 | 8 | – | 16 | 53 | 6.62 | – | – | 2 |

*Also batted*: G.D.Rose (2 matches – cap 1988) 20, 24 (1 ct); A.V.Suppiah (1) 0, 21.

### BOWLING

| | O | M | R | W | Avge | Best | 5wI | 10wM |
|---|---|---|---|---|---|---|---|---|
| R.L.Johnson | 307.1 | 66 | 914 | 43 | 21.25 | 7- 43 | 2 | 1 |
| A.R.Caddick | 247.2 | 53 | 773 | 34 | 22.73 | 6- 84 | 4 | – |
| S.R.G.Francis | 222.3 | 26 | 947 | 28 | 33.82 | 5- 73 | 1 | – |
| M.P.L.Bulbeck | 504 | 86 | 1859 | 53 | 35.07 | 6- 93 | 1 | – |
| I.D.Blackwell | 312.5 | 83 | 830 | 22 | 37.72 | 5- 49 | 1 | – |
| M.Burns | 101.4 | 14 | 444 | 11 | 40.36 | 3- 54 | – | – |
| K.A.Parsons | 197.3 | 29 | 747 | 17 | 43.94 | 3- 44 | – | – |
| P.S.Jones | 239.2 | 43 | 845 | 19 | 44.47 | 6-110 | 1 | 1 |
| K.P.Dutch | 231.2 | 52 | 694 | 11 | 63.09 | 2- 42 | – | – |

*Also bowled*:
| | | | | | | | | |
|---|---|---|---|---|---|---|---|---|
| P.D.Trego | 42 | 3 | 218 | 5 | 43.60 | 3- 65 | – | – |

P.D.Bowler 7-1-23-1; G.D.Rose 24-10-64-0.

The First-Class Averages (pp 121-135) give the records of Somerset players in all first-class county matches (Somerset's other opponents being West Indies A) with the exception of A.R.Caddick and M.E.Trescothick whose full county figures are as above.

# SOMERSET RECORDS

## FIRST-CLASS CRICKET

| | | | | | | |
|---|---|---|---|---|---|---|
| **Highest Total** | For 675-9d | | v | Hampshire | Bath | 1924 |
| | V 811 | | by | Surrey | The Oval | 1899 |
| **Lowest Total** | For 25 | | v | Glos | Bristol | 1947 |
| | V 22 | | by | Glos | Bristol | 1920 |
| **Highest Innings** | For 322 | I.V.A.Richards | v | Warwicks | Taunton | 1985 |
| | V 424 | A.C.MacLaren | for | Lancashire | Taunton | 1895 |

### Highest Partnership for each Wicket

| | | | | | | |
|---|---|---|---|---|---|---|
| 1st | 346 | H.T.Hewett/L.C.H.Palairet | v | Yorkshire | Taunton | 1892 |
| 2nd | 290 | J.C.W.MacBryan/M.D.Lyon | v | Derbyshire | Burton upon T | 1924 |
| 3rd | 319 | P.M.Roebuck/M.D.Crowe | v | Leics | Taunton | 1984 |
| 4th | 310 | P.W.Denning/I.T.Botham | v | Glos | Taunton | 1980 |
| 5th | 235 | J.C.White/C.C.C.Case | v | Glos | Taunton | 1927 |
| 6th | 265 | W.E.Alley/K.E.Palmer | v | Northants | Northampton | 1961 |
| 7th | 279 | R.J.Harden/G.D.Rose | v | Sussex | Taunton | 1997 |
| 8th | 172 | I.V.A.Richards/I.T.Botham | v | Leics | Leicester | 1983 |
| | 172 | A.R.K.Pierson/P.S.Jones | v | N Zealanders | Taunton | 1999 |
| 9th | 183 | C.H.M.Greetham/H.W.Stephenson | v | Leics | Weston-s-Mare | 1963 |
| | 183 | C.J.Tavaré/N.A.Mallender | v | Sussex | Hove | 1990 |
| 10th | 143 | J.J.Bridges/A.H.D.Gibbs | v | Essex | Weston-s-Mare | 1919 |

| | | | | | | |
|---|---|---|---|---|---|---|
| **Best Bowling** | For 10- 49 | E.J.Tyler | v | Surrey | Taunton | 1895 |
| **(Innings)** | V 10- 35 | A.Drake | for | Yorkshire | Weston-s-Mare | 1914 |
| **Best Bowling** | For 16- 83 | J.C.White | v | Worcs | Bath | 1919 |
| **(Match)** | V 17-137 | W.Brearley | for | Lancashire | Manchester | 1905 |

| | | | | |
|---|---|---|---|---|
| **Most Runs – Season** | 2761 | W.E.Alley | (av 58.74) | 1961 |
| **Most Runs – Career** | 21142 | H.Gimblett | (av 36.96) | 1935-54 |
| **Most 100s – Season** | 11 | S.J.Cook | | 1991 |
| **Most 100s – Career** | 49 | H.Gimblett | | 1935-54 |
| **Most Wkts – Season** | 169 | A.W.Wellard | (av 19.24) | 1938 |
| **Most Wkts – Career** | 2166 | J.C.White | (av 18.02) | 1909-37 |
| **Most Career W-K Dismissals** | 1007 | H.W.Stephenson | (698 ct/309 st) | 1948-64 |
| **Most Career Catches in the Field** | 381 | J.C.White | | 1909-37 |

## LIMITED-OVERS CRICKET

| | | | | | | |
|---|---|---|---|---|---|---|
| **Highest Total** | CGT | 413-4 | | v | Devon | Torquay | 1990 |
| | BHC | 349-7 | | v | Ireland | Taunton | 1997 |
| | NL | 360-3 | | v | Glamorgan | Neath | 1990 |
| **Lowest Total** | CGT | 58 | | v | Middlesex | Southgate | 2000 |
| | BHC | 98 | | v | Middlesex | Lord's | 1982 |
| | NL | 58 | | v | Essex | Chelmsford | 1977 |
| **Highest Innings** | CGT | 162* | C.J.Tavaré | v | Devon | Torquay | 1990 |
| | BHC | 177 | S.J.Cook | v | Sussex | Hove | 1990 |
| | NL | 175* | I.T.Botham | v | Northants | Wellingborough | 1986 |
| **Best Bowling** | CGT | 7-15 | R.P.Lefebvre | v | Devon | Torquay | 1990 |
| | BHC | 7-24 | Mushtaq Ahmed | v | Ireland | Taunton | 1997 |
| | NL | 6-24 | I.V.A.Richards | v | Lancashire | Manchester | 1983 |

# SURREY

**Formation of Present Club**: 22 August 1845
**Colours**: Chocolate
**Badge**: Prince of Wales' Feathers
**County Champions (since 1890)**: (18) 1890, 1891, 1892, 1894, 1895, 1899, 1914, 1952, 1953, 1954, 1955, 1956, 1957, 1958, 1971, 1999, 2000, 2002
**Joint Champions**: (1) 1950
**Gillette/NatWest/C & G Trophy Winners**: (1) 1982
**Benson and Hedges Cup Winners**: (3) 1974, 1997, 2001
**National League (Div 1) Winners**: (0); best – 8th 2001
**Sunday League Winners**: (1) 1996
**Match Awards**: CGT 55; BHC 76

**Chief Executive**: P.C.J.Sheldon, Kennington Oval, London, SE11 5SS • Tel: (020) 7582 6660 • Fax: (020) 7735 7769 • E-mail: enquiries@surreyccc.co.uk • Web: www.surreycricket.com

**Cricket Manager/First XI Coach**: K.T.Medlycott. **Captain**: A.J.Hollioake.
**Vice-Captain**: No appointment. **Overseas Players**: Azhar Mahmood and Saqlain Mushtaq. **2003 Beneficiary**: A.J.Stewart (testimonial). **Scorer**: K.R.Booth. ‡ New registration

**AZHAR MAHMOOD** (F.G. No. 1 HS, Islamabad), b Multan, Pakistan 28 Feb 1975. 5'11". RHB, RFM. Islamabad 1993-94. **Tests** (P): 21 (1997-98 to 2001); HS 136 v SA (Johannesburg) 1997-98; BB 4-50 v E (Lord's) 2001. Scored 128* and 50* v SA (Rawalpindi) 1997-98 on debut. **LOI** (P): 124 (1996-97 to 2002-03); HS 67 v I (Adelaide) 1999-00; BB 6-18 v WI (Sharjah) 1999-00. Tours (P): E 2001; A 1999-00; SA 1997-98; I 1998-99; SL 2000-01; Z 1997-98. HS 136 (*see Tests*). Sy HS 64* v Yorks (Leeds) 2002. 50 wkts (0+1): 59 (1996-97). BB 8-61 v Lancs (Oval) 2002. LO HS 100* P v Aus A (Perth) 1999-00. LO BB 6-18 (*see LOI*).

**BATTY, Jonathan** Neil (Wheatley Park S, Oxon; Repton S; Durham U; Keble C, Oxford), b Chesterfield, Derbys 18 Apr 1974. 5'10". RHB, WK. Minor C 1994. Comb U 1995. Oxford U 1996; blue 1996. Surrey debut 1997; cap 2001. Oxfordshire 1993-96. HS 151 v Somerset (Taunton) 2002. BB 1-21. LO HS 40 v Derbys (Oval) 1998 (SL).

‡**BENNING, James** Graham Edward (Beacon S; Chesham S; Caterham S), b Mill Hill, N London 4 May 1983. RHB, RM. Buckinghamshire 2000-01. Surrey staff 2003 – awaiting first-class debut. LO HS 23 Bucks v Worcs CB (Dinton) 2001 (CGT). LO BB v Northants (Croydon) 2002 (NL).

**BICKNELL, Martin** Paul (Robert Haining County SS), b Guildford 14 Jan 1969. Younger brother of D.J.Bicknell (*see NOTTINGHAMSHIRE*). 6'3". RHB, RFM. Debut 1986; cap 1989; benefit 1997. *Wisden* 2000. **Tests**: 2 (1993); HS 14 and BB 3-99 v A (Birmingham) 1993. **LOI**: 7 (1990-91); HS 31* v A (Perth) 1990-91; BB 3-55 v NZ (Christchurch) 1990-91. Tours: A 1990-91; SA 1993-94 (Eng A); Z 1989-90 (Eng A). HS 110* v Kent (Canterbury) 2001. 50 wkts (10); most – 72 (2001). BB 9-45 v CU (Oval) 1988. CC BB 9-47 (16-119 match) v Leics (Guildford) 2000. Awards: BHC 3. LO HS 66* v Northants (Oval) 1991 (NWT). LO BB 7-30 v Glam (Oval) 1999 (NL).

**BROWN, Alistair** Duncan (Caterham S), b Beckenham, Kent 11 Feb 1970. 5'10". RHB, occ LB. Debut 1992; cap 1994; benefit 2002. **LOI**: 16 (1996 to 2001); HS 118 v I (Manchester) 1996. 1000 runs (6); most – 1382 (1993). HS 295* v Leics (Oakham) 2000 – record score (all levels) in Rutland. BB 1-56. Awards: CGT 1; BHC 4. LO HS 268 v Glam (Oval) 2002 (CGT) – world record l-o score (160 balls, 12 sixes, 30 fours). LO BB 3-39 v Notts (Nottingham) 2000 (NL).

**BUTCHER, Mark** Alan (Trinity S; Archbishop Tenison's S, Croydon), b Croydon 23 Aug 1972. Son of A.R.Butcher (Surrey, Glamorgan and England 1972-92); brother of G.P.Butcher (Glamorgan 1994-98; Surrey 1999-2001). 5'11". LHB, RM/OB. Debut 1992; cap 1996. **ECB contracts 2002, 2003. Tests:** 50 (1997 to 2002-03, 1 as captain); HS 173* v A (Leeds) 2001; BB 4-42 v A (Birmingham) 2001. Tours: A 1996-97 (Eng A), 1998-99, 2002-03; SA 1999-00; WI 1997-98; NZ 2001-02; I 2001-02. 1000 runs (6); most – 1604 (1996). HS 259 v Leics (Leicester) 1999. BB 5-86 v Lancs (Manchester) 2000. Awards: CGT 2; BHC 3. LO HS 91 v Somerset (Oval) 1996 (NWT). LO BB 3-23 v Sussex (Oval) 1992 (SL).

**CLARKE, Rikki** (Broadwater SS; Godalming C), b Orsett, Essex 29 Sep 1981. 6'4". RHB, RFM. Debut 2002 – scoring 107* v CU (Cambridge). YC 2002. HS 153* v Somerset (Taunton) 2002. BB 3-41 v Yorks (Guildford) 2002. LO HS 98* v Derbys (Derby) 2002 (NL). LO BB 2-32 v Glos (Bristol) 2002 (NL).

**HOLLIOAKE, Adam** John (St Joseph's C, Sydney; St Patrick's C, Ballarat; St George's C, Weybridge; Surrey Tutorial C), b Melbourne, Australia 5 Sep 1971. Elder brother of the late B.C.Hollioake (Surrey and England 1996-2001). 5'11". RHB, RMF. Debut 1993, scoring 13 and 123 v Derbys (Ilkeston); cap 1995; captain 1997 to date. Qualified for England 1992. **Tests:** 4 (1997 to 1997-98); HS 45 and BB 2-31 v A (Nottingham) 1997 – on debut. **LOI:** 35 (1996 to 1999, 14 as captain); HS 83* v SA (Dhaka) 1998-99; BB 4-23 v P (Birmingham) 1996 – on debut. Tours: A 1996-97 (Eng A – captain); WI 1997-98. 1000 runs (2); most – 1522 (1996). HS 208 v Leics (Oval) 2002. BB 5-62 v Glam (Swansea) 1998. Awards: CGT 2; BHC 1. LO HS 117* v Sussex (Hove) 2002 (CGT). LO BB 5-29 v Durham (Chester-le-St) 2000 (NL).

**MURTAGH, Timothy** James (John Fisher S; St Mary's C), b Lambeth 2 Aug 1981. Nephew of A.J.Murtagh (Hampshire and E Province 1973-7). 6'0". LHB, RFM. British U 2000-02. Surrey debut 2001. HS 22* and BB 6-86 Brit U v P (Nottingham) 2001. Sy HS 22 and Sy BB 5-39 v Leics (Oval) 2002. LO HS 14* v Essex (Chelmsford) 2002 (NL). LO BB 4-31 v Warwks (Croydon) 2001 (NL).

**NEWMAN, Scott** Alexander (Trinity S, Croydon; Coulsdon C; Brighton U), b Epsom 3 Nov 1979. 6'2". LHB, RM. Debut 2002 – scoring 99 v Hants (Oval) 2002. HS 183 v Leics (Oval) 2002. LO HS 49 Surrey CB v Lincs (Bourne) 2001 (CGT).

**ORMOND, James** (St Thomas More S, Nuneaton), b Walsgrave, Coventry, Warwks 20 Aug 1977. 6'3". RHB, RFM. Leicestershire 1995-2001; cap 1999. Surrey debut 2002. **Tests:** 2 (2001 to 2001-02); HS 18 v A (Oval) 2001; BB 1-70. Tours: NZ 2001-02; I 2001-02; SL 1997-98 (Eng A); K 1997-98 (Eng A). HS 50* Le v Warwks (Leicester) 1999. Sy HS 43* v Kent (Canterbury) 2002. 50 wkts (2); most – 52 (1999). BB 6-33 (9-62 match) Le v Somerset (Leicester) 1998. Sy BB 5-62 (10-178 match) v Warwks (Oval) 2002. Awards: BHC 2. LO HS 18* Le v Somerset (Lord's) 2001 (CGT). LO BB 4-12 Le v Middx (Leicester) 1998 (SL).

**RAMPRAKASH, Mark** Ravin (Gayton HS; Harrow Weald SFC), b Bushey, Herts 5 Sep 1969. 5'9". RHB, RM. Middlesex 1987-2000; cap 1990; captain 1997-99. Surrey debut 2001 – scoring 146 v Kent (Oval); cap 2002. YC 1991. **ECB contract 2000. Tests:** 52 (1991 to 2001-02); HS 154 v WI (Bridgetown) 1997-98; BB 1-2. **LOI:** 18 (1991 to 2001-02); HS 51 v WI (Pt-of-Spain) 1997-98; BB 3-28 v Z (Harare) 2001-02. Tours: A 1994-95 (part), 1998-99; SA 1995-96; WI 1991-92 (Eng A), 1993-94, 1997-98; NZ 1991-92, 2001-02; I 1994-95 (Eng A), 2001-02; P 1990-91 (Eng A); SL 1990-91 (Eng A). 1000 runs (12) inc 2000 (1): 2258 (1995). HS 235 M v Yorks (Leeds) 1995. Sy HS 218 v Somerset (Taunton) 2002. BB 3-32 M v Glam (Lord's) 1998. Sy BB – . Awards: CGT 3; BHC 4. LO HS 147* M v Worcs (Lord's) 1990 (SL). LO BB 5-38 M v Leics (Lord's) 1993 (NL).

**SALISBURY, Ian** David Kenneth (Moulton CS), b Northampton 21 Jan 1970. 5'11". RHB, LBG. Sussex 1989-96; cap 1991. Surrey debut 1997; cap 1998. MCC YC. YC 1992. *Wisden* 1992. **Tests**: 15 (1992 to 2000-01); HS 50 v P (Manchester) 1992; BB 4-163 v WI (Georgetown) 1993-94. **LOI**: 4 (1992-93 to 1993-94); HS 5; BB 3-41 v WI (Pt-of-Spain) 1993-94. Tours: WI 1991-92 (Eng A), 1993-94; I 1992-93; 1994-95 (Eng A); P 1990-91 (Eng A), 1995-96 (Eng A), 2000-01; SL 1990-91 (Eng A). HS 100* v Somerset (Oval) 1999. 50 wkts (6); most – 87 (1992). BB 8-60 (12-91 match) v Somerset (Oval) 2000. Awards: CGT 1; BHC 2. LO HS 48* Sx v Glam (Swansea) 1995 (SL). LO BB 5-30 Sx v Leics (Leicester) 1992 (SL).

**SAMPSON, Philip** James (Pretoria BHS, SA), b Manchester 6 Sep 1980. 6'1". RHB, RFM. Debut 2002. Buckinghamshire 1999. HS 42 v CU (Cambridge) 2002 – on debut. CC HS 1*. BB 3-52 v Leics (Oval) 2002. LO HS 16 v Middx (Croydon) 2002 (NL). LO BB 3-42 v Kent (Oval) 2002 (BHC).

**SAQLAIN MUSHTAQ** (Govt Muslim League HS, M.A.O. College, Lahore), b Lahore, Pakistan 29 Dec 1976. Brother of Sibtain Mushtaq (Lahore 1988-89). 5'11". RHB, OB. Islamabad 1994-95. PIA 1994-95 to date. Surrey debut 1997; cap 1998. *Wisden* 1999. **Tests** (P): 47 (1995-96 to 2002-03); HS 101* v NZ (Christchurch) 2000-01; BB 8-164 v E (Lahore) 2000-01 (all eight wickets to fall). **LOI** (P): 168 (1995-96 to 2002-03); HS 37* v A (Brisbane) 1999-00; BB 5-20 v E (Rawalpindi) 2000-01, 2 hat-tricks. Tours (P): E 1996, 2001; A 1995-96, 1996-97, 1999-00; SA 1997-98, 2002-03; WI 1999-00; NZ 2000-01; I 1998-99, SL 1996-97; Z 1997-98, 2002-03; B 1998-99, 2001-02. HS 101* *(see Tests)*. Sy HS 66 v Leics (Oakham) 2000. 50 wkts (5+1); most – 66 (2000). BB 8-65 (11-107 match) v Derbys (Oval) 1988. Took 7-11 (including 7-5 in 34 balls) v Derbys (Oval) 2000. Three hat-tricks, all for Surrey 1997 and 1999 (2). Awards: CGT 2. LO HS 38* v Yorks (Leeds) 2001 (NL). LO BB 5-20 *(see LOI)*.

**SCOTT, Ben** James Matthew (Whitton S, Richmond; Richmond C), b Isleworth, Middx 4 Aug 1981. 5'8". RHB, WK. Staff 2001 – awaiting f-c debut. LO HS 11 Middx CB v Cumb (Southgate) 1999 (NWT).

**SHAHID, Nadeem** (Ipswich S), b Karachi, Pakistan 23 Apr 1969. 6'0". RHB, LB. Essex 1989-94. Surrey debut 1995; cap 1998. Suffolk 1988. 1000 runs (1): 1003 (1990). HS 150 v Sussex (Oval) 2002. BB 3-91 Ex v Surrey (Oval) 1990. Sy BB 3-93 v SA A (Oval) 1996. LO HS 109* v Notts (Nottingham) 2000 (NL). LO BB 3-30 v Bucks (Oval) 1998 (NWT).

**STEWART, Alec** James (Tiffin S), b Merton 8 Apr 1963. Son of M.J.Stewart (Surrey and England 1954-72). 5'11". RHB, WK. Debut 1981; cap 1985; captain 1992-97; benefit 1994; testimonial 2003. *Wisden* 1989. MBE 1998. **ECB contracts 2000, 2001, 2003. Tests**: 126 – Eng record (1989-90 to 2001, 15 as captain); HS 190 v P (Birmingham) 1992. **LOI**: 170 – Eng record (1989-90 to 2002-03, 41 as captain); HS 116 v I (Sharjah) 1997-98. Tours (C=captain): A 1990-91, 1994-95, 1998-99C, 2002-03; SA 1995-96, 1999-00; WI 1989-90, 1993-94, 1997-98; NZ 1991-92, 1996-97; I 1992-93; P 2000-01; SL 1992-93C, 2000-01; Z 1996-97. 1000 runs (8); most – 1665 (1986). HS 271* v Yorks (Oval) 1997. BB 1-7. Held 11 catches (equalling world f-c match record) v Leics (Leicester) 1989. Awards: CGT 5; BHC 6. LO HS 167* v Somerset (Oval) 1994 (SL).

**THORPE, Graham** Paul (Weydon CS; Farnham SFC), b Farnham 1 Aug 1969. 5'10". LHB, RM. Debut 1988; cap 1991; benefit 2000. *Wisden* 1997. **ECB contracts 2001, 2002. Tests**: 77 (1993 to 2002); HS 200* v NZ (Christchurch) 2001-02; scored 114* v A (Nottingham) 1993 on debut. **LOI**: 82 (1993 to 2002, 3 as captain); HS 89 v Z (Brisbane) 1994-95 and 89 v H (Peshawar) 1995-96; BB 2-15 v I (Manchester) 1996. Tours: A 1992-93 (Eng A), 1994-95, 1998-99 *(part)*; SA 1995-96; WI 1991-92 (Eng A), 1993-94, 1997-98; NZ 1996-97, 2001-02; I 2001-02 *(part)*; P 1990-91 (Eng A), 2000-01; SL 1990-91 (Eng A), 2000-01; Z 1989-90 (Eng A). 1000 runs (8); most – 1895 (1992). HS 223* Eng XI v S Aus (Adelaide) 1998-99. Sy HS 222 v Glam (Oval) 1997. BB 4-40 v A (Oval) 1993. CC BB 2-14 v Derbys (Oval) 1996. Awards: CGT 3; BHC 1. LO HS 145* v Lancs (Oval) 1994 (NWT). LO BB 3-21 v Somerset (Oval) 1991 (SL).

**TUDOR, Alex** Jeremy (St Mark's S, Hammersmith; City of Westminster C), b West Brompton, London 23 Oct 1977. 6'5". RHB, RF. Debut 1995; cap 1999. YC 1999. **Tests**: 10 (1998-99 to 2002-03); HS 99* v NZ (Birmingham) 1999 – record score by an England 'night-watchman'; BB 5-44 v A (Nottingham) 2001. **LOI**: 3 (2002); HS 6; BB 2-30 v I (Oval) 2002. Tours: A 1998-99; SA 1999-00; WI 2000-01 (Eng A). HS 116 v Essex (Oval) 2001. BB 7-48 v Lancs (Oval) 2000. LO HS 29* v Essex (Oval) 1995 (SL). LO BB 4-26 v Hants (Oval) 2000 (NL).

**WARD, Ian** James (Millfield S), b Plymouth, Devon 30 Sep 1972. 5'8½". LHB, RM. Surrey 1992, 1996 to date; cap 2000. **Tests**: 5 (200); HS 39 v P (Lord's) 2001 – on debut. Tours (Eng A): WI 2000-01; NZ 1999-00; B 1999-00. 1000 runs (2); most 1759 (2002) – including 114, 112, 156 and 118 in successive innings. HS 168* v Kent (Canterbury) 2002. BB 1-1 (twice). LO HS 97 v Glam (Oval) 2002 (CGT). LO BB 2-27 v Sussex (Hove) 2002 (BHC).

## IN MEMORIAM

**HOLLIOAKE, Benjamin** Caine (Millfield S), b Melbourne, Australia 11 Nov 1977; d Perth 23 Mar 2002. Younger brother of A.J.Hollioake. 6'2". RHB, RFM. Surrey 1996-2001; cap 1999. YC 1997. **Tests**: 2 (1997 to 1998); HS 28 v A (Nottingham) 1997 on debut; BB 2-105 v SL (Oval) 1998. **LOI**: 20 (1997 to 2001-02); HS 63 v A (Lord's) 1997 – on debut; BB 2-37 v Z (Harare) 2001-02. Tours: A 1998-99; SL (Eng A) 1997-98. HS 163 Eng A v SL A (Moratuwa) 1997-98. Sy HS 118 v Yorks (Oval) 2001. BB 5-51 v Glam (Oval) 1999. Awards: BHC 4. LO HS 98 v Kent (Lord's) 1997 (BHC). LO BB 5-10 v Derbys (Oval) 1996 (SL).

## RELEASED/RETIRED
(Having made a first-class County appearance in 2002)

**AMIN, R.M.** – *see LEICESTERSHIRE*.

**CARBERRY, M.A.** – *see KENT*.

**GIDDINS, E.S.H.** – *see HAMPSHIRE*.

**MUSHTAQ AHMED** – *see SUSSEX*.

**RATCLIFFE, Jason** David (Sharman's Cross SS; Solihull SFC), b Solihull, Warwks 19 Jun 1969. Son of D.P.Ratcliffe (Warwks 1957-68). 6'4". RHB, RM. Warwickshire 1988-94. Surrey 1995-2002; cap 1998. No appearances 2001. Tours (Wa): SA 1991-92, 1992-93; Z 1993-94. HS 135 v Worcs (Worcester) 1997. BB 6-48 v SL A (Oval) 1999. BB 3-28 v Kent (Tunbridge W) 1999. Awards: CGT 2. LO HS 105 Wa v Yorks (Leeds) 1993 (NWT). LO BB 4-44 v Essex (Guildford) 2002 (NL).

G.P.Butcher, D.J.Miller and D.M.Ward played in one l-o match without making a f-c appearance in 2002.

# ENGLAND TO TOUR BANGLADESH

England will play their first Tests against Bangladesh when they make a five-week visit there starting on 8 October. The inaugural Test begins in Dhaka on 8 October followed by a second match starting in Chittagong on 29 October. The tour ends with three limited-overs internationals on 7, 10 and 12 November.

# SURREY 2002

## RESULTS SUMMARY

|  | Place | Won | Lost | Tied | Drew | No Result |
|---|---|---|---|---|---|---|
| **County Championship** (1st Division) | **1st** | 10 | 2 |  | 4 |  |
| **All First-Class Matches** |  | 10 | 2 |  | 5 |  |
| **C & G Trophy** | Semi-Finalist |  |  |  |  |  |
| **Benson & Hedges Cup** | 6th in South Division |  |  |  |  |  |
| **NU National League** (2nd Division) | **2nd** | 10 | 5 |  |  | 1 |

## COUNTY CHAMPIONSHIP AVERAGES

### BATTING AND FIELDING

| Cap | | M | I | NO | HS | Runs | Avge | 100 | 50 | Ct/St |
|---|---|---|---|---|---|---|---|---|---|---|
| 1995 | A.J.Hollioake | 9 | 13 | 2 | 208 | 738 | 67.09 | 2 | 5 | 10 |
| 2000 | I.J.Ward | 16 | 29 | 3 | 168* | 1708 | 65.69 | 7 | 7 | 9 |
|  | S.A.Newman | 3 | 5 | – | 183 | 322 | 64.40 | 1 | – | 3 |
| 2002 | M.R.Ramprakash | 14 | 24 | 4 | 218 | 1073 | 53.65 | 3 | 6 | 18 |
| 1994 | A.D.Brown | 16 | 26 | 1 | 188 | 1211 | 50.45 | 5 | 3 | 18 |
| 1985 | A.J.Stewart | 4 | 6 | – | 99 | 301 | 50.16 | – | 3 | 18/2 |
|  | R.Clarke | 9 | 14 | 1 | 153* | 580 | 44.61 | 1 | 4 | 7 |
| 1996 | M.A.Butcher | 6 | 11 | 1 | 116 | 385 | 38.50 | 1 | 2 | 3 |
| 2001 | J.N.Batty | 12 | 22 | 2 | 151 | 740 | 37.00 | 2 | 3 | 41/5 |
| 1998 | N.Shahid | 12 | 19 | 1 | 150 | 647 | 35.94 | 2 | 3 | 23 |
| 1991 | G.P.Thorpe | 4 | 8 | – | 143 | 274 | 34.25 | 1 | – | 1 |
|  | Azhar Mahmood | 3 | 4 | 1 | 64* | 96 | 32.00 | – | 1 | 3 |
| 1989 | M.P.Bicknell | 10 | 14 | 5 | 35* | 258 | 28.66 | – | – | 6 |
| 1998 | Saqlain Mushtaq | 10 | 13 | 2 | 60 | 278 | 25.27 | – | 2 | 4 |
|  | T.J.Murtagh | 3 | 5 | 3 | 22 | 41 | 20.50 | – | – | 2 |
| 1999 | A.J.Tudor | 6 | 9 | – | 61 | 176 | 19.55 | – | 1 | 1 |
| 1998 | I.D.K.Salisbury | 14 | 20 | 2 | 59 | 340 | 18.88 | – | 1 | 11 |
|  | J.Ormond | 15 | 17 | 4 | 43* | 208 | 16.00 | – | – | 6 |
|  | E.S.H.Giddins | 6 | 7 | 4 | 9 | 23 | 7.66 | – | – | 1 |

*Also batted:* M.A.Carberry (1) 10, 24; Mushtaq Ahmed (2) 7, 47, 12 (1 ct); P.J.Sampson (1) 0, 1*.

### BOWLING

|  | O | M | R | W | Avge | Best | 5wI | 10wM |
|---|---|---|---|---|---|---|---|---|
| Azhar Mahmood | 109.2 | 27 | 345 | 20 | 17.25 | 8- 61 | 1 | – |
| T.J.Murtagh | 74.1 | 11 | 276 | 13 | 21.23 | 5- 39 | 1 | – |
| A.J.Tudor | 202.1 | 44 | 739 | 31 | 23.83 | 5- 66 | 1 | – |
| Saqlain Mushtaq | 488.4 | 112 | 1359 | 53 | 25.64 | 6-121 | 3 | 1 |
| M.P.Bicknell | 326 | 78 | 1067 | 34 | 31.38 | 6- 42 | 2 | – |
| I.D.K.Salisbury | 341.3 | 50 | 1192 | 37 | 32.21 | 4- 59 | – | – |
| J.Ormond | 485.1 | 87 | 1780 | 51 | 34.90 | 5- 62 | 2 | 1 |
| E.S.H.Giddins | 208.5 | 41 | 696 | 19 | 36.63 | 4-113 | – | – |
| R.Clarke | 76.3 | 7 | 398 | 10 | 39.80 | 3- 41 | – | – |

*Also bowled:*

| P.J.Sampson | 21 | 4 | 101 | 5 | 20.20 | 3- 52 | – | – |
|---|---|---|---|---|---|---|---|---|
| A.J.Hollioake | 37 | 1 | 178 | 5 | 35.60 | 2- 39 | – | – |
| Mushtaq Ahmed | 105 | 23 | 305 | 8 | 38.12 | 5- 71 | 1 | – |

A.D.Brown 3-0-7-0; M.A.Butcher 8-2-43-0; M.R.Ramprakash 2-0-2-0; N.Shahid 22-1-72-1; I.J.Ward 3-1-5-2.

The First-Class Averages (pp 121-135) give the records of Surrey players in all first-class county matches (Surrey's other opponents being Cambridge UCCE), with the exception of M.A.Butcher, A.J.Stewart, G.P.Thorpe and A.J.Tudor, whose full county figures are as above, and:

T.J.Murtagh 4-6-3-22-47-15.66-0-0-3ct. 95.1-16-322-17-18.94-5/39-1-0.

# SURREY RECORDS

## FIRST-CLASS CRICKET

| Highest Total | For 811 | | v | Somerset | The Oval | 1899 |
|---|---|---|---|---|---|---|
| | V 863 | | by | Lancashire | The Oval | 1990 |
| Lowest Total | For 14 | | v | Essex | Chelmsford | 1983 |
| | V 16 | | by | MCC | Lord's | 1872 |
| Highest Innings | For 357* | R.Abel | v | Somerset | The Oval | 1899 |
| | V 366 | N.H.Fairbrother | for | Lancashire | The Oval | 1990 |

### Highest Partnership for each Wicket

| | | | | | | |
|---|---|---|---|---|---|---|
| 1st | 428 | J.B.Hobbs/A.Sandham | v | Oxford U | The Oval | 1926 |
| 2nd | 371 | J.B.Hobbs/E.G.Hayes | v | Hampshire | The Oval | 1909 |
| 3rd | 413 | D.J.Bicknell/D.M.Ward | v | Kent | Canterbury | 1990 |
| 4th | 448 | R.Abel/T.W.Hayward | v | Yorkshire | The Oval | 1899 |
| 5th | 308 | J.N.Crawford/F.C.Holland | v | Somerset | The Oval | 1908 |
| 6th | 298 | A.Sandham/H.S.Harrison | v | Sussex | The Oval | 1913 |
| 7th | 262 | C.J.Richards/K.T.Medlycott | v | Kent | The Oval | 1987 |
| 8th | 205 | I.A.Greig/M.P.Bicknell | v | Lancashire | The Oval | 1990 |
| 9th | 168 | E.R.T.Holmes/E.W.J.Brooks | v | Hampshire | The Oval | 1936 |
| 10th | 173 | A.Ducat/A.Sandham | v | Essex | Leyton | 1921 |

| Best Bowling | For | 10-43 | T.Rushby | v | Somerset | Taunton | 1921 |
|---|---|---|---|---|---|---|---|
| (Innings) | V | 10-28 | W.P.Howell | for | Australians | The Oval | 1899 |
| Best Bowling | For | 16-83 | G.A.R.Lock | v | Kent | Blackheath | 1956 |
| (Match) | V | 15-57 | W.P.Howell | for | Australians | The Oval | 1899 |

| Most Runs – Season | 3246 | T.W.Hayward | (av 72.13) | 1906 |
|---|---|---|---|---|
| Most Runs – Career | 43554 | J.B.Hobbs | (av 49.72) | 1905-34 |
| Most 100s – Season | 13 | T.W.Hayward | | 1906 |
| | 13 | J.B.Hobbs | | 1925 |
| Most 100s – Career | 144 | J.B.Hobbs | | 1905-34 |
| Most Wkts – Season | 252 | T.Richardson | (av 13.94) | 1895 |
| Most Wkts – Career | 1775 | T.Richardson | (av 17.87) | 1892-1904 |
| Most Career W-K Dismissals | 1221 | H.Strudwick | (1035 ct/186 st) | 1902-27 |
| Most Career Catches in the Field | 605 | M.J.Stewart | | 1954-72 |

## LIMITED-OVERS CRICKET

| Highest Total | CGT | 438-5 | | v | Glamorgan | The Oval | 2002 |
|---|---|---|---|---|---|---|---|
| | BHC | 361-8 | | v | Notts | The Oval | 2001 |
| | NL | 375-4 | | v | Yorkshire | Scarborough | 1994 |
| Lowest Total | CGT | 74 | | v | Kent | The Oval | 1967 |
| | BHC | 89 | | v | Notts | Nottingham | 1984 |
| | NL | 64 | | v | Worcs | Worcester | 1978 |
| Highest Innings | CGT | 268 | A.D.Brown | v | Glamorgan | The Oval | 2002 |
| | BHC | 167* | A.J.Stewart | v | Somerset | The Oval | 1994 |
| | NL | 203 | A.D.Brown | v | Hampshire | Guildford | 1997 |
| Best Bowling | CGT | 7-33 | R.D.Jackman | v | Yorkshire | Harrogate | 1970 |
| | BHC | 5-15 | S.G.Kenlock | v | Ireland | The Oval | 1995 |
| | NL | 7-30 | M.P.Bicknell | v | Glamorgan | The Oval | 1999 |

# SUSSEX

**Formation of Present Club**: 1 March 1839
**Substantial Reorganisation**: August 1857
**Colours**: Dark Blue, Light Blue and Gold
**Badge**: County Arms of Six Martlets
**County Champions**: (0); best – 2nd 1902, 1903, 1932, 1933, 1934, 1953, 1981
**Gillette/NatWest/C & G Trophy Winners**: (4) 1963, 1964, 1978, 1986
**Benson and Hedges Cup Winners**: (0); best – semi-finalists 1982, 1999
**National League (Div 1) Winners**: (0); best – 9th 2000
**Sunday League Winners**: (1) 1982
**Match Awards**: CGT 59; BHC 64

**Chief Executive**: H.H.Griffiths, County Ground, Eaton Road, Hove BN3 3AN • Tel: 01273 827100 • Fax: 01273 771549 • Email: fran@sccc.demon.co.uk • Web: www.sussexcricket.co.uk

**First XI Coach**: P.J.Graves. **Captain**: C.J.Adams. **Vice-Captain**: R.J.Kirtley. **Overseas Players**: M.W.Goodwin and Mushtaq Ahmed. **2003 Beneficiary**: C.J.Adams. **Scorer**: J.F.Hartridge. ‡ New registration

**ADAMS, Christopher** John (Repton S), b Whitwell, Derbyshire 6 May 1970. 6'0". RHB, RM/OB. Derbyshire 1988-97; cap 1992. Sussex debut/cap 1998; captain 1998 to date; benefit 2003. Tests: 5 (1999-00); HS 31 v SA (Cape Town) 1999-00; BB 1-42. LOI: 5 (1998 to 1999-00); HS 42 v SA (Cape Town) 1999-00. Tour: SA 1999-00. 1000 runs (5); most – 1742 (1996). HS 239 De v Hants (Southampton) 1996. Sx HS 217 v Lancs (Manchester) 2002. BB 4-28 v Durham (Chester-le-St) 2001. Awards: CGT 3; BHC 6. LO HS 163 v Middx (Arundel) 1999 (NL). LO BB 5-16 v Middx (Hove) 1998 (SL).

**AMBROSE, Timothy** Raymond (Merewether HS, NSW; TAFE C), b Newcastle, NSW, Australia 1 Dec 1982. ECB qualified. 5'7". RHB, WK. Debut 2001. HS 149 v Yorks (Leeds) 2002. Award: CGT 1. LO HS 95 v Bucks (Beaconsfield) 2002 (CGT).

**COTTEY, Phillip Anthony** (Bishopston CS, Swansea), b Swansea, Glamorgan 2 Jun 1966. 5'4". RHB, OB. Glamorgan 1986-98; cap 1992. Sussex debut/cap 1999. E Transvaal 1991-92. Tours (Gm): SA 1995-96; Z 1990-91, 1994-95. 1000 runs (7); most – 1543 (1996). HS 203 and BB 4-49 Gm v Leics (Swansea) 1996. Sx HS 154 v Essex (Chelmsford) 2000. Sx BB – . LO HS 96 Gm v Sussex (Hove) 1998 (BHC). LO BB 4-56 Gm v Essex (Chelmsford) 1996 (SL).

**DAVIS, Mark** Jeffrey Gronow (Grey HS; Pretoria U), b Port Elizabeth, SA 10 Oct 1971. ECB qualified – British/EU passport. 6'2". RHB, OB. N Transvaal/Northerns 1990-91 to date. MCC 1999 and 2000. Sussex debut 2001; cap 2002. HS 111 v Somerset (Taunton) 2002. BB 8-37 (12-84 match) NT B v W Transvaal (Potchefstroom) 1994-95. Sx BB 6-97 v Surrey (Hove) 2002. Award: BHC 1. LO HS 35 NT v EP (Verwoerdburg) 1994-95 (BHS). LO BB 4-24 v Middx (Richmond) 2001 (NL).

**GOODWIN, Murray** William (Newton Moore HS, Bunbury, WA), b Salisbury, Rhodesia 11 Dec 1972. Younger brother of D.G.Goodwin (Zimbabwe 1986-97 to 1989-90). 5'9". Emigrated to Australia in Nov 1986. Gained Zimbabwean citizenship in Sep 1997. RHB, LB. Western Australia 1994-95 to 1996-97, 2000-01 to date. Mashonaland 1997-98 to 1998-99. Sussex debut/cap 2001. Holland 1997. Tests (Z): 19 (1997-98 to 2000); HS 166* v P (Bulawayo) 1997-98. LOI (Z): 71 (1997-98 to 2000); HS 112* v WI (Chester-le-St) 2000; BB 1-12. Tours: SA 1999-00; WI 1999-00; NZ 1997-98; P 1998-99; SL 1997-98. 1000 (2); most – 1654 (2001). HS 203* v Notts (Nottingham) 2001. BB 2-23 Z v Lahore City (Lahore) 1998-99. Sx BB – . Awards: BHC 2. LO HS 167 WA v NSW (Perth) 2000-01 (MC) – Australian l-o record. LO BB 1-9 Mashonaland v Eng A (Harare) 1998-99.

89

**GREEN, Jeremy** Arthur G., b Haywards Heath 17 Sep 1984. RHB, RMF. LO HS 7 v WI A (Hove) 2002.

**HOPKINSON, Carl** Daniel (Brighton C), b Brighton 14 Sep 1981. 5'11". RHB, RM. Debut 2002. HS 33 and BB 1-35 v Warwks (Hove) 2002 – on debut. LO HS 43 Sussex CB v Glos (Horsham) 2001 (CGT). LO BB 1-2 (NL).

**HUTCHISON, Paul** Michael (Crawshaw HS, Pudsey), b Leeds, Yorks 9 Jun 1977. 6'3". LHB, LFM. Yorkshire 1995-96 (Y in Zim) to 2001; cap 1998. Sussex debut 2002. Tours (Eng A): SL 1997-98; Z 1995-96 (Y); K 1997-98. HS 30 Y v Essex (Scarborough) 1998. Sx HS 20* v Warwks (Hove) 2002. 50 wkts (1): 59 (1998). BB 7-31 Y v Sussex (Hove) 1998. Sx BB 3-146 v Surrey (Oval) 2002. Award: CGT 1. LO HS 12 v Essex (Chelmsford) 2002 (NL). LO BB 4-34 Y v Glos (Gloucester) 1998 (SL).

**INNES, Kevin** John (Weston Favell Upper S), b Wellingborough 24 Sep 1975. 5'10". RHB, RM. 2nd XI debut 1990 (aged 14yr 8m – Northamptonshire record). Northamptonshire 1994-2001. Sussex debut 2002. HS 63 Nh v Lancs (Northampton) 1996. Sx HS 60* v Warwks (Hove) 2002. BB 4-41 v Surrey (Hove) 2002. LO HS 55 Nh v Worcs (Worcester) 2000 (NL). LO BB 4-26 v Hants (Hove) 2002 (NL).

**KIRTLEY, Robert James** (Clifton C), b Eastbourne 10 Jan 1975. 6'0". RHB, RFM. Debut 1995; cap 1998. Mashonaland 1996-97. **LOI**: 9 (2001-02 to 2002-03); HS 1 (twice); BB 2-33 v Z (Harare) 2001-02 – on debut. Tours (Eng A): NZ 1999-00; B 1999-00. HS 59 v Durham (Eastbourne) 1998. 50 wkts (5); most – 75 (2001). BB 7-21 v Hants (Southampton) 1999. Took 5-53 (7-88 match) for Mashonaland v Eng XI (Harare) 1996-97. Award: CGT 1. LO HS 19* v Lancs (Hove) 2002 (NL). LO BB 5-33 v Essex (Chelmsford) 2002 (BHC).

**LEWRY, Jason** David (Durrington HS, Worthing), b Worthing 2 Apr 1971. 6'2". LHB, LFM. Debut 1994; cap 1996; benefit 2002 Tour: Z 1998-99 (Eng A). HS 47 v Glos (Hove) 2001. 50 wkts (4); most – 62 (1998). BB 7-38 (10-113 match) v Derbys (Derby) 1999. 2 hat-tricks (1998, 2001). LO HS 16 v Lancs (Manchester) 2001 (CGT). LO BB 4-29 v Somerset (Bath) 1995 (SL).

**MARTIN-JENKINS, Robin** Simon Christopher (Radley C; Durham U), b Guildford, Surrey 28 Oct 1975. Son of C.D.A.Martin-Jenkins (*Times* Chief Cricket Correspondent/ BBC Commentator). 6'5". RHB, RFM. Debut 1995; cap 2000. British U 1996. 1000 (1): 1008 (2002). HS 205* v Somerset (Taunton) 2002. BB 7-51 v Leics (Horsham) 2002. Award: BHC 1. LO HS 50 v Surrey (Oval) 2002 (NL). LO BB 4-22 v Kent (Canterbury) 2002 (BHC).

**MONTGOMERIE, Richard** Robert (Rugby S; Worcester C, Oxford), b Rugby, Warwks 3 Jul 1971. 5'10½". RHB, OB. Oxford U 1991-94; blue 1991-92-93-94; captain 1994; half blues for rackets and real tennis. Northamptonshire 1991-98; cap 1995. Sussex debut/cap 1999. Tour: Z 1994-95 (Nh). 1000 runs (2): most – 1704 (2001). HS 196 v Hants (Hove) 2002. BB 1-0. Award: CGT 1. LO HS 129* v Z (Hastings) 2000.

**‡MUSHTAQ AHMED** (Mahmoodia HS, Sahiwal), b Sahiwal, Pakistan 28 Jun 1970. 5'5". RHB, LBG. Multan 1986-87 to 1990-91. United Bank 1986-87 to date. Somerset 1993-95, 1997-98; cap 1993. Surrey 2002 (2 matches). *Wisden* 1996. **Tests** (P): 50 (1989-90 to 2000-01); HS 59 v SA (Rawalpindi) 1997-98; BB 7-56 (10-171 match) v NZ (Christchurch) 1995-96. **LOI** (P): 143 (1988-89 to 2000-01); HS 34* v SA (Colombo) 2000-01; BB 5-36 v I (Toronto) 1996-97. Tours (P): E 1992, 1996; A 1989-90, 1991-92, 1992-93, 1995-96, 1996-97, 1999-00; SA 1997-98; WI 1992-93, 1999-00; NZ 1992-93, 1993-94, 1995-96, 2000-01; I 1998-99; SL 1994-95, 1996-97, 2000-01; Z 1997-98. HS 90 and UK BB 7-91 (12-175 match) Somerset v Sussex (Taunton) 1993. 50 wkts (4+2): most – 95 (1995). BB 9-93 Multan v Peshawar (Sahiwal) 1990-91. Awards: NWT 2; BHC 2. LO HS 41 Sm v Durham (Taunton) 1998 (SL). LO BB 7-24 Sm v Ire (Taunton) 1997 (BHC).

**NASH, Christopher** David (Collyers SFC), b Cuckfield 19 May 1983. RHB, OB. Debut 2002. HS 0* and BB 1-81 v Warwks (Birmingham) 2002 – on debut.

**PRIOR, Matthew** James (Brighton C), b Johannesburg, SA, 24 Feb 82. 6'2". RHB, WK. Debut 2001. HS 102* v Hants (Hove) 2002. LO HS 73 v Essex (Horsham) 2002 (NL).

‡**RASHID, Shaun**, b Burnley, Lancs 1 Mar 1977. RHB, RFM. Sussex staff 2003 – awaiting first-class debut. Bedfordshire 2001-02. LO HS 9 Beds v Devon (Exmouth) 2001 (CGT). LO BB 4-30 Beds v Holland (Luton) 2002 (CGT).

**TAYLOR, Billy** Victor (Bitterne Park S, Southampton), b Southampton, Hants 11 Jan 1977. Brother of J.L.Taylor (Wiltshire 1998 to date). 6'3". LHB, RMF. Debut 1999. Wiltshire 1996-98. HS 24* v Glos (Cheltenham) 2001. BB 5-90 v Warwks (Hove) 2002. Awards: CGT 1; BHC 1. LO HS 21* v Notts (Cleethorpes) 1999 (NL). LO BB 5-28 v Middx (Lord's) 2002 (BHC).

**TURK, Neil** Richard Keith (Sackville S, E Grinstead; Exeter U), b Cuckfield 28 Apr 1983. RHB, RM. Awaiting f-c debut. LO HS 36 v Essex (Chelmsford) 2002 (NL).

**YARDY, Michael** Howard (William Parker S, Hastings), b Pembury, Kent 27 Nov 1980. 6'0". LHB, LM. Debut 2000. HS 93 v Surrey (Oval) 2002. BB 1-13. LO HS 59 v Middx (Hove) 2001 (BHC). LO BB 3-30 v Warwks (Hove) 2002 (BHC).

**ZUIDERENT** Bastiaan (*'Bas'*) (Erasmiaans Gymnasium, Rotterdam; Amsterdam U), b Utrecht, Holland 2 Mar 1977. 6'3". RHB, OB. Debut 2001. Holland 1994 to date. **LOI** (H): 13 (1995-96 to 2002-03); HS 54 v E (Peshawar) 1995-96. HS 122 v Notts (Hove) 2001. Award: BHC 1. LO HS 102* v Hants (Southampton) 2001 (BHC).

## IN MEMORIAM

**RASHID, Umer** Bin Abdul (Ealing Green HS; Ealing Tertiary C; Southbank U), b Southampton, Hants 6 Feb 1976; d Concord Falls, Grenada 1 Apr 2002. 6'3". LHB, SLA. Middlesex 1996-98. Sussex 1999-2001; cap 2002 (posthumously). HS 110 v Glam (Colwyn Bay) 2000. BB 5-103 v Northants (Northampton) 2000. LO HS 82 Brit U v Hants (Oxford) 1997. LO BB 5-24 v Glam (Swansea) 1999 (NL).

## RELEASED/RETIRED
(Having made a first-class County appearance in 2002)

**CLAPP, Dominic** Adrian (Lancing C; Worthing SFC), b Southport, Lancs 25 May 1980. 6'0". RHB, RM. Sussex 2002 (one match). 2nd XI debut 1997 when aged 16y 347d. HS 6 v Leics (Horsham) 2002. LO HS 43 v WI A (Hove) 2002. LO BB 3-46 Sussex CB v Herefords (Colwall) 2000 (NWT).

**ROBINSON, Mark** Andrew (Hull GS), b Hull, Yorkshire 23 Nov 1966. 6'3". RHB, RFM. Northamptonshire 1987-90; cap 1990. Canterbury 1988-89. Yorkshire 1991-95; cap 1992. Sussex 1997-2002; cap 1997. Tours (Y): SA 1991-92, 1992-93. Failed to score in 12 successive f-c innings 1990 – world record. HS 27 v Lancs (Manchester) 1997. 50 wkts (2): most – 56 (2001). BB 9-37 (12-124 match) Y v Northants (Harrogate) 1993. Sx BB 6-78 v Northants (Hove) 1999 on Sussex debut. Awards: BHC 2. LO HS 15* v Lancs (Manchester) 2000 (NL). LO BB 4-23 Y v Northants (Leeds) 1993 (SL) and 4-23 v Leics (Leicester) 2000 (NL). Transferred to coaching staff after 2001 season – reappeared in one CC and five 1-o matches in 2002.

J.R.Carpenter, P.M.R.Havell and W.J.House left the staff made no f-c appearances in 2002.

# SUSSEX 2002

## RESULTS SUMMARY

| | Place | Won | Lost | Tied | Drew | No Result |
|---|---|---|---|---|---|---|
| **County Championship** (1st Division) | 6th | 3 | 6 | | 7 | |
| **All First-Class Matches** | | 3 | 6 | | 7 | |
| **C & G Trophy** | Quarter-Finalist | | | | | |
| **Benson & Hedges Cup** | Quarter-Finalist | | | | | |
| **NU National League** (2nd Division) | 8th | 4 | 10 | | | 2 |

## COUNTY CHAMPIONSHIP AVERAGES

### BATTING AND FIELDING

| Cap | | M | I | NO | HS | Runs | Avge | 100 | 50 | Ct/St |
|---|---|---|---|---|---|---|---|---|---|---|
| 1998 | C.J.Adams | 10 | 19 | – | 217 | 848 | 44.63 | 3 | 3 | 2 |
| 2001 | M.W.Goodwin | 16 | 28 | – | 162 | 1179 | 42.10 | 5 | 3 | 13 |
| 2000 | R.S.C.Martin-Jenkins | 16 | 28 | 4 | 205* | 1008 | 42.00 | 1 | 5 | 1 |
| 1999 | R.R.Montgomerie | 16 | 28 | 1 | 196 | 1026 | 38.00 | 2 | 4 | 16 |
| | T.R.Ambrose | 13 | 22 | 1 | 149 | 798 | 38.00 | 2 | 2 | 9 |
| | K.J.Innes | 13 | 22 | 7 | 60* | 478 | 31.86 | – | 2 | 3 |
| 1999 | P.A.Cottey | 13 | 22 | – | 137 | 699 | 31.77 | 3 | 1 | 5 |
| | M.J.Prior | 16 | 27 | 3 | 102* | 741 | 30.87 | 1 | 5 | 39/2 |
| | M.H.Yardy | 10 | 17 | – | 93 | 492 | 28.94 | – | 2 | 11 |
| 2002 | M.J.G.Davis | 15 | 22 | 4 | 111 | 474 | 26.33 | 1 | 2 | 7 |
| 1998 | R.J.Kirtley | 10 | 15 | 3 | 36* | 146 | 12.16 | – | – | 4 |
| | P.M.Hutchison | 3 | 5 | 2 | 20* | 29 | 9.66 | – | – | – |
| 1996 | J.D.Lewry | 10 | 15 | 5 | 21* | 91 | 9.10 | – | – | 5 |
| | B.V.Taylor | 10 | 14 | 2 | 18* | 70 | 5.83 | – | – | 1 |

*Also batted (1 match each):* D.A.Clapp 6; C.D.Hopkinson 33, 9 (2 ct); C.D.Nash 0, 0* (1 ct); M.A.Robinson (cap 1997) 6, 4*; B.Zuiderent 0, 10.

### BOWLING

| | O | M | R | W | Avge | Best | 5wI | 10wM |
|---|---|---|---|---|---|---|---|---|
| R.J.Kirtley | 366 | 90 | 1152 | 50 | 23.04 | 6-107 | 4 | 1 |
| K.J.Innes | 268.3 | 65 | 834 | 29 | 28.75 | 4- 41 | – | – |
| B.V.Taylor | 318.5 | 73 | 1041 | 32 | 32.53 | 5- 90 | 1 | – |
| R.S.C.Martin-Jenkins | 470.2 | 100 | 1477 | 41 | 36.02 | 7- 51 | 2 | – |
| J.D.Lewry | 304.4 | 45 | 1227 | 33 | 37.18 | 5- 88 | 1 | – |
| M.J.G.Davis | 347.2 | 71 | 1081 | 28 | 38.60 | 6- 97 | 1 | – |

*Also bowled:*

| | | | | | | | | |
|---|---|---|---|---|---|---|---|---|
| M.A.Robinson | 40 | 8 | 138 | 5 | 27.60 | 3- 57 | – | – |
| P.M.Hutchison | 79 | 6 | 389 | 6 | 64.83 | 3-146 | – | – |

C.J.Adams 7-1-24-0; T.R.Ambrose 1-0-1-0; P.A.Cottey 16.2-5-33-0; M.W.Goodwin 2-1-1-0; C.D.Hopkinson 7-0-35-1; R.R.Montgomerie 6-2-10-0; C.D.Nash 35-1-171-2; M.H.Yardy 58-9-231-2.

Sussex played no first-class fixtures outside the County Championship in 2002. The First-Class Averages (pp 121-135) give the records of Sussex players in all first-class county matches, with the exception of R.J.Kirtley whose full county figures are as above.

# SUSSEX RECORDS

## FIRST-CLASS CRICKET

| Highest Total | For 705-8d | | v | Surrey | Hastings | 1902 |
|---|---|---|---|---|---|---|
| | V 726 | | by | Notts | Nottingham | 1895 |
| Lowest Total | For 19 | | v | Surrey | Godalming | 1830 |
| | 19 | | v | Notts | Hove | 1873 |
| | V 18 | | by | Kent | Gravesend | 1867 |
| Highest Innings | For 333 | K.S.Duleepsinhji | v | Northants | Hove | 1930 |
| | V 322 | E.Paynter | for | Lancashire | Hove | 1937 |

### Highest Partnership for each Wicket

| 1st | 490 | E.H.Bowley/J.G.Langridge | v | Middlesex | Hove | 1933 |
|---|---|---|---|---|---|---|
| 2nd | 385 | E.H.Bowley/M.W.Tate | v | Northants | Hove | 1921 |
| 3rd | 298 | K.S.Ranjitsinhji/E.H.Killick | v | Lancashire | Hove | 1901 |
| 4th | 326* | J.Langridge/G.Cox | v | Yorkshire | Leeds | 1949 |
| 5th | 297 | J.H.Parks/H.W.Parks | v | Hampshire | Portsmouth | 1937 |
| 6th | 255 | K.S.Duleepsinhji/M.W.Tate | v | Northants | Hove | 1930 |
| 7th | 344 | K.S.Ranjitsinhji/W.Newham | v | Essex | Leyton | 1902 |
| 8th | 291 | R.S.C.Martin-Jenkins/M.J.G.Davis | v | Somerset | Taunton | 2002 |
| 9th | 178 | H.W.Parks/A.F.Wensley | v | Derbyshire | Horsham | 1930 |
| 10th | 156 | G.R.Cox/H.R.Butt | v | Cambridge U | Cambridge | 1908 |

| Best Bowling | For 10- 48 | C.H.G.Bland | v | Kent | Tonbridge | 1899 |
|---|---|---|---|---|---|---|
| (Innings) | V 9- 11 | A.P.Freeman | for | Kent | Hove | 1922 |
| Best Bowling | For 17-106 | G.R.Cox | v | Warwicks | Horsham | 1926 |
| (Match) | V 17- 67 | A.P.Freeman | for | Kent | Hove | 1922 |

| Most Runs – Season | 2850 | J.G.Langridge | (av 64.77) | 1949 |
|---|---|---|---|---|
| Most Runs – Career | 34152 | J.G.Langridge | (av 37.69) | 1928-55 |
| Most 100s – Season | 12 | J.G.Langridge | | 1949 |
| Most 100s – Career | 76 | J.G.Langridge | | 1928-55 |
| Most Wkts – Season | 198 | M.W.Tate | (av 13.47) | 1925 |
| Most Wkts – Career | 2211 | M.W.Tate | (av 17.41) | 1912-37 |
| Most Career W-K Dismissals | 1176 | H.R.Butt | (911 ct/265 st) | 1890-1912 |
| Most Career Catches in the Field | 779 | J.G.Langridge | | 1928-55 |

## LIMITED-OVERS CRICKET

| Highest Total | CGT | 384-9 | | v | Ireland | Belfast | 1996 |
|---|---|---|---|---|---|---|---|
| | BHC | 316-3 | | v | Essex | Chelmsford | 2000 |
| | NL | 312-8 | | v | Hampshire | Portsmouth | 1993 |
| Lowest Total | CGT | 49 | | v | Derbyshire | Chesterfield | 1969 |
| | BHC | 61 | | v | Middlesex | Hove | 1978 |
| | NL | 59 | | v | Glamorgan | Hove | 1996 |
| Highest Innings | CGT | 158 | R.K.Rao | v | Derbyshire | Derby | 1997 |
| | BHC | 157* | M.G.Bevan | v | Essex | Chelmsford | 2000 |
| | NL | 163 | C.J.Adams | v | Middlesex | Arundel | 1999 |
| Best Bowling | CGT | 6- 9 | A.I.C.Dodemaide | v | Ireland | Downpatrick | 1990 |
| | BHC | 5- 8 | Imran Khan | v | Northants | Northampton | 1978 |
| | NL | 7-41 | A.N.Jones | v | Notts | Nottingham | 1986 |

# WARWICKSHIRE

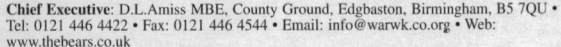

**Formation of Present Club**: 8 April 1882
**Substantial Reorganisation**: 19 January 1884
**Colours**: Dark Blue, Gold and Silver
**Badge**: Bear and Ragged Staff
**County Champions**: (5) 1911, 1951, 1972, 1994, 1995
**Gillette/NatWest/C & G Trophy Winners**: (5) 1966, 1968, 1989, 1993, 1995
**Benson and Hedges Cup Winners**: (2) 1994, 2002
**National League (Div 1) Winners**: (0); best – 3rd 2001, 2002
**Sunday League Winners**: (3) 1980, 1994, 1997
**Match Awards**: CGT 72; BHC 69

**Chief Executive**: D.L.Amiss MBE, County Ground, Edgbaston, Birmingham, B5 7QU • Tel: 0121 446 4422 • Fax: 0121 446 4544 • Email: info@warwk.co.org • Web: www.thebears.co.uk

**Director of Coaching/First XI Coach**: R.J.Inverarity. **Captain**: M.J.Powell.
**Vice-Captain**: D.R.Brown. **Overseas Players**: S.E.Bond and (*tbc*) Z.Khan. **2003**
**Beneficiary**: T.L.Penney. **Scorer**: D.E.Wainwright. ‡ New registration

‡**ALI, Moeen** Munir, b Birmingham 18 Jun 1987. RHB. Warwickshire staff 2003. Awaiting f-c debut.

**BELL, Ian** Ronald (Princethorpe C), b Walsgrave-on-Sowe 11 Apr 1982. 5'9". RHB, RM. Debut 1999; cap 2001. Tour (Eng A): WI 2000-01 (*part*). HS 135 v Derbys (Derby) 2001. BB 1-22. Awards: BHC 2. LO HS 86 v Glam (Birmingham) 2002 (NL).

**BETTS, Melvyn** Morris (Fyndoune CS, Sacriston), b Sacriston, Co Durham 26 Mar 1975. 5'10". RHB, RFM. Durham 1993-2000; cap 1998. Warwickshire debut/cap 2001. Tour: Z 1998-99. HS 57* Du v Sussex (Hove) 1996. Wa HS 56 v Lancs (Birmingham) 2002. BB 9-64 (Durham record; 13-143 match) v Northants (Northampton) 1997. Wa BB 5-22 v Durham (Birmingham) 2001 – on Wa debut. Award: BHC 1. LO HS 21 Du v Hants (Chester-le-St) 1997 (SL). LO BB 4-22 v Somerset (Taunton) 2001 (BHC).

**BOND, Shane** Edward, b Christchurch, NZ 7 Jun 1975. RHB, RF. Canterbury 1996-97 to date. Warwickshire debut 2002. **Tests** (NZ): 8 (2001-02 to 2002-03); HS 17 v WI (St George's) 2001-02; BB 5-78 v WI (Bridgetown) 2001-02. **LOI** (NZ): 26 (2001-02 to 2002-03); HS 31* v I (Auckland) 2002-03; BB 6-23 v A (Pt Elizabeth) 2002-03. Tours (NZ): A 2001-02; WI 2002. WI 2002. HS 66* Canterbury v CD (Blenheim) 2000-01. BB 5-37 Canterbury v ND (Gisborne) 2001-02. Wa HS 29* and Wa BB 5-64 v Somerset (Taunton) 2002. LO HS 31* (*see LOI*). LO BB 6-23 (*see LOI*).

**BROWN, Douglas** Robert (Alloa Academy; W London IHE), b Stirling, Scotland 29 Oct 1969. 6'2". RHB, RFM. Scotland 1989. Warwickshire debut 1991-92 (SA tour); cap 1995. Wellington 1995-96. **LOI**: 9 (1997-98); HS 21 v WI (Bridgetown) 1997-98; BB 2-28 v WI (Sharjah) 1997-98. Tours (Wa): SA 1991-92, 1994-95; SL 1997-98 (Eng A). HS 203 v Sussex (Hove) 2000. 50 wkts (3); most – 81 (1997). BB 8-89 (11-154 match) F-C Counties XI v Pak A (Chelmsford) 1997. Wa BB 7-66 v Durham (Chester-le-St) 1999. Award: BHC 1. LO HS 82* v Yorks (Birmingham) 2002 (NL). LO BB 5-31 v Worcs (Worcester) 1997 (BHC).

**CARTER, Neil** Miller (Hottentots Holland HS; Cape Technicon), b Cape Town, SA 29 Jan 1975. ECB qualified – British passport. 6'2". LHB, LFM. Boland 1999-00 to 2000-01. Warwickshire debut 2001. HS 103 v Sussex (Hove) 2002 – completed maiden hundred off 67 balls. BB 6-63 Boland v GW (Kimberley) 2000-01. Wa BB 5-78 v Worcs (Birmingham) 2001. Award: CGT 1. LO HS 40 v Essex (Birmingham) 2001 (CGT). LO BB 5-31 v Durham (Birmingham) 2002 (NL).

**CLIFFORD, Ian** Jeffrey (Park Hall SFC), b Birmingham 12 Oct 1982. RHB, WK. Debut 2002. HS 7. LO HS 5* (CGT).

**FROST, Tony** (James Brinkley HS; Stoke-on-Trent C), b Stoke-on-Trent, Staffs 17 Nov 1975. 5'11". RHB, WK. Debut 1997; cap 1999. HS 111* v OU (Oxford) 1998. CC HS 103 v Yorks (Birmingham) 2002. LO HS 22* v Kent (Birmingham) 1999.

**GILES, Ashley** Fraser (George Abbot S, Guildford), b Chertsey, Surrey 19 Mar 1973. 6'3". RHB, SLA. Debut 1993; cap 1996. **ECB contracts 2001, 2002, 2003. Tests**: 19 (1998 to 2002-03); HS 45 v SL (Manchester) 2002; BB 5-67 v I (Ahmedabad) 2001-02. **LOI**: 24 (1997 to 2002-03); HS 21* v NZ (Dunedin) 2001-02; BB 5-57 v I (Delhi) 2001-02. Tours: A 1996-97 (Eng A), 2002-03 (*part*); NZ 2001-02; I 2001-02; P 2000-01; SL 1997-98 (Eng A), 2000-01; K 1997-98 (Eng A). HS 128* v Sussex (Hove) 2000. 50 wkts (2); most – 64 (1996). BB 8-90 (12-135 match) v Northants (Northampton) 2000. Awards: CGT 2; BHC 1. LO HS 107 v Derbys (Birmingham) 2000 (NWT). LO BB 5-21 v Norfolk (Birmingham) 1997 (NWT).

**JONES, Huw** Rhys (Trinity S; Warwick S; Brookes U), b Oxford 23 Nov 1980. 5'11". RHB, LB. Oxford UCCE 2001-02. Warwickshire summer contract – awaiting county f-c debut. HS 97 OU v Worcs (Oxford) 2002. LO HS 72 Warwks CB v Leics (Coventry) 2002 (CGT).

**‡KHAN, Zaheer** (KTS HS; RBNB C), b Shrirampur, Maharashtra, India 7 Oct 1978. 6'2". RHB, LFM. Baroda 1999-00 to date. **Tests** (I): 24 (2000-01 to 2002-03); HS 46 v WI (Bridgetown) 2001-02; BB 5-29 v NZ (Hamilton) 2002-03. **LOI** (I): 67 (2000-01 to 2002-03); HS 34* v NZ (Wellington) 2002-03; BB 4-42 v Z (Sharjah) 2000-01, 4-42 v Z (Bulawayo) 2001, and 4-42 v NZ (Pretoria) 2002-03. Tours (I): E 2002; SA 2001-02; WI 2001-02; NZ 2002-03; SL 2001; Z 2001; B 2000-01. HS 48 Baroda v Maharashtra (Poona) 1999-2000. UK HS 14* (*twice*) I v E (Nottingham) 2002. BB 6-25 Baroda v Punjab (Baroda) 2001-02. UK BB 3-90 I v E (Lord's) 2002. LO HS 34* (*see LOI*). LO BB 4-42 (*see LOI*).

**KNIGHT, Nicholas** Verity (Felsted S; Loughborough U), b Watford, Herts 28 Nov 1969. 6'0". LHB, occ RM. Essex 1991-94; cap 1994. Warwickshire debut 1994-95 (SA tour); cap 1995. **Tests**: 17 (1995 to 2001); HS 113 v P (Leeds) 1996. **LOI**: 100 (1996 to 2002-03); HS 125* v P (Nottingham) 1996. Tours: SA 1994-95 (Wa), 1999-00 (*part*); NZ 1996-97; I 1994-95 (Eng A); SL 1997-98 (Eng A – captain); P 1995-96 (Eng A); Z 1996-97; K 1997-98 (Eng A – captain). 1000 runs (3); most – 1520 (2002). HS 255* (carried bat) v Hants (Birmingham) 2002. BB 1-61. Awards: CGT 4; BHC 4. LO HS 151 v Somerset (Birmingham) 1995 (NWT). LO BB 1-14 (SL).

**MEES, Thomas** (Worcester RGS; King Edward VII C, Stourbridge; Brookes U, Oxford), b Wolverhampton, Staffs 8 Jun 1981. 6'3". RHB, RMF. Oxford UCCE 2001-02. Herefordshire 1999. Warwickshire summer contract – awaiting 1st XI debut. HS 13 OU v Worcs (Oxford) 2002. BB 6-64 OU v Middx (Oxford) 2001. Award: CGT 1. LO HS (Wa CB) 4* (CGT). LO BB 3-19 Warwks CB v Cambs (March) 2001 (CGT).

**OSTLER, Dominic** Piers (Princethorpe C; Solihull TC), b Solihull 15 Jul 1970. 6'3". RHB, occ RM. Debut 1990; cap 1991; benefit 1999. Tours: SA 1992-93 (Wa); P 1995-96 (Eng A). 1000 runs (6); most – 1284 (1991). HS 225 v Yorks (Birmingham) 2002. BB 1-46. Awards: CGT 2; BHC 1. LO HS 134* v Glos (Birmingham) 2001 (NL). LO BB 1-4 (NWT).

**PENNEY, Trevor** Lionel (Prince Edward S, Salisbury), b Salisbury, Rhodesia 12 Jun 1968. 6'0". RHB, RM. Qualified for England 1992. Boland 1991-92. Warwickshire debut 1991-92 (SA tour); UK debut v CU (Cambridge) 1992, scoring 102*; cap 1994; benefit 2003. No f-c appearances 2002. Mashonaland 1993-94; 1997-98 to date. Tours (Wa): SA 1991-92, 1992-93, 1994-95; Z 1993-94. 1000 runs (2); most – 1295 (1996). HS 151 v Middx (Lord's) 1992. BB 3-18 Mashonaland v Mashonaland U-24 (Harare) 1993-94. Wa BB 1-40 (Z tour). CC BB – . Awards: CGT 3. LO HS 90 v Cornwall (St Austell) 1996 (NWT). LO BB 1-8 (NWT).

**PIPER, Keith** John (Haringey Cricket C), b Leicester 18 Dec 1969. 5'6". RHB, WK. Warwickshire debut 1989; cap 1992; benefit 2001. Tours (Wa): SA 1991-92, 1992-93, 1994-95; I 1994-95 (Eng A); P 1995-96 (Eng A); Z 1993-94. HS 116* v Durham (Birmingham) 1994. BB 1-57. LO HS 38* v Leics (Birmingham) 1999 (NL).

**POWELL, Michael** James (Lawrence Sheriff S, Rugby), b Bolton, Lancs 5 Apr 1975. 5'11". RHB, RM. Debut 1996; cap 1999; captain 2001 to date. Griqualand West 2001-02. Tour (Eng A): WI 2000-01. 1000 runs (1): 1046 (2000). HS 236 v OU (Oxford) 2001. CC HS 145 v Northants (Northampton) 2000. BB 2-16 v OU (Oxford) 1998. CC BB 2-29 v Somerset (Taunton) 2002. Award: BHC 1. LO HS 101* v Northants (Birmingham) 2002 (BHC). LO BB 5-40 v Kent (Canterbury) 2002 (CGT).

**RICHARDSON, Alan** (Alleyne's HS; Stafford CFE; Durham U), b Newcastle-under-Lyme, Staffs 6 May 1975. 6'2". RHB, RMF. Derbyshire 1995 (one match). Warwickshire debut 1999, cap 2002. Staffordshire 1996-98. HS 91 v Hants (Birmingham) 2002 – adding 214 for 10th wicket with N.V.Knight. Staffordshire 1996-98. HS 91 v Hants (Birmingham) 2002 – adding 214 for 10th wicket with N.V.Knight. BB 8-46 v Sussex (Birmingham) 2002. LO HS 11* v Leics (Birmingham) 1999 (NL). LO BB 5-35 v Staffs (Stone) 2002 (CGT).

**SHEIKH, Mohammad** Avez (Broadway S), b Birmingham 2 Jul 1973. 6'0". LHB, RM. Debut 1997. HS 58* v Northants (Northampton) 2000. BB 4-36 v Hants (Birmingham) 2001. LO HS 36 v Hants (Southampton) 2000 (NL). LO BB 4-17 v Yorks (Birmingham) 2001 (NL).

**SMITH, Neil** Michael Knight (Warwick S), b Birmingham 27 Jul 1967. Son of M.J.K.Smith (Leics, Warwks and England 1951-75). 6'0". RHB, OB. Debut 1987; cap 1993; captain 1999-2000; benefit 2002. MCC YC. **LOI**: 7 (1995-96 to 1996); HS 31 v H (Peshawar) 1995-96; BB 3-29 v UAE (Peshawar) 1995-96. Tours (Wa): SA 1991-92, 1994-95; Z 1993-94. 1000 runs (1): 1002 (1998). HS 161 v Yorks (Leeds) 1989. BB 7-42 v Lancs (Birmingham) 1994. Awards: CGT 1; BHC 2. LO HS 125 v Kent (Canterbury) 1997 (BHC). LO BB 6-33 v Sussex (Birmingham) 1995 (SL).

**SPIRES**, James Ashley S. ('*Jamie*') (Solihull S), b Solihull 12 Nov 1979. 6'0". RHB, SLA. Debut 2001. HS 37* v Sussex (Hove) 2002. BB 5-165 v Yorks (Birmingham) 2002. LO HS – and BB (Warwks CB) 1-33 (CGT).

**TAHIR, Naqaash** (Moseley S; Spring Hill C), b Birmingham 14 Nov 1983. 5'10", RHB, RFM. Staff 2001 – awaiting 1st XI debut.

‡**TROTT, Ian Jonathan** Leonard (Rondebosch BHC; Stellenbosch U), b Cape Town 22 Apr 1981. Step brother of K.C.Jackson. 6'0". RHB, RM. Boland 2002-01. W Province 2001-02. EU/British passport. HS 93 Boland v WP (Cape Town) 2000-01 and 93 WP v Easterns (Cape Town) 2001-02. BB (WP) 1-10. LO HS 108* Boland v North West (Paarl) 2000-01. LO BB 2-32 Boland v EP (Paarl) 1999-00.

**TROUGHTON**, Jamie Oliver ('*Jim*') (Trinity S; Leamington Spa; Birmingham U), b Camden, London 2 Mar 1979. Great-grandson of H.T.Crichton (Warwicks 1908). 5'11". LHB, SLA. Debut 2001, cap 2002. 1000 (1): 1067 (2002). HS 131* v Hants (Southampton) 2002. Awards: CGT 2. LO HS 115* and BB 4-23 Warwks CB v Cumb (Millom) 2001 (CGT).

**WAGG, Graham** Grant (Ashlawn S, Rugby), b Rugby, 28 Apr 1983. 6'0". RHB, LM. Debut 2002 – scoring 42* and 51 v Somerset (Birmingham). HS 51 (*see above*). BB 4-43 v Somerset (Birmingham) 2002 – on debut. LO HS 21 Warwks CB v Leics (Coventry) 2002 (CGT). LO BB 4-50 v Kent (Birmingham) 2002 (NL).

**WAGH, Mark** Anant (King Edward's S, Birmingham; Keble C, Oxford), b Birmingham 20 Oct 1976. 6'2". RHB, OB. Oxford U 1996-98; blue 1996-97-98; captain 1997. Warwickshire debut 1997; cap 2000. British U 1998. Mashonaland A 1998-99. 1000 runs (2): 1277 (2001). HS 315 v Middx (Lord's) 2001. BB 5-137 v Yorks (Birmingham) 2002. LO HS 84 v Worcs (Birmingham) 2002 (NL). LO BB 1-39 (Brit U – BHC).

**WARREN, Nick** Alexander (Wheelers Lane S; Solihull SFC), b Moseley, Birmingham 26 Jun 1982. 5'11". RHB, RMF. Debut 2002 – awaiting CC debut. 2nd XI debut 1998 when aged 16y 76d. HS 11 and BB 2-48 v WI A (Birmingham) 2002. LO HS 2 and LO BB 3-34 v Kent (Canterbury) 2002 (NL). **RELEASED/RETIRED** continued on p 107

# WARWICKSHIRE 2002

## RESULTS SUMMARY

| | Place | Won | Lost | Tied | Drew | No Result |
|---|---|---|---|---|---|---|
| County Championship (1st Division) | 2nd | 7 | 2 | | 7 | |
| All First-Class Matches | | 7 | 3 | | 7 | |
| C & G Trophy | 4th Round | | | | | |
| Benson & Hedges Cup | Winners | | | | | |
| NU National League (1st Division) | 3rd | 9 | 6 | | | 1 |

## COUNTY CHAMPIONSHIP AVERAGES

### BATTING AND FIELDING

| Cap | | M | I | NO | HS | Runs | Avge | 100 | 50 | Ct/St |
|---|---|---|---|---|---|---|---|---|---|---|
| 1995 | N.V.Knight | 10 | 19 | 3 | 255* | 1520 | 95.00 | 5 | 5 | 10 |
| 2002 | J.O.Troughton | 13 | 22 | 3 | 131* | 1052 | 55.36 | 3 | 6 | 8 |
| 1991 | D.P.Ostler | 13 | 23 | 1 | 225 | 1008 | 45.81 | 2 | 5 | 24 |
| | N.M.Carter | 9 | 12 | 5 | 103 | 305 | 43.57 | 1 | 1 | 4 |
| | M.A.Sheikh | 4 | 6 | 2 | 43 | 152 | 38.00 | – | – | 1 |
| 1999 | M.J.Powell | 16 | 29 | 2 | 103 | 858 | 31.77 | 1 | 6 | 12 |
| 1999 | T.Frost | 7 | 11 | 1 | 103 | 308 | 30.80 | 1 | 1 | 6/2 |
| | G.G.Wagg | 4 | 6 | 1 | 51 | 142 | 28.40 | – | 1 | 1 |
| 2000 | M.A.Wagh | 9 | 16 | – | 109 | 417 | 26.06 | 1 | 1 | 2 |
| 1995 | D.R.Brown | 15 | 26 | 4 | 79* | 571 | 25.95 | – | 2 | 9 |
| 1996 | S.M.Pollock | 10 | 18 | 1 | 66 | 425 | 25.00 | – | 4 | 13 |
| 2001 | I.R.Bell | 16 | 28 | 1 | 77 | 658 | 24.37 | – | 3 | 6 |
| 2001 | M.M.Betts | 9 | 16 | 5 | 56 | 259 | 23.54 | – | 1 | 2 |
| 1993 | N.M.K.Smith | 8 | 15 | – | 96 | 337 | 22.46 | – | 2 | 7 |
| 1996 | A.F.Giles | 4 | 6 | – | 68 | 134 | 22.33 | – | 1 | 1 |
| | S.E.Bond | 3 | 4 | 1 | 29* | 64 | 21.33 | – | – | 1 |
| | J.A.S.Spires | 5 | 6 | 3 | 37* | 60 | 20.00 | – | – | 3 |
| 2002 | A.Richardson | 9 | 11 | 4 | 91 | 132 | 18.85 | – | 1 | 4 |
| 1992 | K.J.Piper | 8 | 12 | 2 | 64* | 163 | 16.30 | – | 1 | 14/1 |
| | J.I.Clifford | 4 | 6 | – | 7 | 20 | 3.33 | – | – | 15/1 |

### BOWLING

| | O | M | R | W | Avge | Best | 5wI | 10wM |
|---|---|---|---|---|---|---|---|---|
| G.G.Wagg | 66.5 | 11 | 259 | 12 | 21.58 | 4- 43 | – | – |
| A.Richardson | 279.2 | 56 | 905 | 37 | 24.45 | 8- 46 | 2 | – |
| S.M.Pollock | 301.3 | 101 | 733 | 28 | 26.17 | 4- 37 | – | – |
| A.F.Giles | 215.4 | 33 | 678 | 25 | 27.12 | 7-142 | 3 | 1 |
| S.E.Bond | 95.4 | 23 | 330 | 12 | 27.50 | 5- 64 | 1 | – |
| D.R.Brown | 477.4 | 74 | 1626 | 52 | 31.26 | 7-110 | 2 | – |
| N.M.K.Smith | 126 | 27 | 411 | 12 | 34.25 | 5- 42 | 1 | – |
| J.A.S.Spires | 160.4 | 25 | 556 | 16 | 34.75 | 5-165 | 1 | – |
| M.A.Wagh | 194 | 42 | 566 | 15 | 37.73 | 5-137 | 1 | – |
| N.M.Carter | 228.1 | 35 | 957 | 20 | 47.85 | 4- 46 | – | – |
| M.M.Betts | 248.4 | 34 | 1023 | 20 | 51.15 | 3- 75 | – | – |

*Also bowled:*

| | | | | | | | | |
|---|---|---|---|---|---|---|---|---|
| M.A.Sheikh | 122.3 | 23 | 376 | 5 | 75.20 | 4- 78 | – | – |

I.R.Bell 34-8-89-2; T.Frost 1-0-9-0; D.P.Ostler 1-0-13-0; M.J.Powell 53-7-193-3; J.O.Troughton 16-0-68-0.

The First-Class Averages (pp 121-135) give the records of Warwickshire's players in all first-class county matches (Warwickshire's other opponents being West Indies A), with the exception of T.Mees, whose only first-class appearances were in University matches, and A.F.Giles whose full county figures are as above.

# WARWICKSHIRE RECORDS

## FIRST-CLASS CRICKET

| | | | | | |
|---|---|---|---|---|---|
| **Highest Total** | For 810-4d | | v | Durham | Birmingham | 1994 |
| | V 887 | | by | Yorkshire | Birmingham | 1896 |
| **Lowest Total** | For 16 | | v | Kent | Tonbridge | 1913 |
| | V 15 | | by | Hampshire | Birmingham | 1922 |
| **Highest Innings** | For 501* | B.C.Lara | v | Durham | Birmingham | 1994 |
| | V 322 | I.V.A.Richards | for | Somerset | Taunton | 1985 |

**Highest Partnership for each Wicket**

| | | | | | | |
|---|---|---|---|---|---|---|
| 1st | 377* | N.F.Horner/K.Ibadulla | v | Surrey | The Oval | 1960 |
| 2nd | 465* | J.A.Jameson/R.B.Kanhai | v | Glos | Birmingham | 1974 |
| 3rd | 327 | S.P.Kinneir/W.G.Quaife | v | Lancashire | Birmingham | 1901 |
| 4th | 470 | A.I.Kallicharran/G.W.Humpage | v | Lancashire | Southport | 1982 |
| 5th | 322* | B.C.Lara/K.J.Piper | v | Durham | Birmingham | 1994 |
| 6th | 220 | H.E.Dollery/J.Buckingham | v | Derbyshire | Derby | 1938 |
| 7th | 289 | D.Brown/A.F.Giles | v | Sussex | Hove | 2000 |
| 8th | 228 | A.J.W.Croom/R.E.S.Wyatt | v | Worcs | Dudley | 1925 |
| 9th | 154 | G.W.Stephens/A.J.W.Croom | v | Derbyshire | Birmingham | 1925 |
| 10th | 214 | N.V.Knight/A.Richardson | v | Hampshire | Birmingham | 2002 |

| | | | | | | |
|---|---|---|---|---|---|---|
| **Best Bowling** | For | 10-41 | J.D.Bannister | v | Comb Servs | Birmingham | 1959 |
| **(Innings)** | V | 10-36 | H.Verity | for | Yorkshire | Leeds | 1931 |
| **Best Bowling** | For | 15-76 | S.Hargreave | v | Surrey | The Oval | 1903 |
| **(Match)** | V | 17-92 | A.P.Freeman | for | Kent | Folkestone | 1932 |

| | | | | | |
|---|---|---|---|---|---|
| **Most Runs – Season** | 2417 | M.J.K.Smith | (av 60.42) | | 1959 |
| **Most Runs – Career** | 35146 | D.L.Amiss | (av 41.64) | | 1960-87 |
| **Most 100s – Season** | 9 | A.I.Kallicharran | | | 1984 |
| | 9 | B.C.Lara | | | 1994 |
| **Most 100s – Career** | 78 | D.L.Amiss | | | 1960-87 |
| **Most Wkts – Season** | 180 | W.E.Hollies | (av 15.13) | | 1946 |
| **Most Wkts – Career** | 2201 | W.E.Hollies | (av 20.45) | | 1932-57 |
| **Most Career W-K Dismissals** | 800 | E.J.Smith | (662 ct/138 st) | | 1904-30 |
| **Most Career Catches in the Field** | 422 | M.J.K.Smith | | | 1956-75 |

## LIMITED-OVERS CRICKET

| | | | | | | |
|---|---|---|---|---|---|---|
| **Highest Total** | CGT | 392-5 | | v | Oxfordshire | Birmingham | 1984 |
| | BHC | 369-8 | | v | Minor C | Jesmond | 1996 |
| | NL | 301-6 | | v | Essex | Colchester | 1982 |
| **Lowest Total** | CGT | 98 | | v | Leics | Leicester | 1998 |
| | BHC | 91 | | v | Glos | Bristol | 2002 |
| | NL | 59 | | v | Yorks | Leeds | 2001 |
| **Highest Innings** | CGT | 206 | A.I.Kallicharran | v | Oxfordshire | Birmingham | 1984 |
| | BHC | 137* | T.A.Lloyd | v | Lancashire | Birmingham | 1985 |
| | NL | 134* | D.P.Ostler | v | Glos | Birmingham | 2001 |
| **Best Bowling** | CGT | 6-32 | K.Ibadulla | v | Hampshire | Birmingham | 1965 |
| | | 6-32 | A.I.Kallicharran | v | Oxfordshire | Birmingham | 1984 |
| | BHC | 7-32 | R.G.D.Willis | v | Yorkshire | Birmingham | 1981 |
| | NL | 6-15 | A.A.Donald | v | Yorkshire | Birmingham | 1995 |

# WORCESTERSHIRE

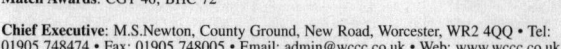

**Formation of Present Club:** 11 March 1865
**Colours:** Dark Green and Black
**Badge:** Shield Argent a Fess between three Pears Sable
**County Championships:** (5) 1964, 1965, 1974, 1988, 1989
**Gillette/NatWest/C & G Trophy Winners:** (1) 1994
**Benson and Hedges Cup Winners:** (1) 1991
**National League (Div 1) Winners:** (0); best – 2nd 1999, 2002
**Sunday League Winners:** (3) 1971, 1987, 1988
**Match Awards:** CGT 46; BHC 72

**Chief Executive:** M.S.Newton, County Ground, New Road, Worcester, WR2 4QQ • Tel: 01905 748474 • Fax: 01905 748005 • Email: admin@wccc.co.uk • Web: www.wccc.co.uk

**Director of Cricket/First XI Coach:** T.M.Moody. **Captain:** B.F.Smith. **Vice-Captain:** S.J.Rhodes. **Overseas Players:** A.J.Hall and M.Hayward. **2003 Beneficiary:** D.A.Leatherdale. **Scorer:** W.Clarke. ‡ New registration

*Worcestershire revised their capping policy in 2002 and now award players with their County Colours when they make their Championship debut.*

**ALI, Kabir** (Moseley CS and SFC), b Moseley, Birmingham 24 Nov 1980. 6'0". RHB, RMF. Debut 1999. 50 wkts (1): 71 (2002). HS 51* v Northants (Northampton) 2002. BB 7-43 (10-88 match) v OU (Oxford) 2002. CC HS 5-22 v Glos (Worcester) 2002. Award: BHC 1. LO HS 27 v Glos (Worcester) 2002 (BHC). LO BB 5-36 v Yorks (Leeds) 2002 (NL).

**ALI, Kadeer** (Handsworth GS), b Moseley, Birmingham 7 Mar 1983. 6'1". RHB, LB. Debut 2000. No f-c appearances 2002. HS 38 v Middx (Worcester) 2001. LO HS 66 Worcs CB v Sussex CB (Kidderminster) 2002 (CGT).

**BATTY, Gareth** Jon (Bingley GS), b Bradford, Yorks 13 Oct 1977. Younger brother of J.D.Batty (Yorkshire and Somerset 1989-96). 5'11". RHB, OB. Yorkshire 1997. Surrey 1999-2001. Worcestershire debut 2002. **LOI:** 2 (2002-03); HS 3 and BB 1-65 v A (Melbourne) 2002-03. HS 74 v Derbys (Worcester) 2002. 50 wkts (1): 56 (2002). BB 6-71 v Essex (Southend) 2002. LO HS 83* Sy v Yorks (Oval) 2001 (NL). LO BB 4-36 Sy v Kent (Canterbury) 2001 (NL) and 4-36 v Notts (Nottingham) 2002 (NL).

**‡FARROW, Jonathan** Colin, b Stockport 22 Feb 1984. RHB, RFM. Cheshire 2002. Worcestershire staff 2003 – awaiting first-class debut. LO HS – . LO BB 2-81 Cheshire v Lincs (Neston) 2002 (CGT).

**‡GUEST, Christopher.** Worcestershire staff 2003 – awaiting first-class debut.

**‡HALL, Andrew** James (Hoerskool Alberton), b Johannesburg, SA 31 Jul 1975. RHB, RFM. Transvaal/Gauteng 1995-96 to 2001-02. Easterns 2001-02 to date. Suffolk 2002. **Tests** (SA): 4 (2001-02 to 2002-03); HS 70 v A (Cape Town) 2001-02 – on debut; BB 3-1 v SL (Jo'burg) 2002-03. **LOI** (SA): 29 (1998-99 to 2002-03); HS 81 v SL (Galle) 2000-01; BB 2-8 v A (Melbourne) 2000-01. HS 153 Easterns v North West (Benoni) 2001-02. BB 5-20 Gauteng v EP (Jo'burg) 1999-00. LO HS 129* Gauteng v Border (E London) 1999-00. LO BB 4-33 Suffolk v Northants (Bury St Edmunds) 2002 (CGT).

**‡HARRITY, Mark** Andrew (Taperoo HS), b Semaphore, S Australia 9 Mar 1974. British passport (English father). 6'4". RHB, LFM. S Australia 1993-94 to date. S Australia to date. HS 19 S Aus v Vic (Melbourne) 2001-02. BB 5-65 S Aus v Tasmania (Hobart) 2002-02. LO HS (S Aus) 6. LO BB 5-42 S Aus v Vic (Adelaide) 1997-98.

**‡HAYWARD, Mornantau** ('*Nantie*') (Daniel Pienaar THS), b Uitenhage, SA 6 Mar 1977. RHB, RF. E Province 1995-96 to date. **Tests** (SA): 14 (1999-00 to 2002-03); HS 14 v A (Melbourne) 2001-02; BB 5-56 v P (Durban) 2002-03. **LOI** (SA): 21 (1998 to 2001-02); HS 4; BB 4-31 v I (Jo'burg) 1999-00. Tours (SA): A 2001-02; I 1999-00; SL 2000-01. HS 55* EP v Boland (Pt Elizabeth) 1997-98. BB 6-31 EP v Easterns (Pt Elizabeth) 1999-00. LO HS 19* EP v WP (Cape Town) 1996-97. LO BB 5-37 EP v KZ-Natal (Durban) 1998-99.

**HICK, Graeme** Ashley (Prince Edward HS, Salisbury), b Salisbury, Rhodesia 23 May 1966. 6'3". RHB, OB. Zimbabwe 1983-84 to 1985-86. Worcestershire debut 1984; cap 1986; benefit 1999; captain 2000-02. N Districts 1987-88 to 1988-89. Queensland 1990-91. *Wisden* 1986. **ECB contract 2000. Tests:** 65 (1991 to 2000-01); HS 178 v I (Bombay) 1992-93; BB 4-126 v NZ (Wellington) 1991-92. Took wicket with third ball in Test cricket. **LOI:** 120 (1991 to 2000-01); HS 126* v SL (Adelaide) 1998-99; BB 5-33 v Z (Harare) 1999-00. Tours: E 1985 (Z); A 1994-95, 1998-99 (*part*); SA 1995-96, 1999-00 (*part*); WI 1993-94; NZ 1991-92; I 1992-93; P 2000-01; SL 1983-84 (Z), 1992-93, 2000-01; Z 1990-91 (Wo), 1996-97 (Wo). 1000 runs (17+1) inc 2000 (3); most – 2713 (1988); youngest to score 2000 (1986). Scored 1019 runs before June 1988, including a record 410 runs in April. Fewest innings for 10,000 runs in county cricket (179). Youngest (24) to score 50 f-c hundreds. Second-youngest (32) to score 100 f-c hundreds. Scored 645 runs without being dismissed (UK record) in 1990. HS 405* (Worcs record and then second highest in UK f-c matches) v Somerset (Taunton) 1988. BB 5-18 v Leics (Worcester) 1995. Awards: CGT 5; BHC 11. LO HS 172* v Devon (Worcester) 1987 (NWT). LO BB 5-19 E v Pak A (Lahore) 1998-99.

**LEATHERDALE, David** Anthony (Pudsey Grangefield S), b Bradford, Yorks 26 Nov 1967. 5'10½". RHB, RM. Debut 1988; cap 1994; benefit 2003. Tours (Wo): Z 1993-94, 1996-97. 1000 runs (1): 1001 (1998). HS 157 v Somerset (Worcester) 1991. BB 5-20 v Glos (Worcester) 1998. Award: BHC 1. LO HS 70* v Yorks (Worcester) 1999 (NL). LO BB 5-9 v Durham (Chester-le-St) 2002 (NL).

**LIPTROT, Christopher** George (The Deanery HS), b Wigan, Lancs 13 Feb 1980. 6'2". LHB, RFM. Debut 1999. HS 61 v Warwks (Birmingham) 1999. BB 6-44 v Warwks (Worcester) 2000. LO HS 15* and LO BB 3-44 v Kent (Canterbury) 2000 (NL).

**MASON, Matthew** Sean (Mazenod C, Lesmurdie, WA), b Claremont, Perth, Australia 20 Mar 1974. ECB qualified – British passport. 6'5". RHB, RFM. W Australia 1996-97 to 1997-98. Worcestershire debut 2002. HS 50 v Derbys (Worcester) 2002. BB 5-50 v Notts (Kidderminster) 2002. LO HS 6 (NL). LO BB 3-33 v Somerset (Taunton) 2002 (BHC).

‡**MITCHELL, Daryl.** Worcestershire staff 2003 – awaiting first-class debut.

‡**MOORE, Stephen** Colin (Exeter U), b Johannesburg, SA 4 Nov 1980. RHB, RM. Worcestershire staff 2003 – awaiting first-class debut.

**PETERS, Stephen** David (Coopers Coborn & Co S), b Harold Wood, Essex 10 Dec 1978. 5'11". RHB, occ LB. Essex 1996-2001, scoring 110 and 12* v CU (Cambridge) on debut. Worcestershire debut 2002. HS 146 v Northants (Northampton) 2002. BB (Ex) 1-19 (not CC). Award: CGT 1. LO HS 73* Ex v Glam (Southend) 2000 (NL).

**PIPE**, David **James** (Queensbury S, Bradford), b Bradford, Yorks 16 Dec 1977. 5'11". RHB, WK. Debut 1998. HS 54 v Warwks (Worcester) 2000 – on CC debut. LO HS 56 Worcs CB v Kent CB (Kidderminster) 2000 (NWT). Held 8 catches v Herts (Hertford) 2001 (CGT) to equal l-o record.

**RHODES, Steven** John (Lapage Middle S; Carlton-Bolling S, Bradford), b Bradford, Yorks 17 Jun 1964. Son of W.E. (Notts 1961-64). 5'7". RHB, WK. Yorkshire 1981-84. Worcestershire debut 1985; cap 1986; benefit 1996. *Wisden* 1994. **Tests:** 11 (1994 to 1994-95); HS 65* v SA (Leeds) 1994. **LOI:** 9 (1989 to 1994-95); HS 56 v SA (Manchester) 1994. Tours: A 1994-95; SA 1993-94 (Eng A); WI 1991-92 (Eng A); SL 1985-86 (Eng B), 1990-91 (Eng A); Z 1989-90 (Eng A), 1990-91 (Wo), 1993-94 (Wo), 1996-97 (Wo – captain). 1000 runs (2); most – 1018 (1995). HS 124 v Notts (Nottingham) 2002. Awards: CGT 1; BHC 2. LO HS 105 v Lancs (Manchester) 1991 (RAC).

**SINGH, Anurag** (King Edward's, Birmingham; Gonville & Caius C, Cambridge), b Kanpur, India 9 Sep 1975. 5'11½". RHB, OB. Warwickshire 1995-2000. Cambridge U 1996-98; blue 1996-97-98; captain 1997-98. British U 1998 (captain). Worcestershire debut 2001. 1000 (2); most – 1167 (2002). HS 187 v Glos (Bristol) 2002. Award: BHC 1. LO HS 123 Brit U v Somerset (Taunton) 1996 (BHC).

**SMITH, Benjamin** Francis (Kibworth HS), b Corby, Northants 3 Apr 1972. 5'9". RHB, RM. Leicestershire 1990-2001; cap 1995. Central Districts 2001-02. Worcestershire debut 2002; captain 2003. Tour (Le): SA 1996-97. 1000 runs (4); most – 1243 (1996). HS 204 Le v Surrey (Oval) 1998. Wo HS 137 v OU (Oxford) 2002 – on Worcs debut. BB (Le) 1-5. Wo BB 1-45. Award: CGT 1. LO HS 115 Le v Somerset (Weston-s-m) 1995 (SL). LO BB (Le) 1-26.

**SOLANKI, Vikram** Singh (Regis S, Wolverhampton), b Udaipur, India 1 Apr 1976. 6'0". RHB, OB. Debut 1995; cap 1998. Tours (Eng A): SA 1999-00 (Eng – *part*); WI 2000-01; NZ 1999-00; Z 1996-97 (Wo), 1998-99; B 1999-00. **LOI**: 8 (1999-00); HS 24 v Z (Bulawayo) 1999-00. 1000 runs (2); most – 1339 (1999). HS 185 Eng A v Bangladesh (Chittagong) 1999-00. Wo HS 171 v Glos (Cheltenham) 1999. BB 5-69 v Middx (Lord's) 1996. Awards: CGT 1; BHC 1. LO HS 120* v Derbys (Derby) 1998 (SL). LO BB 2-40 Eng A v Zim Academy (Harare) 1998-99.

‡**WIGLEY, David** Harry (St Mary's RCS, Menstom, Ilkley), b Bradford, Yorks 26 Oct 1981. RHB, RFM. Yorkshire 2002 (one match). HS 15 and BB 1-71 Y v Surrey (Guildford) 2002 – on debut. LO HS 0 Y v WI A (Leeds) 2002.

### RELEASED/RETIRED
(Having made a first-class County appearance in 2002)

**BICHEL, Andrew** John (Laidley HS; Ipswich C, Queensland), b Laidley, Queensland 27 Aug 1970. RHB, RFM. 5'11". Queensland 1992-93 to date. Worcestershire 2001-02; cap 2001. Tests (A): 11 (1996-97 to 2002-03); HS 49 v E (Sydney) 2002-03; BB 5-60 v WI (Melbourne) 2000-01. **LOI** (A): 46 (1996-97 to 2002-03); HS 64 v NZ (Pt Elizabeth) 2002-03; BB 7-20 v E (Pt Elizabeth) 2002-03. Tours (A): E 1997; Scot 1998 (Aus A); SA 1996-97, 2001-02; WI 1998-99, 2003; P 2002-03 (*Sharjah*). HS 110 (off 110 balls) Q v Vic (Brisbane) 1997-98. Wo HS 78* v Durham (Worcester) 2002. 50 wkts (1+1): most – 66 (2001). BB 9-93 (10-131 match) v Glos (Worcester) 2002. Awards: BHC 3. LO HS 100 v Glam (Cardiff) 2001 (BHC). LO BB 7-20 (*see LOI*).

**DONALD, Allan** Anthony (Grey College HS), b Bloemfontein, SA 20 Oct 1966. 6'2". RHB, RF. OFS/FS 1985-86 to date. Warwickshire 1987-93, 1995, 1997, 1999-2000; cap 1989; benefit 1999. Worcestershire 2002 (one match). *Wisden* 1991. Tests (SA): 72 (1991-92 to 2001-02); HS 37 v WI (Bridgetown) 2001-02; BB 8-71 (11-113 match) v Z (Harare) 1995-96. **LOI** (SA): 164 (1991-92 to 2002-03); HS 12 v SL (Nottingham) 1998; BB 6-23 v K (Nairobi) 1996-97. Tours (SA): E 1994, 1998; A 1993-94, 1997-98, 2001-02; WI 1991-92, 2000-01; NZ 1994-95, 1998-99; I 1996-97, 1999-00; P 1997-98; SL 1993-94; Z 1995-96, 1999-00. HS 55* SA v Tasmania (Devonport) 1997-98. UK HS 44 Wa v Essex (Ilford) 1995. 50 wkts (5); most – 89 (1995). BB 8-37 OFS v Transvaal (Johannesburg) 1986-87. UK BB 7-37 Wa v Durham (Birmingham) 1992. Wo HS 5* and Wo BB 5-77 v Durham (Chester-le-St) 2002 – on Worcs debut. Awards: NWT 4. LO HS 23* v Leics (Leicester) 1989 (BHC). LO BB 6-15 v Yorks (Birmingham) 1995 (SL).

**LEE, Shane** (Oak Flats HS; Wollongong U), b Wollongong, NSW, Australia 8 Aug 1973. 6'2". RHB, RFM. NSW 1992-93 to date. Somerset 1996; cap 1996. Worcestershire 2002. **LOI** (A): 45 (1995-96 to 2000-01); HS 47 v WI (Bridgetown) 1998-99; BB 5-33 v SL (Melbourne) 1998-99. Tour (NSW): E 1995. 1000 runs (1): 1300 (1996). HS 183* NSW v S Aus (Adelaide) 1997-98. UK HS 167* Sm v Worcs (Bath) 1996. Wo HS 48 v Derbys (Derby) 2002. BB 4-20 NSW v Tasmania (Sydney) 1995-96. UK BB 4-52 Sm v Sussex (Hove) 1996. Award: NWT 1. LO HS 115 NSW v WA (N Sydney) 2000-01. LO BB 5-33 (*see LOI*).

**RAWNSLEY, Matthew** James (Shenley Court CS, Birmingham), b Birmingham 8 Jun 1976. 6'2". RHB, SLA. Worcestershire 1996-2002. HS 39 v Hants (Worcester) 2001. BB 6-44 (11-116 match) v OU (Oxford) 1998. CC BB 5-125 v Middx (Southgate) 2000. LO HS 12 v Leics (Worcester) 2001 (CGT). LO BB 5-26 v Kent (Tunbridge W) 1999 (NL).

**SHERIYAR, A.** – *see* KENT.

**WESTON, W.P.C.** – *see* GLOUCESTERSHIRE.

D.N.Catterall, G.S.Kandola, S.R.Lampitt, D.B.Patel, P.R.Pollard, N.W.Round and K.R.Spiring left the staff having made no f-c appearances in 2002.

# WORCESTERSHIRE 2002

## RESULTS SUMMARY

|  | Place | Won | Lost | Tied | Drew | No Result |
|---|---|---|---|---|---|---|
| **County Championship** (2nd Division) | **4th** | 7 | 4 |  | 5 |  |
| **All First-Class Matches** |  | 8 | 4 |  | 6 |  |
| **C & G Trophy** | Quarter-Finalist |  |  |  |  |  |
| **Benson & Hedges Cup** | Semi-Finalist |  |  |  |  |  |
| **NU National League** (1st Division) | **2nd** | 11 | 3 |  | 2 |  |

## COUNTY CHAMPIONSHIP AVERAGES

### BATTING AND FIELDING

| Cap |  | M | I | NO | HS | Runs | Avge | 100 | 50 | Ct/St |
|---|---|---|---|---|---|---|---|---|---|---|
| 1986 | G.A.Hick | 16 | 28 | 4 | 315* | 1262 | 52.58 | 3 | 6 | 28 |
| 1994 | D.A.Leatherdale | 13 | 21 | 4 | 154 | 812 | 47.76 | 2 | 4 | 4 |
| 2002[C] | B.F.Smith | 16 | 28 | 3 | 129 | 1060 | 42.40 | 3 | 6 | 5 |
| 1986 | S.J.Rhodes | 14 | 20 | 5 | 124 | 627 | 41.80 | 1 | 2 | 36/3 |
| 1998 | V.S.Solanki | 14 | 23 | 3 | 153* | 832 | 41.60 | 2 | 4 | 18 |
| 2002[C] | S.D.Peters | 9 | 15 | – | 146 | 617 | 41.13 | 2 | 2 | 6 |
| 2002[C] | A.Singh | 16 | 29 | – | 187 | 1074 | 37.03 | 2 | 6 | 11 |
| 2001 | A.J.Bichel | 9 | 11 | 2 | 78* | 274 | 30.44 | – | 2 | 7 |
| 1995 | W.P.C.Weston | 7 | 13 | 2 | 82 | 311 | 28.27 | – | 3 | 6 |
| 2002[C] | G.J.Batty | 16 | 24 | 2 | 74 | 395 | 17.95 | – | 3 | 9 |
| 2002[C] | M.S.Mason | 6 | 8 | 2 | 50 | 107 | 17.83 | – | 1 | – |
| 2002[C] | Kabir Ali | 15 | 19 | 2 | 51* | 246 | 14.47 | – | 1 | 3 |
| 1997 | A.Sheriyar | 16 | 19 | 8 | 18 | 90 | 8.18 | – | – | 1 |

*Also batted:* A.A.Donald (1 match – 2002[C]) 5\*; S.Lee (2 – 2002[C]) 32, 48; C.G.Liptrot (1 – 2002[C]) 6, 16; D.J.Pipe (2 – 2002[C]) 26, 14, 12 (9 ct, 1 st); M.J.Rawnsley (3 – 2002[C]) 4, 9\*, 7 (2 ct).

### BOWLING

|  | O | M | R | W | Avge | Best | 5wI | 10wM |
|---|---|---|---|---|---|---|---|---|
| A.J.Bichel | 297 | 77 | 902 | 36 | 25.05 | 9-93 | 1 | 1 |
| M.S.Mason | 204.4 | 47 | 581 | 22 | 26.40 | 5-50 | 1 | – |
| Kabir Ali | 497.5 | 116 | 1594 | 60 | 26.56 | 5-32 | 4 | 1 |
| A.Sheriyar | 555.2 | 144 | 1715 | 57 | 30.08 | 6-71 | 4 | – |
| D.A.Leatherdale | 129.3 | 18 | 502 | 16 | 31.37 | 4-23 | – | – |
| G.J.Batty | 571.5 | 152 | 1614 | 51 | 31.64 | 6-71 | 3 | – |

*Also bowled:*
A.A.Donald 24 3 77 5 15.40 5-77 1 –
G.A.Hick 21-5-71-0; S.Lee 0.2-0-8-0; C.G.Liptrot 27-0-141-2; M.J.Rawnsley 80-27-232-2; B.F.Smith 7-0-32-0; V.S.Solanki 39-6-128-0.

The First-Class Averages (pp 121-135) give the records of Worcestershire's players in all first-class county matches (Worcestershire's other opponents being the Indians and Oxford UCCE).

2002[C] Awarded County Colours – a system which replaced capping in 2002.

# WORCESTERSHIRE RECORDS

## FIRST-CLASS CRICKET

| | | | | | | |
|---|---|---|---|---|---|---|
| **Highest Total** | For 670-7d | | v | Somerset | Worcester | 1995 |
| | V 701-4d | | by | Leics | Worcester | 1906 |
| **Lowest Total** | For 24 | | v | Yorkshire | Huddersfield | 1903 |
| | V 30 | | by | Hampshire | Worcester | 1903 |
| **Highest Innings** | For 405* | G.A.Hick | v | Somerset | Taunton | 1988 |
| | V 331* | J.D.B.Robertson | for | Middlesex | Worcester | 1949 |

### Highest Partnership for each Wicket

| | | | | | | |
|---|---|---|---|---|---|---|
| 1st | 309 | F.L.Bowley/H.K.Foster | v | Derbyshire | Derby | 1901 |
| 2nd | 300 | W.P.C.Weston/G.A.Hick | v | Indians | Worcester | 1996 |
| 3rd | 438* | G.A.Hick/T.M.Moody | v | Hampshire | Southampton | 1997 |
| 4th | 281 | J.A.Ormrod/Younis Ahmed | v | Notts | Nottingham | 1979 |
| 5th | 393 | E.G.Arnold/W.B.Burns | v | Warwicks | Birmingham | 1909 |
| 6th | 265 | G.A.Hick/S.J.Rhodes | v | Somerset | Taunton | 1988 |
| 7th | 256 | D.A.Leatherdale/S.J.Rhodes | v | Notts | Nottingham | 2002 |
| 8th | 184 | S.J.Rhodes/S.R.Lampitt | v | Derbyshire | Kidderminster | 1991 |
| 9th | 181 | J.A.Cuffe/R.D.Burrows | v | Glos | Worcester | 1907 |
| 10th | 119 | W.B.Burns/G.A.Wilson | v | Somerset | Worcester | 1906 |

| | | | | | | |
|---|---|---|---|---|---|---|
| **Best Bowling** | For | 9- 23 | C.F.Root | v | Lancashire | Worcester | 1931 |
| **(Innings)** | V | 10- 51 | J.Mercer | for | Glamorgan | Worcester | 1936 |
| **Best Bowling** | For | 15- 87 | A.J.Conway | v | Glos | Moreton-in-M | 1914 |
| **(Match)** | V | 17-212 | J.C.Clay | for | Glamorgan | Swansea | 1937 |

| | | | | |
|---|---|---|---|---|
| **Most Runs – Season** | 2654 | H.H.I.Gibbons | (av 52.03) | 1934 |
| **Most Runs – Career** | 34490 | D.Kenyon | (av 34.18) | 1946-67 |
| **Most 100s – Season** | 10 | G.M.Turner | | 1970 |
| | 10 | G.A.Hick | | 1988 |
| **Most 100s – Career** | 87 | G.A.Hick | | 1984-2001 |
| **Most Wkts – Season** | 207 | C.F.Root | (av 17.52) | 1925 |
| **Most Wkts – Career** | 2143 | R.T.D.Perks | (av 23.73) | 1930-55 |
| **Most Career W-K Dismissals** | 1015† | R.Booth | (868 ct/147 st) | 1946-70 |
| **Most Career Catches in the Field** | 412 | D.W.Richardson | | 1952-67 |

† *S.J.Rhodes (1985-2002) has made 986 dismissals (893 ct; 93 st)*

## LIMITED-OVERS CRICKET

| | | | | | | |
|---|---|---|---|---|---|---|
| **Highest Total** | CGT | 404-3 | | v | Devon | Worcester | 1987 |
| | BHC | 314-5 | | v | Lancashire | Manchester | 1980 |
| | NL | 307-4 | | v | Derbyshire | Worcester | 1975 |
| **Lowest Total** | CGT | 98 | | v | Durham | Chester-le-St | 1968 |
| | BHC | 70 | | v | Glos | Worcester | 2002 |
| | NL | 86 | | v | Yorkshire | Leeds | 1969 |
| **Highest Innings** | CGT | 180* | T.M.Moody | v | Surrey | The Oval | 1994 |
| | BHC | 143* | G.M.Turner | v | Warwicks | Birmingham | 1976 |
| | NL | 160 | T.M.Moody | v | Kent | Worcester | 1991 |
| **Best Bowling** | CGT | 7-19 | N.V.Radford | v | Beds | Bedford | 1991 |
| | BHC | 6- 8 | N.Gifford | v | Minor C (S) | High Wycombe | 1979 |
| | NL | 6-26 | A.P.Pridgeon | v | Surrey | Worcester | 1978 |

# YORKSHIRE

**Formation of Present Club**: 8 January 1863
**Substantial Reorganisation**: 10 December 1891
**Colours**: Dark Blue, Light Blue and Gold
**Badge**: White Rose
**County Championships (since 1890)**: (30) 1893, 1896, 1898, 1900, 1901, 1902, 1905, 1908, 1912, 1919, 1922, 1923, 1924, 1925, 1931, 1932, 1933, 1935, 1937, 1938, 1939, 1946, 1959, 1960, 1962, 1963, 1966, 1967, 1968, 2001
**Joint Champions**: (1) 1949
**Gillette/NatWest/C & G Trophy Winners**: (3) 1965, 1969, 2002
**Benson and Hedges Cup Winners**: (1) 1987
**National League (Div 1) Winners**: (0); best – 2nd 2000
**Sunday League Winners**: (1) 1983
**Match Awards**: CGT 45; BHC 80

**Chief Executive**: C.J.Graves, Headingley Cricket Ground, Leeds, LS6 3BU • Tel: 0113 278 7394 • Fax: 0113 278 4099 • Email: cricket@yorkshireccc.org.uk • Web: www.yorkshireccc.org.uk

**First XI Coaches**: K.Sharp and A.Sidebottom. **Captain** A.McGrath. **Vice-Captain**: no appointment. **Overseas Player**: M.T.G.Elliott. **2003 Beneficiary**: S.Oldham (testimonial). **Scorer**: J.T.Potter.

**BLAKEY, Richard** John (Rastrick GS), b Huddersfield 15 Jan 1967. 5'9". RHB, WK. Debut 1985; cap 1987; benefit 1998. YC 1987. **Tests**: 2 (1992-93); HS 6. **LOI**: 3 (1992 to 1992-93); HS 25 v P (Lord's) 1992 – on debut. Tours: SA 1991-92 (Y); WI 1986-87 (Y); I 1992-93; P 1990-91 (Eng A); SL 1990-91 (Eng A); Z 1989-90 (Eng A), 1995-96 (Y). 1000 runs (6); most – 1361 (1987). HS 221 Eng A v Z (Bulawayo) 1989-90. Y HS 204* v Glos (Leeds) 1987. BB 1-68. Awards: BHC 2. LO HS 130* v Kent (Scarborough) 1991 (SL).

**BRESNAN, Timothy** Thomas (Castleford HS and TC; Pontefract New C), b Pontefract 28 Feb 1985. 6'0". RHB, RMF. Awaiting f-c debut. LO HS 22 v Warwks (Leeds) 2002 (NL). BB 2-27 v Leics (Leicester) 2001 (NL); 2-27 v Kent (Canterbury) 2002 (NL) and 2-27 v Durham (Chester-le-St) 2002 (NL).

**CRAVEN, Victor** John (Harrogate GS), b Harrogate 31 Jul 1980. 6'0". LHB, RM. Debut 2000. HS 72 v Hants (Southampton) 2002. BB 1-25. LO HS 59 v Durham (Leeds) 2002 (NL). BB 1-21 (NL).

**DAWSON, Richard** Kevin James (Batley GS; Exeter U), b Doncaster 4 Aug 1980. 6'3". RHB, OB. British U 2000. Yorkshire debut 2001. Devon 1999-2000. **Tests**: 7 (2000-02 to 2002-03); HS 19* v A (perth) 2002-03; BB 4-134 v I (Chandigarh) 2001-02 – on debut. Tours: A 2002-03; NZ 2001-02; I 2001-02. HS 87 v Kent (Canterbury) 2002. BB 6-82 v Glam (Scarborough) 2001. LO HS 41 v Leics (Scarborough) 2002 (NL). LO BB 4-13 v Derbys (Derby) 2002 (BHC).

**ELLIOTT, Matthew** Thomas Gray (Kyabram Secondary C; La Trobe U), b Chelsea, Victoria, Australia 28 Sep 1971. 6'3". LHB, LM/SLC. Victoria 1992-93 to date. Glamorgan 2000; cap 2000. Yorkshire debut 2002. *Wisden* 1997. **Tests** (A): 20 (1996-97 to 1998-99); HS 199 v E (Leeds) 1997. **LOI** (A): 1 (1997); HS 1 v E (Lord's) 1997. Tours (A): E 1995 (Young A), 1997; SA 1996-97; WI 1998-99. 1000 runs (2+4); most – 1233 (1995-96). HS 203 Vic v Tasmania (Melbourne) 1995-96. UK HS 199 (*see Tests*). Y HS 127 v Warwks (Birmingham) 2002. BB 1-3 (Vic). Y BB 1-64. Awards: CGT 2. LO HS 156 v Dorset (Bournemouth) 2000 (NWT).

**FELLOWS, Gary** Matthew (N Halifax GS), b Halifax 30 Jul 1978. 5'9". RHB, RM. Matabeleland 1996-97. Yorkshire debut 1998. HS 109 v Lancs (Manchester) 2002. BB 3-23 v Essex (Chelmsford) 2001. Award: CGT 1. LO HS 80 * v Surrey (Leeds) 2001 (CGT). LO BB 4-19 v Durham (Leeds) 2002 (NL).

**GOUGH, Darren** (Priory CS, Lundwood), b Barnsley 18 Sep 1970. 5'11". RHB, RF. Debut 1989; cap 1993; benefit 2001. *Wisden* 1998. **ECB contracts 2000, 2001, 2002.** Tests: 56 (1994 to 2001); HS 65 v NZ (Manchester) 1994 – on debut; BB 6-42 v SA (Leeds) 1998; hat-trick v A (Sydney) 1998-99 – first for E v A since 1899. **LOI**: 111 (1994 to 2002); HS 45 v A (Melbourne) 1994-95; BB 5-44 v Z (Sydney) 1994-95 and 5-44 v A (Lord's) 1997. Took wickets with his sixth balls in both Tests and LOIs. Tours: A 1994-95, 1998-99; SA 1991-92 (Y), 1992-93 (Y), 1993-94 (Eng A), 1995-96, 1999-00; NZ 1996-97; P 2000-01; SL 2000-01; Z 1996-97. HS 121 v Warwks (Leeds) 1996. 50 wkts (5); most – 67 (1996). BB 7-28 (10-80 match) v Lancs (Leeds) 1995 (not CC). CC BB 7-42 (10-96 match) v Somerset (Taunton) 1993. 2 hat-tricks (1995, 1998-99); took 4 wkts in 5 balls v Kent (Leeds) 1995. Awards: CGT 2; BHC 1. LO HS 72* v Leics (Leicester) 1991 (SL). LO BB 7-27 v Ire (Leeds) 1997 (NWT).

**GRAY, Andrew** Kenneth Donovan, b Armadale, W Australia 19 May 1974. RHB, OB. Debut 2001. HS 74* v Leics (Scarborough) 2002. BB 4-128 v Surrey (Oval) 2001. LO HS 19* (NL). LO BB 4-34 v Kent (Leeds) 2002 (NL).

**GUY, Simon** Mark (Wickersley CS), b Rotherham 17 Nov 1978. 5'7". RHB, WK. Debut 2000. No 1st appearances 2002. HS 42 v Somerset (Taunton) 2000. LO HS 13 v WI A (Leeds) 2002.

**HAMILTON, Gavin** Mark (Hurstmere SS, Kent), b Broxburn, Scotland 16 Sep 1974. 6'1". LHB, RFM. Scotland 1993-94. Yorkshire debut 1994; cap 1998. **Tests**: 1 (1999-00); HS 0 v SA (Jo'burg) 1999-00. **LOI** (Scot): 5 (1999); HS 76 and BB 2-36 v P (Chester-le-St) 1999. Tours: SA 1999-00; Z 1995-96 (Y). HS 125 v Hants (Leeds) 2000. 50 wkts (1): 59 (1998). BB 7-50 (11-72 match) v Surrey (Leeds) 1998. Match double (79, 70; 5-69, 5-43) v Glam (Cardiff) 1998 – first instance for Yorks since 1964 (R.Illingworth). Award: BHC 1. LO HS 76 (*see LOI*). LO BB 5-16 v Hants (Leeds) 1998 (SL).

**HOGGARD, Matthew** James (Grangefield S, Pudsey), b Leeds 31 Dec 1976. 6'2". RHB, RFM. Debut 1996; cap 2000. Free State 1998-99 to 1999-00. **ECB contracts 2001, 2002, 2003. Tests**: 18 (2000 to 2002-03); HS 32 v I (Nottingham) 2002; BB 7-63 v NZ (Christchurch) 2001-02. **LOI**: 20 (2001-02 to 2002-03); HS 5; BB 5-49 v Z (Harare) 2001-02. Tours: A 2002-03; NZ 2001-02; I 2001-02; P 2000-01; SL 2000-01. HS 32 (*see Tests*). Y HS 21* v Hants (Leeds) 2002. 50 wkts (1): 50 (2000). BB 7-63 (*see Tests*). Y BB 6-51 v Essex (Scarborough) 2001. LO HS 7* (BHC). LO BB 5-28 v Leics (Leicester) 2000 (NL).

**KIRBY, Steven** Paul (Elton HS; Bury C), b Ainsworth, nr Bolton, Lancs 4 Oct 1977. 6'3½". RHB, RF. Leicestershire staff 1998 – no f-c appearances. Debut 2001, sub for M.J.Hoggard (England duty) taking 7-50 v Kent (Leeds). HS 57 v Hants (Leeds) 2002. BB 7-50 (*see above*). LO HS 4* (NL). LO BB 3-35 v Warwks (Leeds) 2001 (NL).

**LUMB, Michael** John (St Stithians C, Jo'burg), b Johannesburg, SA 12 Feb 1980. Son of R.G.Lumb (Yorkshire 1970-84); nephew of A.J.S.Smith (SAU and Natal 1971-72 to 1983-84). 6'0". LHB, RM. Debut 2000. ECB qualified and CC debut 2001. HS 124 v Surrey (Guildford) 2002. BB 2-10 v Kent (Canterbury) 2001. LO HS 73 v Warwks (Birmingham) 2002 (NL).

**McGRATH, Anthony** (Yorkshire Martyrs Collegiate S), b Bradford 6 Oct 1975. 6'2". RHB, RM. Debut 1995; cap 1999; captain 2003. Tours (Eng A): A 1996-97; P 1995-96; Z 1995-96 (Y). HS 165 v Lancs (Leeds) 2002. BB 4-49 v Hants (Southampton) 2002. Awards: CGT 2; BHC 1. LO HS 109* v Minor C (Leeds) 1997 (BHC). LO BB 3-39 v Kent (Leeds) 2002 (NL).

**RICHARDSON, Scott** Andrew (Hulme GS, Oldham; Manchester GS), b Oldham, Lancs 5 Sep 1977. 6'2". RHB, RM. Debut 2000. HS 69 v Kent (Leeds) 2001. LO HS 7 v WI A (Leeds) 2002.

**SIDEBOTTOM, Ryan** Jay (King James's GS, Almondbury), b Huddersfield 15 Jan 1978. Son of A.Sidebottom (Yorks, OFS and England 1973-91). 6'3''. LHB, LFM. Debut 1997; cap 2000. **Tests**: 1 (2001); HS 4 v P (Lord's) 2001; **LOI**: 2 (2001-02); HS 2*; BB 1-42 (twice). Tour (Eng A): WI 2000-01. HS 54 v Glam (Cardiff) 1998. BB 6-16 (11-43 match) v Kent (Leeds) 2000. LO HS 30* v Glam (Leeds) 2002 (NL). LO BB 6-40 v Glam (Cardiff) 1998 (SL).

**SILVERWOOD, Christopher** Eric Wilfred (Garforth CS), b Pontefract 5 Mar 1975. 6'1''. RHB, RFM. Debut 1993; cap 1996. YC 1996. **Tests**: 6 (1996-97 to 2002-03); HS 10 v A (Perth) 2002-03; BB 5-91 v SA (Cape Town) 1999-00. **LOI**: 7 (1996-97 to 2001-02); HS 12 v NZ (Auckland) 1996-97; BB 3-43 v Z (Bulawayo) 2001-02. Tours: A 2002-03 (part); SA 1999-00 (part); WI 1997-98, 2000-01 (Eng A); NZ 1996-97; Z 1995-96 (Y), 1996-97. HS 70 v Essex (Chelmsford) 2001. 50 wkts (2); most – 59 (1999). BB 7-93 (12-148 match) v Kent (Leeds) 1997. Awards: CGT 1; BHC 2. LO HS 61 v Northants (Northampton) 2002 (CGT). LO BB 5-28 v Scot (Leeds) 1996 (BHC).

**TAYLOR, Christopher** Robert (Benton Park HS, Rawdon), b Leeds 21 Feb 1981. 6'4''. RHB, RMF. Debut 2001. HS 52* v Surrey (Leeds) 2002.

**THORNICROFT, Nicholas** David, b York 23 Jan 1985. RHB, RMF. Debut 2002. HS 4* and BB 2-51 v Lancs (Manchester) 2002 – on debut. LO HS 0* (NL). LO BB 2-35 v Warwks (Birmingham) 2002 (NL).

**VAUGHAN, Michael** Paul (Silverdale CS, Sheffield), b Manchester, Lancs 29 Oct 1974. 6'2''. RHB, OB. Debut 1993; cap 1995. **ECB contracts 2000, 2001, 2002, 2003**. **Tests**: 28 (1999-00 to 2002-03); HS 197 and BB 2-71 v I (Nottingham) 2002. Scored Eng record 1,481 runs (avge 61.70) with six hundreds in 2002. **LOI**: 26 (2000-01 to 2002-03); HS 63 v I (Cuttack) 2001-02; BB 4-22 v SL (Manchester) 2002. Tours (C=captain): A 1996-97 (Eng A), 2002-03; SA 1998-99C (Eng A), 1999-00; WI 1997-98, 1994-95 (Eng A), 2001-02; P 2000-01; SL 2000-01; Z 1995-96 (Y), 1998-99C (Eng A). 1000 runs (4); most – 1244 (1995). HS 197 (see Tests). Y HS 183 v Glam (Cardiff) 1996. BB 4-39 v OU (Oxford) 1994. CC BB 4-47 v Somerset (Leeds) 2001. Awards: CGT 2; BHC 2. LO HS 125* v Somerset (Taunton) 2001 (BHC). LO BB 4-22 (see LOI).

**WHITE, Craig** (Flora Hill HS, Bendigo, Australia; Bendigo HS), b Morley 16 Dec 1969. 6'0''. RHB, RFM. Debut 1990; cap 1993; benefit 2002. Victoria 1990-91 (2 matches). **ECB contracts 2000, 2001**. **Tests**: 30 (1994 to 2002-03); HS 121 v I (Ahmedabad) 2001-02; BB 5-32 v WI (Oval) 2000. **LOI**: 51 (1994-95 to 2002-03); HS 57* v A (Melbourne) 2002-03; BB 5-21 v Z (Bulawayo) 1999-00. Tours: A 1994-95, 1996-97 (Eng A), 2002-03; SA 1991-92 (Y), 1992-93 (Y); NZ 1996-97, 2001-02; I 2001-02; P 1995-96 (Eng A), 2000-01; SL 2000-01; Z 1996-97 (part). HS 186 v Lancs (Manchester) 2001. BB 8-55 v Glos (Gloucester) 1998 – inc hat-trick. Hat-trick 1998. Awards: CGT 4; BHC 4. LO HS 148 v Leics (Leicester) 1997 (SL). LO BB 5-19 v Somerset (Scarborough) 2002 (NL).

**WOOD, Matthew** James (Shelley HS & SFC), b Huddersfield 6 Apr 1977. 5'9''. RHB, OB. Debut 1997; cap 2001. 1000 runs (2): most – 1080 (1998). HS 200* v Warwks (Leeds) 1998. Award: BHC 1. LO HS 115* v Derbys (Derby) 2002 (BHC).

## RELEASED/RETIRED
(Having made a first-class County appearance in 2002)

**ELSTUB, Christopher** John (Whitcliffe Mount S and SFC; Leeds Metropolitan U), b Dewsbury 3 Feb 1981. 5'11''. RHB, RMF. Yorkshire 2000-02. British U 2001. HS 18* v Sussex (Arundel) 2002. BB 3-37 v WI (Leeds) 2000. CC BB 2-40 v Lancs (Leeds) 2000. LO HS 4* (NL). LO BB 4-25 v Surrey (Leeds) 2001 (NL).

**KATICH, S.M.** – see HAMPSHIRE.

**LEHMANN, Darren** Scott (Gawler HS), b Gawler, South Australia 5 Feb 1970. 5'10. LHB, SLA. South Australia 1987-88 to 1989-90, 1993-94 to date; captain 1998-99 to date. Victoria 1990-91 to 1992-93. Yorkshire 1997-98, 2000, 2002; cap 1997; captain 2002. *Wisden* 2000. Tests (A): 8 (1997-98 to 2002-03); HS 98 v P (Rawalpindi) 1998-99; BB 1-6. LOI (A): 95 (1996-97 to 2002-03); HS 119 v SL (Perth) 2002-03; BB 3-32 v E (Sydney) 2002-03. Tours (A): E 1991 (Vic); SA 2001-02; WI 2003; I 1997-98; P 1998-99. 1000 runs (4+5); most – 1575 (1997). HS 255 S Aus v Queensland (Adelaide) 1996-97. Y HS 252 v Lancs (Leeds) 2001. BB 4-42 v Kent (Maidstone) 1998. Awards: CGT 1; BHC 5. LO HS 191 v Notts (Scarborough) 2001 (NL). LO BB 4-26 v Devon (Exmouth) 2002 (CGT).

**WIGLEY, D.H.** – *see WORCESTERSHIRE*.

C.T.Brice, J.L.Sadler (*see LEICESTERSHIRE*) and R.A.Stead left the staff having made no f-c appearances in 2002.

---

**WARWICKSHIRE RELEASED/RETIRED** (continued from p 96)
(Having made a first-class County appearance in 2002)

**ALLEN, Alexander** Philip Wortley, b Solihull 13 Oct 1984. RHB, WK. Warwickshire 2002 – no CC appearances. HS 18* v WI A (Birmingham) 2002. LO HS 10 Warwks CB v Herefords (Coventry) 2002 (CGT).

**POLLOCK, Shaun** Maclean (Northwood HS; Durban U), b Port Elizabeth, SA 16 Jul 1973. Son of P.M.Pollock (EP and SA 1958-59 to 1971-72); nephew of R.G.Pollock (EP, Transvaal and SA 1960-61 to 1986-87). 6'3". RHB, RFM. Natal/KZ-Natal 1991-92 to date. Warwickshire 1996 and 2002; cap 1996. Tests (SA): 68 (1995-96 to 2002-03, 26 as captain); HS 111 v SL (Pretoria) 2000-01; BB 7-87 v A (Adelaide) 1997-98. LOI (SA): 186 (1995-96 to 2002-03, 90 as captain); HS 75 v Z (Jo'burg) 1996-97; BB 6-35 v WI (E London) 1998-99. Tours (SA) (C=captain): E 1998; A 1997-98, 2001-02C; WI 2000-01C; NZ 1998-99; I 1999-00; P 1997-98; SL 2000-01C; Z 1999-00, 2001-02C. HS 75 v Z (Jo'burg) 1996-97; BB 6-35 v WI (E London) 1998-99. HS 150* v Glam (Birmingham) 1996. BB 7-33 Natal v Border (E London) 1995-96. Wa BB 6-56 v Middx (Lord's) 2002. Awards: CGT 1; BHC 2. LO HS 111* v Worcs (Worcester) 2002 (NL). LO BB 6-21 BB 6-21 v Leics (Birmingham) 1996 (BHC) – inc 4 wkts in 4 balls on Wa debut.

D.W.Fleming and E.J.Wilson the staff having made no f-c appearances in 2002.

# SCORING OF EXTRAS 2003

The penalty for wides is now **one** run plus other runs scored in all ECB matches. For the past three seasons two runs were awarded for wides in the County and Second XI Championships. The new 20-overs Cup will carry the same penalties as the two surviving county limited-overs competitions.

| COMPETITION | NO-BALL PENALTY | WIDE PENALTY |
|---|---|---|
| Test Matches<br>Limited-Overs Internationals | 1 + other runs scored | 1 + other runs scored |
| County Championship<br>Second XI Championship | 2 + other runs scored | 2 + other runs scored |
| Tourist Matches (First-Class)<br>Tourist Matches (Limited-Overs) | 2 + other runs scored | 1 + other runs scored |
| C & G Trophy<br>National League<br>Twenty 20 Cup | 2 + other runs scored<br>+ for foot fault free hit<br>next ball | 1 + other runs scored |

# YORKSHIRE 2002

## RESULTS SUMMARY

| | Place | Won | Lost | Tied | Drew | No Result |
|---|---|---|---|---|---|---|
| **County Championship** (1st Division) | 9th | 2 | 8 | | 6 | |
| **All First-Class Matches** | | 2 | 8 | | 6 | |
| **C & G Trophy** | Winners | | | | | |
| **Benson & Hedges Cup** | Quarter-Finalist | | | | | |
| **NU National League** (1st Division) | 4th | 8 | 7 | | | 1 |

## COUNTY CHAMPIONSHIP AVERAGES
### BATTING AND FIELDING

| Cap | | M | I | NO | HS | Runs | Avge | 100 | 50 | Ct/St |
|---|---|---|---|---|---|---|---|---|---|---|
| 1997 | D.S.Lehmann | 10 | 18 | 1 | 216 | 1136 | 66.82 | 3 | 7 | 5 |
| | M.T.G.Elliott | 5 | 10 | 1 | 127 | 487 | 54.11 | 1 | 4 | 7 |
| 1987 | R.J.Blakey | 16 | 29 | 7 | 103 | 1041 | 47.31 | 1 | 8 | 29/1 |
| | A.K.D.Gray | 4 | 6 | 1 | 74* | 193 | 38.60 | — | 1 | — |
| 1993 | C.White | 11 | 21 | — | 161 | 794 | 37.80 | 2 | 5 | 5 |
| 1999 | A.McGrath | 14 | 26 | 1 | 165 | 803 | 32.12 | 1 | 3 | 7 |
| | G.M.Fellows | 10 | 18 | — | 109 | 493 | 27.38 | 1 | 1 | 9 |
| | M.J.Lumb | 16 | 30 | 1 | 124 | 777 | 26.79 | 1 | 4 | 8 |
| | V.J.Craven | 11 | 21 | 2 | 72 | 439 | 23.10 | — | 3 | 8 |
| | R.K.J.Dawson | 14 | 23 | 1 | 87 | 496 | 22.54 | — | 2 | 1 |
| | C.R.Taylor | 5 | 9 | 1 | 52* | 150 | 18.75 | — | 2 | 4 |
| 1996 | C.E.W.Silverwood | 12 | 19 | 2 | 44* | 283 | 16.64 | — | — | 3 |
| 2001 | M.J.Wood | 9 | 17 | — | 43 | 201 | 11.82 | — | — | 12 |
| | S.A.Richardson | 2 | 4 | — | 29 | 45 | 11.25 | — | — | 2 |
| | S.P.Kirby | 10 | 17 | 3 | 57 | 141 | 10.07 | — | 1 | — |
| 2000 | R.J.Sidebottom | 13 | 21 | 7 | 28 | 135 | 9.64 | — | — | 4 |
| 1998 | G.M.Hamilton | 2 | 4 | — | 11 | 23 | 5.75 | — | — | — |
| | N.D.Thornicroft | 3 | 6 | 3 | 4* | 9 | 3.00 | — | — | — |

*Also played:* C.J.Elstub (2 matches) 0*, 18*, 4* (1 ct); D.Gough (1 – cap 1993) did not bat; M.J.Hoggard (2 – cap 2000) 5, 2, 21*; S.M.Katich (1) 21, 16 (1 ct); M.P.Vaughan (2 – cap 1995) 3, 19, 54; D.H.Wigley (1) 15, 4*.

### BOWLING

| | O | M | R | W | Avge | Best | 5wI | 10wM |
|---|---|---|---|---|---|---|---|---|
| A.McGrath | 174.3 | 38 | 498 | 18 | 27.66 | 4- 49 | — | — |
| R.J.Sidebottom | 380.5 | 85 | 1190 | 41 | 29.02 | 5- 60 | 1 | — |
| C.E.W.Silverwood | 306.1 | 69 | 985 | 30 | 32.83 | 4- 28 | — | — |
| S.P.Kirby | 331.1 | 68 | 1262 | 37 | 34.10 | 5-129 | 1 | — |
| R.K.J.Dawson | 484.2 | 123 | 1536 | 39 | 39.38 | 5- 42 | 2 | — |
| C.White | 145.1 | 26 | 456 | 10 | 45.60 | 4- 49 | — | — |

*Also bowled:*

| | | | | | | | | |
|---|---|---|---|---|---|---|---|---|
| M.J.Hoggard | 71 | 14 | 268 | 8 | 33.50 | 4- 93 | — | — |
| D.S.Lehmann | 133.2 | 32 | 346 | 9 | 38.44 | 3- 40 | — | — |
| G.M.Fellows | 73.5 | 9 | 315 | 8 | 39.37 | 3- 90 | — | — |
| A.K.D.Gray | 97 | 17 | 297 | 5 | 59.40 | 3- 62 | — | — |

V.J.Craven 15-3-56-1; M.T.G.Elliott 16-1-77-1; C.J.Elstub 41-7-181-1; D.Gough 19-3-85-2; G.M.Hamilton 12-2-65-1; S.M.Katich 2-0-25-0; M.J.Lumb 3-0-16-0; N.D.Thornicroft 61.1-14-248-4; M.P.Vaughan 3.2-0-21-0; D.H.Wigley 20.4-2-116-1.

Yorkshire played no first-class fixtures outside the County Championship in 2002. The First-Class Averages (pp 121-135) give the records of Yorkshire players in all first-class county matches, with the exception of R.K.J.Dawson, M.J.Hoggard, M.P.Vaughan and C.White whose full county figures are as above.

# YORKSHIRE RECORDS

## FIRST-CLASS CRICKET

| | | | | | | |
|---|---|---|---|---|---|---|
| **Highest Total** | For 887 | | v | Warwicks | Birmingham | 1896 |
| | V 681-7d | | by | Leics | Bradford | 1896 |
| **Lowest Total** | For 23 | | v | Hampshire | Middlesbrough | 1965 |
| | V 13 | | by | Notts | Nottingham | 1901 |
| **Highest Innings** | For 341 | G.H.Hirst | v | Leics | Leicester | 1905 |
| | V 318* | W.G.Grace | for | Glos | Cheltenham | 1876 |

### Highest Partnership for each Wicket

| | | | | | | |
|---|---|---|---|---|---|---|
| 1st | 555 | P.Holmes/H.Sutcliffe | v | Essex | Leyton | 1932 |
| 2nd | 346 | W.Barber/M.Leyland | v | Middlesex | Sheffield | 1932 |
| 3rd | 323* | H.Sutcliffe/M.Leyland | v | Glamorgan | Huddersfield | 1928 |
| 4th | 312 | D.Denton/G.H.Hirst | v | Hampshire | Southampton | 1914 |
| 5th | 340 | E.Wainwright/G.H.Hirst | v | Surrey | The Oval | 1899 |
| 6th | 276 | M.Leyland/E.Robinson | v | Glamorgan | Swansea | 1926 |
| 7th | 254 | W.Rhodes/D.C.F.Burton | v | Hampshire | Dewsbury | 1919 |
| 8th | 292 | R.Peel/Lord Hawke | v | Warwicks | Birmingham | 1896 |
| 9th | 192 | G.H.Hirst/S.Haigh | v | Surrey | Bradford | 1898 |
| 10th | 149 | G.Boycott/G.B.Stevenson | v | Warwicks | Birmingham | 1982 |

| | | | | | | |
|---|---|---|---|---|---|---|
| **Best Bowling** | For | 10-10 | H.Verity | v | Notts | Leeds | 1932 |
| **(Innings)** | V | 10-37 | C.V.Grimmett | for | Australians | Sheffield | 1930 |
| **Best Bowling** | For | 17-91 | H.Verity | v | Essex | Leyton | 1933 |
| **(Match)** | V | 17-91 | H.Dean | for | Lancashire | Liverpool | 1913 |

| | | | | | |
|---|---|---|---|---|---|
| **Most Runs – Season** | 2883 | H.Sutcliffe | (av 80.08) | | 1932 |
| **Most Runs – Career** | 38561 | H.Sutcliffe | (av 50.20) | | 1919-45 |
| **Most 100s – Season** | 12 | H.Sutcliffe | | | 1932 |
| **Most 100s – Career** | 112 | H.Sutcliffe | | | 1919-45 |
| **Most Wkts – Season** | 240 | W.Rhodes | (av 12.72) | | 1900 |
| **Most Wkts – Career** | 3608 | W.Rhodes | (av 16.00) | | 1898-1930 |
| **Most Career W-K Dismissals** | 1186 | D.Hunter | (863 ct/323 st) | | 1888-1909 |
| **Most Career Catches in the Field** | 665 | J.Tunnicliffe | | | 1891-1907 |

## LIMITED-OVERS CRICKET

| | | | | | | |
|---|---|---|---|---|---|---|
| **Highest Total** | CGT | 345-5 | | v | Notts | Leeds | 1996 |
| | BHC | 317-5 | | v | Scotland | Leeds | 1986 |
| | NL | 352-6 | | v | Notts | Scarborough | 2001 |
| **Lowest Total** | CGT | 76 | | v | Surrey | Harrogate | 1970 |
| | BHC | 81 | | v | Lancs | Leeds | 2002 |
| | NL | 56 | | v | Warwicks | Birmingham | 1995 |
| **Highest Innings** | CGT | 146 | G.Boycott | v | Surrey | Lord's | 1965 |
| | BHC | 142 | G.Boycott | v | Worcs | Worcester | 1980 |
| | NL | 191 | D.S.Lehmann | v | Notts | Scarborough | 2001 |
| **Best Bowling** | CGT | 7-27 | D.Gough | v | Ireland | Leeds | 1997 |
| | BHC | 6-27 | A.G.Nicholson | v | Minor C (N) | Middlesbrough | 1972 |
| | NL | 7-15 | R.A.Hutton | v | Worcs | Leeds | 1969 |

# FIRST-CLASS UMPIRES 2003

† New Appointment

**BENSON, Mark** Richard (Sutton Valence S), b Shoreham, Sussex 6 Jul 1958. LHB, OB. Kent 1980-95; cap 1981; captain 1991-96 (did not play in 1996); benefit 1991. **Tests:** 1 (1986); HS 30 v I (Birmingham) 1986. **LOI:** 1 (1986; HS 24). 1000 runs (11); most – 1725 (1987). HS 257 K v Hants (Southampton) 1991. BB 2-55 K v Surrey (Dartford) 1986. F-c career: 292 matches; 18387 runs @ 40.23, 48 hundreds; 5 wickets @ 98.60; 140 ct. Appointed 2000.

**BURGESS, Graham** Iefvion (Millfield S), b Glastonbury, Somerset 5 May 1943. RHB, RM. Somerset 1966-79; cap 1968; testimonial 1977. HS 129 Sm v Glos (Taunton) 1973. BB 7-43 (13-75 match) Sm v OU (Oxford) 1975. F-c career: 252 matches; 7129 runs @ 18.90, 2 hundreds; 474 wickets @ 28.57. Appointed 1991.

**CLARKSON, Anthony** (Harrogate GS), b Killinghall, Harrogate, Yorks 5 Sep 1939. RHB, OB. Yorkshire 1963. Somerset 1966-71; cap 1968. Devon. 1000 runs (2); most – 1246 (1970). HS 131 Sm v Northants (Northampton) 1969. BB 3-51 Sm v Essex (Yeovil) 1967. F-c career: 110 matches; 4458 runs @ 25.18, 2 hundreds; 13 wickets @ 28.23. Appointed 1996.

**CONSTANT, David** John, b Bradford-on-Avon, Wilts 9 Nov 1941. LHB, SLA. Kent 1961-63. Leicestershire 1965-68. HS 80 Le v Glos (Bristol) 1966. BB 1-28. F-c career: 61 matches; 1517 runs @ 19.20; 1 wicket @ 36.00. Appointed 1969. Umpired 36 Tests (1971 to 1988) and 33 LOI (1972 to 2001). Represented Gloucestershire at bowls 1984-86.

**COWLEY, Nigel** Geoffrey (Dutchy Manor SS, Mere), b Shaftesbury, Dorset 1 Mar 1953. RHB, OB. Dorset 1972. Hampshire 1974-89; cap 1978; benefit 1988. Glamorgan 1990. 1000 runs (1): 1042 (1984). HS 109* H v Somerset (Taunton) 1977. BB 6-48 H v Leics (Southampton) 1982. F-c career: 271 matches; 7309 runs @ 23.35, 2 hundreds; 437 wickets @ 34.04. Appointed 2000.

**DUDLESTON, Barry** (Stockport S), b Bebington, Cheshire 16 Jul 1945. RHB, SLA. Leicestershire 1966-80; cap 1969; benefit 1980. Gloucestershire 1981-83. Rhodesia 1976-77 to 1979-80. 1000 runs (8); most – 1374 (1970). HS 202 Le v Derbys (Leicester) 1979. BB 4-6 Le v Surrey (Leicester) 1972. F-c career: 295 matches; 14747 runs @ 32.48, 32 hundreds; 47 wickets @ 29.04. Appointed 1984. Umpired 2 Tests (1991 to 1992) and 4 LOI (1992 to 2001).

**EVANS, Jeffery** Howard, b Llanelli, Carms 7 Aug 1954. No f-c appearances. Appointed 2001.

**GOULD, Ian** James (Westgate SS, Slough), b Taplow, Bucks 19 Aug 1957. LHB, WK. Middlesex 1975 to 1980-81, 1996; cap 1977. Auckland 1979-80. Sussex 1981-90; cap 1981; captain 1987; benefit 1990. MCC YC. **LOI:** 18 (1982-83 to 1983; HS 42). Tours: A 1982-83; P 1980-81 (Int); Z 1980-81 (M). HS 128 M v Worcs (Worcester) 1978. BB 3-10 Sx v Surrey (Oval) 1989. Middlesex coach 1991-2000. Reappeared in one match (v OU) 1996. F-c career: 298 matches; 8756 runs @ 26.05, 4 hundreds; 7 wickets @ 52.14; 603 dismissals (536 ct, 67 st). Appointed 2002.

**HAMPSHIRE, John** Harry (Oakwood THS, Rotherham), b Thurnscoe, Yorks 10 Feb 1941. RHB, LB. Son of J. (Yorks 1937); brother of A.W. (Yorks 1975). Yorkshire 1961-81; cap 1963; benefit 1976; captain 1979-80. Leicestershire 1980-81 (tour). Derbyshire 1982-84; cap 1982. Tasmania 1967-68 to 1978-79. **Tests:** 8 (1969 to 1975); 403 runs @ 26.86, HS 107 v WI (Lord's) 1969 on debut (only England player to score hundred at Lord's on Test debut). Tours: A 1970-71; SA 1972-73 (DHR), 1974-75 (DHR); WI 1964-65 (Cav); NZ 1970-71; P 1967-68 (Cwlth XI); SL 1969-70; Z 1980-81 (Le XI). 1000 runs (15); most – 1596 (1978). HS 183* H v Sussex (Hove) 1971. BB 7-52 Y v Glam (Cardiff) 1963. F-c career: 577 matches; 28059 runs @ 34.55, 43 hundreds; 30 wickets @ 54.56; 445 ct. Appointed 1985. Umpired 21 Tests (1989 to 2001-02) and 20 LOI (1989 to 2001). International Panel 1999 to 2001-02.

**HARRIS, Michael** John (*'Pasty'*) (Gerrans S, nr Truro), b St Just-in-Roseland, Cornwall 25 May 1944. RHB, LB, WK. Middlesex 1964-68; cap 1967. Nottinghamshire 1969-82; cap 1970; benefit 1977. E Province 1971-72. Wellington 1975-76. 1000 runs (11); most – 2238 (1971). Equalled Notts record with 9 hundreds in 1971. HS 201* Nt v Glam (Nottingham) 1973. BB 4-16 Nt v Warwks (Nottingham) 1969. F-c career: 344 matches; 19196 runs @ 36.70, 41 hundreds; 79 wickets @ 43.78; 302 dismissals (288 ct, 14 st). Appointed 1998.

**†HARTLEY, Peter** John (Greenhead GS; Bradford C), b Keighley, Yorks 18 Apr 1960. RHB, RMF. Warwickshire 1982. Yorkshire 1985-97; cap 1987; benefit 1996. Hampshire 1998-2000; cap 1998. Tours (Y): SA 1991-92; WI 1986-87; Z 1995-96. HS 127* Y v Lancs (Manchester) 1988. 50 wkts (7); most – 81 (1995). BB 9-41 (inc hat-trick, 4 wkts in 5 balls and 5 in 9; 11-68 match) Y v Derbys (Chesterfield) 1995. Hat-trick 1995. F-c career: 232 matches; 4321 runs @ 19.91, 2 hundreds; 683 wickets @ 30.21. Appointed 2003.

**HOLDER, John** Wakefield (Combermere S), b St George, Barbados 19 Mar 1945. RHB, RFM. Hampshire 1968-72. HS 33 H v Sussex (Hove) 1971. BB 7-79 H v Glos (Gloucester) 1972. Hat-trick 1972. F-c career: 47 matches; 374 runs @ 10.68; 139 wickets @ 24.56. Appointed 1983. Umpired 11 Tests (1988 to 2001) and 19 LOI (1988 to 2001).

**HOLDER, Vanburn** Alonza (Richmond SM), b Deans Village, St Michael, Barbados 8 Oct 1945. RHB, RFM. Barbados 1966-67 to 1977-78. Worcestershire 1968-80; cap 1970; benefit 1979. Shropshire 1981. **Tests** (WI): 40 (1969 to 1978-79); 682 runs @ 14.20, HS 42 v NZ (P-o-S) 1971-72; 109 wkts @ 33.27, BB 6-28 v A (P-o-S) 1977-78. **LOI** (WI): 12. Tours (WI): E 1969, 1973, 1976; A 1975-76; I 1974-75, 1978-79; P 1973-74 (RW), 1974-75; SL 1974-75, 1978-79. HS 122 Barbados v Trinidad (Bridgetown) 1973-74. BB 7-40 Wo v Glam (Cardiff) 1974. F-c career: 311 matches; 3559 runs @ 13.03, 1 hundred; 947 wickets @ 24.48. Appointed 1992.

**JESTY, Trevor** Edward (Privet County SS, Gosport), b Gosport, Hants 2 Jun 1948. RHB, RM. Hampshire 1966-84; cap 1971; benefit 1982. Surrey 1985-87; cap 1985; captain 1985. Lancashire 1987-88 to 1991; cap 1989. Border 1973-74. GW 1974-75 to 1980-81. Canterbury 1979-80. *Wisden* 1982. **LOI:** 10. Tours: WI 1987-88 (La), 1982-83 (Int); Z 1988-89 (La). 1000 runs (10); most – 1645 (1982). HS 248 H v CU (Cambridge) 1984. Scored 122* La v OU (Oxford) 1991 in his final f-c innings. 50 wkts (2); most – 52 (1981). BB 7-75 H v Worcs (Southampton) 1976. F-c career: 490 matches; 21916 runs @ 32.71, 35 hundreds; 585 wickets @ 27.47. Appointed 1994.

**JONES, Allan** Arthur (St John's C, Horsham), b Horley, Surrey 9 Dec 1947. RHB, RFM. Sussex 1966-69. Somerset 1970-75; cap 1972. Middlesex 1976-79; cap 1976. Glamorgan 1980-81. Northern Transvaal 1972-73. Orange Free State 1976-77. HS 33 M v Kent (Canterbury) 1978. BB 9-51 Sm v Sussex (Hove) 1972. F-c career: 214 matches; 799 runs @ 5.39; 549 wickets @ 28.07. Appointed 1985. Umpired 1 LOI (1996).

**KITCHEN, Mervyn** John (Backwell SM, Nailsea), b Nailsea, Somerset 1 Aug 1940. LHB, RM. Somerset 1960-79; cap 1966; testimonial 1973. Tour: Rhodesia 1972-73 (Int W). 1000 runs (7); most – 1730 (1968). HS 189 Sm v Pakistanis (Taunton) 1967. BB 1-4. F-c career: 354 matches; 15230 runs @ 26.25, 17 hundreds; 2 wickets @ 54.50. Appointed 1982. Umpired 20 Tests (1990 to 2000) and 28 LOI (1983 to 2001). International Panel 1995 to 1999.

**LEADBEATER, Barrie** (Harehills SS), b Harehills, Leeds, Yorks 14 Aug 1943. RHB, RM. Yorkshire 1966-79; cap 1969; joint benefit with G.A.Cope 1980. Tour: WI 1969-70 (DN). HS 140* Y v Hants (Portsmouth) 1976. BB 1-1. F-c career: 147 matches; 5373 runs @ 25.34, 1 hundred; 1 wicket @ 5.00. Appointed 1981. Umpired 5 LOI (1983 to 2000).

**LLONG, Nigel** James (Ashford North S), b Ashford, Kent 11 Feb 1969. LHB, OB. Kent 1990-98; cap 1993. Tour: Z 1992-93 (K). HS 130 K v Hants (Canterbury) 1996. BB 5-21 K v Middx (Canterbury) 1996. F-c career: 68 matches; 3024 runs @ 31.17, 6 hundreds; 35 wickets @ 35.97. Appointed 2002.

**LLOYDS, Jeremy** William (Blundells S), b Penang, Malaya 17 Nov 1954. LHB, OB. Somerset 1979-84; cap 1982. Gloucestershire 1985-91; cap 1985. Orange Free State 1983-84 to 1987-88. Tour (Glos): SL 1986-87. 1000 runs (3); most – 1295 (1986). HS 132*

Sm v Northants (Northampton) 1982. BB 7-88 Sm v Essex (Chelmsford) 1982. F-c career: 267 matches; 10679 runs @ 31.04, 10 hundreds; 333 wickets @ 38.86; 229 ct. Appointed 1998. Umpired 2 LOI (2000 to 2001).

**MALLENDER, Neil** Alan (Beverley GS), b Kirk Sandall, Yorks 13 Aug 1961. RHB, RFM. Northamptonshire 1980-86 and 1995-96; cap 1984. Somerset 1987-94; cap 1987; benefit 1994. Otago 1983-84 to 1992-93; captain 1990-91 to 1992-93. **Tests:** 2 (1992); 8 runs @ 2.66, HS 4; 10 wkts @ 21.50, BB 5-50 v P (Leeds) 1992 – on debut. Tour: Z 1994-95 (Nh). HS 100* Otago v CD (Palmerston N) 1991-92. UK HS 87* Sm v Sussex (Hove) 1990. 50 wkts (6); most – 56 (1983). BB 7-27 Otago v Auckland (Auckland) 1984-85. UK BB 7-41 Nh v Derbys (Northampton) 1982. F-c career: 345 matches; 4709 runs @ 17.18, 1 hundred; 937 wickets @ 26.31; 111 ct. Appointed 1999. Umpired 14 LOI (2001 to 2002-03), including 2002-03 World Cup.

**PALMER, Roy** (Southbroom SM, Devizes), b Devizes, Wilts 12 Jul 1942. RHB, RFM. Younger brother of K.E.Palmer (Somerset and England 1955-69). Somerset 1965-70. HS 84 Sm v Leics (Taunton) 1967. BB 6-45 Sm v Middx (Lord's) 1967. F-c career: 74 matches; 1037 runs @ 13.29; 172 wickets @ 31.62. Appointed 1980. Umpired 2 Tests (1992 to 1993) and 8 LOI (1983 to 1995).

**SHARP, George** (Elwick Road SS, Hartlepool), b West Hartlepool, Co Durham 12 Mar 1950. RHB, WK, occ LM. Northamptonshire 1968-85; cap 1973; benefit 1982. HS 98 Nh v Yorks (Northampton) 1983. BB 1-47. F-c career: 306 matches; 6254 runs @ 19.85; 1 wicket @ 70.00; 655 dismissals (565 ct, 90 st). Appointed 1992. Umpired 15 Tests (1996 to 2001-02) and 31 LOI (1995-96 to 2001-02). International Panel 1996 to 2001-02.

**SHEPHERD, David** Robert (Barnstaple GS; St Luke's C, Exeter), b Bideford, Devon 27 Dec 1940. RHB, RM. Gloucestershire 1965-79; cap 1969; joint benefit with J.Davey 1978. Scored 108 on debut (v OU). Devon 1959-64. 1000 runs (2); most – 1079 (1970). HS 153 Gs v Middx (Bristol) 1968. BB 1-1. F-c career: 282 matches; 10672 runs @ 24.47, 12 hundreds; 2 wickets @ 53.00. Appointed 1981. Umpired 69 Tests (1985 to 2002-03) and 127 LOI (1983 to 2002-03), including 1987-88, 1991-92, 1995-96, 1999 and 2002-03 World Cups (3 finals). International Panel 1994 to 2001-02. **Elite Panel 2001-02 to date.**

**STEELE, John** Frederick (Endon SS), b Brown Edge, Staffs 23 Jul 1946. RHB, SLA. Brother of D.S. (Northants, Derbys and England 1963-84). Leicestershire 1970-83; cap 1971; benefit 1983. Glamorgan 1984-86; cap 1984. Natal 1973-74 to 1977-78. Staffordshire 1965-69. Tour: SA 1974-75 (DHR). 1000 runs (6); most – 1347 (1972). HS 195 Le v Derbys (Leicester) 1971. BB 7-29 Natal B v GW (Umzinto) 1973-74 and 7-29 Le v Glos (Leicester) 1980. F-c career: 379 matches; 15054 runs @ 28.95, 21 hundreds; 584 wickets @ 27.04; 413 ct. Appointed 1997.

**WHITEHEAD, Alan** Geoffrey Thomas, b Butleigh, Somerset 28 Oct 1940. LHB, SLA. Somerset 1957-61. HS 15 Sm v Hants (Southampton) 1959 and 15 Sm v Leics (Leicester) 1960. BB 6-74 Sm v Sussex (Eastbourne) 1959. F-c career: 38 matches; 137 runs @ 5.70; 67 wickets @ 34.41. Appointed 1970. Umpired 5 Tests (1982 to 1987) and 14 LOI (1979 to 2001).

**WILLEY, Peter** (Seaham SS), b Sedgefield, Co Durham 6 Dec 1949. RHB, OB. Northamptonshire 1966-83; cap 1971; benefit 1981. Leicestershire 1984-91; cap 1984; captain 1987. E Province 1982-83 to 1984-85. Northumberland 1992. **Tests:** 26 (1976 to 1986); 1184 runs @ 26.90, HS 102* v WI (St John's) 1980-81; 7 wkts @ 65.14, BB 2-73 v WI (Lord's) 1980. **LOI:** 26. Tours: A 1979-80; SA 1972-73 (DHR), 1981-82 (SAB); WI 1980-81, 1985-86; I 1979-80; SL 1977-78 (DHR). 1000 runs (10); most – 1783 (1982). HS 227 Nh v Somerset (Northampton) 1976. 50 wkts (3); most – 52 (1979). BB 7-37 Nh v OU (Oxford) 1975. F-c career: 559 matches; 24361 runs @ 30.56, 44 hundreds; 756 wickets @ 30.95. Appointed 1993. Umpired 24 Tests (1995-96 to 2001) and 31 LOI (1996 to 2002-03), including 1999 and 2002-03 World Cups. International Panel 1996 to 2001-02.

**RESERVE FIRST-CLASS LIST:** †R.J.Bailey, N.L.Bainton, M.Dixon, †S.A.Garratt, A.Hill, †R.K.Illingworth, R.A.Kettleborough, R.T.Robinson, K.Shuttleworth.

**Test Match and LOI statistics to 30 March 2003 inclusive. See page 14 for key to abbreviations.**

# TOURING TEAM FIRST-CLASS REGISTER 2002

## INDIA

| Full Names | Birthdate | Birthplace | Team | Type | F-C Debut |
|---|---|---|---|---|---|
| AGARKAR, Ajit Bhalchandra | 04.12.77 | Bombay | Bombay | RHB/RMF | 1996-97 |
| BANGAR, Sanjay Bapusaheb | 11.10.72 | Beed, Maharashtra | Railways | RHB/RMF | 1993-94 |
| DAS, Shiv Sunder | 05.11.77 | Bhubaneshwar | Orissa | RHB/RM | 1993-94 |
| DRAVID, Rahul | 11.01.73 | Indore | Karnataka | RHB/OB/WK | 1990-91 |
| GANGULY, Sourav Chandidas | 08.07.72 | Calcutta | Bengal | LHB/RM | 1989-90 |
| HARBHAJAN SINGH | 03.07.80 | Jullundur | Punjab | RHB/OB | 1997-98 |
| JAFFER, Wasim | 16.02.78 | Bombay | Bombay | RHB/OB | 1996-97 |
| KAIF, Mohammad | 01.12.80 | Allahabad | Uttar Pradesh | RHB/OB | 1997-98 |
| KHAN, Zaheer | 07.10.78 | Shrirampur | Baroda | RHB/LFM | 1999-00 |
| KUMBLE, Anil | 17.10.70 | Bangalore | Karnataka | RHB/LBG | 1989-90 |
| LAXMAN, Vangipurappu Venkata Sai | 01.11.74 | Hyderabad | Hyderabad | RHB/OB | 1992-93 |
| MONGIA, Dinesh | 17.04.77 | Chandigarh | Punjab | LHB/SLA | 1995-96 |
| NEHRA, Ashish | 29.04.78 | Delhi | Delhi | RHB/LFM | 1997-98 |
| PATEL, Pathiv Ajay | 09.03.85 | Ahmedabad | Gujarat | LHB/WK | 2001-02 |
| RATRA, Ajay | 13.12.81 | Faridabad | Haryana | RHB/WK | 1998-99 |
| SEHWAG, Virender | 20.10.78 | Delhi | Delhi | RHB/OB | 1997-98 |
| TENDULKAR, Sachin Ramesh | 24.04.73 | Bombay | Bombay | RHB/RM-LB | 1988-89 |
| YOHANNAN, Tinu | 18.02.79 | Quilon | Kerala | RHB/RFM | 1999-00 |

## SRI LANKA

| Full Names | Birthdate | Birthplace | Team | Type | F-C Debut |
|---|---|---|---|---|---|
| AMERASINGHE, Merenna Koralage Don Ishara | 05.03.78 | Colombo | Nondescripts | RHB/RFM | 1997-98 |
| ARNOLD, Russel Premakumaran | 25.10.73 | Colombo | Nondescripts | LHB/OB | 1993-94 |
| ATAPATTU, Marvan Samson | 22.11.70 | Kalutara | Sinhalese | RHB/LB | 1988-89 |
| CHANDANA, Umagilya Durage Upul | 07.05.72 | Galle | Tamil Union | RHB/LB | 1991-92 |
| DE SILVA, Karunakalage Sajeewa Chanaka | 11.01.71 | Kalutara | Burgher | LHB/LFM | 1990-91 |
| DE SILVA, Pinnaduwage Aravinda | 17.10.65 | Colombo | Nondescripts | RHB/OB | 1983-84 |
| FERNANDO, Congenige Randhi Dilhara | 19.07.79 | Colombo | Sinhalese | RHB/RFM | 1997-98 |
| FERNANDO, Thudellage Charitha Buddhika | 22.08.80 | Panadura | Panadura | RHB/RMF | 1999-00 |
| JAYASURIYA, Sanath Teran | 30.06.69 | Matara | Bloomfield | LHB/SLA | 1988-89 |
| JAYAWARDENA, Denagamage Proboth Mahela DeSilva | 27.05.77 | Colombo | Sinhalese | RHB/RM | 1995-96 |
| JAYAWARDENA, Hewasan Datchige Asiri Prasanna | 10.09.79 | Colombo | Sinhalese | RHB/WK | 1997-98 |
| MURALITHARAN, Muthiah | 17.04.72 | Kandy | Tamil Union | RHB/OB | 1989-90 |
| PERERA, Panagodage Don Ruchira Laksiri | 06.04.77 | Colombo | Sinhalese | LHB/LFM | 1996-97 |
| SAMARAWEERA, Thilan Thusdara | 22.09.76 | Colombo | Colts | RHB/OB | 1995-96 |
| SANGAKKARA, Kumar | 27.10.77 | Matale | Nondescripts | LHB/WK | 1997-98 |
| TILLEKERATNE, Hashan Prasantha | 14.07.67 | Colombo | Nondescripts | LHB/RM/WK | 1984-85 |
| UPASHANTHA, Kalutarage Eric Amila | 10.06.72 | Kurunegala | Colts | RHB/RM | 1990-91 |
| VAAS, Warnakulasuriya Patabendige Ushantha Chaminda Joseph | 27.01.74 | Mattumagala | Colts | LHB/LFM | 1990-91 |
| WANASINGHE, Wasala Mudiyansclage Pasan Nirmitha | 30.09.70 | Colombo | Galle | RHB/RFM | 1990-91 |
| ZOYSA, Demuni Nuwan Tharanga | 13.05.78 | Colombo | Sinhalese | LHB/LFM | 1996-97 |

## WEST INDIES A

| Full Names | Birthdate | Birthplace | Team | Type | F-C Debut |
|---|---|---|---|---|---|
| BENN, Sulieman Jamaal | 22.07.81 | Haynesville | Barbados | LHB/SLA | 1999-00 |
| BEST, Tino Ia Bertram | 26.08.81 | St Michael | Barbados | RHB/RFM | 2001-02 |
| BLACK, Marlon Ian | 07.06.75 | Trinidad | Trinidad | RHB/RFM | 1993-94 |
| BRAVO, Dwayne James John | 07.10.83 | Santa Cruz | Trinidad | RHB/RM | 2001-02 |
| BREESE, Gareth Rohan | 09.01.76 | Montego Bay | Jamaica | RHB/OB | 1995-96 |
| GANGA, Daren | 14.01.79 | Barrackpore | Trinidad | RHB/OB | 1996-97 |
| GAYLE, Christopher Henry | 21.09.79 | Kingston | Jamaica | LHB/OB | 1998-99 |
| HIBBERT, Keith Hugh | 14.06.80 | St Catherine | Jamaica | RHB/WK | 2000-01 |
| HINDS, Ryan O'Neal | 17.02.81 | Holders Hill | Barbados | LHB/SLA | 1998-99 |
| KING, Reon Dane | 06.10.75 | Geod Fortin | Guyana | RHB/RFM | 1995-96 |
| LAWSON, Jermaine Jay Charles | 13.01.82 | Spanish Town | Jamaica | RHB/RF | 2000-01 |
| MORTON, Runako Shakur | 22.07.78 | Nevis | Leeward Is | RHB/OB | 1996-97 |
| PAGON, Donovan Jomo | 13.09.82 | Kingston | Jamaica | RHB/OB | 2001-02 |
| POWELL, Darren Brentlyle | 15.04.78 | Jamaica | Jamaica | RHB/RFM | 2000-01 |
| SIMMONS, Lendl Mark Platter | 25.01.85 | Port-of-Spain | Trinidad | RHB/RMF/WK | 2001-02 |
| SMITH, Devon Sheldon | 21.10.81 | Grenada | Windward Is | LHB/OB | 1998-99 |

# UNIVERSITY FIRST-CLASS REGISTER 2002

## CAMBRIDGE (‡ Blue 2002)

| Full Names | Birthdate | Birthplace | College | Type | F-C Debut |
|---|---|---|---|---|---|
| CHAPMAN-SMITH, Mark Stuart | 01.09.74 | Auckland, NZ | Hughes Hall | LHB | 2002 |
| ‡HEATH, Duncan Robert | 06.11.81 | Grimsby | Pembroke | RHB/RM | 2002 |
| ‡HEATH, John Alexander | 01.06.78 | Grimsby | Pembroke | RHB/RM | 2002 |
| HUGHES, Toby Roger | 15.02.79 | Stourport-on-Severn | Homerton | RHB/RMF | 2000 |
| JORDISON, John Richard | 18.06.81 | Nottingham | (Anglia U) | RHB/RM | 2002 |
| ‡KUMAR, Vikram Harsh | 21.01.81 | Beckenham | St John's | RHB/WK | 2001 |
| McGRATH, Daniel Edwin Taylor | 13.02.76 | Sydney, Aus | St Edmund's | RHB/RM | 2002 |
| MARSHALL, Simon James | 20.09.82 | Birkenhead | Pembroke | RHB/LB | 2002 |
| ‡MOFFAT, John Stuart David | 18.08.77 | Edinburgh | St Edmund's | RHB | 2002 |
| MOYES, James Robert | 16.12.74 | Workington | Hughes Hall | RHB | 2002 |
| NOBLE, David Jonathan | 08.11.82 | Manchester | Emmanuel | RHB | 2002 |
| ‡PARKER, James William Ralph | 06.11.80 | Durban, SA | St Catharine's | LHB/LM | 2001 |
| SAVILL, Thomas Edward | 16.05.83 | Sheffield | Homerton | RHB/RFM | 2002 |
| ‡SHANKAR, Adrian | 07.05.82 | Ascot | Queens | RHB/OB | 2002 |
| SHARIF, Faisal | 28.10.82 | Forest Gate, London | (Anglia U) | RHB/LB | 2002 |
| ‡SIMCOX, Alexander David | 13.12.79 | Eastbourne | Robinson | RHB | 2001 |

## DURHAM

| Full Names | Birthdate | Birthplace | College | Type | F-C Debut |
|---|---|---|---|---|---|
| BANES, Matthew John | 10.12.79 | Pembury, Kent | Collingwood | RHB/OB | 1999 |
| BISHOP, Justin Edward | 04.01.82 | Bury St Edmunds | John Snow | LHB/LMF | 2002 |
| BROWN, Michael James | 09.02.80 | Burnley | Collingwood | RHB/OB | 1999 |
| BRUCE, James Thomas Anthony | 17.12.79 | London | St Hild & St Bede | RHB/RMF | 2001 |
| CREESE, Matthew Leonard | 13.02.82 | Enfield | George Stephenson | LHB/SLA | 1999 |
| FERLEY, Robert Steven | 04.02.82 | Norwich | Grey | RHB/SLA | 2001 |
| HAZLETON, Marc Alexander | 17.10.80 | Cuckfield | Grey | RHB/RMF | 2002 |
| HOLLINGSWORTH, Andrew Philip | 11.10.79 | Chertsey | St Cuthbert's Soc | RHB/RM | 2002 |
| JEFFERSON, William Ingleby | 25.10.79 | Derby | St Hild & St Bede | RHB/RMF | 2000 |
| KIRBY, William Anthony | 02.06.81 | Hull | Van Mildert | RHB/RM | 2002 |
| LOUDON, Alexander Guy Rushworth | 06.09.80 | Westminster | Collingwood | RHB/OB | 2001 |
| MAIDEN, Alistair Jonathan | 15.09.82 | Stourbridge | Collingwood | RHB | 2002 |
| PHILLIPS, Timothy James | 13.03.81 | Cambridge | St Hild & St Bede | LHB/SLA | 1999 |
| SOUTER, Martin Andrew | 19.02.76 | Guildford | Trevelyan | RHB/RM | 2002 |
| THORBURN, Mark | 11.08.78 | Bath | Collingwood | RHB/RM | 2001 |

## OXFORD (‡ Blue 2002)

| Full Names | Birthdate | Birthplace | College | Type | F-C Debut |
|---|---|---|---|---|---|
| CLARK, Philip Jonathan | 12.08.79 | Khartoum, Sudan | Balliol | RHB/RM | 2002 |
| ‡DALRYMPLE, James William Murray | 21.01.81 | Nairobi, Kenya | St Peter's | RHB/OB | 2001 |
| ‡DALRYMPLE, Simon Hedley | 06.06.83 | Worcester | Christ Church | RHB/RM | 2002 |
| DANIELS, Timothy John | 24.10.80 | Brighton | (Brookes U) | RHB | 2001 |
| ‡EVANS, Patrick Peter | 25.08.81 | London | Keble | RHB | 2002 |
| FLOYD, Matthew Kabir | 30.11.80 | Hampstead | Keble | RHB/OB | 2001 |
| GOFTON, Alan Frederick | 04.10.79 | Chesterfield | Oxford ILP | RHB/RM | 1999 |
| ‡HAWINKELS, Stephen John | 12.03.82 | Cape Town, SA | University | RHB/RM | 2001 |
| ‡HICKS, Thomas Charles | 28.08.79 | Farnborough, Kent | St Catherine's | RHB/OB | 1999 |
| HILSUM, Ian Jack | 29.12.81 | Newport, IOW | (Brookes U) | RHB/LB | 2002 |
| HOWARD, William Oliver Fitzalan | 13.02.81 | Guildford | (Brookes U) | RHB/WK | 2002 |
| JONES, Huw Rhys | 23.11.80 | Oxford | (Brookes U) | RHB/LB | 2001 |
| MEES, Thomas | 08.06.81 | Wolverhampton | (Brookes U) | RHB/RMF | 2001 |
| ‡MILLAR, Neil | 03.02.81 | London | Christ Church | RHB/RM | 2002 |
| PORTER, Joseph James | 05.05.80 | London | (Brookes U) | LHB/SLA | 2000 |
| ‡REDMAYNE, James Richard Studdert | 16.07.79 | London | Trinity | RHB | 2000 |
| ‡SAYERS, Joseph John | 05.11.83 | Leeds | Worcester | LHB/OB | 2002 |
| SHARPE, Toby John | 05.07.81 | London | (Brookes U) | RHB/RMF | 2001 |
| ‡VONWILLER, Benjamin Michael | 16.03.74 | Sydney, Aus | Trinity | RHB/RMF | 2000 |
| ‡WARREN, Charles Christopher Morel | 11.03.79 | Portadown | Worcester | RHB | 2000 |
| ‡WYATT, Alexander August | 23.06.76 | Melbourne, Aus | New | RHB/LB | 2002 |

### BRITISH UNIVERSITIES
(Excluding players listed either above or in the County Register)

| Full Names | Birthdate | Birthplace | University | Type | F-C Debut |
|---|---|---|---|---|---|
| TOURNIER, Mark Andrew | 03.05.71 | Melbourne, Aus | Loughborough | RHB/RFM | 2000 |

# LEADING TEST AGGREGATES 2002

## 1000 RUNS

| | M | I | NO | HS | Runs | Avge | 100 | 50 |
|---|---|---|---|---|---|---|---|---|
| M.P.Vaughan (E) | 14 | 26 | 2 | 197 | 1481 | 61.70 | 6 | 2 |
| S.R.Tendulkar (I) | 16 | 26 | 1 | 193 | 1392 | 55.68 | 4 | 5 |
| R.Dravid (I) | 16 | 26 | 3 | 217 | 1357 | 59.00 | 5 | 5 |
| M.L.Hayden (A) | 11 | 17 | 1 | 197 | 1160 | 72.50 | 6 | 3 |
| S.Chanderpaul (WI) | 14 | 22 | 6 | 140 | 1065 | 66.56 | 4 | 6 |
| R.T.Ponting (A) | 11 | 16 | 1 | 154 | 1064 | 70.93 | 5 | 2 |

## 50 WICKETS

| | M | O | R | W | Avge | Best | 5wI | 10wM |
|---|---|---|---|---|---|---|---|---|
| S.K.Warne (A) | 10 | 479.0 | 1310 | 67 | 19.55 | 7-94 | 3 | 1 |
| Harbhajan Singh (I) | 13 | 594.3 | 1463 | 63 | 23.22 | 7-48 | 5 | – |
| M.Muralitharan (SL) | 8 | 472.4 | 979 | 55 | 17.80 | 9-51 | 5 | 2 |
| Z.Khan (I) | 15 | 479.1 | 1479 | 51 | 29.00 | 5-29 | 2 | – |
| Saqlain Mushtaq (P) | 11 | 441.3 | 1248 | 51 | 24.47 | 7-66 | 2 | 1 |

# THE 2002 FIRST-CLASS SEASON
## STATISTICAL HIGHLIGHTS

**HIGHEST INNINGS TOTALS** († *County record*)

| | | |
|---|---|---|
| 746-9d | Northamptonshire v Gloucestershire | Bristol |
| 671 (-8) | Hampshire v Kent | Canterbury |
| 645-6d† | Durham v Middlesex | Lord's |
| 644 | Sussex v Somerset | Taunton |
| 643-7d | Worcestershire v Durham | Worcester |
| 633-7d | Middlesex v Glamorgan | Cardiff |
| 632 | Northamptonshire v Essex | Northampton |
| 631-6d | Sussex v Hampshire | Hove |
| 628-8d | India v England (3rd Test) | Leeds |
| 617 | England v India (2nd Test) | Nottingham |
| 614-5d | Northamptonshire v Worcestershire | Northampton |
| 608-6d | Surrey v Somerset | Taunton |
| 604 | Cambridge U v Oxford U | Oxford |

*Record University Match total by either team*

| | | |
|---|---|---|
| 601-9d | Warwickshire v Yorkshire | Birmingham |

**HIGHEST FOURTH INNINGS TOTALS**

| | | |
|---|---|---|
| 453 | Somerset (set 454) v West Indies A | Taunton |
| 410-8 | Surrey (set 410) v Kent | Canterbury |
| 405-7 | Warwickshire (set 401) v Sussex | Hove |

**MATCH AGGREGATES OF 1500 RUNS**

| | | |
|---|---|---|
| 1815-28 | Somerset (554, 329-7) v Surrey (608-6d, 324-5d) | Taunton |
| 1665-33 | Warwickshire (601-9d, 232-4) v Yorkshire (351, 481) | Birmingham |
| 1614-26 | Gloucestershire (422, 446-7) v Northamptonshire (746-9d) | Bristol |
| 1575-33 | Northamptonshire (632, 155) v Essex (497-7d, 291-6) | Northampton |
| 1557-38 | Hampshire (327, 390) v Surrey (418, 422-8d) | Southampton |
| 1548-33 | Glamorgan (348, 528-7d) v Northamptonshire (430, 242-6) | Cardiff |

**LOWEST INNINGS TOTALS**

| | | |
|---|---|---|
| 71 | Somerset v Lancashire | Blackpool |
| 77 | Northamptonshire v Worcestershire | Worcester |
| 93 | Middlesex v Essex | Chelmsford |
| 96 | Derbyshire v Durham | Darlington |
| 98 | Hampshire v Somerset | Bath |

**LARGE MARGINS OF VICTORY**

| | | |
|---|---|---|
| Inns & 308 runs | Worcestershire (643-7d) beat Durham (120, 215) | Worcester |
| 483 runs | Surrey (494, 492-9d) beat Leicestershire (361, 142) | The Oval |

**VICTORY AFTER FOLLOWING ON**

| | |
|---|---|
| Warwickshire (293 & 350) beat Surrey (475 & 137) | The Oval |

**TIED MATCH**

| | |
|---|---|
| West Indies A (370 & 266-7d) v Somerset (183 & 453) | Taunton |

**BATSMEN'S MATCH** (Qualification: 1200 runs, average 70 per wicket)

| | | |
|---|---|---|
| 74.26 | Kent (577-7d, 163-4d) v Hampshire (671-8) | Canterbury |

**SEVEN FIFTIES IN AN INNINGS**

| | |
|---|---|
| Northamptonshire (632) v Essex | Northampton |

**SEVEN DUCKS IN AN INNINGS**
Northamptonshire (131) v Derbyshire                                           Derby

**FIRST TO INDIVIDUAL TARGETS**
| **1000 RUNS** | M.E.K.Hussey | Northamptonshire | 19 July |
| **2000 RUNS** | – | *Most 1759 – I.J.Ward (Surrey)* | |
| **100 WICKETS** | – | *Most 83 – M.J.Saggers (Kent),* | |
| | | *K.J.Dean (Derbyshire)* | |

**TRIPLE HUNDREDS**
| G.A.Hick | 315* | Worcestershire v Durham | Worcester |
| M.E.K.Hussey | 310* | Northamptonshire v Gloucestershire | Bristol |

*Highest score conceded by Gloucestershire*

**DOUBLE HUNDREDS** († *County record*)
| Abdul Razzaq | 203* | Middlesex v Glamorgan | Cardiff |
| C.J.Adams | 217 | Sussex v Lancashire | Manchester |
| J.P.Crawley | 272 | Hampshire v Kent | Canterbury |

*On Hampshire debut*

| S.S.Das | 250 | Indians v Essex | Chelmsford |
| M.J.di Venuto | 230 | Derbyshire v Northamptonshire | Derby |
| R.Dravid | 217 | India v England (4th Test) | The Oval |
| A.J.Hollioake | 208 | Surrey v Leicestershire | The Oval |
| R.C.Irani | 207* | Essex v Northamptonshire | Ilford |
| S.P.James | 249 | Glamorgan v Essex | Chelmsford |
| N.V.Knight | (2) | 255* | Warwickshire v Hampshire | Birmingham |
| | | 245* | Warwickshire v Sussex | Birmingham |
| S.G.Law | 218 | Lancashire v Sussex | Manchester |
| D.S.Lehmann | 216 | Yorkshire v Sussex | Arundel |
| M.L.Love | 251† | Durham v Middlesex | Lord's |
| R.S.C.Martin-Jenkins | 205* | Sussex v Somerset | Taunton |
| D.P.Ostler | 225 | Warwickshire v Yorkshire | Birmingham |
| K.P.Pietersen | 254* | Nottinghamshire v Middlesex | Nottingham |
| M.R.Ramprakash | (2) | 218 | Surrey v Somerset | Taunton |
| | | 210* | Surrey v Warwickshire | The Oval |
| R.A.White | 277 | Northamptonshire v Gloucestershire | Northampton |

*The highest maiden first-class hundred in Britain, surpassing 274 by G.A.Davidson for Derbyshire v Lancashire at Manchester in 1896*

**HUNDRED ON FIRST-CLASS DEBUT**
| R.Clarke | 107* | Surrey v Cambridge UCCE | Cambridge |
| J.S.D.Moffat | 169 | Cambridge U v Oxford U | Oxford |

*Hundred in his only first-class match*

**HUNDREDS IN FOUR CONSECUTIVE INNINGS**
I.J.Ward (Surrey) 114 v Warwickshire (Birmingham), 112 & 156 v Hampshire (Southampton), 118 v Leicestershire (The Oval)

**HUNDRED IN EACH INNINGS OF A MATCH**
| M.J.Di Venuto | 192* | 113 | Derbyshire v Middlesex | Lord's |
| M.B.Loye | 105 | 104* | Northamptonshire v Nottinghamshire | Northampton |
| M.P.Maynard | 140 | 118* | Glamorgan v Gloucestershire | Cheltenham |
| I.J.Ward | 112 | 156 | Surrey v Hampshire | Southampton |
| M.J.Wood | 106 | 131 | Somerset v Surrey | Taunton |

## HUNDRED BATTING WITH A RUNNER THROUGHOUT

| | | | |
|---|---|---|---|
| N.V.Knight | 133 | Warwickshire v Surrey | Birmingham |
| D.L.Maddy | 127* | Leicestershire v Surrey | The Oval |

## FASTEST HUNDRED (WALTER LAWRENCE TROPHY)

M.V.Fleming     66 balls     Kent v Sri Lankans     Canterbury

*N.M.Carter scored his maiden first-class hundred off 67 balls for Warwickshire v Sussex at Hove*

## HUNDRED BEFORE LUNCH

| | | Day | | |
|---|---|---|---|---|
| R.A.White | 0*-107* | 1 | Northamptonshire v Gloucestershire | Northampton |
| G.P.Swann | 58*-172* | 3 | Northamptonshire v Gloucestershire | Bristol |

## MOST RUNS IN BOUNDARIES

208 (49⁴, 2⁶) G.A.Hick (315*) Worcestershire v Durham     Worcester

## CARRYING BAT THROUGH COMPLETED INNINGS

| | | | |
|---|---|---|---|
| K.J.Barnett | 182* | Gloucestershire (388) v Middlesex | Southgate |
| M.J.Di Venuto | 192* | Derbyshire (414) v Middlesex | Lord's |
| M.A.Gough | 75* | Durham (187) v Essex | Chester-le-St |
| W.S.Kendall | 53* | Hampshire (146) v Leicestershire | Southampton |
| N.V.Knight (2) | 255* | Warwickshire (367) v Hampshire | Birmingham |
| | 245* | Warwickshire (493) v Sussex | Birmingham |
| R.R.Montgomerie | 122* | Sussex (247) v Leicestershire | Horsham |
| C.M.Spearman | 180* | Gloucestershire (293) v Glamorgan | Cheltenham |
| I.J.Sutcliffe | 125* | Leicestershire (259) v Kent | Canterbury |
| A.J.Swann | 84* | Lancashire (163) v Hampshire | Manchester |

## SLOW DOUBLE HUNDRED

580 min     R.Dravid (217)     India v England (4th Test)     The Oval

## AN HOUR WITHOUT ADDING TO SCORE

60 min on 1     A.McGrath (17)     Yorkshire v Lancashire     Manchester

## LONGEST INNINGS

| | | | |
|---|---|---|---|
| 653 min | M.E.K.Hussey (310*) | Northamptonshire v Gloucestershire | Bristol |
| 629 min | R.Dravid (217) | India v England (4th Test) | The Oval |
| 616 min | N.V.Knight (255*) | Warwickshire v Hampshire | Birmingham |

## NOTABLE PARTNERSHIPS († County record)

**First Wicket**

| | | | |
|---|---|---|---|
| 375† | R.A.White/M.J.Powell | Northamptonshire v Gloucestershire | Northampton |
| 290 | M.E.K.Hussey/M.B.Loye | Northamptonshire v Worcestershire | Northampton |
| 266 | D.P.Fulton/R.W.T.Key | Kent v Hampshire | Canterbury |

**Second Wicket**

| | | | |
|---|---|---|---|
| 252† | M.P.Maynard/D.L.Hemp | Glamorgan v Northamptonshire | Cardiff |
| 251 | M.L.Love/G.J.Muchall | Durham v Middlesex | Lord's |

**Third Wicket**

| | | | |
|---|---|---|---|
| 317 | A.McGrath/D.S.Lehmann | Yorkshire v Lancashire | Leeds |

**Fourth Wicket**

| | | | |
|---|---|---|---|
| 316 | D.J.Bicknell/K.P.Pietersen | Nottinghamshire v Middlesex | Nottingham |

Fifth Wicket

| 320 | E.C.Joyce/Abdul Razzaq | Middlesex v Glamorgan | Cardiff |
|---|---|---|---|
| 282 | A.D.Brown/A.J.Hollioake | Surrey v Leicestershire | The Oval |
| 262 | A.D.Brown/N.Shahid | Surrey v Sussex | The Oval |

Sixth Wicket

| 318 | M.E.K.Hussey/G.P.Swann | Northamptonshire v Gloucestershire | Bristol |
|---|---|---|---|

Seventh Wicket

| 256† | D.A.Leatherdale/S.J.Rhodes | Worcestershire v Nottinghamshire | Nottingham |
|---|---|---|---|
| 207 | R.C.Russell/I.D.Fisher | Gloucestershire v Essex | Gloucester |

Eighth Wicket

| 291† | R.S.C.Martin-Jenkins/<br>M.J.G.Davis | Sussex v Somerset | Taunton |
|---|---|---|---|

Tenth Wicket

| 214† | N.V.Knight/A.Richardson | Warwickshire v Hampshire | Birmingham |
|---|---|---|---|
| 145 | S.G.Law/G.Keedy | Lancashire v Sussex | Manchester |
| 119 | N.M.Carter/J.A.S.Spires | Warwickshire v Sussex | Hove |

## UNUSUAL DISMISSAL

### STUMPED BY A SUBSTITUTE

| G.W.Flower, st J.I.Clifford<br>(sub for T.Frost) | Leicestershire v Warwickshire | Birmingham |
|---|---|---|

## EIGHT OR MORE WICKETS IN AN INNINGS

| Azhar Mahmood | 8- 61 | Surrey v Lancashire | The Oval |
|---|---|---|---|
| A.J.Bichel | 9- 93 | Worcestershire v Gloucestershire | Worcester |
| S.J.Cook | 8- 63 | Middlesex v Northamptonshire | Northampton |
| S.C.G.MacGill | 8-111 | Nottinghamshire v Middlesex | Nottingham |
| A.A.Noffke | 8- 24 | Middlesex v Derbyshire | Derby |
| A.Richardson | 8- 46 | Warwickshire v Sussex | Birmingham |
| G.J.Smith | 8- 53 | Nottinghamshire v Essex | Nottingham |
| P.C.R.Tufnell | 8- 66 | Middlesex v Gloucestershire | Cheltenham |

## TEN OR MORE WICKETS IN A MATCH

| Kabir Ali | (2) | 10- 88 | Worcestershire v Oxford UCCE | Oxford |
|---|---|---|---|---|
| | | 10- 66 | Worcestershire v Gloucestershire | Bristol |
| A.J.Bichel | | 10-131 | Worcestershire v Gloucestershire | Worcester |
| M.E.Cassar | | 10-134 | Northamptonshire v Gloucestershire | Bristol |
| G.Chapple | | 10-127 | Lancashire v Sussex | Hove |
| D.G.Cork | | 10-126 | Derbyshire v Durham | Derby |
| K.J.Dean | (2) | 10-109 | Derbyshire v Glamorgan | Derby |
| | | 10-125 | Derbyshire v Middlesex | Derby |
| A.F.Giles | | 12-216 | Warwickshire v Kent | Birmingham |
| A.J.Harris | (2) | 11-122 | Nottinghamshire v Northamptonshire | Nottingham |
| | | 10-171 | Nottinghamshire v Worcestershire | Nottingham |
| I.J.Harvey | | 11-154 | Gloucestershire v Essex | Gloucester |
| R.L.Johnson | | 10- 75 | Somerset v Hampshire | Bath |
| P.S.Jones | | 10-156 | Somerset v Warwickshire | Birmingham |
| M.S.Kasprowicz | | 11-105 | Glamorgan v Durham | Chester-le-St |
| R.J.Kirtley | | 10- 90 | Sussex v Yorkshire | Leeds |
| J.Lewis | | 12-131 | Gloucestershire v Worcestershire | Worcester |
| S.C.G.MacGill | | 14-165 | Nottinghamshire v Middlesex | Nottingham |
| D.E.Malcolm | | 10-148 | Leicestershire v Yorkshire | Leicester |
| A.A.Noffke | | 12-108 | Middlesex v Derbyshire | Derby |
| J.Ormond | | 10-178 | Surrey v Warwickshire | The Oval |
| Saqlain Mushtaq | | 11-180 | Surrey v Hampshire | The Oval |

| G.J.Smith | 11- 74 | Nottinghamshire v Essex | Nottingham |
| J.P.Stephenson | 10-104 | Essex v Worcestershire | Worcester |
| G.P.Swann | 10-238 | Northamptonshire v Derbyshire | Northampton |
| S.D.Thomas | 10- 83 | Glamorgan v Durham | Cardiff |

## OUTSTANDING ANALYSIS
| N.C.Phillips | 4-4-0-3 | Durham v Derbyshire | Darlington |

## HAT-TRICKS
| J.Srinath | | Leicestershire v Surrey | The Oval |

## 200 RUNS CONCEDED IN AN INNINGS
| S.D.Udal | 47-7-213-4 | Hampshire v Surrey | The Oval |

*Hampshire record*

## 60 OVERS IN AN INNINGS
| M.Muralitharan | 64-12-143-5 | Sri Lanka v England (2nd Test) | Birmingham |
| M.Muralitharan | 60-20-137-3 | Sri Lanka v England (3rd Test) | Manchester |

## SIX OR MORE WICKET-KEEPING DISMISSALS IN AN INNINGS
| R.C.Russell | 6 ct | Gloucestershire v Durham | Bristol |

## NINE OR MORE WICKET-KEEPING DISMISSALS IN A MATCH
| A.J.Stewart | 9 ct 1 st | Surrey v Lancashire | The Oval |
| R.C.Russell | 9 ct | Gloucestershire v Durham | Bristol |

## NO BYES CONCEDED IN TOTAL OF 550 OR MORE
| 749-9d | R.C.Russell | Gloucestershire v Northamptonshire | Bristol |

*World record total without byes*

| 644 | R.J.Turner | Somerset v Sussex | Taunton |
| 643-7d | A.Pratt | Durham v Worcestershire | Worcester |
| 632 | A.Flower | Essex v Northamptonshire | Northampton |
| 608-6d | R.J.Turner | Somerset v Surrey | Taunton |

*N.D.Burns (Leicestershire) conceded no byes v Surrey (494 & 492-9d) at The Oval*

## FIVE OR MORE CATCHES IN AN INNINGS IN THE FIELD
| M.E.K.Hussey | | Northamptonshire v Oxford UCCE | Oxford |

## SEVEN OR MORE CATCHES IN A MATCH IN THE FIELD
| M.E.K.Hussey | | Northamptonshire v Oxford UCCE | Oxford |

## SIXTY EXTRAS IN AN INNINGS (Excluding Penalties)
| | B | LB | W | NB | | |
|---|---|---|---|---|---|---|
| 64 | 13 | 11 | 16 | 24 | Worcestershire (523-6d) v Oxford UCCE | Oxford |
| 64 | 23 | 24 | 9 | 8 | Yorkshire (515-5d) v Lancashire | Leeds |
| 64 | 1 | 15 | 8 | 40 | Gloucestershire (577-9d) v Derbyshire | Bristol |
| 62 | 17 | 10 | 21 | 14 | Lancashire (425) v Sussex | Hove |
| 60 | 16 | 12 | 2 | 30 | Leicestershire (523) v Warwickshire | Leicester |
| 60 | 12 | 14 | – | 34 | Gloucestershire (438) v Glamorgan | Cheltenham |

*Under ECB regulations (Test matches excluded), two extras were scored for each no-ball, in addition to any runs scored off that ball, and two extras were also scored for each wide. There were a further 25 instances of 50-59 extras in an innings.*

# 2002 FIRST-CLASS AVERAGES

These averages involve the 486 cricketers who appeared in the 177 first-class matches played by 27 teams in the British Isles during the 2002 season.

'Cap' denotes the season in which the player was awarded a 1st XI cap by the county he represented in 2002. 2002$^C$ (Worcestershire) denotes awarded his county colours.

Team abbreviations: BU – British Universities; CU – Cambridge University/Cambridge UCCE; De – Derbyshire; Du – Durham; DU – Durham UCCE; E – England; Ex – Essex; Gm – Glamorgan; Gs – Gloucestershire; H – Hampshire; I – India(ns); K – Kent; La – Lancashire; Le – Leicestershire; M – Middlesex; MCC – Marylebone Cricket Club; Nh – Northamptonshire; Nt – Nottinghamshire; OU – Oxford University/Oxford UCCE; SL – Sri Lanka(ns); Sm – Somerset; Sy – Surrey; Sx – Sussex; Wa – Warwickshire; WIA – West Indies A; Wo – Worcestershire; Y – Yorkshire.

† Left-handed batsman.

## BATTING AND FIELDING

| | Cap | M | I | NO | HS | Runs | Avge | 100 | 50 | Ct/St |
|---|---|---|---|---|---|---|---|---|---|---|
| Abdul Razzaq (M) | 2002 | 6 | 9 | 3 | 203* | 364 | 60.66 | 1 | – | 1 |
| Adams, C.J.(Sx) | 1998 | 10 | 19 | – | 217 | 848 | 44.63 | 3 | 3 | 2 |
| †Adams, J.H.K.(BU/H) | – | 3 | 5 | 1 | 48 | 88 | 22.00 | – | – | 3 |
| Afzaal, U.(Nt/MCC) | 2000 | 18 | 32 | 4 | 134 | 1275 | 45.53 | 5 | 6 | 12 |
| Agarkar, A.B.(I) | – | 7 | 9 | 1 | 109* | 244 | 30.50 | 1 | – | – |
| Aldred, P.(De) | 1999 | 2 | 3 | 1 | 29 | 40 | 20.00 | – | – | – |
| Ali, Kabir (Wo) | 2002$^C$ | 17 | 21 | 4 | 51* | 271 | 15.94 | – | 1 | 3 |
| Ali, S.M.B.(De) | – | 15 | 24 | 2 | 53 | 333 | 15.13 | – | 1 | 5 |
| Allen, A.P.W.(Wa) | – | 1 | 1 | 1 | 18* | 18 | – | – | – | – |
| Alleyne, D.(M) | – | 3 | 3 | 1 | 49* | 93 | 46.50 | – | – | 8 |
| Alleyne, M.W.(Gs) | 1990 | 14 | 25 | 3 | 142* | 555 | 25.22 | 1 | 2 | 12 |
| Ambrose, T.R.(Sx) | – | 13 | 22 | 1 | 149 | 798 | 38.00 | 2 | 2 | 9 |
| Amerasinghe, M.K.D.I.(SL) | – | 3 | 1 | – | 0 | 0 | 0.00 | – | – | – |
| Amin, R.M.(Sy) | – | 1 | – | – | – | – | – | – | – | – |
| †Anderson, J.M.(La) | – | 13 | 16 | 8 | 16 | 58 | 7.25 | – | – | 2 |
| Anderson, R.S.G.(Nh) | – | 5 | 10 | – | 51 | 166 | 16.60 | – | 1 | – |
| †Arnold, R.P.(SL) | – | 9 | 12 | – | 112 | 518 | 43.16 | 2 | 3 | 5 |
| Atapattu, M.S.(SL) | – | 7 | 12 | 1 | 185 | 522 | 47.45 | 2 | 1 | 1 |
| Atri, V.(Nt) | – | 1 | 1 | – | 98 | 98 | 98.00 | – | 1 | 2 |
| Averis, J.M.M.(Gs) | 2001 | 5 | 8 | – | 43 | 83 | 10.37 | – | – | 3 |
| Aymes, A.N.(H) | 1991 | 5 | 7 | 2 | 22* | 52 | 10.40 | – | – | 16/1 |
| Azhar Mahmood (Sy) | – | 3 | 4 | 1 | 64* | 96 | 32.00 | – | 1 | 3 |
| Bailey, T.M.B.(Nh) | – | 17 | 25 | 4 | 68 | 457 | 21.76 | – | 4 | 43/6 |
| Ball, M.C.J.(Gs) | 1996 | 7 | 10 | 3 | 63 | 117 | 16.71 | – | 1 | 5 |
| Banes, M.J.(DU) | – | 3 | 5 | – | 69 | 178 | 35.60 | – | 1 | 1 |
| Bangar, S.B.(I) | – | 7 | 11 | 1 | 74 | 291 | 29.10 | – | 3 | 2 |
| Barnett, K.J.(De) | 1999 | 8 | 15 | 3 | 182* | 641 | 53.41 | 3 | 1 | 1 |
| Bassano, C.W.G.(De) | 2002 | 14 | 26 | 1 | 152 | 1063 | 42.52 | 1 | 8 | 13 |
| Batty, G.J.(Wo) | 2002$^C$ | 18 | 27 | 4 | 74 | 491 | 21.34 | – | 3 | 9 |
| Batty, J.N.(Sy) | 2001 | 13 | 23 | 2 | 151 | 742 | 35.33 | 2 | 3 | 41/5 |
| Bell, I.R.(Wa) | 2001 | 16 | 28 | 1 | 77 | 658 | 24.37 | – | 3 | 6 |
| †Benn, S.J. (WIA) | – | 3 | 5 | – | 31 | 75 | 15.00 | – | – | 4 |
| Best, T.Le B.(WIA) | – | 3 | 1 | – | 8 | 8 | 8.00 | – | – | – |
| Betts, M.M.(Wa) | 2001 | 9 | 16 | 5 | 56 | 259 | 23.54 | – | 1 | 2 |
| †Bevan, M.G.(Le) | 2002 | 9 | 14 | 3 | 146 | 697 | 63.36 | 2 | 4 | 4 |
| Bichel, A.J.(Wo) | 2001 | 9 | 11 | 2 | 78* | 274 | 30.44 | – | 2 | 7 |
| †Bicknell, D.J.(Nt) | 2000 | 13 | 23 | – | 112 | 734 | 31.91 | 2 | 5 | 5 |
| Bicknell, M.P.(Sy) | 1989 | 10 | 14 | 5 | 35* | 258 | 28.66 | – | – | 6 |
| †Bishop, J.E.(DU/Ex) | – | 6 | 9 | 2 | 23* | 69 | 9.85 | – | – | 2 |
| Black, M.I.(WIA) | – | 4 | 4 | – | 16 | 33 | 8.25 | – | – | 2 |
| †Blackwell, I.D.(Sm) | 2001 | 14 | 23 | – | 114 | 879 | 38.21 | 3 | 3 | 4 |

121

| F-C | Cap | M | I | NO | HS | Runs | Avge | 100 | 50 | Ct/St |
|---|---|---|---|---|---|---|---|---|---|---|
| Blain, J.A.R.(Nh) | – | 7 | 9 | 2 | 17* | 47 | 6.71 | – | – | 2 |
| Blakey, R.J.(Y) | 1987 | 16 | 29 | 7 | 103 | 1041 | 47.31 | 1 | 8 | 29/1 |
| Bloomfield, T.F.(M) | 2001 | 3 | 3 | 2 | 31* | 57 | 57.00 | – | – | 1 |
| †Boje, N.(Nt) | – | 9 | 16 | 2 | 84 | 409 | 29.21 | – | 2 | 10 |
| Bond, S.E.(Wa) | – | 3 | 4 | 1 | 29* | 64 | 21.33 | – | – | 1 |
| Bopara, R.S.(Ex) | – | 4 | 7 | 1 | 48 | 165 | 27.50 | – | – | 6 |
| Bowler, P.D.(Sm) | 1995 | 14 | 25 | 2 | 94 | 766 | 33.30 | – | 7 | 22 |
| Brandy, D.G.(Le) | – | 2 | 3 | – | 23 | 28 | 9.33 | – | – | 1 |
| Bravo, D.J.J.(WIA) | – | 6 | 11 | 3 | 77* | 350 | 43.75 | – | 3 | 4 |
| Breese, G.R.(WIA) | – | 2 | 3 | 1 | 54* | 92 | 46.00 | – | 1 | – |
| Bridge, G.D.(Du) | – | 10 | 15 | 2 | 49 | 184 | 14.15 | – | – | 4 |
| Brophy, G.L.(Nh) | – | 4 | 8 | 3 | 110 | 246 | 49.20 | 1 | 1 | 5 |
| Brown, A.D.(Sy) | 1994 | 16 | 26 | 2 | 188 | 1211 | 50.45 | 5 | 3 | 18 |
| Brown, D.R.(Wa) | 1995 | 16 | 28 | 4 | 79* | 671 | 27.95 | – | 3 | 9 |
| Brown, J.F.(Nh) | 2000 | 8 | 11 | 5 | 19 | 64 | 10.66 | – | – | 2 |
| Brown, M.J.(DU/BU) | – | 4 | 6 | – | 57 | 145 | 24.16 | – | 1 | 6 |
| Brown, S.J.E.(Du) | 1998 | 1 | – | – | – | – | – | – | – | – |
| Bruce, J.T.A.(DU) | – | 3 | 3 | 2 | 8* | 8 | 8.00 | – | – | 1 |
| †Bulbeck, M.P.L.(Sm) | 2002 | 16 | 27 | 7 | 53* | 359 | 17.95 | – | 1 | 3 |
| Burns, M.(Sm) | 1999 | 16 | 30 | 2 | 99 | 1047 | 37.39 | – | 9 | 14 |
| †Burns, N.D.(Le) | 2001 | 16 | 24 | 2 | 101 | 720 | 32.72 | 1 | 5 | 61/2 |
| †Butcher, M.A.(Sy/E) | 1996 | 13 | 21 | 1 | 123 | 936 | 46.80 | 3 | 5 | 8 |
| †Byas, D.(La) | 2002 | 15 | 25 | 2 | 101 | 684 | 29.73 | 1 | 4 | 15 |
| Caddick, A.R.(Sm/E) | 1992 | 10 | 14 | 2 | 16 | 89 | 7.41 | – | – | 2 |
| †Carberry, M.A.(Sy) | – | 2 | 4 | 1 | 153* | 223 | 74.33 | 1 | – | 2 |
| †Carter, N.M.(Wa) | – | 9 | 12 | 5 | 103 | 305 | 43.57 | 1 | 1 | 4 |
| Cassar, M.E.(Nh) | – | 7 | 9 | 1 | 101* | 343 | 42.87 | 1 | 3 | 4 |
| Chandana, U.D.U.(SL) | – | 3 | 3 | – | 1 | 1 | 0.33 | – | – | 1 |
| †Chapman-Smith, M.S.(CU) | – | 1 | 2 | – | 7 | 10 | 5.00 | – | – | – |
| Chapple, G.(La) | 1994 | 16 | 23 | 1 | 65 | 493 | 22.40 | – | 4 | 6 |
| †Cherry, D.D.(Gm) | – | 5 | 8 | – | 47 | 129 | 16.12 | – | – | 4 |
| Chilton, M.J.(La) | 2002 | 17 | 29 | 1 | 107 | 761 | 27.17 | 1 | 4 | 15 |
| Clapp, D.A.(Sx) | – | 1 | 1 | – | 6 | 6 | 6.00 | – | – | – |
| Clark, P.J.(OU) | – | 1 | 2 | 1 | 2* | 2 | 2.00 | – | – | – |
| †Clarke, A.J.(Ex) | – | 2 | 4 | 1 | 31 | 42 | 14.00 | – | – | 1 |
| Clarke, R.(Sy) | – | 10 | 16 | 2 | 153* | 711 | 50.78 | 2 | 4 | 9 |
| Clifford, J.I.(Wa) | – | 4 | 6 | – | 7 | 20 | 3.33 | – | – | 15/1 |
| †Clinton, R.S.(Ex) | – | 5 | 8 | 1 | 107 | 242 | 34.57 | 1 | 1 | 2 |
| Clough, G.D.(Nt) | – | 1 | 1 | – | 5 | 5 | 5.00 | – | – | – |
| Collingwood, P.D.(Du) | 1998 | 7 | 12 | – | 190 | 636 | 53.00 | 1 | 4 | 5 |
| †Cook, J.W.(Nh) | – | 15 | 24 | 3 | 90 | 746 | 35.52 | – | 4 | 4 |
| Cook, S.J.(M) | – | 15 | 18 | 2 | 43* | 267 | 16.68 | – | – | 4 |
| Cork, D.G.(De/E) | 1993 | 11 | 16 | – | 80 | 487 | 30.43 | – | 5 | 12 |
| Cosker, D.A.(Gm) | 2000 | 10 | 13 | 2 | 37 | 115 | 10.45 | – | – | 8 |
| Cottey, P.A.(Sx) | 1999 | 13 | 22 | – | 137 | 699 | 31.77 | 3 | 1 | 5 |
| Cousins, D.M.(Nh) | 2000 | 11 | 16 | 7 | 23* | 103 | 11.44 | – | – | 4 |
| Cowan, A.P.(Ex) | 1997 | 10 | 15 | 2 | 60* | 305 | 23.46 | – | 2 | 6 |
| Cox, J.(Sm) | 1999 | 13 | 25 | 2 | 176 | 724 | 31.47 | 1 | 3 | 6 |
| †Craven, V.J.(Y) | – | 11 | 21 | 2 | 72 | 439 | 23.10 | – | 3 | 8 |
| Crawley, J.P.(H/E) | 2002 | 15 | 25 | 4 | 272 | 1130 | 53.80 | 2 | 7 | 8 |
| †Creese, M.L.(DU) | – | 1 | 1 | – | 8 | 8 | 8.00 | – | – | – |
| Croft, R.D.B.(Gm) | 1992 | 17 | 24 | 3 | 101* | 747 | 35.57 | 1 | 5 | 8 |
| Crowe, C.D.(Le) | – | 12 | 16 | 4 | 34 | 172 | 14.33 | – | – | 4 |
| Cunliffe, R.J.(Le) | – | 5 | 10 | 1 | 30 | 121 | 13.44 | – | – | 1 |
| Currie, M.R.(La) | – | 1 | 2 | 1 | 48* | 50 | 50.00 | – | – | – |
| Dagnall, C.E.(Le) | – | 4 | 5 | 1 | 16 | 33 | 8.25 | – | – | 1 |
| †Dakin, J.M.(Ex) | – | 14 | 20 | 3 | 57 | 359 | 21.11 | – | 1 | 3 |
| Dale, A.(Gm) | 1992 | 16 | 24 | 1 | 127* | 859 | 37.34 | 2 | 3 | 7 |

| F-C | Cap | M | I | NO | HS | Runs | Avge | 100 | 50 | Ct/St |
|---|---|---|---|---|---|---|---|---|---|---|
| Daley, J.A.(Du) | 1999 | 3 | 6 | 1 | 59* | 130 | 26.00 | – | 1 | 1 |
| Dalrymple, J.W.M.(OU/BU/M) | – | 8 | 14 | 1 | 148 | 535 | 41.15 | 2 | 1 | 2 |
| Dalrymple, S.H.(OU) | – | 1 | 2 | 1 | 15* | 27 | 27.00 | – | – | 2 |
| Daniels, T.J.(OU) | – | 2 | 4 | – | 16 | 18 | 4.50 | – | – | 4/1 |
| Das, S.S.(I) | – | 3 | 5 | – | 250 | 349 | 69.80 | 1 | 1 | 2 |
| Davies, A.M.(Du) | – | 14 | 24 | 7 | 33 | 184 | 10.82 | – | – | 3 |
| †Davies, A.P.(Gm) | – | 5 | 6 | – | 30 | 58 | 9.66 | – | – | – |
| Davis, M.J.G.(Sx) | 2002 | 15 | 22 | 4 | 111 | 474 | 26.33 | 1 | 2 | 7 |
| Dawson, R.K.J.(Y/MCC) | – | 15 | 24 | 1 | 87 | 511 | 22.21 | – | 2 | 2 |
| †Dean, K.J.(De/MCC) | 1998 | 17 | 26 | 9 | 54* | 347 | 20.41 | – | 2 | 6 |
| DeFreitas, P.A.J.(Le) | 1986 | 16 | 23 | 2 | 114 | 609 | 29.00 | 1 | 3 | 10 |
| †De Silva, K.S.C.(SL) | – | 1 | – | – | – | – | – | – | – | – |
| De Silva, P.A.(SL) | – | 8 | 12 | 2 | 88 | 500 | 50.00 | – | 6 | – |
| †Di Venuto, M.J.(De) | 2000 | 15 | 28 | 3 | 230 | 1538 | 61.52 | 4 | 7 | 29 |
| Donald, A.A.(Wo) | 2002c | 1 | 1 | 1 | 5* | 5 | – | – | – | – |
| †Dowman, M.P.(De) | 2000 | 8 | 14 | – | 71 | 298 | 21.28 | – | 1 | 6 |
| Dravid, R.(I) | – | 7 | 9 | 1 | 217 | 773 | 96.62 | 3 | 3 | 14 |
| †Driver, R.C.(La) | – | 5 | 8 | 2 | 56 | 113 | 18.83 | – | 1 | 5 |
| Dumelow, N.R.C.(De) | – | 2 | 3 | – | 56 | 80 | 26.66 | – | 1 | 1 |
| Durston, W.J.(Sm) | – | 1 | 2 | – | 55 | 81 | 40.50 | – | 1 | 1 |
| Dutch, K.P.(Sm) | 2001 | 16 | 27 | 3 | 74 | 432 | 18.00 | – | 2 | 20 |
| Ealham, M.A.(K) | 1992 | 14 | 24 | 7 | 83* | 594 | 34.94 | – | 3 | 14 |
| †Edwards, N.J.(Sm) | – | 1 | 2 | – | 31 | 58 | 29.00 | – | – | 1 |
| †Elliott, M.T.G.(Y) | – | 5 | 10 | 1 | 127 | 487 | 54.11 | 1 | 4 | 7 |
| Elstub, C.J.(Y) | – | 2 | 3 | 3 | 18* | 22 | – | – | – | 1 |
| Evans, P.P.(OU) | – | 1 | 1 | – | 16 | 16 | 16.00 | – | – | 2 |
| †Fairbrother, N.H.(La) | 1985 | 12 | 19 | 1 | 101 | 406 | 22.55 | 1 | – | 10 |
| Fellows, G.M.(Y) | – | 10 | 18 | – | 109 | 493 | 27.38 | 1 | 1 | 9 |
| Ferley, R.S.(DU/BU) | – | 4 | 5 | 2 | 37* | 96 | 32.00 | – | – | 1 |
| Fernando, C.R.D.(SL) | – | 3 | 3 | 1 | 6* | 13 | 6.50 | – | – | – |
| Fernando, T.C.B.(SL) | – | 5 | 6 | 3 | 20* | 60 | 20.00 | – | – | 1 |
| †Fisher, I.D.(Gs) | – | 16 | 26 | 3 | 103* | 568 | 24.69 | 1 | 4 | 8 |
| Fleming, M.V.(K) | 1990 | 5 | 8 | 1 | 102 | 211 | 30.14 | 1 | – | – |
| Flintoff, A.(La/E) | 1998 | 7 | 10 | – | 137 | 284 | 28.40 | 1 | 1 | 8 |
| †Flower, A.(Ex) | 2002 | 16 | 29 | 6 | 172* | 1151 | 50.04 | 2 | 6 | 35/1 |
| Flower, G.W.(Le) | 2002 | 1 | 2 | – | 75 | 82 | 41.00 | – | 1 | 1 |
| Floyd, M.K.(OU) | – | 2 | 4 | – | 7 | 9 | 2.25 | – | – | 1 |
| Foster, J.S.(Ex) | 2001 | 4 | 4 | – | 36 | 80 | 20.00 | – | – | 9/1 |
| †Francis, J.D.(BU/H) | – | 10 | 17 | – | 82 | 391 | 23.00 | – | 3 | 6 |
| Francis, S.R.G.(Sm) | – | 10 | 16 | 8 | 17 | 67 | 8.37 | – | – | – |
| †Franks, P.J.(Nt) | 1999 | 10 | 14 | 2 | 67 | 301 | 25.08 | – | 3 | 2 |
| Fraser, A.R.C.(M) | 1988 | 2 | 2 | – | 20 | 36 | 18.00 | – | – | – |
| †Frost, T.(Wa) | 1999 | 7 | 11 | 1 | 103 | 308 | 30.80 | 1 | 1 | 6/2 |
| Fulton, D.P.(K/MCC) | 1998 | 17 | 33 | 2 | 177 | 1358 | 43.80 | 4 | 4 | 33 |
| Gait, A.I.(De) | – | 17 | 33 | – | 175 | 983 | 30.71 | 3 | 8 | 14 |
| Gallian, J.E.R.(Nt) | 1998 | 16 | 29 | 3 | 171 | 1087 | 41.80 | 4 | 6 | 16 |
| Ganga, D.(WIA) | – | 5 | 8 | 2 | 139* | 325 | 54.16 | 2 | – | 3 |
| †Ganguly, S.C.(I) | – | 7 | 11 | 1 | 128 | 477 | 47.70 | 1 | 4 | 3 |
| Gannon, B.W.(Gs) | – | 7 | 8 | 4 | 14 | 31 | 7.75 | – | – | 1 |
| †Gayle, C.H.(WIA) | – | 3 | 5 | – | 94 | 236 | 47.20 | – | 3 | 3 |
| Gazzard, C.M.(Sm) | – | 1 | 2 | – | 24 | 31 | 15.50 | – | – | 3/1 |
| Giddins, E.S.H.(Sy) | – | 7 | 7 | 4 | 9 | 23 | 7.66 | – | – | 1 |
| Gidman, A.P.R.(Gs) | – | 10 | 17 | 1 | 117 | 558 | 34.87 | 1 | 4 | 5 |
| Giles, A.F.(Wa/E) | – | 9 | 12 | – | 68 | 264 | 22.00 | – | 1 | 3 |
| Gofton, A.F.(OU) | – | 1 | 2 | – | 25 | 41 | 20.50 | – | – | – |
| Golding, J.M.(K) | – | 4 | 5 | 3 | 32 | 113 | 56.50 | – | – | – |
| Goodwin, M.W.(Sx) | 2001 | 16 | 28 | – | 162 | 1179 | 42.10 | 5 | 3 | 13 |
| Gough, D.(Y) | 1993 | 1 | – | – | – | – | – | – | – | – |

123

| F-C | Cap | M | I | NO | HS | Runs | Avge | 100 | 50 | Ct/St |
|---|---|---|---|---|---|---|---|---|---|---|
| Gough, M.A.(Du) | – | 8 | 14 | 2 | 103 | 616 | 51.33 | 1 | 3 | 6 |
| Grant, J.B.(Ex) | – | 11 | 12 | 4 | 30 | 64 | 8.00 | – | – | – |
| Gray, A.K.D.(Y) | – | 4 | 6 | 1 | 74* | 193 | 38.60 | – | 1 | – |
| Grayson, A.P.(Ex) | 1996 | 7 | 9 | – | 105 | 309 | 34.33 | 1 | 1 | 7 |
| Greenidge, C.G.(Nh) | – | 15 | 19 | 2 | 46 | 160 | 9.41 | – | – | 7 |
| Grove, J.O.(Le) | – | 2 | 4 | – | 6 | 13 | 3.25 | – | – | – |
| †Gunter, N.E.L.(De) | – | 2 | 3 | – | 18 | 18 | 6.00 | – | – | 3 |
| Habib, A.(Ex) | 2002 | 15 | 25 | 3 | 123 | 964 | 43.81 | 2 | 8 | 12 |
| Hamblin, J.R.C.(H) | – | 5 | 9 | – | 50 | 162 | 18.00 | – | 1 | 4 |
| †Hamilton, G.M.(Y) | 1998 | 2 | 4 | – | 11 | 23 | 5.75 | – | – | – |
| Hancock, T.H.C.(Gs) | 1998 | 9 | 17 | 3 | 112 | 406 | 29.00 | 1 | 2 | 1 |
| Harbhajan Singh (I) | – | 8 | 10 | 2 | 54 | 218 | 27.25 | – | 1 | 1 |
| Hardinges, M.A.(Gs) | – | 1 | 1 | – | 172 | 172 | 172.00 | 1 | – | – |
| Harmison, S.J.(Du/E) | 1999 | 11 | 18 | 3 | 19* | 88 | 5.86 | – | – | 4 |
| Harris, A.J.(Nt) | 2000 | 14 | 20 | 7 | 41* | 151 | 11.61 | – | – | 6 |
| Harrison, D.S.(Gm) | – | 1 | 1 | – | 0 | 0 | 0.00 | – | – | – |
| Harvey, I.J.(Gs) | 1999 | 6 | 10 | 1 | 123 | 390 | 43.33 | 1 | 2 | 6 |
| Hatch, N.G.(Du) | – | 4 | 4 | 2 | 6* | 12 | 6.00 | – | – | 2 |
| Hawinkels, S.J.(OU) | – | 2 | 4 | – | 78 | 166 | 41.50 | – | 1 | 1 |
| Haynes, J.J.(La) | – | 3 | 4 | 1 | 53 | 70 | 23.33 | – | 1 | 4 |
| Hazleton, M.A.(DU) | – | 1 | 2 | – | 11 | 16 | 8.00 | – | – | 2 |
| Heath, D.R.(CU) | – | 4 | 7 | 1 | 75 | 88 | 14.66 | – | 1 | 2 |
| Heath, J.A.(CU) | – | 2 | 2 | – | 35 | 36 | 18.00 | – | – | – |
| Hegg, W.K.(La) | 1989 | 16 | 23 | 2 | 62 | 416 | 19.80 | – | 1 | 44/2 |
| †Hemp, D.L.(Gm) | 1994 | 12 | 20 | 2 | 108 | 505 | 28.05 | 1 | 2 | 6 |
| †Hewitt, J.P.(K) | – | 1 | 1 | 1 | 48* | 48 | – | – | – | – |
| Hewson, D.R.(De) | – | 11 | 20 | 1 | 102* | 393 | 20.68 | 1 | 1 | 7 |
| Hibbert, K.H.(WIA) | – | 4 | 6 | 2 | 83* | 140 | 35.00 | – | 1 | 8 |
| Hick, G.A.(Wo) | 1986 | 18 | 30 | 4 | 315* | 1453 | 55.88 | 4 | 6 | 30 |
| Hicks, T.C.(OU) | – | 3 | 6 | 1 | 38 | 58 | 11.60 | – | – | 2 |
| .Hilsum, I.J.(OU) | – | 2 | 4 | – | 23 | 56 | 14.00 | – | – | 1 |
| †Hinds, R.O.(WIA) | – | 5 | 9 | 2 | 75 | 289 | 41.28 | – | 3 | 2 |
| Hockley, J.B.(K) | – | 5 | 9 | 1 | 46 | 82 | 10.25 | – | – | 1 |
| Hodge, B.J.(Du) | – | 4 | 8 | – | 73 | 284 | 35.50 | – | 2 | 3 |
| Hogg, K.W.(La) | – | 7 | 9 | – | 50 | 109 | 12.11 | – | 1 | 5 |
| Hoggard, M.J.(Y/E) | 2000 | 9 | 11 | 5 | 32 | 95 | 15.83 | – | – | 3 |
| Hollingsworth, A.P.(DU) | – | 3 | 4 | 1 | 42* | 72 | 24.00 | – | – | 1 |
| Holliaoke, A.J.(Sy) | 1995 | 9 | 13 | 2 | 208 | 738 | 67.09 | 2 | 5 | 10 |
| †Holloway, P.C.L.(Sm) | 1997 | 7 | 13 | – | 88 | 428 | 32.92 | – | 3 | 4 |
| Hopkinson, C.D.(Sx) | – | 1 | 2 | – | 33 | 42 | 21.00 | – | – | 2 |
| Howard, W.O.F.(OU) | – | 1 | 2 | – | 1 | 1 | 0.50 | – | – | 1 |
| Hughes, J.(Gm) | – | 7 | 10 | 1 | 74 | 225 | 25.00 | – | 1 | 2 |
| Hughes, T.R.(CU) | – | 2 | 4 | 2 | 10 | 12 | 6.00 | – | – | – |
| Hunt, T.A.(M) | – | 2 | 1 | – | 3 | 3 | 3.00 | – | – | – |
| Hunter, I.D.(Du) | – | 8 | 12 | 1 | 65 | 204 | 18.54 | – | 1 | 2 |
| Hussain, N.(Ex/E) | 1989 | 8 | 12 | – | 155 | 483 | 40.25 | 2 | 2 | 8 |
| †Hussey, M.E.K.(Nh) | 2001 | 13 | 23 | 2 | 310* | 1442 | 68.66 | 5 | 4 | 21 |
| †Hutchison, P.M.(Sx) | – | 3 | 5 | 2 | 20* | 29 | 9.66 | – | – | 1 |
| Hutton, B.L.(M) | – | 11 | 19 | 1 | 116 | 518 | 28.77 | 1 | 4 | 19 |
| Hyam, B.J.(Ex) | 1999 | 1 | 2 | 1 | 16* | 28 | 28.00 | – | – | –/2 |
| †Ilott, M.C.(Ex) | 1993 | 6 | 5 | 3 | 28 | 45 | 22.50 | – | – | 4 |
| Innes, K.J.(Sx) | – | 13 | 22 | 7 | 60* | 478 | 31.86 | – | 2 | 3 |
| Inness, M.W.H.(Nh) | – | 4 | 4 | 1 | 25 | 66 | 22.00 | – | – | 5 |
| Irani, R.C.(Ex) | 1994 | 12 | 19 | 3 | 207* | 977 | 61.06 | 3 | 1 | – |
| Jaffer, W.(I) | – | 7 | 13 | 1 | 53 | 290 | 24.16 | – | 2 | 9 |
| James, S.P.(Gm) | 1992 | 14 | 22 | 1 | 249 | 1111 | 52.90 | 4 | 3 | 7 |
| †Jayasuriya, S.T.(SL) | – | 8 | 12 | – | 57 | 322 | 26.83 | – | 3 | 3 |
| Jayawardena, D.P.M.D.(SL) | – | 6 | 11 | 2 | 125* | 567 | 63.00 | 3 | 1 | 4 |

| F-C | Cap | M | I | NO | HS | Runs | Avge | 100 | 50 | Ct/St |
|---|---|---|---|---|---|---|---|---|---|---|
| Jayawardena, H.A.P.W.(SL) | – | 2 | 2 | 1 | 12* | 19 | 19.00 | – | – | 1 |
| Jefferson, W.I.(Du/BU/Ex) | 2002 | 15 | 29 | 4 | 165* | 815 | 32.60 | 2 | 2 | 17 |
| †Johnson, N.C.(H) | 2001 | 17 | 29 | 1 | 117 | 857 | 31.74 | 1 | 6 | 27 |
| Johnson, P.(Nt) | 1986 | 14 | 25 | 3 | 96 | 662 | 30.09 | – | 5 | 7 |
| Johnson, R.L.(Sm) | 2001 | 9 | 17 | 4 | 61 | 290 | 22.30 | – | 1 | 2 |
| Jones, G.O.(K) | – | 4 | 4 | 1 | 76* | 162 | 54.00 | – | 1 | 5 |
| Jones, H.R.(OU) | – | 3 | 6 | – | 97 | 130 | 21.66 | – | 1 | 3 |
| Jones, I.(M) | – | 1 | 1 | – | 29 | 29 | 29.00 | – | – | – |
| Jones, P.S.(Sm) | 2001 | 7 | 8 | 3 | 37* | 76 | 15.20 | – | – | – |
| †Jones, S.P.(Gm/MCC/E) | 2002 | 13 | 18 | 6 | 44 | 218 | 18.16 | – | – | 5 |
| Jordison, J.R.(CU) | – | 1 | 2 | – | 17 | 28 | 14.00 | – | – | – |
| †Joyce, E.C.(M) | 2002 | 18 | 27 | 3 | 129 | 1267 | 52.79 | 4 | 6 | 17 |
| Kaif, M.(I/Le) | 2002 | 2 | 4 | 1 | 77 | 140 | 46.66 | – | 1 | – |
| Kasprowicz, M.S.(Gm) | 2002 | 12 | 19 | 7 | 72* | 352 | 29.33 | – | 1 | 7 |
| Katich, S.M.(Y) | – | 1 | 2 | – | 21 | 37 | 18.50 | – | – | 1 |
| †Keedy, G.(La) | 2000 | 16 | 22 | 8 | 57 | 219 | 15.64 | – | 1 | 4 |
| Keegan, C.B.(M) | – | 9 | 10 | – | 24 | 58 | 5.80 | – | – | 3 |
| Kendall, W.S.(H) | 1999 | 17 | 31 | 2 | 88 | 705 | 24.31 | – | 4 | 12 |
| Kenway, D.A.(H) | 2001 | 8 | 15 | 2 | 54 | 238 | 18.30 | – | 1 | 15 |
| Kerr, J.I.D.(De) | – | 7 | 12 | 2 | 68 | 299 | 29.90 | – | 3 | 2 |
| Key, R.W.T.(K/MCC/E) | 2001 | 17 | 31 | 1 | 160 | 1255 | 41.83 | 3 | 6 | 12 |
| Khan, A.(K) | – | 16 | 19 | 5 | 58 | 213 | 15.21 | – | 1 | 5 |
| Khan, R.M.(De) | – | 1 | 1 | – | 91 | 91 | 91.00 | – | 1 | – |
| Khan, Z.(I) | – | 4 | 5 | 3 | 14* | 44 | 22.00 | – | – | – |
| Killeen, N.(Du) | 1999 | 15 | 22 | 5 | 27* | 178 | 10.47 | – | – | 5 |
| King, R.D.(WIA) | – | 4 | 5 | 4 | 8 | 11 | 11.00 | – | – | – |
| Kirby, S.P.(Y) | – | 10 | 17 | 3 | 57 | 141 | 10.07 | – | 1 | – |
| Kirby, W.A.(DU) | – | 2 | 4 | 1 | 37 | 78 | 26.00 | – | – | 2 |
| Kirtley, R.J.(Sx/MCC) | 1998 | 11 | 15 | 3 | 36* | 146 | 12.16 | – | – | 4 |
| †Klusener, L.(Nt) | – | 1 | 2 | – | 42 | 42 | 21.00 | – | – | 1 |
| †Knight, N.V.(Wa) | 1995 | 10 | 19 | 3 | 255* | 1520 | 95.00 | 5 | 5 | 10 |
| †Koenig, S.G.(M) | 2002 | 18 | 29 | 2 | 141* | 1251 | 46.33 | 4 | 7 | 6 |
| Krikken, K.M.(De) | 1992 | 9 | 16 | 1 | 48 | 169 | 11.26 | – | – | 26 |
| Kumar, V.H.(CU) | – | 4 | 7 | 1 | 64 | 114 | 16.28 | – | 1 | 3/1 |
| Kumble, A.(I) | – | 5 | 5 | – | 47 | 77 | 15.40 | – | – | – |
| Laney, J.S.(H) | 1996 | 7 | 13 | – | 89 | 289 | 22.23 | – | 1 | 7 |
| Laraman, A.W.(M) | – | 11 | 13 | 3 | 82* | 330 | 33.00 | – | 1 | 3 |
| Law, D.R.(Du) | 2001 | 6 | 10 | 1 | 72* | 253 | 28.11 | – | 2 | 2 |
| Law, S.G.(La) | 2002 | 15 | 26 | 3 | 218 | 1216 | 52.86 | 2 | 6 | 21 |
| Lawson, J.J.C.(WIA) | – | 4 | 4 | – | 17 | 37 | 9.25 | – | – | – |
| Laxman, V.V.S.(I) | – | 8 | 13 | 1 | 85 | 502 | 41.83 | – | 3 | 5 |
| Leatherdale, D.A.(Wo) | 1994 | 14 | 23 | 4 | 154 | 823 | 43.31 | 2 | 4 | 4 |
| Lee, S.(Wo) | 2002c | 2 | 2 | – | 48 | 80 | 40.00 | – | – | 1 |
| †Lehmann, D.S.(Y) | 1997 | 10 | 18 | 1 | 216 | 1136 | 66.82 | 3 | 7 | 5 |
| Lewis, J.(Gs) | 1998 | 16 | 25 | 6 | 57 | 273 | 14.36 | – | 1 | 6 |
| Lewis, J.J.B.(Du) | 1998 | 11 | 18 | 1 | 102 | 402 | 23.64 | 1 | 2 | 2 |
| †Lewry, J.D.(Sx) | 1996 | 10 | 15 | 5 | 21* | 91 | 9.10 | – | – | 1 |
| †Liptrot, C.G.(Wo) | 2002c | 2 | 3 | – | 16 | 32 | 10.66 | – | – | 2 |
| Lloyd, G.D.(La) | 1992 | 7 | 13 | 1 | 80 | 449 | 37.41 | – | 5 | 4 |
| Logan, R.J.(Nt) | – | 13 | 19 | 4 | 32 | 143 | 9.53 | – | – | 5 |
| Loudon, A.G.R.(DU) | – | 3 | 5 | – | 35 | 54 | 10.80 | – | – | 5 |
| Love, M.L.(Du) | 2001 | 6 | 8 | 1 | 251 | 576 | 82.28 | 2 | 2 | 3 |
| Loye, M.B.(Nh) | 1994 | 13 | 22 | 1 | 139 | 768 | 36.57 | 4 | 1 | 7 |
| Lucas, D.S.(Nt) | – | 1 | 1 | – | 49 | 49 | 49.00 | – | – | – |
| †Lumb, M.J.(Y) | – | 16 | 30 | 1 | 124 | 777 | 26.79 | 1 | 4 | 8 |
| †Lungley, T.(De) | – | 7 | 13 | – | 44 | 168 | 12.92 | – | – | 4 |
| McGarry, A.C.(Ex) | – | 3 | 4 | 2 | 11* | 16 | 8.00 | – | – | 1 |
| MacGill, S.C.G.(Nt) | 2002 | 6 | 7 | 1 | 22 | 48 | 8.00 | – | – | 5 |

125

| F-C | Cap | M | I | NO | HS | Runs | Avge | 100 | 50 | Ct/St |
|---|---|---|---|---|---|---|---|---|---|---|
| McGrath, A.(Y) | 1999 | 14 | 26 | 1 | 165 | 803 | 32.12 | 1 | 3 | 7 |
| McGrath, D.E.T.(CU) | – | 1 | 1 | – | 0 | 0 | 0.00 | – | – | – |
| McMahon, P.J.(Nt) | – | 2 | 3 | – | 15 | 15 | 5.00 | – | – | – |
| Maddy, D.L.(Le) | 1996 | 16 | 29 | 4 | 156 | 1187 | 47.48 | 2 | 8 | 22 |
| Mahmood, S.I.(La) | – | 1 | 1 | – | 18 | 18 | 18.00 | – | – | – |
| Maiden, A.J.(DU) | – | 1 | 1 | – | 0 | 0 | 0.00 | – | – | – |
| Malcolm, D.E.(Le) | – | 16 | 22 | 8 | 44 | 138 | 9.85 | – | – | 4 |
| Malik, M.N.(Nt) | – | 7 | 7 | 1 | 18 | 32 | 5.33 | – | – | 1 |
| Marshall, S.J.(CU) | – | 4 | 7 | – | 99 | 182 | 26.00 | – | 1 | 1 |
| Martin, P.J.(La) | 1994 | 12 | 16 | 5 | 117* | 422 | 38.36 | 1 | 1 | 4 |
| Martin-Jenkins, R.S.C.(Sx) | 2000 | 16 | 28 | 4 | 205* | 1008 | 42.00 | 1 | 5 | 1 |
| Mascarenhas, A.D.(H) | 1998 | 16 | 26 | 2 | 94 | 574 | 23.91 | – | 2 | 8 |
| Mason, M.S.(Wo) | 2002ᶜ | 7 | 8 | 2 | 50 | 107 | 17.83 | – | 1 | 1 |
| Masters, D.D.(K) | – | 8 | 7 | – | 68 | 117 | 16.71 | – | 1 | 3 |
| Maynard, M.P.(Gm) | 1987 | 13 | 20 | 1 | 151 | 1058 | 55.68 | 3 | 6 | 14 |
| Mees, T.(OU) | – | 2 | 4 | – | 13 | 20 | 5.00 | – | – | – |
| Middlebrook, J.D.(Ex) | – | 18 | 28 | 4 | 67 | 417 | 17.37 | – | 1 | 7 |
| Millar, N.(OU) | – | 3 | 6 | – | 67 | 203 | 33.83 | – | 2 | 2 |
| Moffat, J.S.D.(CU) | – | 1 | 1 | – | 169 | 169 | 169.00 | 1 | – | 4 |
| †Mongia, D.(I) | – | 1 | 2 | – | 87 | 114 | 57.00 | – | 1 | 1 |
| Montgomerie, R.R.(Sx) | 1999 | 16 | 28 | 1 | 196 | 1026 | 38.00 | 2 | 4 | 16 |
| †Morris, A.C.(H) | 2001 | 2 | 2 | – | 24 | 36 | 18.00 | – | – | – |
| Morton, R.S.(WIA) | – | 5 | 8 | – | 79 | 218 | 27.25 | – | 2 | 4 |
| Moyes, J.R.(CU) | – | 3 | 5 | – | 35 | 51 | 10.20 | – | – | 6 |
| Muchall, G.J.(Du) | – | 15 | 25 | – | 127 | 613 | 24.52 | 1 | 3 | 14 |
| Mullally, A.D.(H/E) | 2000 | 13 | 16 | 5 | 23 | 54 | 4.90 | – | – | 1 |
| Muralitharan, M.(SL) | – | 2 | 3 | 1 | 6 | 6 | 3.00 | – | – | 1 |
| †Murtagh, T.J.(BU/Sy) | – | 5 | 7 | 3 | 22 | 50 | 12.50 | – | – | 3 |
| Mushtaq Ahmed (Sy) | – | 2 | 3 | – | 47 | 66 | 22.00 | – | – | 1 |
| †Mustard, P.(Du) | – | 1 | 1 | – | 75 | 75 | 75.00 | – | 1 | 2 |
| Napier, G.R.(Ex) | – | 9 | 13 | 2 | 54* | 230 | 20.90 | – | 1 | 6 |
| Nash, C.D.(Sx) | – | 1 | 1 | 1 | 0* | 0 | – | – | – | – |
| Nash, D.C.(M) | 2000 | 15 | 19 | 5 | 100 | 646 | 46.14 | 1 | 4 | 36/1 |
| Nehra, A.(I) | – | 4 | 3 | – | 19 | 19 | 6.33 | – | – | – |
| †Newman, S.A.(Sy) | – | 3 | 5 | – | 183 | 322 | 64.40 | 1 | 1 | 3 |
| †Nixon, P.A.(K) | 2000 | 16 | 30 | 7 | 103 | 865 | 37.60 | 1 | 6 | 49/4 |
| Noble, D.J.(CU) | – | 4 | 6 | 2 | 21 | 61 | 15.25 | – | – | – |
| Noffke, A.A.(M) | – | 8 | 10 | 1 | 76 | 203 | 22.55 | – | 1 | 3 |
| Noon, W.M.(Nt) | – | 1 | 1 | – | 15 | 15 | 15.00 | – | – | 1 |
| Ormond, J.(Sy) | – | 15 | 17 | 4 | 43* | 208 | 16.00 | – | – | 6 |
| Ostler, D.P.(Wa) | 1991 | 14 | 25 | 1 | 225 | 1039 | 43.29 | 2 | 5 | 24 |
| Pagon, D.J.(WIA) | – | 4 | 6 | – | 18 | 37 | 6.16 | – | – | – |
| †Panesar, M.S.(BU/Nh) | – | 6 | 6 | 2 | 2* | 4 | 1.00 | – | – | 3 |
| †Parker, J.W.R.(CU) | – | 4 | 7 | – | 86 | 284 | 40.57 | – | 2 | 1 |
| Parkin, O.T.(Gm) | – | 3 | 3 | – | 16 | 23 | 7.66 | – | – | 1 |
| Parsons, K.A.(Sm) | 1999 | 15 | 26 | 2 | 68 | 581 | 24.20 | – | 4 | 16 |
| Patel, M.M.(K) | 1994 | 16 | 20 | 6 | 82 | 561 | 40.07 | – | 5 | 9 |
| †Patel, P.A.(I) | – | 5 | 8 | 2 | 32 | 97 | 16.16 | – | – | 5 |
| Patel, S.R.(Nt) | – | 1 | 1 | – | 35 | 35 | 35.00 | – | – | – |
| Pattison, I.(Du) | – | 3 | 6 | – | 27 | 61 | 10.16 | – | – | 2 |
| Paynter, D.E.(Nh) | – | 2 | 4 | 1 | 20 | 32 | 10.66 | – | – | 2 |
| †Pearson, J.A.(Gs) | – | 3 | 6 | 1 | 51 | 114 | 22.80 | – | 1 | 2 |
| †Penberthy, A.L.(Nh) | 1994 | 16 | 25 | 3 | 130* | 909 | 41.31 | 2 | 5 | 9 |
| Peng, N.(Du) | 2001 | 12 | 21 | – | 108 | 508 | 24.19 | 1 | 2 | 3 |
| †Perera, P.D.R.L.(SL) | – | 2 | 4 | 2 | 5* | 15 | 7.50 | – | – | 2 |
| Peters, S.D.(Wo) | 2002ᶜ | 10 | 16 | – | 146 | 667 | 41.68 | 2 | 3 | 6 |
| Pettini, M.L.(Ex) | – | 3 | 6 | – | 64 | 157 | 26.16 | – | 1 | 2 |
| Phillips, B.J.(Nh) | – | 1 | 1 | – | 17 | 17 | 17.00 | – | – | – |

| F-C | Cap | M | I | NO | HS | Runs | Avge | 100 | 50 | Ct/St |
|---|---|---|---|---|---|---|---|---|---|---|
| Phillips, N.C.(Du) | 2001 | 10 | 16 | 6 | 58* | 226 | 22.60 | – | 1 | 4 |
| †Phillips, T.J.(DU/Ex) | – | 8 | 13 | 3 | 75 | 281 | 28.10 | – | 1 | 6 |
| Pietersen, K.P.(Nt) | 2002 | 12 | 17 | 3 | 254* | 871 | 62.21 | 4 | – | 12 |
| Pipe, D.J.(Wo) | 2002ᶜ | 3 | 4 | – | 26 | 64 | 16.00 | – | – | 12/1 |
| Piper, K.J.(Wa) | 1992 | 8 | 12 | 2 | 64* | 163 | 16.30 | – | 1 | 14/1 |
| Pollock, S.M.(Wa) | 1996 | 10 | 18 | 1 | 66 | 425 | 25.00 | – | 4 | 13 |
| †Porter, J.J.(OU/BU) | – | 3 | 5 | – | 37 | 123 | 24.60 | – | – | 4 |
| Pothas, N.(H) | – | 16 | 26 | 1 | 99 | 597 | 23.88 | – | 5 | 30/4 |
| Powell, D.B.(WIA) | – | 3 | 3 | 1 | 11 | 19 | 9.50 | – | – | 2 |
| Powell, M.J.(Gm) | 2000 | 16 | 26 | 3 | 135 | 1152 | 50.08 | 3 | 7 | 7 |
| Powell, M.J.(Nh) | – | 3 | 5 | 1 | 108* | 289 | 72.25 | 2 | – | 6 |
| Powell, M.J.(Wa) | 1999 | 17 | 31 | 2 | 103 | 872 | 30.06 | 1 | 6 | 13 |
| †Pratt, A.(Du) | 2001 | 17 | 29 | 2 | 93 | 556 | 20.59 | – | 3 | 42/3 |
| †Pratt, G.J.(Du) | – | 16 | 27 | – | 78 | 746 | 27.62 | – | 4 | 12 |
| Prior, M.J.(Sx) | – | 16 | 27 | 3 | 102* | 741 | 30.87 | 1 | 5 | 39/2 |
| Prittipaul, L.R.(H) | – | 3 | 6 | – | 32 | 45 | 7.50 | – | – | 1 |
| Pyemont, J.P.(De) | – | 4 | 7 | – | 43 | 121 | 17.28 | – | – | 1 |
| Ramprakash, M.R.(Sy) | 2002 | 15 | 25 | 4 | 218 | 1194 | 56.85 | 4 | 6 | 6 |
| Randall, S.J.(Nt) | – | 2 | 3 | – | 8 | 13 | 4.33 | – | – | 1 |
| Ratcliffe, J.D.(Sy) | – | 1 | 2 | 1 | 13 | 16 | 16.00 | – | – | – |
| Ratra, A.(I) | – | 7 | 11 | 2 | 101* | 183 | 20.33 | 1 | – | 14/2 |
| Rawnsley, M.J.(Wo) | 2002ᶜ | 4 | 3 | 1 | 9* | 20 | 10.00 | – | – | 2 |
| Read, C.M.W.(Nt/MCC) | 1999 | 18 | 28 | 5 | 127 | 797 | 34.65 | 1 | 4 | 66/2 |
| Redmayne, J.R.S.(OU) | – | 2 | 4 | 1 | 75* | 106 | 35.33 | – | 1 | – |
| Rees, T.M.(La) | – | 1 | 1 | – | 16 | 16 | 16.00 | – | – | 1 |
| Rhodes, S.J.(Wo) | 1986 | 15 | 22 | 6 | 124 | 636 | 39.75 | 1 | 2 | 37/4 |
| Richardson, A.(Wa) | 2002 | 10 | 12 | 4 | 91 | 132 | 16.50 | – | 1 | 5 |
| Richardson, S.A.(Y) | – | 2 | 4 | – | 29 | 45 | 11.25 | – | – | 2 |
| Roberts, T.W.(La) | – | 2 | 2 | – | 2 | 2 | 1.00 | – | – | 1 |
| Robinson, D.D.J.(Ex) | 1997 | 18 | 34 | 2 | 175 | 1474 | 46.06 | 5 | 6 | 17 |
| Robinson, M.A.(Sx) | 1997 | 1 | 2 | 1 | 6 | 10 | 10.00 | – | – | 1 |
| Rollins, A.S.(Nh) | – | 6 | 12 | 1 | 107 | 460 | 41.81 | 1 | 2 | 6 |
| Rose, G.D.(Sm) | 1988 | 3 | 4 | 2 | 32 | 84 | 21.00 | – | – | 1 |
| †Russell, R.C.(Gs) | 1985 | 17 | 28 | 6 | 119* | 991 | 45.04 | 3 | 5 | 39/2 |
| Saggers, M.J.(K) | 2001 | 16 | 19 | 6 | 16* | 73 | 5.61 | – | – | 6 |
| Sales, D.J.G.(Nh) | 1999 | 14 | 22 | – | 179 | 551 | 25.04 | 1 | 3 | 11 |
| Salisbury, I.D.K.(Sy) | 1998 | 14 | 20 | 2 | 59 | 340 | 18.88 | – | 1 | 11 |
| Samaraweera, T.T.(SL) | – | 5 | 5 | – | 57 | 101 | 20.20 | – | 1 | 3 |
| Sampson, P.J.(Sy) | – | 2 | 3 | 1 | 42 | 43 | 21.50 | – | – | – |
| †Sangakkara, K.C.(SL) | – | 9 | 15 | 2 | 113 | 345 | 26.53 | 1 | 1 | 12/1 |
| Saqlain Mushtaq (Sy) | 1998 | 10 | 13 | 2 | 60 | 278 | 25.27 | – | 2 | 4 |
| Savill, T.E.(CU/Nt) | – | 4 | 6 | 2 | 18* | 58 | 14.50 | – | – | 2 |
| †Sayers, J.J.(OU) | – | 4 | 8 | – | 55 | 152 | 19.00 | – | 1 | 1 |
| †Schofield, C.P.(La) | 2002 | 7 | 9 | 1 | 91 | 262 | 32.75 | – | 2 | 4 |
| Schofield, J.E.K.(H) | – | 1 | 2 | 1 | 18* | 18 | 18.00 | – | – | – |
| Sehwag, V.(I) | – | 8 | 13 | – | 142 | 640 | 49.23 | 3 | 1 | 13 |
| †Selwood, S.A.(De) | – | 10 | 19 | – | 99 | 457 | 24.05 | – | 2 | 1 |
| Shafayat, B.M.(Nt) | – | 7 | 13 | 1 | 104 | 450 | 37.50 | 1 | 2 | 5 |
| Shah, O.A.(M/MCC) | 2000 | 17 | 26 | 3 | 172* | 1084 | 47.13 | 3 | 6 | 5 |
| Shahid, N.(Sy) | 1998 | 13 | 20 | 1 | 150 | 712 | 37.47 | 2 | 3 | 24 |
| Shankar, A.(CU) | – | 4 | 7 | – | 143 | 167 | 23.85 | 1 | – | 4 |
| Sharif, F.(CU) | – | 2 | 3 | – | 36 | 46 | 15.33 | – | – | 2 |
| †Sharif, Z.K.(Ex) | – | 2 | 1 | – | 42 | 42 | 42.00 | – | – | 1 |
| Sharpe, T.J.(OU) | – | 3 | 6 | 2 | 7* | 12 | 3.00 | – | – | 2 |
| †Sheikh, M.A.(Wa) | – | 5 | 8 | 2 | 43 | 178 | 29.66 | – | – | 1 |
| Sheriyar, A.(Wo) | 1997 | 18 | 20 | 9 | 18 | 107 | 9.72 | – | – | 1 |
| †Sidebottom, R.J.(Y) | 2000 | 13 | 21 | 7 | 28 | 135 | 9.64 | – | – | 4 |
| Sillence, R.J.(Gs) | – | 5 | 7 | – | 101 | 167 | 23.85 | 1 | – | 2 |

| F-C | Cap | M | I | NO | HS | Runs | Avge | 100 | 50 | Ct/St |
|---|---|---|---|---|---|---|---|---|---|---|
| Silverwood, C.E.W.(Y) | 1996 | 12 | 19 | 2 | 44* | 283 | 16.64 | – | – | 3 |
| Simcox, A.D.(CU) | – | 4 | 7 | 1 | 30 | 72 | 12.00 | – | – | 2 |
| Simmons, L.M.P.(WIA) | – | 5 | 8 | 1 | 81 | 176 | 25.14 | – | 1 | 7/2 |
| Singh, A.(Wo) | 2002[c] | 18 | 32 | – | 187 | 1167 | 36.46 | 2 | 6 | 11 |
| Smethurst, M.P.(La) | – | 4 | 4 | 2 | 13 | 32 | 16.00 | – | – | 1 |
| Smith, A.M.(Gs) | 1995 | 9 | 13 | 6 | 21 | 92 | 13.14 | – | – | 3 |
| Smith, B.F.(Wo) | 2002[c] | 18 | 30 | 3 | 137 | 1202 | 44.51 | 4 | 6 | 6 |
| †Smith, D.S.(WIA) | – | 6 | 10 | – | 181 | 465 | 46.50 | 1 | 2 | 4 |
| Smith, E.T.(K) | 2001 | 17 | 32 | 2 | 154 | 1239 | 41.30 | 2 | 8 | 4 |
| Smith, G.J.(Nt) | 2001 | 15 | 20 | 7 | 39* | 243 | 18.69 | – | – | 4 |
| Smith, N.M.K.(Wa) | 1993 | 8 | 15 | – | 96 | 337 | 22.46 | – | 2 | 7 |
| Smith, R.A.(H) | 1985 | 15 | 25 | 1 | 104 | 832 | 34.66 | 2 | 3 | 6 |
| Smith, W.R.(Nt) | – | 1 | 1 | 1 | 38* | 38 | – | – | – | – |
| Snape, J.N.(Gs) | 1999 | 5 | 8 | – | 28 | 117 | 14.62 | – | – | 2 |
| Solanki, V.S.(Wo) | 1998 | 16 | 26 | 4 | 153* | 944 | 42.90 | 2 | 5 | 18 |
| Souter, M.A.(DU) | – | 1 | 1 | – | 1 | 1 | 1.00 | – | – | – |
| Spearman, C.M.(Gs) | 2002 | 17 | 34 | 4 | 180* | 1444 | 48.13 | 5 | 7 | 16 |
| Spires, J.A.S.(Wa) | – | 6 | 7 | 3 | 37* | 70 | 17.50 | – | – | 3 |
| Srinath, J.(Le) | 2002 | 5 | 7 | – | 52 | 98 | 14.00 | – | 1 | 2 |
| Stemp, R.D.(Le) | – | 1 | 2 | 1 | 8* | 8 | 8.00 | – | – | – |
| Stephenson, J.P.(Ex) | 1989 | 13 | 24 | 8 | 100* | 562 | 35.12 | 1 | 2 | 7 |
| Stevens, D.I.(Le/MCC) | 2002 | 17 | 29 | 3 | 125 | 850 | 32.69 | 1 | 6 | 16 |
| Stewart, A.J.(Sy/E) | 1985 | 11 | 16 | 2 | 123 | 751 | 53.64 | 1 | 5 | 33/5 |
| †Strauss, A.J.(M/MCC) | 2001 | 17 | 27 | 2 | 141 | 1202 | 48.08 | 3 | 5 | 16 |
| †Stubbings, S.D.(De) | 2001 | 11 | 20 | 1 | 128 | 428 | 22.52 | 1 | 1 | 5 |
| Suppiah, A.V.(Sm) | – | 2 | 4 | – | 21 | 27 | 6.75 | – | – | 1 |
| †Sutcliffe, I.J.(Le) | 1997 | 16 | 29 | 3 | 125* | 1088 | 41.84 | 2 | 5 | 4 |
| Sutton, L.D.(De) | 2002 | 10 | 19 | 1 | 80 | 400 | 22.22 | – | 3 | 30/1 |
| Swann, A.J.(La) | 2002 | 18 | 31 | 2 | 128 | 1073 | 37.00 | 2 | 6 | 12 |
| Swann, G.P.(Nh) | 1999 | 11 | 16 | – | 183 | 539 | 33.68 | 2 | 1 | 5 |
| Symington, M.J.(Du) | – | 10 | 16 | 2 | 42 | 224 | 16.00 | – | – | 6 |
| Symonds, A.(K) | 1999 | 12 | 24 | 2 | 118 | 858 | 39.00 | 2 | 4 | 16 |
| †Taylor, B.V.(Sx) | – | 10 | 14 | 2 | 18* | 70 | 5.83 | – | – | 1 |
| Taylor, C.G.(Gs) | 2001 | 15 | 29 | 2 | 126 | 664 | 24.59 | 1 | 3 | 15 |
| Taylor, C.R.(Y) | – | 5 | 9 | 1 | 52* | 150 | 18.75 | – | 2 | 4 |
| Tendulkar, S.R.(I) | – | 6 | 8 | – | 193 | 573 | 71.62 | 2 | 2 | 2 |
| †Thomas, I.J.(Gm) | – | 9 | 15 | 1 | 76 | 273 | 19.50 | – | 2 | 2 |
| †Thomas, S.D.(Gm) | 1997 | 16 | 22 | 1 | 47 | 274 | 13.04 | – | – | 4 |
| Thorburn, M.(DU) | – | 3 | 3 | – | 12 | 16 | 5.33 | – | – | 1 |
| Thornicroft, N.D.(Y) | – | 3 | 6 | 3 | 4* | 9 | 3.00 | – | – | – |
| †Thorpe, A.M.(Du) | – | 7 | 13 | – | 95 | 271 | 20.84 | – | 2 | 5 |
| †Thorpe, G.P.(Sy/E) | 1991 | 8 | 14 | – | 143 | 526 | 37.57 | 2 | 1 | 6 |
| †Tillekeratne, H.P.(SL) | – | 8 | 13 | 5 | 81 | 366 | 45.75 | – | 2 | 8 |
| †Tomlinson, J.A.(BU/H) | – | 6 | 10 | 5 | 23 | 34 | 6.80 | – | – | 2 |
| Tournier, M.A.(BU) | – | 1 | 1 | 1 | 10* | 10 | – | – | – | – |
| †Tredwell, J.C.(K) | – | 4 | 6 | – | 61 | 161 | 26.83 | – | 2 | 8 |
| Trego, P.D.(Sm) | – | 4 | 8 | 1 | 140 | 270 | 38.57 | 1 | – | 2 |
| Tremlett, C.T.(H) | – | 11 | 14 | 6 | 40* | 180 | 22.50 | – | – | 4 |
| †Trescothick, M.E.(Sm/E) | 1999 | 6 | 11 | 2 | 161 | 622 | 69.11 | 2 | 4 | 5 |
| Trott, B.J.(K) | – | 3 | 3 | – | 26 | 27 | 9.00 | – | – | – |
| †Troughton, J.O.(Wa) | 2002 | 14 | 24 | 3 | 131* | 1067 | 50.80 | 3 | 6 | 8 |
| Tudor, A.J.(Sy/E) | 1999 | 10 | 14 | – | 61 | 222 | 15.85 | – | 1 | 2 |
| Tufnell, P.C.R.(M) | 1990 | 14 | 15 | 8 | 45 | 89 | 12.71 | – | – | 3 |
| Turner, R.J.(Sm) | 1994 | 16 | 27 | 4 | 83* | 691 | 30.04 | – | 4 | 50/1 |
| Udal, S.D.(H) | 1992 | 17 | 26 | 6 | 88 | 516 | 25.80 | – | 1 | 9 |
| Upashantha, K.E.A.(SL) | – | 5 | 6 | – | 25 | 43 | 7.16 | – | – | 1 |
| †Vaas, W.P.U.C.J.(SL) | – | 5 | 7 | 1 | 50* | 138 | 23.00 | – | 1 | 2 |
| Vaughan, M.P.(Y/E) | 1995 | 9 | 15 | 2 | 197 | 976 | 75.07 | 4 | 3 | 5 |

**F-C**

| | Cap | M | I | NO | HS | Runs | Avge | 100 | 50 | Ct/St |
|---|---|---|---|---|---|---|---|---|---|---|
| Vonwiller, B.M.(OU) | – | 1 | 1 | 1 | 4* | 4 | – | – | – | 1 |
| Wagg, G.G.(Wa) | – | 5 | 8 | 2 | 51 | 161 | 26.83 | – | 1 | 1 |
| Wagh, M.A.(Wa) | 2000 | 10 | 18 | – | 109 | 503 | 27.94 | 1 | 2 | 3 |
| †Walker, G.W.(Le) | – | 1 | 2 | 1 | 37* | 44 | 44.00 | – | – | 1 |
| †Walker, M.J.(K) | 2000 | 12 | 23 | 3 | 46 | 382 | 19.10 | – | – | 3 |
| †Wallace, M.A.(Gm) | – | 17 | 25 | 4 | 106* | 553 | 26.33 | 1 | 2 | 58/3 |
| Wanasinghe, W.M.P.N.(SL) | – | 1 | 1 | 1 | 6* | 6 | – | – | – | – |
| †Ward, I.J.(Sy) | 2000 | 17 | 31 | 3 | 168* | 1759 | 62.82 | 7 | 7 | 10 |
| Ward, T.R.(Le) | 2001 | 14 | 24 | – | 89 | 554 | 23.08 | – | 4 | 7 |
| Warn, C.J.(De) | – | 1 | 1 | – | 1 | 1 | 1.00 | – | – | – |
| Warren, C.C.M.(OU) | – | 2 | 3 | – | 8 | 12 | 4.00 | – | – | 3 |
| Warren, N.A.(Wa) | – | 1 | 1 | – | 13 | 13 | 13.00 | – | – | – |
| Warren, R.J.(Nh) | 1995 | 6 | 11 | 1 | 150* | 369 | 36.90 | 1 | 1 | 1 |
| Waugh, M.E.(Ex) | 1989 | 2 | 3 | – | 117 | 242 | 80.66 | 1 | 1 | 4 |
| Waugh, S.R.(K) | 2002 | 4 | 6 | 1 | 146 | 224 | 44.80 | 1 | – | 3 |
| †Weekes, P.N.(M) | 1993 | 18 | 25 | 6 | 127* | 990 | 52.10 | 4 | 3 | 23 |
| Welch, G.(De) | 2001 | 14 | 23 | 5 | 64 | 460 | 25.55 | – | 3 | 8 |
| Wells, V.J.(Le) | 1994 | 11 | 17 | 2 | 150 | 558 | 37.20 | 1 | 3 | 9 |
| Welton, G.E.(Nt) | – | 16 | 28 | 2 | 115 | 954 | 36.69 | 1 | 6 | 16 |
| Weston, R.M.S.(M) | 2001 | 9 | 11 | 2 | 72 | 237 | 26.33 | – | 2 | 4 |
| †Weston, W.P.C.(Wo) | 1995 | 8 | 15 | 2 | 82 | 315 | 24.23 | – | 3 | 7 |
| Wharf, A.G.(Gm) | 2000 | 3 | 2 | – | 6 | 6 | 3.00 | – | – | – |
| †Wharton, L.J.(De) | – | 14 | 23 | 12 | 16 | 83 | 7.54 | – | – | 7 |
| Whiley, M.J.A.(Le) | – | 7 | 9 | 2 | 13* | 41 | 5.85 | – | – | 1 |
| White, C.(Y/E) | 1993 | 13 | 24 | 2 | 161 | 947 | 43.04 | 2 | 7 | 6 |
| White, G.W.(H) | 1998 | 8 | 14 | 2 | 36 | 234 | 19.50 | – | 6 | 6 |
| White, R.A.(Nh) | – | 4 | 7 | 1 | 277 | 556 | 92.66 | 1 | 3 | 1 |
| Wigley, D.H.(Y) | – | 1 | 2 | 1 | 15 | 19 | 19.00 | – | – | – |
| Windows, M.G.N.(Gs) | 1998 | 17 | 31 | 2 | 145 | 1062 | 36.62 | 2 | 7 | 6 |
| Wood, J.(La) | – | 8 | 11 | – | 64 | 185 | 16.81 | – | 1 | 2 |
| Wood, M.J.(Sm) | – | 15 | 28 | – | 196 | 971 | 34.67 | 3 | 5 | 5 |
| Wood, M.J.(Y) | 2001 | 9 | 17 | – | 43 | 201 | 11.82 | – | – | 12 |
| Wright, A.S.(Le) | – | 5 | 8 | 1 | 28 | 94 | 13.42 | – | – | 1 |
| Wyatt, A.A.(OU) | – | 2 | 3 | 1 | 10* | 18 | 9.00 | – | – | – |
| †Yardy, M.H.(Sx) | – | 10 | 17 | – | 93 | 492 | 28.94 | – | 2 | 11 |
| Yates, G.(La) | 1994 | 2 | 2 | – | 14 | 17 | 8.50 | – | – | – |
| Yohannan, T.(I) | – | 4 | 3 | 3 | 4* | 4 | – | – | – | – |
| †Zoysa, D.N.T.(SL) | – | 4 | 5 | 1 | 28 | 29 | 7.25 | – | – | 2 |
| Zuiderent, B.(Sx) | – | 1 | 2 | – | 10 | 10 | 5.00 | – | – | – |

## BOWLING

See BATTING and FIELDING section for details of matches, caps and teams

| | Cat | O | M | R | W | Avge | Best | 5wI | 10wM |
|---|---|---|---|---|---|---|---|---|---|
| Abdul Razzaq | RFM | 206.3 | 25 | 757 | 26 | 29.11 | 7-133 | 2 | – |
| Adams, C.J. | RM/OB | 7 | 1 | 24 | 0 | | | | |
| Adams, J.H.K. | LM | 21 | 4 | 102 | 2 | 51.00 | 2- 81 | – | – |
| Afzaal, U. | SLA | 63.3 | 20 | 180 | 4 | 45.00 | 3- 32 | – | – |
| Agarkar, A.B. | RFM | 162.3 | 32 | 640 | 14 | 45.71 | 4- 55 | – | – |
| Aldred, P. | RM | 73.2 | 19 | 211 | 5 | 42.20 | 2- 30 | – | – |
| Ali, Kabir | RMF | 547.1 | 129 | 1781 | 71 | 25.08 | 7- 43 | 5 | 2 |
| Ali, S.M.B. | LFM | 405 | 63 | 1708 | 47 | 36.34 | 3- 48 | – | – |
| Alleyne, M.W. | RM | 266 | 59 | 876 | 17 | 51.52 | 3- 76 | – | – |
| Ambrose, T.R. | (WK) | 1 | 0 | 1 | 0 | | | | |
| Amerasinghe, M.K.D.I. | RFM | 26 | 2 | 159 | 3 | 53.00 | 3- 46 | – | – |
| Amin, R.M. | SLA | 24 | 8 | 55 | 2 | 27.50 | 2- 40 | – | – |
| Anderson, J.M. | RF | 326.4 | 61 | 1114 | 50 | 22.28 | 6- 23 | 3 | – |
| Anderson, R.S.G. | RMF | 143 | 29 | 550 | 9 | 61.11 | 4- 97 | – | – |

| F-C | Cat | O | M | R | W | Avge | Best | 5wI | 10wM |
|---|---|---|---|---|---|---|---|---|---|
| Arnold, R.P. | OB | 4 | 1 | 7 | 0 | | | – | – |
| Averis, J.M.M. | RMF | 128 | 33 | 432 | 13 | 33.23 | 5- 51 | 1 | – |
| Azhar Mahmood | RMF | 109.2 | 27 | 345 | 20 | 17.25 | 8- 61 | 1 | – |
| Ball, M.C.J. | OB | 287 | 66 | 876 | 23 | 38.08 | 6- 54 | 1 | – |
| Banes, M.J. | OB | 3 | 0 | 13 | 0 | | | – | – |
| Bangar, S.B. | RMF | 132.5 | 25 | 395 | 14 | 28.21 | 4- 40 | – | – |
| Barnett, K.J. | RM/LB | 22.4 | 6 | 74 | 2 | 37.00 | 1- 7 | – | – |
| Batty, G.J. | OB | 613.1 | 162 | 1733 | 56 | 30.94 | 6- 71 | 3 | – |
| Bell, I.R. | RM | 34 | 8 | 89 | 2 | 44.50 | 1- 22 | – | – |
| Benn, S.J. | SLA | 98 | 20 | 322 | 7 | 46.00 | 2- 52 | – | – |
| Best, T.Le B. | RFM | 69.4 | 14 | 249 | 6 | 41.50 | 2- 40 | – | – |
| Betts, M.M. | RFM | 248.4 | 34 | 1023 | 20 | 51.15 | 3- 75 | – | – |
| Bevan, M.G. | SLC | 33 | 1 | 118 | 3 | 39.33 | 3- 25 | – | – |
| Bichel, A.J. | RFM | 297 | 77 | 902 | 36 | 25.05 | 9- 93 | 1 | 1 |
| Bicknell, M.P. | RFM | 326 | 78 | 1067 | 34 | 31.38 | 6- 42 | 2 | – |
| Bishop, J.E. | LMF | 120 | 17 | 470 | 11 | 42.72 | 3- 59 | – | – |
| Black, M.I. | RFM | 113.1 | 32 | 344 | 14 | 24.57 | 4- 32 | – | – |
| Blackwell, I.D. | SLA | 312.5 | 83 | 830 | 22 | 37.72 | 5- 49 | 1 | – |
| Blain, J.A.R. | RMF | 192.4 | 21 | 909 | 16 | 56.81 | 4-144 | – | – |
| Bloomfield, T.F. | RMF | 93.1 | 20 | 340 | 7 | 48.57 | 3- 45 | – | – |
| Boje, N. | SLA | 238 | 58 | 671 | 27 | 24.85 | 6-128 | 2 | – |
| Bond, S.E. | RF | 95.4 | 23 | 330 | 12 | 27.50 | 5- 64 | 1 | – |
| Bopara, R.S. | RM | 16 | 1 | 74 | 1 | 74.00 | 1- 43 | – | – |
| Bowler, P.D. | OB | 7 | 1 | 23 | 1 | 23.00 | 1- 20 | – | – |
| Brandy, D.G. | RMF | 17 | 0 | 114 | 2 | 57.00 | 2- 86 | – | – |
| Bravo, D.J.J. | RM | 5 | 0 | 17 | 0 | | | – | – |
| Bridge, G.D. | SLA | 248.5 | 61 | 761 | 21 | 36.23 | 4- 50 | – | – |
| Brown, A.D. | LB | 3 | 0 | 7 | 0 | | | – | – |
| Brown, D.R. | RFM | 493.4 | 75 | 1716 | 52 | 33.00 | 7-110 | 2 | – |
| Brown, J.F. | OB | 352.5 | 76 | 1138 | 28 | 40.64 | 4- 88 | – | – |
| Brown, S.J.E. | LFM | 18.4 | 3 | 65 | 2 | 32.50 | 2- 65 | – | – |
| Bruce, J.T.A. | RMF | 48 | 6 | 178 | 5 | 35.60 | 2- 76 | – | – |
| Bulbeck, M.P.L. | LMF | 534 | 93 | 1940 | 58 | 33.44 | 6- 93 | 1 | – |
| Burns, M. | RM | 101.4 | 14 | 444 | 11 | 40.36 | 3- 54 | – | – |
| Butcher, M.A. | RM | 12 | 3 | 60 | 0 | | | – | – |
| Caddick, A.R. | RFM | 423.3 | 87 | 1313 | 48 | 27.35 | 6- 84 | 4 | – |
| Carter, N.M. | LFM | 228.1 | 35 | 957 | 20 | 47.85 | 4- 46 | – | – |
| Cassar, M.E. | RMF | 113.3 | 18 | 464 | 16 | 29.00 | 6- 34 | 1 | 1 |
| Chandana, U.D.U. | LB | 35 | 9 | 109 | 2 | 54.50 | 1- 45 | – | – |
| Chapple, G. | RFM | 539.3 | 128 | 1594 | 54 | 29.51 | 6- 30 | 3 | 1 |
| Cherry, D.D. | RM | 3 | 3 | 0 | 0 | | | – | – |
| Chilton, M.J. | RM | 71 | 17 | 226 | 3 | 75.33 | 1- 10 | – | – |
| Clark, P.J. | RM | 17 | 1 | 92 | 1 | 92.00 | 1- 72 | – | – |
| Clarke, A.J. | RM | 36.3 | 5 | 113 | 7 | 16.14 | 5- 54 | 1 | – |
| Clarke, R. | RFM | 94.3 | 15 | 451 | 11 | 41.00 | 3- 41 | – | – |
| Clough, G.D. | RM | 13 | 1 | 61 | 2 | 30.50 | 2- 61 | – | – |
| Collingwood, P.D. | RMF | 96.4 | 24 | 258 | 10 | 25.80 | 4- 31 | – | – |
| Cook, J.W. | RM | 132 | 31 | 474 | 9 | 52.66 | 2- 7 | – | – |
| Cook, S.J. | RM | 367.2 | 71 | 1305 | 48 | 27.18 | 8- 63 | 2 | – |
| Cork, D.G. | RFM | 403.4 | 101 | 1210 | 64 | 18.90 | 6- 51 | 5 | 1 |
| Cosker, D.A. | SLA | 317.5 | 60 | 1012 | 20 | 50.60 | 4-135 | – | – |
| Cottey, P.A. | OB | 16.2 | 5 | 33 | 0 | | | – | – |
| Cousins, D.M. | RMF | 311.2 | 67 | 1024 | 22 | 46.54 | 4- 75 | – | – |
| Cowan, A.P. | RFM | 276.1 | 70 | 843 | 31 | 27.19 | 5- 68 | 1 | – |
| Craven, V.J. | RM | 15 | 3 | 56 | 1 | 56.00 | 1- 25 | – | – |
| Creese, G.R. | OB | 29.5 | 2 | 103 | 3 | 34.33 | 1- 6 | – | – |
| Creese, M.L. | SLA | 3 | 0 | 9 | 0 | | | – | – |
| Croft, R.D.B. | OB | 619 | 138 | 1701 | 40 | 42.52 | 5- 71 | 1 | – |

| F-C | Cat | O | M | R | W | Avge | Best | 5wI | 10wM |
|-----|-----|---|---|---|---|------|------|-----|------|
| Crowe, C.D. | OB | 193.2 | 51 | 593 | 16 | 37.06 | 4- 63 | – | – |
| Cunliffe, R.J. | RM | 1.1 | 0 | 3 | 0 | | | | |
| Dagnall, C.E. | RM | 91 | 24 | 270 | 7 | 38.57 | 3- 55 | – | – |
| Dakin, J.M. | RM | 360.2 | 77 | 1233 | 40 | 30.82 | 4- 17 | – | – |
| Dale, A. | RMF | 125 | 25 | 459 | 6 | 76.50 | 1- 15 | – | – |
| Dalrymple, J.W.M. | OB | 122.4 | 20 | 467 | 6 | 77.83 | 4-152 | – | – |
| Das, S.S. | OB | 2 | 0 | 8 | 0 | | | | |
| Davies, A.M. | RM | 357.5 | 106 | 942 | 36 | 26.16 | 5- 61 | 1 | – |
| Davies, A.P. | RMF | 116.2 | 14 | 420 | 15 | 28.00 | 5- 79 | 1 | – |
| Davis, M.J.G. | OB | 347.2 | 71 | 1081 | 28 | 38.60 | 6- 97 | 1 | – |
| Dawson, R.K.J. | OB | 488.5 | 104 | 1551 | 40 | 38.77 | 5- 42 | 2 | – |
| Dean, K.J. | LMF | 590 | 148 | 1951 | 83 | 23.50 | 7- 42 | 3 | 2 |
| DeFreitas, P.A.J. | RFM | 566.4 | 150 | 1594 | 51 | 31.25 | 6-101 | 2 | – |
| De Silva, P.A. | OB | 42 | 7 | 142 | 2 | 71.00 | 1- 34 | – | – |
| Donald, A.A. | RFM | 24 | 3 | 77 | 5 | 15.40 | 5- 77 | 1 | – |
| Dowman, M.P. | RMF | 72 | 24 | 223 | 10 | 22.30 | 4- 28 | – | – |
| Driver, R.C. | RM | 105 | 28 | 331 | 12 | 27.58 | 5- 70 | 1 | – |
| Dumelow, N.R.C. | OB | 30 | 5 | 145 | 0 | | | | |
| Durston, W.J. | SLA | 14 | 0 | 65 | 1 | 65.00 | 1- 25 | – | – |
| Dutch, K.P. | OB | 268.3 | 59 | 852 | 15 | 56.80 | 3-104 | – | – |
| Ealham, M.A. | RMF | 351 | 107 | 954 | 28 | 34.07 | 3- 22 | – | – |
| Elliott, M.T.G. | LM | 16 | 1 | 77 | 1 | 77.00 | 1- 64 | – | – |
| Elstub, C.J. | RMF | 41 | 7 | 181 | 1 | 181.00 | 1- 16 | – | – |
| Fairbrother, N.H. | LM | 6 | 0 | 27 | 0 | | | | |
| Fellows, G.M. | RM | 73.5 | 9 | 315 | 8 | 39.37 | 3- 90 | – | – |
| Ferley, R.S. | SLA | 87 | 20 | 303 | 8 | 37.87 | 4- 83 | – | – |
| Fernando, C.R.D. | RFM | 49.2 | 5 | 230 | 5 | 46.00 | 3-154 | – | – |
| Fernando, T.C.B. | RMF | 113.5 | 14 | 524 | 10 | 52.40 | 4- 72 | – | – |
| Fisher, I.D. | SLA | 514 | 103 | 1725 | 32 | 53.90 | 5- 87 | 1 | – |
| Fleming, M.V. | RM | 102 | 19 | 292 | 6 | 48.66 | 4- 68 | – | – |
| Flintoff, A. | RFM | 251 | 53 | 768 | 14 | 54.85 | 2- 22 | – | – |
| Flower, A. | (WK) | 6 | 0 | 19 | 0 | | | | |
| Flower, G.W. | SLA | 35 | 12 | 98 | 6 | 16.33 | 4- 66 | – | – |
| Francis, J.D. | SLA | 2 | 1 | 1 | 1 | 1.00 | 1- 1 | – | – |
| Francis, S.R.G. | RMF | 222.3 | 26 | 947 | 28 | 33.82 | 5- 73 | 1 | – |
| Franks, P.J. | RMF | 234.5 | 53 | 813 | 32 | 25.40 | 5- 51 | 1 | – |
| Fraser, A.R.C. | RMF | 72 | 26 | 190 | 7 | 27.14 | 5- 61 | 1 | – |
| Frost, T. | (WK) | 1 | 0 | 9 | 0 | | | | |
| Ganga, D. | OB | 1 | 0 | 1 | 0 | | | | |
| Ganguly, S.C. | RMF | 21 | 4 | 95 | 5 | 19.00 | 3- 10 | – | – |
| Gannon, B.W. | RMF | 162 | 36 | 626 | 15 | 41.73 | 3- 41 | – | – |
| Gayle, S.C. | OB | 24 | 2 | 89 | 4 | 22.25 | 2- 30 | – | – |
| Giddins, E.S.H. | RFM | 232.5 | 49 | 736 | 22 | 33.45 | 4-113 | – | – |
| Gidman, A.P.R. | RM | 99 | 16 | 442 | 10 | 44.20 | 3- 33 | – | – |
| Giles, A.F. | SLA | 419.1 | 67 | 1222 | 36 | 33.94 | 7-142 | 3 | 1 |
| Gofton, A.F. | RM | 18 | 1 | 83 | 1 | 83.00 | 1- 59 | – | – |
| Golding, J.M. | RMF | 60.1 | 10 | 195 | 6 | 32.50 | 4- 76 | – | – |
| Goodwin, M.W. | RM/LB | 2 | 1 | 1 | 0 | | | | |
| Gough, D. | RF | 19 | 3 | 85 | 2 | 42.50 | 2- 85 | – | – |
| Gough, M.A. | OB | 41 | 9 | 132 | 2 | 66.00 | 2- 22 | – | – |
| Grant, J.B. | RFM | 267.5 | 50 | 1086 | 33 | 32.90 | 5- 38 | 1 | – |
| Gray, A.K.D. | OB | 97 | 17 | 297 | 5 | 59.40 | 3- 62 | – | – |
| Grayson, A.P. | SLA | 70 | 18 | 176 | 8 | 22.00 | 3- 21 | – | – |
| Greenidge, C.G. | RMF | 431 | 67 | 1681 | 53 | 31.71 | 6- 40 | 3 | – |
| Grove, J.O. | RMF | 35 | 6 | 152 | 1 | 152.00 | 1- 75 | – | – |
| Gunter, N.E.L. | RFM | 51.1 | 18 | 153 | 8 | 19.12 | 4- 14 | – | – |
| Hamblin, J.R.C. | RMF | 81 | 9 | 373 | 6 | 62.16 | 2- 44 | – | – |
| Hamilton, G.M. | RFM | 12 | 2 | 65 | 1 | 65.00 | 1- 48 | – | – |

| F-C | Cat | O | M | R | W | Avge | Best | 5wI | 10wM |
|---|---|---|---|---|---|---|---|---|---|
| Harbhajan Singh | OB | 243.2 | 43 | 773 | 28 | 27.60 | 7- 83 | 2 | – |
| Hardinges, M.A. | RMF | 12 | 2 | 45 | 0 | | | | |
| Harmison, S.J. | RF | 324.2 | 75 | 1001 | 33 | 30.33 | 5- 65 | 1 | – |
| Harris, A.J. | RM | 413.4 | 93 | 1475 | 67 | 22.01 | 7- 54 | 3 | 2 |
| Harrison, D.S. | RM | 39 | 6 | 132 | 3 | 44.00 | 2- 79 | – | – |
| Harvey, I.J. | RM | 152.2 | 29 | 533 | 28 | 19.03 | 6- 68 | 3 | 1 |
| Hatch, N.G. | RM | 123.5 | 26 | 444 | 9 | 49.33 | 4- 61 | – | – |
| Hawinkels, S.J. | RM | 23 | 1 | 130 | 2 | 65.00 | 1- 44 | – | – |
| Hazleton, M.A. | RMF | 10 | 2 | 58 | 0 | | | | |
| Heath, D.R. | RM | 72.3 | 20 | 230 | 6 | 38.33 | 3- 28 | – | – |
| Heath, J.A. | RM | 16 | 7 | 31 | 0 | | | | |
| Hewitt, J.P. | RM | 26 | 5 | 92 | 0 | | | | |
| Hewson, D.R. | RM | 13 | 4 | 33 | 0 | | | | |
| Hick, G.A. | OB | 24 | 7 | 79 | 0 | | | | |
| Hicks, T.C. | OB | 84.5 | 12 | 324 | 4 | 81.00 | 1- 56 | – | – |
| Hilsum, I.J. | LB | 5 | 1 | 20 | 0 | | | | |
| Hinds, R.O. | SLA | 105.1 | 18 | 338 | 10 | 33.80 | 3- 54 | – | – |
| Hodge, B.J. | OB | 22.4 | 4 | 102 | 1 | 102.00 | 1- 28 | – | – |
| Hogg, K.W. | RFM | 175 | 41 | 621 | 19 | 32.68 | 5- 48 | 1 | – |
| Hoggard, M.J. | RFM | 364 | 71 | 1250 | 36 | 34.72 | 5- 92 | 1 | – |
| Hollingsworth, A.P. | RM | 23 | 4 | 86 | 4 | 21.50 | 3- 35 | – | – |
| Hollioake, A.J. | RMF | 37 | 1 | 178 | 5 | 35.60 | 2- 39 | – | – |
| Hopkinson, C.D. | RM | 7 | 0 | 35 | 1 | 35.00 | 1- 35 | – | – |
| Hughes, T.R. | RMF | 45 | 7 | 178 | 1 | 178.00 | 1- 49 | – | – |
| Hunt, T.A. | RMF | 37.4 | 3 | 189 | 4 | 47.25 | 3- 43 | – | – |
| Hunter, I.D. | RMF | 206 | 42 | 775 | 20 | 38.75 | 3- 44 | – | – |
| Hutchison, P.M. | LFM | 79 | 6 | 389 | 6 | 64.83 | 3-146 | – | – |
| Hutton, B.L. | RMF | 83 | 20 | 262 | 9 | 29.11 | 4- 37 | – | – |
| Ilott, M.C. | LFM | 193.5 | 45 | 639 | 16 | 39.93 | 4- 67 | – | – |
| Innes, K.J. | RM | 268.3 | 65 | 834 | 29 | 28.75 | 4- 41 | – | – |
| Inness, M.W.H. | LFM | 116.4 | 25 | 429 | 15 | 28.60 | 7- 90 | 1 | – |
| Irani, R.C. | RMF | 227.5 | 72 | 591 | 29 | 20.37 | 6- 71 | 1 | – |
| Jaffer, W. | OB | 4 | 0 | 16 | 0 | | | | |
| Jayasuriya, S.T. | SLA | 45 | 10 | 130 | 0 | | | | |
| Jayawardena, D.P.M.D. | RM | 13 | 1 | 59 | 1 | 59.00 | 1- 45 | – | – |
| Johnson, N.C. | RFM | 242.2 | 52 | 814 | 22 | 37.00 | 3- 22 | – | – |
| Johnson, P. | RM | 1.2 | 0 | 12 | 0 | | | | |
| Johnson, R.L. | RMF | 307.1 | 66 | 914 | 43 | 21.25 | 7- 43 | 2 | 1 |
| Jones, I. | RFM | 22.3 | 3 | 100 | 4 | 25.00 | 3- 72 | – | – |
| Jones, P.S. | RMF | 239.2 | 43 | 845 | 19 | 44.47 | 6-110 | 1 | 1 |
| Jones, S.P. | RF | 323.5 | 53 | 1101 | 40 | 27.52 | 6- 45 | 2 | – |
| Jordison, J.R. | RM | 29 | 6 | 96 | 1 | 96.00 | 1- 61 | – | – |
| Joyce, E.C. | RM | 18 | 2 | 74 | 1 | 74.00 | 1- 20 | – | – |
| Kaif, M. | OB | 7 | 0 | 43 | 0 | | | | |
| Kasprowicz, M.S. | RFM | 418.4 | 78 | 1413 | 53 | 26.66 | 6- 47 | 4 | 1 |
| Katich, S.M. | SLC | 2 | 0 | 25 | 0 | | | | |
| Keedy, G. | SLA | 437.4 | 102 | 1313 | 33 | 39.78 | 5-122 | 1 | – |
| Keegan, C.B. | RFM | 211.5 | 32 | 855 | 19 | 45.00 | 4- 47 | – | – |
| Kendall, W.S. | RM | 63.4 | 14 | 186 | 3 | 62.00 | 1- 8 | – | – |
| Kenway, D.A. | RM | 1 | 0 | 8 | 0 | | | | |
| Kerr, J.I.D. | RMF | 147.2 | 29 | 652 | 16 | 40.75 | 4- 32 | – | – |
| Khan, A. | RFM | 485 | 75 | 2004 | 63 | 31.80 | 6- 52 | 4 | – |
| Khan, R.M. | OB | 3 | 0 | 15 | 0 | | | | |
| Khan, Z. | LFM | 147 | 32 | 483 | 11 | 43.90 | 3- 90 | – | – |
| Killeen, N. | RFM | 391.1 | 108 | 1165 | 37 | 31.48 | 4- 26 | – | – |
| King, R.D. | RFM | 151 | 31 | 451 | 16 | 28.18 | 4- 48 | – | – |
| Kirby, S.P. | RFM | 331.1 | 68 | 1262 | 37 | 34.10 | 5-129 | 1 | – |
| Kirtley, R.J. | RFM | 379 | 94 | 1199 | 53 | 22.62 | 6-107 | 4 | 1 |

**F-C**

| | Cat | O | M | R | W | Avge | Best | 5wI | 10wM |
|---|---|---|---|---|---|---|---|---|---|
| Klusener, L. | RMF | 20 | 4 | 88 | 1 | 88.00 | 1- 88 | – | – |
| Kumble, A. | LBG | 212 | 51 | 607 | 22 | 27.59 | 4- 58 | – | – |
| Laraman, A.W. | RFM | 262.4 | 47 | 920 | 27 | 34.07 | 4- 55 | – | – |
| Law, D.R. | RFM | 85 | 17 | 330 | 7 | 47.14 | 3- 41 | – | – |
| Law, S.G. | RM/LB | 24.4 | 5 | 72 | 1 | 72.00 | 1- 24 | – | – |
| Lawson, J.J.C. | RF | 123.4 | 19 | 484 | 18 | 26.88 | 6- 76 | 1 | – |
| Leatherdale, D.A. | RM | 140.3 | 22 | 535 | 16 | 33.43 | 4- 23 | – | – |
| Lee, S. | RM | 0.2 | 0 | 8 | 0 | | | | |
| Lehmann, D.S. | SLA | 133.2 | 32 | 346 | 9 | 38.44 | 3- 40 | – | – |
| Lewis, J. | RMF | 536.1 | 137 | 1662 | 44 | 37.77 | 6- 54 | 2 | 1 |
| Lewry, J.D. | LFM | 304.4 | 45 | 1227 | 33 | 37.18 | 5- 88 | 1 | – |
| Liptrot, C.G. | RFM | 49 | 5 | 210 | 4 | 52.50 | 2- 51 | – | – |
| Logan, R.J. | RMF | 319.3 | 71 | 1191 | 35 | 34.02 | 4- 64 | – | – |
| Loudon, A.G.R. | OB | 52.1 | 10 | 190 | 4 | 47.50 | 2- 60 | – | – |
| Loye, M.B. | OB | 2 | 1 | 1 | 0 | | | | |
| Lucas, D.S. | LFM | 29 | 11 | 56 | 2 | 28.00 | 1- 21 | – | – |
| Lumb, M.J. | RM | 3 | 0 | 16 | 0 | | | | |
| Lungley, T. | RMF | 117.4 | 32 | 416 | 17 | 24.47 | 3- 43 | – | – |
| McGarry, A.C. | RFM | 56.5 | 9 | 228 | 2 | 114.00 | 2- 23 | – | – |
| MacGill, S.C.G. | LBG | 227.4 | 37 | 930 | 40 | 23.25 | 8-111 | 4 | 1 |
| McGrath, A. | RM | 174.3 | 38 | 498 | 18 | 27.66 | 4- 49 | – | – |
| McGrath, D.E.T. | RM | 46 | 9 | 148 | 6 | 24.66 | 3- 49 | – | – |
| McMahon, P.J. | OB | 22.5 | 2 | 103 | 2 | 51.50 | 2- 22 | – | – |
| Maddy, D.L. | RM/OB | 334.3 | 78 | 1025 | 43 | 23.83 | 5- 37 | 2 | – |
| Mahmood, S.I. | RMF | 2 | 1 | 6 | 0 | | | | |
| Malcolm, D.E. | RF | 477.5 | 79 | 1826 | 60 | 30.43 | 7- 76 | 4 | 1 |
| Malik, M.N. | RFM | 146.4 | 29 | 562 | 22 | 25.54 | 5- 67 | 1 | – |
| Marshall, S.J. | LB | 215.2 | 42 | 657 | 10 | 65.70 | 6-128 | 1 | – |
| Martin, P.J. | RFM | 452 | 143 | 1126 | 53 | 21.24 | 5- 54 | 1 | – |
| Martin-Jenkins, R.S.C. | RFM | 470.2 | 100 | 1477 | 41 | 36.02 | 7- 51 | 2 | – |
| Mascarenhas, A.D. | RMF | 420.5 | 144 | 1141 | 37 | 30.83 | 5- 87 | 1 | – |
| Mason, M.S. | RMF | 224.4 | 55 | 613 | 22 | 27.86 | 5- 50 | 1 | – |
| Masters, D.D. | RMF | 243.1 | 46 | 864 | 23 | 37.56 | 4- 36 | – | – |
| Maynard, M.P. | RM | 1 | 0 | 5 | 0 | | | | |
| Mees, T. | RMF | 64 | 10 | 270 | 8 | 33.75 | 4- 55 | – | – |
| Middlebrook, J.D. | OB | 555.2 | 121 | 1736 | 38 | 45.68 | 4- 38 | – | – |
| Millar, N. | RM | 48 | 2 | 226 | 2 | 113.00 | 1- 48 | – | – |
| Mongia, D. | SLC | 1 | 0 | 7 | 0 | | | | |
| Montgomery, R.R. | OB | 6 | 2 | 10 | 0 | | | | |
| Morris, A.C. | RMF | 29 | 5 | 112 | 0 | | | | |
| Muchall, G.J. | RM | 43 | 6 | 194 | 4 | 48.50 | 2- 52 | – | – |
| Mullally, A.D. | LFM | 463.2 | 145 | 1156 | 46 | 25.13 | 6- 56 | 1 | – |
| Muralitharan, M. | OB | 126 | 32 | 297 | 8 | 37.12 | 5-143 | 1 | – |
| Murtagh, T.J. | RFM | 122.1 | 23 | 424 | 17 | 24.94 | 5- 39 | 1 | – |
| Mushtaq Ahmed | LBG | 105 | 23 | 305 | 8 | 38.12 | 5- 71 | 1 | – |
| Napier, G.R. | RM | 172 | 33 | 639 | 20 | 31.95 | 3- 47 | – | – |
| Nash, C.D. | OB | 35 | 1 | 171 | 2 | 85.50 | 1- 81 | – | – |
| Nehra, A. | LMF | 114 | 14 | 473 | 11 | 43.00 | 4- 85 | – | – |
| Nixon, P.A. | (WK) | 0.3 | 0 | 8 | 0 | | | | |
| Noble, D.J. | RMF | 133 | 24 | 480 | 9 | 53.33 | 3- 66 | – | – |
| Noffke, A.A. | RFM | 305.1 | 57 | 1128 | 45 | 25.06 | 8- 24 | 3 | 1 |
| Ormond, J. | RFM | 485.1 | 87 | 1780 | 51 | 34.90 | 5- 62 | 2 | 1 |
| Ostler, D.P. | RM | 1 | 0 | 13 | 0 | | | | |
| Panesar, M.S. | SLA | 190.5 | 55 | 554 | 17 | 32.58 | 4- 42 | – | – |
| Parker, J.W.R. | LM | 8 | 0 | 39 | 0 | | | | |
| Parkin, O.T. | RFM | 83.4 | 19 | 247 | 7 | 35.28 | 2- 47 | – | – |
| Parsons, K.A. | RM | 216.3 | 30 | 830 | 21 | 39.52 | 3- 44 | – | – |
| Patel, M.M. | SLA | 525.3 | 152 | 1206 | 36 | 33.50 | 5- 56 | 1 | – |

| F-C | Cat | O | M | R | W | Avge | Best | 5wI | 10wM |
|---|---|---|---|---|---|---|---|---|---|
| Patel, P.A. | (WK) | 3 | 0 | 9 | 0 | | | – | – |
| Pattison, I. | RM | 35 | 9 | 159 | 4 | 39.75 | 3- 41 | – | – |
| Penberthy, A.L. | RM | 292 | 76 | 833 | 17 | 49.00 | 3- 21 | – | – |
| Peng, N. | OB | 1 | 0 | 2 | 0 | | | – | – |
| Perera, P.D.R.L. | LFM | 115 | 13 | 433 | 17 | 25.47 | 4- 66 | – | – |
| Phillips, B.J. | RFM | 17 | 5 | 41 | 4 | 10.25 | 3- 28 | – | – |
| Phillips, N.C. | OB | 210 | 47 | 671 | 21 | 31.95 | 4-103 | – | – |
| Phillips, T.J. | SLA | 209.5 | 32 | 844 | 18 | 46.88 | 4-102 | – | – |
| Pietersen, K.P. | OB | 62 | 13 | 226 | 5 | 45.20 | 2- 54 | – | – |
| Pollock, S.M. | RFM | 301.3 | 101 | 733 | 28 | 26.17 | 4- 37 | – | – |
| Porter, J.J. | SLA | 13 | 0 | 72 | 2 | 36.00 | 1- 34 | – | – |
| Powell, D.B. | RFM | 81 | 19 | 303 | 10 | 30.30 | 3- 55 | – | – |
| Powell, M.J.(Gm) | RSM | 6 | 0 | 21 | 0 | | | – | – |
| Powell, M.J.(Wa) | RM | 57 | 7 | 210 | 3 | 70.00 | 2- 29 | – | – |
| Pratt, G.J. | (WK) | 2.3 | 0 | 12 | 0 | | | – | – |
| Prittipaul, L.R. | RM/OB | 38.3 | 10 | 108 | 3 | 36.00 | 2- 43 | – | – |
| Pyemont, J.P. | OB | 15.3 | 2 | 70 | 1 | 70.00 | 1- 37 | – | – |
| Ramprakash, M.R. | RM | 8 | 1 | 23 | 0 | | | – | – |
| Randall, S.J. | OB | 33 | 6 | 140 | 0 | | | – | – |
| Ratcliffe, J.D. | RM | 6 | 4 | 14 | 1 | 14.00 | 1- 0 | – | – |
| Rawnsley, M.J. | SLA | 93 | 28 | 274 | 2 | 137.00 | 1- 26 | – | – |
| Richardson, A. | RMF | 300.2 | 64 | 951 | 38 | 25.02 | 8- 46 | 2 | – |
| Roberts, T.W. | OB | 2 | 0 | 6 | 0 | | | – | – |
| Robinson, D.D.J. | RMF | 9 | 1 | 54 | 0 | | | – | – |
| Robinson, M.A. | RFM | 40 | 8 | 138 | 5 | 27.60 | 3- 57 | – | – |
| Rose, G.D. | RM | 30 | 10 | 95 | 0 | | | – | – |
| Saggers, M.J. | RMF | 571 | 111 | 1786 | 83 | 21.51 | 6- 39 | 6 | – |
| Salisbury, I.D.K. | LBG | 341.3 | 50 | 1192 | 37 | 32.21 | 4- 59 | – | – |
| Samaraweera, T.T. | OB | 43 | 5 | 178 | 1 | 178.00 | 1- 63 | – | – |
| Sampson, P.J. | RFM | 44 | 11 | 160 | 7 | 22.85 | 3- 52 | – | – |
| Saqlain Mushtaq | OB | 488.4 | 112 | 1359 | 53 | 25.64 | 6-121 | 3 | 1 |
| Savill, T.E. | RFM | 86 | 10 | 422 | 8 | 52.75 | 2- 42 | – | – |
| Sayers, J.J. | OB | 3 | 1 | 12 | 0 | | | – | – |
| Schofield, C.P. | LB | 122.2 | 27 | 331 | 18 | 18.38 | 4- 35 | – | – |
| Schofield, J.E.K. | RMF | 53 | 14 | 192 | 6 | 32.00 | 3- 94 | – | – |
| Sehwag, V. | OB | 65.4 | 8 | 232 | 4 | 58.00 | 2- 52 | – | –' |
| Selwood, S.A. | SLA | 13 | 3 | 67 | 2 | 33.50 | 1- 8 | – | – |
| Shafayat, B.M. | RMF | 14 | 0 | 52 | 0 | | | – | – |
| Shah, O.A. | OB | 2 | 0 | 15 | 0 | | | – | – |
| Shahid, N. | LB | 22 | 1 | 72 | 1 | 72.00 | 1- 55 | – | – |
| Sharif, F. | LB | 42.3 | 2 | 180 | 1 | 180.00 | 1- 81 | – | – |
| Sharif, Z.K. | LB | 31 | 0 | 164 | 4 | 41.00 | 4- 98 | – | – |
| Sharpe, T.J. | RMF | 95 | 18 | 400 | 8 | 50.00 | 3- 70 | – | – |
| Sheikh, M.A. | RM | 130.3 | 25 | 396 | 6 | 66.00 | 4- 78 | – | – |
| Sheriyar, A. | LFM | 616.2 | 160 | 1905 | 66 | 28.86 | 6- 71 | 5 | – |
| Sidebottom, R.J. | LFM | 380.5 | 85 | 1190 | 41 | 29.02 | 5- 60 | 1 | – |
| Sillence, R.J. | RMF | 100 | 11 | 449 | 13 | 34.53 | 5- 63 | 1 | – |
| Silverwood, C.E.W. | RFM | 306.1 | 68 | 985 | 30 | 32.83 | 4- 28 | – | – |
| Smethurst, M.P. | RM | 110 | 20 | 471 | 9 | 52.33 | 3- 68 | – | – |
| Smith, A.M. | LMF | 270 | 55 | 916 | 31 | 29.54 | 5- 69 | 1 | – |
| Smith B.F. | RM | 17 | 2 | 77 | 1 | 77.00 | 1- 45 | – | – |
| Smith, G.J. | LFM | 400.1 | 85 | 1275 | 48 | 26.56 | 8- 53 | 1 | 1 |
| Smith, N.M.K. | OB | 126 | 27 | 411 | 12 | 34.25 | 5- 42 | 1 | – |
| Snape, J.N. | OB | 50 | 6 | 179 | 2 | 89.50 | 2- 54 | – | – |
| Solanki, V.S. | OB | 39 | 6 | 128 | 0 | | | – | – |
| Souter, M.A. | RM | 20 | 5 | 83 | 1 | 83.00 | 1- 54 | – | – |
| Spires, J.A.S. | SLA | 171.4 | 29 | 613 | 18 | 34.05 | 5-165 | 1 | – |
| Srinath, J. | RFM | 179.2 | 29 | 561 | 30 | 18.70 | 5- 25 | 2 | – |

**F-C**

| | Cat | O | M | R | W | Avge | Best | 5wI | 10wM |
|---|---|---|---|---|---|---|---|---|---|
| Stemp, R.D. | SLA | 17 | 2 | 59 | 1 | 59.00 | 1- 18 | – | – |
| Stephenson, J.P. | RM | 295.4 | 59 | 1082 | 48 | 22.54 | 7- 44 | 1 | 1 |
| Stevens, D.I. | RM | 49 | 3 | 201 | 1 | 201.00 | 1-125 | – | – |
| Suppiah, A.V. | SLA | 15 | 4 | 55 | 3 | 18.33 | 3- 46 | – | – |
| Sutcliffe, I.J. | OB | 7 | 0 | 39 | 0 | | | – | – |
| Swann, A.J. | RM/OB | 8 | 1 | 40 | 0 | | | – | – |
| Swann, G.P. | OB | 270.5 | 60 | 884 | 31 | 28.51 | 6-126 | 1 | 1 |
| Symington, M.J. | RM | 147 | 29 | 590 | 17 | 34.70 | 4- 27 | – | – |
| Symonds, A. | RMF/OB | 187.2 | 34 | 602 | 13 | 46.30 | 6-105 | 1 | – |
| Taylor, B.V. | RMF | 318.5 | 73 | 1041 | 32 | 32.53 | 5- 90 | 1 | – |
| Taylor, C.G. | OB | 10 | 1 | 36 | 0 | | | – | – |
| Tendulkar, S.R. | RM/OB/LB | 10 | 0 | 33 | 0 | | | – | – |
| Thomas, I.J. | OB | 6.1 | 0 | 30 | 1 | 30.00 | 1- 26 | – | – |
| Thomas, S.D. | RFM | 467.1 | 66 | 1637 | 52 | 31.48 | 7- 33 | 3 | 1 |
| Thorburn, M. | RMF | 53 | 12 | 244 | 7 | 34.85 | 2- 60 | – | – |
| Thornicroft, N.D. | RMF | 61.1 | 14 | 248 | 4 | 62.00 | 2- 51 | – | – |
| Thorpe, A.M. | RM | 8 | 0 | 32 | 0 | | | – | – |
| Tillekeratne, H.P. | OB | 5 | 1 | 33 | 0 | | | – | – |
| Tomlinson, J.A. | LFM | 168.3 | 14 | 748 | 12 | 62.33 | 2- 55 | – | – |
| Tournier, M.A. | RFM | 34 | 4 | 125 | 6 | 20.83 | 5- 88 | 1 | – |
| Tredwell, J.C. | OB | 124.2 | 29 | 358 | 10 | 35.80 | 4-103 | – | – |
| Trego, P.D. | RM | 63 | 6 | 357 | 5 | 71.40 | 3- 65 | – | – |
| Tremlett, C.T. | RMF | 336 | 83 | 1061 | 36 | 29.47 | 5- 57 | 2 | – |
| Trott, B.J. | RFM | 58 | 8 | 260 | 7 | 37.14 | 3- 83 | – | – |
| Troughton, J.O. | SLA | 18 | 0 | 89 | 0 | | | – | – |
| Tudor, A.J. | RF | 322 | 74 | 1124 | 42 | 26.76 | 5- 66 | 1 | – |
| Tufnell, P.C.R. | SLA | 514.5 | 104 | 1390 | 45 | 30.88 | 8- 66 | 4 | – |
| Udal, S.D. | OB | 627.1 | 146 | 1858 | 56 | 33.17 | 5- 56 | 4 | – |
| Upashantha, K.E.A. | RMF | 57 | 5 | 341 | 6 | 56.83 | 3- 85 | – | – |
| Vaas, W.P.U.C.J. | LFM | 186.1 | 30 | 543 | 9 | 60.33 | 3- 79 | – | – |
| Vaughan, M.P. | OB | 59.2 | 10 | 185 | 4 | 46.25 | 2- 71 | – | – |
| Vonwiller, B.M. | RMF | 15 | 2 | 80 | 2 | 40.00 | 2- 80 | – | – |
| Wagg, G.G. | LM | 82.5 | 13 | 343 | 12 | 28.58 | 4- 43 | – | – |
| Wagh, M.A. | OB | 203 | 43 | 604 | 15 | 40.26 | 5-137 | 1 | – |
| Walker, G.W. | SLA | 13 | 2 | 50 | 0 | | | – | – |
| Walker, M.J. | RM | 24.3 | 4 | 98 | 0 | | | – | – |
| Ward, I.J. | RM | 9.4 | 3 | 19 | 3 | 6.33 | 1- 7 | – | – |
| Ward, T.R. | OB | 11 | 0 | 47 | 1 | 47.00 | 1- 32 | – | – |
| Warren, N.A. | RMF | 20 | 3 | 90 | 2 | 45.00 | 2- 48 | – | – |
| Waugh, M.E. | OB | 4 | 1 | 14 | 0 | | | – | – |
| Waugh, S.R. | RM | 3 | 0 | 15 | 0 | | | – | – |
| Weekes, P.N. | OB | 397 | 61 | 1198 | 21 | 57.04 | 3- 27 | – | – |
| Welch, G. | RM | 486.1 | 157 | 1409 | 55 | 25.61 | 6- 60 | 2 | – |
| Wells, V.J. | RMF | 155 | 41 | 421 | 19 | 22.15 | 5- 39 | 1 | – |
| Wharf, A.G. | RMF | 86 | 9 | 266 | 7 | 38.00 | 4- 71 | – | – |
| Wharton, L.J. | SLA | 208.5 | 45 | 695 | 25 | 27.80 | 6- 62 | 2 | – |
| Whiley, M.J.A. | LMF | 175.4 | 28 | 803 | 16 | 50.18 | 3- 60 | – | – |
| White, C. | RFM | 193.5 | 33 | 634 | 15 | 42.26 | 4- 49 | – | – |
| White, G.W. | LB | 12.1 | 1 | 64 | 1 | 64.00 | 1- 17 | – | – |
| White, R.A. | LB | 26.4 | 3 | 91 | 5 | 18.20 | 2- 30 | – | – |
| Wigley, D.H. | LFM | 20.4 | 2 | 116 | 1 | 116.00 | 1- 71 | – | – |
| Windows, M.G.N. | LM | 3.2 | 0 | 20 | 0 | | | – | – |
| Wood, J. | RFM | 180.5 | 34 | 631 | 18 | 35.05 | 4- 17 | – | – |
| Wyatt, A.A. | LB | 49 | 7 | 181 | 2 | 90.50 | 1- 33 | – | – |
| Yardy, M.H. | LM | 58 | 9 | 231 | 2 | 115.50 | 1- 17 | – | – |
| Yates, G. | OB | 29 | 7 | 76 | 0 | | | – | – |
| Yohannan, T. | RFM | 73 | 16 | 293 | 5 | 58.60 | 1- 27 | – | – |
| Zoysa, D.N.T. | LFM | 110.2 | 15 | 421 | 10 | 42.10 | 3- 93 | – | – |

# COUNTY CHAMPIONSHIP 2002
# FRIZZELL FINAL TABLES

## DIVISION 1

| | | P | W | L | D | Bonus Points Bat | Bonus Points Bowl | Deduct Points | Total Points |
|---|---|---|---|---|---|---|---|---|---|
| 1 | SURREY (4) | 16 | 10 | 2 | 4 | 59 | 48 | 0.25 | 242.75 |
| 2 | Warwickshire (-) | 16 | 7 | 2 | 7 | 42 | 44 | 0.00 | 198.00 |
| 3 | Kent (3) | 16 | 7 | 4 | 5 | 48 | 44 | 0.50 | 195.50 |
| 4 | Lancashire (6) | 16 | 6 | 4 | 6 | 33 | 43 | 0.00 | 172.00 |
| 5 | Leicestershire (5) | 16 | 5 | 5 | 6 | 42 | 46 | 1.00 | 171.00 |
| 6 | Sussex (-) | 16 | 3 | 6 | 7 | 43 | 47 | 0.00 | 154.00 |
| 7 | Hampshire (-) | 16 | 2 | 5 | 9 | 35 | 44 | 8.00 | 131.00 |
| 8 | Somerset (2) | 16 | 1 | 7 | 8 | 39 | 44 | 0.25 | 126.75 |
| 9 | Yorkshire (1) | 16 | 2 | 8 | 6 | 35 | 45 | 3.25 | 124.75 |

## DIVISION 2

| | | P | W | L | D | Bonus Points Bat | Bonus Points Bowl | Deduct Points | Total Points |
|---|---|---|---|---|---|---|---|---|---|
| 1 | ESSEX (-) | 16 | 10 | 3 | 3 | 42 | 46 | 1.00 | 219.00 |
| 2 | Middlesex (5) | 16 | 7 | 3 | 6 | 61 | 43 | 0.25 | 211.75 |
| 3 | Nottinghamshire (7) | 16 | 8 | 5 | 3 | 47 | 48 | 1.25 | 201.75 |
| 4 | Worcestershire (6) | 16 | 7 | 4 | 5 | 53 | 43 | 0.00 | 200.00 |
| 5 | Glamorgan (-) | 16 | 5 | 5 | 6 | 41 | 44 | 0.00 | 169.00 |
| 6 | Derbyshire (9) | 16 | 7 | 7 | 2 | 37 | 48 | 9.25 | 167.75 |
| 7 | Northamptonshire (-) | 16 | 5 | 7 | 4 | 46 | 41 | 0.50 | 162.50 |
| 8 | Gloucestershire (4) | 16 | 2 | 7 | 7 | 42 | 44 | 1.50 | 136.50 |
| 9 | Durham (8) | 16 | 1 | 11 | 4 | 21 | 42 | 0.25 | 90.75 |

2001 final positions for that division are shown in brackets.

## SCORING OF CHAMPIONSHIP POINTS 2002

(a) For a win, 12 points, plus any points scored in the first innings (*increased to 14 in 2003*).

(b) In a tie, each side to score six points, plus any points scored in the first innings.

(c) In a drawn match, each side to score four points, plus any points scored in the first innings (see also paragraph (f) below).

(d) If the scores are equal in a drawn match, the side batting in the fourth innings to score six points plus any points scored in the first innings, and the opposing side to score four points plus any points scored in the first innings.

(e) **First Innings Points** (awarded only for performances **in the first 130 overs** of each first innings and retained whatever the result of the match):-
  • A maximum of five batting points to be available as under:-
    200 to 249 runs – 1 point; 250 to 299 runs – 2 points; 300 to 349 runs – 3 points;
    350 to 399 runs – 4 points; 400 runs or over – 5 points.
  • A maximum of three bowling points to be available as under:-
    3 to 5 wickets taken – 1 point; 6 to 8 wickets taken – 2 points; 9 to 10 wickets taken – 3 points.

(f) If play starts when less than eight hours playing time remains (in which event a one innings match shall be played as provided for in First Class Playing Condition 18), no first innings points shall be scored. The side winning on the one innings to score 12 points. In a tie, each side to score six points. In a drawn match, each side to score four points. If the scores are equal in a drawn match, the side batting in the second innings to score six points and the opposing side to score four points.

(g) If a match is abandoned without a ball being bowled, each side to score four points.

(h) The side which has the highest aggregate of points gained at the end of the season shall be the Champion County of their respective Division. Should any sides in the Championship table be equal on points, the following tie-breakers will be applied in the order stated: most wins, least losses, team achieving most points in contests between teams level on points, most wickets taken, most runs scored. At the end of the season, the top three teams from the Second Division will be promoted and the bottom three teams from the First Division will be relegated.

# COUNTY CHAMPIONS

The English County Championship was not officially constituted until December 1889. Prior to that date there was no generally accepted method of awarding the title; although the 'least matches lost' method existed, it was not consistently applied. Rules governing playing qualifications were agreed in 1873 and the first unofficial points system 15 years later.

Research has produced a list of champions dating back to 1826, but at least seven different versions exist for the period from 1864 to 1889 (see *The Wisden Book of Cricket Records*). Only from 1890 can any authorised list of county champions commence.

That first official Championship was contested between eight counties: Gloucestershire, Kent, Lancashire, Middlesex, Nottinghamshire, Surrey, Sussex and Yorkshire. The remaining counties were admitted in the following seasons: 1891 – Somerset, 1895 – Derbyshire, Essex, Hampshire, Leicestershire and Warwickshire, 1899 – Worcestershire, 1905 – Northamptonshire, 1921 – Glamorgan, and 1992 – Durham.

The Championship pennant was introduced by the 1951 champions, Warwickshire, and the Lord's Taverners' Trophy was first presented in 1973. The first sponsors, Schweppes (1977 to 1983), were succeeded by Britannic Assurance (1984 to 1998), PPP Healthcare (1999-2000), CricInfo (2001) and Frizzell (2002 to date). Based on their previous season's positions, the 18 counties were separated into two divisions in 2001.

| | | | | | | |
|---|---|---|---|---|---|---|
| 1890 | Surrey | 1930 | Lancashire | 1970 | Kent | |
| 1891 | Surrey | 1931 | Yorkshire | 1971 | Surrey | |
| 1892 | Surrey | 1932 | Yorkshire | 1972 | Warwickshire | |
| 1893 | Yorkshire | 1933 | Yorkshire | 1973 | Hampshire | |
| 1894 | Surrey | 1934 | Lancashire | 1974 | Worcestershire | |
| 1895 | Surrey | 1935 | Yorkshire | 1975 | Leicestershire | |
| 1896 | Yorkshire | 1936 | Derbyshire | 1976 | Middlesex | |
| 1897 | Lancashire | 1937 | Yorkshire | 1977 | Kent | |
| 1898 | Yorkshire | 1938 | Yorkshire | 1977 | Middlesex | |
| 1899 | Surrey | 1939 | Yorkshire | 1978 | Kent | |
| 1900 | Yorkshire | 1946 | Yorkshire | 1979 | Essex | |
| 1901 | Yorkshire | 1947 | Middlesex | 1980 | Middlesex | |
| 1902 | Yorkshire | 1948 | Glamorgan | 1981 | Nottinghamshire | |
| 1903 | Middlesex | 1949 | Middlesex | 1982 | Middlesex | |
| 1904 | Lancashire | 1949 | Yorkshire | 1983 | Essex | |
| 1905 | Yorkshire | 1950 | Lancashire | 1984 | Essex | |
| 1906 | Kent | 1950 | Surrey | 1985 | Middlesex | |
| 1907 | Nottinghamshire | 1951 | Warwickshire | 1986 | Essex | |
| 1908 | Yorkshire | 1952 | Surrey | 1987 | Nottinghamshire | |
| 1909 | Kent | 1953 | Surrey | 1988 | Worcestershire | |
| 1910 | Kent | 1954 | Surrey | 1989 | Worcestershire | |
| 1911 | Warwickshire | 1955 | Surrey | 1990 | Middlesex | |
| 1912 | Yorkshire | 1956 | Surrey | 1991 | Essex | |
| 1913 | Kent | 1957 | Surrey | 1992 | Essex | |
| 1914 | Surrey | 1958 | Surrey | 1993 | Middlesex | |
| 1919 | Yorkshire | 1959 | Yorkshire | 1994 | Warwickshire | |
| 1920 | Middlesex | 1960 | Yorkshire | 1995 | Warwickshire | |
| 1921 | Middlesex | 1961 | Hampshire | 1996 | Leicestershire | |
| 1922 | Yorkshire | 1962 | Yorkshire | 1997 | Glamorgan | |
| 1923 | Yorkshire | 1963 | Yorkshire | 1998 | Leicestershire | |
| 1924 | Yorkshire | 1964 | Worcestershire | 1999 | Surrey | |
| 1925 | Yorkshire | 1965 | Worcestershire | 2000 | Surrey | |
| 1926 | Lancashire | 1966 | Yorkshire | 2001 | Yorkshire | |
| 1927 | Lancashire | 1967 | Yorkshire | 2002 | Surrey | |
| 1928 | Lancashire | 1968 | Yorkshire | | | |
| 1929 | Nottinghamshire | 1969 | Glamorgan | | | |

# COUNTY CHAMPIONSHIP RESULTS 2002

## DIVISION 1

|  | HANTS | KENT | LANCS | LEICS | SOM'T | SURREY | SUSSEX | WARWKS | YORKS |
|---|---|---|---|---|---|---|---|---|---|
| **HANTS** | – | So'ton H 8w | So'ton La 111 | So'ton Le I/9 | So'ton H 4w | So'ton Sy 123 | So'ton Drawn | So'ton Drawn | So'ton Y 7w |
| **KENT** | Cant Drawn | – | Cant K 6w | Cant Drawn | Cant K 153 | Cant Sy 2w | Tun W K 4w | Maid Drawn | Cant K 4w |
| **LANCS** | Man Drawn | L'pool K 6w | – | Man La 1w | B'pool La 336 | Man Drawn | Man Drawn | Man Drawn | Man Y 150 |
| **LEICS** | Leics Drawn | Leics K 6w | Leics Drawn | – | Leics Le I/18 | Leics Sy 7w | Leics Le 8w | Leics Le 7w | Leics Le 5w |
| **SOM'T** | Bath Drawn | Taunton Drawn | Taunton La 8w | Taunton Drawn | – | Taunton Drawn | Taunton Sx I/1 | Taunton Drawn | Taunton Sm 7w |
| **SURREY** | Oval Sy I/60 | Oval Sy 9w | Oval Sy 3w | Oval Sy 483 | Oval Drawn | – | Oval Sy 10w | Oval Wa 26 | Guild Sy 6w |
| **SUSSEX** | Hove Drawn | Hove Drawn | Hove La 7w | Horsham Drawn | Hove Drawn | Hove Sx 4w | – | Hove Wa 3w | Arundel Drawn |
| **WARWKS** | B'ham Drawn | B'ham Wa 10w | B'ham La 6w | B'ham Wa 144 | B'ham Wa 88 | B'ham Drawn | B'ham Wa 208 | | B'ham Wa 6w |
| **YORKS** | Leeds Drawn | Leeds K 8w | Leeds Drawn | Scar Drawn | Scar Drawn | Leeds Sy I/168 | Leeds Sx I/94 | Leeds Drawn | – |

## DIVISION 2

|  | DERBYS | DURHAM | ESSEX | GLAM | GLOS | MIDDX | N'HANTS | NOTTS | WORCS |
|---|---|---|---|---|---|---|---|---|---|
| **DERBYS** | – | Derby De 2 | Derby Ex 140 | Derby De 9w | Derby Drawn | Derby M 73 | Derby De 8w | Derby Nt 1w | Derby Wo 9w |
| **DURHAM** | Dar'ton Du 89 | – | C-le-St Ex 10w | C-le-St Gm 10w | C-le-St Drawn | C-le-St M 10w | C-le-St Nh 7w | C-le-St Nt 8w | C-le-St Drawn |
| **ESSEX** | Chelms Ex 6w | Colch'r Ex 4w | – | Chelms Drawn | Chelms Drawn | Ilford Ex 6w | Chelms Ex 7w | Chelms Drawn | S'end Wo 8w |
| **GLAM** | Cardiff De 163 | Cardiff Gm 5w | Swansea Gm 8w | – | Cardiff Drawn | Cardiff M 8w | Cardiff Drawn | Col Bay Drawn | Cardiff Drawn |
| **GLOS** | Bristol Drawn | Bristol Gs 10w | Glos Ex 3w | Chelt Gm 2w | – | Chelt Drawn | Bristol Drawn | Bristol Gs 7w | Bristol Wo 304 |
| **MIDDX** | Lord's De 204 | Lord's Drawn | S'gate Drawn | Lord's Drawn | S'gate M 5w | – | Lord's Drawn | Lord's M I/31 | Lord's Drawn |
| **N'HANTS** | No'ton De 177 | No'ton Nh 1w | No'ton Ex 4w | No'ton Nh 8w | No'ton Nh I/59 | No'ton M I/2 | – | No'ton Nh 6w | No'ton Drawn |
| **NOTTS** | N'ham De 4w | N'ham Drawn | N'ham Nt 7w | N'ham Nt 7w | N'ham Nt I/84 | N'ham Nt I/73 | N'ham Nt 7w | – | N'ham Nt 114 |
| **WORCS** | Worcs Wo 1w | Worcs Wo I/308 | Worcs Ex 5w | Worcs Gm 110 | Worcs Wo 206 | Worcs M 6w | Worcs Wo 8w | Kidd Drawn | – |

# COUNTY CHAMPIONSHIP RESULTS 2003

KEEP YOUR OWN RECORD (see page 138)

## DIVISION 1

|         | ESSEX   | KENT   | LANCS  | LEICS  | MIDDX  | NOTTS   | SURREY | SUSSEX | WARWKS |
|---------|---------|--------|--------|--------|--------|---------|--------|--------|--------|
| **ESSEX**  | –       | Chelms | Chelms | S'end  | Chelms | Chelms  | Chelms | Colch'r| Chelms |
| **KENT**   | Cant    | –      | Cant   | Cant   | Cant   | Maid    | Cant   | Tun W  | Cant   |
| **LANCS**  | Man     | B'pool | –      | L'pool | Man    | Man     | Man    | Man    | Man    |
| **LEICS**  | Leics   | Leics  | Leics  | –      | Leics  | Leics   | Leics  | Leics  | Leics  |
| **MIDDX**  | Lord's  | Lord's | Lord's | S'gate | –      | Lord's  | Lord's | Lord's | S'gate |
| **NOTTS**  | N'ham   | N'ham  | N'ham  | N'ham  | N'ham  | –       | N'ham  | N'ham  | N'ham  |
| **SURREY** | Oval    | Oval   | Oval   | Oval   | Guild  | Whit S  | –      | Oval   | Oval   |
| **SUSSEX** | Arundel | Hove   | Hove   | Hove   | Hove   | Horsham | Hove   | –      | Hove   |
| **WARWKS** | B'ham   | B'ham  | B'ham  | B'ham  | B'ham  | B'ham   | B'ham  | B'ham  | –      |

## DIVISION 2

|          | DERBYS  | DURHAM  | GLAM    | GLOS    | HANTS   | N'HANTS | SOM'T   | WORCS   | YORKS   |
|----------|---------|---------|---------|---------|---------|---------|---------|---------|---------|
| **DERBYS**  | –       | Derby   | Derby   | Derby   | Derby   | Derby   | Derby   | Derby   | Derby   |
| **DURHAM**  | C-le-St | –       | C-le-St | C-le-St | C-le-St | C-le-St | C-le-St | C-le-St | C-le-St |
| **GLAM**    | Swansea | Cardiff | –       | Cardiff | Cardiff | Cardiff | Cardiff | Cardiff | Col Bay |
| **GLOS**    | Bristol | Bristol | Bristol | –       | Bristol | Glos    | Bristol | Chelt   | Chelt   |
| **HANTS**   | So'ton  | So'ton  | So'ton  | So'ton  | –       | So'ton  | So'ton  | So'ton  | So'ton  |
| **N'HANTS** | No'ton  | No'ton  | No'ton  | No'ton  | No'ton  | –       | No'ton  | No'ton  | No'ton  |
| **SOM'T**   | Taunton | Taunton | Taunton | Taunton | Taunton | Taunton | –       | Bath    | Taunton |
| **WORCS**   | Worcs   | Worcs   | Worcs   | Worcs   | Worcs   | Worcs   | Worcs   | –       | Worcs   |
| **YORKS**   | Leeds   | Leeds   | Leeds   | Leeds   | Scar    | Leeds   | Leeds   | Scar    | –       |

# NATWEST TRIANGULAR SERIES 2002

### Nottingham 27 June (floodlight)

**Toss: England. ENGLAND** beat **SRI LANKA** by 44 runs. England 293-6 (50 overs) (A.J.Stewart 83, A.Flintoff 50* off 25 balls – England record). Sri Lanka 249-9 (50 overs) (R.S.Kaluwitharana 52; A.Flintoff 3-49). Award: A.Flintoff.

### Lord's 29 June

**Toss: England. INDIA** beat **ENGLAND** by six wickets. England 271-7 (50 overs) (M.E.Trescothick 86, N.Hussain 54; Yuvraj Singh 3-39). India 272-4 (48.5 overs) (R.Dravid 73*, V.Sehwag 71, Yuvraj Singh 64*; A.F.Giles 3-39). Award: Yuvraj Singh.

### The Oval 30 June

**Toss: Sri Lanka. INDIA** beat **SRI LANKA** by four wickets. Sri Lanka 202-8 (50 overs) (D.P.M.D.Jayawardena 62; A.B.Agarkar 3-44, Z.Khan 3-48). India 203-6 (45.2 overs). Award: A.B.Agarkar.

### Leeds 2 July

**Toss: England. ENGLAND** beat **SRI LANKA** by three wickets. Sri Lanka 240-7 (32 overs) (S.T.Jayasuriya 112; D.Gough 3-45). England 241-7 (31.2 overs) (M.E.Trescothick 82). Award: S.T.Jayasuriya.

### Chester-le-Street 4 July (floodlit)

**Toss: India.** MATCH ABANDONED – NO RESULT. India 285-4 (50 overs) (S.R.Tendulkar 105*, R.Dravid 82). England 53-1 (12.3 overs). No award.

### Birmingham 6 July

**Toss: India. INDIA** beat **SRI LANKA** by four wickets. Sri Lanka 187 (48.2 overs) (M.S.Atapattu 50). India 188-6 (48.1 overs) (R.Dravid 64). Award: R.Dravid.

### Manchester 7 July

**Toss: Sri Lanka. SRI LANKA** beat **ENGLAND** by 23 runs. Sri Lanka 229 (49.4 overs) (K.C.Sangakkara 70; M.P.Vaughan 4-22). England 206 (47.4 overs) (S.T.Jayasuriya 3-38). Award: K.C.Sangakkara.

### The Oval 9 July

**Toss: India. ENGLAND** beat **INDIA** by 64 runs. England 229-8 (32 overs) (R.C.Irani 53, A.Flintoff 51; Z.Khan 3-53). India 165 (29.1 overs) (R.C.Irani 5-26). Award: R.C.Irani.

### Bristol 11 July (floodlit)

**Toss: India. INDIA** beat **SRI LANKA** by 63 runs. India 304 (50 overs) (S.R.Tendulkar 113). Sri Lanka 241 (44.1 overs) (K.C.Sangakkara 66, M.S.Atapattu 53; Harbhajan Singh 4-46). Award: S.R.Tendulkar.

|           | Played | Won | Lost | No Result | Bonus | Points | NRR    |
|-----------|--------|-----|------|-----------|-------|--------|--------|
| India     | 6      | 4   | 1    | 1         | 1     | 19     | 0.175  |
| England   | 6      | 3   | 2    | 1         | 1     | 15     | 0.386  |
| Sri Lanka | 6      | 1   | 3    | —         | 0     | 4      | –0.441 |

### Final – Lord's 13 July

**Toss: England. INDIA** beat **ENGLAND** by two wickets. England 325-5 (50 overs) (N.Hussain 115, M.E.Trescothick 109; Z.Khan 3-62). India 326-8 (49.3 overs) (M.Kaif 87*, Yuvraj Singh 69, S.C.Ganguly 60). Award: M.Kaif. Series Award: M.E.Trescothick.

# CHELTENHAM & GLOUCESTER TROPHY 2002 RESULTS CHART

| THIRD ROUND 24, 29, 30 May | FOURTH ROUND 18 June | QUARTER-FINALS 16, 17 July | SEMI-FINALS 31 July – 4 August | FINAL 31 August |
|---|---|---|---|---|
| Yorkshire CB† | | | | |
| SOMERSET | SOMERSET† | | | |
| Kent CB† | | SOMERSET† | | |
| HAMPSHIRE | Hampshire | | | |
| Cornwall† | | | SOMERSET† | |
| WORCESTERSHIRE | WORCESTERSHIRE | | | |
| Ireland† | | Worcestershire (£11,500) | | |
| NOTTINGHAMSHIRE | Nottinghamshire† | | | |
| Norfolk† | | | | Somerset (£27,000) |
| KENT | KENT† | | | |
| Staffordshire† | | KENT† | | |
| WARWICKSHIRE | Warwickshire | | | |
| Shropshire† | | | Kent (£16,500) | |
| GLOUCESTERSHIRE | GLOUCESTERSHIRE† | | | |
| Wales MC† | | Gloucestershire (£11,500) | | |
| DURHAM | Durham | | | |
| Buckinghamshire† | | | | |
| SUSSEX | SUSSEX | | | |
| Warwickshire CB† | | Sussex† (£11,500) | | |
| LEICESTERSHIRE | Leicestershire† | | | |
| Scotland† | | | Surrey (£16,500) | |
| SURREY | SURREY† | | | |
| Lincolnshire† | | SURREY | | |
| GLAMORGAN | Glamorgan | | | |
| Derbyshire | | | | YORKSHIRE (£53,000) |
| LANCASHIRE† | Lancashire | | | |
| Middlesex | | Essex† (£11,500) | | |
| ESSEX† | ESSEX† | | | |
| Suffolk† | | | YORKSHIRE† | |
| NORTHAMPTONSHIRE | Northamptonshire† | | | |
| Devon† | | YORKSHIRE | | |
| YORKSHIRE | YORKSHIRE | | | |

† Home team. Winning teams are in capitals. Prize-money shown in brackets.

# 2002 C & G TROPHY FINAL

## SOMERSET v YORKSHIRE

At Lord's, London on 31 August
Result: **YORKSHIRE won by six wickets**
Toss: Somerset. Award: M.T.G.Elliott.

| SOMERSET | | Runs | Balls | 4/6 | Fall |
|---|---|---|---|---|---|
| P.D.Bowler | c Blakey b Hoggard | 67 | 89 | 6 | 3-159 |
| M.E.Trescothick | c Vaughan b Hoggard | 27 | 25 | 4/1 | 1- 41 |
| * J.Cox | lbw b McGrath | 34 | 49 | 5 | 2-122 |
| M.Burns | lbw b Hoggard | 21 | 41 | 2 | 4-171 |
| I.D.Blackwell | b Sidebottom | 12 | 16 | 1 | 5-191 |
| K.A.Parsons | c Sidebottom b Hoggard | 41 | 46 | 3 | 8-250 |
| † R.J.Turner | c White b Sidebottom | 20 | 26 | – | 6-230 |
| R.L.Johnson | b Hoggard | 2 | 3 | – | 7-233 |
| K.P.Dutch | not out | 13 | 7 | 2 | |
| A.R.Caddick | not out | 0 | 1 | – | |
| P.S.Jones | | | | | |
| Extras | (B 1, LB 6, W 6, NB 6) | 19 | | | |
| **Total** | (50 overs; 8 wickets; 207 minutes) | **256** | | | |

| YORKSHIRE | | Runs | Balls | 4/6 | Fall |
|---|---|---|---|---|---|
| C.White | c Turner b Johnson | 12 | 14 | 1 | 1- 19 |
| M.J.Wood | b Johnson | 19 | 38 | 2 | 3- 64 |
| C.E.W.Silverwood | b Johnson | 0 | 3 | – | 2- 19 |
| M.T.G.Elliott | not out | 128 | 125 | 16 | |
| M.P.Vaughan | lbw b Jones | 31 | 56 | – | 4-157 |
| A.McGrath | not out | 46 | 53 | 4 | |
| G.M.Fellows | | | | | |
| *†R.J.Blakey | | | | | |
| R.K.J.Dawson | | | | | |
| R.J.Sidebottom | | | | | |
| M.J.Hoggard | | | | | |
| Extras | (LB 7, W 15, NB 2) | 24 | | | |
| **Total** | (48 overs; 4 wickets; 199 minutes) | **260** | | | |

| YORKS | O | M | R | W | SOMERSET | O | M | R | W |
|---|---|---|---|---|---|---|---|---|---|
| Silverwood | 8 | 1 | 30 | 0 | Caddick | 9 | 0 | 53 | 0 |
| Hoggard | 10 | 0 | 65 | 5 | Johnson | 10 | 2 | 51 | 3 |
| Sidebottom | 9 | 0 | 49 | 2 | Parsons | 6 | 0 | 31 | 0 |
| McGrath | 9 | 0 | 37 | 1 | Jones | 9 | 0 | 45 | 1 |
| Dawson | 10 | 0 | 48 | 0 | Dutch | 8 | 0 | 43 | 0 |
| Vaughan | 4 | 0 | 20 | 0 | Blackwell | 6 | 0 | 30 | 0 |

Scores after 15 overs: Somerset 82-1; Yorkshire 67-3.

Umpires: J.W.Holder and G.Sharp.

# CHELTENHAM & GLOUCESTER TROPHY
# PRINCIPAL RECORDS 1963-2002
### (Including Gillette Cup and NatWest Trophy Matches)

| | | | | | |
|---|---|---|---|---|---|
| **Highest Total** | 438-5 | | Surrey v Glamorgan | The Oval | 2002 |
| **Highest Total in a Final** | 322-5 | | Warwicks v Sussex | Lord's | 1993 |
| **Highest Total Batting Second** | 429 | | Glamorgan v Surrey | The Oval | 2002 |
| **Highest Total to Win Batting Second** | 329-5 | | Sussex v Derbyshire | Derby | 1997 |
| **Lowest Total** | 39 | | Ireland v Sussex | Hove | 1985 |
| **Lowest Total in a Final** | 57 | | Essex v Lancashire | Lord's | 1996 |
| **Lowest Total to Win Batting First** | 98 | | Worcs v Durham | Chester-le-St | 1968 |

| | | | | | |
|---|---|---|---|---|---|
| **Highest Score** | 268 | A.D.Brown | Surrey v Glamorgan | The Oval | 2002 |
| **Fastest Hundred** | 36 balls | G.D.Rose | Somerset v Devon | Torquay | 1990 |
| **Most Hundreds** | 8 | R.A.Smith | Hampshire | | 1985-99 |
| **Most Runs** | 2547 | (av 48.98) | G.A.Gooch | Essex | 1973-96 |

**Highest Partnership for each Wicket**

| | | | | | |
|---|---|---|---|---|---|
| 1st | 311 | A.J.Wright/N.J.Trainor | Glos v Scotland | Bristol | 1997 |
| 2nd | 286 | I.S.Anderson/A.Hill | Derbys v Cornwall | Derby | 1986 |
| 3rd | 309* | T.S.Curtis/T.M.Moody | Worcs v Surrey | The Oval | 1994 |
| 4th | 234* | D.Lloyd/C.H.Lloyd | Lancashire v Glos | Manchester | 1978 |
| 5th | 166 | M.A.Lynch/G.R.J.Roope | Surrey v Sussex | The Oval | 1982 |
| 6th | 226 | N.J.Llong/M.V.Fleming | Kent v Cheshire | Bowdon | 1999 |
| 7th | 160* | C.J.Richards/I.R.Payne | Surrey v Lincs | Sleaford | 1983 |
| 8th | 112 | A.L.Penberthy/J.E.Emburey | Northants v Lancs | Manchester | 1996 |
| 9th | 87 | M.A.Nash/A.E.Cordle | Glamorgan v Lincs | Swansea | 1974 |
| 10th | 81 | S.Turner/R.E.East | Essex v Yorkshire | Leeds | 1982 |

| | | | | | |
|---|---|---|---|---|---|
| **Best Bowling** | 8-21 | M.A.Holding | Derbys v Sussex | Hove | 1988 |
| | 8-31 | D.L.Underwood | Kent v Scotland | Edinburgh | 1987 |
| **Most Wickets** | 88 | (av 14.35) | A.A.Donald | Warwks/Worcs | 1987-02 |

**Most Wicket-Keeping Dismissals in an Innings**

| | | | | | |
|---|---|---|---|---|---|
| | 8 (8ct) | D.J.Pipe | Worcs v Herts | Hertford | 2001 |

**Most Match Wins: 83 – Lancashire.**          **Most Cup/Trophy Wins: 7 – Lancashire**

## GILLETTE CUP WINNERS

| | | | | | |
|---|---|---|---|---|---|
| 1963 | Sussex | 1970 | Lancashire | 1977 | Middlesex |
| 1964 | Sussex | 1971 | Lancashire | 1978 | Sussex |
| 1965 | Yorkshire | 1972 | Lancashire | 1979 | Somerset |
| 1966 | Warwickshire | 1973 | Gloucestershire | 1980 | Middlesex |
| 1967 | Kent | 1974 | Kent | | |
| 1968 | Warwickshire | 1975 | Lancashire | | |
| 1969 | Yorkshire | 1976 | Northamptonshire | | |

## NATWEST TROPHY WINNERS

| | | | | | |
|---|---|---|---|---|---|
| 1981 | Derbyshire | 1988 | Middlesex | 1995 | Warwickshire |
| 1982 | Surrey | 1989 | Warwickshire | 1996 | Lancashire |
| 1983 | Somerset | 1990 | Lancashire | 1997 | Essex |
| 1984 | Middlesex | 1991 | Hampshire | 1998 | Lancashire |
| 1985 | Essex | 1992 | Northamptonshire | 1999 | Gloucestershire |
| 1986 | Sussex | 1993 | Warwickshire | 2000 | Gloucestershire |
| 1987 | Nottinghamshire | 1994 | Worcestershire | | |

## CHELTENHAM & GLOUCESTER TROPHY WINNERS

| | | | |
|---|---|---|---|
| 2001 | Somerset | 2002 | Yorkshire |

# NORWICH UNION NATIONAL LEAGUE 2002

## FIRST DIVISION

| | P | W | L | T | NR | Pts | NRR |
|---|---|---|---|---|---|---|---|
| 1 Glamorgan (-) | 16 | 12 | 3 | 1 | – | 50 | 8.36 |
| 2 Worcestershire (-) | 16 | 11 | 3 | – | 2 | 48 | 10.69 |
| 3 Warwickshire (3) | 16 | 9 | 6 | – | 1 | 38 | 8.41 |
| 4 Yorkshire (6) | 16 | 8 | 7 | – | 1 | 34 | 1.44 |
| 5 Kent (1) | 16 | 7 | 8 | 1 | – | 30 | 5.85 |
| 6 Leicestershire (2) | 16 | 7 | 8 | – | 1 | 30 | 3.52 |
| 7 Somerset (4) | 16 | 5 | 10 | – | 1 | 22 | –3.53 |
| 8 Durham (-) | 16 | 5 | 11 | – | – | 20 | –21.17 |
| 9 Nottinghamshire (5) | 16 | 3 | 11 | – | 2 | 16 | –11.28 |

## SECOND DIVISION

| | P | W | L | T | NR | Pts | NRR |
|---|---|---|---|---|---|---|---|
| 1 Gloucestershire (-) | 16 | 10 | 4 | – | 2 | 44 | 12.75 |
| 2 Surrey (-) | 16 | 10 | 5 | – | 1 | 42 | 6.53 |
| 3 Essex (7) | 16 | 10 | 6 | – | – | 40 | 3.94 |
| 4 Derbyshire (9) | 16 | 8 | 7 | – | 1 | 34 | –0.98 |
| 5 Lancashire (6) | 16 | 7 | 7 | – | 2 | 32 | –6.99 |
| 6 Northamptonshire (-) | 16 | 7 | 8 | – | 1 | 30 | 7.63 |
| 7 Hampshire (4) | 16 | 6 | 9 | – | 1 | 26 | –2.81 |
| 8 Sussex (5) | 16 | 4 | 10 | – | 2 | 20 | –7.42 |
| 9 Middlesex (8) | 16 | 4 | 10 | – | 2 | 20 | –12.51 |

Win = 4 points. Tie (T)/No Result (NR) = 2 points. Positions of counties finishing equal on points are decided by most wins or, if equal, by higher net run-rate (NRR – overall run-rate in all matches, i.e. total runs scored x 100 divided by balls received, minus the run-rate of its opponents in those same matches). Horizontal rules segregate the counties relegated and promoted for the 2003 competition.

2001 final positions for that division are shown in brackets.

HIGHEST BATTING AGGREGATE: 654 runs – B.F.Smith (Worcestershire)
HIGHEST BOWLING AGGREGATE: 30 Wickets – E.S.H.Giddins (Surrey) and N.Killeen (Durham)

## SUNDAY LEAGUE CHAMPIONS

| | | | | | |
|---|---|---|---|---|---|
| 1969 | Lancashire | 1979 | Somerset | 1989 | Lancashire |
| 1970 | Lancashire | 1980 | Warwickshire | 1990 | Derbyshire |
| 1971 | Worcestershire | 1981 | Essex | 1991 | Nottinghamshire |
| 1972 | Kent | 1982 | Sussex | 1992 | Middlesex |
| 1973 | Kent | 1983 | Yorkshire | 1993 | Glamorgan |
| 1974 | Leicestershire | 1984 | Essex | 1994 | Warwickshire |
| 1975 | Hampshire | 1985 | Essex | 1995 | Kent |
| 1976 | Kent | 1986 | Hampshire | 1996 | Surrey |
| 1977 | Leicestershire | 1987 | Worcestershire | 1997 | Warwickshire |
| 1978 | Hampshire | 1988 | Worcestershire | 1998 | Lancashire |

## NATIONAL LEAGUE CHAMPIONS

| | | | |
|---|---|---|---|
| 1999 | Lancashire | 2001 | Kent |
| 2000 | Gloucestershire | 2002 | Glamorgan |

# NATIONAL (SUNDAY) LEAGUE 1969-2002
## PRINCIPAL RECORDS

| | | | | | |
|---|---|---|---|---|---|
| **Highest Total** | | 375-4 | Surrey v Yorkshire | Scarborough | 1994 |
| **Highest Total Batting Second** | | 317-6 | Surrey v Notts | The Oval | 1993 |
| **Lowest Total** | | 23 | Middlesex v Yorks | Leeds | 1974 |
| **Highest Score** | 203 | A.D.Brown | Surrey v Hampshire | Guildford | 1997 |
| **Fastest Hundred** | 44 balls | M.A.Ealham | Kent v Derbyshire | Maidstone | 1995 |

**Highest Partnership for each Wicket**

| | | | | | |
|---|---|---|---|---|---|
| 1st | 239 | G.A.Gooch/B.R.Hardie | Essex v Notts | Nottingham | 1985 |
| 2nd | 273 | G.A.Gooch/K.S.McEwan | Essex v Notts | Nottingham | 1983 |
| 3rd | 223 | S.J.Cook/G.D.Rose | Somerset v Glam | Neath | 1990 |
| 4th | 219 | C.G.Greenidge/C.L.Smith | Hampshire v Surrey | Southampton | 1987 |
| 5th | 220* | C.C.Lewis/P.A.Nixon | Leics v Kent | Canterbury | 1999 |
| 6th | 137 | M.P.Speight/I.D.K.Salisbury | Sussex v Surrey | Guildford | 1996 |
| 7th | 132 | K.R.Brown/N.F.Williams | Middx v Somerset | Lord's | 1988 |
| 8th | 110* | C.L.Cairns/B.N.French | Notts v Surrey | The Oval | 1993 |
| 9th | 105 | D.G.Moir/R.W.Taylor | Derbyshire v Kent | Derby | 1984 |
| 10th | 82 | G.Chapple/P.J.Martin | Lancashire v Worcs | Manchester | 1996 |
| **Best Bowling** | 8-26 | K.D.Boyce | Essex v Lancashire | Manchester | 1971 |
| | 7-15 | R.A.Hutton | Yorkshire v Worcs | Leeds | 1969 |
| | 7-16 | S.D.Thomas | Glamorgan v Surrey | Swansea | 1998 |
| | 7-30 | M.P.Bicknell | Surrey v Glamorgan | The Oval | 1999 |
| | 7-39 | A.Hodgson | Northants v Somerset | Northampton | 1976 |
| | 7-41 | A.N.Jones | Sussex v Notts | Nottingham | 1986 |
| **Four Wkts in Four Balls** | | A.Ward | Derbyshire v Sussex | Derby | 1970 |
| | | V.C.Drakes | Notts v Derbys | Nottingham | 1999 |

**Most Wicket-Keeping Dismissals in an Innings**

| | | | | | |
|---|---|---|---|---|---|
| 7 (6ct, 1st) | | R.W.Taylor | Derbyshire v Lancs | Manchester | 1975 |

**Most Catches in an Innings**

| | | | | | |
|---|---|---|---|---|---|
| 5 | | J.M.Rice | Hampshire v Warwicks | Southampton | 1978 |

# BENSON & HEDGES CUP 2002
## FINAL GROUP TABLES

| *MID/WEST/WALES* | *P* | *W* | *L* | *NR* | *Points* | *Run-Rate* |
|---|---|---|---|---|---|---|
| Gloucestershire | 5 | 4 | 1 | – | 8 | 1.33 |
| Worcestershire | 5 | 4 | 1 | – | 8 | –0.06 |
| Warwickshire | 5 | 3 | 2 | – | 6 | 0.01 |
| Northamptonshire | 5 | 3 | 2 | – | 6 | 1.51 |
| Glamorgan | 5 | – | 4 | 1 | 1 | –1.74 |
| Somerset | 5 | – | 4 | 1 | 1 | –2.39 |

| *NORTH* | *P* | *W* | *L* | *NR* | *Points* | *Run-Rate* |
|---|---|---|---|---|---|---|
| Leicestershire | 5 | 4 | – | 1 | 9 | 0.46 |
| Yorkshire | 5 | 3 | 2 | – | 6 | 0.45 |
| Lancashire | 5 | 2 | 2 | 1 | 5 | 1.35 |
| Nottinghamshire | 5 | 2 | 3 | – | 4 | –0.71 |
| Durham | 5 | 2 | 3 | – | 4 | –0.54 |
| Derbyshire | 5 | – | 3 | 2 | 2 | –1.46 |

| *SOUTH* | *P* | *W* | *L* | *NR* | *Points* | *Run-Rate* |
|---|---|---|---|---|---|---|
| Essex | 5 | 4 | – | 1 | 9 | 0.48 |
| Sussex | 5 | 4 | 1 | – | 8 | 0.61 |
| Kent | 5 | 2 | 3 | – | 4 | –0.48 |
| Hampshire | 5 | 2 | 3 | – | 4 | –0.42 |
| Middlesex | 5 | 1 | 3 | 1 | 3 | 0.37 |
| Surrey | 5 | 1 | 4 | – | 2 | –0.29 |

# 2002 – THE FINAL B & H CUP FINAL

## ESSEX v WARWICKSHIRE

At Lord's, London on 22 June.
Result: **WARWICKSHIRE won by five wickets.**
Toss: Warwickshire. Award: I.R.Bell.

| ESSEX | | Runs | Balls | 4/6 | Fall |
|---|---|---|---|---|---|
| N.Hussain | c Piper b Pollock | 0 | 2 | – | 1- 0 |
| D.D.J.Robinson | c Brown b Carter | 18 | 36 | 3 | 4- 40 |
| G.R.Napier | run out | 17 | 18 | 2/1 | 2- 33 |
| J.P.Stephenson | b Carter | 0 | 1 | – | 3- 33 |
| † A.Flower | c Piper b Smith | 30 | 44 | 3 | 6- 86 |
| * R.C.Irani | c Smith b Brown | 8 | 33 | – | 5- 61 |
| A.Habib | c Knight b Giles | 19 | 42 | – | 7-109 |
| A.P.Grayson | not out | 38 | 66 | – | |
| J.M.Dakin | c Powell b Brown | 12 | 32 | – | 8-134 |
| A.P.Cowan | not out | 27 | 28 | 1 | |
| A.J.Clarke | | | | | |
| Extras | (LB 4, W 4, NB 4) | 12 | | | |
| **Total** | (50 overs; 8 wickets; 192 minutes) | 181 | | | |

| WARWICKSHIRE | | Runs | Balls | 4/6 | Fall |
|---|---|---|---|---|---|
| * M.J.Powell | c Flower b Cowan | 11 | 18 | 2 | 1- 19 |
| N.V.Knight | c Flower b Irani | 9 | 20 | – | 2- 21 |
| I.R.Bell | not out | 65 | 89 | 7 | |
| J.O.Troughton | c Flower b Napier | 37 | 33 | 8 | 3-105 |
| S.M.Pollock | c Dakin b Irani | 34 | 31 | 5 | 4-158 |
| T.L.Penney | lbw b Stephenson | 0 | 3 | – | 5-159 |
| D.R.Brown | not out | 12 | 24 | – | |
| N.M.K.Smith | | | | | |
| A.F.Giles | | | | | |
| † K.J.Piper | | | | | |
| N.M.Carter | | | | | |
| Extras | (LB 6, W 8) | 14 | | | |
| **Total** | (36.2 overs; 5 wickets; 148 minutes) | 182 | | | |

| WARWICKS | O | M | R | W | ESSEX | O | M | R | W |
|---|---|---|---|---|---|---|---|---|---|
| Pollock | 10 | 1 | 32 | 1 | Irani | 10 | 2 | 40 | 2 |
| Carter | 10 | 1 | 45 | 2 | Cowan | 8 | 0 | 37 | 1 |
| Brown | 10 | 0 | 32 | 2 | Clarke | 2 | 0 | 20 | 0 |
| Giles | 10 | 1 | 28 | 1 | Dakin | 2 | 0 | 22 | 0 |
| Smith | 10 | 0 | 40 | 1 | Grayson | 4 | 0 | 11 | 0 |
| | | | | | Napier | 5.2 | 0 | 31 | 1 |
| | | | | | Stephenson | 5 | 0 | 15 | 1 |

Scores after 15 overs: Essex 53-4; Warwickshire: 83-2.

Umpires: B.Dudleston and J.H.Hampshire.

# BENSON AND HEDGES CUP

## RESULTS CHART 2002

| QUARTER-FINALS | SEMI-FINALS | FINAL |
|---|---|---|
| *21, 22 May* | *6, 7 June* | *22 June* |

LANCASHIRE
Leicestershire† (£10,500)          } Lancashire† (£15,500)

Sussex† (£10,500)
WARWICKSHIRE                       } WARWICKSHIRE (£52,000)

Gloucestershire† (£10,500)
WORCESTERSHIRE                     } Worcestershire (£15,500)

ESSEX†
Yorkshire (£10,500)                } ESSEX†                   } Essex (£26,000)

*† Home team. Winning teams are in capitals. Prize-money in brackets.*

## PRINCIPAL RECORDS 1972-2002

| | | | | | |
|---|---|---|---|---|---|
| **Highest Total** | | 388-7 | Essex v Scotland | Chelmsford | 1992 |
| **Highest Total Batting Second** | | 318-5 | Lancashire v Leics | Manchester | 1995 |
| **Lowest Total** | | 50 | Hampshire v Yorks | Leeds | 1991 |
| **Highest Score** | 198* | G.A.Gooch | Essex v Sussex | Hove | 1982 |
| **Fastest Hundred** | 62 min | M.A.Nash | Glamorgan v Hants | Swansea | 1976 |
| **Highest Partnership for each Wicket** | | | | | |
| 1st | 252 | V.P.Terry/C.L.Smith | Hants v Combined U | Southampton | 1990 |
| 2nd | 285* | C.G.Greenidge/D.R.Turner | Hants v Minor C (S) | Amersham | 1973 |
| 3rd | 271 | C.J.Adams/M.G.Bevan | Sussex v Essex | Chelmsford | 2000 |
| 4th | 207 | R.C.Russell/A.J.Wright | Glos v British U | Bristol | 1998 |
| 5th | 160 | A.J.Lamb/D.J.Capel | Northants v Leics | Northampton | 1986 |
| 6th | 167* | M.G.Bevan/R.J.Blakey | Yorkshire v Lancs | Manchester | 1996 |
| 7th | 149* | J.D.Love/C.M.Old | Yorks v Scotland | Bradford | 1981 |
| 8th | 109 | R.E.East/N.Smith | Essex v Northants | Chelmsford | 1977 |
| 9th | 83 | P.G.Newman/M.A.Holding | Derbyshire v Notts | Nottingham | 1985 |
| 10th | 80* | D.L.Bairstow/M.Johnson | Yorkshire v Derbys | Derby | 1981 |
| **Best Bowling** | 7-12 | W.W.Daniel | Middx v Minor C (E) | Ipswich | 1978 |
| | 7-22 | J.R.Thomson | Middx v Hampshire | Lord's | 1981 |
| | 7-24 | Mushtaq Ahmed | Somerset v Ireland | Taunton | 1997 |
| | 7-32 | R.G.D.Willis | Warwicks v Yorks | Birmingham | 1981 |
| **Four Wickets in Four Balls** | | S.M.Pollock | Warwicks v Leics | Birmingham | 1996 |
| **Most Wicket-Keeping Dismissals in an Innings** | | | | | |
| 8 (8ct) | | D.J.S.Taylor | Somerset v Combined U | Taunton | 1982 |
| **Most Catches in an Innings** | | | | | |
| 5 | | V.J.Marks | Combined U v Kent | Oxford | 1976 |

## BENSON AND HEDGES CUP WINNERS

| | | | | | |
|---|---|---|---|---|---|
| 1972 | Leicestershire | 1983 | Middlesex | 1994 | Warwickshire |
| 1973 | Kent | 1984 | Lancashire | 1995 | Lancashire |
| 1974 | Surrey | 1985 | Leicestershire | 1996 | Lancashire |
| 1975 | Leicestershire | 1986 | Middlesex | 1997 | Surrey |
| 1976 | Kent | 1987 | Yorkshire | 1998 | Essex |
| 1977 | Gloucestershire | 1988 | Hampshire | 1999 | Gloucestershire |
| 1978 | Kent | 1989 | Nottinghamshire | 2000 | Gloucestershire |
| 1979 | Essex | 1991 | Worcestershire | 2001 | Surrey |
| 1980 | Northamptonshire | 1992 | Hampshire | 2002 | Warwickshire |
| 1981 | Somerset | 1990 | Lancashire | | |
| 1982 | Somerset | 1993 | Derbyshire | | |

# MINOR COUNTIES CHAMPIONSHIP

## FINAL TABLES 2002

| | P | W | L | D | NR | Bonus Points Bat | Bonus Points Bowl | Total Points |
|---|---|---|---|---|---|---|---|---|
| **EASTERN DIVISION** | | | | | | | | |
| NORFOLK | 6 | 3 | – | 3 | – | 11 | 22 | 93 |
| Suffolk | 6 | 2 | 1 | 2 | 1 | 15 | 17 | 78† |
| Cambridgeshire | 6 | 2 | – | 4 | – | 10 | 19 | 77 |
| Bedfordshire | 6 | 2 | 1 | 3 | – | 11 | 20 | 75 |
| Staffordshire | 6 | 2 | 1 | 3 | – | 11 | 17 | 72 |
| Lincolnshire | 6 | 1 | 1 | 4 | – | 20 | 16 | 68 |
| Northumberland | 6 | 1 | 2 | 3 | – | 10 | 20 | 58 |
| Hertfordshire | 6 | 1 | 4 | 1 | – | 16 | 18 | 54 |
| Buckinghamshire | 6 | 1 | 2 | 2 | 1 | 4 | 18 | 52† |
| Cumberland | 6 | – | 3 | 3 | – | 6 | 21 | 39 |
| **WESTERN DIVISION** | | | | | | | | |
| HEREFORDSHIRE | 6 | 5 | – | 1 | – | 14 | 22 | 120 |
| Devon | 6 | 5 | – | 1 | – | 16 | 19 | 119 |
| Oxfordshire | 6 | 3 | 1 | 2 | – | 8 | 24 | 88 |
| Cornwall | 6 | 3 | 2 | 1 | – | 8 | 23 | 83 |
| Berkshire | 6 | 2 | 2 | 2 | – | 12 | 23 | 75 |
| Cheshire | 6 | 1 | 2 | 3 | – | 17 | 17 | 62 |
| Shropshire | 6 | 1 | 3 | 2 | – | 11 | 22 | 57 |
| Dorset | 6 | – | 4 | 2 | – | 12 | 24 | 44 |
| Wiltshire | 6 | – | 3 | 3 | – | 8 | 21 | 41 |
| Wales MC | 6 | – | 3 | 3 | – | 8 | 12 | 32 |

† Includes six points for a match abandoned without a ball bowled.

## CHAMPIONSHIP FINAL

At Luctonians CC, Kingsland on 8, 9, 10 September: **HEREFORDSHIRE drew with NORFOLK**. Herefordshire 302 (70 overs; H.V.Patel 84, C.W.Boroughs 90, C.Brown 4-98) and 245-3 dec (P.S.Lazenbury 77, I.Dawood 70*). Norfolk 217-8 closed (70 overs; K.E.Cooper 5-64) and 97-8 (C.R.Borrett 51, K.E.Cooper 4-26).

## ECB 38-COUNTY CUP FINAL

At Worcester on 3 September: **WARWICKSHIRE CRICKET BOARD beat DEVON by two wickets**. Devon 261-8 closed (50 overs; M.P.Hunt 65, G.T.J.Townsend 51, M.A.Sheikh 4-37). Warwickshire CB 266-8 (49.1 overs; I.J.Westwood 67, N.V.Humphrey 57, A.J.Procter 4-35).

## MINOR COUNTIES RECORDS

| | | | | | |
|---|---|---|---|---|---|
| **Highest Total** | 621 | | Surrey II v Devon | The Oval | 1928 |
| **Lowest Total** | 14 | | Cheshire v Staffs | Stoke | 1909 |
| **Highest Score** | 282 | E.Garnett | Berkshire v Wiltshire | Reading | 1908 |
| **Most Runs – Season** | 1212 | A.F.Brazier | Surrey II | | 1949 |
| **Record Partnership:** | | | | | |
| 2nd wicket | 388* | T.H.Clark and A.F.Brazier | Surrey II v Sussex II | The Oval | 1949 |
| **Best Bowling – Innings** | 10- 11 | S.Turner | Cambs v Cumberland | Penrith | 1987 |
| – Match | 18-100 | N.W.Harding | Kent II v Wiltshire | Swindon | 1937 |
| **Most Wickets – Season** | 119 | S.F.Barnes | Staffordshire | | 1906 |

# MINOR COUNTIES CHAMPIONS

| | | | |
|---|---|---|---|
| 1895 | Norfolk / Durham / Worcestershire | 1931 Leicestershire II | 1972 Bedfordshire |
| 1896 | Worcestershire | 1932 Buckinghamshire | 1973 Shropshire |
| 1897 | Worcestershire | 1933 *Undecided* | 1974 Oxfordshire |
| 1898 | Worcestershire | 1934 Lancashire II | 1975 Hertfordshire |
| 1899 | Northamptonshire / Buckinghamshire | 1935 Middlesex II | 1976 Durham |
| 1900 | Glamorgan / Durham / Northamptonshire | 1936 Hertfordshire | 1977 Suffolk |
| 1901 | Durham | 1937 Lancashire II | 1978 Devon |
| 1902 | Wiltshire | 1938 Buckinghamshire | 1979 Suffolk |
| 1903 | Northamptonshire | 1939 Surrey II | 1980 Durham |
| 1904 | Northamptonshire | 1946 Suffolk | 1981 Durham |
| 1905 | Norfolk | 1947 Yorkshire II | 1982 Oxfordshire |
| 1906 | Staffordshire | 1948 Lancashire II | 1983 Hertfordshire |
| 1907 | Lancashire II | 1949 Lancashire II | 1984 Durham |
| 1908 | Staffordshire | 1950 Surrey II | 1985 Cheshire |
| 1909 | Wiltshire | 1951 Kent II | 1986 Cumberland |
| 1910 | Norfolk | 1952 Buckinghamshire | 1987 Buckinghamshire |
| 1911 | Staffordshire | 1953 Berkshire | 1988 Cheshire |
| 1912 | *In abeyance* | 1954 Surrey II | 1989 Oxfordshire |
| 1913 | Norfolk | 1955 Surrey II | 1990 Hertfordshire |
| 1920 | Staffordshire | 1956 Kent II | 1991 Staffordshire |
| 1921 | Staffordshire | 1957 Yorkshire II | 1992 Staffordshire |
| 1922 | Buckinghamshire | 1958 Yorkshire II | 1993 Staffordshire |
| 1923 | Buckinghamshire | 1959 Warwickshire II | 1994 Devon |
| 1924 | Berkshire | 1960 Lancashire II | 1995 Devon |
| 1925 | Buckinghamshire | 1961 Somerset II | 1996 Devon |
| 1926 | Durham | 1962 Warwickshire II | 1997 Devon |
| 1927 | Staffordshire | 1963 Cambridgeshire | 1998 Staffordshire |
| 1928 | Berkshire | 1964 Lancashire II | 1999 Cumberland |
| 1929 | Oxfordshire | 1965 Somerset II | 2000 Dorset |
| 1930 | Durham | 1966 Lincolnshire | 2001 Cheshire / Lincolnshire |
| | | 1967 Cheshire | 2002 Herefordshire / Norfolk |
| | | 1968 Yorkshire II | |
| | | 1969 Buckinghamshire | |
| | | 1970 Bedfordshire | |
| | | 1971 Yorkshire II | |

## LEADING CHAMPIONSHIP BATTING AVERAGES
### (Qualifications: 8 innings; average 30.00)

| | | M | I | NO | HS | Runs | Avge | 100 | 50 |
|---|---|---|---|---|---|---|---|---|---|
| P.M.Roebuck | Devon | 6 | 9 | 6 | 93* | 237 | 79.00 | – | 1 |
| M.A.Fell | Lincolnshire | 5 | 8 | 3 | 92 | 393 | 78.60 | – | 4 |
| C.W.Boroughs | Herefordshire | 7 | 10 | 4 | 96* | 446 | 74.33 | – | 5 |
| S.T.Knox | Cumberland | 5 | 8 | 2 | 125* | 436 | 72.66 | 2 | 3 |
| P.D.Atkins | Buckinghamshire | 5 | 9 | 4 | 113* | 351 | 70.20 | 1 | 3 |
| R.W.J.Howitt | Lincolnshire | 6 | 10 | 1 | 153* | 624 | 69.33 | 2 | 3 |
| C.S.Knightley | Oxfordshire | 5 | 9 | 3 | 91 | 393 | 65.50 | – | 4 |
| S.A.Kellett | Cambridgeshire | 6 | 11 | 3 | 150* | 516 | 64.50 | 2 | 1 |
| J.A.Knott | Bedfordshire | 6 | 11 | 3 | 69 | 460 | 57.50 | – | 6 |
| T.J.Mason | Shropshire | 6 | 12 | 2 | 146* | 574 | 57.40 | 2 | 3 |
| G.F.Archer | Staffordshire | 5 | 10 | 2 | 111 | 452 | 56.50 | 2 | 1 |
| I.Dawood | Herefordshire | 7 | 11 | 3 | 148* | 438 | 54.75 | 1 | 2 |
| B.Parker | Northumberland | 4 | 8 | 2 | 120* | 326 | 54.33 | 1 | 1 |
| P.S.Lazenbury | Herefordshire | 7 | 12 | 1 | 143 | 585 | 53.18 | 2 | 2 |
| B.J.Thompson | Oxfordshire | 4 | 8 | 3 | 125 | 262 | 52.40 | 1 | 1 |
| B.P.Price | Cornwall | 5 | 8 | 2 | 74* | 311 | 51.83 | – | 4 |
| O.A.Dawkins | Wales MC | 6 | 12 | 2 | 164 | 501 | 50.10 | 3 | – |
| D.J.Roberts | Bedfordshire | 5 | 10 | 2 | 126* | 394 | 49.25 | 1 | 3 |
| S.G.Cordingley | Hertfordshire | 5 | 10 | 1 | 133* | 434 | 48.22 | 1 | 3 |

| | | M | I | NO | HS | Runs | Avge | 100 | 50 |
|---|---|---|---|---|---|---|---|---|---|
| J.Trower | Lincolnshire | 6 | 10 | – | 86 | 478 | 47.80 | – | 7 |
| S.C.Goldsmith | Norfolk | 7 | 14 | 1 | 167 | 559 | 43.00 | 1 | 2 |
| A.Farooque | Herefordshire | 5 | 8 | 3 | 85 | 212 | 42.40 | – | 2 |
| M.I.Humphries | Staffordshire | 6 | 10 | 5 | 59* | 211 | 42.20 | – | 1 |
| S.Dean | Staffordshire | 6 | 12 | – | 133 | 492 | 41.00 | 1 | 1 |
| C.J.Rogers | Norfolk | 7 | 14 | – | 153 | 561 | 40.07 | 2 | 3 |
| S.Chapman | Northumberland | 4 | 8 | 1 | 103 | 280 | 40.00 | 1 | 1 |
| D.N.Leech | Cheshire | 6 | 9 | 2 | 152* | 279 | 39.85 | 1 | 1 |
| N.J.Wilton | Berkshire | 5 | 8 | 1 | 79 | 278 | 39.71 | – | 2 |
| D.M.Ward | Hertfordshire | 4 | 8 | – | 92 | 317 | 39.62 | – | 4 |
| A.Shankar | Bedfordshire | 5 | 9 | – | 104 | 356 | 39.55 | 1 | – |
| T.G.Sharp | Cornwall | 6 | 8 | – | 99 | 314 | 39.25 | – | 2 |
| J.B.R.Jones | Shropshire | 6 | 11 | 3 | 64* | 311 | 38.87 | – | 5 |
| D.J.Cowley | Dorset | 4 | 8 | – | 151 | 311 | 38.87 | 1 | 1 |
| G.D.Franklin | Staffordshire | 4 | 8 | – | 151 | 306 | 38.25 | 1 | 1 |
| R.I.Dawson | Devon | 6 | 12 | – | 76* | 381 | 38.10 | – | 4 |
| R.J.Catley | Suffolk | 5 | 8 | 1 | 96 | 264 | 37.71 | – | 2 |
| Baqar Rizvi | Wiltshire | 4 | 8 | – | 59 | 300 | 37.50 | – | 2 |
| S.W.D.Rintoul | Dorset | 6 | 12 | 1 | 139 | 411 | 37.36 | 1 | 3 |
| G.A.White | Cumberland | 5 | 9 | 1 | 138 | 297 | 37.12 | 1 | 1 |
| C.R.Borrett | Norfolk | 6 | 12 | 2 | 77* | 366 | 36.60 | – | 4 |
| M.J.Marvell | Shropshire | 5 | 10 | 1 | 103* | 329 | 36.55 | 1 | 2 |
| C.R.J.Budd | Wiltshire | 5 | 10 | – | 112 | 348 | 34.80 | 1 | 3 |
| O.E.Burford | Lincolnshire | 6 | 9 | 3 | 91* | 203 | 33.83 | – | 2 |
| C.Amos | Norfolk | 7 | 14 | – | 180 | 467 | 33.35 | 1 | 1 |
| R.J.Rowe | Wiltshire | 6 | 12 | – | 96 | 399 | 33.25 | – | 3 |
| P.J.Deakin | Dorset | 5 | 10 | 1 | 92* | 297 | 33.00 | – | 3 |
| H.V.Patel | Hertfordshire | 6 | 11 | – | 93 | 352 | 32.00 | – | 1 |
| A.R.Roberts | Bedfordshire | 6 | 11 | 3 | 79 | 255 | 31.87 | – | 1 |
| Ajaz Akhtar | Cambridgeshire | 6 | 9 | 2 | 63 | 219 | 31.28 | – | 1 |
| M.G.Miller | Dorset | 4 | 8 | 2 | 79 | 186 | 31.00 | – | 2 |
| T.C.Z.Lamb | Dorset | 6 | 11 | 1 | 103 | 307 | 30.70 | 1 | 1 |
| M.H.James | Hertfordshire | 6 | 12 | 1 | 115 | 333 | 30.27 | 1 | 1 |
| C.Jones | Cambridgeshire | 6 | 10 | 1 | 73* | 271 | 30.11 | – | 2 |

## LEADING CHAMPIONSHIP BOWLING AVERAGES
### (Qualification: 20 wickets)

| | | O | M | R | W | Avge | BB | 5w | 10w |
|---|---|---|---|---|---|---|---|---|---|
| K.E.Cooper | Hertfordshire | 220.2 | 73 | 482 | 52 | 9.26 | 7- 49 | 5 | 2 |
| N.A.Denning | Berkshire | 165 | 49 | 457 | 34 | 13.44 | 8- 66 | 3 | 1 |
| K.A.Arnold | Oxfordshire | 197 | 54 | 474 | 32 | 14.81 | 6- 75 | 1 | 1 |
| I.E.Bishop | Devon | 220.2 | 69 | 524 | 34 | 15.41 | 5- 55 | 2 | – |
| M.A.E.Richards | Devon | 170.3 | 67 | 334 | 21 | 15.90 | 6- 46 | 1 | 1 |
| D.Follett | Staffordshire | 109.4 | 18 | 404 | 25 | 16.16 | 7- 67 | 3 | 1 |
| K.J.Nash | Wiltshire | 102.1 | 21 | 325 | 20 | 16.25 | 5- 33 | 2 | – |
| A.R.Roberts | Bedfordshire | 181.4 | 66 | 343 | 20 | 17.15 | 7- 85 | 1 | 1 |
| A.P.O'Connor | Shropshire | 130 | 32 | 419 | 23 | 18.21 | 6- 66 | 3 | – |
| J.R.Wilson | Dorset | 178 | 73 | 401 | 22 | 18.22 | 4- 16 | – | – |
| A.J.Procter | Devon | 214.2 | 74 | 421 | 22 | 19.13 | 4- 35 | – | – |
| P.M.Such | Cambridgeshire | 291.3 | 85 | 684 | 34 | 20.11 | 6- 75 | 4 | 1 |
| C.Brown | Norfolk | 216 | 58 | 627 | 30 | 20.90 | 5- 49 | 1 | – |
| C.E.Shreck | Cornwall | 232 | 48 | 875 | 41 | 21.34 | 7-100 | 5 | 1 |
| A.R.Clarke | Buckinghamshire | 228 | 58 | 650 | 30 | 21.66 | 5- 50 | 3 | – |
| S.R.Walbridge | Dorset | 229 | 59 | 594 | 27 | 22.00 | 6- 38 | 2 | 1 |
| T.M.Smith | Suffolk | 171 | 42 | 559 | 24 | 23.29 | 6- 86 | 1 | – |
| S.C.Goldsmith | Norfolk | 165 | 34 | 526 | 22 | 23.90 | 4- 13 | – | – |
| Ajaz Akhtar | Cambridgeshire | 219.2 | 72 | 542 | 22 | 24.63 | 6- 61 | 1 | – |
| M.W.Patterson | Bedfordshire | 173.1 | 43 | 539 | 20 | 26.95 | 5- 57 | 1 | – |
| P.J.Lawson | Cumberland | 141.2 | 20 | 545 | 20 | 27.25 | 5- 85 | 1 | – |
| S.Rashid | Bedfordshire | 174.4 | 34 | 665 | 23 | 28.91 | 4- 94 | – | – |
| B.J.Frazer | Hertfordshire | 207.5 | 29 | 766 | 26 | 29.46 | 7- 36 | 2 | 1 |

# SECOND XI CHAMPIONSHIP 2002
# FINAL TABLE

| | P | W | L | D | T | Bonus Points Bat | Bonus Points Bowl | Total Points | Avge |
|---|---|---|---|---|---|---|---|---|---|
| 1 KENT (6) | 10 | 6 | 2 | 2 | – | 22 | 35 | 137 | 13.70 |
| 2 Derbyshire (18) | 12 | 5 | 1 | 6 | – | 38 | 37 | 159 | 13.25 |
| 3 Yorkshire (2) | 12 | 5 | 1 | 6 | – | 34 | 39 | 157 | 13.08 |
| 4 Glamorgan (16) | 11 | 4 | 1 | 6 | – | 32 | 34 | 138 | 12.55 |
| 5 Warwickshire (8) | 12 | 4 | 1 | 6 | – | 26 | 36 | †146 | 12.17 |
| 6 Northamptonshire (5) | 15 | 6 | 3 | 6 | – | 34 | 47 | 177 | 11.80 |
| 7 Lancashire (9) | 13 | 4 | 2 | 7 | – | 29 | 37 | 142 | 10.92 |
| 8 Hampshire (1) | 11 | 2 | 4 | 4 | – | 32 | 28 | †112 | 10.18 |
| 9 Durham (10) | 11 | 3 | 3 | 5 | – | 21 | 29 | 106 | 9.64 |
| 10 Middlesex (11) | 11 | 2 | 3 | 6 | – | 28 | 29 | 105 | 9.55 |
| 11 Surrey (7) | 13 | 1 | 3 | 9 | – | 32 | 41 | 121 | 9.31 |
| 12 Worcestershire (13) | 11 | 2 | 6 | 3 | – | 29 | 35 | 100 | 9.09 |
| 13 Nottinghamshire (3) | 15 | 3 | 4 | 8 | – | 23 | 45 | 136 | 9.07 |
| 14 Sussex (17) | 12 | 3 | 6 | 3 | – | 27 | 31 | 106 | 8.83 |
| 15 Somerset (15) | 10 | 2 | 3 | 5 | – | 15 | 25 | 84 | 8.40 |
| 16 Gloucestershire (4) | 11 | 1 | 4 | 5 | 1 | 12 | 29 | 79 | 7.18 |
| 17 Leicestershire (12) | 12 | 1 | 6 | 5 | – | 17 | 36 | 85 | 7.08 |
| 18 Essex (14) | 10 | 1 | 4 | 5 | – | 10 | 21 | 63 | 6.30 |

Win = 12 points, plus any first-innings points.
Tie = 6 points, plus any first-innings points.
Draw = 4 points, plus any first-innings points.
† Includes 2 extra draw points in match where scores were level.
2001 final positions are shown in brackets.

## ECB SECOND XI AWARDS 2002

No awards were made.

## SECOND XI CHAMPIONS

| | | | | | |
|---|---|---|---|---|---|
| 1959 | Gloucestershire | 1974 | Middlesex | 1989 | Middlesex |
| 1960 | Northamptonshire | 1975 | Surrey | 1990 | Sussex |
| 1961 | Kent | 1976 | Kent | 1991 | Yorkshire |
| 1962 | Worcestershire | 1977 | Yorkshire | 1992 | Surrey |
| 1963 | Worcestershire | 1978 | Sussex | 1993 | Middlesex |
| 1964 | Lancashire | 1979 | Warwickshire | 1994 | Somerset |
| 1965 | Glamorgan | 1980 | Glamorgan | 1995 | Hampshire |
| 1966 | Surrey | 1981 | Hampshire | 1996 | Warwickshire |
| 1967 | Hampshire | 1982 | Worcestershire | 1997 | Lancashire |
| 1968 | Surrey | 1983 | Leicestershire | 1998 | Northamptonshire |
| 1969 | Kent | 1984 | Yorkshire | 1999 | Middlesex |
| 1970 | Kent | 1985 | Nottinghamshire | 2000 | Middlesex |
| 1971 | Hampshire | 1986 | Lancashire | 2001 | Hampshire |
| 1972 | Nottinghamshire | 1987 | Kent/Yorkshire | 2002 | Kent |
| 1973 | Essex | 1988 | Surrey | | |

# YOUNG CRICKETER OF THE YEAR

This annual award, made by The Cricket Writers' Club (founded 1946), is currently restricted to players qualified for England, Andrew Symonds meeting that requirement at the time of his award, and under the age of 23 on 1st May. In 1986 their ballot resulted in a dead heat. To 9 April 2003 their selections have gained a tally of 1,783 England caps (shown in brackets).

| | | | |
|---|---|---|---|
| 1950 | R.Tattersall (16) | 1977 | I.T.Botham (102) |
| 1951 | P.B.H.May (66) | 1978 | D.I.Gower (117) |
| 1952 | F.S.Trueman (67) | 1979 | P.W.G.Parker (1) |
| 1953 | M.C.Cowdrey (114) | 1980 | G.R.Dilley (41) |
| 1954 | P.J.Loader (13) | 1981 | M.W.Gatting (79) |
| 1955 | K.F.Barrington (82) | 1982 | N.G.Cowans (19) |
| 1956 | B.Taylor | 1983 | N.A.Foster (29) |
| 1957 | M.J.Stewart (8) | 1984 | R.J.Bailey (4) |
| 1958 | A.C.D.Ingleby-Mackenzie | 1985 | D.V.Lawrence (5) |
| 1959 | G.Pullar (28) | 1986 | A.A.Metcalfe |
| 1960 | D.A.Allen (39) | | J.J.Whitaker (1) |
| 1961 | P.H.Parfitt (37) | 1987 | R.J.Blakey |
| 1962 | P.J.Sharpe (12) | 1988 | M.P.Maynard (4) |
| 1963 | G.Boycott (108) | 1989 | N.Hussain (81) |
| 1964 | J.M.Brearley (39) | 1990 | M.A.Atherton (115) |
| 1965 | A.P.E.Knott (95) | 1991 | M.R.Ramprakash (52) |
| 1966 | D.L.Underwood (86) | 1992 | I.D.K.Salisbury (15) |
| 1967 | A.W.Greig (58) | 1993 | M.N.Lathwell (2) |
| 1968 | R.M.H.Cottam (4) | 1994 | J.P.Crawley (37) |
| 1969 | A.Ward (5) | 1995 | A.Symonds |
| 1970 | C.M.Old (46) | 1996 | C.E.W.Silverwood (6) |
| 1971 | J.Whitehouse | 1997 | B.C.Hollioake (2) |
| 1972 | D.R.Owen-Thomas | 1998 | A.Flintoff (21) |
| 1973 | M.Hendrick (30) | 1999 | A.J.Tudor (10) |
| 1974 | P.H.Edmonds (51) | 2000 | P.J.Franks |
| 1975 | A.Kennedy | 2001 | O.A.Shah |
| 1976 | G.Miller (34) | 2002 | R.Clarke |

# THE PROFESSIONAL CRICKETER'S ASSOCIATION
## PLAYER OF THE YEAR

Introduced in 1970, this annual award is voted by members of the PCA. Michael Vaughan was the recipient for 2002.

| | | | |
|---|---|---|---|
| 1970 | M.J.Procter | 1986 | C.A.Walsh |
| | J.D.Bond | 1987 | R:J.Hadlee |
| 1971 | L.R.Gibbs | 1988 | G.A.Hick |
| 1972 | A.M.E.Roberts | 1989 | S.J.Cook |
| 1973 | P.G.Lee | 1990 | G.A.Gooch |
| 1974 | B.Stead | 1991 | Waqar Younis |
| 1975 | Zaheer Abbas | 1992 | C.A.Walsh |
| 1976 | P.G.Lee | 1993 | S.L.Watkin |
| 1977 | M.J.Procter | 1994 | B.C.Lara |
| 1978 | J.K.Lever | 1995 | D.G.Cork |
| 1979 | J.K.Lever | 1996 | P.V.Simmons |
| 1980 | R.D.Jackman | 1997 | S.P.James |
| 1981 | R.J.Hadlee | 1998 | M.B.Loye |
| 1982 | M.D.Marshall | 1999 | S.G.Law |
| 1983 | K.S.McEwan | 2000 | M.E.Trescothick |
| 1984 | R.J.Hadlee | 2001 | D.P.Fulton |
| 1985 | N.V.Radford | 2002 | M.P.Vaughan |

# FIRST-CLASS CAREER RECORDS

Compiled by **PHILIP BAILEY**

The following career records are for all players who appeared in first-class or limited-overs cricket during the 2002 season and are complete to the end of that season. Some players who did not appear in 2002 but may do so in 2003 are also included.

## BATTING AND FIELDING

'1000' denotes instances of scoring 1000 runs in a season. Where these have been achieved outside the British Isles they are shown after a plus sign.

| | M | I | NO | HS | Runs | Avge | 100 | 50 | 1000 | Ct/St |
|---|---|---|---|---|---|---|---|---|---|---|
| Abdul Razzaq | 64 | 95 | 15 | 203* | 2730 | 34.12 | 7 | 13 | – | 16 |
| Adams, C.J. | 241 | 395 | 29 | 239 | 13784 | 37.66 | 33 | 68 | 5 | 281 |
| Adams, J.H.K. | 3 | 5 | 1 | 48 | 88 | 22.00 | – | – | – | 3 |
| Afzaal, U. | 122 | 211 | 19 | 151* | 6215 | 32.36 | 12 | 35 | 3 | 60 |
| Agarkar, A.B. | 41 | 53 | 9 | 109* | 1120 | 25.45 | 2 | 4 | – | 12 |
| Aldred, P. | 60 | 81 | 12 | 83 | 806 | 11.68 | – | 1 | – | 34 |
| Ali, Kabir | 32 | 42 | 8 | 51* | 633 | 18.61 | – | 3 | – | 8 |
| Ali, Kadeer | 9 | 15 | 0 | 38 | 78 | 5.20 | – | – | – | 3 |
| Ali, S.M.B. | 70 | 89 | 22 | 92 | 1036 | 15.46 | – | 4 | – | 24 |
| Allen, A.P.W. | 1 | 1 | 1 | 18* | 18 | – | – | – | – | – |
| Alleyne, D. | 5 | 7 | 1 | 49* | 148 | 24.66 | – | – | – | 12 |
| Alleyne, M.W. | 314 | 516 | 48 | 256 | 14512 | 31.00 | 22 | 69 | 6 | 258/3 |
| Ambrose, T.R. | 15 | 25 | 1 | 149 | 890 | 37.08 | 2 | 3 | – | 12 |
| Amerasinghe, M.K.D.I. | 46 | 43 | 24 | 46 | 141 | 7.42 | – | – | – | 13 |
| Amin, R.M. | 15 | 18 | 8 | 12 | 35 | 3.50 | – | – | – | 6 |
| Anderson, J.M. | 13 | 16 | 8 | 16 | 58 | 7.25 | – | – | – | 2 |
| Anderson, R.S.G. | 37 | 49 | 5 | 67* | 637 | 14.47 | – | 2 | – | 7 |
| Angel, J. | 108 | 139 | 40 | 84* | 1299 | 13.12 | – | 4 | – | 27 |
| Arnold, R.P. | 131 | 195 | 18 | 217* | 7801 | 44.07 | 21 | 35 | 0+1 | 120 |
| Atapattu, M.S. | 179 | 265 | 46 | 253* | 11085 | 50.61 | 36 | 39 | 0+3 | 124 |
| Atri, V. | 1 | 1 | 0 | 98 | 98 | 98.00 | – | 1 | – | 2 |
| Averis, J.M.M. | 39 | 56 | 11 | 43 | 500 | 11.11 | – | – | – | 9 |
| Aymes, A.N. | 215 | 314 | 79 | 133 | 7338 | 31.22 | 8 | 38 | – | 516/44 |
| Azhar Mahmood | 82 | 131 | 17 | 136 | 3101 | 27.20 | 4 | 15 | – | 57 |
| Bailey, T.M.B. | 35 | 47 | 7 | 96* | 851 | 21.27 | – | 5 | – | 65/8 |
| Ball, M.C.J. | 162 | 249 | 46 | 71 | 3949 | 19.45 | – | 13 | – | 195 |
| Banes, M.J. | 10 | 16 | 1 | 69 | 349 | 23.26 | – | 3 | – | 3 |
| Bangar, S.B. | 72 | 116 | 10 | 212 | 4022 | 37.94 | 7 | 21 | – | 69 |
| Barnett, K.J. | 479 | 784 | 76 | 239* | 28593 | 40.38 | 61 | 153 | 16 | 284 |
| Bassano, C.W.G. | 22 | 40 | 3 | 186* | 1586 | 42.86 | 3 | 10 | 1 | 18 |
| Batty, G.J. | 21 | 33 | 5 | 74 | 589 | 21.03 | – | 3 | – | 11 |
| Batty, J.N. | 82 | 113 | 17 | 151 | 2383 | 24.82 | 3 | 9 | – | 202/30 |
| Bell, I.R. | 29 | 47 | 4 | 135 | 1544 | 35.90 | 3 | 7 | – | 19 |
| Benn, S.J. | 17 | 30 | 2 | 78 | 601 | 21.46 | – | 3 | – | 18 |
| Best, T.Le B. | 8 | 9 | 4 | 12* | 41 | 8.20 | – | – | – | 3 |
| Betts, M.M. | 89 | 132 | 31 | 57* | 1308 | 12.95 | – | 3 | – | 32 |
| Bevan, M.G. | 206 | 344 | 61 | 203* | 15985 | 56.48 | 55 | 71 | 3 | 113 |
| Bichel, A.J. | 98 | 128 | 11 | 110 | 2441 | 20.86 | 1 | 10 | – | 52 |
| Bicknell, D.J. | 256 | 449 | 38 | 235* | 15842 | 38.54 | 39 | 67 | 7 | 94 |
| Bicknell, M.P. | 253 | 307 | 76 | 110* | 5350 | 23.16 | 1 | 22 | – | 89 |
| Bishop, J.E. | 16 | 22 | 4 | 23* | 160 | 8.88 | – | – | – | 2 |
| Black, M.I. | 39 | 50 | 18 | 21* | 201 | 6.28 | – | – | – | 6 |
| Blackwell, I.D. | 68 | 102 | 4 | 122 | 2952 | 30.12 | 8 | 12 | – | 27 |

153

| F-C | M | I | NO | HS | Runs | Avge | 100 | 50 | 1000 | Ct/St |
|---|---|---|---|---|---|---|---|---|---|---|
| Blain, J.A.R. | 16 | 20 | 7 | 34 | 144 | 11.07 | – | – | – | 5 |
| Blakey, R.J. | 335 | 535 | 85 | 221 | 14206 | 31.56 | 12 | 86 | 6 | 746/56 |
| Bloomfield, T.F. | 52 | 57 | 24 | 31* | 279 | 8.45 | – | – | – | 6 |
| Boje, N. | 122 | 180 | 31 | 116 | 4764 | 31.97 | 5 | 27 | – | 75 |
| Bond, S.E. | 30 | 36 | 13 | 66* | 342 | 14.86 | – | 1 | – | 13 |
| Bopara, R.S. | 4 | 7 | 1 | 48 | 165 | 27.50 | – | – | – | 6 |
| Bowler, P.D. | 293 | 500 | 52 | 241* | 18056 | 40.30 | 42 | 93 | 9 | 210/1 |
| Brandy, D.G. | 2 | 3 | 0 | 23 | 28 | 9.33 | – | – | – | 1 |
| Brant, S.A. | 3 | 3 | 2 | 19* | 35 | 35.00 | – | – | – | 3 |
| Bravo, D.J.J. | 11 | 20 | 3 | 122 | 730 | 42.94 | 1 | 5 | – | 10 |
| Breese, G.R. | 33 | 51 | 8 | 124 | 1156 | 26.88 | 1 | 7 | – | 24 |
| Bressington, A.N. | 6 | 6 | 3 | 17* | 42 | 14.00 | – | – | – | 3 |
| Bridge, G.D. | 18 | 30 | 4 | 49 | 320 | 12.30 | – | – | – | 10 |
| Brophy, G.L. | 27 | 46 | 6 | 185 | 1276 | 31.90 | 2 | 6 | – | 78/5 |
| Brown, A.D. | 170 | 267 | 26 | 295* | 10567 | 43.84 | 32 | 40 | 6 | 180/1 |
| Brown, D.R. | 146 | 222 | 29 | 203 | 5482 | 28.40 | 3 | 31 | – | 93 |
| Brown, J.F. | 48 | 61 | 27 | 35* | 203 | 5.97 | – | – | – | 11 |
| Brown, M.J. | 11 | 19 | 4 | 60* | 396 | 26.40 | – | 3 | – | 10 |
| Brown, S.J.E. | 159 | 221 | 72 | 69 | 1796 | 12.05 | – | 2 | – | 42 |
| Bruce, J.T.A. | 6 | 6 | 3 | 14* | 27 | 9.00 | – | – | – | 1 |
| Brunnschweiler, I. | 2 | 4 | 1 | 19 | 33 | 11.00 | – | – | – | 9 |
| Bryant, J.D.C. | 44 | 81 | 11 | 149 | 2535 | 36.21 | 5 | 13 | – | 36 |
| Bulbeck, M.P.L. | 47 | 62 | 24 | 76* | 821 | 21.60 | – | 2 | – | 9 |
| Burns, M. | 111 | 177 | 8 | 221 | 5298 | 31.34 | 5 | 37 | 1 | 106/7 |
| Burns, N.D. | 205 | 307 | 65 | 166 | 7376 | 30.47 | 7 | 40 | – | 478/38 |
| Butcher, G.P. | 53 | 78 | 12 | 101* | 1841 | 27.89 | 1 | 12 | – | 19 |
| Butcher, M.A. | 190 | 328 | 25 | 259 | 11772 | 38.85 | 22 | 66 | 6 | 178 |
| Byas, D. | 283 | 474 | 44 | 213 | 15082 | 35.07 | 29 | 83 | 5 | 366 |
| Caddick, A.R. | 196 | 263 | 49 | 92 | 3097 | 14.47 | – | 5 | – | 64 |
| Cairns, C.L. | 190 | 297 | 35 | 126 | 9254 | 35.32 | 11 | 61 | 1 | 70 |
| Carberry, M.A. | 8 | 14 | 1 | 153* | 534 | 41.07 | 1 | 1 | – | 8 |
| Carpenter, J.R. | 13 | 24 | 0 | 65 | 383 | 15.95 | – | 2 | – | 5 |
| Carter, N.M. | 24 | 31 | 8 | 103 | 449 | 19.52 | 1 | 1 | – | 8 |
| Cassar, M.E. | 63 | 98 | 12 | 121 | 2155 | 25.05 | 2 | 12 | – | 20 |
| Catterall, D.N. | 4 | 5 | 0 | 60 | 157 | 31.40 | – | 1 | – | 1 |
| Cawdron, M.J. | 18 | 26 | 4 | 42 | 333 | 15.13 | – | – | – | 3 |
| Chandana, U.D.U. | 107 | 137 | 12 | 194 | 4148 | 33.18 | 8 | 23 | – | 93 |
| Chapman-Smith, M.S. | 1 | 2 | 0 | 7 | 10 | 5.00 | – | – | – | – |
| Chapple, G. | 146 | 199 | 48 | 155 | 3278 | 21.70 | 2 | 12 | – | 46 |
| Cherry, D.D. | 6 | 9 | 0 | 47 | 140 | 15.55 | – | – | – | 4 |
| Chilton, M.J. | 63 | 104 | 6 | 107 | 2725 | 27.80 | 4 | 12 | – | 56 |
| Clapp, D.A. | 1 | 1 | 0 | 6 | 6 | 6.00 | – | – | – | – |
| Clark, P.J. | 1 | 2 | 1 | 2* | 2 | 2.00 | – | – | – | – |
| Clarke, A.J. | 2 | 4 | 1 | 31 | 42 | 14.00 | – | – | – | 1 |
| Clarke, R. | 10 | 16 | 2 | 153* | 711 | 50.78 | 2 | 4 | – | 9 |
| Clifford, J.I. | 4 | 6 | 0 | 7 | 20 | 3.33 | – | – | – | 15/1 |
| Clinton, R.S. | 13 | 23 | 2 | 107 | 525 | 25.00 | 1 | 2 | – | 4 |
| Clough, D.M. | 6 | 9 | 0 | 33 | 61 | 6.77 | – | – | – | 2 |
| Collingwood, P.D. | 91 | 157 | 10 | 190 | 4730 | 32.17 | 8 | 26 | 1 | 92 |
| Cook, J.W. | 35 | 57 | 5 | 137 | 1639 | 31.51 | 2 | 9 | – | 13 |
| Cook, S.J. | 42 | 55 | 8 | 93* | 885 | 18.82 | – | 2 | – | 12 |
| Cork, D.G. | 206 | 305 | 41 | 200* | 6712 | 25.42 | 5 | 39 | – | 145 |
| Cosker, D.A. | 93 | 109 | 29 | 49 | 867 | 10.83 | – | – | – | 63 |
| Cottey, P.A. | 251 | 406 | 51 | 203 | 12908 | 36.36 | 27 | 66 | 7 | 167 |
| Cousins, D.M. | 50 | 74 | 22 | 29* | 559 | 10.75 | – | – | – | 12 |
| Cowan, A.P. | 100 | 149 | 28 | 94 | 2178 | 18.00 | – | 9 | – | 48 |

154

| F-C | M | I | NO | HS | Runs | Avge | 100 | 50 | 1000 | Ct/St |
|---|---|---|---|---|---|---|---|---|---|---|
| Cox, J. | 209 | 369 | 26 | 245 | 15294 | 44.58 | 44 | 66 | 2+2 | 90 |
| Craven, V.J. | 21 | 36 | 4 | 72 | 723 | 22.59 | – | 5 | – | 16 |
| Crawley, J.P. | 252 | 412 | 40 | 286 | 17660 | 47.47 | 42 | 97 | 8 | 170 |
| Creese, M.L. | 2 | 2 | 0 | 8 | 12 | 6.00 | – | – | – | – |
| Croft, R.D.B. | 266 | 386 | 75 | 143 | 7927 | 25.48 | 3 | 37 | – | 134 |
| Crowe, C.D. | 38 | 49 | 10 | 44* | 581 | 14.89 | – | – | – | 18 |
| Cunliffe, R.J. | 67 | 113 | 7 | 190* | 2542 | 23.98 | 3 | 10 | – | 53 |
| Currie, M.R. | 1 | 2 | 1 | 48* | 50 | 50.00 | – | – | – | – |
| Dagnall, C.E. | 10 | 9 | 3 | 16 | 45 | 7.50 | – | – | – | 1 |
| Dakin, J.M. | 63 | 91 | 9 | 190 | 2316 | 28.24 | 5 | 11 | – | 19 |
| Dale, A. | 229 | 373 | 31 | 214* | 11688 | 34.17 | 22 | 56 | 4 | 92 |
| Daley, J.A. | 94 | 164 | 13 | 159* | 4272 | 28.29 | 4 | 20 | – | 44 |
| Dalrymple, J.W.M. | 13 | 24 | 2 | 148 | 738 | 33.54 | 2 | 2 | – | 10 |
| Dalrymple, S.H. | 1 | 2 | 1 | 15* | 27 | 27.00 | – | – | – | 2 |
| Daniels, T.J. | 3 | 5 | 0 | 16 | 18 | 3.60 | – | – | – | 5/3 |
| Das, S.S. | 92 | 158 | 7 | 253 | 6445 | 42.68 | 16 | 32 | – | 103 |
| Davies, A.M. | 14 | 24 | 7 | 33 | 184 | 10.82 | – | – | – | 3 |
| Davies, A.P. | 18 | 22 | 3 | 40 | 222 | 11.68 | – | – | – | 3 |
| Davis, M.J.G. | 100 | 155 | 25 | 111 | 2427 | 18.66 | 1 | 7 | – | 58 |
| Dawes, J.H. | 34 | 43 | 13 | 26 | 252 | 8.40 | – | – | – | 7 |
| Dawson, R.K.J. | 31 | 46 | 5 | 87 | 737 | 17.97 | – | 2 | – | 9 |
| De Silva, K.S.C. | 101 | 123 | 40 | 74 | 941 | 11.33 | – | 1 | – | 53 |
| De Silva, P.A. | 220 | 343 | 33 | 267 | 15000 | 48.38 | 43 | 71 | 1+1 | 108 |
| Dean, K.J. | 73 | 96 | 34 | 54* | 794 | 12.80 | – | 2 | – | 13 |
| DeFreitas, P.A.J. | 339 | 481 | 45 | 123* | 10042 | 23.03 | 9 | 51 | – | 120 |
| Di Venuto, M.J. | 154 | 267 | 15 | 230 | 10566 | 41.92 | 21 | 66 | 3 | 155 |
| Donald, A.A. | 308 | 359 | 136 | 55* | 2688 | 12.05 | – | 1 | – | 112 |
| Dowman, M.P. | 101 | 178 | 11 | 149 | 4648 | 27.83 | 9 | 18 | 1 | 56 |
| Dravid, R. | 172 | 277 | 38 | 217 | 13609 | 56.94 | 37 | 71 | 1+3 | 191/1 |
| Driver, R.C. | 25 | 43 | 6 | 64 | 686 | 18.54 | – | 2 | – | 13 |
| Dumelow, N.R.C. | 11 | 18 | 1 | 61 | 384 | 22.58 | – | 3 | – | 3 |
| Durston, W.J. | 1 | 2 | 0 | 55 | 81 | 40.50 | – | 1 | – | 1 |
| Dutch, K.P. | 59 | 84 | 9 | 118 | 1459 | 19.45 | 1 | 8 | – | 61 |
| Ealham, M.A. | 175 | 279 | 47 | 153* | 7229 | 31.15 | 6 | 45 | 1 | 78 |
| Edwards, N.J. | 1 | 2 | 0 | 31 | 58 | 29.00 | – | – | – | 1 |
| Elliott, M.T.G. | 136 | 252 | 20 | 203 | 11503 | 49.58 | 35 | 55 | 2+4 | 161 |
| Elstub, C.J. | 7 | 9 | 7 | 18* | 34 | 17.00 | – | – | – | 2 |
| Elworthy, S. | 128 | 187 | 26 | 89 | 3257 | 20.22 | – | 9 | – | 42 |
| Evans, P.P. | 1 | 1 | 0 | 16 | 16 | 16.00 | – | – | – | 1 |
| Fairbrother, N.H. | 366 | 580 | 80 | 366 | 20612 | 41.22 | 47 | 104 | 10 | 290 |
| Fellows, G.M. | 42 | 66 | 6 | 109 | 1450 | 24.16 | 1 | 5 | – | 22 |
| Ferley, R.S. | 8 | 10 | 3 | 37* | 137 | 19.57 | – | – | – | 2 |
| Fernando, C.R.D. | 45 | 43 | 9 | 42 | 224 | 6.58 | – | – | – | 19 |
| Fernando, T.C.B. | 32 | 43 | 10 | 81 | 634 | 19.21 | – | 2 | – | 11 |
| Fisher, I.D. | 40 | 58 | 12 | 103* | 1113 | 24.19 | 1 | 6 | – | 9 |
| Fleming, D.W. | 112 | 134 | 38 | 71* | 1437 | 14.96 | – | 4 | – | 54 |
| Fleming, M.V. | 219 | 348 | 43 | 138 | 9206 | 30.18 | 11 | 42 | – | 83 |
| Flintoff, A. | 96 | 150 | 10 | 160 | 4551 | 32.50 | 9 | 22 | – | 113 |
| Flower, A. | 144 | 241 | 50 | 232* | 10385 | 54.37 | 30 | 52 | 1 | 289/21 |
| Flower, G.W. | 132 | 233 | 20 | 243* | 8155 | 38.28 | 16 | 45 | – | 119 |
| Floyd, M.K. | 5 | 10 | 1 | 128* | 183 | 20.33 | 1 | – | – | 1 |
| Foster, J.S. | 36 | 53 | 7 | 103 | 1236 | 26.86 | 1 | 6 | – | 78/11 |
| Francis, J.D. | 12 | 21 | 2 | 82 | 522 | 27.47 | – | 4 | – | 7 |
| Francis, S.R.G. | 26 | 38 | 18 | 30* | 158 | 7.90 | – | – | – | 1 |
| Franks, P.J. | 81 | 119 | 21 | 85 | 2163 | 22.07 | – | 11 | – | 32 |
| Fraser, A.R.C. | 290 | 344 | 82 | 92 | 2934 | 11.19 | – | 2 | – | 54 |

| F-C | M | I | NO | HS | Runs | Avge | 100 | 50 | 1000 | Ct/St |
|---|---|---|---|---|---|---|---|---|---|---|
| Frost, T. | 38 | 56 | 7 | 111* | 1220 | 24.89 | 2 | 4 | – | 83/7 |
| Fulton, D.P. | 142 | 250 | 16 | 208* | 8543 | 36.50 | 20 | 34 | 2 | 218 |
| Gait, A.I. | 36 | 68 | 1 | 175 | 1920 | 28.65 | 3 | 13 | – | 33 |
| Gallian, J.E.R. | 157 | 274 | 26 | 312 | 9211 | 37.14 | 22 | 42 | 3 | 128 |
| Ganga, D. | 63 | 108 | 9 | 151* | 3095 | 31.26 | 7 | 13 | – | 40 |
| Ganguly, S.C. | 160 | 253 | 33 | 200* | 9774 | 44.42 | 17 | 61 | – | 118 |
| Gannon, B.W. | 31 | 36 | 16 | 28 | 187 | 9.35 | – | – | – | 8 |
| Gayle, C.H. | 70 | 125 | 13 | 259* | 4897 | 43.72 | 11 | 24 | 0+1 | 68 |
| Gazzard, C.M. | 1 | 2 | 0 | 24 | 31 | 15.50 | – | – | – | 3/1 |
| Giddins, E.S.H. | 144 | 171 | 73 | 34 | 524 | 5.34 | – | – | – | 22 |
| Gidman, A.P.R. | 10 | 17 | 1 | 117 | 558 | 34.87 | 1 | 4 | – | 5 |
| Giles, A.F. | 124 | 168 | 35 | 128* | 3550 | 26.69 | 3 | 14 | – | 56 |
| Gofton, A.F. | 13 | 19 | 3 | 47* | 281 | 17.56 | – | – | – | – |
| Golding, J.M. | 11 | 16 | 7 | 32 | 224 | 24.88 | – | – | – | 2 |
| Goodwin, M.W. | 96 | 169 | 13 | 203* | 6936 | 44.46 | 21 | 30 | 2 | 66 |
| Gough, D. | 193 | 260 | 50 | 121 | 3379 | 16.09 | 1 | 12 | – | 41 |
| Gough, M.A. | 54 | 94 | 3 | 123 | 2368 | 26.02 | 2 | 11 | – | 49 |
| Grant, J.B. | 26 | 31 | 13 | 36* | 154 | 8.55 | – | – | – | 6 |
| Gray, A.K.D. | 7 | 10 | 1 | 74* | 197 | 21.88 | – | 1 | – | 2 |
| Grayson, A.P. | 165 | 270 | 23 | 189 | 7902 | 31.99 | 15 | 38 | 4 | 116 |
| Greenidge, C.G. | 20 | 24 | 2 | 46 | 189 | 8.59 | – | – | – | 10 |
| Grove, J.O. | 24 | 31 | 9 | 33 | 204 | 9.27 | – | – | – | 2 |
| Gunter, N.E.L. | 2 | 3 | 0 | 18 | 18 | 6.00 | – | – | – | 3 |
| Guy, S.M. | 7 | 11 | 3 | 42 | 148 | 18.50 | – | – | – | 21/2 |
| Habib, A. | 118 | 175 | 26 | 215 | 6650 | 44.63 | 17 | 34 | 2 | 59 |
| Hall, A.J. | 44 | 62 | 11 | 153 | 1831 | 35.90 | 2 | 14 | – | 25 |
| Hamblin, J.R.C. | 6 | 10 | 0 | 50 | 167 | 16.70 | – | 1 | – | 4 |
| Hamilton, G.M. | 80 | 107 | 20 | 125 | 2253 | 25.89 | 1 | 14 | – | 27 |
| Hancock, T.H.C. | 159 | 279 | 19 | 220* | 7143 | 27.47 | 7 | 42 | 1 | 96 |
| Harbhajan Singh | 75 | 100 | 24 | 84 | 1469 | 19.32 | – | 5 | – | 29 |
| Hardinges, M.A. | 8 | 8 | 0 | 172 | 232 | 29.00 | 1 | – | – | 2 |
| Harmison, S.J. | 69 | 99 | 25 | 36 | 628 | 8.48 | – | – | – | 13 |
| Harris, A.J. | 80 | 114 | 31 | 41* | 775 | 9.33 | – | – | – | 26 |
| Harrison, D.S. | 4 | 5 | 0 | 27 | 56 | 11.20 | – | – | – | – |
| Harrity, M.A. | 70 | 85 | 43 | 19 | 220 | 5.23 | – | – | – | 25 |
| Harvey, I.J. | 105 | 175 | 14 | 136 | 5193 | 32.25 | 8 | 30 | – | 76 |
| Hatch, N.G. | 13 | 20 | 10 | 24 | 141 | 14.10 | – | – | – | 3 |
| Hawinkels, S.J. | 3 | 6 | 0 | 78 | 194 | 32.33 | – | 1 | – | 1 |
| Haynes, J.J. | 14 | 21 | 4 | 80 | 418 | 24.58 | – | 3 | – | 32/2 |
| Hayward, M. | 60 | 60 | 24 | 55* | 538 | 14.94 | – | 1 | – | 20 |
| Hazelton, M.A. | 1 | 2 | 0 | 11 | 16 | 8.00 | – | – | – | 2 |
| Heath, D.R. | 4 | 7 | 1 | 75 | 88 | 14.66 | – | 1 | – | 2 |
| Heath, J.A. | 2 | 2 | 0 | 35 | 36 | 18.00 | – | – | – | – |
| Hegg, W.K. | 305 | 446 | 83 | 134 | 9984 | 27.50 | 7 | 50 | – | 747/81 |
| Hemp, D.L. | 173 | 288 | 26 | 186* | 8970 | 34.23 | 18 | 46 | 3 | 113 |
| Hewitt, J.P. | 61 | 82 | 13 | 75 | 1264 | 18.31 | – | 3 | – | 23 |
| Hewson, D.R. | 62 | 114 | 8 | 168 | 2565 | 24.19 | 3 | 14 | – | 30 |
| Hibbert, K.H. | 23 | 35 | 4 | 83* | 694 | 22.38 | – | 3 | – | 50/4 |
| Hick, G.A. | 440 | 725 | 69 | 405* | 35246 | 53.72 | 121 | 133 | 17+1 | 552 |
| Hicks, T.C. | 19 | 26 | 3 | 58 | 359 | 15.60 | – | 2 | – | 18 |
| Hilsum, I.J. | 2 | 4 | 0 | 23 | 56 | 14.00 | – | – | – | 1 |
| Hinds, R.O. | 36 | 59 | 8 | 166 | 1596 | 31.29 | 1 | 11 | – | 21 |
| Hockley, J.B. | 19 | 30 | 2 | 74 | 423 | 15.10 | – | 1 | – | 9 |
| Hodge, B.J. | 90 | 167 | 17 | 140 | 5930 | 39.53 | 16 | 28 | 0+1 | 49 |
| Hogg, K.W. | 8 | 10 | 0 | 50 | 128 | 12.80 | – | 1 | – | 5 |
| Hoggard, M.J. | 70 | 85 | 29 | 32 | 384 | 6.85 | – | – | – | 14 |

156

| F-C | M | I | NO | HS | Runs | Avge | 100 | 50 | 1000 | Ct/St |
|---|---|---|---|---|---|---|---|---|---|---|
| Hollingsworth, A.P. | 3 | 4 | 1 | 42* | 72 | 24.00 | – | – | – | 1 |
| Hollioake, A.J. | 148 | 225 | 19 | 208 | 8276 | 40.17 | 15 | 50 | 2 | 140 |
| Holloway, P.C.L. | 126 | 213 | 28 | 168 | 5786 | 31.27 | 9 | 31 | – | 86/1 |
| Hopkinson, C.D. | 1 | 2 | 0 | 33 | 42 | 21.00 | – | – | – | 2 |
| House, W.J. | 37 | 57 | 8 | 136 | 1443 | 29.44 | 2 | 8 | – | 21 |
| Howard, W.O.F. | 1 | 2 | 0 | 1 | 1 | 0.50 | – | – | – | 1 |
| Hughes, J. | 8 | 12 | 1 | 74 | 312 | 28.36 | – | 1 | – | 2 |
| Hughes, T.R. | 11 | 12 | 4 | 13* | 38 | 4.75 | – | – | – | 1 |
| Hunt, T.A. | 2 | 1 | 0 | 3 | 3 | 3.00 | – | – | – | – |
| Hunter, I.D. | 19 | 30 | 4 | 65 | 486 | 18.69 | – | 2 | – | 6 |
| Hussain, N. | 303 | 491 | 48 | 207 | 18555 | 41.88 | 47 | 94 | 5 | 331 |
| Hussey, M.E.K. | 112 | 203 | 15 | 329* | 9500 | 50.53 | 24 | 40 | 2 | 107 |
| Hutchison, P.M. | 47 | 50 | 27 | 30 | 229 | 9.95 | – | – | – | 9 |
| Hutton, B.L. | 44 | 72 | 5 | 139 | 1833 | 27.35 | 4 | 9 | – | 52 |
| Hyam, B.J. | 61 | 97 | 12 | 63 | 1409 | 16.57 | – | 3 | – | 168/13 |
| Ilott, M.C. | 192 | 245 | 52 | 60 | 2830 | 14.66 | – | 4 | – | 54 |
| Innes, K.J. | 34 | 54 | 13 | 63 | 1000 | 24.39 | – | 3 | – | 13 |
| Inness, M.W.H. | 45 | 47 | 17 | 27 | 143 | 4.76 | – | – | – | 17 |
| Irani, R.C. | 173 | 285 | 35 | 207* | 9438 | 37.75 | 18 | 50 | 5 | 64 |
| Jaffer, W. | 68 | 110 | 12 | 314* | 4756 | 48.53 | 10 | 29 | 0+1 | 73 |
| James, S.P. | 244 | 422 | 33 | 309* | 15875 | 40.80 | 47 | 58 | 9 | 172 |
| Jarvis, P.W. | 215 | 268 | 67 | 80 | 3373 | 16.78 | – | 10 | – | 67 |
| Jayasuriya, S.T. | 189 | 290 | 28 | 340 | 10558 | 40.29 | 22 | 51 | – | 122 |
| Jayawardena, D.P.M.D. | 97 | 151 | 14 | 274 | 7178 | 52.39 | 21 | 33 | 0+1 | 112 |
| Jayawardena, H.A.P.W. | 58 | 84 | 9 | 101 | 1609 | 21.45 | 1 | 7 | – | 140/31 |
| Jefferson, W.I. | 20 | 37 | 4 | 165* | 1021 | 30.93 | 2 | 3 | – | 20 |
| Johnson, N.C. | 147 | 229 | 27 | 150 | 6928 | 34.29 | 9 | 50 | 1 | 196 |
| Johnson, P. | 371 | 624 | 60 | 187 | 20534 | 36.40 | 40 | 119 | 9 | 236/1 |
| Johnson, R.L. | 115 | 164 | 22 | 69 | 2422 | 17.05 | – | 6 | – | 47 |
| Jones, G.O. | 5 | 5 | 1 | 76* | 167 | 41.75 | – | 1 | – | 6 |
| Jones, H.R. | 5 | 10 | 1 | 97 | 220 | 24.44 | – | 2 | – | 5 |
| Jones, I. | 4 | 5 | 1 | 35 | 107 | 26.75 | – | – | – | – |
| Jones, P.S. | 61 | 72 | 21 | 105 | 832 | 16.31 | 1 | 1 | – | 14 |
| Jones, S.P. | 39 | 48 | 13 | 46 | 393 | 11.22 | – | – | – | 8 |
| Jordison, J.R. | 1 | 2 | 0 | 17 | 28 | 14.00 | – | – | – | – |
| Joyce, E.C. | 30 | 46 | 5 | 129 | 1787 | 43.58 | 6 | 7 | 1 | 31 |
| Kaif, M. | 44 | 69 | 9 | 136 | 2559 | 42.65 | 5 | 16 | – | 25 |
| Kasprowicz, M.S. | 166 | 218 | 48 | 92 | 3052 | 17.95 | – | 9 | – | 63 |
| Katich, S.M. | 74 | 131 | 21 | 228* | 5383 | 48.93 | 16 | 24 | 1+2 | 76 |
| Keedy, G. | 94 | 111 | 57 | 57 | 663 | 12.27 | – | 1 | – | 25 |
| Keegan, C.B. | 16 | 20 | 2 | 30* | 103 | 5.72 | – | – | – | 4 |
| Kendall, W.S. | 123 | 203 | 24 | 201 | 6193 | 34.59 | 9 | 31 | 3 | 105 |
| Kenway, D.A. | 62 | 110 | 13 | 166 | 3050 | 31.44 | 4 | 16 | 1 | 59/1 |
| Kerr, J.I.D. | 65 | 95 | 18 | 80 | 1693 | 21.98 | – | 8 | – | 18 |
| Key, R.W.T. | 87 | 149 | 4 | 160 | 4620 | 31.86 | 10 | 24 | 2 | 56 |
| Khan, A. | 17 | 19 | 5 | 58 | 213 | 15.21 | – | 1 | – | 5 |
| Khan, R.M. | 2 | 3 | 0 | 91 | 109 | 36.33 | – | 1 | – | – |
| Khan, Z. | 43 | 55 | 10 | 48 | 638 | 14.17 | – | – | – | 18 |
| Killeen, N. | 60 | 86 | 17 | 48 | 807 | 11.69 | – | – | – | 17 |
| King, R.D. | 67 | 83 | 29 | 30 | 326 | 6.03 | – | – | – | 7 |
| Kirby, S.P. | 20 | 27 | 5 | 57 | 190 | 8.63 | – | 1 | – | 4 |
| Kirby, W.A. | 2 | 4 | 1 | 37 | 78 | 26.00 | – | – | – | 2 |
| Kirtley, R.J. | 104 | 146 | 41 | 59 | 1115 | 10.61 | – | 2 | – | 33 |
| Klusener, L. | 109 | 150 | 31 | 174 | 4047 | 34.00 | 6 | 20 | – | 64 |
| Knight, N.V. | 176 | 293 | 30 | 255* | 11544 | 43.89 | 29 | 53 | 3 | 241 |
| Koenig, S.G. | 93 | 160 | 7 | 155 | 5893 | 38.51 | 11 | 32 | 1 | 51 |

157

| F-C | M | I | NO | HS | Runs | Avge | 100 | 50 | 1000 | Ct/St |
|---|---|---|---|---|---|---|---|---|---|---|
| Krikken, K.M. | 213 | 321 | 60 | 104 | 5710 | 21.87 | 1 | 25 | – | 525/31 |
| Kumar, V.H. | 8 | 14 | 1 | 86* | 313 | 24.07 | – | 2 | – | 5/1 |
| Kumble, A. | 172 | 223 | 43 | 154* | 4292 | 23.84 | 6 | 15 | – | 81 |
| Lampitt, S.R. | 236 | 311 | 74 | 122 | 5649 | 23.83 | 1 | 20 | – | 148 |
| Laney, J.S. | 87 | 153 | 5 | 112 | 4414 | 29.82 | 5 | 26 | 1 | 72 |
| Laraman, A.W. | 14 | 14 | 3 | 82* | 359 | 32.63 | – | 1 | – | 5 |
| Law, D.R. | 102 | 160 | 7 | 115 | 3171 | 20.72 | 2 | 14 | – | 54 |
| Law, S.G. | 259 | 432 | 47 | 263 | 19122 | 49.66 | 56 | 92 | 6+1 | 292 |
| Lawson, J.J.C. | 17 | 22 | 5 | 25 | 168 | 9.88 | – | – | – | 7 |
| Laxman, V.V.S. | 120 | 195 | 21 | 353 | 10112 | 58.11 | 32 | 38 | 0+4 | 128/1 |
| Leatherdale, D.A. | 210 | 339 | 41 | 157 | 9839 | 33.01 | 14 | 52 | 1 | 149 |
| Lee, S. | 93 | 151 | 22 | 183* | 5071 | 39.31 | 12 | 24 | – | 74 |
| Lehmann, D.S. | 209 | 356 | 23 | 255 | 18909 | 56.78 | 61 | 86 | 4+5 | 112 |
| Lewis, J. | 102 | 152 | 31 | 62 | 1479 | 12.22 | – | 3 | – | 25 |
| Lewis, J.J.B. | 151 | 267 | 22 | 210* | 8026 | 32.75 | 14 | 46 | 3 | 92 |
| Lewry, J.D. | 101 | 141 | 32 | 47 | 1056 | 9.68 | – | – | – | 22 |
| Liptrot, C.G. | 29 | 36 | 11 | 61 | 303 | 12.12 | – | 1 | – | 9 |
| Lloyd, G.D. | 203 | 323 | 28 | 241 | 11279 | 38.23 | 24 | 64 | 5 | 140 |
| Logan, R.J. | 31 | 44 | 7 | 37* | 357 | 9.64 | – | – | – | 11 |
| Loudon, A.G.R. | 5 | 7 | 0 | 39 | 96 | 13.71 | – | – | – | 6 |
| Love, M.L. | 123 | 212 | 17 | 251 | 9412 | 48.26 | 22 | 46 | 1+2 | 143 |
| Loye, M.B. | 151 | 243 | 22 | 322* | 8349 | 37.77 | 21 | 35 | 3 | 75 |
| Lucas, D.S. | 22 | 28 | 8 | 49 | 436 | 21.80 | – | – | – | 3 |
| Lumb, M.J. | 21 | 39 | 3 | 124 | 1063 | 29.52 | 2 | 6 | – | 8 |
| Lungley, T. | 14 | 24 | 4 | 47 | 276 | 13.80 | – | – | – | 4 |
| McCoubrey, A.G.A.M. | 2 | 2 | 1 | 1* | 1 | 1.00 | – | – | – | |
| McGarry, A.C. | 13 | 16 | 11 | 11* | 22 | 4.40 | – | – | – | 3 |
| MacGill, S.C.G. | 75 | 102 | 21 | 53 | 777 | 9.59 | – | 1 | – | 45 |
| McGrath, A. | 116 | 199 | 13 | 165 | 5520 | 29.67 | 9 | 24 | – | 70 |
| McGrath, D.E.T. | 1 | 1 | 0 | 0 | 0 | 0.00 | – | – | – | |
| McLean, N.A.M. | 100 | 158 | 22 | 70 | 1811 | 13.31 | – | 2 | – | 27 |
| McMahon, P.J. | 2 | 3 | 0 | 15 | 15 | 5.00 | – | – | – | |
| Maddy, D.L. | 154 | 247 | 15 | 202 | 7465 | 32.17 | 16 | 35 | 3 | 156 |
| Mahmood, S.I. | 1 | 1 | 0 | 18 | 18 | 18.00 | – | – | – | |
| Maiden, A.J. | 1 | 1 | 0 | 0 | 0 | 0.00 | – | – | – | |
| Malcolm, D.E. | 300 | 362 | 113 | 51 | 1958 | 7.86 | – | 2 | – | 45 |
| Malik, M.N. | 12 | 13 | 6 | 18 | 44 | 6.28 | – | – | – | 1 |
| Marshall, S.J. | 4 | 7 | 0 | 99 | 182 | 26.00 | – | 1 | – | 1 |
| Martin, P.J. | 192 | 227 | 59 | 133 | 3415 | 20.32 | 2 | 7 | – | 47 |
| Martin-Jenkins, R.S.C. | 69 | 112 | 14 | 205* | 2944 | 30.04 | 2 | 15 | 1 | 16 |
| Mascarenhas, A.D. | 86 | 128 | 13 | 104 | 2678 | 23.28 | 2 | 13 | – | 34 |
| Mason, M.S. | 10 | 13 | 3 | 50 | 117 | 11.70 | – | 1 | – | 2 |
| Masters, D.D. | 28 | 30 | 9 | 68 | 196 | 9.33 | – | 1 | – | 9 |
| Maunders, J.K. | 1 | 2 | 0 | 9 | 13 | 6.50 | – | – | – | 1 |
| Maynard, M.P. | 363 | 589 | 57 | 243 | 22576 | 42.43 | 51 | 123 | 12 | 346/7 |
| Mees, T. | 4 | 6 | 0 | 13 | 28 | 4.66 | – | – | – | 1 |
| Middlebrook, J.D. | 41 | 59 | 7 | 84 | 902 | 17.34 | – | 2 | – | 21 |
| Millar, N. | 8 | 12 | 1 | 67 | 290 | 26.36 | – | 2 | – | 3 |
| Moffat, J.S.D. | 1 | 1 | 0 | 169 | 169 | 169.00 | 1 | – | – | |
| Mongia, D. | 61 | 89 | 9 | 308* | 4182 | 52.27 | 13 | 15 | 0+1 | 75 |
| Montgomerie, R.R. | 164 | 288 | 27 | 196 | 9534 | 36.52 | 23 | 46 | 4 | 153 |
| Morris, A.C. | 60 | 78 | 12 | 65 | 1325 | 20.07 | – | 7 | – | 32 |
| Morton, R.S. | 34 | 56 | 4 | 110 | 1736 | 33.38 | 3 | 13 | – | 41 |
| Moyes, J.R. | 3 | 5 | 0 | 35 | 51 | 10.20 | – | – | – | 6 |
| Muchall, G.J. | 15 | 25 | 0 | 127 | 613 | 24.52 | 1 | 3 | – | 14 |
| Mullally, A.D. | 212 | 238 | 62 | 75 | 1510 | 8.57 | – | 2 | – | 41 |

| F-C | M | I | NO | HS | Runs | Avge | 100 | 50 | 1000 | Ct/St |
|-----|---|---|----|----|------|------|-----|----|----|-------|
| Muralitharan, M. | 148 | 177 | 55 | 67 | 1364 | 11.18 | – | 1 | – | 79 |
| Murtagh, T.J. | 8 | 11 | 5 | 22* | 86 | 14.33 | – | – | – | 3 |
| Mushtaq Ahmed | 206 | 261 | 32 | 90 | 3267 | 14.26 | – | 11 | – | 94 |
| Mustard, P. | 1 | 1 | 0 | 75 | 75 | 75.00 | – | 1 | – | 2 |
| Napier, G.R. | 25 | 37 | 4 | 104 | 843 | 25.54 | 1 | 3 | – | 16 |
| Nash, C.D. | 1 | 2 | 1 | 0* | 0 | 0.00 | – | – | – | 1 |
| Nash, D.C. | 86 | 119 | 22 | 114 | 3002 | 30.94 | 4 | 15 | – | 171/14 |
| Nehra, A. | 49 | 56 | 17 | 25 | 266 | 6.82 | – | – | – | 14 |
| Nel, A. | 35 | 39 | 16 | 44 | 262 | 11.39 | – | – | – | 11 |
| Newell, K. | 72 | 123 | 14 | 135 | 2930 | 26.88 | 5 | 11 | – | 25 |
| Newman, S.A. | 3 | 5 | 0 | 183 | 322 | 64.40 | 1 | 1 | – | 3 |
| Nixon, P.A. | 236 | 339 | 77 | 134* | 8482 | 32.37 | 13 | 36 | 1 | 619/50 |
| Noble, D.J. | 4 | 6 | 2 | 21 | 61 | 15.25 | – | – | – | – |
| Noffke, A.A. | 28 | 31 | 6 | 76 | 610 | 24.40 | – | 2 | – | 10 |
| Noon, W.M. | 90 | 141 | 22 | 83 | 2489 | 20.91 | – | 12 | – | 188/20 |
| Ormond, J. | 80 | 94 | 22 | 50* | 997 | 13.84 | – | 1 | – | 18 |
| Ostler, D.P. | 200 | 328 | 25 | 225 | 10737 | 35.43 | 16 | 66 | 6 | 256 |
| Pagon, D.J. | 6 | 9 | 0 | 110 | 193 | 21.44 | 1 | – | – | – |
| Panesar, M.S. | 8 | 9 | 4 | 10 | 19 | 3.80 | – | – | – | 3 |
| Parker, J.W.R. | 5 | 9 | 0 | 86 | 411 | 45.66 | – | 3 | – | 1 |
| Parkin, O.T. | 40 | 47 | 20 | 24* | 226 | 8.37 | – | – | – | 11 |
| Parsons, K.A. | 107 | 174 | 17 | 193* | 4285 | 27.29 | 5 | 23 | – | 98 |
| Patel, M.M. | 160 | 214 | 44 | 82 | 2925 | 17.20 | – | 11 | – | 88 |
| Patel, P.A. | 12 | 16 | 3 | 74 | 346 | 26.61 | – | 3 | – | 21/3 |
| Patel, S.R. | 1 | 1 | 0 | 35 | 35 | 35.00 | – | – | – | – |
| Pattison, I. | 3 | 6 | 0 | 27 | 61 | 10.16 | – | – | – | 2 |
| Paynter, D.E. | 2 | 4 | 1 | 20 | 32 | 10.66 | – | – | – | 2 |
| Pearson, J.A. | 3 | 6 | 1 | 57 | 114 | 22.80 | – | 1 | – | 2 |
| Penberthy, A.L. | 179 | 267 | 29 | 132* | 7119 | 29.91 | 10 | 40 | – | 108 |
| Peng, N. | 33 | 58 | 2 | 108 | 1290 | 23.03 | 2 | 6 | – | 17 |
| Penney, T.L. | 157 | 246 | 45 | 151 | 7954 | 39.57 | 15 | 36 | 2 | 93/2 |
| Perera, P.D.R.L. | 52 | 52 | 26 | 33* | 224 | 8.61 | – | – | – | 25 |
| Peters, S.D. | 72 | 118 | 15 | 146 | 2912 | 28.27 | 4 | 13 | – | 52 |
| Pettini, M.L. | 4 | 8 | 0 | 64 | 199 | 24.87 | – | 2 | – | 3 |
| Phillips, B.J. | 28 | 40 | 4 | 100* | 601 | 16.69 | 1 | 2 | – | 8 |
| Phillips, N.C. | 64 | 96 | 22 | 58* | 1171 | 15.82 | – | 4 | – | 35 |
| Phillips, T.J. | 17 | 25 | 3 | 75 | 388 | 17.63 | – | 1 | – | 7 |
| Pietersen, K.P. | 37 | 56 | 9 | 254* | 2399 | 51.04 | 8 | 8 | 1 | 36 |
| Pipe, D.J. | 11 | 16 | 0 | 54 | 251 | 15.68 | – | 1 | – | 18/3 |
| Piper, K.J. | 195 | 268 | 44 | 116* | 4481 | 20.00 | 2 | 14 | – | 490/33 |
| Pollock, S.M. | 133 | 194 | 36 | 150* | 5242 | 33.17 | 6 | 27 | – | 94 |
| Porter, J.J. | 12 | 21 | 1 | 93 | 522 | 26.10 | – | 4 | – | 7 |
| Pothas, N. | 102 | 159 | 26 | 165 | 4486 | 33.72 | 7 | 22 | – | 267/26 |
| Powell, D.B. | 16 | 18 | 3 | 38 | 120 | 8.00 | – | – | – | 8 |
| Powell, M.J. (Gm) | 86 | 140 | 15 | 200* | 4862 | 38.89 | 11 | 25 | 2 | 46 |
| Powell, M.J. (Nh) | 4 | 7 | 1 | 108* | 291 | 48.50 | 2 | – | – | 6 |
| Powell, M.J. (Wa) | 90 | 147 | 5 | 236 | 4492 | 31.63 | 8 | 25 | 1 | 72 |
| Pratt, A. | 43 | 71 | 8 | 93 | 1263 | 20.04 | – | 6 | – | 102/10 |
| Pratt, G.J. | 20 | 34 | 0 | 78 | 838 | 24.64 | – | 4 | – | 14 |
| Pretorius, D. | 34 | 40 | 9 | 43 | 275 | 8.87 | – | – | – | 8 |
| Prior, M.J. | 32 | 51 | 5 | 102* | 1174 | 25.52 | 1 | 6 | – | 78/4 |
| Prittipaul, L.R. | 14 | 21 | 0 | 152 | 508 | 24.19 | 1 | 2 | – | 8 |
| Pyemont, J.P. | 38 | 58 | 4 | 124 | 1126 | 20.85 | 1 | 5 | – | 22 |
| Ramprakash, M.R. | 325 | 537 | 66 | 235 | 21779 | 46.23 | 60 | 108 | 12 | 187 |
| Randall, S.J. | 10 | 15 | 2 | 28 | 116 | 8.92 | – | – | – | 5 |
| Ratcliffe, J.D. | 136 | 244 | 14 | 135 | 6561 | 28.52 | 5 | 38 | – | 68 |

| F-C | M | I | NO | HS | Runs | Avge | 100 | 50 | 1000 | Ct/St |
|---|---|---|---|---|---|---|---|---|---|---|
| Ratra, A. | 36 | 59 | 10 | 115* | 1211 | 24.71 | 2 | 7 | – | 72/14 |
| Rawnsley, M.J. | 46 | 56 | 9 | 39 | 522 | 11.10 | – | – | – | 23 |
| Read, C.M.W. | 99 | 150 | 24 | 160 | 3330 | 26.42 | 2 | 15 | – | 284/9 |
| Redmayne, J.R.S. | 6 | 10 | 2 | 75* | 245 | 30.62 | – | 2 | – | – |
| Rees, T.M. | 1 | 1 | 0 | 16 | 16 | 16.00 | – | – | – | 1 |
| Rhodes, J.N. | 148 | 234 | 26 | 172 | 8167 | 39.26 | 17 | 45 | – | 120 |
| Rhodes, S.J. | 412 | 583 | 155 | 124 | 14097 | 32.93 | 12 | 68 | 2 | 1057/118 |
| Richardson, A. | 43 | 39 | 18 | 91 | 208 | 9.90 | – | 1 | – | 15 |
| Richardson, S.A. | 10 | 17 | 2 | 69 | 274 | 18.26 | – | 2 | – | 8 |
| Roberts, T.W. | 5 | 7 | 0 | 49 | 110 | 15.71 | – | – | – | 2 |
| Robinson, D.D.J. | 125 | 220 | 11 | 200 | 6557 | 31.37 | 15 | 29 | 1 | 104 |
| Robinson, M.A. | 229 | 259 | 112 | 27 | 590 | 4.01 | – | – | – | 41 |
| Rollins, A.S. | 129 | 233 | 20 | 210 | 7331 | 34.41 | 13 | 40 | 3 | 109/1 |
| Rose, G.D. | 251 | 347 | 63 | 191 | 8737 | 30.76 | 11 | 41 | 1 | 117 |
| Russell, R.C. | 452 | 672 | 140 | 129* | 16395 | 30.81 | 11 | 86 | 1 | 1158/124 |
| Saggers, M.J. | 59 | 74 | 21 | 61* | 477 | 9.00 | – | 1 | – | 13 |
| Sales, D.J.G. | 90 | 141 | 10 | 303* | 4375 | 33.39 | 9 | 19 | 1 | 66 |
| Salisbury, I.D.K. | 261 | 336 | 68 | 100* | 5201 | 19.40 | 1 | 18 | – | 171 |
| Samaraweera, T.T. | 87 | 106 | 31 | 123* | 3361 | 44.81 | 6 | 22 | – | 68 |
| Sampson, P.J. | 2 | 3 | 1 | 42 | 43 | 21.50 | – | – | – | – |
| Sangakkara, K.C. | 72 | 110 | 8 | 230 | 3437 | 33.69 | 5 | 18 | – | 156/13 |
| Saqlain Mushtaq | 137 | 191 | 50 | 101* | 2302 | 16.32 | 1 | 8 | – | 53 |
| Savill, T.E. | 4 | 6 | 2 | 18* | 58 | 14.50 | – | – | – | 2 |
| Sayers, J.J. | 4 | 8 | 0 | 55 | 152 | 19.00 | – | 1 | – | 1 |
| Schofield, C.P. | 56 | 77 | 12 | 91 | 1834 | 28.21 | – | 15 | – | 31 |
| Schofield, J.E.K. | 4 | 7 | 3 | 21* | 43 | 10.75 | – | – | – | 1 |
| Sehwag, V. | 47 | 69 | 3 | 274 | 3693 | 55.95 | 13 | 16 | 0+1 | 51 |
| Selwood, S.A. | 12 | 23 | 0 | 99 | 500 | 21.73 | – | 2 | – | 2 |
| Shafayat, B.M. | 10 | 19 | 1 | 104 | 681 | 37.83 | 1 | 4 | – | 5 |
| Shah, O.A. | 95 | 156 | 11 | 203 | 5075 | 35.00 | 12 | 24 | 2 | 61 |
| Shahid Afridi | 65 | 109 | 3 | 164 | 3279 | 30.93 | 7 | 16 | – | 46 |
| Shahid, N. | 141 | 223 | 26 | 150 | 6268 | 31.81 | 9 | 33 | 1 | 149 |
| Shankar, A. | 4 | 7 | 0 | 143 | 167 | 23.85 | 1 | – | – | 4 |
| Sharif, F.I. | 2 | 3 | 0 | 36 | 46 | 15.33 | – | – | – | 2 |
| Sharif, Z.K. | 3 | 3 | 0 | 42 | 59 | 19.66 | – | – | – | 1 |
| Sharpe, T.J. | 5 | 8 | 4 | 7* | 12 | 3.00 | – | – | – | 2 |
| Shaw, A.D. | 76 | 102 | 16 | 140 | 1873 | 21.77 | 1 | 9 | – | 180/14 |
| Sheikh, M.A. | 14 | 19 | 4 | 58* | 401 | 26.73 | – | 1 | – | 1 |
| Sheriyar, A. | 127 | 134 | 50 | 21 | 683 | 8.13 | – | – | – | 19 |
| Shoaib Akhtar | 83 | 108 | 40 | 59* | 739 | 10.86 | – | 1 | – | 29 |
| Sidebottom, R.J. | 51 | 68 | 22 | 54 | 502 | 10.91 | – | 1 | – | 19 |
| Sillence, R.J. | 6 | 9 | 0 | 101 | 173 | 19.22 | 1 | – | – | 4 |
| Silverwood, C.E.W. | 122 | 161 | 32 | 70 | 2013 | 15.60 | – | 5 | – | 26 |
| Simcox, A.D. | 7 | 12 | 2 | 30 | 128 | 12.80 | – | – | – | 5 |
| Simmons, L.M.P. | 8 | 14 | 3 | 81 | 338 | 30.72 | – | 1 | – | 9/2 |
| Singh, A. | 79 | 130 | 5 | 187 | 4050 | 32.40 | 8 | 17 | 2 | 31 |
| Smethurst, M.P. | 30 | 35 | 13 | 66 | 227 | 10.31 | – | 1 | – | 5 |
| Smith, A.M. | 143 | 190 | 54 | 61 | 1686 | 12.39 | – | 4 | – | 29 |
| Smith, B.F. | 214 | 330 | 40 | 204 | 11449 | 39.47 | 28 | 50 | 4 | 109 |
| Smith, D.S. | 32 | 58 | 2 | 181 | 1974 | 35.25 | 2 | 12 | – | 27 |
| Smith, E.T. | 96 | 163 | 9 | 190 | 5800 | 37.66 | 11 | 29 | 3 | 27 |
| Smith, G.J. | 100 | 124 | 47 | 68 | 1088 | 14.12 | – | 2 | – | 19 |
| Smith, N.M.K. | 199 | 281 | 34 | 161 | 6645 | 26.90 | 4 | 34 | 1 | 71 |
| Smith, R.A. | 416 | 702 | 86 | 209* | 25633 | 41.61 | 61 | 126 | 11 | 224 |
| Smith, W.R. | 1 | 1 | 1 | 38* | 38 | – | – | – | – | – |
| Snape, J.N. | 90 | 134 | 23 | 131 | 3240 | 29.18 | 3 | 19 | – | 62 |

160

| F-C | M | I | NO | HS | Runs | Avge | 100 | 50 | 1000 | Ct/St |
|---|---|---|---|---|---|---|---|---|---|---|
| Solanki, V.S. | 142 | 235 | 18 | 185 | 7826 | 36.06 | 14 | 42 | 2 | 176 |
| Souter, M.A. | 1 | 1 | 0 | 1 | 1 | 1.00 | – | – | – | 1 |
| Spearman, C.M. | 102 | 185 | 12 | 180* | 6333 | 36.60 | 14 | 31 | 1 | 99 |
| Spires, J.A.S. | 7 | 7 | 3 | 37* | 70 | 17.50 | – | – | – | 3 |
| Srinath, J. | 141 | 182 | 31 | 76 | 2115 | 14.00 | – | 7 | – | 61 |
| Stemp, R.D. | 166 | 198 | 64 | 66 | 1657 | 12.36 | – | 3 | – | 68 |
| Stephenson, J.P. | 294 | 498 | 53 | 202* | 14409 | 32.37 | 25 | 74 | 5 | 181 |
| Stevens, D.I. | 54 | 89 | 5 | 130 | 2166 | 25.78 | 2 | 12 | – | 37 |
| Stewart, A.J. | 428 | 705 | 77 | 271* | 25085 | 39.94 | 48 | 138 | 8 | 669/31 |
| Strauss, A.J. | 63 | 106 | 6 | 176 | 3909 | 39.09 | 7 | 19 | 2 | 35 |
| Stubbings, S.D. | 52 | 95 | 5 | 135* | 2604 | 28.93 | 5 | 11 | 1 | 18 |
| Suppiah, A.V. | 2 | 4 | 0 | 21 | 27 | 6.75 | – | – | – | 1 |
| Sutcliffe, I.J. | 121 | 192 | 16 | 203 | 5735 | 32.58 | 9 | 29 | 2 | 58 |
| Sutton, L.D. | 38 | 68 | 8 | 140* | 1536 | 25.60 | 2 | 6 | – | 69/2 |
| Swann, A.J. | 62 | 101 | 4 | 154 | 2838 | 29.25 | 7 | 13 | 1 | 40 |
| Swann, G.P. | 85 | 126 | 7 | 183 | 3238 | 27.21 | 4 | 13 | – | 53 |
| Symington, M.J. | 13 | 19 | 4 | 42 | 276 | 18.40 | – | – | – | 7 |
| Symonds, A. | 145 | 245 | 21 | 254* | 9141 | 40.80 | 26 | 37 | 2 | 103 |
| Taylor, B.V. | 20 | 25 | 7 | 24* | 128 | 7.11 | – | – | – | 2 |
| Taylor, C.G. | 39 | 71 | 5 | 196 | 2086 | 31.60 | 5 | 6 | – | 29 |
| Taylor, C.R. | 8 | 15 | 1 | 52* | 210 | 15.00 | – | 2 | – | 5 |
| Tendulkar, S.R. | 191 | 295 | 29 | 233* | 16448 | 61.83 | 54 | 76 | 1+3 | 130 |
| Thomas, I.J. | 19 | 32 | 4 | 82 | 653 | 23.32 | – | 4 | – | 9 |
| Thomas, S.D. | 143 | 193 | 37 | 138 | 3059 | 19.60 | 1 | 13 | – | 47 |
| Thorburn, M. | 5 | 5 | 1 | 12 | 35 | 8.75 | – | – | – | 1 |
| Thornicroft, N.D. | 3 | 6 | 3 | 4* | 9 | 3.00 | – | – | – | – |
| Thorpe, A.M. | 7 | 13 | 0 | 95 | 271 | 20.84 | – | 2 | – | 5 |
| Thorpe, G.P. | 290 | 485 | 66 | 223* | 18625 | 44.45 | 43 | 100 | 8 | 260 |
| Tillekeratne, H.P. | 208 | 290 | 70 | 204* | 11029 | 50.13 | 32 | 49 | – | 241/7 |
| Tomlinson, J.A. | 6 | 10 | 5 | 23 | 34 | 6.80 | – | – | – | 2 |
| Tournier, M.A. | 3 | 3 | 1 | 13 | 23 | 11.50 | – | – | – | – |
| Tredwell, J.C. | 5 | 7 | 0 | 61 | 171 | 24.42 | – | 2 | – | 8 |
| Trego, P.D. | 14 | 21 | 3 | 140 | 521 | 28.94 | 1 | 1 | – | 5 |
| Tremlett, C.T. | 19 | 25 | 10 | 40* | 296 | 19.73 | – | – | – | 6 |
| Trescothick, M.E. | 138 | 234 | 11 | 190 | 7589 | 34.03 | 12 | 44 | – | 140 |
| Trott, B.J. | 22 | 20 | 6 | 26 | 85 | 6.07 | – | – | – | 5 |
| Trott, I.J.L. | 17 | 32 | 3 | 93 | 800 | 27.58 | – | 7 | – | 13 |
| Troughton, J.O. | 15 | 26 | 4 | 131* | 1099 | 49.95 | 3 | 6 | 1 | 8 |
| Tudor, A.J. | 82 | 108 | 24 | 116 | 1831 | 21.79 | 1 | 5 | – | 22 |
| Tufnell, P.C.R. | 316 | 349 | 136 | 67* | 2066 | 9.69 | – | 1 | – | 106 |
| Turner, R.J. | 209 | 323 | 55 | 144 | 8255 | 30.80 | 9 | 42 | 2 | 555/40 |
| Udal, S.D. | 200 | 286 | 52 | 117* | 5293 | 22.61 | 1 | 22 | – | 92 |
| Upashantha, K.E.A. | 103 | 123 | 7 | 82 | 2328 | 20.06 | – | 15 | – | 69 |
| Vaas, W.P.U.C.J. | 104 | 128 | 27 | 74* | 2006 | 19.86 | – | 10 | – | 28 |
| Van der Gucht, C.G. | 2 | 2 | 1 | 38 | 38 | 38.00 | – | – | – | – |
| Vaughan, M.P. | 176 | 308 | 17 | 197 | 10791 | 37.08 | 26 | 47 | 4 | 84 |
| Vonwiller, B.M. | 3 | 3 | 2 | 4* | 5 | 5.00 | – | – | – | 3 |
| Wagg, G.G. | 5 | 8 | 2 | 51 | 161 | 26.83 | – | 1 | – | 1 |
| Wagh, M.A. | 92 | 148 | 13 | 315 | 5074 | 37.58 | 13 | 20 | 2 | 38 |
| Walker, G.W. | 1 | 2 | 1 | 37* | 44 | 44.00 | – | – | – | 1 |
| Walker, M.J. | 99 | 165 | 18 | 275* | 4212 | 28.65 | 7 | 14 | – | 59 |
| Wallace, M.A. | 33 | 50 | 9 | 106* | 1057 | 25.78 | 1 | 6 | – | 107/4 |
| Wanasinghe, W.M.P.N. | 79 | 133 | 13 | 136 | 3574 | 29.78 | 6 | 18 | – | 30 |
| Ward, D.M. | 156 | 246 | 34 | 294* | 8139 | 38.39 | 16 | 33 | 2 | 122/3 |
| Ward, I.J. | 97 | 165 | 15 | 168* | 6067 | 40.44 | 14 | 36 | 2 | 56 |
| Ward, T.R. | 239 | 410 | 22 | 235* | 13433 | 34.62 | 28 | 76 | 6 | 219 |

| F-C | M | I | NO | HS | Runs | Avge | 100 | 50 | 1000 | Ct/St |
|---|---|---|---|---|---|---|---|---|---|---|
| Warn, C.J. | 1 | 1 | 0 | 1 | 1 | 1.00 | – | – | – | 3 |
| Warren, C.C.M. | 8 | 14 | 2 | 40* | 149 | 12.41 | – | – | – | 5 |
| Warren, N.A. | 1 | 2 | 1 | 11 | 13 | 13.00 | – | – | – | – |
| Warren, R.J. | 110 | 180 | 21 | 201* | 5767 | 36.27 | 10 | 31 | 1 | 106/3 |
| Waugh, M.E. | 346 | 553 | 70 | 229* | 25715 | 53.24 | 81 | 126 | 5+1 | 417 |
| Waugh, S.R. | 319 | 492 | 81 | 216* | 21351 | 51.94 | 68 | 88 | 2 | 251 |
| Weekes, P.N. | 178 | 276 | 36 | 171* | 8109 | 33.78 | 15 | 37 | 1 | 169 |
| Welch, G. | 108 | 161 | 25 | 84* | 2866 | 21.07 | – | 12 | – | 41 |
| Wells, V.J. | 184 | 285 | 21 | 224 | 8894 | 33.68 | 17 | 44 | 2 | 123 |
| Welton, G.E. | 61 | 110 | 5 | 200* | 2727 | 25.97 | 2 | 14 | – | 37 |
| Weston, R.M.S. | 60 | 100 | 6 | 156 | 2634 | 28.02 | 6 | 9 | – | 37 |
| Weston, W.P.C. | 170 | 299 | 31 | 205 | 9132 | 34.07 | 17 | 47 | 4 | 89 |
| Wharf, A.G. | 46 | 62 | 8 | 101* | 914 | 16.92 | 2 | 3 | – | 22 |
| Wharton, L.J. | 32 | 50 | 25 | 16 | 127 | 5.08 | – | – | – | 10 |
| Whiley, M.J.A. | 13 | 18 | 4 | 13* | 43 | 3.07 | – | – | – | 2 |
| White, C. | 211 | 331 | 43 | 186 | 9129 | 31.69 | 14 | 44 | – | 140 |
| White, G.W. | 128 | 223 | 21 | 156 | 6195 | 30.66 | 9 | 30 | 1 | 107/2 |
| White, R.A. | 6 | 11 | 1 | 277 | 593 | 59.30 | 1 | 3 | – | 3 |
| Wigley, D.H. | 1 | 2 | 1 | 15 | 19 | 19.00 | – | – | – | – |
| Windows, M.G.N. | 129 | 229 | 17 | 184 | 7358 | 34.70 | 15 | 39 | 3 | 73 |
| Wood, J. | 104 | 153 | 21 | 64 | 1647 | 12.47 | – | 3 | – | 25 |
| Wood, M.J. (Sm) | 22 | 40 | 0 | 196 | 1500 | 37.50 | 4 | 9 | – | 7 |
| Wood, M.J. (Y) | 72 | 123 | 10 | 200* | 3228 | 28.56 | 9 | 13 | 2 | 55 |
| Wright, A.S. | 6 | 10 | 1 | 30 | 124 | 13.77 | – | – | – | 1 |
| Wyatt, A.A. | 2 | 3 | 1 | 10* | 18 | 9.00 | – | – | – | – |
| Yardy, M.H. | 31 | 54 | 7 | 93 | 1352 | 28.76 | – | 7 | – | 20 |
| Yates, G. | 82 | 107 | 36 | 134* | 1789 | 25.19 | 3 | 5 | – | 38 |
| Yohannan, T. | 17 | 15 | 10 | 21* | 48 | 9.60 | – | – | – | 9 |
| Zoysa, D.N.T. | 50 | 57 | 14 | 60* | 621 | 14.44 | – | 2 | – | 9 |
| Zuiderent, B. | 18 | 29 | 1 | 122 | 629 | 22.46 | 1 | 3 | – | 18 |

## BOWLING

'50wS' denotes instances of taking 50 or more wickets in a season. Where these have been achieved outside the British Isles they are shown after a plus sign.

| | Runs | Wkts | Avge | Best | 5wI | 10wM | 50wS |
|---|---|---|---|---|---|---|---|
| Abdul Razzaq | 6233 | 210 | 29.68 | 7- 51 | 8 | 2 | – |
| Adams, C.J. | 1854 | 41 | 45.21 | 4- 28 | – | – | – |
| Adams, J.H.K. | 102 | 2 | 51.00 | 2- 81 | – | – | – |
| Afzaal, U. | 3333 | 66 | 50.50 | 4-101 | – | – | – |
| Agarkar, A.B. | 3319 | 115 | 28.86 | 6- 72 | 4 | – | – |
| Aldred, P. | 4562 | 132 | 34.56 | 7-101 | 5 | 1 | 1 |
| Ali, Kabir | 2903 | 108 | 26.87 | 7- 43 | 6 | 2 | 1 |
| Ali, Kadeer | 57 | 0 | | | – | – | – |
| Ali, S.M.B. | 7061 | 226 | 31.24 | 6- 37 | 11 | 2 | 0+1 |
| Alleyne, M.W. | 12885 | 394 | 32.70 | 6- 49 | 8 | – | 1 |
| Ambrose, T.R. | 1 | 0 | | | – | – | – |
| Amerasinghe, M.K.D.I. | 2848 | 141 | 20.19 | 5- 28 | 6 | 1 | 0+1 |
| Amin, R.M. | 1108 | 27 | 41.03 | 4- 87 | – | – | – |
| Anderson, J.M. | 1114 | 50 | 22.28 | 6- 23 | 3 | – | 1 |
| Anderson, R.S.G. | 3251 | 118 | 27.55 | 6- 34 | 8 | 1 | 1 |
| Angel, J. | 10920 | 449 | 24.32 | 6- 52 | 15 | 1 | – |
| Arnold, R.P. | 3919 | 141 | 27.79 | 7- 84 | 4 | – | – |
| Atapattu, M.S. | 692 | 19 | 36.42 | 3- 19 | – | – | – |
| Averis, J.M.M. | 4011 | 89 | 45.06 | 5- 51 | 3 | – | – |
| Aymes, A.N. | 438 | 6 | 73.00 | 2-101 | – | – | – |

| F-C | Runs | Wkts | Avge | Best | 5wI | 10wM | 50wS |
|---|---|---|---|---|---|---|---|
| Azhar Mahmood | 6948 | 295 | 23.55 | 8- 61 | 12 | 3 | 0+1 |
| Ball, M.C.J. | 11735 | 317 | 37.01 | 8- 46 | 11 | 1 | – |
| Banes, M.J. | 175 | 3 | 58.33 | 3- 65 | – | – | – |
| Bangar, S.B. | 3974 | 103 | 38.58 | 5- 17 | 2 | – | – |
| Barnett, K.J. | 7108 | 188 | 37.80 | 6- 28 | 3 | – | – |
| Bassano, C.W.G. | 11 | 0 | | | | | |
| Batty, G.J. | 1861 | 60 | 31.01 | 6- 71 | 3 | – | 1 |
| Batty, J.N. | 61 | 1 | 61.00 | 1- 21 | – | – | – |
| Bell, I.R. | 129 | 3 | 43.00 | 1- 22 | – | – | – |
| Benn, S.J. | 1945 | 65 | 29.92 | 5- 51 | 3 | – | – |
| Best, T.Le B. | 662 | 23 | 28.78 | 5- 37 | 1 | – | – |
| Betts, M.M. | 8250 | 282 | 29.25 | 9- 64 | 12 | 2 | – |
| Bevan, M.G. | 5164 | 115 | 44.90 | 6- 82 | 1 | 1 | – |
| Bichel, A.J. | 10093 | 414 | 24.37 | 9- 93 | 21 | 4 | 1+1 |
| Bicknell, D.J. | 789 | 23 | 34.30 | 3- 7 | – | – | – |
| Bicknell, M.P. | 22748 | 932 | 24.40 | 9- 45 | 37 | 4 | 10 |
| Bishop, J.E. | 1565 | 38 | 41.18 | 5-148 | 1 | – | – |
| Black, M.I. | 3331 | 120 | 27.75 | 6- 23 | 3 | – | – |
| Blackwell, I.D. | 4082 | 93 | 43.89 | 5- 49 | 3 | – | – |
| Blain, J.A.R. | 1864 | 36 | 51.77 | 6- 42 | 1 | – | – |
| Blakey, R.J. | 68 | 1 | 68.00 | 1- 68 | – | – | – |
| Bloomfield, T.F. | 4808 | 148 | 32.48 | 5- 36 | 6 | – | 1 |
| Boje, N. | 10320 | 329 | 31.36 | 6- 31 | 15 | 1 | – |
| Bond, S.E. | 2693 | 101 | 26.66 | 5- 37 | 6 | – | – |
| Bopara, R.S. | 74 | 1 | 74.00 | 1- 43 | – | – | – |
| Bowler, P.D. | 2041 | 34 | 60.02 | 3- 25 | – | – | – |
| Brandy, D.G. | 114 | 2 | 57.00 | 2- 86 | – | – | – |
| Brant, S.A. | 126 | 7 | 18.00 | 3- 23 | – | – | – |
| Bravo, D.J.J. | 133 | 2 | 66.50 | 2- 28 | – | – | – |
| Breese, G.R. | 2116 | 99 | 21.37 | 7- 60 | 7 | 2 | – |
| Bressington, A.N. | 446 | 16 | 27.87 | 4- 36 | – | – | – |
| Bridge, G.D. | 1284 | 40 | 32.10 | 6- 84 | 1 | – | – |
| Brown, A.D. | 432 | 1 | 432.00 | 1- 56 | – | – | – |
| Brown, D.R. | 11052 | 401 | 27.56 | 8- 89 | 15 | 4 | 3 |
| Brown, J.F. | 5571 | 182 | 30.60 | 7- 78 | 9 | 3 | 1 |
| Brown, S.J.E. | 15800 | 550 | 28.72 | 7- 51 | 36 | 2 | 7 |
| Bruce, J.T.A. | 389 | 5 | 77.80 | 2- 76 | – | – | – |
| Bryant, J.D.C. | 29 | 1 | 29.00 | 1- 22 | – | – | – |
| Bulbeck, M.P.L. | 4615 | 152 | 30.36 | 6- 93 | 4 | 1 | 2 |
| Burns, M. | 2074 | 49 | 42.32 | 6- 54 | 1 | – | – |
| Burns, N.D. | 8 | 0 | | | | | |
| Butcher, G.P. | 2390 | 63 | 37.93 | 7- 77 | 2 | – | – |
| Butcher, M.A. | 3874 | 116 | 33.39 | 5- 86 | 1 | – | – |
| Byas, D. | 727 | 12 | 60.58 | 3- 55 | – | – | – |
| Caddick, A.R. | 21327 | 863 | 24.71 | 9- 32 | 60 | 14 | 8 |
| Cairns, C.L. | 16415 | 597 | 27.49 | 8- 47 | 29 | 6 | 3 |
| Carpenter, J.R. | 81 | 1 | 81.00 | 1- 50 | – | – | – |
| Carter, N.M. | 2363 | 69 | 34.24 | 6- 63 | 3 | – | – |
| Cassar, M.E. | 2751 | 91 | 30.23 | 6- 34 | 3 | 1 | – |
| Catterall, D.N. | 308 | 11 | 28.00 | 4- 50 | – | – | – |
| Cawdron, M.J. | 1298 | 53 | 24.49 | 6- 25 | 5 | 1 | – |
| Chandana, U.D.U. | 6198 | 274 | 22.62 | 7- 80 | 10 | – | – |
| Chapple, G. | 12319 | 438 | 28.12 | 6- 30 | 18 | 1 | 4 |
| Cherry, D.D. | 0 | 0 | | | | | |
| Chilton, M.J. | 397 | 5 | 79.40 | 1- 1 | – | – | – |
| Clark, P.J. | 92 | 1 | 92.00 | 1- 72 | – | – | – |

| F-C | Runs | Wkts | Avge | Best | 5wI | 10wM | 50wS |
|---|---|---|---|---|---|---|---|
| Clarke, A.J. | 113 | 7 | 16.14 | 5- 54 | 1 | – | – |
| Clarke, R. | 451 | 11 | 41.00 | 3- 41 | – | – | – |
| Clinton, R.S. | 30 | 2 | 15.00 | 2- 30 | – | – | – |
| Clough, G.D. | 425 | 8 | 53.12 | 3- 69 | – | – | – |
| Collingwood, P.D. | 2401 | 61 | 39.36 | 4- 31 | – | – | – |
| Cook, J.W. | 605 | 10 | 60.50 | 2- 7 | – | – | – |
| Cook, S.J. | 3290 | 106 | 31.03 | 8- 63 | 2 | – | – |
| Cork, D.G. | 17570 | 672 | 26.14 | 9- 43 | 25 | 3 | 6 |
| Cosker, D.A. | 8203 | 223 | 36.78 | 6-140 | 2 | – | – |
| Cottey, P.A. | 895 | 16 | 55.93 | 4- 49 | – | – | – |
| Cousins, D.M. | 4656 | 152 | 30.63 | 8-102 | 4 | – | 1 |
| Cowan, A.P. | 8773 | 270 | 32.49 | 6- 47 | 8 | – | 1 |
| Cox, J. | 323 | 4 | 80.75 | 3- 46 | – | – | – |
| Craven, V.J. | 140 | 1 | 140.00 | 1- 25 | – | – | – |
| Crawley, J.P. | 201 | 1 | 201.00 | 1- 90 | – | – | – |
| Creese, M.L. | 107 | 1 | 107.00 | 1- 37 | – | – | – |
| Croft, R.D.B. | 26103 | 716 | 36.45 | 8- 66 | 31 | 5 | 5 |
| Crowe, C.D. | 1925 | 57 | 33.77 | 4- 47 | – | – | – |
| Cunliffe, R.J. | 3 | 0 | | | | | |
| Dagnall, C.E. | 818 | 30 | 27.26 | 6- 50 | 1 | – | – |
| Dakin, J.M. | 3983 | 114 | 34.93 | 4- 17 | – | – | – |
| Dale, A. | 8073 | 214 | 37.72 | 6- 18 | 4 | – | – |
| Daley, J.A. | 81 | 1 | 81.00 | 1- 12 | – | – | – |
| Dalrymple, J.W.M. | 1045 | 16 | 65.31 | 4- 86 | – | – | – |
| Das, S.S. | 122 | 3 | 40.66 | 1- 0 | – | – | – |
| Davies, A.M. | 942 | 36 | 26.16 | 5- 61 | 1 | – | – |
| Davies, A.P. | 1364 | 40 | 34.10 | 5- 79 | 1 | – | – |
| Davis, M.J.G. | 6768 | 193 | 35.06 | 8- 37 | 5 | 1 | – |
| Dawes, J.H. | 3180 | 132 | 24.09 | 7- 98 | 4 | 1 | – |
| Dawson, R.K.J. | 3108 | 79 | 39.34 | 6- 82 | 4 | – | – |
| De Silva, K.S.C. | 7366 | 330 | 22.32 | 7- 73 | 18 | 2 | 0+1 |
| De Silva, P.A. | 3763 | 129 | 29.17 | 7- 24 | 8 | 1 | – |
| Dean, K.J. | 6676 | 291 | 22.94 | 8- 52 | 14 | 4 | 2 |
| DeFreitas, P.A.J. | 31896 | 1145 | 27.85 | 7- 21 | 57 | 5 | 13 |
| Di Venuto, M.J. | 406 | 5 | 81.20 | 1- 0 | – | – | – |
| Donald, A.A. | 26937 | 1187 | 22.69 | 8- 37 | 66 | 9 | 5 |
| Dowman, M.P. | 1394 | 35 | 39.82 | 4- 28 | – | – | – |
| Dravid, R. | 273 | 5 | 54.60 | 2- 16 | – | – | – |
| Driver, R.C. | 408 | 14 | 29.14 | 5- 70 | 1 | – | – |
| Dumelow, N.R.C. | 868 | 14 | 62.00 | 4- 81 | – | – | – |
| Durston, W.J. | 65 | 1 | 65.00 | 1- 25 | – | – | – |
| Dutch, K.P. | 3311 | 88 | 37.62 | 6- 62 | 1 | – | – |
| Ealham, M.A. | 11120 | 387 | 28.73 | 8- 36 | 16 | 1 | – |
| Elliott, M.T.G. | 640 | 10 | 64.00 | 1- 3 | – | – | – |
| Elstub, C.J. | 421 | 11 | 38.27 | 3- 37 | – | – | – |
| Elworthy, S. | 12514 | 456 | 27.44 | 7- 65 | 17 | 4 | 0+1 |
| Fairbrother, N.H. | 500 | 7 | 71.42 | 2- 91 | – | – | – |
| Fellows, G.M. | 1180 | 30 | 39.33 | 3- 23 | – | – | – |
| Ferley, R.S. | 640 | 15 | 42.66 | 4- 83 | – | – | – |
| Fernando, C.R.D. | 3387 | 122 | 27.76 | 6- 29 | 5 | – | – |
| Fernando, T.C.B. | 2561 | 87 | 29.43 | 6- 39 | 3 | 1 | – |
| Fisher, I.D. | 3109 | 75 | 41.45 | 5- 35 | 3 | – | – |
| Flanagan, I.N. | 51 | 1 | 51.00 | 1- 50 | – | – | – |
| Fleming, D.W. | 10508 | 376 | 27.94 | 7- 90 | 13 | 1 | – |
| Fleming, M.V. | 10415 | 290 | 35.91 | 5- 51 | 2 | – | – |
| Flintoff, A. | 3824 | 107 | 35.73 | 5- 24 | 1 | – | – |

| F-C | Runs | Wkts | Avge | Best | 5wI | 10wM | 50wS |
|---|---|---|---|---|---|---|---|
| Flower, A. | 217 | 4 | 54.25 | 1- 1 | – | – | – |
| Flower, G.W. | 4346 | 117 | 37.14 | 7- 31 | 2 | – | – |
| Foster, J.S. | 6 | 0 | | | | | |
| Francis, J.D. | 35 | 2 | 17.50 | 1- 1 | – | – | – |
| Francis, S.R.G. | 2179 | 53 | 41.11 | 5- 73 | 1 | – | – |
| Franks, P.J. | 7247 | 265 | 27.34 | 7- 56 | 9 | – | 2 |
| Fraser, A.R.C. | 24277 | 886 | 27.40 | 8- 53 | 36 | 5 | 7 |
| Frost, T. | 15 | 0 | | | | | |
| Fulton, D.P. | 112 | 1 | 112.00 | 1- 37 | – | – | – |
| Gallian, J.E.R. | 3825 | 94 | 40.69 | 6-115 | 1 | – | – |
| Ganga, D. | 98 | 1 | 98.00 | 1- 7 | – | – | – |
| Ganguly, S.C. | 4474 | 117 | 38.23 | 6- 46 | 3 | – | – |
| Gannon, B.W. | 2730 | 85 | 32.11 | 6- 80 | 3 | – | – |
| Gayle, C.H. | 1410 | 38 | 37.10 | 4- 86 | – | – | – |
| Giddins, E.S.H. | 13226 | 465 | 28.44 | 6- 47 | 22 | 2 | 4 |
| Gidman, A.P.R. | 442 | 10 | 44.20 | 3- 33 | – | – | – |
| Giles, A.F. | 10430 | 379 | 27.51 | 8- 90 | 19 | 3 | 2 |
| Gofton, A.F. | 807 | 11 | 73.36 | 3- 41 | – | – | – |
| Golding, J.M. | 637 | 14 | 45.50 | 4- 76 | – | – | – |
| Goodwin, M.W. | 338 | 7 | 48.28 | 2- 23 | – | – | – |
| Gough, D. | 18712 | 707 | 26.46 | 7- 28 | 27 | 3 | 5 |
| Gough, M.A. | 1241 | 27 | 45.96 | 5- 66 | 1 | – | – |
| Grant, J.B. | 2066 | 56 | 36.89 | 5- 38 | 1 | – | – |
| Gray, A.K.D. | 578 | 15 | 38.53 | 4-128 | – | – | – |
| Grayson, A.P. | 5418 | 127 | 42.66 | 5- 20 | 1 | – | – |
| Greenidge, C.G. | 2018 | 65 | 31.04 | 6- 40 | 4 | – | 1 |
| Grove, J.O. | 2025 | 42 | 48.21 | 5- 90 | 1 | – | – |
| Gunter, N.E.L. | 153 | 8 | 19.12 | 4- 14 | – | – | – |
| Guy, S.M. | 8 | 0 | | | | | |
| Habib, A. | 52 | 0 | | | | | |
| Hall, A.J. | 3212 | 123 | 26.11 | 5- 20 | 5 | – | – |
| Hamblin, J.R.C. | 461 | 7 | 65.85 | 2- 44 | – | – | – |
| Hamilton, G.M. | 6067 | 239 | 25.38 | 7- 50 | 9 | 2 | 1 |
| Hancock, T.H.C. | 1658 | 44 | 37.68 | 3- 5 | – | – | – |
| Harbhajan Singh | 8022 | 314 | 25.54 | 8- 84 | 19 | 3 | 0+1 |
| Hardinges, M.A. | 499 | 10 | 49.90 | 2- 16 | – | – | – |
| Harmison, S.J. | 6754 | 216 | 31.26 | 6-111 | 5 | – | 2 |
| Harris, A.J. | 8465 | 276 | 30.67 | 7- 54 | 12 | 3 | 2 |
| Harrison, D.S. | 241 | 4 | 60.25 | 2- 79 | – | – | – |
| Harrity, M.A. | 7273 | 192 | 37.88 | 5- 65 | 2 | – | – |
| Harvey, I.J. | 7962 | 295 | 26.98 | 7- 44 | 13 | 2 | – |
| Hatch, N.G. | 1311 | 35 | 37.45 | 4- 61 | – | – | – |
| Hawinkels, S.J. | 133 | 2 | 66.50 | 1- 44 | – | – | – |
| Hayward, M. | 5997 | 210 | 28.55 | 6- 31 | 6 | 2 | – |
| Hazelton, M.A. | 58 | 0 | | | | | |
| Heath, D.R. | 230 | 6 | 38.33 | 3- 28 | – | – | – |
| Heath, J.A. | 31 | 0 | | | | | |
| Hegg, W.K. | 7 | 0 | | | | | |
| Hemp, D.L. | 778 | 17 | 45.76 | 3- 23 | – | – | – |
| Hewitt, J.P. | 4948 | 170 | 29.10 | 6- 14 | 5 | – | – |
| Hewson, D.R. | 77 | 1 | 77.00 | 1- 7 | – | – | – |
| Hick, G.A. | 10205 | 231 | 44.17 | 5- 18 | 5 | 1 | – |
| Hicks, T.C. | 1960 | 41 | 47.80 | 5- 54 | 2 | – | – |
| Hilsum, I.J. | 20 | 0 | | | | | |
| Hinds, R.O. | 1464 | 58 | 25.24 | 9- 68 | 2 | 1 | – |
| Hockley, J.B. | 233 | 3 | 77.66 | 1- 21 | – | – | – |

| F-C | Runs | Wkts | Avge | Best | 5wI | 10wM | 50wS |
|---|---|---|---|---|---|---|---|
| Hodge, B.J. | 1497 | 37 | 40.45 | 4-17 | – | – | – |
| Hogg, K.W. | 651 | 22 | 29.59 | 5-48 | 1 | – | – |
| Hoggard, M.J. | 6540 | 262 | 24.96 | 7-63 | 10 | – | 1 |
| Hollingsworth, A.P. | 86 | 4 | 21.50 | 3-35 | – | – | – |
| Hollioake, A.J. | 4337 | 108 | 40.15 | 5-62 | 1 | – | – |
| Holloway, P.C.L. | 69 | 0 | | | | | |
| Hopkinson, C.D. | 35 | 1 | 35.00 | 1-35 | – | – | – |
| House, W.J. | 964 | 4 | 241.00 | 1-34 | – | – | – |
| Hughes, T.R. | 863 | 17 | 50.76 | 3-55 | – | – | – |
| Hunt, T.A. | 189 | 4 | 47.25 | 3-43 | – | – | – |
| Hunter, I.D. | 1703 | 42 | 40.54 | 4-55 | – | – | – |
| Hussain, N. | 323 | 2 | 161.50 | 1-38 | – | – | – |
| Hussey, M.E.K. | 269 | 5 | 53.80 | 2-21 | – | – | – |
| Hutchison, P.M. | 3951 | 161 | 24.54 | 7-31 | 7 | 1 | 1 |
| Hutton, B.L. | 838 | 18 | 46.55 | 4-37 | – | – | – |
| Hyam, B.J. | 8 | 0 | | | | | |
| Ilott, M.C. | 17537 | 633 | 27.70 | 9-19 | 27 | 3 | 6 |
| Innes, K.J. | 1951 | 67 | 29.11 | 4-41 | – | – | – |
| Inness, M.W.H. | 4064 | 163 | 24.93 | 7-19 | 6 | 2 | – |
| Irani, R.C. | 9762 | 330 | 29.58 | 6-71 | 9 | – | 1 |
| Jaffer, W. | 59 | 2 | 29.50 | 2-18 | – | – | – |
| James, S.P. | 3 | 0 | | | | | |
| Jarvis, P.W. | 18914 | 654 | 28.92 | 7-55 | 22 | 3 | 4 |
| Jayasuriya, S.T. | 4170 | 129 | 32.32 | 5-43 | 1 | – | – |
| Jayawardena, D.P.M.D. | 1416 | 49 | 28.89 | 5-72 | 1 | – | – |
| Johnson, N.C. | 7190 | 222 | 32.38 | 5-79 | 2 | – | – |
| Johnson, P. | 617 | 6 | 102.83 | 1- 9 | – | – | – |
| Johnson, R.L. | 10181 | 384 | 26.51 | 10-45 | 14 | 3 | 4 |
| Jones, G.O. | 4 | 0 | | | | | |
| Jones, I. | 441 | 10 | 44.10 | 3-72 | – | – | – |
| Jones, P.S. | 5983 | 166 | 36.04 | 6-67 | 4 | 1 | 1 |
| Jones, S.P. | 3483 | 93 | 37.45 | 6-45 | 3 | – | – |
| Jordison, J.R. | 96 | 1 | 96.00 | 1-61 | – | – | – |
| Joyce, E.C. | 176 | 1 | 176.00 | 1-20 | – | – | – |
| Kaif, M. | 488 | 16 | 30.50 | 3- 4 | – | – | – |
| Kasprowicz, M.S. | 17441 | 654 | 26.66 | 7-36 | 37 | 4 | 3+3 |
| Katich, S.M. | 1085 | 20 | 54.25 | 3-21 | – | – | – |
| Keedy, G. | 8445 | 231 | 36.55 | 6-56 | 7 | 2 | – |
| Keegan, C.B. | 1443 | 37 | 39.00 | 4-47 | – | – | – |
| Kendall, W.S. | 639 | 13 | 49.15 | 3-37 | – | – | – |
| Kenway, D.A. | 150 | 3 | 50.00 | 1- 5 | – | – | – |
| Kerr, J.I.D. | 5210 | 129 | 40.38 | 7-23 | 2 | – | – |
| Key, R.W.T. | 40 | 0 | | | | | |
| Khan, A. | 2050 | 64 | 32.03 | 6-52 | 4 | – | 1 |
| Khan, R.M. | 15 | 0 | | | | | |
| Khan, Z. | 4903 | 164 | 29.89 | 6-25 | 9 | 3 | – |
| Killeen, N. | 5003 | 176 | 28.42 | 7-85 | 6 | – | 1 |
| King, R.D. | 5700 | 227 | 25.11 | 7-82 | 9 | 1 | – |
| Kirby, S.P. | 2242 | 84 | 26.69 | 7-50 | 4 | 1 | – |
| Kirtley, R.J. | 10036 | 403 | 24.90 | 7-21 | 24 | 4 | 5 |
| Klusener, L. | 8071 | 303 | 26.63 | 8-34 | 11 | 3 | – |
| Knight, N.V. | 191 | 1 | 191.00 | 1-61 | – | – | – |
| Koenig, S.G. | 67 | 1 | 67.00 | 1- 0 | – | – | – |
| Krikken, K.M. | 121 | 1 | 121.00 | 1-54 | – | – | – |
| Kumble, A. | 18903 | 787 | 24.01 | 10-74 | 53 | 14 | 1+1 |
| Lampitt, S.R. | 17224 | 601 | 28.65 | 7-45 | 20 | – | 7 |

| F-C | Runs | Wkts | Avge | Best | 5wI | 10wM | 50wS |
|---|---|---|---|---|---|---|---|
| Laney, J.S. | 224 | 2 | 112.00 | 1- 24 | – | – | – |
| Laraman, A.W. | 995 | 33 | 30.15 | 4- 33 | – | – | – |
| Law, D.R. | 6647 | 201 | 33.06 | 6- 53 | 8 | – | – |
| Law, S.G. | 4029 | 82 | 49.13 | 5- 39 | 1 | – | – |
| Lawson, J.J.C. | 1448 | 47 | 30.80 | 6- 76 | 1 | – | – |
| Laxman, V.V.S. | 659 | 18 | 36.61 | 3- 11 | – | – | – |
| Leatherdale, D.A. | 3969 | 127 | 31.25 | 5- 20 | 2 | – | – |
| Lee, S. | 6078 | 150 | 40.52 | 4- 20 | – | – | – |
| Lehmann, D.S. | 2565 | 64 | 40.07 | 4- 42 | – | – | – |
| Lewis, J. | 9287 | 338 | 27.47 | 8- 95 | 15 | 2 | 3 |
| Lewis, J.J.B. | 121 | 1 | 121.00 | 1- 73 | – | – | – |
| Lewry, J.D. | 9716 | 363 | 26.76 | 7- 38 | 21 | 3 | 4 |
| Liptrot, C.G. | 2165 | 66 | 32.80 | 6- 44 | 2 | – | – |
| Lloyd, G.D. | 440 | 2 | 220.00 | 1- 4 | – | – | – |
| Logan, R.J. | 3197 | 97 | 32.95 | 6- 93 | 4 | – | – |
| Loudon, A.G.R. | 276 | 7 | 39.42 | 3- 86 | – | – | – |
| Love, M.L. | 5 | 1 | 5.00 | 1- 5 | – | – | – |
| Loye, M.B. | 44 | 0 | | | | | |
| Lucas, D.S. | 1909 | 52 | 36.71 | 5-104 | 1 | – | – |
| Lumb, M.J. | 26 | 2 | 13.00 | 2- 10 | – | – | – |
| Lungley, T. | 984 | 35 | 28.11 | 3- 10 | – | – | – |
| McCoubrey, A.G.A.M. | 137 | 5 | 27.40 | 3- 38 | – | – | – |
| McGarry, A.C. | 1241 | 22 | 56.40 | 3- 29 | – | – | – |
| MacGill, S.C.G. | 9292 | 326 | 28.50 | 8-111 | 18 | 3 | 0+1 |
| McGrath, A. | 1079 | 36 | 29.97 | 4- 49 | – | – | – |
| McGrath, D.E.T. | 148 | 6 | 24.66 | 3- 49 | – | – | – |
| McLean, N.A.M. | 9036 | 330 | 27.38 | 7- 28 | 11 | 1 | 1 |
| McMahon, P.J. | 103 | 2 | 51.50 | 2- 22 | – | – | – |
| Maddy, D.L. | 2914 | 98 | 29.73 | 5- 37 | 3 | – | – |
| Mahmood, S.I. | 6 | 0 | | | | | |
| Malcolm, D.E. | 31615 | 1040 | 30.39 | 9- 57 | 45 | 9 | 9 |
| Malik, M.N. | 976 | 32 | 30.50 | 5- 57 | 2 | – | – |
| Marshall, S.J. | 657 | 10 | 65.70 | 6-128 | 1 | – | – |
| Martin, P.J. | 15063 | 555 | 27.14 | 8- 32 | 16 | 1 | 4 |
| Martin-Jenkins, R.S.C. | 5307 | 168 | 31.58 | 7- 51 | 4 | – | – |
| Mascarenhas, A.D. | 5534 | 176 | 31.44 | 6- 26 | 5 | – | – |
| Mason, M.S. | 862 | 26 | 33.15 | 5- 50 | 1 | – | – |
| Masters, D.D. | 2304 | 78 | 29.53 | 6- 27 | 3 | – | – |
| Maynard, M.P. | 866 | 6 | 144.33 | 3- 21 | – | – | – |
| Mees, T. | 492 | 15 | 32.80 | 6- 64 | 1 | – | – |
| Middlebrook, J.D. | 3194 | 87 | 36.71 | 6- 82 | 1 | 1 | – |
| Millar, N. | 365 | 4 | 91.25 | 2- 50 | – | – | – |
| Mongia, D. | 261 | 4 | 65.25 | 1- 0 | – | – | – |
| Montgomerie, R.R. | 99 | 1 | 99.00 | 1- 0 | – | – | – |
| Morris, A.C. | 4119 | 156 | 26.40 | 5- 39 | 5 | 1 | 2 |
| Morton, R.S. | 153 | 4 | 38.25 | 3- 17 | – | – | – |
| Muchall, G.J. | 194 | 4 | 48.50 | 2- 52 | – | – | – |
| Mullally, A.D. | 18558 | 673 | 27.60 | 9- 93 | 30 | 4 | 5 |
| Muralitharan, M. | 16256 | 835 | 19.46 | 9- 51 | 73 | 23 | 2+4 |
| Murtagh, T.J. | 544 | 25 | 21.76 | 6- 86 | 2 | – | – |
| Mushtaq Ahmed | 22822 | 872 | 26.17 | 9- 93 | 59 | 16 | 4+2 |
| Napier, G.R. | 1277 | 37 | 34.51 | 3- 47 | – | – | – |
| Nash, C.D. | 171 | 2 | 85.50 | 1- 81 | – | – | – |
| Nash, D.C. | 19 | 1 | 19.00 | 1- 8 | – | – | – |
| Nehra, A. | 4795 | 187 | 25.64 | 7- 14 | 10 | 4 | – |
| Nel, A. | 2600 | 130 | 20.00 | 6- 25 | 7 | – | – |

| F-C | Runs | Wkts | Avge | Best | 5wI | 10wM | 50wS |
|---|---|---|---|---|---|---|---|
| Newell, K. | 1023 | 24 | 42.62 | 4- 61 | – | – | – |
| Nixon, P.A. | 22 | 0 | | | | | |
| Noble, D.J. | 480 | 9 | 53.33 | 3- 66 | – | – | – |
| Noffke, A.A. | 3143 | 114 | 27.57 | 8- 24 | 6 | 1 | – |
| Noon, W.M. | 34 | 0 | | | | | |
| Ormond, J. | 7711 | 278 | 27.73 | 6- 33 | 15 | 1 | 2 |
| Ostler, D.P. | 262 | 1 | 262.00 | 1- 46 | – | – | – |
| Panesar, M.S. | 912 | 28 | 32.57 | 4- 11 | – | – | – |
| Parker, J.W.R. | 47 | 0 | | | | | |
| Parkin, O.T. | 2992 | 107 | 27.96 | 5- 24 | 2 | – | – |
| Parsons, K.A. | 3552 | 84 | 42.28 | 5- 13 | 2 | – | – |
| Patel, M.M. | 14484 | 470 | 30.81 | 8- 96 | 23 | 9 | 3 |
| Patel, P.A. | 9 | 0 | | | | | |
| Pattison, I. | 159 | 4 | 39.75 | 3- 41 | – | – | – |
| Penberthy, A.L. | 8997 | 231 | 38.94 | 5- 37 | 4 | – | – |
| Peng, N. | 2 | 0 | | | | | |
| Penney, T.L. | 184 | 6 | 30.66 | 3- 18 | – | – | – |
| Perera, P.D.R.L. | 3985 | 141 | 28.26 | 7- 40 | 2 | – | – |
| Peters, S.D. | 19 | 1 | 19.00 | 1- 19 | – | – | – |
| Phillips, B.J. | 1955 | 69 | 28.33 | 5- 47 | 2 | – | – |
| Phillips, N.C. | 5561 | 124 | 44.84 | 6- 97 | 4 | 1 | – |
| Phillips, T.J. | 1704 | 32 | 53.25 | 4- 42 | – | – | – |
| Pietersen, K.P. | 1755 | 37 | 47.43 | 4-141 | – | – | – |
| Piper, K.J. | 60 | 1 | 60.00 | 1- 57 | – | – | – |
| Pollock, S.M. | 10694 | 484 | 22.09 | 7- 33 | 20 | 2 | – |
| Porter, J.J. | 206 | 6 | 34.33 | 3- 50 | – | – | – |
| Pothas, N. | 5 | 0 | | | | | |
| Powell, D.B. | 1161 | 47 | 24.70 | 5- 28 | 2 | – | – |
| Powell, M.J. (Gm) | 132 | 2 | 66.00 | 2- 39 | – | – | – |
| Powell, M.J. (Wa) | 534 | 10 | 53.40 | 2- 16 | – | – | – |
| Pratt, G.J. | 12 | 0 | | | | | |
| Pretorius, D. | 3282 | 139 | 23.61 | 6- 49 | 6 | – | – |
| Prittipaul, L.R. | 194 | 3 | 64.66 | 2- 43 | – | – | – |
| Pyemont, J.P. | 743 | 12 | 61.91 | 4-101 | – | – | – |
| Ramprakash, M.R. | 2064 | 32 | 64.50 | 3- 32 | – | – | – |
| Randall, S.J. | 951 | 8 | 118.87 | 2- 64 | – | – | – |
| Ratcliffe, J.D. | 911 | 27 | 33.74 | 6- 48 | 1 | – | – |
| Ratra, A. | 1 | 0 | | | | | |
| Rawnsley, M.J. | 3283 | 74 | 44.36 | 6- 44 | 3 | 1 | – |
| Read, C.M.W. | 25 | 0 | | | | | |
| Rhodes, J.N. | 65 | 1 | 65.00 | 1- 13 | – | – | – |
| Rhodes, S.J. | 30 | 0 | | | | | |
| Richardson, A. | 3573 | 127 | 28.13 | 8- 46 | 4 | 1 | – |
| Roberts, T.W. | 6 | 0 | | | | | |
| Robinson, D.D.J. | 153 | 0 | | | | | |
| Robinson, M.A. | 17807 | 584 | 30.49 | 9- 37 | 13 | 2 | 2 |
| Rollins, A.S. | 122 | 1 | 122.00 | 1- 19 | – | – | – |
| Rose, G.D. | 17963 | 604 | 29.74 | 7- 47 | 15 | 1 | 5 |
| Russell, R.C. | 68 | 1 | 68.00 | 1- 4 | – | – | – |
| Saggers, M.J. | 5446 | 243 | 22.41 | 7- 79 | 13 | – | 3 |
| Sales, D.J.G. | 163 | 9 | 18.11 | 4- 25 | – | – | – |
| Salisbury, I.D.K. | 23280 | 727 | 32.02 | 8- 60 | 34 | 6 | 6 |
| Samaraweera, T.T. | 6265 | 288 | 21.75 | 6- 55 | 14 | 2 | 0+2 |
| Sampson, P.J. | 160 | 7 | 22.85 | 3- 52 | – | – | – |
| Sangakkara, K.C. | 5 | 0 | | | | | |
| Saqlain Mushtaq | 13660 | 637 | 21.44 | 8- 65 | 50 | 13 | 5+1 |

| F-C | Runs | Wkts | Avge | Best | 5wI | 10wM | 50wS |
|---|---|---|---|---|---|---|---|
| Savill, T.E. | 422 | 8 | 52.75 | 2- 42 | – | – | – |
| Sayers, J.J. | 12 | 0 | | | | | |
| Schofield, C.P. | 4626 | 155 | 29.84 | 6-120 | 4 | – | – |
| Schofield, J.E.K. | 477 | 19 | 25.10 | 4- 51 | – | – | – |
| Sehwag, V. | 1761 | 48 | 36.68 | 4- 32 | – | – | – |
| Selwood, S.A. | 67 | 2 | 33.50 | 1- 8 | – | – | – |
| Shafayat, B.M. | 52 | 0 | | | | | |
| Shah, O.A. | 627 | 17 | 36.88 | 3- 33 | – | – | – |
| Shahid Afridi | 3829 | 139 | 27.54 | 6-101 | 5 | – | – |
| Shahid, N. | 2071 | 44 | 47.06 | 3- 91 | – | – | – |
| Sharif, F.I. | 180 | 1 | 180.00 | 1- 81 | – | – | – |
| Sharif, Z.K. | 187 | 4 | 46.75 | 4- 98 | – | – | – |
| Sharpe, T.J. | 550 | 9 | 61.11 | 3- 70 | – | – | – |
| Shaw, A.D. | 7 | 0 | | | | | |
| Sheikh, M.A. | 838 | 21 | 39.90 | 4- 36 | – | – | – |
| Sheriyar, A. | 12875 | 442 | 29.12 | 7-130 | 21 | 3 | 4 |
| Shoaib Akhtar | 7818 | 273 | 28.63 | 6- 11 | 18 | – | 0+1 |
| Sidebottom, R.J. | 3719 | 144 | 25.82 | 6- 16 | 6 | 1 | – |
| Sillence, R.J. | 549 | 18 | 30.50 | 5- 63 | 2 | – | – |
| Silverwood, C.E.W. | 10513 | 391 | 26.88 | 7- 93 | 18 | 1 | 2 |
| Simmons, L.M.P. | 54 | 6 | 9.00 | 3- 6 | – | – | – |
| Singh, A. | 111 | 0 | | | | | |
| Smethurst, M.P. | 2380 | 85 | 28.00 | 7- 37 | 3 | – | 1 |
| Smith, A.M. | 12133 | 487 | 24.91 | 8- 73 | 21 | 5 | 5 |
| Smith, B.F. | 350 | 3 | 116.66 | 1- 5 | – | – | – |
| Smith, E.T. | 45 | 0 | | | | | |
| Smith, G.J. | 8531 | 304 | 28.06 | 8- 53 | 10 | 2 | 1 |
| Smith, N.M.K. | 13560 | 370 | 36.64 | 7- 42 | 18 | – | – |
| Smith, R.A. | 993 | 14 | 70.92 | 2- 11 | – | – | – |
| Snape, J.N. | 4559 | 97 | 47.00 | 5- 65 | 1 | – | – |
| Solanki, V.S. | 3300 | 72 | 45.83 | 5- 69 | 3 | 1 | – |
| Souter, M.A. | 83 | 1 | 83.00 | 1- 54 | – | – | – |
| Spearman, C.M. | 55 | 1 | 55.00 | 1- 37 | – | – | – |
| Spires, J.A.S. | 768 | 20 | 38.40 | 5-165 | 1 | – | – |
| Srinath, J. | 13674 | 523 | 26.14 | 9- 76 | 23 | 3 | 1 |
| Stemp, R.D. | 13554 | 385 | 35.20 | 6- 37 | 14 | 1 | – |
| Stephenson, J.P. | 12335 | 380 | 32.46 | 7- 44 | 11 | 1 | – |
| Stevens, D.I. | 254 | 2 | 127.00 | 1- 5 | – | – | – |
| Stewart, A.J. | 423 | 3 | 141.00 | 1- 7 | – | – | – |
| Strauss, A.J. | 16 | 0 | | | | | |
| Stubbings, S.D. | 77 | 0 | | | | | |
| Suppiah, A.V. | 55 | 3 | 18.33 | 3- 46 | – | – | – |
| Sutcliffe, I.J. | 318 | 8 | 39.75 | 2- 21 | – | – | – |
| Swann, A.J. | 286 | 5 | 57.20 | 2- 30 | – | – | – |
| Swann, G.P. | 7032 | 221 | 31.81 | 6- 41 | 9 | 2 | 1 |
| Symington, M.J. | 805 | 24 | 33.54 | 4- 27 | – | – | – |
| Symonds, A. | 4796 | 126 | 38.06 | 6-105 | 1 | – | – |
| Taylor, B.V. | 1812 | 48 | 37.75 | 5- 90 | 1 | – | – |
| Taylor, C.G. | 172 | 3 | 57.33 | 3-126 | – | – | – |
| Tendulkar, S.R. | 2993 | 51 | 58.68 | 3- 10 | – | – | – |
| Thomas, I.J. | 32 | 1 | 32.00 | 1- 26 | – | – | – |
| Thomas, S.D. | 13867 | 448 | 30.95 | 8- 50 | 18 | 1 | 5 |
| Thorburn, M. | 403 | 9 | 44.77 | 2- 50 | – | – | – |
| Thornicroft, N.D. | 248 | 4 | 62.00 | 2- 51 | – | – | – |
| Thorpe, A.M. | 32 | 0 | | | | | |
| Thorpe, G.P. | 1305 | 25 | 52.20 | 4- 40 | – | – | – |

| F-C | Runs | Wkts | Avge | Best | 5wI | 10wM | 50wS |
|---|---|---|---|---|---|---|---|
| Tillekeratne, H.P. | 1280 | 39 | 32.82 | 4- 37 | – | – | – |
| Tomlinson, J.A. | 748 | 12 | 62.33 | 2- 55 | – | – | – |
| Tournier, M.A. | 309 | 9 | 34.33 | 5- 88 | 1 | – | – |
| Tredwell, J.C. | 481 | 12 | 40.08 | 4-103 | – | – | – |
| Trego, P.D. | 1203 | 27 | 44.55 | 4- 84 | – | – | – |
| Tremlett, C.T. | 1553 | 62 | 25.04 | 5- 57 | 2 | – | – |
| Trescothick, M.E. | 1438 | 36 | 39.94 | 4- 36 | – | – | – |
| Trott, B.J. | 1812 | 65 | 27.87 | 6- 13 | 4 | 1 | – |
| Trott, I.J.L. | 220 | 4 | 55.00 | 1- 10 | – | – | – |
| Troughton, J.O. | 106 | 0 | | | | | |
| Tudor, A.J. | 6996 | 261 | 26.80 | 7- 48 | 13 | – | – |
| Tufnell, P.C.R. | 31026 | 1057 | 29.35 | 8- 29 | 53 | 6 | 9 |
| Turner, R.J. | 58 | 0 | | | | | |
| Udal, S.D. | 19105 | 562 | 33.99 | 8- 50 | 29 | 4 | 7 |
| Upashantha, K.E.A. | 6966 | 274 | 25.42 | 8- 65 | 6 | – | 0+1 |
| Vaas, W.P.U.C.J. | 9141 | 373 | 24.50 | 7- 71 | 16 | 2 | 0+2 |
| Van der Gucht, C.G. | 138 | 4 | 34.50 | 3- 75 | – | – | – |
| Vaughan, M.P. | 4910 | 112 | 43.83 | 4- 39 | – | – | – |
| Vonwiller, B.M. | 217 | 5 | 43.40 | 2- 59 | – | – | – |
| Wagg, G.G. | 343 | 12 | 28.58 | 4- 43 | – | – | – |
| Wagh, M.A. | 2803 | 58 | 48.32 | 5-137 | 1 | – | – |
| Walker, G.W. | 50 | 0 | | | | | |
| Walker, M.J. | 488 | 8 | 61.00 | 1- 3 | – | – | – |
| Wanasinghe, W.M.P.N. | 4443 | 169 | 26.28 | 6- 36 | 6 | – | – |
| Ward, D.M. | 113 | 2 | 56.50 | 2- 66 | – | – | – |
| Ward, I.J. | 121 | 3 | 40.33 | 1- 1 | – | – | – |
| Ward, T.R. | 694 | 9 | 77.11 | 2- 10 | – | – | – |
| Warren, N.A. | 90 | 2 | 45.00 | 2- 48 | – | – | – |
| Warren, R.J. | 0 | 0 | | | | | |
| Waugh, M.E. | 8208 | 208 | 39.46 | 6- 68 | 3 | – | – |
| Waugh, S.R. | 7814 | 243 | 32.15 | 6- 51 | 5 | – | – |
| Weekes, P.N. | 9135 | 224 | 40.78 | 8- 39 | 4 | – | – |
| Welch, G. | 9276 | 283 | 32.77 | 6- 30 | 9 | 1 | 2 |
| Wells, V.J. | 7405 | 280 | 26.44 | 5- 18 | 5 | – | – |
| Welton, G.E. | 5 | 0 | | | | | |
| Weston, R.M.S. | 104 | 2 | 52.00 | 1- 15 | – | – | – |
| Weston, W.P.C. | 640 | 4 | 160.00 | 2- 39 | – | – | – |
| Wharf, A.G. | 3657 | 109 | 33.55 | 5- 63 | 2 | – | – |
| Wharton, L.J. | 1803 | 45 | 40.06 | 6- 62 | 3 | – | – |
| Whiley, M.J.A. | 1235 | 20 | 61.75 | 3- 60 | – | – | – |
| White, C. | 10067 | 362 | 27.80 | 8- 55 | 10 | – | – |
| White, G.W. | 629 | 12 | 52.41 | 3- 23 | – | – | – |
| White, R.A. | 98 | 5 | 19.60 | 2- 30 | – | – | – |
| Wigley, D.H. | 116 | 1 | 116.00 | 1- 71 | – | – | – |
| Windows, M.G.N. | 131 | 2 | 65.50 | 1- 6 | – | – | – |
| Wood, J. | 9690 | 287 | 33.76 | 7- 58 | 11 | – | 1 |
| Wood, M.J. (Sm) | 30 | 0 | | | | | |
| Wood, M.J. (Y) | 16 | 0 | | | | | |
| Wyatt, A.A. | 181 | 2 | 90.50 | 1- 33 | – | – | – |
| Yardy, M.H. | 376 | 3 | 125.33 | 1- 13 | – | – | – |
| Yates, G. | 7025 | 184 | 38.17 | 6- 64 | 5 | – | – |
| Yohannan, T. | 1514 | 40 | 37.85 | 6-117 | 2 | – | – |
| Zoysa, D.N.T. | 3352 | 123 | 27.25 | 7- 58 | 2 | – | – |

# LEADING CURRENT PLAYERS

The leading career batting/bowling averages and wicket-keeping/fielding aggregates among players currently registered for first-class county cricket. All figures are to the end of the 2002 English season.

## BATTING

(Qualification: 100 innings)

| | Runs | Avge |
|---|---|---|
| A.Flower | 10385 | 54.37 |
| G.A.Hick | 35246 | 53.72 |
| M.E.K.Hussey | 9500 | 50.53 |
| S.G.Law | 19122 | 49.66 |
| M.T.G.Elliott | 11503 | 49.58 |
| S.M.Katich | 5383 | 48.93 |
| M.L.Love | 9412 | 48.26 |
| J.P.Crawley | 17660 | 47.47 |
| M.R.Ramprakash | 21779 | 46.23 |
| A.Habib | 6650 | 44.63 |
| J.Cox | 15294 | 44.58 |
| M.W.Goodwin | 6936 | 44.46 |
| G.P.Thorpe | 18625 | 44.45 |
| N.V.Knight | 11544 | 43.89 |
| A.D.Brown | 10567 | 43.84 |
| M.P.Maynard | 22576 | 42.43 |
| M.J.Di Venuto | 10566 | 41.92 |
| N.Hussain | 18555 | 41.88 |
| R.A.Smith | 25633 | 41.61 |
| S.P.James | 15875 | 40.809 |
| A.Symonds | 9141 | 40.808 |
| I.J.Ward | 6067 | 40.44 |
| P.D.Bowler | 18056 | 40.30 |
| A.J.Hollioake | 8276 | 40.17 |
| A.J.Stewart | 25085 | 39.94 |
| T.L.Penney | 7954 | 39.57 |
| B.J.Hodge | 5930 | 39.53 |
| B.F.Smith | 11449 | 39.47 |
| J.N.Rhodes | 8167 | 39.26 |
| A.J.Strauss | 3909 | 39.09 |
| M.J.Powell (Gm) | 4862 | 38.89 |
| M.A.Butcher | 11772 | 38.85 |
| D.J.Bicknell | 15842 | 38.54 |
| S.G.Koenig | 5893 | 38.51 |

## BOWLING

(Qualification: 100 wickets)

| | Wkts | Avge |
|---|---|---|
| A.Nel | 130 | 20.00 |
| Saqlain Mushtaq | 637 | 21.44 |
| M.J.Saggers | 243 | 22.41 |
| K.J.Dean | 291 | 22.94 |
| Azhar Mahmood | 295 | 23.55 |
| D.Pretorius | 139 | 23.61 |
| M.P.Bicknell | 932 | 24.40 |
| P.M.Hutchison | 161 | 24.54 |
| A.R.Caddick | 863 | 24.71 |
| R.J.Kirtley | 403 | 24.90 |
| A.M.Smith | 487 | 24.91 |
| M.W.H.Inness | 163 | 24.93 |
| M.J.Hoggard | 262 | 24.96 |
| G.M.Hamilton | 239 | 25.38 |
| Harbhajan Singh | 314 | 25.54 |
| R.J.Sidebottom | 144 | 25.82 |
| A.J.Hall | 123 | 26.11 |
| D.G.Cork | 672 | 26.14 |
| Mushtaq Ahmed | 872 | 26.17 |
| A.C.Morris | 156 | 26.40 |
| V.J.Wells | 280 | 26.44 |
| D.Gough | 707 | 26.46 |
| R.L.Johnson | 384 | 26.51 |
| S.E.Bond | 101 | 26.663 |
| M.S.Kasprowicz | 654 | 26.668 |
| J.D.Lewry | 363 | 26.76 |
| A.J.Tudor | 261 | 26.80 |
| Ali, Kabir | 108 | 26.87 |
| C.E.W.Silverwood | 391 | 26.88 |
| I.J.Harvey | 295 | 26.98 |
| P.J.Martin | 555 | 27.14 |
| P.J.Franks | 265 | 27.34 |
| N.A.M.McLean | 330 | 27.38 |
| J.Lewis | 338 | 27.47 |
| C.L.Cairns | 597 | 27.49 |

## WICKET-KEEPING

| | Total | Ct | St |
|---|---|---|---|
| R.C.Russell | 1282 | 1158 | 124 |
| S.J.Rhodes | 1175 | 1057 | 118 |
| W.K.Hegg | 828 | 747 | 81 |
| R.J.Blakey | 802 | 746 | 56 |
| A.J.Stewart | 700 | 669 | 31 |
| P.A.Nixon | 669 | 619 | 50 |
| R.J.Turner | 595 | 555 | 40 |
| K.M.Krikken | 556 | 525 | 31 |
| K.J.Piper | 523 | 490 | 33 |

## FIELDING

| | Ct |
|---|---|
| G.A.Hick | 552 |
| M.P.Maynard | 346 |
| N.Hussain | 331 |
| S.G.Law | 292 |
| C.J.Adams | 281 |
| M.W.Alleyne | 258 |
| D.P.Ostler | 256 |

# LIMITED-OVERS CAREER RECORDS
Compiled by **PHILIP BAILEY**

The following career records, to the end of the 2002 season, include all players currently registered with first-class counties. These records are restricted to performances in limited-overs matches of 'List A' status as defined by the Association of Cricket Statisticians and Historians. The following matches qualify for List A status and are included in the figures that follow: Limited-Overs Internationals; Other international matches (e.g. Commonwealth Games, 'A' team internationals); Premier domestic limited-overs tournaments in Test status countries; Official tourist matches against the main first-class teams.

The following matches do not qualify for inclusion: World Cup warm-up games; Tourist matches against first-class teams outside the major domestic competitions (e.g. Universities, Minor Counties, etc.); Festival and pre-season friendly games.

| | M | Runs | Avge | HS | 100 | 50 | Wkts | Avge | Best | Ct/St |
|---|---|---|---|---|---|---|---|---|---|---|
| Abdul Razzaq | 145 | 2465 | 25.41 | 87* | – | 13 | 194 | 26.00 | 6-35 | 20 |
| Adams, C.J. | 274 | 8652 | 39.68 | 163 | 16 | 55 | 32 | 37.93 | 5-16 | 135 |
| Adams, J.H.K. | 3 | 28 | 9.33 | 17 | – | – | 0 | – | – | 2 |
| Afzaal, U. | 81 | 2086 | 36.59 | 95* | – | 17 | 31 | 27.12 | 3- 8 | 20 |
| Agarkar, A.B. | 134 | 970 | 17.96 | 67* | – | 1 | 211 | 26.47 | 4-25 | 43 |
| Aldred, P. | 83 | 367 | 11.83 | 39* | – | – | 94 | 29.47 | 4-30 | 14 |
| Ali, Kabir | 54 | 188 | 9.89 | 27 | – | – | 82 | 20.81 | 5-36 | 10 |
| Ali, Kadeer | 5 | 181 | 36.20 | 66 | – | 2 | 0 | – | – | – |
| Ali, S.M.B | 28 | 72 | 8.00 | 19 | – | – | 31 | 31.77 | 4-34 | 5 |
| Allen, A.P.W. | 1 | 10 | 10.00 | 10 | – | – | – | – | – | 1 |
| Alleyne, D. | 22 | 234 | 11.70 | 58 | – | 1 | – | – | – | 19/6 |
| Alleyne, M.W. | 390 | 7828 | 28.05 | 134* | 5 | 33 | 365 | 29.54 | 5-27 | 161/1 |
| Ambrose, T.R. | 26 | 621 | 27.00 | 95 | – | 5 | – | – | – | 23/3 |
| Amin, R.M. | 4 | 0 | – | 0* | – | – | 2 | 48.50 | 2-43 | – |
| Anderson, J.M. | 5 | 5 | – | 5* | – | – | 9 | 23.77 | 3-42 | 1 |
| Anderson, R.S.G. | 26 | 110 | 7.33 | 22 | – | – | 21 | 44.04 | 3-28 | 1 |
| Angel, J. | 82 | 107 | 8.23 | 19* | – | – | 96 | 29.30 | 5-16 | 7 |
| Atri, V. | 1 | 0 | 0.00 | 0 | – | – | – | – | – | – |
| Averis, J.M.M. | 92 | 262 | 10.07 | 23* | – | – | 139 | 23.41 | 5-20 | 13 |
| Aymes, A.N. | 221 | 2210 | 23.26 | 73* | – | 6 | – | – | – | 215/53 |
| Azhar Mahmood | 176 | 1983 | 18.88 | 100* | 1 | 5 | 171 | 34.26 | 6-18 | 58 |
| Bailey, T.M.B. | 49 | 418 | 19.00 | 52 | – | 1 | – | – | – | 46/21 |
| Baker, T.M. | 6 | 66 | 33.00 | 63 | – | 1 | 5 | 38.80 | 2-13 | 3 |
| Ball, M.C.J. | 220 | 1472 | 13.75 | 51 | – | 1 | 202 | 33.11 | 5-42 | 101 |
| Banes, M.J. | 2 | 106 | 53.00 | 82 | – | 1 | 1 | 11.00 | 1-11 | 2 |
| Barnett, K.J. | 522 | 15520 | 35.03 | 136 | 17 | 92 | 112 | 25.97 | 6-24 | 173 |
| Bassano, C.W.G. | 25 | 458 | 21.80 | 61 | – | 2 | – | – | – | 5 |
| Batty, G.J. | 49 | 733 | 22.21 | 83* | – | 4 | 32 | 38.59 | 4-36 | 18 |
| Batty, J.N. | 80 | 546 | 13.00 | 40 | – | – | – | – | – | 77/12 |
| Bell, I.R. | 26 | 828 | 37.63 | 86 | – | 7 | 0 | – | – | 8 |
| Benning, J.G.E. | 3 | 53 | 17.66 | 23 | – | – | 3 | 28.00 | 2-58 | 1 |
| Betts, M.M. | 75 | 303 | 10.10 | 21 | – | – | 89 | 30.48 | 4-22 | 12 |
| Bevan, M.G. | 349 | 12686 | 59.00 | 157* | 12 | 99 | 93 | 33.07 | 5-29 | 110 |
| Bichel, A.J. | 122 | 1203 | 20.74 | 100 | 1 | 2 | 162 | 26.58 | 5-19 | 40 |
| Bicknell, D.J. | 222 | 7268 | 38.45 | 135* | 10 | 50 | 3 | 27.33 | 1-11 | 54 |
| Bicknell, M.P. | 307 | 1432 | 15.56 | 66* | – | 1 | 402 | 24.56 | 7-30 | 72 |
| Bishop, J.E. | 21 | 57 | 6.33 | 16* | – | – | 24 | 28.16 | 3-33 | 3 |
| Blackwell, I.D. | 101 | 2043 | 24.32 | 97 | – | 14 | 70 | 34.28 | 4-24 | 29 |
| Blain, J.A.R. | 24 | 50 | 7.14 | 11 | – | – | 39 | 26.56 | 5-24 | 5 |
| Blakey, R.J. | 360 | 7363 | 32.01 | 130* | 3 | 37 | – | – | – | 352/55 |
| Bloomfield, T.F. | 49 | 67 | 6.70 | 15 | – | – | 43 | 36.11 | 4-17 | 10 |
| Boje, N. | 178 | 2460 | 27.03 | 129 | 2 | 9 | 167 | 31.90 | 5-21 | 55 |
| Bond, S.E. | 36 | 179 | 17.90 | 30* | – | – | 48 | 26.83 | 5-25 | 7 |
| Bopara, R.S. | 3 | 1 | 0.33 | 1 | – | – | – | – | – | – |
| Bowler, P.D. | 318 | 9246 | 31.99 | 138* | 7 | 71 | 13 | 40.84 | 3-31 | 119/2 |

| L-O | M | Runs | Avge | HS | 100 | 50 | Wkts | Avge | Best | Ct/St |
|---|---|---|---|---|---|---|---|---|---|---|
| Brandy, D.G. | 2 | 50 | 25.00 | 35 | – | – | – | – | – | – |
| Brant, S.A. | 1 | – | – | – | – | – | 1 | 33.00 | 1-33 | 1 |
| Bresnan, T.T. | 25 | 88 | 12.57 | 22 | – | – | 18 | 35.27 | 2-27 | 4 |
| Bressington, A.N. | 8 | 141 | 23.50 | 54 | – | 1 | 8 | 32.25 | 3-21 | 5 |
| Bridge, G.D. | 28 | 240 | 20.00 | 50* | – | 1 | 29 | 31.48 | 3-22 | 6 |
| Brignull, D.S. | 3 | 16 | 8.00 | 9* | – | – | 6 | 22.83 | 2-35 | 1 |
| Brophy, G.L. | 26 | 337 | 19.82 | 54 | – | 2 | – | – | – | 24/4 |
| Brown, A.D. | 287 | 8402 | 31.94 | 268 | 16 | 34 | 9 | 34.00 | 3-39 | 90 |
| Brown, D.R. | 221 | 3450 | 21.97 | 82* | – | 20 | 256 | 26.27 | 5-31 | 55 |
| Brown, J.F. | 56 | 55 | 5.50 | 16 | – | – | 53 | 35.60 | 4-26 | 9 |
| Brown, M.J. | 1 | 18 | 18.00 | 18 | – | – | – | – | – | – |
| Brown, S.J.E. | 113 | 217 | 6.57 | 18 | – | – | 132 | 30.77 | 6-30 | 23 |
| Brunnschweiler, I. | 3 | 37 | 18.50 | 37 | – | – | – | – | – | 5 |
| Bryant, J.D.C. | 43 | 1331 | 38.02 | 105* | 1 | 10 | – | – | – | 13 |
| Bulbeck, M.P.L. | 31 | 117 | 10.63 | 24* | – | – | 35 | 29.34 | 5-18 | 5 |
| Burns, M. | 176 | 3843 | 26.14 | 115* | 2 | 26 | 51 | 28.47 | 4-39 | 74/12 |
| Burns, N.D. | 231 | 2799 | 20.28 | 90* | – | 8 | – | – | – | 238/48 |
| Butcher, G.P. | 68 | 693 | 16.50 | 48 | – | – | 28 | 47.17 | 4-32 | 6 |
| Butcher, M.A. | 148 | 2948 | 27.81 | 91 | – | 17 | 49 | 44.79 | 3-23 | 47 |
| Byas, D. | 332 | 8116 | 28.67 | 116* | 5 | 46 | 25 | 26.36 | 3-19 | 139 |
| Caddick, A.R. | 202 | 615 | 9.91 | 39 | – | – | 263 | 25.95 | 6-30 | 32 |
| Cairns, C.L. | 314 | 7768 | 31.70 | 143 | 9 | 39 | 360 | 27.01 | 6-37 | 89 |
| Carberry, M.A. | 12 | 91 | 9.10 | 20 | – | – | – | – | – | 5 |
| Carpenter, J.R. | 57 | 827 | 22.97 | 64* | – | 5 | 0 | – | – | 29 |
| Carter, N.M. | 40 | 203 | 10.68 | 40 | – | – | 60 | 23.61 | 5-31 | 6 |
| Cassar, M.E. | 68 | 1695 | 28.72 | 134 | 4 | 8 | 34 | 33.79 | 4-29 | 19 |
| Catterall, D.N. | 14 | 49 | 9.80 | 21* | – | – | 5 | 70.60 | 2-35 | 3 |
| Cawdron, M.J. | 60 | 303 | 14.42 | 50 | – | 1 | 60 | 32.65 | 4-17 | 6 |
| Chapple, G. | 182 | 904 | 13.10 | 81* | – | 4 | 197 | 30.00 | 6-18 | 37 |
| Chilton, M.J. | 70 | 1675 | 28.38 | 102 | 2 | 8 | 26 | 25.26 | 5-26 | 18 |
| Clapp, D.A. | 3 | 57 | 19.00 | 43 | – | – | 3 | 15.33 | 3-46 | – |
| Clarke, A.J. | 25 | 22 | 3.14 | 9 | – | – | 31 | 23.09 | 4-30 | 6 |
| Clarke, R. | 18 | 388 | 25.86 | 98* | – | 4 | 10 | 43.50 | 2-32 | 7 |
| Clifford, J.I. | 5 | 9 | 4.50 | 5* | – | – | – | – | – | 7/1 |
| Clinton, R.S. | 13 | 153 | 21.85 | 56 | – | 1 | 0 | – | – | 2 |
| Clough, G.D. | 27 | 98 | 9.80 | 24 | – | – | 22 | 38.95 | 2-33 | 7 |
| Coleman, A.J. | 4 | 29 | – | 14* | – | – | 0 | – | – | 2 |
| Collingwood, P.D. | 152 | 3584 | 28.44 | 118* | 1 | 22 | 89 | 34.02 | 4-31 | 68 |
| Compton, N.R.D. | 5 | 129 | 64.50 | 86* | – | 1 | – | – | – | – |
| Cook, J.W. | 56 | 1276 | 26.04 | 130 | 2 | 5 | 30 | 23.23 | 4-35 | 18 |
| Cook, S.J. | 67 | 574 | 13.34 | 50 | – | 1 | 72 | 30.59 | 3-16 | 10 |
| Cork, D.G. | 202 | 2886 | 21.06 | 93 | – | 16 | 256 | 27.41 | 6-21 | 79 |
| Cosker, D.A. | 92 | 235 | 8.10 | 27* | – | – | 101 | 30.29 | 4-17 | 29 |
| Cottey, P.A. | 256 | 4559 | 24.51 | 96 | – | 26 | 21 | 37.14 | 4-56 | 84 |
| Cousins, D.M. | 95 | 190 | 7.91 | 21 | – | – | 120 | 26.07 | 5-22 | 20 |
| Cowan, A.P. | 135 | 976 | 13.94 | 45 | – | – | 167 | 27.59 | 5-14 | 45 |
| Cox, J. | 147 | 4357 | 31.57 | 114 | 3 | 32 | 4 | 36.00 | 3-28 | 53 |
| Craven, V.J. | 16 | 275 | 17.18 | 59 | – | 2 | 1 | 21.00 | 1-21 | 7 |
| Crawley, J.P. | 221 | 5952 | 30.36 | 114 | 5 | 35 | 0 | – | – | 61/4 |
| Creese, M.L. | 2 | 47 | 23.50 | 34 | – | – | 2 | 39.50 | 2-35 | – |
| Croft, R.D.B. | 306 | 4394 | 22.76 | 119 | 2 | 19 | 317 | 31.61 | 6-20 | 75 |
| Crowe, C.D. | 33 | 151 | 16.77 | 23* | – | – | 29 | 30.58 | 4-30 | 5 |
| Cunliffe, R.J. | 91 | 1983 | 27.16 | 137* | 3 | 11 | – | – | – | 25 |
| Currie, M.R. | 3 | 118 | 39.33 | 94 | – | 1 | – | – | – | 1 |
| Dagnall, C.E. | 26 | 89 | 14.83 | 28 | – | – | 36 | 21.77 | 4-34 | 2 |
| Dakin, J.M. | 164 | 2403 | 20.36 | 179 | 2 | 2 | 133 | 29.39 | 5-30 | 33 |
| Dale, A. | 281 | 6238 | 29.01 | 110 | 2 | 31 | 237 | 30.99 | 6-22 | 59 |
| Daley, J.A. | 68 | 1639 | 30.92 | 105 | 1 | 10 | 0 | – | – | 11 |

173

| L-O | M | Runs | Avge | HS | 100 | 50 | Wkts | Avge | Best | Ct/St |
|---|---|---|---|---|---|---|---|---|---|---|
| Dalrymple, J.W.M. | 21 | 341 | 24.35 | 52 | – | 1 | 18 | 27.77 | 4-14 | 10 |
| Davies, A.M. | 34 | 117 | 7.31 | 31* | – | – | 35 | 27.42 | 4-13 | 7 |
| Davies, A.P. | 43 | 96 | 12.00 | 24 | – | – | 62 | 24.08 | 5-19 | 6 |
| Davis, M.J.G. | 111 | 515 | 13.91 | 35 | – | – | 98 | 37.95 | 4-24 | 26 |
| Dawes, J.H. | 10 | 1 | – | 1* | – | – | 17 | 21.94 | 3-26 | 1 |
| Dawson, R.K.J. | 36 | 166 | 7.90 | 41 | – | – | 37 | 27.43 | 4-13 | 9 |
| Dean, K.J. | 88 | 187 | 11.00 | 16* | – | – | 104 | 28.60 | 5-32 | 17 |
| DeFreitas, P.A.J. | 448 | 4736 | 18.64 | 75* | – | 11 | 510 | 27.85 | 5-13 | 93 |
| Denning, N.A. | 3 | 1 | – | 1* | – | – | 4 | 29.75 | 3-22 | – |
| Di Venuto, M.J. | 162 | 4632 | 32.16 | 173* | 4 | 25 | 1 | 31.20 | 1-10 | 52 |
| Donald, A.A. | 428 | 521 | 8.14 | 23* | – | – | 649 | 21.45 | 6-15 | 67 |
| Dowman, M.P. | 139 | 2578 | 20.95 | 92 | – | 10 | 58 | 29.94 | 3-21 | 31 |
| Driver, R.C. | 20 | 235 | 13.05 | 61* | – | 2 | 1 | 227.00 | 1-17 | 1 |
| Dumelow, N.R.C. | 20 | 355 | 20.88 | 52 | – | 1 | 19 | 33.57 | 3-24 | 1 |
| Durston, W.J. | 4 | 75 | 18.75 | 50 | – | 1 | 2 | 47.00 | 1-32 | – |
| Dutch, K.P. | 130 | 1598 | 19.25 | 64 | – | 5 | 136 | 26.26 | 6-40 | 53 |
| Ealham, M.A. | 324 | 5166 | 24.95 | 112 | 1 | 22 | 363 | 27.59 | 6-53 | 79 |
| Elliott, M.T.G. | 85 | 2738 | 37.50 | 156 | 9 | 12 | 0 | – | – | 33 |
| Elstub, C.J. | 10 | 6 | – | 4* | – | – | 12 | 24.16 | 4-25 | – |
| Elworthy, S. | 198 | 1929 | 22.17 | 116* | 1 | 6 | 240 | 26.87 | 4-14 | 39 |
| Fairbrother, N.H. | 505 | 14761 | 41.69 | 145 | 9 | 107 | 3 | 64.33 | 1-17 | 185 |
| Farrow, S.J.C. | 2 | – | – | – | – | – | 2 | 54.50 | 2-81 | – |
| Fellows, G.M. | 92 | 1333 | 21.50 | 80* | – | 6 | 22 | 35.68 | 4-19 | 24 |
| Ferley, R.S. | 2 | 6 | 6.00 | 6 | – | – | 3 | 14.33 | 3-20 | – |
| Fisher, I.D. | 31 | 78 | 7.09 | 20 | – | – | 32 | 25.59 | 3-20 | 6 |
| Flanagan, I.N. | 2 | 48 | 24.00 | 45 | – | – | 0 | – | – | – |
| Fleming, D.W. | 150 | 320 | 11.42 | 29 | – | – | 214 | 25.53 | 5-24 | 26 |
| Fleming, M.V. | 314 | 6161 | 24.74 | 125 | 4 | 28 | 377 | 25.71 | 5-27 | 81 |
| Flintoff, A. | 163 | 3627 | 27.27 | 143 | 3 | 20 | 125 | 23.63 | 4-11 | 60 |
| Flower, A. | 283 | 8780 | 35.54 | 142* | 4 | 71 | 0 | – | – | 224/46 |
| Flower, G.W. | 235 | 6886 | 32.32 | 142* | 8 | 40 | 115 | 35.70 | 4-32 | 88 |
| Foster, J.S. | 37 | 387 | 20.36 | 56* | – | 1 | – | – | – | 48/11 |
| Francis, J.D. | 16 | 528 | 48.00 | 103* | 1 | 4 | – | – | – | 3 |
| Francis, S.R.G. | 26 | 111 | 15.85 | 27 | – | – | 21 | 42.47 | 4-60 | 6 |
| Franks, P.J. | 91 | 706 | 19.08 | 60 | – | 1 | 123 | 26.28 | 6-27 | 12 |
| Fraser, A.R.C. | 336 | 865 | 11.68 | 38* | – | – | 392 | 26.49 | 5-32 | 56 |
| Frost, T. | 37 | 146 | 13.27 | 22* | – | – | – | – | – | 32/4 |
| Fulton, D.P. | 68 | 1322 | 20.33 | 82 | – | 5 | 0 | – | – | 36 |
| Gait, A.I. | 20 | 517 | 27.21 | 138* | 1 | 1 | – | – | – | 4 |
| Gallian, J.E.R. | 164 | 4678 | 31.82 | 134 | 7 | 27 | 52 | 32.75 | 5-15 | 55 |
| Gannon, B.W. | 2 | 3 | 3.00 | 2 | – | – | 3 | 23.66 | 2-29 | – |
| Gazzard, C.M. | 1 | 16 | 16.00 | 16 | – | – | – | – | – | 2 |
| Giddins, E.S.H. | 187 | 107 | 2.74 | 13* | – | – | 223 | 28.14 | 5-20 | 35 |
| Gidman, A.P.R. | 19 | 251 | 17.92 | 48 | – | – | 5 | 46.80 | 3-46 | 5 |
| Giles, A.F. | 166 | 1569 | 19.61 | 107 | 1 | 3 | 216 | 23.47 | 5-21 | 49 |
| Golding, J.M. | 39 | 373 | 19.63 | 47* | – | – | 46 | 25.54 | 4-42 | 8 |
| Goodwin, M.W. | 164 | 4808 | 32.93 | 167 | 6 | 30 | 4 | 43.71 | 1- 9 | 48 |
| Gough, D. | 296 | 1555 | 12.74 | 72* | – | 1 | 430 | 24.00 | 7-27 | 52 |
| Gough, M.A. | 45 | 922 | 24.91 | 132 | 1 | 3 | 19 | 42.52 | 3-26 | 12 |
| Grant, J.B. | 18 | 38 | 9.50 | 14 | – | – | 17 | 30.00 | 3-10 | 4 |
| Gray, A.K.D. | 10 | 45 | 9.00 | 19* | – | – | 9 | 25.55 | 4-34 | 1 |
| Grayson, A.P. | 222 | 3000 | 19.86 | 82* | – | 9 | 199 | 31.86 | 4-25 | 62 |
| Green, J.A.G. | 1 | 7 | 7.00 | 7 | – | – | – | – | – | 1 |
| Greenidge, C.G. | 34 | 66 | 6.00 | 20 | – | – | 32 | 38.03 | 3-22 | 11 |
| Grove, J.O. | 36 | 42 | 5.25 | 13 | – | – | 38 | 32.71 | 4-36 | 8 |
| Gunter, N.E.L. | 3 | 5 | 2.50 | 5 | – | – | 0 | – | – | – |
| Guy, S.M. | 1 | 13 | 13.00 | 13 | – | – | – | – | – | – |
| Habib, A. | 140 | 2620 | 26.73 | 111 | 1 | 11 | 2 | 7.50 | 2- 5 | 51 |

**L-O**

| | M | Runs | Avge | HS | 100 | 50 | Wkts | Avge | Best | Ct/St |
|---|---|---|---|---|---|---|---|---|---|---|
| Hall, A.J. | 94 | 2189 | 33.16 | 129* | 1 | 13 | 82 | 30.80 | 4-33 | 24 |
| Hamblin, J.R.C. | 25 | 261 | 15.35 | 61 | – | 1 | 21 | 35.28 | 4-29 | 7 |
| Hamilton, G.M. | 108 | 1281 | 22.87 | 76 | – | 4 | 128 | 24.42 | 5-16 | 16 |
| Hancock, T.H.C. | 193 | 3678 | 21.26 | 110 | – | 16 | 47 | 24.72 | 6-58 | 62 |
| Harbhajan Singh | 77 | 423 | 13.21 | 46 | – | – | 105 | 26.69 | 5-43 | 30 |
| Hardinges, M.A. | 23 | 238 | 14.00 | 65 | – | 1 | 17 | 34.47 | 4-19 | 8 |
| Harmison, S.J. | 41 | 48 | 4.36 | 11* | – | – | 40 | 38.07 | 4-43 | 5 |
| Harris, A.J. | 104 | 150 | 6.25 | 16* | – | – | 133 | 29.88 | 5-35 | 22 |
| Harrison, D.S. | 8 | 66 | 22.00 | 37* | – | – | 9 | 31.22 | 5-26 | 2 |
| Harrity, M.A. | 37 | 13 | 4.33 | 6 | – | – | 59 | 23.71 | 5-42 | 8 |
| Harvey, I.J. | 187 | 3538 | 24.06 | 92 | – | 18 | 300 | 20.33 | 5-19 | 57 |
| Hatch, N.G. | 11 | 38 | 19.00 | 20* | – | – | 14 | 27.14 | 3-26 | 2 |
| Haynes, J.J. | 12 | 120 | 24.00 | 59* | – | 1 | – | – | – | 16/3 |
| Hayward, M. | 76 | 103 | 9.36 | 19* | – | – | 110 | 26.95 | 5-37 | 15 |
| Hegg, W.K. | 357 | 2917 | 20.83 | 81 | – | 5 | – | – | – | 398/54 |
| Hemp, D.L. | 177 | 3589 | 24.92 | 121 | 5 | 17 | 8 | 20.87 | 4-32 | 64 |
| Hewitt, J.P. | 78 | 326 | 11.64 | 32* | – | – | 69 | 33.66 | 4-24 | 24 |
| Hewson, D.R. | 44 | 731 | 20.30 | 64 | – | 3 | 0 | – | – | 11 |
| Hick, G.A. | 552 | 19349 | 42.61 | 172* | 36 | 125 | 224 | 29.17 | 5-19 | 256 |
| Hockley, J.B. | 57 | 1329 | 26.58 | 121 | 1 | 6 | 1 | 35.00 | 1-35 | 20 |
| Hodd, A.J. | 2 | 4 | 2.00 | 3 | – | – | – | – | – | 3 |
| Hodge, B.J. | 74 | 2330 | 36.40 | 118* | 2 | 17 | 9 | 46.22 | 2-25 | 29 |
| Hodgkinson, R. | 1 | – | – | – | – | – | 2 | 18.00 | 2-36 | – |
| Hogg, K.W. | 22 | 109 | 15.57 | 24 | – | – | 27 | 19.81 | 4-20 | 6 |
| Hoggard, M.J. | 87 | 39 | 3.00 | 7* | – | – | 135 | 21.69 | 5-28 | 11 |
| Hollioake, A.J. | 251 | 5157 | 28.18 | 117* | 2 | 25 | 315 | 23.13 | 5-29 | 80 |
| Holloway, P.C.L. | 133 | 2751 | 27.51 | 117 | 3 | 17 | – | – | – | 53/8 |
| Hopkinson, C.D. | 7 | 91 | 18.20 | 43 | – | – | 2 | 53.00 | 1- 2 | 7 |
| House, W.J. | 97 | 1501 | 20.01 | 93 | – | 3 | 31 | 30.06 | 5-58 | 22 |
| Hughes, J. | 1 | 9 | 9.00 | 9 | – | – | – | – | – | – |
| Hunkin, C.A. | 4 | 31 | 15.50 | 21* | – | – | 3 | 56.66 | 2-43 | 1 |
| Hunt, T.A. | 4 | 0 | 0.00 | 0 | – | – | 2 | 56.00 | 1-24 | 1 |
| Hunter, I.D. | 46 | 213 | 9.26 | 39 | – | – | 50 | 31.66 | 4-29 | 10 |
| Hussain, N. | 334 | 9680 | 36.25 | 136* | 8 | 67 | – | – | – | 153 |
| Hussey, M.E.K. | 94 | 3368 | 43.74 | 114* | 4 | 26 | 7 | 19.28 | 3-52 | 45 |
| Hutchison, P.M. | 37 | 31 | 5.16 | 12 | – | – | 48 | 20.60 | 4-34 | 7 |
| Hutton, B.L. | 49 | 765 | 21.85 | 77 | – | 5 | 27 | 32.48 | 5-45 | 22 |
| Hyam, B.J. | 45 | 356 | 13.69 | 37 | – | – | – | – | – | 33/6 |
| Ilott, M.C. | 185 | 797 | 12.07 | 56* | – | 2 | 232 | 26.39 | 5-21 | 31 |
| Innes, K.J. | 73 | 707 | 22.80 | 55 | – | 2 | 68 | 32.20 | 4-26 | 19 |
| Inness, M.W.H. | 14 | 4 | 2.00 | 2* | – | – | 9 | 54.33 | 2-28 | 2 |
| Irani, R.C. | 230 | 5265 | 29.91 | 124 | 3 | 31 | 286 | 24.71 | 5-26 | 58 |
| James, S.P. | 238 | 7040 | 34.50 | 135 | 7 | 49 | – | – | – | 60 |
| Jarvis, P.W. | 276 | 1322 | 12.35 | 63 | – | 1 | 399 | 24.22 | 6-27 | 50 |
| Jefferson, W.I. | 17 | 540 | 33.75 | 111* | 2 | 2 | – | – | – | 9 |
| Johnson, N.C. | 210 | 6414 | 36.03 | 146* | 12 | 37 | 150 | 34.48 | 4-19 | 113 |
| Johnson, P. | 385 | 10135 | 31.47 | 167* | 13 | 57 | 1 | 23.00 | 1- 2 | 113 |
| Johnson, R.L. | 138 | 873 | 12.12 | 45* | – | – | 158 | 31.66 | 5-50 | 17 |
| Jones, G.O. | 14 | 200 | 18.18 | 39 | – | – | – | – | – | 3/1 |
| Jones, H.R. | 3 | 88 | 29.33 | 72 | – | 1 | – | – | – | – |
| Jones, I. | 10 | 17 | 8.50 | 6 | – | – | 12 | 25.91 | 3-14 | 4 |
| Jones, P.S. | 103 | 256 | 11.13 | 27 | – | – | 154 | 25.53 | 5-23 | 17 |
| Jones, S.P. | 5 | 17 | 17.00 | 12* | – | – | 1 | 175.00 | 1-39 | – |
| Joyce, E.C. | 39 | 780 | 24.37 | 73 | – | 3 | – | – | – | 12 |
| Kaif, M. | 56 | 2115 | 49.18 | 120 | 1 | 20 | 26 | 25.92 | 4-23 | 22 |
| Kandola, G.S. | 4 | 101 | 33.66 | 53 | – | 1 | – | – | – | – |
| Kasprowicz, M.S. | 140 | 711 | 13.67 | 40 | – | – | 177 | 28.07 | 5-60 | 26 |
| Katich, S.M. | 75 | 2356 | 37.39 | 118 | 2 | 19 | 6 | 30.16 | 3-21 | 32 |

| L-O | M | Runs | Avge | HS | 100 | 50 | Wkts | Avge | Best | Ct/St |
|---|---|---|---|---|---|---|---|---|---|---|
| Keedy, G. | 15 | 13 | 6.50 | 10* | – | – | 15 | 31.93 | 5-30 | 1 |
| Keegan, C.B. | 35 | 130 | 10.83 | 24 | – | – | 52 | 24.80 | 5-17 | 6 |
| Kendall, W.S. | 112 | 1866 | 21.95 | 110* | 1 | 5 | 4 | 48.75 | 2-48 | 48 |
| Kenway, D.A. | 73 | 1764 | 26.72 | 93* | – | 11 | – | – | – | 36/6 |
| Kerr, J.I.D. | 113 | 769 | 13.25 | 65* | – | 2 | 124 | 30.08 | 4-28 | 18 |
| Key, R.W.T. | 76 | 2117 | 32.56 | 114 | 1 | 18 | – | – | – | 11 |
| Khan, A. | 12 | 49 | 7.00 | 21 | – | – | 10 | 43.50 | 2-38 | 3 |
| Khan, R.M. | 1 | 29 | 29.00 | 29 | – | – | – | – | – | – |
| Khan, Z. | 66 | 240 | 12.00 | 32* | – | – | 91 | 29.71 | 4-38 | 17 |
| Killeen, N. | 128 | 447 | 9.12 | 32 | – | – | 179 | 24.50 | 6-31 | 23 |
| Kirby, S.P. | 10 | 6 | 1.50 | 4* | – | – | 10 | 45.10 | 3-35 | 1 |
| Kirtley, R.J. | 125 | 251 | 10.45 | 19* | – | – | 191 | 22.09 | 5-33 | 40 |
| Klusener, L. | 192 | 4438 | 41.09 | 142* | 3 | 24 | 219 | 29.00 | 6-49 | 49 |
| Knight, N.V. | 321 | 9840 | 36.71 | 151 | 19 | 50 | 2 | 44.50 | 1-14 | 133 |
| Koenig, S.G. | 49 | 900 | 19.14 | 116 | 2 | 1 | – | – | – | 8 |
| Krikken, K.M. | 201 | 1671 | 18.77 | 55 | – | 1 | – | – | – | 195/44 |
| Lampitt, S.R. | 301 | 2080 | 18.24 | 54 | – | 1 | 370 | 24.52 | 6-26 | 88 |
| Laney, J.S. | 124 | 2903 | 24.39 | 153 | 2 | 11 | 0 | – | – | 30 |
| Laraman, A.W. | 23 | 133 | 12.09 | 28 | – | – | 33 | 20.45 | 6-42 | 6 |
| Law, D.R. | 146 | 2275 | 21.06 | 82 | – | 6 | 79 | 33.78 | 3-26 | 28 |
| Law, S.G. | 293 | 8642 | 33.62 | 163 | 19 | 37 | 89 | 35.33 | 5-26 | 120 |
| Leatherdale, D.A. | 268 | 4044 | 21.39 | 70* | – | 17 | 131 | 22.66 | 5- 9 | 109 |
| Lee, S. | 145 | 2862 | 28.62 | 115 | 4 | 13 | 162 | 26.45 | 5-33 | 72 |
| Lehmann, D.S. | 274 | 9735 | 44.25 | 191 | 15 | 67 | 100 | 26.30 | 4-26 | 83 |
| Lewis, J. | 99 | 410 | 12.42 | 33* | – | – | 113 | 30.40 | 4-22 | 19 |
| Lewis, J.J.B. | 181 | 3781 | 29.31 | 102 | 1 | 20 | 0 | – | – | 30 |
| Lewry, J.D. | 60 | 150 | 7.14 | 16 | – | – | 76 | 28.17 | 4-29 | 9 |
| Liptrot, C.G. | 8 | 23 | 23.00 | 15* | – | – | 8 | 24.87 | 3-44 | 2 |
| Lloyd, G.D. | 294 | 5994 | 28.67 | 134 | 3 | 29 | 1 | 103.00 | 1-23 | 67 |
| Logan, R.J. | 29 | 108 | 9.00 | 24 | – | – | 32 | 36.71 | 5-24 | 9 |
| Loudon, A.G.R. | 4 | 85 | 28.33 | 53 | – | 1 | 0 | – | – | 4 |
| Love, M.L. | 97 | 2885 | 33.94 | 127* | 3 | 15 | 0 | – | – | 44 |
| Loye, M.B. | 189 | 5426 | 33.70 | 124* | 6 | 34 | – | – | – | 41 |
| Lucas, D.S. | 27 | 53 | 7.57 | 19* | – | – | 33 | 31.63 | 4-27 | 3 |
| Lumb, M.J. | 34 | 603 | 22.33 | 73 | – | 2 | – | – | – | 11 |
| Lungley, T. | 26 | 177 | 14.75 | 45 | – | – | 39 | 21.28 | 4-28 | 3 |
| McCoubrey, A.G.A.M. | 4 | 13 | 4.33 | 11 | – | – | 3 | 28.33 | 2-20 | – |
| McGarry, A.C. | 15 | 2 | 1.00 | 1 | – | – | 10 | 35.70 | 2-20 | 1 |
| MacGill, S.C.G. | 46 | 63 | 5.72 | 18 | – | – | 88 | 20.60 | 5-40 | 14 |
| McGrath, A. | 155 | 4000 | 32.52 | 109* | 3 | 22 | 19 | 32.42 | 3-39 | 49 |
| McLean, N.A.M. | 134 | 1043 | 13.72 | 50* | – | 1 | 161 | 28.07 | 5-26 | 23 |
| Maddy, D.L. | 220 | 5224 | 29.85 | 151 | 6 | 29 | 128 | 27.13 | 4-16 | 77 |
| Mahmood, S.I. | 2 | 11 | 11.00 | 11 | – | – | 0 | – | – | – |
| Malcolm, D.E. | 185 | 313 | 5.21 | 42 | – | – | 249 | 27.61 | 7-35 | 21 |
| Malik, M.N. | 20 | 30 | 10.00 | 11 | – | – | 10 | 66.00 | 2-34 | 4 |
| Martin, P.J. | 226 | 450 | 12.85 | 35* | – | – | 314 | 22.61 | 5-16 | 40 |
| Martin-Jenkins, R.S.C. | 103 | 812 | 12.11 | 50 | – | 1 | 107 | 29.21 | 4-22 | 23 |
| Mascarenhas, A.D. | 117 | 1697 | 19.50 | 79 | – | 11 | 144 | 23.72 | 5-27 | 30 |
| Mason, M.S. | 16 | 14 | 3.50 | 6 | – | – | 24 | 24.20 | 3-33 | 2 |
| Masters, D.D. | 34 | 82 | 6.30 | 12* | – | – | 21 | 52.09 | 5-20 | 4 |
| Maunders, J.K. | 3 | 66 | 22.00 | 49 | – | – | 0 | – | – | 1 |
| Maynard, M.P. | 398 | 12226 | 35.64 | 151* | 14 | 74 | 3 | 94.66 | 1-13 | 172/5 |
| Mees, T. | 4 | 4 | 4.00 | 4* | – | – | 3 | 48.00 | 3-19 | – |
| Middlebrook, J.D. | 39 | 156 | 9.75 | 19 | – | – | 33 | 27.96 | 4-33 | 11 |
| Miller, D.J. | 1 | 1 | 1.00 | 1 | – | – | – | – | – | – |
| Montgomerie, R.R. | 145 | 4718 | 37.14 | 129* | 4 | 34 | 0 | – | – | 33 |
| Morris, A.C. | 42 | 285 | 17.81 | 48* | – | 1 | 39 | 26.23 | 5-32 | 9 |
| Muchall, G.J. | 11 | 250 | 25.00 | 81 | – | 1 | 0 | – | – | 5 |

176

| L-O | M | Runs | Avge | HS | 100 | 50 | Wkts | Avge | Best | Ct/St |
|---|---|---|---|---|---|---|---|---|---|---|
| Mullally, A.D. | 272 | 478 | 7.02 | 38 | – | – | 324 | 27.47 | 6-38 | 38 |
| Murtagh, T.J. | 20 | 57 | 7.12 | 14* | – | – | 26 | 30.88 | 4-31 | 5 |
| Mushtaq Ahmed | 308 | 1383 | 11.52 | 41 | – | – | 383 | 27.78 | 7-24 | 54 |
| Mustard, P. | 5 | 14 | 4.66 | 8 | – | – | – | – | – | 7/3 |
| Napier, G.R. | 67 | 889 | 17.43 | 79 | – | 5 | 39 | 27.23 | 6-29 | 20 |
| Nash, D.C. | 85 | 977 | 21.23 | 67 | – | 3 | – | – | – | 77/15 |
| Nel, A. | 54 | 92 | 13.14 | 17* | – | – | 78 | 21.39 | 6-27 | 12 |
| New, T.J. | 2 | 9 | 4.50 | 6 | – | – | – | – | – | – |
| Newell, K. | 125 | 2520 | 24.23 | 129 | 1 | 10 | 40 | 37.50 | 5-33 | 20 |
| Newman, S.A. | 9 | 195 | 21.66 | 49 | – | – | – | – | – | 1 |
| Nixon, P.A. | 265 | 4252 | 23.75 | 101 | 1 | 17 | – | – | – | 279/59 |
| Noffke, A.A. | 28 | 144 | 20.57 | 58 | – | 1 | 36 | 29.91 | 4-32 | 8 |
| Noon, W.M. | 118 | 751 | 13.90 | 46 | – | – | – | – | – | 89/27 |
| Ormond, J. | 86 | 276 | 10.22 | 18* | – | – | 109 | 24.11 | 4-12 | 18 |
| Ostler, D.P. | 264 | 7153 | 33.11 | 134* | 3 | 50 | 1 | 14.00 | 1- 4 | 94 |
| Panesar, M.S. | 1 | 16 | – | 16* | – | – | 0 | – | – | – |
| Parkin, O.T. | 95 | 77 | 3.50 | 14* | – | – | 123 | 26.15 | 5-28 | 22 |
| Parsons, K.A. | 166 | 3157 | 27.93 | 121 | 1 | 15 | 96 | 36.82 | 4-43 | 66 |
| Parsons, M. | 2 | 0 | 0.00 | 0 | – | – | 3 | 32.00 | 3-70 | – |
| Patel, M.M. | 77 | 229 | 9.16 | 27* | – | – | 78 | 31.32 | 3-22 | 23 |
| Patel, S.R. | 3 | 18 | 18.00 | 18 | – | – | 3 | 14.66 | 2-14 | – |
| Pattison, I. | 5 | 57 | 19.00 | 48* | – | – | 3 | 39.00 | 1-25 | 2 |
| Paynter, D.E. | 3 | 133 | 44.33 | 104 | 1 | – | 1 | 73.00 | 1-27 | – |
| Pearson, J.A. | 3 | 7 | 2.33 | 7 | – | – | 1 | 29.00 | 1-29 | 1 |
| Penberthy, A.L. | 248 | 4077 | 25.32 | 81* | – | 24 | 251 | 30.25 | 5-29 | 63 |
| Peng, N | 49 | 1146 | 24.91 | 121 | 3 | 4 | – | – | – | 12 |
| Penney, T.L. | 248 | 4329 | 27.92 | 90 | – | 17 | 1 | 21.00 | 1- 8 | 94/1 |
| Peters, S.D. | 90 | 1388 | 18.26 | 73* | – | 7 | – | – | – | 21 |
| Pettini, M.L. | 12 | 196 | 19.60 | 75 | – | 2 | – | – | – | 4 |
| Phillips, B.J. | 28 | 62 | 7.75 | 29 | – | – | 35 | 19.94 | 4-25 | 9 |
| Phillips, N.C. | 101 | 542 | 10.03 | 38* | – | – | 114 | 29.20 | 4-13 | 30 |
| Phillips, T.J. | 7 | 20 | 5.00 | 6 | – | – | 6 | 34.83 | 2-36 | 2 |
| Pietersen, K.P. | 49 | 1198 | 39.93 | 147 | 2 | 5 | 22 | 56.81 | 3-39 | 25 |
| Pipe, D.J. | 15 | 284 | 23.66 | 56 | – | 2 | – | – | – | 16/5 |
| Piper, K.J. | 218 | 943 | 14.96 | 38* | – | – | – | – | – | 231/50 |
| Pollock, S.M. | 282 | 3232 | 23.94 | 111* | 1 | 14 | 397 | 22.03 | 6-21 | 98 |
| Pope, S.P. | 5 | 22 | 5.50 | 15 | – | – | – | – | – | 10/1 |
| Pothas, N. | 128 | 2135 | 34.43 | 101 | 1 | 11 | – | – | – | 119/23 |
| Powell, M.J. (Gm) | 102 | 2091 | 25.50 | 86 | – | 9 | – | – | – | 33 |
| Powell, M.J. (Nh) | 2 | 66 | 33.00 | 64 | – | 1 | – | – | – | – |
| Powell, M.J. (Wa) | 80 | 1491 | 25.27 | 101* | 1 | 5 | 25 | 28.80 | 5-40 | 37 |
| Pratt, A. | 55 | 685 | 21.40 | 86 | – | 3 | – | – | – | 51/19 |
| Pratt, G.J. | 24 | 501 | 25.05 | 89 | – | 4 | – | – | – | 7 |
| Pretorius, D. | 32 | 26 | 2.88 | 7* | – | – | 49 | 23.97 | 4-39 | 3 |
| Prior, M.J. | 30 | 260 | 11.81 | 73 | – | 1 | – | – | – | 18/4 |
| Prittipaul, L.R. | 38 | 406 | 15.61 | 61 | – | 1 | 14 | 38.14 | 3-33 | 11 |
| Pyemont, J.P. | 23 | 301 | 13.68 | 50 | – | 1 | – | – | – | 10 |
| Ramprakash, M.R. | 309 | 9684 | 38.73 | 147* | 9 | 63 | 44 | 27.13 | 5-38 | 107 |
| Randall, S.J. | 14 | 96 | 19.20 | 25 | – | – | 11 | 48.00 | 3-44 | 4 |
| Rashid, S. | 6 | 11 | – | 9* | – | – | 15 | 16.93 | 4-30 | 1 |
| Ratcliffe, J.D. | 110 | 1856 | 23.20 | 105 | 1 | 10 | 40 | 31.07 | 4-44 | 28 |
| Rawnsley, M.J. | 52 | 76 | 4.47 | 12 | – | – | 50 | 30.50 | 5-26 | 11 |
| Read, C.M.W. | 121 | 1566 | 21.16 | 69 | – | 3 | – | – | – | 136/30 |
| Rees, T.M. | 1 | 7 | – | 7* | – | – | – | – | – | – |
| Rhodes, J.N. | 334 | 8119 | 33.27 | 121 | 2 | 46 | 2 | 22.50 | 1- 2 | 146 |
| Rhodes, S.J. | 438 | 4022 | 19.15 | 105 | 1 | 5 | 0 | – | – | 491/120 |
| Richardson, A. | 29 | 40 | 5.71 | 11* | – | – | 30 | 30.86 | 5-35 | 5 |
| Richardson, S.A. | 1 | 7 | 7.00 | 7 | – | – | – | – | – | – |

| L-O | M | Runs | Avge | HS | 100 | 50 | Wkts | Avge | Best | Ct/St |
|---|---|---|---|---|---|---|---|---|---|---|
| Roberts, T.W. | 9 | 130 | 16.25 | 55 | – | 1 | 0 | – | – | 2 |
| Robinson, D.D.J. | 150 | 3414 | 25.86 | 137* | 3 | 17 | 1 | 26.00 | 1- 7 | 40 |
| Robinson, M.A. | 242 | 158 | 3.16 | 15* | – | – | 256 | 30.27 | 4-23 | 25 |
| Rollins, A.S. | 101 | 1911 | 22.22 | 126* | 2 | 8 | 0 | – | – | 40 |
| Rose, G.D. | 295 | 5044 | 23.79 | 148 | 2 | 24 | 303 | 29.65 | 4-16 | 68 |
| Round, N.W. | 7 | 215 | 35.83 | 66 | – | 1 | 2 | 44.50 | 2-28 | 2 |
| Russell, R.C. | 460 | 6439 | 24.39 | 119* | 2 | 25 | – | – | – | 449/91 |
| Sadler, J.L. | 2 | 28 | 14.00 | 19 | – | – | – | – | – | – |
| Saggers, M.J. | 66 | 180 | 10.58 | 34* | – | – | 96 | 24.12 | 5-22 | 18 |
| Sales, D.J.G. | 127 | 3072 | 29.53 | 93 | – | 21 | 0 | – | – | 51 |
| Salisbury, I.D.K. | 225 | 1325 | 12.99 | 48* | – | – | 225 | 32.43 | 5-30 | 76 |
| Sampson, P.J. | 9 | 28 | 7.00 | 16 | – | – | 8 | 38.75 | 3-42 | 3 |
| Saqlain Mushtaq | 272 | 1126 | 11.85 | 38* | – | – | 429 | 21.92 | 5-20 | 74 |
| Schofield, C.P. | 63 | 629 | 18.50 | 52 | – | 1 | 77 | 23.27 | 5-31 | 16 |
| Schofield, J.E.K. | 1 | – | – | – | – | – | 1 | 22.00 | 1-22 | – |
| Scott, B.J.M. | 2 | 15 | 7.50 | 11 | – | – | – | – | – | – |
| Scott, G.M. | 3 | 130 | 43.33 | 100 | 1 | – | 4 | 26.75 | 2-32 | 2 |
| Sehwag, V. | 81 | 2106 | 31.43 | 125 | 2 | 14 | 44 | 35.61 | 4-17 | 32 |
| Selwood, S.A. | 23 | 599 | 33.27 | 93 | – | 5 | 1 | 56.00 | 1-48 | 6 |
| Shafayat, B.M. | 22 | 394 | 20.73 | 66 | – | 1 | 8 | 24.75 | 4-35 | 8 |
| Shah, O.A. | 133 | 3150 | 28.89 | 134 | 4 | 15 | 8 | 31.12 | 2- 2 | 39 |
| Shahid Afridi | 214 | 5277 | 26.12 | 112 | 4 | 32 | 181 | 35.41 | 5-36 | 74 |
| Shahid, N. | 167 | 2922 | 24.76 | 109* | 2 | 12 | 5 | 50.80 | 3-30 | 51 |
| Shaw, A.D. | 85 | 759 | 15.48 | 48 | – | – | – | – | – | 59/17 |
| Sheikh, M.A. | 66 | 199 | 9.47 | 36 | – | – | 76 | 26.05 | 4-17 | 13 |
| Sheriyar, A. | 110 | 121 | 8.06 | 19 | – | – | 124 | 27.48 | 4-18 | 7 |
| Shoaib Akhtar | 81 | 109 | 7.26 | 36 | – | – | 130 | 21.58 | 6-16 | 17 |
| Shreck, C.E. | 8 | 12 | 6.00 | 9 | – | – | 17 | 19.58 | 5-19 | 3 |
| Sidebottom, R.J. | 92 | 188 | 9.89 | 30* | – | – | 91 | 30.85 | 6-40 | 20 |
| Sillence, R.J. | 6 | 101 | 20.20 | 82 | – | 1 | 8 | 13.75 | 4-35 | – |
| Silverwood, C.E.W. | 157 | 779 | 14.16 | 61 | – | 4 | 211 | 23.34 | 5-28 | 25 |
| Singh, A. | 82 | 1960 | 25.12 | 123 | 1 | 15 | – | – | – | 23 |
| Smethurst, M.P. | 26 | 26 | 5.20 | 10* | – | – | 21 | 35.71 | 4-46 | 4 |
| Smith, A.M. | 228 | 487 | 10.58 | 26* | – | – | 268 | 26.26 | 6-39 | 45 |
| Smith, B.F. | 273 | 6913 | 30.18 | 115 | 2 | 44 | 1 | 97.00 | 1-26 | 88 |
| Smith, E.T. | 42 | 732 | 20.33 | 87 | – | 4 | – | – | – | 6 |
| Smith, G.J. | 87 | 118 | 6.55 | 16* | – | – | 130 | 23.62 | 5-11 | 10 |
| Smith, N.M.K. | 320 | 4936 | 21.55 | 125 | 2 | 25 | 298 | 27.32 | 6-33 | 97 |
| Smith, R.A. | 434 | 14629 | 41.09 | 167* | 27 | 79 | 3 | 5.33 | 2-13 | 158 |
| Smith, W.R. | 3 | 25 | 12.50 | 16 | – | – | – | – | – | – |
| Snape, J.N. | 188 | 2457 | 22.96 | 104* | 1 | 8 | 157 | 28.49 | 5-32 | 69 |
| Solanki, V.S. | 181 | 3774 | 26.57 | 120* | 3 | 21 | 10 | 45.40 | 2-40 | 61 |
| Spearman, C.M. | 155 | 3796 | 25.47 | 126 | 3 | 23 | 0 | – | – | 42 |
| Spires, J.A.S. | 1 | – | – | – | – | – | 3 | 33.00 | 1-33 | – |
| Srinath, J. | 261 | 1089 | 10.89 | 53 | – | 1 | 366 | 26.39 | 5-23 | 48 |
| Stemp, R.D. | 153 | 226 | 7.79 | 29* | – | – | 161 | 31.42 | 4-25 | 30 |
| Stephenson, J.P. | 314 | 7251 | 29.35 | 142 | 8 | 38 | 268 | 26.31 | 6-33 | 116 |
| Stevens, D.I. | 87 | 2094 | 27.92 | 133 | 2 | 13 | 6 | 38.16 | 2-26 | 27 |
| Stewart, A.J. | 485 | 14344 | 35.41 | 167* | 19 | 90 | 0 | – | – | 424/45 |
| Strauss, A.J. | 67 | 1385 | 23.08 | 90 | – | 10 | – | – | – | 13 |
| Stubbings, S.D. | 62 | 1025 | 19.71 | 98* | – | 4 | – | – | – | 7 |
| Suppiah, A.V. | 5 | 115 | 23.00 | 70 | – | 1 | 2 | 49.00 | 2-36 | 3 |
| Sutcliffe, I.J. | 84 | 2278 | 30.37 | 105* | 3 | 15 | – | – | – | 17 |
| Sutton, L.D. | 48 | 610 | 16.05 | 60 | – | 2 | – | – | – | 34/5 |
| Swann, A.J. | 38 | 884 | 31.57 | 83* | – | 6 | 0 | – | – | 5 |
| Swann, G.P. | 97 | 1338 | 19.39 | 83 | – | 7 | 83 | 30.66 | 5-35 | 27 |
| Symington, M.J. | 20 | 167 | 11.92 | 34 | – | – | 9 | 58.66 | 2-11 | 7 |
| Symonds, A. | 208 | 4582 | 26.63 | 95 | – | 23 | 137 | 27.64 | 6-14 | 91 |

| L-O | M | Runs | Avge | HS | 100 | 50 | Wkts | Avge | Best | Ct/St |
|---|---|---|---|---|---|---|---|---|---|---|
| Taylor, B.V. | 61 | 93 | 6.20 | 21* | – | – | 88 | 21.15 | 5-28 | 10 |
| Taylor, C.G. | 64 | 744 | 16.53 | 93 | – | 2 | – | – | – | 19 |
| Thomas, I.J. | 24 | 638 | 27.73 | 72 | – | 4 | – | – | – | 9 |
| Thomas, S.D. | 129 | 1167 | 15.98 | 71* | – | 1 | 164 | 26.57 | 7-16 | 23 |
| Thornicroft, N.D. | 4 | 0 | – | 0* | – | – | 3 | 36.00 | 2-35 | 1 |
| Thorpe, A.M. | 4 | 83 | 20.75 | 53 | – | 1 | 2 | 33.50 | 2-49 | – |
| Thorpe, G.P. | 330 | 10089 | 39.41 | 145* | 8 | 75 | 16 | 40.56 | 3-21 | 151 |
| Tomlinson, J.A. | 11 | 11 | 2.75 | 6 | – | – | 11 | 33.18 | 2-15 | 1 |
| Tredwell, J.C. | 25 | 231 | 16.50 | 71 | – | 2 | 24 | 27.83 | 3- 7 | 9 |
| Trego, P.D. | 21 | 129 | 9.21 | 24 | – | – | 18 | 30.83 | 3-14 | 3 |
| Tremlett, C.T. | 34 | 153 | 9.56 | 30* | – | – | 48 | 22.54 | 4-25 | 7 |
| Trescothick, M.E. | 181 | 5503 | 35.73 | 137 | 12 | 23 | 55 | 26.58 | 4-50 | 63 |
| Trott, B.J. | 23 | 6 | 1.20 | 2* | – | – | 31 | 27.51 | 5-18 | 3 |
| Trott, I.J.L. | 27 | 709 | 30.82 | 108* | 1 | 4 | 5 | 16.80 | 2-32 | 8 |
| Troughton, J.O. | 20 | 614 | 38.37 | 115* | 1 | 2 | 7 | 11.85 | 4-23 | 5 |
| Tudor, A.J. | 60 | 327 | 10.90 | 29* | – | – | 85 | 23.88 | 4-26 | 14 |
| Tufnell, P.C.R. | 93 | 125 | 8.92 | 18 | – | – | 103 | 32.30 | 5-28 | 17 |
| Turk, N.R.K. | 2 | 56 | 28.00 | 36 | – | – | 0 | – | – | – |
| Turner, R.J. | 208 | 3126 | 25.83 | 70 | – | 9 | – | – | – | 214/30 |
| Udal, S.D. | 284 | 2017 | 15.63 | 78 | – | 8 | 316 | 30.64 | 5-43 | 91 |
| Van der Gucht C.G. | 3 | 4 | 2.00 | 3 | – | – | 5 | 19.00 | 3-35 | – |
| Vaughan, M.P. | 186 | 4366 | 26.46 | 125* | 1 | 24 | 64 | 27.45 | 4-22 | 55 |
| Wagg, G.G. | 5 | 23 | 7.66 | 21 | – | – | 9 | 17.55 | 4-50 | 2 |
| Wagh, M.A. | 37 | 708 | 21.45 | 84 | – | 4 | 3 | 77.00 | 1-39 | 1 |
| Walker, M.J. | 163 | 3581 | 26.92 | 117 | 2 | 20 | 18 | 22.83 | 4-24 | 39 |
| Wallace, M.A. | 26 | 250 | 15.62 | 39 | – | – | – | – | – | 28/9 |
| Ward, D.M. | 236 | 5414 | 30.58 | 112 | 5 | 33 | 0 | – | – | 101/3 |
| Ward, I.J. | 118 | 2713 | 27.13 | 97 | – | 18 | 2 | 66.00 | 2-27 | 25 |
| Ward, T.R. | 310 | 8814 | 30.18 | 131 | 9 | 58 | 10 | 35.10 | 3-20 | 75 |
| Warn, C.J. | 5 | 89 | 44.50 | 52* | – | 1 | – | – | – | 9/2 |
| Warren, N.A. | 3 | 2 | 1.00 | 2 | – | – | 3 | 36.00 | 3-34 | 2 |
| Warren, R.J. | 145 | 2614 | 24.20 | 100* | 1 | 12 | – | – | – | 119/10 |
| Waugh, M.E. | 415 | 14156 | 39.21 | 173 | 27 | 84 | 172 | 33.22 | 5-24 | 188 |
| Waugh, S.R. | 419 | 11019 | 36.97 | 140* | 11 | 63 | 257 | 33.45 | 4-32 | 145 |
| Webley, T. | 2 | 12 | 6.00 | 8 | – | – | – | – | – | – |
| Weekes, P.N. | 251 | 4747 | 26.08 | 143* | 3 | 22 | 273 | 27.73 | 4-17 | 107 |
| Welch, G. | 156 | 1564 | 17.97 | 71 | – | 4 | 134 | 35.90 | 6-31 | 17 |
| Wells, V.J. | 256 | 5511 | 25.63 | 201 | 4 | 26 | 237 | 27.27 | 6-25 | 72 |
| Welton, G.E. | 50 | 967 | 21.02 | 104* | 1 | 4 | – | – | – | 16 |
| Weston, R.M.S. | 50 | 865 | 19.65 | 80* | – | 4 | – | – | – | 10 |
| Weston, W.P.C. | 128 | 2157 | 20.94 | 134 | 2 | 7 | 1 | 2.00 | 1- 2 | 29 |
| Wharf, A.G. | 57 | 368 | 15.33 | 38* | – | – | 55 | 36.30 | 4-29 | 9 |
| Wharton, L.J. | 28 | 43 | 21.50 | 11* | – | – | 26 | 32.19 | 3-23 | 3 |
| Whiley, M.J.A. | 21 | 28 | 28.00 | 14* | – | – | 17 | 38.52 | 2-20 | 5 |
| White, C. | 281 | 5477 | 25.83 | 148 | 3 | 22 | 300 | 25.14 | 5-19 | 82 |
| White, G.W. | 126 | 2398 | 21.22 | 76 | – | 15 | 1 | 90.00 | 1-45 | 41 |
| White, R.A. | 5 | 70 | 14.00 | 18 | – | – | 2 | 18.50 | 2-18 | – |
| Wigley, D.H. | 1 | 0 | 0.00 | 0 | – | – | 0 | – | – | – |
| Windows, M.G.N. | 166 | 3403 | 25.02 | 117 | 3 | 12 | 0 | – | – | 54 |
| Wood, J. | 138 | 598 | 10.87 | 28* | – | – | 152 | 30.57 | 5-49 | 19 |
| Wood, M.J. (Sm) | 26 | 487 | 22.13 | 88* | – | 3 | – | – | – | 6 |
| Wood, M.J. (Y) | 73 | 1380 | 25.09 | 115* | 2 | 6 | – | – | – | 28 |
| Wright, A.S. | 12 | 245 | 30.62 | 112 | 1 | 1 | 0 | – | – | 2 |
| Wright, L.J. | 1 | 16 | 16.00 | 16 | – | – | – | – | – | – |
| Yardy, M.H. | 33 | 348 | 15.13 | 59 | – | 2 | 22 | 35.95 | 3-30 | 12 |
| Yates, G. | 169 | 661 | 14.36 | 38 | – | – | 157 | 32.26 | 4-34 | 39 |
| Zuiderent, B. | 48 | 967 | 22.48 | 102* | 1 | 7 | 0 | – | – | 17 |

# LIMITED-OVERS INTERNATIONALS
# CAREER RECORDS

These records, complete to the end of the 2003 World Cup, include all players registered for county cricket in 2003 at the time of going to press, plus those who have appeared in LOI matches since 1 October 2001.

## ENGLAND – BATTING AND FIELDING

|  | M | I | NO | HS | Runs | Avge | 100 | 50 | Ct/St |
|---|---|---|---|---|---|---|---|---|---|
| C.J.Adams | 5 | 4 | – | 42 | 71 | 17.75 | – | – | 3 |
| M.W.Alleyne | 10 | 8 | 1 | 53 | 151 | 21.57 | – | 1 | 3 |
| J.M.Anderson | 14 | 9 | 2 | 8 | 18 | 2.57 | – | – | 2 |
| G.J.Batty | 2 | 2 | – | 3 | 3 | 1.50 | – | – | 2 |
| M.P.Bicknell | 7 | 6 | 2 | 31* | 96 | 24.00 | – | – | 2 |
| I.D.Blackwell | 14 | 14 | 1 | 82 | 252 | 19.38 | – | 1 | 5 |
| R.J.Blakey | 3 | 2 | – | 25 | 25 | 12.50 | – | – | 2/1 |
| A.D.Brown | 16 | 16 | – | 118 | 354 | 22.12 | 1 | 1 | 6 |
| D.R.Brown | 9 | 8 | 4 | 21 | 99 | 24.75 | – | – | 1 |
| A.R.Caddick | 54 | 38 | 18 | 36 | 249 | 12.45 | – | – | 9 |
| P.D.Collingwood | 38 | 37 | 10 | 100 | 874 | 32.37 | 1 | 5 | 18 |
| D.G.Cork | 32 | 21 | 3 | 31* | 180 | 10.00 | – | – | 6 |
| J.P.Crawley | 13 | 12 | 1 | 73 | 235 | 21.36 | – | 2 | 1/1 |
| R.D.B.Croft | 50 | 36 | 12 | 32 | 345 | 14.37 | – | – | 11 |
| P.A.J.DeFreitas | 103 | 66 | 23 | 67 | 690 | 16.04 | – | 1 | 26 |
| M.A.Ealham | 64 | 45 | 4 | 45 | 716 | 17.46 | – | – | 9 |
| A.Flintoff | 52 | 44 | 3 | 84 | 1019 | 24.85 | – | 6 | 19 |
| J.S.Foster | 11 | 6 | 3 | 13 | 41 | 13.66 | – | – | 13/7 |
| P.J.Franks | 1 | 1 | – | 4 | 4 | 4.00 | – | – | 1 |
| A.F.Giles | 24 | 15 | 5 | 21* | 114 | 11.40 | – | – | 8 |
| D.Gough | 111 | 71 | 29 | 45 | 455 | 10.83 | – | – | 17 |
| A.P.Grayson | 2 | 2 | – | 6 | 6 | 3.00 | – | – | 1 |
| S.J.Harmison | 5 | 2 | 1 | 7 | 9 | 9.00 | – | – | 3 |
| G.A.Hick | 120 | 118 | 15 | 126* | 3846 | 37.33 | 5 | 27 | 64 |
| M.J.Hoggard | 20 | 5 | 2 | 5 | 10 | 3.33 | – | – | 3 |
| A.J.Hollioake | 35 | 30 | 6 | 83* | 606 | 25.25 | – | 3 | 13 |
| N.Hussain | 88 | 87 | 10 | 115 | 2332 | 30.28 | 1 | 16 | 40 |
| R.C.Irani | 31 | 30 | 5 | 53 | 360 | 14.40 | – | 1 | 6 |
| R.J.Kirtley | 9 | 2 | – | 1 | 2 | 1.00 | – | – | 5 |
| N.V.Knight | 100 | 100 | 10 | 125* | 3637 | 40.41 | 5 | 25 | 44 |
| D.L.Maddy | 8 | 6 | – | 53 | 113 | 18.83 | – | 1 | 1 |
| D.E.Malcolm | 10 | 5 | 2 | 4 | 9 | 3.00 | – | – | 1 |
| P.J.Martin | 20 | 13 | 7 | 6 | 38 | 6.33 | – | – | 1 |
| M.P.Maynard | 14 | 12 | 1 | 41 | 156 | 14.18 | – | – | 4 |
| A.D.Mullally | 50 | 25 | 10 | 20 | 86 | 5.73 | – | – | 8 |
| M.R.Ramprakash | 18 | 18 | 4 | 51 | 376 | 26.85 | – | 1 | 8 |
| C.M.W.Read | 9 | 6 | 2 | 26* | 70 | 17.50 | – | – | 11/2 |
| S.J.Rhodes | 9 | 8 | 2 | 56 | 107 | 17.83 | – | 1 | 9/2 |
| R.C.Russell | 40 | 31 | 7 | 50 | 423 | 17.62 | – | 1 | 41/6 |
| I.D.K.Salisbury | 4 | 2 | 1 | 5 | 7 | 7.00 | – | – | 1 |
| O.A.Shah | 15 | 15 | 2 | 62 | 283 | 21.76 | – | 2 | 6 |
| R.J.Sidebottom | 2 | 1 | 1 | 2* | 2 | – | – | – | – |
| C.E.W.Silverwood | 7 | 4 | – | 12 | 17 | 4.25 | – | – | 1 |
| N.M.K.Smith | 7 | 6 | 1 | 31 | 100 | 20.00 | – | – | 1 |
| R.A.Smith | 71 | 70 | 8 | 167* | 2419 | 39.01 | 4 | 15 | 26 |
| J.N.Snape | 10 | 7 | 3 | 38 | 118 | 29.50 | – | – | 5 |
| V.S.Solanki | 8 | 7 | 1 | 24 | 96 | 16.00 | – | – | 2 |
| A.J.Stewart | 170 | 162 | 14 | 116 | 4677 | 31.60 | 4 | 28 | 159/15 |
| G.P.Swann | 1 | – | – | – | – | – | – | – | – |
| G.P.Thorpe | 82 | 77 | 13 | 89 | 2380 | 37.18 | – | 21 | 42 |
| M.E.Trescothick | 61 | 61 | 1 | 137 | 2161 | 36.01 | 4 | 12 | 22 |

## ENGLAND – BATTING AND FIELDING (continued)

| | M | I | NO | HS | Runs | Avge | 100 | 50 | Ct/St |
|---|---|---|---|---|---|---|---|---|---|
| A.J.Tudor | 3 | 2 | 1 | 6 | 9 | 9.00 | – | – | 1 |
| P.C.R.Tufnell | 20 | 10 | 9 | 5* | 15 | 15.00 | – | – | 4 |
| S.D.Udal | 10 | 6 | 4 | 11* | 35 | 17.50 | – | – | 1 |
| M.P.Vaughan | 26 | 25 | 1 | 63 | 564 | 23.50 | – | 5 | 6 |
| V.J.Wells | 9 | 7 | – | 39 | 141 | 20.14 | – | – | 7 |
| C.White | 51 | 41 | 5 | 57* | 568 | 15.77 | – | 1 | 12 |

## ENGLAND – BOWLING

| | O | R | W | Avge | Best | 4wI | R/Over |
|---|---|---|---|---|---|---|---|
| M.W.Alleyne | 61 | 280 | 10 | 28.00 | 3-27 | – | 4.59 |
| J.M.Anderson | 120.2 | 598 | 23 | 26.00 | 4-25 | 2 | 4.96 |
| G.J.Batty | 20 | 120 | 1 | 120.00 | 1-65 | – | 6.00 |
| M.P.Bicknell | 68.5 | 347 | 13 | 26.69 | 3-55 | – | 5.04 |
| I.D.Blackwell | 95 | 415 | 14 | 29.64 | 3-26 | – | 4.36 |
| A.D.Brown | 1 | 5 | 0 | – | – | – | 5.00 |
| D.R.Brown | 54 | 305 | 7 | 43.57 | 2-28 | – | 5.65 |
| A.R.Caddick | 489.3 | 1965 | 69 | 28.47 | 4-19 | 3 | 4.01 |
| P.D.Collingwood | 111.1 | 665 | 16 | 41.56 | 4-38 | 1 | 5.98 |
| D.G.Cork | 295.2 | 1368 | 41 | 33.36 | 3-27 | – | 4.63 |
| R.D.B.Croft | 411 | 1743 | 45 | 38.73 | 3-51 | – | 4.24 |
| P.A.J.DeFreitas | 952 | 3775 | 115 | 32.82 | 4-35 | 1 | 3.97 |
| M.A.Ealham | 537.5 | 2197 | 67 | 32.79 | 5-15 | 3 | 4.08 |
| A.Flintoff | 277.2 | 1263 | 44 | 28.70 | 4-17 | 1 | 4.55 |
| P.J.Franks | 9 | 48 | 0 | – | – | – | 5.33 |
| A.F.Giles | 178 | 866 | 24 | 36.08 | 5-57 | 1 | 4.86 |
| D.Gough | 1015.1 | 4380 | 174 | 25.17 | 5-44 | 9 | 4.31 |
| A.P.Grayson | 15 | 60 | 3 | 20.00 | 3-40 | – | 4.00 |
| S.J.Harmison | 38.4 | 228 | 5 | 45.60 | 2-39 | – | 5.89 |
| G.A.Hick | 206 | 1026 | 30 | 34.20 | 5-33 | 1 | 4.98 |
| M.J.Hoggard | 162.4 | 817 | 27 | 30.25 | 5-49 | 1 | 5.02 |
| A.J.Hollioake | 201.2 | 1019 | 32 | 31.84 | 4-23 | 2 | 5.06 |
| R.C.Irani | 213.5 | 989 | 24 | 41.20 | 5-26 | 2 | 4.63 |
| R.J.Kirtley | 76.2 | 420 | 7 | 60.00 | 2-33 | – | 5.50 |
| D.E.Malcolm | 87.4 | 404 | 16 | 25.25 | 3-40 | – | 4.61 |
| P.J.Martin | 174.4 | 806 | 27 | 29.85 | 4-44 | 1 | 4.61 |
| A.D.Mullally | 449.5 | 1728 | 63 | 27.42 | 4-18 | 2 | 3.84 |
| M.R.Ramprakash | 22 | 108 | 4 | 27.00 | 3-28 | – | 4.91 |
| I.D.K.Salisbury | 31 | 177 | 5 | 35.40 | 3-41 | – | 5.71 |
| R.J.Sidebottom | 14 | 84 | 2 | 42.00 | 1-42 | – | 6.00 |
| C.E.W.Silverwood | 51 | 244 | 6 | 40.66 | 3-43 | – | 4.78 |
| N.M.K.Smith | 43.3 | 190 | 6 | 31.66 | 3-29 | – | 4.37 |
| J.N.Snape | 88.1 | 403 | 13 | 31.00 | 3-43 | – | 4.57 |
| G.P.Swann | 5 | 24 | 0 | – | – | – | 4.80 |
| G.P.Thorpe | 20 | 97 | 2 | 48.50 | 2-15 | – | 4.85 |
| M.E.Trescothick | 7.4 | 45 | 2 | 22.50 | 2- 7 | – | 5.87 |
| A.J.Tudor | 21.1 | 136 | 4 | 34.00 | 2-30 | – | 6.42 |
| P.C.R.Tufnell | 170 | 699 | 19 | 36.78 | 4-22 | 1 | 4.11 |
| S.D.Udal | 95 | 371 | 8 | 46.37 | 2-37 | – | 3.91 |
| M.P.Vaughan | 48.4 | 242 | 8 | 30.25 | 4-22 | 1 | 4.97 |
| V.J.Wells | 36.4 | 189 | 8 | 23.62 | 3-30 | – | 5.15 |
| C.White | 394 | 1725 | 65 | 26.53 | 5-21 | 2 | 4.37 |

## AUSTRALIA – BATTING AND FIELDING

| | M | I | NO | HS | Runs | Avge | 100 | 50 | Ct/St |
|---|---|---|---|---|---|---|---|---|---|
| M.G.Bevan | 205 | 173 | 60 | 108* | 6176 | 54.65 | 6 | 41 | 65 |
| A.J.Bichel | 46 | 25 | 9 | 64 | 347 | 21.68 | – | 1 | 13 |
| N.W.Bracken | 11 | – | – | – | – | – | – | – | 3 |
| R.J.Campbell | 2 | 2 | – | 38 | 54 | 27.00 | – | – | 4/1 |
| M.J.Clarke | 1 | 1 | – | 39* | 39 | – | – | – | – |
| M.J.Di Venuto | 9 | 9 | – | 89 | 241 | 26.77 | – | 2 | 1 |

## AUSTRALIA – BATTING AND FIELDING (continued)

| | M | I | NO | HS | Runs | Avge | 100 | 50 | Ct/St |
|---|---|---|---|---|---|---|---|---|---|
| M.T.G.Elliot | 1 | 1 | 0 | 1 | 1 | 1.00 | – | – | – |
| A.C.Gilchrist | 162 | 157 | 6 | 154 | 5225 | 34.60 | 8 | 31 | 233/37 |
| J.N.Gillespie | 50 | 24 | 8 | 26 | 166 | 10.37 | – | – | 2 |
| I.J.Harvey | 49 | 37 | 10 | 47* | 495 | 18.33 | – | – | 13 |
| N.M.Hauritz | 5 | 2 | 2 | 11* | 13 | – | – | – | 2 |
| M.L.Hayden | 65 | 62 | 9 | 146 | 2286 | 43.13 | 2 | 16 | 20 |
| G.B.Hogg | 25 | 16 | 7 | 71* | 169 | 18.77 | – | 1 | 7 |
| M.S.Kasprowicz | 16 | 8 | 6 | 28* | 62 | 31.00 | – | – | 3 |
| S.M.Katich | 1 | – | – | – | – | – | – | – | – |
| S.G.Law | 54 | 51 | 5 | 110 | 1237 | 26.89 | 1 | 7 | 12 |
| B.Lee | 65 | 27 | 8 | 51* | 295 | 15.52 | – | 1 | 13 |
| D.S.Lehmann | 95 | 85 | 19 | 119 | 2509 | 38.01 | 3 | 13 | 19 |
| S.C.G.MacGill | 3 | 2 | 1 | 1 | 1 | 1.00 | – | – | 2 |
| G.D.McGrath | 179 | 49 | 26 | 11 | 91 | 3.95 | – | – | 22 |
| J.P.Maher | 21 | 16 | 3 | 95 | 378 | 29.07 | – | 1 | 13 |
| D.R.Martyn | 123 | 103 | 33 | 144* | 2932 | 41.88 | 4 | 16 | 47 |
| R.T.Ponting | 168 | 165 | 22 | 145 | 5995 | 41.92 | 13 | 31 | 65 |
| A.Symonds | 63 | 43 | 9 | 143* | 1088 | 32.00 | 1 | 4 | 27 |
| S.K.Warne | 193 | 106 | 28 | 55 | 1016 | 13.02 | – | 1 | 80 |
| S.R.Watson | 23 | 15 | 7 | 77* | 288 | 36.00 | – | 1 | 6 |
| M.E.Waugh | 244 | 236 | 20 | 173 | 8500 | 39.35 | 18 | 50 | 108 |
| S.R.Waugh | 325 | 288 | 58 | 120* | 7569 | 32.90 | 3 | 45 | 111 |
| B.A.Williams | 6 | 1 | 1 | 13* | 13 | – | – | – | – |

## AUSTRALIA – BOWLING

| | O | R | W | Avge | Best | 4wI | R/Over |
|---|---|---|---|---|---|---|---|
| M.G.Bevan | 327.4 | 1655 | 36 | 45.97 | 3-36 | – | 5.05 |
| A.J.Bichel | 385.5 | 1675 | 60 | 27.91 | 7-20 | 3 | 4.34 |
| N.W.Bracken | 87.3 | 357 | 14 | 25.50 | 3-21 | – | 4.08 |
| M.J.Clarke | 7 | 24 | 1 | 24.00 | 1-24 | – | 3.42 |
| J.N.Gillespie | 448.3 | 1930 | 79 | 24.43 | 5-22 | 4 | 4.30 |
| I.J.Harvey | 381.4 | 1783 | 55 | 32.41 | 4-28 | 2 | 4.67 |
| N.M.Hauritz | 39 | 185 | 7 | 26.42 | 4-39 | 1 | 4.74 |
| M.L.Hayden | 1 | 18 | 0 | – | – | – | 18.00 |
| G.B.Hogg | 196.5 | 881 | 28 | 31.46 | 3-37 | – | 4.47 |
| M.S.Kasprowicz | 136.1 | 709 | 22 | 32.22 | 3-50 | – | 5.20 |
| S.G.Law | 134.3 | 635 | 12 | 52.91 | 2-22 | – | 4.72 |
| B.Lee | 560.3 | 2642 | 122 | 21.65 | 5-27 | 8 | 4.71 |
| D.S.Lehmann | 210.1 | 986 | 33 | 29.87 | 3-32 | – | 4.69 |
| S.C.G.MacGill | 30 | 105 | 6 | 17.50 | 4-19 | 1 | 3.50 |
| G.D.McGrath | 1579.4 | 6160 | 277 | 22.23 | 7-15 | 13 | 3.89 |
| D.R.Martyn | 132.2 | 704 | 12 | 58.66 | 2-21 | – | 5.32 |
| R.T.Ponting | 25 | 104 | 3 | 34.66 | 1-12 | – | 4.16 |
| A.Symonds | 314.2 | 1537 | 46 | 33.41 | 4-11 | 2 | 4.88 |
| S.K.Warne | 1766.4 | 7514 | 291 | 25.82 | 5-33 | 13 | 4.25 |
| S.R.Watson | 136.5 | 632 | 18 | 35.11 | 3-27 | – | 4.61 |
| M.E.Waugh | 614.3 | 2938 | 85 | 34.56 | 5-24 | 2 | 4.78 |
| S.R.Waugh | 1480.3 | 6764 | 195 | 34.68 | 4-33 | 3 | 4.56 |
| B.A.Williams | 57 | 209 | 7 | 29.85 | 2-22 | – | 3.66 |

## SOUTH AFRICA – BATTING AND FIELDING

| | M | I | NO | HS | Runs | Avge | 100 | 50 | Ct/St |
|---|---|---|---|---|---|---|---|---|---|
| P.R.Adams | 17 | 8 | 4 | 15* | 33 | 8.25 | – | – | 4 |
| D.M.Benkenstein | 23 | 20 | 3 | 69 | 305 | 17.94 | – | 1 | 3 |
| N.Boje | 88 | 55 | 12 | 129 | 1197 | 27.83 | 2 | 3 | 26 |
| M.V.Boucher | 143 | 99 | 25 | 70 | 1816 | 24.54 | – | 13 | 201/10 |
| A.C.Dawson | 6 | 2 | 1 | 6 | 10 | 10.00 | – | – | – |
| H.H.Dippenaar | 56 | 47 | 7 | 93 | 1695 | 42.37 | – | 15 | 19 |
| A.A.Donald | 164 | 40 | 18 | 12 | 94 | 4.27 | – | – | 28 |
| S.Elworthy | 39 | 16 | 8 | 23 | 100 | 12.50 | – | – | 9 |

**SOUTH AFRICA – BATTING AND FIELDING (continued)**

| | M | I | NO | HS | Runs | Avge | 100 | 50 | Ct/St |
|---|---|---|---|---|---|---|---|---|---|
| H.H.Gibbs | 123 | 123 | 9 | 153 | 4213 | 36.95 | 12 | 16 | 54 |
| A.J.Hall | 29 | 24 | 4 | 81 | 457 | 22.85 | – | 1 | 11 |
| M.Hayward | 21 | 5 | 1 | 4 | 12 | 3.00 | – | – | 4 |
| C.W.Henderson | 4 | – | – | – | – | – | – | – | – |
| J.H.Kallis | 174 | 166 | 28 | 113* | 5965 | 43.22 | 8 | 42 | 75 |
| J.M.Kemp | 14 | 6 | 2 | 46 | 70 | 17.50 | – | – | 6 |
| J.C.Kent | 2 | – | – | – | – | – | – | – | – |
| G.Kirsten | 185 | 185 | 19 | 188* | 6798 | 40.95 | 13 | 45 | 62/1 |
| L.Klusener | 154 | 124 | 46 | 103* | 3381 | 43.34 | 2 | 19 | 31 |
| C.K.Langeveldt | 4 | 1 | – | 3 | 3 | 3.00 | – | – | – |
| N.D.McKenzie | 51 | 44 | 7 | 131* | 1320 | 35.67 | 2 | 6 | 15 |
| A.Nel | 7 | 2 | 2 | 3* | 3 | – | – | – | 2 |
| M.Ntini | 68 | 14 | 5 | 14 | 40 | 4.44 | – | – | 19 |
| J.L.Ontong | 16 | 10 | 1 | 32 | 87 | 9.66 | – | – | 8 |
| R.J.Peterson | 7 | 2 | – | 11 | 16 | 8.00 | – | – | 1 |
| S.M.Pollock | 186 | 122 | 42 | 75 | 1893 | 23.66 | – | 7 | 78 |
| N.Pothas | 3 | 1 | – | 24 | 24 | 24.00 | – | – | 4/1 |
| A.G.Prince | 1 | 1 | – | 14* | 14 | – | – | – | – |
| J.N.Rhodes | 245 | 220 | 51 | 121 | 5935 | 35.11 | 2 | 33 | 105 |
| G.C.Smith | 22 | 22 | 1 | 99 | 864 | 41.14 | – | 6 | 10 |
| E.L.R.Stewart | 6 | 6 | 2 | 23* | 61 | 15.25 | – | – | 5 |
| R.Telemachus | 33 | 12 | 3 | 13 | 32 | 3.55 | – | – | 2 |
| M.van Jaarsveld | 2 | 1 | – | 42 | 42 | 42.00 | – | – | 1 |
| M.Zondeki | 5 | 2 | 2 | 3* | 4 | – | – | – | 2 |

## SOUTH AFRICA – BOWLING

| | O | R | W | Avge | Best | 4wI | R/Over |
|---|---|---|---|---|---|---|---|
| P.R.Adams | 130.5 | 590 | 23 | 25.65 | 3-26 | – | 4.50 |
| D.M.Benkenstein | 10.5 | 44 | 4 | 11.00 | 3- 5 | – | 4.06 |
| N.Boje | 559.2 | 2509 | 75 | 33.45 | 5-21 | 3 | 4.48 |
| A.C.Dawson | 52 | 251 | 7 | 35.85 | 3-36 | – | 4.82 |
| A.A.Donald | 1426.5 | 5926 | 272 | 21.78 | 6-23 | 13 | 4.15 |
| S.Elworthy | 283.4 | 1235 | 44 | 28.06 | 3-17 | – | 4.35 |
| A.J.Hall | 97.4 | 444 | 13 | 34.15 | 2- 8 | – | 4.54 |
| M.Hayward | 165.3 | 858 | 21 | 40.85 | 4-31 | 1 | 5.18 |
| C.W.Henderson | 36.1 | 132 | 7 | 18.85 | 4-17 | 1 | 3.64 |
| J.H.Kallis | 1088.2 | 5070 | 167 | 30.35 | 5-30 | 4 | 4.65 |
| J.M.Kemp | 91 | 418 | 17 | 24.58 | 3-20 | – | 4.59 |
| J.C.Kent | 8 | 57 | 0 | – | – | – | 7.12 |
| G.Kirsten | 5 | 23 | 0 | – | – | – | 4.60 |
| L.Klusener | 1095.4 | 5140 | 175 | 29.37 | 6-49 | 7 | 4.69 |
| C.K.Langeveldt | 29.3 | 121 | 6 | 20.16 | 4-21 | 1 | 4.10 |
| N.D.McKenzie | 7.4 | 27 | 0 | – | – | – | 3.52 |
| A.Nel | 59.5 | 241 | 10 | 24.10 | 3-20 | – | 4.03 |
| M.Ntini | 575.4 | 2389 | 99 | 24.13 | 5-31 | 5 | 4.14 |
| J.L.Ontong | 84 | 345 | 7 | 49.28 | 3-30 | – | 4.10 |
| R.J.Peterson | 51 | 232 | 3 | 77.33 | 2-39 | – | 4.54 |
| S.M.Pollock | 1624.4 | 6121 | 268 | 22.83 | 6-35 | 13 | 3.76 |
| J.N.Rhodes | 2.2 | 4 | 0 | – | – | – | 1.71 |
| G.C.Smith | 11.1 | 59 | 1 | 59.00 | 1-24 | – | 5.28 |
| R.Telemachus | 283.4 | 1352 | 49 | 27.59 | 4-43 | 1 | 4.76 |
| M.van Jaarsveld | 0.1 | – | 1 | 0.00 | 1- 0 | – | 0.00 |
| M.Zondeki | 34 | 149 | 4 | 37.25 | 1-17 | – | 4.38 |

## WEST INDIES – BATTING AND FIELDING

| | M | I | NO | HS | Runs | Avge | 100 | 50 | Ct/St |
|---|---|---|---|---|---|---|---|---|---|
| M.I.Black | 5 | 2 | – | 4 | 4 | 2.00 | – | – | – |
| D.Brown | 3 | 2 | 1 | 9 | 10 | 10.00 | – | – | – |
| S.Chanderpaul | 132 | 123 | 16 | 150 | 3913 | 36.57 | 3 | 25 | 38 |
| P.T.Collins | 23 | 7 | 3 | 10* | 26 | 6.50 | – | – | 8 |

## WEST INDIES – BATTING AND FIELDING (continued)

| | M | I | NO | HS | Runs | Avge | 100 | 50 | Ct/St |
|---|---|---|---|---|---|---|---|---|---|
| C.D.Collymore | 32 | 13 | 7 | 13* | 42 | 7.00 | – | – | 5 |
| C.E.Cuffy | 41 | 22 | 8 | 17* | 62 | 4.42 | – | – | 5 |
| M.Dillon | 80 | 39 | 16 | 21* | 178 | 7.73 | – | – | 16 |
| V.C.Drakes | 23 | 9 | 4 | 25 | 67 | 13.40 | – | – | 4 |
| D.Ganga | 28 | 27 | 1 | 71 | 691 | 26.57 | – | 8 | 8 |
| C.H.Gayle | 68 | 66 | 1 | 152 | 2356 | 36.24 | 5 | 15 | 31 |
| R.O.Hinds | 11 | 8 | 3 | 18* | 93 | 18.60 | – | – | 2 |
| W.W.Hinds | 70 | 66 | 3 | 116* | 1666 | 26.44 | 1 | 11 | 20 |
| C.L.Hooper | 227 | 206 | 43 | 113* | 5761 | 35.34 | 7 | 29 | 120 |
| R.D.Jacobs | 118 | 97 | 25 | 80* | 1710 | 23.75 | – | 9 | 139/24 |
| B.C.Lara | 209 | 204 | 21 | 169 | 7797 | 42.60 | 16 | 49 | 85 |
| J.J.C.Lawson | 6 | 1 | – | 3 | 3 | 3.00 | – | – | – |
| N.C.McGarrell | 17 | 10 | 2 | 19 | 60 | 7.50 | – | – | 9 |
| N.A.M.McLean | 45 | 34 | 8 | 50* | 314 | 12.07 | – | 1 | 8 |
| R.S.Morton | 2 | 2 | – | 16 | 19 | 9.50 | – | – | 1 |
| M.V.Nagamootoo | 24 | 18 | 6 | 33 | 162 | 13.50 | – | – | 6 |
| D.B.Powell | 1 | – | – | – | – | – | – | – | – |
| R.L.Powell | 64 | 59 | 7 | 124 | 1361 | 26.17 | 1 | 6 | 30 |
| M.N.Samuels | 40 | 39 | 5 | 108* | 1101 | 32.38 | 1 | 9 | 7 |
| R.R.Sarwan | 34 | 33 | 10 | 102* | 1281 | 55.69 | 1 | 6 | 11 |

## WEST INDIES – BOWLING

| | O | R | W | Avge | Best | 4wI | R/Over |
|---|---|---|---|---|---|---|---|
| M.I.Black | 38 | 196 | 0 | – | – | – | 5.16 |
| D.Brown | 25 | 124 | 5 | 24.80 | 3-21 | – | 4.96 |
| S.Chanderpaul | 118 | 606 | 14 | 43.28 | 3-18 | – | 5.13 |
| P.T.Collins | 205.5 | 946 | 30 | 31.53 | 3-18 | – | 4.59 |
| C.D.Collymore | 263.3 | 1109 | 38 | 29.18 | 5-51 | 2 | 4.20 |
| C.E.Cuffy | 358.5 | 1436 | 41 | 35.02 | 4-24 | 1 | 4.00 |
| M.Dillon | 684.5 | 3083 | 104 | 29.64 | 5-51 | 5 | 4.50 |
| V.C.Drakes | 190.2 | 875 | 42 | 20.83 | 5-33 | 5 | 4.59 |
| D.Ganga | 0.1 | 4 | 0 | – | – | – | 24.00 |
| C.H.Gayle | 357.4 | 1647 | 55 | 29.94 | 4-19 | 2 | 4.60 |
| R.O.Hinds | 57.1 | 317 | 6 | 52.83 | 2-19 | – | 5.54 |
| W.W.Hinds | 38.5 | 204 | 10 | 20.40 | 3-35 | – | 5.25 |
| C.L.Hooper | 1595.3 | 6957 | 193 | 36.04 | 4-34 | 3 | 4.36 |
| B.C.Lara | 7.1 | 46 | 4 | 11.50 | 2- 5 | – | 6.42 |
| J.J.C.Lawson | 45 | 217 | 9 | 24.11 | 4-57 | 1 | 4.82 |
| N.C.McGarrell | 143.1 | 681 | 15 | 45.40 | 3-32 | – | 4.76 |
| N.A.M.McLean | 353.2 | 1729 | 46 | 37.58 | 3-21 | – | 4.89 |
| M.V.Nagamootoo | 198.1 | 998 | 18 | 55.44 | 4-32 | 1 | 5.03 |
| D.B.Powell | 10 | 34 | 1 | 34.00 | 1-34 | – | 3.40 |
| R.L.Powell | 34.3 | 220 | 5 | 44.00 | 2- 5 | – | 6.37 |
| M.N.Samuels | 175 | 884 | 26 | 34.00 | 3-25 | – | 5.05 |
| R.R.Sarwan | 3 | 23 | 0 | – | – | – | 7.66 |

## NEW ZEALAND – BATTING AND FIELDING

| | M | I | NO | HS | Runs | Avge | 100 | 50 | Ct/St |
|---|---|---|---|---|---|---|---|---|---|
| A.R.Adams | 27 | 22 | 7 | 45 | 332 | 22.13 | – | – | 3 |
| N.J.Astle | 174 | 171 | 10 | 122* | 5540 | 34.40 | 13 | 32 | 69 |
| S.E.Bond | 26 | 13 | 6 | 31* | 122 | 17.42 | – | – | 8 |
| I.G.Butler | 9 | 5 | 3 | 6 | 3 | 3.00 | – | – | 4 |
| C.L.Cairns | 162 | 148 | 15 | 115 | 3886 | 29.21 | 4 | 20 | 53 |
| S.P.Fleming | 197 | 190 | 17 | 134* | 5402 | 31.22 | 4 | 33 | 98 |
| J.E.C.Franklin | 24 | 16 | 3 | 25* | 116 | 8.92 | – | – | 7 |
| C.Z.Harris | 225 | 194 | 59 | 130 | 4072 | 30.16 | 1 | 15 | 88 |
| M.N.Hart | 13 | 8 | – | 16 | 61 | 7.62 | – | – | 7 |
| R.G.Hart | 2 | 1 | – | 0 | 0 | 0.00 | – | – | 1 |
| P.A.Hitchcock | 8 | 3 | 2 | 7 | 11 | 11.00 | – | – | 2 |
| M.J.Horne | 50 | 48 | – | 74 | 980 | 20.41 | – | 5 | 12 |

| | M | I | NO | HS | Runs | Avge | 100 | 50 | Ct/St |
|---|---|---|---|---|---|---|---|---|---|
| B.B.McCullum | 21 | 16 | 2 | 37 | 193 | 13.78 | – | – | 29/1 |
| C.D.McMillan | 130 | 124 | 6 | 105 | 3089 | 26.17 | 2 | 17 | 32 |
| K.D.Mills | 17 | 11 | 4 | 23* | 79 | 11.28 | – | – | 3 |
| D.J.Nash | 81 | 53 | 13 | 42 | 624 | 15.60 | – | – | 25 |
| C.J.Nevin | 27 | 26 | – | 74 | 607 | 23.34 | – | 4 | 14/3 |
| J.D.P.Oram | 37 | 30 | 4 | 59 | 412 | 15.84 | – | 1 | 9 |
| A.C.Parore | 179 | 161 | 32 | 108 | 3314 | 25.69 | 1 | 14 | 116/25 |
| M.H.Richardson | 4 | 4 | – | 26 | 42 | 10.50 | – | – | 1 |
| M.S.Sinclair | 33 | 32 | 2 | 118* | 806 | 26.86 | 2 | 4 | 8 |
| S.B.Styris | 59 | 48 | 8 | 141 | 980 | 24.50 | 1 | 3 | 16 |
| C.M.Spearman | 51 | 50 | – | 86 | 936 | 18.72 | – | 5 | 15 |
| S.B.Styris | 59 | 48 | 8 | 141 | 980 | 24.50 | 1 | 3 | 16 |
| D.R.Tuffey | 46 | 28 | 12 | 20* | 123 | 7.68 | – | – | 12 |
| D.L.Vettori | 106 | 69 | 22 | 30 | 533 | 11.34 | – | – | 26 |
| L.Vincent | 51 | 50 | 7 | 60* | 1013 | 23.55 | – | 4 | 20 |
| B.G.K.Walker | 11 | 7 | 4 | 16* | 47 | 15.66 | – | – | 5 |

## NEW ZEALAND – BOWLING

| | O | R | W | Avge | Best | 4wI | R/Over |
|---|---|---|---|---|---|---|---|
| A.R.Adams | 218.4 | 1091 | 42 | 25.97 | 5-22 | 3 | 4.98 |
| N.J.Astle | 735.3 | 3412 | 95 | 35.91 | 4-43 | 1 | 4.63 |
| S.E.Bond | 223.2 | 961 | 49 | 19.61 | 6-23 | 5 | 4.30 |
| I.G.Butler | 56.3 | 328 | 6 | 54.66 | 2-32 | – | 5.80 |
| C.L.Cairns | 1054.2 | 4968 | 156 | 31.84 | 5-42 | 3 | 4.71 |
| S.P.Fleming | 4.5 | 28 | 1 | 28.00 | 1- 8 | – | 5.79 |
| J.E.C.Franklin | 175 | 907 | 20 | 45.35 | 3-44 | – | 5.18 |
| C.Z.Harris | 1658.4 | 7130 | 195 | 36.56 | 5-42 | 3 | 4.29 |
| M.N.Hart | 95.2 | 373 | 13 | 28.69 | 5-22 | 1 | 3.91 |
| P.A.Hitchcock | 52 | 226 | 10 | 22.60 | 3-30 | – | 4.34 |
| C.D.McMillan | 230.3 | 1219 | 37 | 32.94 | 3-20 | – | 5.28 |
| K.D.Mills | 131 | 513 | 22 | 23.31 | 3-30 | – | 3.91 |
| D.J.Nash | 569.2 | 2622 | 64 | 40.96 | 4-38 | 1 | 4.60 |
| J.D.P.Oram | 247.1 | 1132 | 40 | 28.30 | 5-26 | 2 | 4.57 |
| C.M.Spearman | 0.3 | 6 | 0 | – | – | – | 12.00 |
| S.B.Styris | 390 | 1918 | 55 | 34.87 | 6-25 | 3 | 4.91 |
| D.R.Tuffey | 341 | 1561 | 53 | 29.45 | 4-24 | 1 | 4.57 |
| D.L.Vettori | 788.2 | 3482 | 84 | 41.45 | 4-24 | 2 | 4.41 |
| L.Vincent | 0.2 | 3 | 0 | – | – | – | 9.00 |
| B.G.K.Walker | 73 | 417 | 8 | 52.12 | 2-43 | – | 5.71 |

## INDIA – BATTING AND FIELDING

| | M | I | NO | HS | Runs | Avge | 100 | 50 | Ct/St |
|---|---|---|---|---|---|---|---|---|---|
| A.B.Agarkar | 110 | 69 | 23 | 95 | 781 | 16.97 | – | 2 | 38 |
| H.K.Badani | 29 | 27 | 6 | 100 | 655 | 31.19 | 1 | 3 | 9 |
| L.Balaji | 1 | – | – | – | – | – | – | – | – |
| S.B.Bangar | 11 | 11 | 2 | 57* | 161 | 17.88 | – | 1 | 4 |
| R.V.Bharadwaj | 10 | 9 | 4 | 41* | 136 | 27.20 | – | – | 4 |
| S.S.Das | 4 | 4 | 1 | 30 | 39 | 13.00 | – | – | – |
| D.Dasgupta | 5 | 4 | 1 | 24* | 51 | 17.00 | – | – | 2/1 |
| R.Dravid | 207 | 190 | 24 | 153 | 6498 | 39.14 | 8 | 44 | 125/10 |
| S.C.Ganguly | 229 | 221 | 18 | 183 | 8720 | 42.95 | 22 | 50 | 81 |
| Harbhajan Singh | 73 | 39 | 11 | 46 | 338 | 12.07 | – | – | 20 |
| Harvinder Singh | 16 | 5 | 1 | 3* | 6 | 1.50 | – | – | 6 |
| M.Kaif | 48 | 39 | 8 | 111* | 899 | 29.00 | 1 | 4 | 22 |
| M.Kartik | 5 | 2 | – | 11 | 13 | 6.50 | – | – | 2 |
| Z.Khan | 67 | 35 | 13 | 34* | 252 | 11.45 | – | – | 17 |
| A.Kumble | 241 | 120 | 40 | 26 | 842 | 10.52 | – | – | 80 |
| V.V.S.Laxman | 51 | 49 | 3 | 101 | 1250 | 27.17 | 1 | 9 | 20 |
| D.Mongia | 43 | 38 | 3 | 159* | 925 | 26.42 | 1 | 2 | 19 |
| A.Nehra | 39 | 14 | 9 | 24 | 47 | 9.40 | – | – | 6 |

## LOI

### INDIA – BATTING AND FIELDING (continued)

|  | M | I | NO | HS | Runs | Avge | 100 | 50 | Ct/St |
|---|---|---|---|---|---|---|---|---|---|
| P.A.Patel | 1 | 1 | – | 13 | 13 | 13.00 | – | – | – |
| B.K.V.Prasad | 161 | 63 | 32 | 19 | 221 | 7.12 | – | – | 37 |
| A.Ratra | 12 | 8 | 1 | 30 | 90 | 12.85 | – | – | 11/5 |
| Sarandeep Singh | 3 | 3 | 1 | 19 | 28 | 14.00 | – | – | 1 |
| V.Sehwag | 68 | 66 | 6 | 126 | 2079 | 34.65 | 5 | 10 | 24 |
| R.S.Sodhi | 18 | 14 | 3 | 67 | 280 | 25.45 | – | 2 | 9 |
| J.Srinath | 229 | 121 | 38 | 53 | 883 | 10.63 | – | 1 | 32 |
| S.R.Tendulkar | 314 | 305 | 30 | 186* | 12219 | 44.43 | 34 | 62 | 97 |
| J.P.Yadav | 2 | 1 | – | 0 | 0 | 0.00 | – | – | 3 |
| T.Yohannan | 3 | 2 | 2 | 5* | 7 | – | – | – | – |
| Yuvraj Singh | 70 | 60 | 8 | 98* | 1529 | 29.40 | – | 12 | 22 |

### INDIA – BOWLING

|  | O | R | W | Avge | Best | 4wI | R/Over |
|---|---|---|---|---|---|---|---|
| A.B.Agarkar | 930.3 | 4769 | 166 | 28.72 | 4-25 | 7 | 5.12 |
| H.K.Badani | 15 | 74 | 2 | 37.00 | 1- 7 | – | 4.93 |
| L.Balaji | 4 | 44 | 0 | – | – | – | 11.00 |
| S.B.Bangar | 54 | 292 | 5 | 58.40 | 2-39 | – | 5.40 |
| R.V.Bharadwaj | 62 | 307 | 16 | 19.18 | 3-34 | – | 4.95 |
| R.Dravid | 31 | 170 | 4 | 42.50 | 2-43 | – | 5.48 |
| S.C.Ganguly | 600 | 2988 | 85 | 35.15 | 5-16 | 3 | 4.98 |
| Harbhajan Singh | 656 | 2746 | 94 | 29.21 | 5-43 | 3 | 4.18 |
| Harvinder Singh | 114.2 | 609 | 24 | 25.37 | 3-44 | – | 5.32 |
| M.Kartik | 47 | 236 | 4 | 59.00 | 3-36 | – | 5.02 |
| Z.Khan | 565.4 | 2654 | 104 | 25.51 | 4-42 | 5 | 4.69 |
| A.Kumble | 2152.3 | 9129 | 308 | 29.63 | 6-12 | 10 | 4.24 |
| V.V.S.Laxman | 7 | 40 | 0 | – | – | – | 5.71 |
| D.Mongia | 49.3 | 261 | 8 | 32.62 | 3-31 | – | 5.27 |
| A.Nehra | 321.4 | 1448 | 45 | 32.17 | 6-23 | 2 | 4.50 |
| B.K.V.Prasad | 1354.5 | 6332 | 196 | 32.30 | 5-27 | 4 | 4.67 |
| Sarandeep Singh | 23 | 114 | 1 | 114.00 | 1-49 | – | 4.95 |
| V.Sehwag | 237.4 | 1241 | 28 | 44.32 | 3-25 | – | 5.22 |
| R.S.Sodhi | 77 | 365 | 5 | 73.00 | 2-31 | – | 4.74 |
| J.Srinath | 1989.1 | 8847 | 315 | 28.08 | 5-23 | 10 | 4.44 |
| S.R.Tendulkar | 1053.5 | 5232 | 112 | 46.71 | 5-32 | 4 | 4.96 |
| J.P.Yadav | 6 | 36 | 0 | – | – | – | 6.00 |
| T.Yohannan | 20 | 122 | 5 | 24.40 | 3-33 | – | 6.10 |
| Yuvraj Singh | 162.3 | 787 | 23 | 34.21 | 4- 6 | 1 | 4.84 |

### PAKISTAN – BATTING AND FIELDING

|  | M | I | NO | HS | Runs | Avge | 100 | 50 | Ct/St |
|---|---|---|---|---|---|---|---|---|---|
| Abdul Razzaq | 124 | 106 | 22 | 112 | 2288 | 27.23 | 1 | 12 | 17 |
| Azhar Mahmood | 124 | 94 | 20 | 67 | 1309 | 17.68 | – | 3 | 37 |
| Danish Kaneria | 1 | 1 | 1 | 3* | 3 | – | – | – | – |
| Faisal Iqbal | 9 | 7 | 2 | 100* | 167 | 33.40 | 1 | – | 1 |
| Imran Nazir | 53 | 53 | 2 | 105* | 1271 | 24.92 | 1 | 8 | 15 |
| Inzamam-ul-Haq | 290 | 272 | 38 | 137* | 8957 | 38.27 | 8 | 64 | 87 |
| Kamran Akmal | 7 | 6 | 2 | 44 | 141 | 35.25 | – | – | 5 |
| Misbah-ul-Haq | 8 | 7 | 2 | 50* | 215 | 43.00 | – | 2 | 4 |
| Mohammad Sami | 19 | 8 | 5 | 4* | 10 | 3.33 | – | – | 5 |
| Mohammad Zahid | 11 | 4 | 2 | 7* | 15 | 7.50 | – | – | 1 |
| Mushtaq Ahmed | 143 | 76 | 34 | 34* | 399 | 9.50 | – | – | 30 |
| Naved Latif | 9 | 9 | – | 113 | 255 | 28.33 | 1 | – | 2 |
| Rashid Latif | 149 | 103 | 28 | 79 | 1474 | 19.65 | – | 3 | 156/35 |
| Saeed Anwar | 247 | 244 | 19 | 194 | 8823 | 39.21 | 20 | 43 | 42 |
| Salim Elahi | 40 | 40 | 2 | 135 | 1373 | 36.13 | 4 | 7 | 9 |
| Saqlain Mushtaq | 168 | 97 | 38 | 37* | 708 | 12.00 | – | – | 40 |
| Shahid Afridi | 176 | 171 | 7 | 109 | 3887 | 23.70 | 3 | 22 | 65 |
| Shoaib Akhtar | 81 | 36 | 22 | 43 | 170 | 12.14 | – | – | 13 |
| Shoaib Malik | 31 | 21 | 4 | 115 | 514 | 30.23 | 2 | – | 12 |

**PAKISTAN – BATTING AND FIELDING (continued)**

| | M | I | NO | HS | Runs | Avge | 100 | 50 | Ct/St |
|---|---|---|---|---|---|---|---|---|---|
| Taufiq Umar | 9 | 9 | – | 76 | 271 | 30.11 | – | 2 | 5 |
| Waqar Younis | 262 | 139 | 45 | 37 | 969 | 10.30 | – | – | 35 |
| Wasim Akram | 356 | 280 | 55 | 86 | 3717 | 16.52 | – | 6 | 88 |
| Younis Khan | 75 | 72 | 10 | 90 | 1907 | 30.75 | – | 14 | 34 |
| Yousuf Youhana | 127 | 121 | 18 | 141* | 4330 | 42.03 | 8 | 24 | 31 |

## PAKISTAN – BOWLING

| | O | R | W | Avge | Best | 4wI | R/Over |
|---|---|---|---|---|---|---|---|
| Abdul Razzaq | 915.4 | 4057 | 154 | 26.34 | 6-35 | 7 | 4.43 |
| Azhar Mahmood | 919.3 | 4181 | 112 | 37.33 | 6-18 | 5 | 4.54 |
| Danish Kaneria | 7 | 43 | 0 | – | – | | 6.14 |
| Faisal Iqbal | 3 | 33 | 0 | – | – | | 11.00 |
| Imran Nazir | 4.1 | 19 | 1 | 19.00 | 1- 3 | – | 4.56 |
| Inzamam-ul-Haq | 9.4 | 64 | 3 | 21.33 | 1- 0 | – | 6.61 |
| Mohammad Sami | 144.5 | 725 | 25 | 29.00 | 4-41 | 2 | 5.00 |
| Mohammad Zahid | 85.2 | 391 | 10 | 39.10 | 2-20 | – | 4.58 |
| Mushtaq Ahmed | 1247.1 | 5296 | 161 | 32.89 | 5-36 | 4 | 4.24 |
| Naved Latif | 8 | 51 | 0 | – | – | | 6.37 |
| Saeed Anwar | 40.2 | 191 | 6 | 31.83 | 2- 9 | – | 4.73 |
| Saqlain Mushtaq | 1453.4 | 6223 | 288 | 21.60 | 5-20 | 17 | 4.28 |
| Shahid Afridi | 1118.5 | 5152 | 131 | 39.32 | 5-40 | 1 | 4.60 |
| Shoaib Akhtar | 612.5 | 2815 | 133 | 21.16 | 6-16 | 5 | 4.59 |
| Shoaib Malik | 189.1 | 863 | 23 | 37.52 | 3-37 | – | 4.56 |
| Taufiq Umar | 11 | 77 | 1 | 77.00 | 1-49 | – | 7.00 |
| Waqar Younis | 2116.2 | 9919 | 416 | 23.84 | 7-36 | 27 | 4.68 |
| Wasim Akram | 3031 | 11812 | 502 | 23.52 | 5-15 | 23 | 3.89 |
| Younis Khan | 15 | 99 | 1 | 99.00 | 1-24 | – | 6.60 |

## SRI LANKA – BATTING AND FIELDING

| | M | I | NO | HS | Runs | Avge | 100 | 50 | Ct/St |
|---|---|---|---|---|---|---|---|---|---|
| R.P.Arnold | 119 | 104 | 27 | 103 | 2797 | 36.32 | 1 | 19 | 38 |
| M.S.Atapattu | 190 | 188 | 24 | 132* | 6346 | 38.69 | 10 | 45 | 52 |
| U.D.U.Chandana | 103 | 79 | 10 | 64 | 1507 | 15.31 | – | 2 | 61 |
| P.A.de Silva | 308 | 296 | 30 | 145 | 9284 | 34.90 | 11 | 64 | 95 |
| H.D.P.K.Dharmasena | 129 | 76 | 29 | 69* | 1040 | 22.12 | – | 4 | 34 |
| T.M.Dilshan | 17 | 14 | 3 | 53 | 282 | 25.63 | – | 2 | 8 |
| K.H.R.K.Fernando | 5 | 3 | 2 | 23* | 40 | 40.00 | – | – | 1 |
| C.R.D.Fernando | 54 | 23 | 13 | 13* | 81 | 8.10 | – | – | 11 |
| T.C.B.Fernando | 14 | 9 | 5 | 4* | 15 | 3.75 | – | – | 3 |
| P.W.Gunaratne | 23 | 8 | 3 | 15* | 36 | 7.20 | – | – | 3 |
| D.A.Gunawardana | 42 | 42 | – | 132 | 1222 | 29.09 | 1 | 7 | 9 |
| S.T.Jayasuriya | 297 | 289 | 12 | 189 | 8966 | 32.36 | 16 | 54 | 99 |
| D.P.M.D.Jayawardena | 140 | 131 | 12 | 128 | 3607 | 30.31 | 6 | 17 | 67 |
| R.S.Kaluwitharana | 179 | 171 | 13 | 102* | 3504 | 22.17 | 2 | 22 | 127/71 |
| M.K.G.C.P.Lakshitha | 7 | 2 | 1 | 4 | 7 | 7.00 | – | – | – |
| D.K.Liyanage | 16 | 11 | 2 | 43 | 144 | 16.00 | – | – | 6 |
| J.Mubarak | 6 | 6 | – | 15 | 48 | 8.00 | – | – | 6 |
| M.Muralitharan | 213 | 98 | 41 | 18 | 343 | 6.01 | – | – | 89 |
| M.N.Nawaz | 3 | 3 | 1 | 15* | 31 | 15.50 | – | – | – |
| R.A.P.Nissanka | 15 | 8 | 2 | 7* | 22 | 3.66 | – | – | 2 |
| A.S.A.Perera | 20 | 13 | 2 | 56* | 195 | 17.72 | – | 1 | 4 |
| T.T.Samaraweera | 14 | 11 | 1 | 33 | 175 | 17.50 | – | – | 2 |
| K.C.Sangakkara | 85 | 78 | 10 | 85 | 1827 | 26.86 | – | 9 | 68/19 |
| L.P.C.Silva | 10 | 8 | – | 55 | 134 | 16.75 | – | 1 | 2 |
| H.P.Tillekeratne | 197 | 165 | 40 | 104 | 3704 | 29.63 | 2 | 13 | 86/6 |
| W.P.U.C.J.Vaas | 220 | 151 | 51 | 50* | 1447 | 14.47 | – | 1 | 44 |
| G.P.Wickremasinghe | 134 | 64 | 24 | 32 | 344 | 8.60 | – | – | 26 |
| D.N.T.Zoysa | 67 | 34 | 15 | 32 | 230 | 12.10 | – | – | 10 |

# LOI

## SRI LANKA – BOWLING

| | O | R | W | Avge | Best | 4wI | R/Over |
|---|---|---|---|---|---|---|---|
| R.P.Arnold . | 324.4 | 1554 | 35 | 44.40 | 3-47 | – | 4.78 |
| M.S.Atapattu | 8.3 | 41 | 0 | – | – | – | 4.82 |
| U.D.U.Chandana | 693.5 | 3215 | 98 | 32.80 | 4-31 | 3 | 4.63 |
| P.A.de Silva | 858 | 4177 | 106 | 39.40 | 4-30 | 2 | 4.86 |
| H.D.P.K.Dharmasena | 1065 | 4580 | 133 | 34.43 | 4-37 | 1 | 4.30 |
| K.H.R.K.Fernando | 28 | 118 | 5 | 23.60 | 3-12 | – | 4.21 |
| C.R.D.Fernando | 383.3 | 2014 | 72 | 27.97 | 4-48 | 1 | 5.25 |
| T.C.B.Fernando | 99.4 | 508 | 14 | 36.28 | 5-67 | 1 | 5.09 |
| P.W.Gunaratne | 159.5 | 908 | 27 | 33.62 | 4-44 | 1 | 5.68 |
| S.T.Jayasuriya | 1807.4 | 8703 | 244 | 35.66 | 6-29 | 9 | 4.81 |
| D.P.M.D.Jayawardena | 88.4 | 502 | 7 | 71.71 | 2-56 | – | 5.66 |
| M.K.G.C.P.Lakshitha | 50 | 254 | 8 | 31.75 | 2-34 | – | 5.08 |
| D.K.Liyanage | 107 | 510 | 10 | 51.00 | 3-49 | – | 4.77 |
| J.Mubarak | 5 | 29 | 0 | – | – | – | 5.80 |
| M.Muralitharan | 1919.5 | 7341 | 321 | 22.86 | 7-30 | 15 | 3.82 |
| R.A.P.Nissanka | 108.3 | 628 | 16 | 39.25 | 4-12 | 1 | 5.78 |
| A.S.A.Perera | 96.3 | 522 | 13 | 40.15 | 2-25 | – | 5.41 |
| T.T.Samaraweera | 112 | 509 | 10 | 50.90 | 3-34 | – | 4.54 |
| H.P.Tillekeratne | 30 | 141 | 6 | 23.50 | 1- 3 | – | 4.70 |
| W.P.U.C.J.Vaas | 1791.3 | 7544 | 278 | 27.13 | 8-19 | 7 | 4.21 |
| G.P.Wickremasinghe | 953.2 | 4322 | 109 | 39.65 | 4-48 | 1 | 4.53 |
| D.N.T.Zoysa | 514.4 | 2378 | 73 | 32.57 | 4-28 | 2 | 4.62 |

## ZIMBABWE – BATTING AND FIELDING

| | M | I | NO | HS | Runs | Avge | 100 | 50 | Ct/St |
|---|---|---|---|---|---|---|---|---|---|
| A.M.Blignaut | 23 | 20 | 3 | 63* | 368 | 21.64 | – | 4 | 5 |
| G.B.Brent | 39 | 30 | 11 | 24 | 174 | 9.15 | – | – | 8 |
| A.D.R.Campbell | 187 | 183 | 14 | 131* | 5178 | 30.63 | 7 | 30 | 77 |
| S.V.Carlisle | 98 | 95 | 8 | 121* | 2372 | 27.26 | 2 | 8 | 34 |
| A.D.R.Campbell | 188 | 184 | 14 | 131* | 5185 | 30.50 | 7 | 30 | 77 |
| D.D.Ebrahim | 43 | 40 | 2 | 121 | 785 | 20.65 | 1 | 1 | 6 |
| S.M.Ervine | 16 | 13 | 3 | 61* | 192 | 19.20 | – | 1 | 1 |
| C.N.Evans | 53 | 47 | 5 | 96* | 764 | 18.19 | – | 2 | 12 |
| A.Flower | 213 | 208 | 16 | 145 | 6786 | 35.34 | 4 | 55 | 141/32 |
| G.W.Flower | 199 | 194 | 16 | 142* | 5986 | 33.62 | 6 | 35 | 76 |
| T.J.Friend | 40 | 29 | 5 | 91 | 416 | 17.33 | – | 2 | 13 |
| M.W.Goodwin | 71 | 70 | 3 | 112* | 1818 | 27.13 | 2 | 8 | 20 |
| T.R.Gripper | 5 | 5 | – | 26 | 41 | 8.20 | – | – | 3 |
| D.T.Hondo | 21 | 10 | 5 | 15* | 40 | 8.00 | – | – | 4 |
| D.A.Marillier | 40 | 34 | 4 | 56* | 460 | 15.33 | – | 2 | 10 |
| S.Matsikenyeri | 3 | 3 | 1 | 1* | 2 | 1.00 | – | – | – |
| M.Mbangwa | 29 | 13 | 6 | 11 | 34 | 4.85 | – | – | 3 |
| B.A.Murphy | 31 | 17 | 8 | 20* | 72 | 8.00 | – | – | 11 |
| W.Mwayenga | 1 | – | – | – | – | – | – | – | – |
| M.L.Nkala | 35 | 21 | 3 | 36 | 157 | 8.72 | – | – | 5 |
| H.K.Olonga | 50 | 27 | 14 | 31 | 95 | 7.30 | – | – | 13 |
| R.W.Price | 2 | 1 | – | 7 | 7 | 7.00 | – | – | – |
| B.G.Rogers | 2 | 2 | – | 13 | 13 | 6.50 | – | – | 1 |
| R.W.Sims | 2 | 1 | 1 | 7* | 7 | – | – | – | 1 |
| P.A.Strang | 95 | 73 | 24 | 47 | 1090 | 22.24 | – | – | 30 |
| H.H.Streak | 157 | 130 | 45 | 79* | 2132 | 25.08 | – | 7 | 37 |
| D.P.Viljoen | 53 | 43 | 7 | 63* | 512 | 14.22 | – | 2 | 18 |
| T.Taibu | 28 | 21 | 9 | 53 | 246 | 20.50 | – | 1 | 19/2 |
| M.A.Vermeulen | 10 | 10 | 2 | 79 | 258 | 32.25 | – | 2 | 3 |
| G.J.Whittall | 147 | 142 | 22 | 83 | 2705 | 22.54 | – | 11 | 35 |
| C.B.Wishart | 80 | 72 | 7 | 172* | 1576 | 24.24 | 2 | 4 | 24 |

## ZIMBABWE – BOWLING

|  | O | R | W | Avge | Best | 4wI | R/Over |
|---|---|---|---|---|---|---|---|
| A.M.Blignaut | 176.4 | 820 | 18 | 45.55 | 2-24 | – | 4.64 |
| G.B.Brent | 320 | 1630 | 45 | 36.22 | 4-53 | 1 | 5.09 |
| A.D.R.Campbell | 84.5 | 434 | 12 | 36.16 | 2-20 | – | 5.11 |
| D.D.Ebrahim | 0.3 | 6 | 0 | – | – | – | 12.00 |
| S.M.Ervine | 112.4 | 660 | 14 | 47.14 | 3-29 | – | 5.85 |
| C.N.Evans | 160.4 | 848 | 21 | 40.38 | 3-11 | – | 5.27 |
| A.Flower | 5 | 23 | 0 | – | – | – | 4.60 |
| G.W.Flower | 808.3 | 3731 | 97 | 38.46 | 4-32 | 2 | 4.61 |
| T.J.Friend | 306.1 | 1674 | 36 | 46.50 | 4-55 | 1 | 5.46 |
| M.W.Goodwin | 41.2 | 210 | 4 | 52.50 | 1-12 | – | 5.08 |
| T.R.Gripper | 10 | 22 | 0 | – | – | – | 2.20 |
| D.T.Hondo | 146.5 | 853 | 27 | 31.59 | 4-37 | 3 | 5.80 |
| D.A.Marillier | 229.2 | 1079 | 29 | 37.20 | 4-38 | 1 | 4.70 |
| S.Matsikenyeri | 2 | 13 | 0 | – | – | – | 6.50 |
| M.Mbangwa | 228.1 | 1140 | 11 | 103.63 | 2-24 | – | 4.99 |
| B.A.Murphy | 237 | 1130 | 29 | 38.96 | 3-43 | – | 4.76 |
| W.Mwayenga | 9 | 74 | 0 | – | – | – | 8.22 |
| M.L.Nkala | 212.3 | 1245 | 18 | 69.16 | 3-12 | – | 5.85 |
| H.K.Olonga | 343.1 | 1977 | 58 | 34.08 | 6-19 | 4 | 5.76 |
| R.W.Price | 14 | 65 | 0 | – | – | – | 4.64 |
| B.G.Rogers | 4 | 30 | 0 | – | – | – | 7.50 |
| R.W.Sims | 19 | 109 | 0 | – | – | – | 5.73 |
| P.A.Strang | 725.1 | 3174 | 96 | 33.06 | 5-21 | 4 | 4.38 |
| H.H.Streak | 1311.3 | 6002 | 190 | 31.58 | 5-32 | 6 | 4.57 |
| D.P.Viljoen | 345.5 | 1639 | 44 | 37.25 | 3-20 | – | 4.74 |
| G.J.Whittall | 676.4 | 3480 | 88 | 39.54 | 4-35 | 1 | 5.14 |
| C.B.Wishart | 2 | 12 | 0 | – | – | – | 6.00 |

## BANGLADESH – BATTING AND FIELDING

|  | M | I | NO | HS | Runs | Avge | 100 | 50 | Ct/St |
|---|---|---|---|---|---|---|---|---|---|
| Akram Khan | 40 | 40 | 2 | 65 | 914 | 24.05 | – | 5 | 8 |
| Al Sahariar | 27 | 27 | 1 | 62* | 358 | 13.76 | – | 2 | 7 |
| Alok Kapali | 17 | 16 | 2 | 89* | 308 | 22.00 | – | 1 | 5 |
| Aminul Islam | 39 | 39 | 5 | 70 | 794 | 23.35 | – | 3 | 13 |
| Anwar Hossain Monir | 1 | 1 | 1 | 0* | 0 | – | – | – | – |
| Anwar Hossain Piju | 1 | 1 | – | 42 | 42 | 42.00 | – | – | – |
| Ehsanul Haque | 6 | 6 | – | 20 | 57 | 9.50 | – | – | – |
| Enamul Haque | 29 | 26 | 5 | 32 | 236 | 11.23 | – | – | 6 |
| Fahim Muntasir | 3 | 3 | 1 | 5 | 6 | 3.00 | – | – | 1 |
| Habibul Bashar | 29 | 29 | – | 74 | 548 | 18.89 | – | 6 | 6 |
| Hannan Sarkar | 7 | 7 | – | 25 | 62 | 8.85 | – | – | 2 |
| Hasibul Hussain | 28 | 22 | 3 | 21* | 161 | 8.47 | – | – | 6 |
| Javed Omar | 24 | 24 | 3 | 85* | 530 | 25.23 | – | 4 | 6 |
| Khaled Mahmud | 38 | 35 | – | 50 | 509 | 14.54 | – | 1 | 9 |
| Khaled Masud | 57 | 52 | 10 | 54* | 752 | 17.90 | – | 3 | 40/9 |
| Mashrafe Mortaza | 5 | 5 | – | 28 | 48 | 9.60 | – | – | 1 |
| Mazharul Haque | 1 | 1 | – | 3 | 3 | 3.00 | – | – | – |
| Mehrab Hossain | 15 | 15 | – | 101 | 413 | 27.53 | 1 | 2 | 5 |
| Mohammed Ashraful | 16 | 16 | 1 | 56 | 242 | 16.13 | – | 1 | 3 |
| Mohammed Rafique | 40 | 38 | 4 | 77 | 434 | 12.76 | – | 1 | 9 |
| Mohammed Sharif | 8 | 8 | 5 | 13* | 47 | 15.66 | – | – | 1 |
| Monjurul Islam | 32 | 20 | 12 | 13 | 47 | 5.87 | – | – | 8 |
| Naimur Rahman | 29 | 27 | 2 | 47 | 488 | 19.52 | – | – | 7 |
| Rafiqul Islam | 1 | 1 | – | 0 | 0 | 0.00 | – | – | – |
| Sanwar Hossain | 20 | 20 | 2 | 52 | 224 | 12.44 | – | 1 | 9 |
| Talha Jubair | 6 | 5 | 3 | 4* | 5 | 2.50 | – | – | 1 |
| Tapash Baisya | 14 | 12 | 5 | 35* | 80 | 11.42 | – | – | 3 |
| Tareq Aziz | 3 | 2 | 1 | 7* | 7 | 7.00 | – | – | 1 |
| Tushar Imran | 16 | 15 | – | 65 | 334 | 22.26 | – | 2 | 1 |

LOI                    **BANGLADESH – BOWLING**

|  | O | R | W | Avge | Best | 4wI | R/Over |
|---|---|---|---|---|---|---|---|
| Akram Khan | 19.3 | 138 | 0 | – | – | – | 7.07 |
| Aminul Islam | 68.4 | 411 | 7 | 58.71 | 3-57 | – | 5.99 |
| Alok Kapali | 60 | 325 | 3 | 108.33 | 1- 3 | – | 5.41 |
| Anwar Hossain Monir | 8 | 45 | 0 | – | – | – | 5.62 |
| Ehsanul Haque | 23.3 | 113 | 3 | 37.66 | 2-34 | – | 4.80 |
| Enamul Haque | 206.2 | 1083 | 19 | 57.00 | 2-40 | – | 5.24 |
| Fahim Muntasir | 28.1 | 111 | 0 | – | – | – | 3.94 |
| Habibul Bashar | 29.1 | 142 | 1 | 142.00 | 1-31 | – | 4.86 |
| Hasibul Hussain | 206.1 | 1187 | 28 | 42.39 | 4-56 | 1 | 5.76 |
| Khaled Mahmud | 290.2 | 1422 | 37 | 38.43 | 3-31 | – | 4.89 |
| Mashrafe Mortaza | 40.2 | 192 | 6 | 32.00 | 2-26 | – | 4.76 |
| Mazharul Haque | 0.4 | 4 | 0 | – | – | – | 6.00 |
| Mehrab Hossain | 3 | 32 | 0 | – | – | – | 10.66 |
| Mohammed Ashraful | 38.3 | 242 | 7 | 34.57 | 3-26 | – | 6.28 |
| Mohammed Rafique | 319.2 | 1526 | 29 | 52.62 | 3-56 | – | 4.77 |
| Mohammed Sharif | 73.2 | 371 | 9 | 41.22 | 3-40 | – | 5.05 |
| Monjurul Islam | 249.2 | 1219 | 24 | 50.79 | 3-37 | – | 4.88 |
| Naimur Rahman | 182.2 | 905 | 10 | 90.50 | 2-51 | – | 4.96 |
| Sanwar Hossain | 33.3 | 167 | 6 | 27.83 | 3-49 | – | 4.98 |
| Talha Jubair | 34 | 255 | 6 | 42.50 | 4-65 | 1 | 7.50 |
| Tapash Baisya | 94 | 532 | 12 | 44.33 | 3-50 | – | 5.65 |
| Tareq Aziz | 28.3 | 126 | 4 | 31.50 | 3-19 | – | 4.42 |

## KENYA – BATTING AND FIELDING

|  | M | I | NO | HS | Runs | Avge | 100 | 50 | Ct/St |
|---|---|---|---|---|---|---|---|---|---|
| J.Ababu | 3 | 2 | – | 17 | 28 | 14.00 | – | – | 1 |
| J.O.Angara | 16 | 10 | 5 | 6 | 23 | 4.60 | – | – | 2 |
| S.K.Gupta | 10 | 10 | 1 | 41 | 121 | 13.44 | – | – | – |
| J.K.Kamande | 15 | 11 | 4 | 32* | 134 | 19.14 | – | – | 6 |
| A.Y.Karim | 34 | 24 | 6 | 53 | 228 | 12.66 | – | 1 | 6 |
| H.S.Modi | 50 | 43 | 6 | 78* | 903 | 24.40 | – | 5 | 8 |
| C.O.Obuya | 25 | 20 | 3 | 29 | 236 | 13.88 | – | – | 6 |
| D.O.Obuya | 20 | 20 | 2 | 34 | 154 | 8.55 | – | – | 19/4 |
| K.O.Obuya | 58 | 57 | 1 | 144 | 1401 | 25.01 | 2 | 8 | 22/13 |
| T.M.Odoyo | 58 | 55 | 7 | 53 | 1031 | 21.47 | – | 2 | 16 |
| M.O.Odumbe | 58 | 56 | 5 | 83 | 1296 | 25.41 | – | 10 | 9 |
| P.O.Ongondo | 17 | 15 | 3 | 36 | 127 | 10.58 | – | – | 1 |
| L.N.Onyango | 5 | 5 | 2 | 23 | 30 | 10.00 | – | – | 1 |
| B.J.Patel | 19 | 13 | 1 | 44 | 247 | 20.58 | – | – | 4 |
| R.D.Shah | 42 | 42 | – | 71 | 1092 | 26.00 | – | 10 | 11 |
| A.O.Suji | 41 | 32 | 6 | 67 | 314 | 12.07 | – | 1 | 13 |
| M.A.Suji | 58 | 47 | 21 | 16* | 222 | 8.53 | – | – | 10 |
| S.O.Tikolo | 60 | 58 | 2 | 106* | 1654 | 29.53 | 1 | 14 | 19 |
| A.V.Vadher | 18 | 16 | 6 | 73* | 278 | 27.80 | – | 2 | 6 |

## KENYA – BOWLING

|  | O | R | W | Avge | Best | 4wI | R/Over |
|---|---|---|---|---|---|---|---|
| J.Ababu | 16 | 75 | 1 | 75.00 | 1-26 | – | 4.69 |
| J.O.Angara | 90 | 517 | 13 | 39.76 | 3-10 | – | 5.74 |
| J.K.Kamande | 38.3 | 240 | 3 | 80.00 | 1-16 | – | 6.23 |
| A.Y.Karim | 261.2 | 1114 | 27 | 41.25 | 5-33 | 1 | 4.26 |
| H.S.Modi | 3.1 | 27 | 0 | – | – | – | 8.52 |
| C.O.Obuya | 193 | 1000 | 20 | 50.00 | 5-24 | 1 | 5.18 |
| K.O.Obuya | 1 | 5 | 0 | – | – | – | 5.00 |
| T.M.Odoyo | 414.2 | 2045 | 54 | 37.87 | 4-28 | 1 | 4.93 |
| M.O.Odumbe | 346.5 | 1666 | 39 | 42.71 | 4-38 | 1 | 4.80 |
| P.O.Ongondo | 92.2 | 441 | 5 | 88.20 | 2-44 | – | 4.77 |
| L.N.Onyango | 13.3 | 130 | 1 | 130.00 | 1-45 | – | 9.63 |
| B.J.Patel | 16.1 | 108 | 2 | 54.00 | 1-15 | – | 6.67 |

**LOI**

## KENYA – BOWLING (continued)

| | O | R | W | Avge | Best | 4wI | R/Over |
|---|---|---|---|---|---|---|---|
| R.D.Shah | 10 | 72 | 0 | – | – | – | 7.20 |
| A.O.Suji | 165.5 | 863 | 11 | 78.45 | 2-24 | – | 5.20 |
| M.A.Suji | 443 | 1954 | 41 | 47.65 | 4-24 | 1 | 4.41 |
| S.O.Tikolo | 255.5 | 1315 | 37 | 35.54 | 3-14 | – | 5.14 |

## CANADA – BATTING AND FIELDING

| | M | I | NO | HS | Runs | Avge | 100 | 50 | Ct/St |
|---|---|---|---|---|---|---|---|---|---|
| A.Bagai | 6 | 6 | 1 | 28* | 56 | 11.20 | – | – | 8/2 |
| I.S.Billcliff | 6 | 6 | – | 71 | 147 | 24.50 | – | 1 | – |
| D.Chumney | 5 | 5 | – | 28 | 68 | 13.60 | – | – | – |
| A.Codrington | 5 | 5 | – | 16 | 28 | 5.60 | – | – | – |
| J.M.Davison | 6 | 6 | – | 111 | 226 | 37.66 | 1 | 1 | 1 |
| N.A.de Groot | 6 | 6 | – | 17 | 44 | 7.33 | – | – | – |
| J.V.Harris | 6 | 6 | – | 31 | 91 | 15.16 | – | – | 1 |
| N.Ifill | 3 | 2 | – | 9 | 16 | 8.00 | – | – | 1 |
| D.Joseph | 4 | 3 | 3 | 9* | 13 | – | – | – | – |
| I.Maraj | 6 | 6 | 1 | 53* | 98 | 19.60 | – | 1 | 2 |
| A.Patel | 2 | 1 | – | 25 | 25 | 25.00 | – | – | – |
| A.M.Samad | 1 | 1 | – | 12 | 12 | 12.00 | – | – | – |
| A.F.Sattaur | 3 | 3 | – | 13 | 20 | 6.66 | – | – | 2 |
| B.B.Seebaran | 4 | 3 | 2 | 4* | 4 | 4.00 | – | – | 1 |
| S.Thuraisingham | 3 | 3 | – | 13 | 25 | 8.33 | – | – | – |

## CANADA – BOWLING

| | O | R | W | Avge | Best | 4wI | R/Over |
|---|---|---|---|---|---|---|---|
| A.Codrington | 25 | 129 | 6 | 21.50 | 5-27 | 1 | 5.16 |
| J.M.Davison | 42 | 187 | 10 | 18.70 | 3-15 | – | 4.45 |
| N.A.de Groot | 13.3 | 88 | 3 | 29.33 | 2-45 | – | 6.51 |
| N.Ifill | 12 | 88 | 0 | – | – | – | 7.33 |
| D.Joseph | 31 | 170 | 5 | 34.00 | 2-42 | – | 5.48 |
| I.Maraj | 4.3 | 22 | 0 | – | – | – | 4.88 |
| A.Patel | 10 | 73 | 3 | 24.33 | 3-41 | – | 7.30 |
| B.B.Seebaran | 18 | 130 | 1 | 130.00 | 1-61 | – | 7.22 |
| S.Thuraisingham | 18.4 | 109 | 4 | 27.25 | 2-53 | – | 5.83 |

## HOLLAND – BATTING AND FIELDING

| | M | I | NO | HS | Runs | Avge | 100 | 50 | Ct/St |
|---|---|---|---|---|---|---|---|---|---|
| T.B.M.de Leede | 13 | 13 | 1 | 58* | 243 | 20.25 | – | 1 | 3 |
| J.J.Esmeijer | 6 | 5 | 1 | 7 | 10 | 2.50 | – | – | 3 |
| V.D.Grandia | 1 | 1 | – | 0 | 0 | 0.00 | – | – | – |
| J.F.Kloppenburg | 6 | 6 | – | 121 | 165 | 27.50 | 1 | – | 1 |
| R.P.Lefebvre | 11 | 11 | 1 | 45 | 171 | 28.50 | – | – | 4 |
| H.J.C.Mol | 5 | 4 | – | 23 | 38 | 9.50 | – | – | 1 |
| M.A.K.Raja | 5 | 4 | 1 | 5 | 9 | 3.00 | – | – | 1 |
| E.Schiferli | 8 | 8 | – | 22 | 90 | 11.25 | – | – | 1 |
| R.H.Scholte | 5 | 5 | – | 12 | 39 | 7.80 | – | – | – |
| J.Smits | 6 | 5 | 2 | 26 | 58 | 19.33 | – | – | 4/1 |
| N.A.Statham | 2 | 2 | – | 7 | 7 | 3.50 | – | – | – |
| D.L.S.van Bunge | 8 | 7 | – | 62 | 139 | 19.85 | – | 1 | 2 |
| K-J.J.van Noortwijk | 9 | 9 | 2 | 134* | 322 | 46.00 | 1 | 1 | – |
| R.F.van Oosterom | 3 | 3 | 2 | 5* | 7 | 7.00 | – | – | 2 |
| L.P.van Troost | 8 | 8 | 1 | 26 | 112 | 16.00 | – | – | – |
| B.Zuiderent | 13 | 13 | 1 | 54 | 133 | 11.08 | – | 1 | 12 |

**LOI**                    **HOLLAND – BOWLING**

|                | O    | R   | W  | Avge  | Best  | 4wI | R/Over |
|----------------|------|-----|----|-------|-------|-----|--------|
| T.B.M.de Leede | 82.5 | 488 | 11 | 44.36 | 4-35  | 1   | 5.89   |
| J.J.Esmeijer   | 38   | 208 | 0  | –     | –     | –   | 5.47   |
| V.D.Grandia    | 5    | 40  | 1  | 40.00 | 1-40  | –   | 8.00   |
| J.F.Kloppenburg| 40.2 | 191 | 8  | 23.87 | 4-42  | 1   | 4.73   |
| R.P.Lefebvre   | 89   | 346 | 9  | 38.44 | 2-38  | –   | 3.88   |
| H.J.C.Mol      | 13   | 89  | 2  | 44.50 | 1-24  | –   | 6.84   |
| M.A.K.Raja     | 35.1 | 204 | 8  | 25.50 | 4-42  | 1   | 5.80   |
| E.Schiferli    | 60   | 327 | 4  | 81.75 | 2-43  | –   | 5.45   |
| D.L.S.van Bunge| 12   | 85  | 5  | 17.00 | 3-16  | –   | 7.08   |
| L.P.van Troost | 8    | 48  | 0  | –     | –     | –   | 6.00   |

**NAMIBIA – BATTING AND FIELDING**

|                 | M | I | NO | HS  | Runs | Avge  | 100 | 50 | Ct/St |
|-----------------|---|---|----|-----|------|-------|-----|----|-------|
| A.J-B.Burger    | 6 | 6 | –  | 85  | 199  | 33.16 | –   | 1  | –     |
| L.J.Burger      | 6 | 6 | 1  | 5   | 11   | 2.20  | –   | –  | 6     |
| S.F.Burger      | 2 | 2 | –  | 6   | 11   | 5.50  | –   | –  | 1     |
| M.Karg          | 3 | 2 | –  | 41  | 45   | 22.50 | –   | –  | 1     |
| D.Keulder       | 6 | 6 | –  | 52  | 132  | 22.00 | –   | 1  | 3     |
| B.L.Kotze       | 5 | 4 | 1  | 24* | 27   | 9.00  | –   | –  | 1     |
| D.B.Kotze       | 6 | 6 | 1  | 27  | 82   | 16.40 | –   | –  | 3     |
| J.L.Louw        | 1 | – | –  | –   | –    | –     | –   | –  | 1     |
| B.G.Murgatroyd  | 6 | 6 | –  | 52  | 90   | 15.00 | –   | 1  | –     |
| G.Snyman        | 5 | 4 | –  | 5   | 5    | 1.25  | –   | –  | –     |
| S.J.Swanepoel   | 5 | 5 | –  | 23  | 43   | 8.60  | –   | –  | –     |
| B.O.van Rooi    | 3 | 3 | 2  | 17  | 26   | 26.00 | –   | –  | 1     |
| M.van Schoor    | 5 | 5 | 1  | 24  | 58   | 14.50 | –   | –  | 4     |
| R.J.van Vuuren  | 5 | 5 | 2  | 14  | 26   | 8.66  | –   | –  | –     |
| R.Walters       | 2 | 2 | –  | 0   | 0    | 0.00  | –   | –  | –     |

**NAMIBIA – BOWLING**

|                | O  | R   | W | Avge   | Best | 4wI | R/Over |
|----------------|----|-----|---|--------|------|-----|--------|
| A.J-B.Burger   | 16 | 104 | 3 | 34.66  | 1-18 | –   | 6.50   |
| L.J.Burger     | 55 | 297 | 6 | 49.50  | 3-39 | –   | 5.40   |
| S.F.Burger     | 11 | 67  | 0 | –      | –    | –   | 6.09   |
| B.L.Kotze      | 43 | 276 | 3 | 92.00  | 2-51 | –   | 6.41   |
| D.B.Kotze      | 47 | 256 | 2 | 128.00 | 1-32 | –   | 5.44   |
| J.L.Louw       | 10 | 60  | 1 | 60.00  | 1-60 | –   | 6.00   |
| G.Snyman       | 48 | 281 | 6 | 46.83  | 3-69 | –   | 5.85   |
| B.O.van Rooi   | 20 | 119 | 1 | 119.00 | 1-24 | –   | 5.95   |
| R.J.van Vuuren | 50 | 298 | 8 | 37.25  | 5-43 | 1   | 5.96   |

**SCOTLAND – BATTING AND FIELDING**

|              | M | I | NO | HS | Runs | Avge  | 100 | 50 | Ct/St |
|--------------|---|---|----|----|------|-------|-----|----|-------|
| J.A.R.Blain  | 5 | 5 | 1  | 9  | 15   | 3.75  | –   | –  | 1     |
| G.M.Hamilton | 5 | 5 | 1  | 76 | 217  | 54.25 | –   | 2  | 1     |

**SCOTLAND – BOWLING**

|              | O    | R   | W  | Avge  | Best | 4wI | R/Over |
|--------------|------|-----|----|-------|------|-----|--------|
| J.A.R.Blain  | 37.1 | 210 | 10 | 21.00 | 4-37 | 1   | 5.65   |
| G.M.Hamilton | 35.4 | 149 | 3  | 49.66 | 2-36 | –   | 4.18   |

# TEST CAREER RECORDS

Complete to 9 April 2003, these records include all players registered for county cricket in 2003 at the time of going to press, plus those who have played Test cricket since 1 October 2001.

## ENGLAND – BATTING AND FIELDING

| | M | I | NO | HS | Runs | Avge | 100 | 50 | Ct/St |
|---|---|---|---|---|---|---|---|---|---|
| C.J.Adams | 5 | 8 | – | 31 | 104 | 13.00 | – | – | 6 |
| U.Afzaal | 3 | 6 | 1 | 54 | 83 | 16.60 | – | 1 | – |
| M.P.Bicknell | 2 | 4 | – | 14 | 26 | 6.50 | – | – | – |
| R.J.Blakey | 2 | 4 | – | 6 | 7 | 1.75 | – | – | 2 |
| M.A.Butcher | 50 | 93 | 3 | 173* | 2969 | 32.98 | 6 | 12 | 44 |
| A.R.Caddick | 62 | 95 | 12 | 49* | 861 | 10.37 | – | – | 21 |
| D.G.Cork | 37 | 56 | 8 | 59 | 864 | 18.00 | – | 3 | 18 |
| J.P.Crawley | 37 | 61 | 9 | 156* | 1800 | 34.61 | 4 | 9 | 29 |
| R.D.B.Croft | 21 | 34 | 8 | 37* | 421 | 16.19 | – | – | 10 |
| R.K.J.Dawson | 7 | 13 | 3 | 19* | 114 | 11.40 | – | – | 3 |
| P.A.J.DeFreitas | 44 | 68 | 5 | 88 | 934 | 14.82 | – | 4 | 14 |
| M.A.Ealham | 8 | 13 | 3 | 53* | 210 | 21.00 | – | 2 | 4 |
| A.Flintoff | 21 | 33 | – | 137 | 643 | 19.48 | 1 | 2 | 14 |
| J.S.Foster | 7 | 12 | 3 | 48 | 226 | 25.11 | – | – | 17/1 |
| J.E.R.Gallian | 3 | 6 | – | 28 | 74 | 12.33 | – | – | 1 |
| E.S.H.Giddins | 4 | 7 | 3 | 7 | 10 | 2.50 | – | – | – |
| A.F.Giles | 19 | 28 | 5 | 45 | 324 | 14.08 | – | – | 13 |
| D.Gough | 56 | 83 | 18 | 65 | 806 | 12.40 | – | 2 | 12 |
| A.Habib | 2 | 3 | – | 19 | 26 | 8.66 | – | – | – |
| G.M.Hamilton | 1 | 2 | – | 0 | 0 | 0.00 | – | – | – |
| S.J.Harmison | 5 | 9 | 2 | 20* | 50 | 7.14 | – | – | 1 |
| W.K.Hegg | 2 | 4 | – | 15 | 30 | 7.50 | – | – | 8 |
| G.A.Hick | 65 | 114 | 6 | 178 | 3383 | 31.32 | 6 | 18 | 90 |
| M.J.Hoggard | 18 | 26 | 10 | 32 | 106 | 6.62 | – | – | 5 |
| A.J.Hollioake | 4 | 6 | – | 45 | 65 | 10.83 | – | – | 4 |
| N.Hussain | 81 | 144 | 13 | 207 | 4866 | 37.14 | 12 | 27 | 57 |
| R.C.Irani | 3 | 5 | – | 41 | 86 | 17.20 | – | – | 2 |
| S.P.James | 2 | 4 | – | 36 | 71 | 17.75 | – | – | – |
| S.P.Jones | 2 | 1 | – | 44 | 44 | 44.00 | – | – | – |
| R.W.T.Key | 6 | 11 | – | 52 | 222 | 20.18 | – | 1 | 3 |
| N.V.Knight | 17 | 30 | – | 113 | 719 | 23.96 | 1 | 4 | 26 |
| D.L.Maddy | 3 | 4 | – | 24 | 46 | 11.50 | – | – | 4 |
| D.E.Malcolm | 40 | 58 | 19 | 29 | 236 | 6.05 | – | – | 7 |
| P.J.Martin | 8 | 13 | – | 29 | 115 | 8.84 | – | – | 6 |
| M.P.Maynard | 4 | 8 | – | 35 | 87 | 10.87 | – | – | 3 |
| A.D.Mullally | 19 | 27 | 4 | 24 | 127 | 5.52 | – | – | 6 |
| J.Ormond | 2 | 4 | 1 | 18 | 38 | 12.66 | – | – | – |
| M.M.Patel | 2 | 2 | – | 27 | 45 | 22.50 | – | – | 2 |
| M.R.Ramprakash | 52 | 92 | 6 | 154 | 2350 | 27.32 | 2 | 12 | 39 |
| C.M.W.Read | 3 | 4 | – | 37 | 38 | 9.50 | – | – | 10/1 |
| S.J.Rhodes | 11 | 17 | 5 | 65* | 294 | 24.50 | – | 1 | 46/3 |
| R.C.Russell | 54 | 86 | 16 | 128* | 1897 | 27.10 | 2 | 6 | 153/12 |
| I.D.K.Salisbury | 15 | 25 | 3 | 50 | 368 | 16.72 | – | 1 | 5 |
| C.P.Schofield | 2 | 3 | – | 57 | 67 | 22.33 | – | 1 | – |
| R.J.Sidebottom | 1 | 1 | – | 4 | 4 | 4.00 | – | – | – |
| C.E.W.Silverwood | 6 | 7 | 3 | 10 | 29 | 7.25 | – | – | 2 |
| A.M.Smith | 1 | 2 | 1 | 4* | 4 | 4.00 | – | – | – |
| R.A.Smith | 62 | 112 | 15 | 175 | 4236 | 43.67 | 9 | 28 | 39 |
| J.P.Stephenson | 1 | 2 | – | 25 | 36 | 18.00 | – | – | – |
| A.J.Stewart | 126 | 225 | 21 | 190 | 8187 | 40.13 | 15 | 43 | 247/13 |
| G.P.Thorpe | 77 | 140 | 18 | 200* | 5109 | 41.87 | 11 | 30 | 86 |

## ENGLAND – BATTING AND FIELDING (continued)

|  | M | I | NO | HS | Runs | Avge | 100 | 50 | Ct/St |
|---|---|---|---|---|---|---|---|---|---|
| M.E.Trescothick | 31 | 59 | 4 | 161 | 2213 | 40.23 | 3 | 15 | 26 |
| A.J.Tudor | 10 | 16 | 4 | 99* | 229 | 19.08 | – | 1 | 3 |
| P.C.R.Tufnell | 42 | 59 | 29 | 22* | 153 | 5.10 | – | – | 12 |
| M.P.Vaughan | 28 | 49 | 3 | 197 | 2343 | 50.93 | 8 | 5 | 17 |
| I.J.Ward | 5 | 9 | 1 | 39 | 129 | 16.12 | – | – | 1 |
| C.White | 30 | 50 | 7 | 121 | 1052 | 24.46 | 1 | 5 | 14 |

## ENGLAND – BOWLING

|  | O | R | W | Avge | Best | 5wI | 10wM |
|---|---|---|---|---|---|---|---|
| C.J.Adams | 20 | 59 | 1 | 59.00 | 1- 42 | – | – |
| U.Afzaal | 9 | 49 | 1 | 49.00 | 1- 49 | – | – |
| M.P.Bicknell | 87 | 263 | 4 | 65.75 | 3- 99 | – | – |
| M.A.Butcher | 119.2 | 412 | 10 | 41.20 | 4- 42 | – | – |
| A.R.Caddick | 2259.4 | 6999 | 234 | 29.91 | 7- 46 | 13 | 1 |
| D.G.Cork | 1279.4 | 3906 | 131 | 29.81 | 7- 43 | 5 | – |
| R.D.B.Croft | 769.5 | 1825 | 49 | 37.24 | 5- 95 | 1 | – |
| R.K.J.Dawson | 186 | 677 | 11 | 61.54 | 4-134 | – | – |
| P.A.J.DeFreitas | 1639.4 | 4700 | 140 | 33.57 | 7- 70 | 4 | – |
| M.A.Ealham | 176.4 | 488 | 17 | 28.70 | 4- 21 | – | – |
| A.Flintoff | 541.5 | 1556 | 33 | 47.15 | 4- 50 | – | – |
| J.E.R.Gallian | 14 | 62 | 0 |  |  |  |  |
| E.S.H.Giddins | 74 | 240 | 12 | 20.00 | 5- 15 | 1 | – |
| A.F.Giles | 829.3 | 2102 | 55 | 38.21 | 5- 67 | 2 | – |
| D.Gough | 1917.1 | 6288 | 228 | 27.57 | 6- 42 | 9 | – |
| G.M.Hamilton | 15 | 63 | 0 |  |  |  |  |
| S.J.Harmison | 181.3 | 575 | 14 | 41.07 | 3- 57 | – | – |
| G.A.Hick | 509.3 | 1306 | 23 | 56.78 | 4-126 | – | – |
| M.J.Hoggard | 678.4 | 2261 | 66 | 34.25 | 7- 63 | 2 | – |
| A.J.Hollioake | 24 | 67 | 2 | 33.50 | 2- 31 | – | – |
| N.Hussain | 5 | 15 | 0 |  |  |  |  |
| R.C.Irani | 32 | 112 | 3 | 37.33 | 1- 22 | – | – |
| S.P.Jones | 45 | 161 | 5 | 32.20 | 2- 61 | – | – |
| D.L.Maddy | 14 | 40 | 0 |  |  |  |  |
| D.E.Malcolm | 1413.2 | 4748 | 128 | 37.09 | 9- 57 | 5 | 2 |
| P.J.Martin | 242 | 580 | 17 | 34.11 | 4- 60 | – | – |
| A.D.Mullally | 754.1 | 1812 | 58 | 31.24 | 5-105 | 1 | – |
| J.Ormond | 62 | 185 | 2 | 92.50 | 1- 70 | – | – |
| M.M.Patel | 46 | 180 | 1 | 180.00 | 1-101 | – | – |
| M.R.Ramprakash | 149.1 | 477 | 4 | 119.25 | 1- 2 | – | – |
| I.D.K.Salisbury | 415.2 | 1539 | 20 | 76.95 | 4-163 | – | – |
| C.P.Schofield | 18 | 73 | 0 |  |  |  |  |
| R.J.Sidebottom | 20 | 64 | 0 |  |  |  |  |
| C.E.W.Silverwood | 138 | 444 | 11 | 40.36 | 5- 91 | 1 | – |
| A.M.Smith | 23 | 89 | 0 |  |  |  |  |
| R.A.Smith | 4 | 6 | 0 |  |  |  |  |
| A.J.Stewart | 3.2 | 13 | 0 |  |  |  |  |
| G.P.Thorpe | 23 | 37 | 0 |  |  |  |  |
| M.E.Trescothick | 20 | 52 | 1 | 52.00 | 1- 34 | – | – |
| A.J.Tudor | 252 | 963 | 28 | 34.39 | 5- 44 | 1 | – |
| P.C.R.Tufnell | 1881.2 | 4560 | 121 | 37.68 | 7- 47 | 5 | 2 |
| M.P.Vaughan | 90 | 310 | 4 | 77.50 | 2- 71 | – | – |
| C.White | 659.5 | 2220 | 59 | 37.62 | 5- 32 | 3 | – |

## AUSTRALIA – BATTING AND FIELDING

|  | M | I | NO | HS | Runs | Avge | 100 | 50 | Ct/St |
|---|---|---|---|---|---|---|---|---|---|
| A.J.Bichel | 11 | 14 | 1 | 49 | 175 | 13.46 | – | – | 7 |
| M.T.G.Elliott | 20 | 34 | 1 | 199 | 1171 | 35.48 | 3 | 4 | 13 |

## AUSTRALIA – BATTING AND FIELDING (continued)

| | M | I | NO | HS | Runs | Avge | 100 | 50 | Ct/St |
|---|---|---|---|---|---|---|---|---|---|
| A.C.Gilchrist | 39 | 56 | 11 | 204* | 2615 | 58.11 | 7 | 14 | 155/13 |
| J.N.Gillespie | 39 | 49 | 16 | 46 | 466 | 14.12 | – | – | 10 |
| M.L.Hayden | 38 | 64 | 4 | 203 | 3096 | 51.60 | 12 | 10 | 37 |
| M.S.Kasprowicz | 17 | 23 | 5 | 25 | 234 | 13.00 | – | – | 6 |
| S.M.Katich | 1 | 2 | 1 | 15 | 15 | 15.00 | – | – | 1 |
| J.L.Langer | 59 | 97 | 5 | 250 | 4077 | 44.31 | 13 | 16 | 37 |
| S.G.Law | 1 | 1 | 1 | 54* | 54 | – | – | 1 | 1 |
| B.Lee | 27 | 28 | 5 | 62* | 498 | 21.65 | – | 2 | 3 |
| D.S.Lehmann | 8 | 12 | 1 | 98 | 325 | 29.54 | – | 2 | 5 |
| M.L.Love | 2 | 4 | 2 | 62* | 95 | 47.50 | – | 1 | 4 |
| S.C.G.MacGill | 19 | 25 | 2 | 43 | 230 | 10.00 | – | – | 12 |
| G.D.McGrath | 91 | 102 | 35 | 39 | 431 | 6.43 | – | – | 29 |
| D.R.Martyn | 33 | 52 | 9 | 133 | 2000 | 46.51 | 5 | 13 | 15 |
| R.T.Ponting | 64 | 101 | 12 | 197 | 4264 | 47.91 | 14 | 17 | 80 |
| S.K.Warne | 107 | 146 | 13 | 99 | 2238 | 16.82 | – | 8 | 86 |
| M.E.Waugh | 128 | 209 | 17 | 153* | 8029 | 41.81 | 20 | 47 | 181 |
| S.R.Waugh | 156 | 245 | 42 | 200 | 10039 | 49.45 | 29 | 46 | 108 |

## AUSTRALIA – BOWLING

| | O | R | W | Avge | Best | 5wI | 10wM |
|---|---|---|---|---|---|---|---|
| A.J.Bichel | 289.4 | 974 | 31 | 31.41 | 5-60 | 1 | – |
| M.T.G.Elliott | 2 | 4 | 0 | | | | |
| J.N.Gillespie | 1267.3 | 3814 | 146 | 26.12 | 7-37 | 6 | – |
| M.L.Hayden | 9 | 40 | 0 | | | | |
| M.S.Kasprowicz | 556.2 | 1739 | 47 | 37.00 | 7-36 | 2 | – |
| J.L.Langer | 1 | 3 | 0 | | | | |
| S.G.Law | 3 | 9 | 0 | | | | |
| B.Lee | 862.2 | 3023 | 102 | 29.63 | 5-47 | 4 | – |
| D.S.Lehmann | 22 | 56 | 2 | 28.00 | 1- 6 | – | – |
| S.C.G.MacGill | 858.5 | 2537 | 94 | 26.98 | 7-50 | 5 | 1 |
| G.D.McGrath | 3595.5 | 9056 | 422 | 21.45 | 8-38 | 23 | 3 |
| D.R.Martyn | 33 | 98 | 2 | 49.00 | 1- 0 | – | – |
| R.T.Ponting | 64.5 | 165 | 4 | 41.25 | 1- 0 | – | – |
| S.K.Warne | 4979.2 | 12624 | 491 | 25.71 | 8-71 | 23 | 6 |
| M.E.Waugh | 808.5 | 2429 | 59. | 41.16 | 5-40 | 1 | – |
| S.R.Waugh | 1223.5 | 3240 | 91 | 35.60 | 5-28 | 3 | – |

## SOUTH AFRICA – BATTING AND FIELDING

| | M | I | NO | HS | Runs | Avge | 100 | 50 | Ct/St |
|---|---|---|---|---|---|---|---|---|---|
| P.R.Adams | 36 | 44 | 12 | 35 | 261 | 8.15 | – | – | 21 |
| N.Boje | 21 | 30 | 5 | 85 | 586 | 23.44 | – | 2 | 8 |
| M.V.Boucher | 58 | 78 | 10 | 125 | 2031 | 29.86 | 3 | 12 | 221/6 |
| H.H.Dippenaar | 17 | 25 | – | 100 | 552 | 22.08 | 1 | 2 | 9 |
| A.A.Donald | 72 | 94 | 33 | 37 | 652 | 10.68 | – | – | 18 |
| S.Elworthy | 4 | 5 | 1 | 48 | 72 | 18.00 | – | – | 1 |
| H.H.Gibbs | 43 | 72 | 3 | 228 | 3069 | 44.47 | 8 | 11 | 30 |
| A.J.Hall | 4 | 6 | 1 | 70 | 144 | 28.80 | – | 1 | 2 |
| M.Hayward | 14 | 14 | 7 | 14 | 62 | 8.85 | – | – | 1 |
| C.W.Henderson | 7 | 7 | – | 30 | 65 | 9.28 | – | – | 2 |
| J.H.Kallis | 66 | 107 | 18 | 189* | 4486 | 50.40 | 11 | 25 | 65 |
| G.Kirsten | 89 | 155 | 12 | 275 | 6133 | 42.88 | 16 | 29 | 78 |
| L.Klusener | 48 | 68 | 11 | 174 | 1904 | 33.40 | 4 | 8 | 33 |
| N.D.McKenzie | 28 | 45 | 3 | 120 | 1501 | 35.73 | 2 | 10 | 31 |
| A.Nel | 3 | 2 | – | 7 | 7 | 3.50 | – | – | – |
| M.Ntini | 29 | 27 | 7 | 23 | 162 | 8.10 | – | – | 8 |
| J.L.Ontong | 1 | 2 | – | 32 | 41 | 20.50 | – | – | – |
| S.M.Pollock | 68 | 96 | 23 | 111 | 2442 | 33.45 | 2 | 11 | 46 |

**TEST**    ## SOUTH AFRICA – BATTING AND FIELDING (continued)

| | M | I | NO | HS | Runs | Avge | 100 | 50 | Ct/St |
|---|---|---|---|---|---|---|---|---|---|
| D.Pretorius | 1 | 2 | 1 | 5* | 5 | 5.00 | – | – | – |
| A.G.Prince | 7 | 11 | – | 49 | 185 | 16.81 | – | – | 3 |
| J.N.Rhodes | 52 | 80 | 9 | 117 | 2532 | 35.66 | 3 | 17 | 34 |
| G.C.Smith | 8 | 12 | 1 | 200 | 606 | 55.09 | 2 | 2 | 14 |
| D.J.Terbrugge | 6 | 6 | 5 | 4* | 14 | 14.00 | – | – | 4 |
| M.van Jaarsveld | 3 | 3 | 1 | 39* | 53 | 26.50 | – | – | 4 |

## SOUTH AFRICA – BOWLING

| | O | R | W | Avge | Best | 5wI | 10wM |
|---|---|---|---|---|---|---|---|
| P.R.Adams | 1164.1 | 3353 | 106 | 31.63 | 6- 55 | 1 | – |
| N.Boje | 629.3 | 1640 | 53 | 30.94 | 5- 62 | 2 | – |
| A.A.Donald | 2586.3 | 7344 | 330 | 22.25 | 8- 71 | 20 | 3 |
| S.Elworthy | 144.3 | 444 | 13 | 34.15 | 4- 66 | – | – |
| A.J.Hall | 62.1 | 191 | 7 | 27.28 | 3- 1 | – | – |
| M.Hayward | 427.3 | 1417 | 50 | 28.34 | 5- 56 | 1 | – |
| C.W.Henderson | 327 | 928 | 22 | 42.18 | 4-116 | – | – |
| J.H.Kallis | 1465.3 | 3919 | 137 | 28.60 | 6- 67 | 3 | – |
| G.Kirsten | 56.1 | 141 | 2 | 70.50 | 1- 0 | – | – |
| L.Klusener | 1114.5 | 2924 | 78 | 37.48 | 8- 64 | 1 | – |
| N.D.McKenzie | 9 | 54 | 0 | | | | |
| A.Nel | 85.3 | 289 | 8 | 36.12 | 4- 53 | – | – |
| M.Ntini | 892.4 | 2688 | 93 | 28.90 | 6- 66 | 2 | – |
| J.L.Ontong | 2 | 10 | 0 | | | | |
| S.M.Pollock | 2518 | 5759 | 278 | 20.71 | 7- 87 | 14 | 1 |
| D.Pretorius | 25 | 132 | 1 | 132.00 | 1- 60 | – | – |
| J.N.Rhodes | 2 | 5 | 0 | | | | |
| G.C.Smith | 4 | 12 | 0 | | | | |
| D.J.Terbrugge | 146.4 | 424 | 20 | 21.20 | 5- 46 | 1 | – |

## WEST INDIES – BATTING AND FIELDING

| | M | I | NO | HS | Runs | Avge | 100 | 50 | Ct/St |
|---|---|---|---|---|---|---|---|---|---|
| M.I.Black | 6 | 11 | 3 | 6 | 21 | 2.62 | – | – | – |
| G.R.Breese | 1 | 2 | – | 5 | 5 | 2.50 | – | – | 1 |
| S.L.Campbell | 52 | 93 | 4 | 208 | 2882 | 32.38 | 4 | 18 | 46 |
| S.Chanderpaul | 63 | 103 | 15 | 140 | 3898 | 44.29 | 6 | 28 | 26 |
| P.T.Collins | 17 | 26 | 4 | 24 | 149 | 6.77 | – | – | 2 |
| C.E.Cuffy | 15 | 23 | 9 | 15 | 58 | 4.14 | – | – | 5 |
| M.Dillon | 30 | 54 | 2 | 43 | 371 | 7.13 | – | – | 15 |
| V.C.Drakes | 2 | 2 | – | 26 | 41 | 20.50 | – | – | – |
| D.Ganga | 17 | 29 | – | 89 | 666 | 22.96 | – | 3 | 12 |
| C.H.Gayle | 28 | 47 | 2 | 204 | 1588 | 35.28 | 2 | 9 | 39 |
| R.O.Hinds | 4 | 8 | 1 | 62 | 162 | 23.14 | – | 1 | – |
| W.W.Hinds | 29 | 51 | 1 | 165 | 1638 | 32.76 | 3 | 10 | 27 |
| C.L.Hooper | 102 | 173 | 15 | 233 | 5762 | 36.46 | 13 | 27 | 115 |
| R.D.Jacobs | 47 | 82 | 16 | 118 | 1880 | 28.48 | 2 | 10 | 157/8 |
| B.C.Lara | 90 | 157 | 4 | 375 | 7572 | 49.49 | 18 | 37 | 116 |
| J.J.C.Lawson | 4 | 5 | – | 6 | 14 | 2.80 | – | – | – |
| N.C.McGarrell | 4 | 6 | 2 | 33 | 61 | 15.25 | – | – | 5 |
| N.A.M.McLean | 19 | 32 | 2 | 46 | 368 | 12.26 | – | – | 5 |
| J.R.Murray | 33 | 45 | 4 | 101* | 918 | 22.39 | 1 | 3 | 99/5 |
| M.V.Nagamootoo | 5 | 8 | 1 | 68 | 185 | 26.42 | – | 1 | 2 |
| D.B.Powell | 4 | 5 | – | 16 | 19 | 3.80 | – | – | 1 |
| D.Ramnarine | 12 | 21 | 4 | 35* | 106 | 6.23 | – | – | 8 |
| M.N.Samuels | 15 | 26 | 2 | 104 | 776 | 32.33 | 1 | 5 | 6 |
| A.Sanford | 7 | 10 | 1 | 12 | 35 | 3.88 | –, | – | – |
| R.R.Sarwan | 29 | 51 | 5 | 119 | 1720 | 37.39 | 1 | 14 | 16 |

**WEST INDIES – BATTING AND FIELDING (continued)**

|  | M | I | NO | HS | Runs | Avge | 100 | 50 | Ct/St |
|---|---|---|---|---|---|---|---|---|---|
| C.E.L.Stuart | 6 | 9 | 2 | 12* | 24 | 3.42 | – | – | 2 |
| S.C.Williams | 31 | 52 | 3 | 128 | 1183 | 24.14 | 1 | 3 | 27 |

## WEST INDIES – BOWLING

|  | O | R | W | Avge | Best | 5wI | 10wM |
|---|---|---|---|---|---|---|---|
| M.I.Black | 159 | 597 | 12 | 49.75 | 4- 83 | – | – |
| G.R.Breese | 31.2 | 135 | 2 | 67.50 | 2-108 | – | – |
| S.Chanderpaul | 240 | 718 | 8 | 89.75 | 1- 2 | – | – |
| P.T.Collins | 648.4 | 1955 | 54 | 36.20 | 6- 76 | 2 | – |
| C.E.Cuffy | 561 | 1455 | 43 | 33.83 | 4- 82 | – | – |
| M.Dillon | 1139.3 | 3403 | 112 | 30.38 | 5- 71 | 2 | – |
| V.C.Drakes | 54 | 155 | 11 | 14.09 | 4- 61 | – | – |
| C.H.Gayle | 125.2 | 310 | 8 | 38.75 | 3- 25 | – | – |
| R.O.Hinds | 36 | 119 | 0 |  |  | – | – |
| W.W.Hinds | 34.3 | 107 | 4 | 26.75 | 2- 23 | – | – |
| C.L.Hooper | 2298 | 5635 | 114 | 49.42 | 5- 26 | 4 | – |
| B.C.Lara | 10 | 28 | 0 |  |  | – | – |
| J.J.C.Lawson | 119.5 | 341 | 15 | 22.73 | 6- 3 | 1 | – |
| N.C.McGarrell | 202 | 453 | 17 | 26.64 | 4- 23 | – | – |
| N.A.M.McLean | 549.5 | 1873 | 44 | 42.56 | 3- 53 | – | – |
| M.V.Nagamootoo | 249 | 637 | 12 | 53.08 | 3-119 | – | – |
| D.B.Powell | 128.2 | 354 | 12 | 29.50 | 3- 36 | – | – |
| D.Ramnarine | 582.3 | 1383 | 45 | 30.73 | 5- 78 | 1 | – |
| M.N.Samuels | 91.5 | 260 | 4 | 65.00 | 2- 49 | – | – |
| A.Sanford | 234.1 | 794 | 20 | 39.70 | 3- 20 | – | – |
| R.R.Sarwan | 38 | 138 | 3 | 46.00 | 2- 1 | – | – |
| C.E.L.Stuart | 186 | 628 | 20 | 31.40 | 3- 33 | – | – |
| S.C.Williams | 3 | 19 | 0 |  |  | – | – |

## NEW ZEALAND – BATTING AND FIELDING

|  | M | I | NO | HS | Runs | Avge | 100 | 50 | Ct/St |
|---|---|---|---|---|---|---|---|---|---|
| A.R.Adams | 1 | 2 | – | 11 | 18 | 9.00 | – | – | 1 |
| N.J.Astle | 57 | 98 | 8 | 222 | 3420 | 38.00 | 8 | 16 | 51 |
| M.D.Bell | 13 | 23 | 1 | 105 | 484 | 22.00 | 1 | 2 | 10 |
| S.E.Bond | 8 | 8 | 3 | 17 | 42 | 8.40 | – | – | 4 |
| I.G.Butler | 4 | 6 | 1 | 26 | 50 | 10.00 | – | – | 3 |
| C.L.Cairns | 55 | 92 | 5 | 126 | 2853 | 32.79 | 4 | 20 | 14 |
| C.J.Drum | 5 | 5 | 2 | 4 | 10 | 3.33 | – | – | 4 |
| S.P.Fleming | 73 | 126 | 7 | 174* | 4295 | 36.09 | 4 | 33 | 111 |
| C.Z.Harris | 23 | 42 | 4 | 71 | 777 | 20.44 | – | 5 | 14 |
| R.G.Hart | 5 | 9 | 3 | 57* | 153 | 25.50 | – | 1 | 12/1 |
| M.J.Horne | 33 | 61 | 2 | 157 | 1714 | 29.05 | 4 | 5 | 17 |
| C.D.McMillan | 44 | 73 | 7 | 142 | 2619 | 39.68 | 5 | 16 | 19 |
| C.S.Martin | 11 | 11 | 4 | 7 | 12 | 1.71 | – | – | 4 |
| D.J.Nash | 32 | 45 | 14 | 89* | 729 | 23.51 | – | 4 | 13 |
| S.B.O'Connor | 19 | 27 | 9 | 20 | 105 | 5.83 | – | – | 6 |
| J.D.P.Oram | 2 | 3 | 1 | 26* | 29 | 14.50 | – | – | 2 |
| A.C.Parore | 78 | 128. | 19 | 110 | 2865 | 26.28 | 2 | 14 | 197/7 |
| M.H.Richardson | 22 | 37 | 2 | 143 | 1651 | 47.17 | 2 | 13 | 17 |
| M.S.Sinclair | 18 | 30 | 5 | 214 | 1079 | 43.16 | 3 | 1 | 16 |
| C.M.Spearman | 19 | 37 | 2 | 112 | 922 | 26.34 | 1 | 3 | 21 |
| S.B.Styris | 3 | 5 | 1 | 107 | 206 | 51.50 | 1 | 1 | 5 |
| D.R.Tuffey | 12 | 16 | 3 | 31 | 137 | 10.53 | – | – | 7 |
| D.L.Vettori | 44 | 64 | 10 | 90 | 878 | 16.25 | – | 4 | 22 |
| L.Vincent | 11 | 20 | 1 | 104 | 558 | 29.36 | 1 | 5 | 11 |
| B.G.K.Walker | 5 | 8 | 2 | 27* | 118 | 19.66 | – | – | 7 |

**TEST**

## NEW ZEALAND – BOWLING

| | O | R | W | Avge | Best | 5wI | 10wM |
|---|---|---|---|---|---|---|---|
| A.R.Adams | 31.4 | 105 | 6 | 17.50 | 3-44 | – | – |
| N.J.Astle | 773.5 | 1711 | 36 | 47.52 | 2-22 | – | – |
| S.E.Bond | 242.3 | 851 | 38 | 22.39 | 5-78 | 2 | – |
| I.G.Butler | 109.3 | 455 | 14 | 32.50 | 4-60 | – | – |
| C.L.Cairns | 1740.5 | 5675 | 197 | 28.80 | 7-27 | 12 | 1 |
| C.J.Drum | 134.2 | 482 | 16 | 30.12 | 3-36 | – | – |
| C.Z.Harris | 426.4 | 1170 | 16 | 73.12 | 2-16 | – | – |
| M.J.Horne | 11 | 26 | 0 | | | | |
| C.D.McMillan | 384.5 | 1174 | 27 | 43.48 | 3-48 | – | – |
| C.S.Martin | 326 | 1176 | 34 | 34.58 | 5-71 | 1 | – |
| D.J.Nash | 1032.4 | 2649 | 93 | 28.48 | 6-27 | 3 | 1 |
| S.B.O'Connor | 611.1 | 1724 | 53 | 32.52 | 5-51 | 1 | – |
| J.D.P.Oram | 48.5 | 122 | 11 | 11.09 | 4-41 | – | – |
| M.H.Richardson | 10 | 17 | 1 | 17.00 | 1-16 | – | – |
| M.S.Sinclair | 4 | 13 | 0 | | | | |
| S.B.Styris | 38 | 150 | 5 | 30.00 | 3-28 | – | – |
| D.R.Tuffey | 349.5 | 1145 | 45 | 25.44 | 6-54 | 1 | – |
| D.L.Vettori | 1774 | 4707 | 139 | 33.86 | 7-87 | 7 | 1 |
| B.G.K.Walker | 111.3 | 399 | 5 | 79.80 | 2-92 | – | – |

## INDIA – BATTING AND FIELDING

| | M | I | NO | HS | Runs | Avge | 100 | 50 | Ct/St |
|---|---|---|---|---|---|---|---|---|---|
| A.B.Agarkar | 16 | 25 | 2 | 109* | 356 | 15.47 | 1 | – | 3 |
| S.B.Bangar | 12 | 18 | 2 | 100* | 470 | 29.37 | 1 | 3 | 4 |
| S.S.Das | 23 | 40 | 2 | 110 | 1326 | 34.89 | 2 | 9 | 34 |
| D.Dasgupta | 8 | 13 | 1 | 100 | 344 | 28.66 | 1 | 2 | 13 |
| R.Dravid | 69 | 118 | 13 | 217 | 5614 | 53.46 | 14 | 28 | 87 |
| S.C.Ganguly | 67 | 112 | 11 | 173 | 4100 | 40.59 | 9 | 20 | 51 |
| Harbhajan Singh | 33 | 49 | 10 | 66 | 513 | 13.15 | – | 2 | 14 |
| W.Jaffer | 7 | 13 | – | 86 | 261 | 20.07 | – | 3 | 12 |
| Z.Khan | 24 | 33 | 6 | 46 | 249 | 9.25 | – | – | 8 |
| A.Kumble | 76 | 99 | 19 | 88 | 1388 | 17.35 | – | 3 | 35 |
| V.V.S.Laxman | 44 | 72 | 7 | 281 | 2687 | 41.33 | 4 | 15 | 51 |
| A.Nehra | 13 | 20 | 9 | 19 | 76 | 6.90 | – | – | 2 |
| P.A.Patel | 7 | 11 | 3 | 47 | 170 | 21.25 | – | – | 12/2 |
| A.Ratra | 6 | 10 | 1 | 115* | 163 | 18.11 | 1 | – | 11/2 |
| Sarandeep Singh | 3 | 2 | 1 | 39* | 43 | 43.00 | – | – | 1 |
| V.Sehwag | 14 | 21 | – | 147 | 872 | 41.52 | 3 | 4 | 16 |
| I.R.Siddiqui | 1 | 2 | 1 | 24 | 29 | 29.00 | – | – | 1 |
| J.Srinath | 67 | 92 | 21 | 76 | 1009 | 14.21 | – | 4 | 22 |
| S.R.Tendulkar | 105 | 169 | 16 | 217 | 8811 | 57.58 | 31 | 35 | 68 |
| T.Yohannan | 3 | 4 | 4 | 8* | 13 | – | – | – | 1 |

## INDIA – BOWLING

| | O | R | W | Avge | Best | 5wI | 10wM |
|---|---|---|---|---|---|---|---|
| A.B.Agarkar | 504.4 | 1630 | 35 | 46.57 | 3-43 | – | – |
| S.B.Bangar | 127 | 343 | 7 | 49.00 | 2-23 | – | – |
| S.S.Das | 11 | 35 | 0 | | | | |
| R.Dravid | 20 | 39 | 1 | 39.00 | 1-18 | – | – |
| S.C.Ganguly | 343.2 | 1154 | 23 | 50.17 | 3-28 | – | – |
| Harbhajan Singh | 1450.5 | 3830 | 144 | 26.59 | 8-84 | 11 | 2 |
| W.Jaffer | 11 | 18 | 2 | 9.00 | 2-18 | – | – |
| Z.Khan | 759.2 | 2435 | 73 | 33.35 | 5-29 | 2 | – |
| A.Kumble | 3965 | 9768 | 349 | 27.98 | 10-74 | 20 | 4 |
| V.V.S.Laxman | 42 | 100 | 1 | 100.00 | 1-32 | – | – |
| A.Nehra | 446.3 | 1404 | 37 | 37.94 | 4-72 | – | – |
| A.Ratra | 1 | 1 | 0 | | | | |

## INDIA – BOWLING (continued)

| | O | R | W | Avge | Best | 5wI | 10wM |
|---|---|---|---|---|---|---|---|
| Sarandeep Singh | 113 | 340 | 10 | 34.00 | 4-136 | – | – |
| V.Sehwag | 40 | 152 | 2 | 76.00 | 1- 27 | – | – |
| I.R.Siddiqui | 19 | 48 | 1 | 48.00 | 1- 32 | – | – |
| J.Srinath | 2517.2 | 7196 | 236 | 30.49 | 8- 86 | 10 | 1 |
| S.R.Tendulkar | 381 | 1220 | 27 | 45.18 | 3- 10 | – | – |
| T.Yohannan | 81 | 256 | 5 | 51.20 | 2- 56 | – | – |

## PAKISTAN – BATTING AND FIELDING

| | M | I | NO | HS | Runs | Avge | 100 | 50 | Ct/St |
|---|---|---|---|---|---|---|---|---|---|
| Abdul Razzaq | 24 | 38 | 4 | 134 | 1001 | 29.44 | 3 | 4 | 7 |
| Azhar Mahmood | 21 | 34 | 4 | 136 | 900 | 30.00 | 3 | 1 | 14 |
| Danish Kaneria | 10 | 12 | 7 | 15 | 45 | 9.00 | – | – | 3 |
| Faisal Iqbal | 10 | 18 | 1 | 83 | 403 | 23.70 | – | 3 | 7 |
| Hasan Raza | 5 | 7 | 1 | 68 | 213 | 35.50 | – | 2 | 1 |
| Imran Farhat | 4 | 7 | – | 63 | 162 | 23.14 | – | 1 | 4 |
| Imran Nazir | 8 | 13 | – | 131 | 427 | 32.84 | 2 | 1 | 4 |
| Inzamam-ul-Haq | 85 | 140 | 13 | 329 | 6214 | 48.92 | 17 | 32 | 66 |
| Irfan Fazil | 1 | 2 | 1 | 3 | 4 | 4.00 | – | – | 2 |
| Kamran Akmal | 4 | 7 | – | 56 | 139 | 19.85 | – | 1 | 13/1 |
| Misbah-ul-Haq | 4 | 8 | – | 28 | 107 | 13.37 | – | – | 1 |
| Mohammad Sami | 9 | 14 | 9 | 22 | 66 | 13.20 | – | – | – |
| Mohammad Zahid | 5 | 6 | 1 | 6* | 7 | 1.40 | – | – | – |
| Mushtaq Ahmed | 50 | 70 | 15 | 59 | 636 | 11.56 | – | 2 | 22 |
| Naved Latif | 1 | 2 | – | 20 | 20 | 10.00 | – | – | – |
| Rashid Latif | 34 | 53 | 8 | 150 | 1277 | 28.37 | 1 | 6 | 102/10 |
| Saeed Anwar | 55 | 91 | 2 | 188* | 4052 | 45.52 | 11 | 25 | 18 |
| Salim Elahi | 13 | 24 | 1 | 72 | 436 | 18.95 | – | 1 | 10/1 |
| Saqlain Mushtaq | 47 | 74 | 14 | 101* | 902 | 15.03 | 1 | 2 | 15 |
| Shadab Kabir | 5 | 7 | – | 55 | 148 | 21.14 | – | 1 | 11 |
| Shahid Afridi | 14 | 25 | 1 | 141 | 780 | 32.50 | 2 | 4 | 8 |
| Shoaib Akhtar | 25 | 37 | 10 | 37 | 229 | 8.48 | – | – | 7 |
| Shoaib Malik | 2 | 2 | – | 21 | 34 | 17.00 | – | – | 1 |
| Taufiq Umar | 13 | 23 | 1 | 135 | 968 | 44.00 | 3 | 5 | 12 |
| Waqar Younis | 87 | 120 | 21 | 45 | 1010 | 10.20 | – | – | 18 |
| Wasim Akram | 104 | 147 | 19 | 257* | 2898 | 22.64 | 3 | 7 | 43 |
| Younis Khan | 27 | 45 | 2 | 153 | 1646 | 38.27 | 5 | 9 | 29 |
| Yousuf Youhana | 43 | 71 | 5 | 204* | 3149 | 47.71 | 10 | 17 | 43 |

## PAKISTAN – BOWLING

| | O | R | W | Avge | Best | 5wI | 10wM |
|---|---|---|---|---|---|---|---|
| Abdul Razzaq | 561.1 | 1584 | 48 | 33.00 | 4- 24 | – | – |
| Azhar Mahmood | 502.3 | 1402 | 39 | 35.94 | 4- 50 | – | – |
| Danish Kaneria | 354.4 | 1058 | 42 | 25.19 | 7- 77 | 4 | 1 |
| Faisal Iqbal | 1 | 7 | 0 | | | | |
| Hasan Raza | 1 | 1 | 0 | | | | |
| Inzamam-ul-Haq | 1.3 | 8 | 0 | | | | |
| Irfan Fazil | 8 | 65 | 2 | 32.50 | 1- 30 | – | – |
| Mohammad Sami | 314.3 | 1007 | 25 | 40.28 | 5- 36 | 1 | – |
| Mohammad Zahid | 132 | 502 | 15 | 33.46 | 7- 66 | 1 | 1 |
| Mushtaq Ahmed | 2037.4 | 5901 | 183 | 32.24 | 7- 56 | 10 | 3 |
| Rashid Latif | 2 | 10 | 0 | | | | |
| Saeed Anwar | 8 | 23 | 0 | | | | |
| Saqlain Mushtaq | 2274.3 | 5932 | 205 | 28.93 | 8-164 | 13 | 3 |
| Shadab Kabir | 1 | 9 | 0 | | | | |
| Shahid Afridi | 221.5 | 661 | 21 | 31.47 | 5- 52 | 1 | – |
| Shoaib Akhtar | 711.4 | 2392 | 88 | 27.18 | 6- 11 | 5 | – |
| Shoaib Malik | 20.1 | 81 | 2 | 40.50 | 2- 18 | – | – |

## PAKISTAN – BOWLING (continued)

| | O | R | W | Avge | Best | 5wI | 10wM |
|---|---|---|---|---|---|---|---|
| Taufiq Umar | 11 | 36 | 0 | | | | |
| Waqar Younis | 2704 | 8788 | 373 | 23.56 | 7- 76 | 22 | 5 |
| Wasim Akram | 3771.1 | 9779 | 414 | 23.62 | 7-119 | 25 | 5 |
| Younis Khan | 37 | 139 | 1 | 139.00 | 1- 47 | – | – |
| Yousuf Youhana | 1 | 3 | 0 | | | | |

## SRI LANKA – BATTING AND FIELDING

| | M | I | NO | HS | Runs | Avge | 100 | 50 | Ct/St |
|---|---|---|---|---|---|---|---|---|---|
| R.P.Arnold | 43 | 67 | 4 | 123 | 1804 | 28.63 | 3 | 10 | 49 |
| M.S.Atapattu | 61 | 107 | 12 | 223 | 3611 | 38.01 | 10 | 11 | 38 |
| M.R.C.N.Bandaratilake | 7 | 9 | 1 | 25 | 93 | 11.62 | – | – | – |
| U.D.U.Chandana | 7 | 9 | 1 | 92 | 224 | 28.00 | – | 1 | 4 |
| P.A.de Silva | 93 | 159 | 11 | 267 | 6361 | 42.97 | 20 | 22 | 43 |
| W.R.S.de Silva | 2 | 3 | 1 | 5* | 10 | 10.00 | – | – | – |
| C.R.D.Fernando | 13 | 19 | 5 | 15 | 84 | 6.00 | – | – | 5 |
| K.H.R.K.Fernando | 2 | 4 | – | 24 | 38 | 9.50 | – | – | 1 |
| T.C.B.Fernando | 9 | 8 | 3 | 45 | 132 | 26.40 | – | – | 4 |
| S.T.Jayasuriya | 76 | 128 | 12 | 340 | 4789 | 41.28 | 10 | 22 | 58 |
| D.P.M.D.Jayawardena | 47 | 75 | 5 | 242 | 3351 | 47.87 | 9 | 16 | 57 |
| H.A.P.W.Jayawardena | 3 | 2 | – | 5 | 5 | 2.50 | – | – | 5/2 |
| M.K.G.C.P.Lakshitha | 2 | 3 | – | 40 | 42 | 14.00 | – | – | 1 |
| J.Mubarak | 2 | 4 | – | 48 | 118 | 29.50 | – | – | 4 |
| M.Muralitharan | 78 | 99 | 38 | 67 | 746 | 12.22 | – | 1 | 37 |
| M.N.Nawaz | 1 | 2 | 1 | 78* | 99 | 99.00 | – | 1 | – |
| P.D.R.L.Perera | 8 | 9 | 6 | 11* | 33 | 11.00 | – | – | 2 |
| T.T.Samaraweera | 10 | 10 | 3 | 123* | 581 | 83.00 | 2 | 4 | 7 |
| K.C.Sangakkara | 26 | 42 | 3 | 230 | 1874 | 48.05 | 4 | 9 | 74/6 |
| H.P.Tillekeratne | 73 | 115 | 24 | 204* | 4025 | 44.23 | 10 | 18 | 111/2 |
| K.E.A.Upashanta | 2 | 3 | – | 6 | 10 | 3.33 | – | – | – |
| W.P.U.C.J.Vaas | 64 | 90 | 14 | 74* | 1460 | 19.21 | – | 6 | 18 |
| M.G.Vandort | 2 | 3 | – | 140 | 237 | 79.00 | 1 | 1 | 1 |
| D.N.T.Zoysa | 24 | 31 | 3 | 28 | 236 | 8.42 | – | – | 3 |

## SRI LANKA – BOWLING

| | O | R | W | Avge | Best | 5wI | 10wM |
|---|---|---|---|---|---|---|---|
| R.P.Arnold | 221.2 | 589 | 11 | 53.54 | 3- 76 | – | – |
| M.S.Atapattu | 8 | 24 | 1 | 24.00 | 1- 9 | – | – |
| M.R.C.N.Bandaratilake | 287 | 698 | 23 | 30.34 | 5- 36 | 1 | – |
| U.D.U.Chandana | 167.2 | 549 | 18 | 30.50 | 6-179 | 1 | – |
| P.A.de Silva | 432.3 | 1208 | 29 | 41.65 | 3- 30 | – | – |
| W.R.S.de Silva | 48 | 146 | 7 | 20.85 | 4- 35 | – | – |
| C.R.D.Fernando | 329.1 | 1258 | 33 | 38.12 | 5- 42 | 2 | – |
| K.H.R.K.Fernando | 39 | 108 | 4 | 27.00 | 3- 63 | – | – |
| T.C.B.Fernando | 211.4 | 792 | 18 | 44.00 | 4- 27 | – | – |
| S.T.Jayasuriya | 902.1 | 2258 | 69 | 32.72 | 5- 43 | 1 | – |
| D.P.M.D.Jayawardena | 70.2 | 214 | 4 | 53.50 | 2- 32 | – | – |
| M.K.G.C.P.Lakshitha | 48 | 158 | 5 | 31.60 | 2- 33 | – | – |
| J.Mubarak | 2 | 6 | 0 | | | | |
| M.Muralitharan | 4357.5 | 10281 | 437 | 23.52 | 9- 51 | 36 | 11 |
| P.D.R.L.Perera | 188.2 | 661 | 17 | 38.88 | 3- 40 | – | – |
| T.T.Samaraweera | 120.4 | 336 | 11 | 30.54 | 4- 49 | – | – |
| H.P.Tillekeratne | 11.4 | 24 | 0 | | | | |
| K.E.A.Upashanta | 51 | 200 | 4 | 50.00 | 2- 41 | – | – |
| W.P.U.C.J.Vaas | 2363.2 | 6244 | 206 | 30.31 | 7- 71 | 7 | 2 |
| D.N.T.Zoysa | 556.4 | 1587 | 44 | 36.06 | 4- 76 | – | – |

**TEST**　　**ZIMBABWE – BATTING AND FIELDING**

| | M | I | NO | HS | Runs | Avge | 100 | 50 | Ct/St |
|---|---|---|---|---|---|---|---|---|---|
| A.M.Blignaut | 8 | 14 | 1 | 92 | 323 | 24.84 | – | 2 | 9 |
| G.B.Brent | 4 | 6 | – | 25 | 35 | 5.83 | – | – | 1 |
| A.D.R.Campbell | 60 | 109 | 4 | 103 | 2858 | 27.21 | 2 | 18 | 60 |
| S.V.Carlisle | 27 | 47 | 4 | 77 | 1129 | 26.25 | – | 7 | 24 |
| D.D.Ebrahim | 14 | 26 | 1 | 94 | 658 | 26.32 | – | 5 | 9 |
| A.Flower | 63 | 112 | 19 | 232* | 4794 | 51.54 | 12 | 27 | 151/9 |
| G.W.Flower | 63 | 116 | 5 | 201* | 3359 | 30.26 | 6 | 15 | 41 |
| T.J.Friend | 10 | 15 | 3 | 81 | 339 | 28.25 | – | 2 | 1 |
| M.W.Goodwin | 19 | 37 | 4 | 166* | 1414 | 42.84 | 3 | 8 | 10 |
| T.R.Gripper | 14 | 27 | 1 | 112 | 548 | 21.07 | 1 | 3 | 12 |
| N.B.Mahwire | 1 | 2 | – | 4 | 7 | 3.50 | – | – | – |
| D.A.Marillier | 5 | 7 | 1 | 73 | 185 | 30.83 | – | 2 | 2 |
| H.Masakadza | 7 | 14 | 1 | 119 | 347 | 26.69 | 1 | 1 | – |
| B.A.Murphy | 11 | 15 | 3 | 30 | 123 | 10.25 | – | – | 11 |
| M.L.Nkala | 7 | 9 | 2 | 47 | 114 | 16.28 | – | – | 3 |
| H.K.Olonga | 30 | 45 | 11 | 24 | 184 | 5.41 | – | – | 10 |
| R.W.Price | 10 | 17 | 4 | 18 | 59 | 4.53 | – | – | 2 |
| G.J.Rennie | 23 | 46 | 1 | 93 | 1023 | 22.73 | – | 7 | 13 |
| H.H.Streak | 51 | 82 | 14 | 87 | 1429 | 21.01 | – | 8 | 14 |
| T.Taibu | 6 | 12 | 1 | 51* | 184 | 16.72 | – | 1 | 9 |
| M.A.Vermeulen | 1 | 2 | – | 26 | 28 | 14.00 | – | – | – |
| B.T.Watambwa | 6 | 8 | 5 | 4* | 11 | 3.66 | – | – | – |
| G.J.Whittall | 46 | 82 | 7 | 203* | 2207 | 29.42 | 4 | 10 | 19 |
| C.B.Wishart | 21 | 38 | 1 | 114 | 760 | 20.54 | 1 | 4 | 9 |

**ZIMBABWE – BOWLING**

| | O | R | W | Avge | Best | 5wI | 10wM |
|---|---|---|---|---|---|---|---|
| A.M.Blignaut | 276.3 | 922 | 29 | 31.79 | 5- 73 | 3 | – |
| G.B.Brent | 136.2 | 314 | 7 | 44.85 | 3- 21 | – | – |
| A.D.R.Campbell | 11 | 28 | 0 | | | | |
| A.Flower | 0.3 | 4 | 0 | | | | |
| G.W.Flower | 561 | 1529 | 25 | 61.16 | 4- 41 | – | – |
| T.J.Friend | 307.2 | 995 | 23 | 43.26 | 5- 31 | 1 | – |
| M.W.Goodwin | 19.5 | 69 | 0 | | | | |
| T.R.Gripper | 76.4 | 296 | 3 | 98.66 | 2- 91 | – | – |
| N.B.Mahwire | 28.5 | 118 | 1 | 118.00 | 1- 58 | – | – |
| D.A.Marillier | 102.4 | 322 | 11 | 29.27 | 4- 57 | – | – |
| H.Masakadza | 4 | 12 | 1 | 12.00 | 1- 9 | – | – |
| B.A.Murphy | 358.5 | 1113 | 18 | 61.83 | 3- 32 | – | – |
| M.L.Nkala | 177 | 525 | 8 | 65.62 | 3- 82 | – | – |
| H.K.Olonga | 750.2 | 2620 | 68 | 38.52 | 5- 70 | 2 | – |
| R.W.Price | 512.1 | 1399 | 34 | 41.14 | 5-181 | 2 | – |
| G.J.Rennie | 21 | 84 | 1 | 84.00 | 1- 40 | – | – |
| H.H.Streak | 1872.4 | 4858 | 180 | 26.98 | 6- 87 | 6 | – |
| B.T.Watambwa | 155.1 | 490 | 14 | 35.00 | 4- 64 | – | – |
| G.J.Whittall | 781 | 2088 | 51 | 40.94 | 4- 18 | – | – |

**BANGLADESH – BATTING AND FIELDING**

| | M | I | NO | HS | Runs | Avge | 100 | 50 | Ct/St |
|---|---|---|---|---|---|---|---|---|---|
| Akram Khan | 6 | 12 | – | 44 | 194 | 16.16 | – | – | 2 |
| Al Sahariar | 14 | 28 | – | 71 | 647 | 23.10 | – | 4 | 10 |
| Alamgir Kabir | 1 | 2 | – | 0 | 0 | 0.00 | – | – | – |
| Alok Kapali | 5 | 10 | 1 | 85 | 307 | 34.11 | – | 2 | 3 |
| Aminul Islam | 13 | 26 | 1 | 145 | 530 | 21.20 | 1 | 2 | 5 |
| Anwar Piju Hossain | 1 | 2 | – | 12 | 14 | 7.00 | – | – | – |
| Ehsanul Haque | 1 | 2 | – | 5 | 7 | 3.50 | – | – | – |
| Enamul Haque | 9 | 17 | 4 | 24* | 168 | 12.92 | – | – | 1 |

| | M | I | NO | HS | Runs | Avge | 100 | 50 | Ct/St |
|---|---|---|---|---|---|---|---|---|---|
| Fahim Muntasir | 3 | 6 | – | 33 | 52 | 8.66 | – | – | 1 |
| Habibul Bashar | 17 | 34 | 1 | 108 | 1039 | 31.48 | 1 | 9 | 11 |
| Hannan Sarkar | 5 | 10 | – | 65 | 226 | 22.60 | – | 2 | – |
| Hasibul Hussain | 5 | 10 | 1 | 31 | 97 | 10.77 | – | – | 1 |
| Javed Omar | 10 | 20 | 1 | 85* | 450 | 23.68 | – | 3 | 1 |
| Khaled Mahmud | 3 | 5 | – | 45 | 65 | 13.00 | – | – | 1 |
| Khaled Masud | 16 | 30 | 5 | 33 | 407 | 16.28 | – | – | 25/1 |
| Manjural Islam | 14 | 27 | 8 | 21 | 69 | 3.63 | – | – | 4 |
| Mashrafe Mortaza | 4 | 7 | – | 29 | 51 | 7.28 | – | – | 2 |
| Mehrab Hossain | 7 | 14 | – | 71 | 208 | 14.85 | – | 1 | 5 |
| Mohammed Ashraful | 9 | 18 | 1 | 114 | 385 | 22.64 | 1 | 1 | 4 |
| Mohammed Rafique | 2 | 4 | 1 | 22 | 62 | 20.66 | – | – | 1 |
| Mohammed Sharif | 8 | 16 | 2 | 24* | 86 | 6.14 | – | – | 5 |
| Naimur Rahman | 8 | 15 | 1 | 48 | 210 | 15.00 | – | – | 4 |
| Rafiqul Islam | 1 | 2 | – | 6 | 7 | 3.50 | – | – | – |
| Sanwar Hossain | 7 | 14 | – | 49 | 265 | 18.92 | – | 1 | 1 |
| Talha Jubair | 6 | 12 | 6 | 5* | 21 | 3.50 | – | – | – |
| Tapash Baisya | 5 | 10 | 1 | 52* | 81 | 9.00 | – | 1 | 1 |
| Tushar Imran | 3 | 6 | – | 28 | 52 | 8.66 | – | – | 1 |

## BANGLADESH – BOWLING

| | O | R | W | Avge | Best | 5wI | 10wM |
|---|---|---|---|---|---|---|---|
| Alamgir Kabir | 15 | 82 | 0 | | | | |
| Alok Kapali | 78.3 | 327 | 2 | 163.50 | 2-122 | – | – |
| Aminul Islam | 33 | 149 | 1 | 149.00 | 1- 66 | – | – |
| Ehsanul Haque | 3 | 18 | 0 | | | | |
| Enamul Haque | 338.4 | 946 | 18 | 52.55 | 4-136 | – | – |
| Fahim Muntasir | 96 | 342 | 5 | 68.40 | 3-131 | – | – |
| Habibul Bashar | 31 | 156 | 0 | | | | |
| Hasibul Hussain | 130 | 571 | 6 | 95.16 | 2-125 | – | – |
| Javed Omar | 1 | 12 | 0 | | | | |
| Khaled Mahmud | 36 | 141 | 1 | 141.00 | 1- 40 | – | – |
| Manjural Islam | 397 | 1328 | 24 | 55.33 | 6- 81 | 1 | – |
| Mashrafe Mortaza | 104.4 | 374 | 12 | 31.16 | 4-106 | – | – |
| Mohammed Ashraful | 68 | 312 | 3 | 104.00 | 2- 57 | – | – |
| Mohammed Rafique | 76 | 205 | 3 | 68.33 | 3-117 | – | – |
| Mohammed Sharif | 225.3 | 911 | 14 | 65.07 | 4- 98 | – | – |
| Naimur Rahman | 220.1 | 718 | 12 | 59.83 | 6-132 | 1 | – |
| Sanwar Hossain | 30 | 136 | 3 | 45.33 | 1- 9 | – | – |
| Talha Jubair | 162.4 | 676 | 14 | 48.28 | 3-135 | – | – |
| Tapash Baisya | 142.3 | 594 | 11 | 54.00 | 4- 72 | – | – |

# ENGLAND'S TEST MATCH SCHEDULE

| 2003 | May | Host Zimbabwe | 2004 | Dec | Tour South Africa |
|---|---|---|---|---|---|
| | Jul | Host South Africa | 2005 | May | Host Bangladesh |
| | Oct | Tour Bangladesh | | Jun | Host Australia |
| | Nov | Tour Sri Lanka | | Nov | Tour Pakistan |
| 2004 | Feb | Tour West Indies | 2006 | Feb | Tour India |
| | May | Host New Zealand | | May | Host Sri Lanka |
| | Jul | Host West Indies | | Jul | Host Pakistan |
| | Nov | Tour Zimbabwe | | Dec | Tour Australia |

# FIRST-CLASS CRICKET RECORDS

To 21 September 2002 inclusive

## TEAM RECORDS

### HIGHEST INNINGS TOTALS

| | | | |
|---|---|---|---|
| 1107 | Victoria v New South Wales | Melbourne | 1926-27 |
| 1059 | Victoria v Tasmania | Melbourne | 1922-23 |
| 952-6d | Sri Lanka v India | Colombo | 1997-98 |
| 951-7d | Sind v Baluchistan | Karachi | 1973-74 |
| 944-6d | Hyderabad v Andhra | Secunderabad | 1993-94 |
| 918 | New South Wales v South Australia | Sydney | 1900-01 |
| 912-8d | Holkar v Mysore | Indore | 1945-46 |
| 910-6d | Railways v Dera Ismail Khan | Lahore | 1964-65 |
| 903-7d | England v Australia | The Oval | 1938 |
| 887 | Yorkshire v Warwickshire | Birmingham | 1896 |
| 863 | Lancashire v Surrey | The Oval | 1990 |
| 860-6d | Tamil Nadu v Goa | Panjim | 1988-89 |

Excluding penalty runs in India, there have been 30 innings totals of 800 runs or more in first-class cricket. Tamil Nadu's total of 860-6d was boosted to 912 by 52 penalty runs.

### HIGHEST SECOND INNINGS TOTAL

| | | | |
|---|---|---|---|
| 770 | New South Wales v South Australia | Adelaide | 1920-21 |

### HIGHEST FOURTH INNINGS TOTAL

| | | | |
|---|---|---|---|
| 654-5 | England v South Africa | Durban | 1938-39 |

### HIGHEST MATCH AGGREGATE

| | | | |
|---|---|---|---|
| 2376 | Maharashtra v Bombay | Poona | 1948-49 |

### RECORD MARGIN OF VICTORY

| | | |
|---|---|---|
| Innings and 851 runs: Railways v Dera Ismail Khan | Lahore | 1964-65 |

### MOST RUNS IN A DAY

| | | | |
|---|---|---|---|
| 721 | Australians v Essex | Southend | 1948 |

### MOST HUNDREDS IN AN INNINGS

| | | | |
|---|---|---|---|
| 6 | Holkar v Mysore | Indore | 1945-46 |

### LOWEST INNINGS TOTALS

| | | | |
|---|---|---|---|
| 12 | †Oxford University v MCC and Ground | Oxford | 1877 |
| 12 | Northamptonshire v Gloucestershire | Gloucester | 1907 |
| 13 | Auckland v Canterbury | Auckland | 1877-78 |
| 13 | Nottinghamshire v Yorkshire | Nottingham | 1901 |
| 14 | Surrey v Essex | Chelmsford | 1983 |
| 15 | MCC v Surrey | Lord's | 1839 |
| 15 | †Victoria v MCC | Melbourne | 1903-04 |
| 15 | †Northamptonshire v Yorkshire | Northampton | 1908 |
| 15 | Hampshire v Warwickshire | Birmingham | 1922 |

*† Batted one man short*
There have been 27 instances of a team being dismissed for under 20.

## LOWEST MATCH AGGREGATE BY ONE TEAM

34 (16 and 18)  Border v Natal                      East London            1959-60

## LOWEST COMPLETED MATCH AGGREGATE BY BOTH TEAMS

105  MCC v Australians                              Lord's                 1878

## FEWEST RUNS IN AN UNINTERRUPTED DAY'S PLAY

95  Australia (80) v Pakistan (15-2)               Karachi                1956-57

## TIED MATCHES

Before 1949 a match was considered to be tied if the scores were level after the fourth innings, even if the side batting last had wickets in hand when play ended. Law 22 was amended in 1948 and since then a match has been tied only when the scores are level after the fourth innings has been completed. There have been 54 tied first-class matches, five of which would not have qualified under the current law. The most recent is:

West Indies A (370 & 266-7d) v Somerset (183 & 453)     Taunton            2002

## BATTING RECORDS
## HIGHEST INDIVIDUAL INNINGS

| | | | |
|---|---|---|---|
| 501* | B.C.Lara | Warwickshire v Durham | Birmingham | 1994 |
| 499 | Hanif Mohammed | Karachi v Bahawalpur | Karachi | 1958-59 |
| 452* | D.G.Bradman | New South Wales v Queensland | Sydney | 1929-30 |
| 443* | B.B.Nimbalkar | Maharashtra v Kathiawar | Poona | 1948-49 |
| 437 | W.H.Ponsford | Victoria v Queensland | Melbourne | 1927-28 |
| 429 | W.H.Ponsford | Victoria v Tasmania | Melbourne | 1922-23 |
| 428 | Aftab Baloch | Sind v Baluchistan | Karachi | 1973-74 |
| 424 | A.C.MacLaren | Lancashire v Somerset | Taunton | 1895 |
| 405* | G.A.Hick | Worcestershire v Somerset | Taunton | 1988 |
| 394 | Naved Latif | Sargodha v Gujranwala | Gujranwala | 2000-01 |
| 385 | B.Sutcliffe | Otago v Canterbury | Christchurch | 1952-53 |
| 383 | C.W.Gregory | New South Wales v Queensland | Brisbane | 1906-07 |
| 377 | S.V.Manjrekar | Bombay v Hyderabad | Bombay | 1990-91 |
| 375 | B.C.Lara | West Indies v England | St John's | 1993-94 |
| 369 | D.G.Bradman | South Australia v Tasmania | Adelaide | 1935-36 |
| 366 | N.H.Fairbrother | Lancashire v Surrey | The Oval | 1990 |
| 366 | M.V.Sridhar | Hyderabad v Andhra | Secunderabad | 1993-94 |
| 365* | C.Hill | South Australia v NSW | Adelaide | 1900-01 |
| 365* | G.St A.Sobers | West Indies v Pakistan | Kingston | 1957-58 |
| 364 | L.Hutton | England v Australia | The Oval | 1938 |
| 359* | V.M.Merchant | Bombay v Maharashtra | Bombay | 1943-44 |
| 359 | R.B.Simpson | New South Wales v Queensland | Brisbane | 1963-64 |
| 357* | R.Abel | Surrey v Somerset | The Oval | 1899 |
| 357 | D.G.Bradman | South Australia v Victoria | Melbourne | 1935-36 |
| 356 | B.A.Richards | South Australia v W Australia | Perth | 1970-71 |
| 355* | G.R.Marsh | W Australia v S Australia | Perth | 1989-90 |
| 355 | B.Sutcliffe | Otago v Auckland | Dunedin | 1949-50 |
| 353 | W.V.S.Laxman | Hyderabad v Karnataka | Bangalore | 1999-00 |
| 352 | W.H.Ponsford | Victoria v New South Wales | Melbourne | 1926-27 |
| 350 | Rashid Israr | Habib Bank v National Bank | Lahore | 1976-77 |

There have been 136 triple hundreds in first-class cricket, W.V.Raman (313) and Arjan Kripal Singh (302*) for Tamil Nadu v Goa at Panjim in 1988-89 providing the only instance of two batsmen scoring 300 in the same innings.

## MOST HUNDREDS IN SUCCESSIVE INNINGS

| | | | |
|---|---|---|---|
| 6 | C.B.Fry | Sussex and Rest of England | 1901 |
| 6 | D.G.Bradman | South Australia and D.G.Bradman's XI | 1938-39 |
| 6 | M.J.Procter | Rhodesia | 1970-71 |

## TWO DOUBLE HUNDREDS IN A MATCH

| 244 | 202* | A.E.Fagg | Kent v Essex | Colchester | 1938 |

## TRIPLE HUNDRED AND HUNDRED IN A MATCH

| 333 | 123 | G.A.Gooch | England v India | Lord's | 1990 |

## DOUBLE HUNDRED AND HUNDRED IN A MATCH MOST TIMES

| 4 | Zaheer Abbas | Gloucestershire | 1976-81 |

## TWO HUNDREDS IN A MATCH MOST TIMES

| 8 | Zaheer Abbas | Gloucestershire and PIA | 1976-82 |
| 7 | W.R.Hammond | Gloucestershire, England and MCC | 1927-45 |

## MOST HUNDREDS IN A SEASON

| 18 | D.C.S.Compton | 1947 | 16 | J.B.Hobbs | 1925 |

## 100 HUNDREDS IN A CAREER

|  | Total | | 100th Hundred | |
| --- | --- | --- | --- | --- |
|  | Hundreds | Inns | Season | Inns |
| J.B.Hobbs | 197 | 1315 | 1923 | 821 |
| E.H.Hendren | 170 | 1300 | 1928-29 | 740 |
| W.R.Hammond | 167 | 1005 | 1935 | 679 |
| C.P.Mead | 153 | 1340 | 1927 | 892 |
| G.Boycott | 151 | 1014 | 1977 | 645 |
| H.Sutcliffe | 149 | 1088 | 1932 | 700 |
| F.E.Woolley | 145 | 1532 | 1929 | 1031 |
| L.Hutton | 129 | 814 | 1951 | 619 |
| G.A.Gooch | 128 | 990 | 1992-93 | 820 |
| W.G Grace | 126 | 1493 | 1895 | 1113 |
| D.C.S.Compton | 123 | 839 | 1952 | 552 |
| T.W.Graveney | 122 | 1223 | 1964 | 940 |
| G.A.Hick | 121 | 725 | 1998 | 574 |
| D.G.Bradman | 117 | 338 | 1947-48 | 295 |
| I.V.A.Richards | 114 | 796 | 1988-89 | 658 |
| Zaheer Abbas | 108 | 768 | 1982-83 | 658 |
| A.Sandham | 107 | 1000 | 1935 | 871 |
| M.C.Cowdrey | 107 | 1130 | 1973 | 1035 |
| T.W.Hayward | 104 | 1138 | 1913 | 1076 |
| G.M.Turner | 103 | 792 | 1982 | 779 |
| J.H.Edrich | 103 | 979 | 1977 | 945 |
| L.E.G.Ames | 102 | 951 | 1950 | 915 |
| G.E.Tyldesley | 102 | 961 | 1934 | 919 |
| D.L.Amiss | 102 | 1139 | 1986 | 1081 |

**MOST 400s:**    2 – W.H.Ponsford
**MOST 300s or more:**    6 – D.G.Bradman; 4 – W.R.Hammond
**MOST 200s or more:**    37 – D.G.Bradman; 36 – W.R.Hammond; 22 – E.H.Hendren

## MOST RUNS IN A MONTH

| 1294 (avge 92.42) | L.Hutton | Yorkshire | June 1949 |

## MOST RUNS IN A SEASON

| Runs | | | I | NO | HS | Avge | 100 | Season |
|---|---|---|---|---|---|---|---|---|
| 3816 | D.C.S.Compton | Middlesex | 50 | 8 | 246 | 90.85 | 18 | 1947 |
| 3539 | W.J.Edrich | Middlesex | 52 | 8 | 267* | 80.43 | 12 | 1947 |
| 3518 | T.W.Hayward | Surrey | 61 | 8 | 219 | 66.37 | 13 | 1906 |

The feat of scoring 3000 runs in a season has been achieved 28 times, the most recent instance being by W.E.Alley (3019) in 1961. The highest aggregate in a season since 1969 is 2755 by S.J.Cook in 1991.

## 1000 RUNS IN A SEASON MOST TIMES

28    W.G.Grace (Gloucestershire), F.E.Woolley (Kent)

## HIGHEST BATTING AVERAGE IN A SEASON

(Qualification: 12 innings)

| Avge | | | I | NO | HS | Runs | 100 | Season |
|---|---|---|---|---|---|---|---|---|
| 115.66 | D.G.Bradman | Australians | 26 | 5 | 278 | 2429 | 13 | 1938 |
| 104.66 | D.R.Martyn | Australians | 14 | 5 | 176* | 942 | 5 | 2001 |
| 102.53 | G.Boycott | Yorkshire | 20 | 5 | 175* | 1538 | 6 | 1979 |
| 102.00 | W.A.Johnston | Australians | 17 | 16 | 28* | 102 | – | 1953 |
| 101.70 | G.A.Gooch | Essex | 30 | 3 | 333 | 2746 | 12 | 1990 |
| 100.12 | G.Boycott | Yorkshire | 30 | 5 | 233 | 2503 | 13 | 1971 |

## FASTEST HUNDRED AGAINST AUTHENTIC BOWLING

| 35 min | P.G.H.Fender | Surrey v Northamptonshire | Northampton | 1920 |
|---|---|---|---|---|

## FASTEST DOUBLE HUNDRED

| 113 min | R.J.Shastri | Bombay v Baroda | Bombay | 1984-85 |
|---|---|---|---|---|

## FASTEST TRIPLE HUNDRED

| 181 min | D.C.S.Compton | MCC v NE Transvaal | Benoni | 1948-49 |
|---|---|---|---|---|

## MOST SIXES IN AN INNINGS

| 16 | A.Symonds | Gloucestershire v Glamorgan | Abergavenny | 1995 |
|---|---|---|---|---|

## MOST SIXES IN A MATCH

| 20 | A.Symonds | Gloucestershire v Glamorgan | Abergavenny | 1995 |
|---|---|---|---|---|

## MOST SIXES IN A SEASON

| 80 | I.T.Botham | Somerset and England | | 1985 |
|---|---|---|---|---|

## MOST FOURS IN AN INNINGS

| 72 | B.C.Lara | Warwickshire v Durham | Birmingham | 1994 |
|---|---|---|---|---|

## MOST RUNS OFF ONE OVER

| 36 | G.St A.Sobers | Nottinghamshire v Glamorgan | Swansea | 1968 |
|---|---|---|---|---|
| 36 | R.J.Shastri | Bombay v Baroda | Bombay | 1984-85 |

Both batsmen hit for six all six balls of overs bowled by M.A.Nash and Tilak Raj respectively.

## MOST RUNS IN A DAY

| 390* | B.C.Lara | Warwickshire v Durham | Birmingham | 1994 |
|---|---|---|---|---|

There have been 19 instances of a batsman scoring 300 or more runs in a day.

# LONGEST INNINGS

1015 min  R.Nayyar (271)  Himachal Pradesh v Jammu & Kashmir Chamba  1999-00

## HIGHEST PARTNERSHIPS FOR EACH WICKET

**First Wicket**

| | | | |
|---|---|---|---|
| 561 | Waheed Mirza/Mansoor Akhtar | Karachi W v Quetta | Karachi | 1976-77 |
| 555 | P.Holmes/H.Sutcliffe | Yorkshire v Essex | Leyton | 1932 |
| 554 | J.T.Brown/J.Tunnicliffe | Yorkshire v Derbys | Chesterfield | 1898 |

**Second Wicket**

| | | | |
|---|---|---|---|
| 576 | S.T.Jayasuriya/R.S.Mahanama | Sri Lanka v India | Colombo (RPS) | 1997-98 |
| 475 | Zahir Alam/L.S.Rajput | Assam v Tripura | Gauhati | 1991-92 |
| 465* | J.A.Jameson/R.B.Kanhai | Warwickshire v Glos | Birmingham | 1974 |

**Third Wicket**

| | | | |
|---|---|---|---|
| 467 | A.H.Jones/M.D.Crowe | N Zealand v Sri Lanka | Wellington | 1990-91 |
| 456 | Khalid Irtiza/Aslam Ali | United Bank v Multan | Karachi | 1975-76 |
| 451 | Mudassar Nazar/Javed Miandad | Pakistan v India | Hyderabad | 1982-83 |
| 445 | P.E.Whitelaw/W.N.Carson | Auckland v Otago | Dunedin | 1936-37 |
| 438* | G.A.Hick/T.M.Moody | Worcestershire v Hants | Southampton | 1997 |

**Fourth Wicket**

| | | | |
|---|---|---|---|
| 577 | V.S.Hazare/Gul Mahomed | Baroda v Holkar | Baroda | 1946-47 |
| 574* | C.L.Walcott/F.M.M.Worrell | Barbados v Trinidad | Port-of-Spain | 1945-46 |
| 502* | F.M.M.Worrell/J.D.C.Goddard | Barbados v Trinidad | Bridgetown | 1943-44 |
| 470 | A.I.Kallicharran/G.W.Humpage | Warwickshire v Lancs | Southport | 1982 |

**Fifth Wicket**

| | | | |
|---|---|---|---|
| 464* | M.E.Waugh/S.R.Waugh | NSW v W Australia | Perth | 1990-91 |
| 405 | S.G.Barnes/D.G.Bradman | Australia v England | Sydney | 1946-47 |
| 401 | M.B.Loye/D.Ripley | Northants v Glamorgan | Northampton | 1998 |

**Sixth Wicket**

| | | | |
|---|---|---|---|
| 487* | G.A.Headley/C.C.Passailaigue | Jamaica v Tennyson's | Kingston | 1931-32 |
| 428 | W.W.Armstrong/M.A.Noble | Australians v Sussex | Hove | 1902 |
| 411 | R.M.Poore/E.G.Wynyard | Hampshire v Somerset | Taunton | 1899 |

**Seventh Wicket**

| | | | |
|---|---|---|---|
| 460 | Bhupinder Singh jr/P.Dharmani | Punjab v Delhi | Delhi | 1994-95 |
| 347 | D.St E.Atkinson/C.C.Depeiza | W Indies v Australia | Bridgetown | 1954-55 |
| 344 | K.S.Ranjitsinhji/W.Newham | Sussex v Essex | Leyton | 1902 |

**Eighth Wicket**

| | | | |
|---|---|---|---|
| 433 | V.T.Trumper/A.Sims | Australians v C'bury | Christchurch | 1913-14 |
| 313 | Wasim Akram/Saqlain Mushtaq | Pakistan v Zimbabwe | Sheikhupura | 1996-97 |
| 292 | R.Peel/Lord Hawke | Yorkshire v Warwicks | Birmingham | 1896 |

**Ninth Wicket**

| | | | |
|---|---|---|---|
| 283 | J.Chapman/A.Warren | Derbys v Warwicks | Blackwell | 1910 |
| 268 | J.B.Commins/N.Boje | SA 'A' v Mashonaland | Harare | 1994-95 |
| 251 | J.W.H.T.Douglas/S.N.Hare | Essex v Derbyshire | Leyton | 1921 |

**Tenth Wicket**

| | | | |
|---|---|---|---|
| 307 | A.F.Kippax/J.E.H.Hooker | NSW v Victoria | Melbourne | 1928-29 |
| 249 | C.T.Sarwate/S.N.Banerjee | Indians v Surrey | The Oval | 1946 |
| 235 | F.E.Woolley/A.Fielder | Kent v Worcs | Stourbridge | 1909 |

## 35000 RUNS IN A CAREER

| | *Career* | *I* | *NO* | *HS* | *Runs* | *Avge* | *100* |
|---|---|---|---|---|---|---|---|
| J.B.Hobbs | 1905-34 | 1315 | 106 | 316* | **61237** | 50.65 | 197 |
| F.E.Woolley | 1906-38 | 1532 | 85 | 305* | **58969** | 40.75 | 145 |
| E.H.Hendren | 1907-38 | 1300 | 166 | 301* | **57611** | 50.80 | 170 |
| C.P.Mead | 1905-36 | 1340 | 185 | 280* | **55061** | 47.67 | 153 |
| W.G.Grace | 1865-1908 | 1493 | 105 | 344 | **54896** | 39.55 | 126 |
| W.R.Hammond | 1920-51 | 1005 | 104 | 336* | **50551** | 56.10 | 167 |
| H.Sutcliffe | 1919-45 | 1088 | 123 | 313 | **50138** | 51.95 | 149 |
| G.Boycott | 1962-86 | 1014 | 162 | 261* | **48426** | 56.83 | 151 |
| T.W.Graveney | 1948-71/72 | 1223 | 159 | 258 | **47793** | 44.91 | 122 |
| G.A.Gooch | 1973-2000 | 990 | 75 | 333 | **44846** | 49.01 | 128 |
| T.W.Hayward | 1893-1914 | 1138 | 96 | 315* | **43551** | 41.79 | 104 |
| D.L.Amiss | 1960-87 | 1139 | 126 | 262* | **43423** | 42.86 | 102 |
| M.C.Cowdrey | 1950-76 | 1130 | 134 | 307 | **42719** | 42.89 | 107 |
| A.Sandham | 1911-37/38 | 1000 | 79 | 325 | **41284** | 44.82 | 107 |
| L.Hutton | 1934-60 | 814 | 91 | 364 | **40140** | 55.51 | 129 |
| M.J.K.Smith | 1951-75 | 1091 | 139 | 204 | **39832** | 41.84 | 69 |
| W.Rhodes | 1898-1930 | 1528 | 237 | 267* | **39802** | 30.83 | 58 |
| J.H.Edrich | 1956-78 | 979 | 104 | 310* | **39790** | 45.47 | 103 |
| R.E.S.Wyatt | 1923-57 | 1141 | 157 | 232 | **39405** | 40.04 | 85 |
| D.C.S.Compton | 1936-64 | 839 | 88 | 300 | **38942** | 51.85 | 123 |
| G.E.Tyldesley | 1909-36 | 961 | 106 | 256* | **38874** | 45.46 | 102 |
| J.T.Tyldesley | 1895-1923 | 994 | 62 | 295* | **37897** | 40.60 | 86 |
| K.W.R.Fletcher | 1962-88 | 1167 | 170 | 228* | **37665** | 37.77 | 63 |
| C.G.Greenidge | 1970-92 | 889 | 75 | 273* | **37354** | 45.88 | 92 |
| J.W.Hearne | 1909-36 | 1025 | 116 | 285* | **37252** | 40.98 | 96 |
| L.E.G.Ames | 1926-51 | 951 | 95 | 295 | **37248** | 43.51 | 102 |
| D.Kenyon | 1946-67 | 1159 | 59 | 259 | **37002** | 33.63 | 74 |
| W.J.Edrich | 1934-58 | 964 | 92 | 267* | **36965** | 42.39 | 86 |
| J.M.Parks | 1949-76 | 1227 | 172 | 205* | **36673** | 34.76 | 51 |
| M.W.Gatting | 1975-98 | 861 | 123 | 258 | **36549** | 49.52 | 94 |
| D.Denton | 1894-1920 | 1163 | 70 | 221 | **36479** | 33.37 | 69 |
| G.H.Hirst | 1891-1929 | 1215 | 151 | 341 | **36323** | 34.13 | 60 |
| I.V.A.Richards | 1971/72-93 | 796 | 63 | 322 | **36212** | 49.40 | 114 |
| A.Jones | 1957-83 | 1168 | 72 | 204* | **36049** | 32.89 | 56 |
| W.G.Quaife | 1894-1928 | 1203 | 185 | 255* | **36012** | 35.37 | 72 |
| R.E.Marshall | 1945/46-72 | 1053 | 59 | 228* | **35725** | 35.94 | 68 |
| G.A.Hick | 1983/84-2002 | 725 | 69 | 405* | **35246** | 53.72 | 121 |
| G.Gunn | 1902-32 | 1061 | 82 | 220 | **35208** | 35.96 | 62 |

## BOWLING RECORDS
## ALL TEN WICKETS IN AN INNINGS

This feat has been achieved 78 times in first-class matches (excluding 12-a-side fixtures).

**Three Times:** A.P.Freeman (1929, 1930, 1931)

**Twice:** V.E.Walker (1859, 1865); H.Verity (1931, 1932); J.C.Laker (1956)

**Instances since 1945:**

| | | | |
|---|---|---|---|
| W.E.Hollies | Warwickshire v Notts | Birmingham | 1946 |
| J.M.Sims | East v West | Kingston on Thames | 1948 |
| J.K.R.Graveney | Gloucestershire v Derbyshire | Chesterfield | 1949 |
| T.E.Bailey | Essex v Lancashire | Clacton | 1949 |
| R.Berry | Lancashire v Worcestershire | Blackpool | 1953 |
| S.P.Gupte | President's XI v Combined XI | Bombay | 1954-55 |
| J.C.Laker | Surrey v Australians | The Oval | 1956 |

| K.Smales | Nottinghamshire v Glos | Stroud | 1956 |
| G.A.R.Lock | Surrey v Kent | Blackheath | 1956 |
| J.C.Laker | England v Australia | Manchester | 1956 |
| P.M.Chatterjee | Bengal v Assam | Jorhat | 1956-57 |
| J.D.Bannister | Warwicks v Combined Services | Birmingham (M & B) | 1959 |
| A.J.G.Pearson | Cambridge U v Leicestershire | Loughborough | 1961 |
| N.I.Thomson | Sussex v Warwickshire | Worthing | 1964 |
| P.J.Allan | Queensland v Victoria | Melbourne | 1965-66 |
| I.J.Brayshaw | Western Australia v Victoria | Perth | 1967-68 |
| Shahid Mahmood | Karachi Whites v Khairpur | Karachi | 1969-70 |
| E.E.Hemmings | International XI v W Indians | Kingston | 1982-83 |
| P.Sunderam | Rajasthan v Vidarbha | Jodhpur | 1985-86 |
| S.T.Jefferies | Western Province v OFS | Cape Town | 1987-88 |
| Imran Adil | Bahawalpur v Faisalabad | Faisalabad | 1989-90 |
| G.P.Wickremasinghe | Sinhalese v Kalutara | Colombo | 1991-92 |
| R.L.Johnson | Middlesex v Derbyshire | Derby | 1994 |
| Naeem Akhtar | Rawalpindi B v Peshawar | Peshawar | 1995-96 |
| A.Kumble | India v Pakistan | Delhi | 1998-99 |
| D.S.Mohanty | East Zone v South Zone | Agartala | 2000-01 |

## MOST WICKETS IN A MATCH

| 19 | J.C.Laker | England v Australia | Manchester | 1956 |

## MOST WICKETS IN A SEASON

| Wkts | | Season | Matches | Overs | Mdns | Runs | Avge |
|---|---|---|---|---|---|---|---|
| 304 | A.P.Freeman | 1928 | 37 | 1976.1 | 423 | 5489 | 18.05 |
| 298 | A.P.Freeman | 1933 | 33 | 2039 | 651 | 4549 | 15.26 |

The feat of taking 250 wickets in a season has been achieved on 12 occasions, the last instance being by A.P.Freeman in 1933. 200 or more wickets in a season have been taken on 59 occasions, the last being by G.A.R.Lock (212 wickets, average 12.02) in 1957.

The highest aggregates of wickets taken in a season since the reduction of County Championship matches in 1969 are as follows:

| Wkts | | Season | Matches | Overs | Mdns | Runs | Avge |
|---|---|---|---|---|---|---|---|
| 134 | M.D.Marshall | 1982 | 22 | 822 | 225 | 2108 | 15.73 |
| 131 | L.R.Gibbs | 1971 | 23 | 1024.1 | 295 | 2475 | 18.89 |
| 125 | F.D.Stephenson | 1988 | 22 | 819.1 | 196 | 2289 | 18.31 |
| 121 | R.D.Jackman | 1980 | 23 | 746.2 | 220 | 1864 | 15.40 |

Since 1969 there have been 49 instances of bowlers taking 100 wickets in a season.

## MOST HAT-TRICKS IN A CAREER

| 7 | D.V.P.Wright |
| 6 | T.W.J.Goddard, C.W.L.Parker |
| 5 | S.Haigh, V.W.C.Jupp, A.E.G.Rhodes, F.A.Tarrant |

## 2000 WICKETS IN A CAREER

| | Career | Runs | Wkts | Avge | 100w |
|---|---|---|---|---|---|
| W.Rhodes | 1898-1930 | 69993 | **4187** | 16.71 | 23 |
| A.P.Freeman | 1914-36 | 69577 | **3776** | 18.42 | 17 |
| C.W.L.Parker | 1903-35 | 63817 | **3278** | 19.46 | 16 |
| J.T.Hearne | 1888-1923 | 54352 | **3061** | 17.75 | 15 |
| T.W.J.Goddard | 1922-52 | 59116 | **2979** | 19.84 | 16 |
| W.G.Grace | 1865-1908 | 51545 | **2876** | 17.92 | 10 |
| A.S.Kennedy | 1907-36 | 61034 | **2874** | 21.23 | 15 |
| D.Shackleton | 1948-69 | 53303 | **2857** | 18.65 | 20 |
| G.A.R.Lock | 1946-70/71 | 54709 | **2844** | 19.23 | 14 |

| | Career | Runs | Wkts | Avge | 100w |
|---|---|---|---|---|---|
| F.J.Titmus | 1949-82 | 63313 | **2830** | 22.37 | 16 |
| M.W.Tate | 1912-37 | 50571 | **2784** | 18.16 | 13+1 |
| G.H.Hirst | 1891-1929 | 51282 | **2739** | 18.72 | 15 |
| C.Blythe | 1899-1914 | 42136 | **2506** | 16.81 | 14 |
| D.L.Underwood | 1963-87 | 49993 | **2465** | 20.28 | 10 |
| W.E.Astill | 1906-39 | 57783 | **2431** | 23.76 | 9 |
| J.C.White | 1909-37 | 43759 | **2356** | 18.57 | 14 |
| W.E.Hollies | 1932-57 | 48656 | **2323** | 20.94 | 14 |
| F.S.Trueman | 1949-69 | 42154 | **2304** | 18.29 | 12 |
| J.B.Statham | 1950-68 | 36999 | **2260** | 16.37 | 13 |
| R.T.D.Perks | 1930-55 | 53771 | **2233** | 24.07 | 16 |
| J.Briggs | 1879-1900 | 35431 | **2221** | 15.95 | 12 |
| D.J.Shepherd | 1950-72 | 47302 | **2218** | 21.32 | 12 |
| E.G.Dennett | 1903-26 | 42571 | **2147** | 19.82 | 12 |
| T.Richardson | 1892-1905 | 38794 | **2104** | 18.43 | 10 |
| T.E.Bailey | 1945-67 | 48170 | **2082** | 23.13 | 9 |
| R.Illingworth | 1951-83 | 42023 | **2072** | 20.28 | 10 |
| F.E.Woolley | 1906-38 | 41066 | **2068** | 19.85 | 8 |
| N.Gifford | 1960-88 | 48731 | **2068** | 23.56 | 4 |
| G.Geary | 1912-38 | 41339 | **2063** | 20.03 | 11 |
| D.V.P.Wright | 1932-57 | 49307 | **2056** | 23.98 | 10 |
| J.A.Newman | 1906-30 | 51111 | **2032** | 25.15 | 9 |
| A.Shaw | 1864-97 | 24580 | **2026+1** | 12.12 | 9 |
| S.Haigh | 1895-1913 | 32091 | **2012** | 15.94 | 11 |

## ALL-ROUND RECORDS

### THE 'DOUBLE'

**3000 runs and 100 wickets:** J.H.Parks (1937)

**2000 runs and 200 wickets:** G.H.Hirst (1906)

**2000 runs and 100 wickets:** F.E.Woolley (4), J.W.Hearne (3), W.G.Grace (2), G.H.Hirst (2), W.Rhodes (2), T.E.Bailey, D.E.Davies, G.L.Jessop, V.W.C.Jupp, J.Langridge, F.A.Tarrant, C.L.Townsend, L.F.Townsend.

**1000 runs and 200 wickets:** M.W.Tate (3), A.E.Trott (2), A.S.Kennedy

**Most Doubles:** 16 – W.Rhodes; 14 – G.H.Hirst; 10 – V.W.C.Jupp

**Double in Debut Season:** D.B.Close (1949) – aged 18, the youngest to achieve this feat.

The feat of scoring 1000 runs and taking 100 wickets in a season has been achieved on 305 occasions, R.J.Hadlee (1984) and F.D.Stephenson (1988) being the only players to complete the 'double' since the reduction of County Championship matches in 1969.

## WICKET-KEEPING RECORDS

### EIGHT DISMISSALS IN AN INNINGS

| 9 | (8ct, 1st) | Tahir Rashid | Habib Bank v PACO | Gujranwala | 1992-93 |
|---|---|---|---|---|---|
| 9 | (7ct, 2st) | W.R.James | Matabeleland v Mashonaland CD | Bulawayo | 1995-96 |
| 8 | (8ct) | A.T.W.Grout | Queensland v W Australia | Brisbane | 1959-60 |
| 8 | (8ct) | D.E.East | Essex v Somerset | Taunton | 1985 |
| 8 | (8ct) | S.A.Marsh | Kent v Middlesex | Lord's | 1991 |
| 8 | (6ct, 2st) | T.J.Zoehrer | Australians v Surrey | The Oval | 1993 |
| 8 | (7ct, 1st) | D.S.Berry | Victoria v South Australia | Melbourne | 1996-97 |
| 8 | (7ct, 1st) | Y.S.S.Mendis | Bloomfield v Kurunegala Youth | Colombo | 2000-01 |
| 8 | (7ct, 1st) | S.Nath | Assam v Tripura (*on debut*) | Gauhati | 2001-02 |

## TWELVE DISMISSALS IN A MATCH

| | | | | |
|---|---|---|---|---|
| 13 | (11ct, 2st) | W.R.James | Matabeleland v Mashonaland CD | Bulawayo | 1995-96 |
| 12 | (8ct, 4st) | E.Pooley | Surrey v Sussex | The Oval | 1868 |
| 12 | (9ct, 3st) | D.Tallon | Queensland v NSW | Sydney | 1938-39 |
| 12 | (9ct, 3st) | H.B.Taber | NSW v South Australia | Adelaide | 1968-69 |

## MOST DISMISSALS IN A SEASON

128 (79ct, 49st) L.E.G.Ames            1929

## 1000 DISMISSALS IN A CAREER

| | Career | Dismissals | Ct | St |
|---|---|---|---|---|
| R.W.Taylor | 1960-88 | **1649** | 1473 | 176 |
| J.T.Murray | 1952-75 | **1527** | 1270 | 257 |
| H.Strudwick | 1902-27 | **1497** | 1242 | 255 |
| A.P.E.Knott | 1964-85 | **1344** | 1211 | 133 |
| F.H.Huish | 1895-1914 | **1310** | 933 | 377 |
| B.Taylor | 1949-73 | **1294** | 1083 | 211 |
| R.C.Russell | 1981-2002 | **1282** | 1158 | 124 |
| D.Hunter | 1889-1909 | **1253** | 906 | 347 |
| H.R.Butt | 1890-1912 | **1228** | 953 | 275 |
| J.H.Board | 1891-1914/15 | **1207** | 852 | 355 |
| H.Elliott | 1920-47 | **1206** | 904 | 302 |
| J.M.Parks | 1949-76 | **1181** | 1088 | 93 |
| S.J.Rhodes | 1981-2002 | **1175** | 1057 | 118 |
| R.Booth | 1951-70 | **1126** | 948 | 178 |
| L.E.G.Ames | 1926-51 | **1121** | 703 | 418 |
| D.L.Bairstow | 1970-90 | **1099** | 961 | 138 |
| G.Duckworth | 1923-47 | **1096** | 753 | 343 |
| H.W.Stephenson | 1948-64 | **1082** | 748 | 334 |
| J.G.Binks | 1955-75 | **1071** | 895 | 176 |
| T.G.Evans | 1939-69 | **1066** | 816 | 250 |
| A.Long | 1960-80 | **1046** | 922 | 124 |
| G.O.Dawkes | 1937-61 | **1043** | 895 | 148 |
| R.W.Tolchard | 1965-83 | **1037** | 912 | 125 |
| W.L.Cornford | 1921-47 | **1017** | 675 | 342 |

## FIELDING RECORDS

### MOST CATCHES IN AN INNINGS

| | | | | |
|---|---|---|---|---|
| 7 | M.J.Stewart | Surrey v Northamptonshire | Northampton | 1957 |
| 7 | A.S.Brown | Gloucestershire v Nottinghamshire | Nottingham | 1966 |

### MOST CATCHES IN A MATCH

| | | | | |
|---|---|---|---|---|
| 10 | W.R.Hammond | Gloucestershire v Surrey | Cheltenham | 1928 |

### MOST CATCHES IN A SEASON

| | | | | | |
|---|---|---|---|---|---|
| 78 | W.R.Hammond | 1928 | 77 | M.J.Stewart | 1957 |

### 750 CATCHES IN A CAREER

| | | | | | |
|---|---|---|---|---|---|
| 1018 | F.E.Woolley | 1906-38 | 784 | J.G.Langridge | 1928-55 |
| 887 | W.G.Grace | 1865-1908 | 764 | W.Rhodes | 1898-1930 |
| 830 | G.A.R.Lock | 1946-70/71 | 758 | C.A.Milton | 1948-74 |
| 819 | W.R.Hammond | 1920-51 | 754 | E.H.Hendren | 1907-38 |
| 813 | D.B.Close | 1949-86 | | | |

# LIMITED-OVERS INTERNATIONALS RESULTS

## 1970-71 to 30 March 2003

| | Opponents | Matches | Won | | | | | | | | | | | | | | | | | | Tied | NR |
|---|---|---|---|---|---|---|---|---|---|---|---|---|---|---|---|---|---|---|---|---|---|---|
| | | | E | A | SA | WI | NZ | I | P | SL | Z | B | C | EA | H | K | N | SC | UAE | | |
| **England** | Australia | 77 | 31 | 44 | – | – | – | – | – | – | – | – | – | – | – | – | – | – | – | 1 | 1 |
| | South Africa | 23 | 7 | – | 16 | – | – | – | – | – | – | – | – | – | – | – | – | – | – | – | – |
| | West Indies | 61 | 26 | – | – | 32 | – | – | – | – | – | – | – | – | – | – | – | – | – | – | 3 |
| | New Zealand | 52 | 25 | – | – | – | 23 | – | – | – | – | – | – | – | – | – | – | – | – | 1 | 3 |
| | India | 48 | 23 | – | – | – | – | 23 | – | – | – | – | – | – | – | – | – | – | – | – | 2 |
| | Pakistan | 50 | 29 | – | – | – | – | – | 20 | – | – | – | – | – | – | – | – | – | – | – | 1 |
| | Sri Lanka | 30 | 18 | – | – | – | – | – | – | 12 | – | – | – | – | – | – | – | – | – | – | – |
| | Zimbabwe | 22 | 15 | – | – | – | – | – | – | – | 7 | – | – | – | – | – | – | – | – | – | – |
| | Bangladesh | 1 | 1 | – | – | – | – | – | – | – | – | 0 | – | – | – | – | – | – | – | – | – |
| | Canada | 1 | 1 | – | – | – | – | – | – | – | – | – | 0 | – | – | – | – | – | – | – | – |
| | East Africa | 1 | 1 | – | – | – | – | – | – | – | – | – | – | 0 | – | – | – | – | – | – | – |
| | Holland | 2 | 2 | – | – | – | – | – | – | – | – | – | – | – | 0 | – | – | – | – | – | – |
| | Kenya | 1 | 1 | – | – | – | – | – | – | – | – | – | – | – | – | 0 | – | – | – | – | – |
| | Namibia | 1 | 1 | – | – | – | – | – | – | – | – | – | – | – | – | – | 0 | – | – | – | – |
| | U A Emirates | 1 | 1 | – | – | – | – | – | – | – | – | – | – | – | – | – | – | – | 0 | – | – |
| **Australia** | South Africa | 56 | – | 29 | 24 | – | – | – | – | – | – | – | – | – | – | – | – | – | – | – | 3 |
| | West Indies | 98 | – | 43 | – | 52 | – | – | – | – | – | – | – | – | – | – | – | – | – | 2 | 1 |
| | New Zealand | 86 | – | 58 | – | – | 25 | – | – | – | – | – | – | – | – | – | – | – | – | – | 3 |
| | India | 69 | – | 41 | – | – | – | 25 | – | – | – | – | – | – | – | – | – | – | – | – | 3 |
| | Pakistan | 67 | – | 37 | – | – | – | – | 26 | – | – | – | – | – | – | – | – | – | – | 1 | 3 |
| | Sri Lanka | 50 | – | 33 | – | – | – | – | – | 15 | – | – | – | – | – | – | – | – | – | – | 2 |
| | Zimbabwe | 20 | – | 19 | – | – | – | – | – | – | 1 | – | – | – | – | – | – | – | – | – | – |
| | Bangladesh | 3 | – | 3 | – | – | – | – | – | – | – | 0 | – | – | – | – | – | – | – | – | – |
| | Canada | 1 | – | 1 | – | – | – | – | – | – | – | – | 0 | – | – | – | – | – | – | – | – |
| | Holland | 2 | – | 1 | – | – | – | – | – | – | – | – | – | – | 0 | – | – | – | – | – | – |
| | Kenya | 4 | – | 4 | – | – | – | – | – | – | – | – | – | – | – | 0 | – | – | – | – | – |
| | Namibia | 1 | – | 1 | – | – | – | – | – | – | – | – | – | – | – | – | 0 | – | – | – | – |
| | Scotland | 1 | – | 1 | – | – | – | – | – | – | – | – | – | – | – | – | – | – | 0 | – | – |
| **S Africa** | West Indies | 27 | – | – | 18 | 9 | – | – | – | – | – | – | – | – | – | – | – | – | – | – | – |
| | N Zealand | 34 | – | – | 22 | – | 9 | – | – | – | – | – | – | – | – | – | – | – | – | – | 3 |
| | India | 43 | – | – | 27 | – | – | 15 | – | – | – | – | – | – | – | – | – | – | – | – | – |
| | Pakistan | 36 | – | – | 25 | – | – | – | 11 | – | – | – | – | – | – | – | – | – | – | – | – |
| | Sri Lanka | 34 | – | – | 18 | – | – | – | – | 14 | – | – | – | – | – | – | – | – | – | 1 | 1 |
| | Zimbabwe | 15 | – | – | 12 | – | – | – | – | – | 2 | – | – | – | – | – | – | – | – | – | 1 |
| | Bangladesh | 4 | – | – | 4 | – | – | – | – | – | – | 0 | – | – | – | – | – | – | – | – | – |
| | Canada | 1 | – | – | 1 | – | – | – | – | – | – | – | 0 | – | – | – | – | – | – | – | – |
| | Holland | 1 | – | – | 1 | – | – | – | – | – | – | – | – | – | 0 | – | – | – | – | – | – |
| | Kenya | 8 | – | – | 8 | – | – | – | – | – | – | – | – | – | – | 0 | – | – | – | – | – |
| | U A Emirates | 1 | – | – | 1 | – | – | – | – | – | – | – | – | – | – | – | – | – | 0 | – | – |
| **W Indies** | New Zealand | 36 | – | – | – | 22 | 11 | – | – | – | – | – | – | – | – | – | – | – | – | – | 3 |
| | India | 76 | – | – | – | 46 | – | 28 | – | – | – | – | – | – | – | – | – | – | – | 1 | 1 |
| | Pakistan | 98 | – | – | – | 60 | – | – | 36 | – | – | – | – | – | – | – | – | – | – | 2 | 1 |
| | Sri Lanka | 36 | – | – | – | 22 | – | – | – | 13 | – | – | – | – | – | – | – | – | – | – | 1 |
| | Zimbabwe | 19 | – | – | – | 14 | – | – | – | – | 5 | – | – | – | – | – | – | – | – | – | 2 |
| | Bangladesh | 7 | – | – | – | 5 | – | – | – | – | – | 0 | – | – | – | – | – | – | – | – | – |
| | Canada | 1 | – | – | – | 1 | – | – | – | – | – | – | 0 | – | – | – | – | – | – | – | – |
| | Kenya | 6 | – | – | – | 5 | – | – | – | – | – | – | – | – | – | 1 | – | – | – | – | – |
| | Scotland | 1 | – | – | – | 1 | – | – | – | – | – | – | – | – | – | – | – | – | 0 | – | – |
| **N Zealand** | India | 69 | – | – | – | – | 32 | 34 | – | – | – | – | – | – | – | – | – | – | – | – | 3 |
| | Pakistan | 64 | – | – | – | – | 22 | – | 40 | – | – | – | – | – | – | – | – | – | – | 1 | 1 |
| | Sri Lanka | 53 | – | – | – | – | 27 | – | – | 23 | – | – | – | – | – | – | – | – | – | 1 | 2 |
| | Zimbabwe | 26 | – | – | – | – | 17 | – | – | – | 7 | – | – | – | – | – | – | – | – | 1 | 1 |
| | Bangladesh | 4 | – | – | – | – | 4 | – | – | – | – | 0 | – | – | – | – | – | – | – | – | – |
| | Canada | 1 | – | – | – | – | 1 | – | – | – | – | – | 0 | – | – | – | – | – | – | – | – |
| | East Africa | 1 | – | – | – | – | 1 | – | – | – | – | – | – | 0 | – | – | – | – | – | – | – |
| | Holland | 1 | – | – | – | – | 1 | – | – | – | – | – | – | – | 0 | – | – | – | – | – | – |
| | Scotland | 1 | – | – | – | – | 1 | – | – | – | – | – | – | – | – | – | – | – | 0 | – | – |
| | U A Emirates | 1 | – | – | – | – | 1 | – | – | – | – | – | – | – | – | – | – | – | 0 | – | – |
| **India** | Pakistan | 86 | – | – | – | – | – | 30 | 52 | – | – | – | – | – | – | – | – | – | – | – | 4 |
| | Sri Lanka | 76 | – | – | – | – | – | 40 | – | 29 | – | – | – | – | – | – | – | – | – | – | 7 |
| | Zimbabwe | 43 | – | – | – | – | – | 33 | – | – | 8 | – | – | – | – | – | – | – | – | 2 | – |
| | Bangladesh | 8 | – | – | – | – | – | 8 | – | – | – | – | – | – | – | – | – | – | – | – | – |

212

| | Opponents | Matches | E | A | SA | WI | NZ | I | P | SL | Z | B | C | EA | H | K | N | SC | UAE | Tied | NR |
|---|---|---|---|---|---|---|---|---|---|---|---|---|---|---|---|---|---|---|---|---|---|---|
| | East Africa | 1 | – | – | – | – | – | 1 | – | – | | | | – | | – | | | | | |
| | Holland | 1 | – | – | – | – | – | 1 | – | | | | | | – | | – | | | | |
| | Kenya | 12 | – | – | – | – | – | 10 | | | | | | | – | | | – | | | |
| | Namibia | 1 | – | – | – | – | – | 1 | | | | | | | | | – | | | | |
| | U A Emirates | 1 | – | – | – | – | – | 1 | | | | | | | | | | – | | | |
| **Pakistan** | Sri Lanka | 96 | – | – | – | – | – | – | 58 | 35 | | | | | | | | | – | 1 | 2 |
| | Zimbabwe | 30 | – | – | – | | | | 26 | – | 2 | | | | | | | – | | 1 | 1 |
| | Bangladesh | 11 | – | – | – | | | | 10 | – | 1 | | | | | | | | | 1 | 1 |
| | Holland | 3 | – | – | – | | | | 3 | | | | | – | | | | | | | |
| | Kenya | 3 | – | – | – | | | | 3 | | | | | | – | | | | | | |
| | Namibia | 1 | – | – | – | | | | 1 | | | | | | | | – | | | | |
| | Scotland | 1 | – | – | – | | | | 1 | | | | | | | | | – | | | |
| | U A Emirates | 2 | – | – | – | | | | 1 | | | | | | | | – | | | | 1 |
| **Sri Lanka** | Zimbabwe | 28 | – | – | – | | | | – | 22 | 5 | | | | | | | | | | 1 |
| | Bangladesh | 10 | – | – | | | | | | 10 | – | 0 | | | | | | | | | |
| | Canada | 1 | – | – | | | | | | 1 | – | | 0 | | | | | | | | |
| | Holland | 1 | – | – | | | | | | 1 | | | | | – | | | | | | |
| | Kenya | 4 | – | – | | | | | | 3 | – | | | | – | 1 | | | | | |
| **Zimbabwe** | Bangladesh | 10 | – | | | | | | | | 10 | 0 | | | | | | | | | |
| | Holland | 1 | – | | | | | | | | 1 | | | | – | | | | | | |
| | Kenya | 15 | – | | | | | | | | 12 | – | | | 1 | | | | | | 2 |
| | Namibia | 1 | – | | | | | | | | 1 | | | | | – | | | | | |
| **Bangladesh** | Canada | 1 | – | | | | | | | | | 0 | 1 | | | | | | | | |
| | Kenya | 7 | – | | | | | | | | | 1 | | | 6 | | | | | | |
| | Scotland | 1 | – | | | | | | | | | 1 | | | | | 6 | | | | |
| **Holland** | U A Emirates | 1 | – | | | | | | | | | | | | 1 | | – | | | | |
| | Namibia | 1 | – | | | | | | | | | | | | 1 | | – | | | | |
| **Kenya** | Canada | 1 | – | | | | | | | | | | | | | 0 | | – | | | |
| **1993** | | 182 | 315 | 177 | 269 | 175 | 250 | 290 | 178 | 61 | 3 | 1 | 0 | 2 | 12 | 0 | 0 | 1 | | 19 | 59 |

## MERIT TABLE OF ALL L-O INTERNATIONALS
### 1970-71 to 30 March 2003

| | Matches | Won | Lost | Tied | No Result | % Won (exc NR) |
|---|---|---|---|---|---|---|
| South Africa | 283 | 177 | 96 | 4 | 6 | 63.89 |
| Australia | 534 | 315 | 199 | 7 | 13 | 60.46 |
| West Indies | 466 | 269 | 181 | 5 | 11 | 59.12 |
| Pakistan | 548 | 290 | 241 | 6 | 12 | 54.10 |
| England | 371 | 182 | 177 | 2 | 10 | 50.41 |
| India | 534 | 250 | 260 | 3 | 21 | 48.73 |
| Sri Lanka | 419 | 178 | 222 | 3 | 16 | 44.16 |
| New Zealand | 429 | 175 | 231 | 4 | 19 | 42.68 |
| Zimbabwe | 230 | 61 | 159 | 4 | 6 | 27.23 |
| Kenya | 61 | 12 | 47 | – | 2 | 20.33 |
| Associate Members | 43 | 3 | 40 | – | – | 6.97 |
| Bangladesh | 67 | 3 | 62 | – | 2 | 4.61 |

## TEAM RECORDS
### HIGHEST TOTALS

| | | | | |
|---|---|---|---|---|
| 398-5 | (50 overs) | Sri Lanka v Kenya | Kandy | 1995-96 |
| 376-2 | (50 overs) | India v New Zealand | Hyderabad, India | 1999-00 |
| 373-6 | (50 overs) | India v Sri Lanka | Taunton | 1999 |
| 371-9 | (50 overs) | Pakistan v Sri Lanka | Nairobi | 1996-97 |
| 363-3 | (50 overs) | South Africa v Zimbabwe | Bulawayo | 2001-02 |
| 363-7 | (55 overs) | England v Pakistan | Nottingham | 1992 |
| 360-4 | (50 overs) | West Indies v Sri Lanka | Karachi | 1987-88 |
| 359-2 | (50 overs) | Australia v India | Johannesburg | 2002-03 |
| 354-3 | (50 overs) | South Africa v Kenya | Cape Town | 2001-02 |
| 351-3 | (50 overs) | India v Kenya | Paarl | 2001-02 |

The highest for New Zealand is 349-9 (v India, Rajkot, 1999-00); for Zimbabwe is 340-2 (v Namibia, Harare, 2002-03); for Bangladesh 272-8 (v Zimbabwe, Bulawayo, 2000-01); and for Kenya 347-3 (v Bangladesh, Nairobi, 1997-98).

## HIGHEST TOTALS BATTING SECOND

| | | | | | |
|---|---|---|---|---|---|
| **WINNING:** | 330-7 | (49.1 overs) | Australia v South Africa | Port Elizabeth | 2001-02 |
| **LOSING:** | 329 | (49.3 overs) | Sri Lanka v West Indies | Sharjah | 1995-96 |

## HIGHEST MATCH AGGREGATE

| | | | | |
|---|---|---|---|---|
| 664-19 | (99.4 overs) | Sri Lanka (349-9) v Pakistan (315) | Singapore | 1995-96 |

## LARGEST RUNS MARGINS OF VICTORY

| | | | |
|---|---|---|---|
| 256 runs | Australia beat Namibia | Potschefstroom | 2002-03 |
| 245 runs | Sri Lanka beat India | Sharjah | 2000-01 |
| 233 runs | Pakistan v Bangladesh | Dhaka | 1999-00 |
| 232 runs | Australia beat Sri Lanka | Adelaide | 1984-85 |
| 224 runs | Australia beat Pakistan | Nairobi | 2002 |
| 217 runs | Pakistan beat Sri Lanka | Sharjah | 2001-02 |
| 208 runs | South Africa v Kenya | Cape Town | 2001-02 |
| 206 runs | New Zealand beat Australia | Adelaide | 1985-86 |
| 206 runs | Sri Lanka beat Holland | Colombo (RPS) | 2002-03 |
| 202 runs | England beat India | Lord's | 1975 |
| 202 runs | South Africa beat Kenya | Nairobi | 1996-97 |
| 202 runs | Zimbabwe beat Kenya | Dhaka | 1998-99 |

## LOWEST TOTALS (Excluding reduced innings)

| | | | | |
|---|---|---|---|---|
| 36 | (18.4 overs) | Canada v Sri Lanka | Paarl | 2002-03 |
| 38 | (15.4 overs) | Zimbabwe v Sri Lanka | Colombo (SSC) | 2001-02 |
| 43 | (19.5 overs) | Pakistan v West Indies | Cape Town | 1992-93 |
| 45 | (40.3 overs) | Canada v England | Manchester | 1979 |
| 45 | (14.0 overs) | Namibia v Australia | Potschefstroom | 2002-03 |
| 54 | (26.3 overs) | India v Sri Lanka | Sharjah | 1986-87 |
| 55 | (28.3 overs) | Sri Lanka v West Indies | Sharjah | 1980-81 |
| 63 | (25.5 overs) | India v Australia | Sydney | 1980-81 |
| 64 | (35.5 overs) | New Zealand v Pakistan | Sharjah | 1985-86 |
| 68 | (31.3 overs) | Scotland v West Indies | Leicester | 1999 |
| 69 | (28.0 overs) | South Africa v Australia | Sydney | 1993-94 |
| 70 | (25.2 overs) | Australia v England | Birmingham | 1977 |
| 70 | (26.3 overs) | Australia v New Zealand | Adelaide | 1985-86 |

The lowest for England is 86 (v A, Manchester, 2001); for West Indies 87 (v A, Sydney, 1992-93); for Bangladesh 76 (v SL, Colombo (SSC), 2002), and for Kenya 84 (v A, Nairobi, 2002).

## LOWEST MATCH AGGREGATE

| | | | | |
|---|---|---|---|---|
| 73-11 | (23.2 overs) | Canada (36) v Sri Lanka (37-1) | Paarl | 2002-03 |
| 78-11 | (20 overs) | Zimbabwe (38) v Sri Lanka (40-1) | Colombo (SSC) | 2001-02 |

## BATTING RECORDS
## HIGHEST INDIVIDUAL INNINGS

| | | | | |
|---|---|---|---|---|
| 194 | Saeed Anwar | Pakistan v India | Madras | 1996-97 |
| 189* | I.V.A.Richards | West Indies v England | Manchester | 1984 |
| 189 | S.T.Jayasuriya | Sri Lanka v India | Sharjah | 2000-01 |
| 188* | G.Kirsten | South Africa v UAE | Rawalpindi | 1995-96 |
| 186* | S.R.Tendulkar | India v New Zealand | Hyderabad | 1999-00 |
| 183 | S.C.Ganguly | India v Sri Lanka | Taunton | 1999 |
| 181 | I.V.A.Richards | West Indies v Sri Lanka | Karachi | 1987-88 |
| 175* | Kapil Dev | India v Zimbabwe | Tunbridge Wells | 1983 |
| 173 | M.E.Waugh | Australia v West Indies | Melbourne | 2000-01 |
| 172* | C.B.Wishart | Zimbabwe v Namibia | Harare | 2002-03 |
| 171* | G.M.Turner | New Zealand v East Africa | Birmingham | 1975 |
| 169* | D.J.Callaghan | South Africa v New Zealand | Pretoria | 1994-95 |
| 169 | B.C.Lara | West Indies v Sri Lanka | Sharjah | 1995-96 |
| 167* | R.A.Smith | England v Australia | Birmingham | 1993 |
| 161 | A.C.Hudson | South Africa v Holland | Rawalpindi | 1995-96 |
| 159* | D.Mongia | India v Zimbabwe | Gauhati | 2001-02 |
| 158 | D.I.Gower | England v New Zealand | Brisbane | 1982-83 |

214

| | | | | | |
|---|---|---|---|---|---|
| 154 | A.C.Gilchrist | Australia v Sri Lanka | | Melbourne | 1998-99 |
| 153* | I.V.A.Richards | West Indies v Australia | | Melbourne | 1979-80 |
| 153* | M.Azharuddin | India v Zimbabwe | | Cuttack | 1997-98 |
| 153* | S.C.Ganguly | India v New Zealand | | Gwalior | 1999-00 |
| 153 | B.C.Lara | West Indies v Pakistan | | Sharjah | 1993-94 |
| 153 | R.Dravid | India v New Zealand | | Hyderabad | 1999-00 |
| 153 | H.H.Gibbs | South Africa v Bangladesh | | Potchefstroom | 2002-03 |
| 152* | D.L.Haynes | West Indies v India | | Georgetown | 1988-89 |
| 152 | C.H.Gayle | West Indies v Kenya | | Nairobi | 2001-02 |
| 152 | S.R.Tendulkar | India v Namibia | | Pietermaritzburg | 2002-03 |
| 151* | S.T.Jayasuriya | Sri Lanka v India | | Bombay | 1996-97 |
| 150 | S.Chanderpaul | West Indies v South Africa | | East London | 1998-99 |

The highest for Bangladesh is 101 by Mehrab Hossain (v Z, Dhaka, 1998-99), and for Kenya 144 by K.O.Obuya (v B, Nairobi, 1997-98).

## HUNDRED ON DEBUT

| | | | | |
|---|---|---|---|---|
| D.L.Amiss | 103 | England v Australia | Manchester | 1972 |
| D.L.Haynes | 148 | West Indies v Australia | St John's | 1977-78 |
| A.Flower | 115* | Zimbabwe v Sri Lanka | New Plymouth | 1991-92 |
| Salim Elahi | 102* | Pakistan v Sri Lanka | Gujranwala | 1995-96 |

Shahid Afridi scored 102 for P v SL, Nairobi, 1996-97, in his second match having not batted in his first.

| | | | | | |
|---|---|---|---|---|---|
| **Fastest 100** | 37 balls | Shahid Afridi (102) | P v SL | Nairobi | 1996-97 |
| **Fastest 50** | 17 balls | S.T.Jayasuriya (76) | SL v P | Singapore | 1995-96 |

## CARRYING BAT THROUGH COMPLETED INNINGS (ALL OUT)

| | | |
|---|---|---|
| G.W.Flower | 84* | Zimbabwe (205) v England | Sydney | 1994-95 |
| Saeed Anwar | 103* | Pakistan (219) v Zimbabwe | Harare | 1994-95 |
| N.V.Knight | 125* | England (246) v Pakistan | Nottingham | 1996 |
| R.D.Jacobs | 49* | West Indies (110) v Australia | Manchester | 1999 |
| D.R.Martyn | 116* | Australia (191) v New Zealand | Auckland | 1999-00 |
| H.H.Gibbs | 59* | South Africa (101) v Pakistan | Sharjah | 1999-00 |
| A.J.Stewart | 100* | England (192) v West Indies | Nottingham | 2000 |
| Javed Omar | 33* | Bangladesh (103) v Zimbabwe | Harare | 2000-01 |

## 5000 RUNS IN A CAREER

| | | LOI | I | NO | HS | Runs | Avge | 100 | 50 |
|---|---|---|---|---|---|---|---|---|---|
| S.R.Tendulkar | I | 314 | 305 | 30 | 186* | **12219** | 44.43 | 34 | 62 |
| M.Azharuddin | I | 334 | 308 | 54 | 153* | 9378 | 36.92 | 7 | 58 |
| P.A.de Silva | SL | 308 | 296 | 30 | 145 | 9284 | 34.90 | 11 | 64 |
| S.T.Jayasuriya | SL | 297 | 289 | 12 | 189 | 8966 | 32.36 | 16 | 54 |
| Inzamam-ul-Haq | P | 290 | 272 | 38 | 137* | 8957 | 38.27 | 8 | 64 |
| Saeed Anwar | P | 247 | 244 | 19 | 194 | 8823 | 39.21 | 20 | 43 |
| S.C.Ganguly | I | 229 | 221 | 18 | 183 | 8720 | 42.95 | 22 | 50 |
| D.L.Haynes | WI | 238 | 237 | 28 | 152* | 8648 | 41.37 | 17 | 57 |
| M.E.Waugh | A | 244 | 236 | 20 | 173 | 8500 | 39.35 | 18 | 50 |
| B.C.Lara | WI | 209 | 204 | 21 | 169 | 7797 | 42.60 | 16 | 49 |
| S.R.Waugh | A | 335 | 288 | 58 | 120* | 7569 | 32.90 | 3 | 45 |
| A.Ranatunga | SL | 269 | 255 | 47 | 131* | 7454 | 35.83 | 4 | 49 |
| Javed Miandad | P | 233 | 218 | 41 | 119* | 7381 | 41.70 | 8 | 50 |
| Salim Malik | P | 283 | 256 | 38 | 102 | 7171 | 32.89 | 5 | 47 |
| G.Kirsten | SA | 185 | 185 | 19 | 188* | 6798 | 40.95 | 13 | 45 |
| A.Flower | Z | 213 | 208 | 16 | 145 | 6786 | 35.34 | 4 | 55 |
| I.V.A.Richards | WI | 187 | 167 | 24 | 189* | 6721 | 47.00 | 11 | 45 |
| Ijaz Ahmed | P | 250 | 232 | 29 | 139* | 6564 | 32.33 | 10 | 37 |
| A.R.Border | A | 273 | 252 | 39 | 127* | 6524 | 30.62 | 3 | 39 |
| R.Dravid | I | 207 | 190 | 24 | 153 | 6498 | 39.14 | 8 | 44 |
| M.S.Atapattu | SL | 190 | 188 | 24 | 132* | 6346 | 38.69 | 10 | 45 |
| R.B.Richardson | WI | 224 | 217 | 30 | 122 | 6248 | 33.41 | 5 | 44 |
| M.G.Bevan | A | 205 | 173 | 60 | 108* | 6176 | 54.65 | 6 | 41 |
| D.M.Jones | A | 164 | 161 | 25 | 145 | 6068 | 44.61 | 7 | 46 |
| R.T.Ponting | A | 168 | 165 | 22 | 145 | **5995** | 41.92 | 13 | 31 |

215

| | | LOI | I | NO | HS | Runs | Avge | 100 | 50 |
|---|---|---|---|---|---|---|---|---|---|
| G.W.Flower | Z | 199 | 194 | 16 | 142* | 5986 | 33.62 | 6 | 35 |
| J.H.Kallis | SA | 174 | 166 | 28 | 113* | 5965 | 43.22 | 8 | 42 |
| D.C.Boon | A | 181 | 177 | 16 | 122 | 5964 | 37.04 | 5 | 37 |
| J.N.Rhodes | SA | 245 | 220 | 51 | 121 | 5935 | 35.11 | 2 | 33 |
| Ramiz Raja | P | 198 | 197 | 15 | 119* | 5841 | 32.09 | 9 | 31 |
| C.L.Hooper | WI | 227 | 206 | 43 | 113* | 5761 | 35.34 | 7 | 29 |
| W.J.Cronje | SA | 188 | 175 | 31 | 112 | 5565 | 38.64 | 2 | 39 |
| N.J.Astle | NZ | 174 | 171 | 10 | 122* | 5540 | 34.40 | 13 | 32 |
| S.P.Fleming | NZ | 197 | 190 | 17 | 134* | 5402 | 31.22 | 4 | 33 |
| A.Jadeja | I | 196 | 179 | 36 | 119 | 5359 | 37.47 | 6 | 30 |
| A.C.Gilchrist | A | 162 | 157 | 6 | 154 | 5225 | 34.60 | 8 | 31 |
| A.D.R.Campbell | Z | 188 | 184 | 14 | 131* | 5185 | 30.50 | 7 | 30 |
| R.S.Mahanama | SL | 213 | 198 | 23 | 119* | 5162 | 29.49 | 4 | 35 |
| C.G.Greenidge | WI | 128 | 127 | 13 | 133* | 5134 | 45.03 | 11 | 31 |

The most for England is 4677 in 162 innings by A.J.Stewart; for Bangladesh 914 (40) by Akram Khan; and for Kenya 1654 (58) by S.O.Tikolo.

## 16 HUNDREDS

| | | Inns | 100 | E | A | SA | WI | NZ | I | P | SL | Z | B | K | N |
|---|---|---|---|---|---|---|---|---|---|---|---|---|---|---|---|
| S.R.Tendulkar | I | 305 | 34 | 1 | 6 | 3 | 2 | 3 | – | 2 | 7 | 5 | – | 4 | 1 |
| S.C.Ganguly | I | 221 | 22 | 1 | 1 | 3 | – | 2 | – | 3 | 4 | 3 | 1 | 3 | 1 |
| Saeed Anwar | P | 244 | 20 | – | 1 | – | 2 | 4 | 4 | – | 7 | 2 | – | – | |
| M.E.Waugh | A | 236 | 18 | 1 | – | 2 | 3 | 2 | 3 | – | 2 | 2 | – | 1 | |
| D.L.Haynes | WI | 237 | 17 | 2 | 6 | 1 | – | 2 | 4 | 1 | 1 | – | – | | |
| B.C.Lara | WI | 204 | 16 | 1 | 3 | 2 | – | 2 | 2 | 1 | 4 | – | – | 1 | |
| S.T.Jayasuriya | SL | 289 | 16 | 1 | 1 | 2 | 2 | 3 | 2 | 3 | – | 2 | – | – | 1 |

The most for England is 8 in 122 innings by G.A.Gooch; for South Africa 13 (185) by G.Kirsten; for New Zealand 13 (171) by N.J.Astle; and for Zimbabwe 7 (184) by A.D.R.Campbell.

## HIGHEST PARTNERSHIP FOR EACH WICKET

| | | | | | |
|---|---|---|---|---|---|
| 1st | 258 | S.C.Ganguly/S.R.Tendulkar | India v Kenya | Paarl | 2001-02 |
| 2nd | 331 | S.R.Tendulkar/R.Dravid | India v New Zealand | Hyderabad (Ind) | 1999-00 |
| 3rd | 237* | R.Dravid/S.R.Tendulkar | India v Kenya | Bristol | 1999 |
| 4th | 275* | M.Azharuddin/A.Jadeja | India v England | Cuttack | 1997-98 |
| 5th | 223 | M.Azharuddin/A.Jadeja | India v Sri Lanka | Colombo (RPS) | 1997-98 |
| 6th | 161 | M.O.Odumbe/A.V.Vadher | Kenya v Sri Lanka | Southampton | 1999 |
| 7th | 130 | A.Flower/H.H.Streak | Zimbabwe v England | Harare | 2001-02 |
| 8th | 119 | P.R.Reiffel/S.K.Warne | Australia v South Africa | Port Elizabeth | 1993-94 |
| 9th | 126* | Kapil Dev/S.M.H.Kirmani | India v Zimbabwe | Tunbridge Wells | 1983 |
| 10th | 106* | I.V.A.Richards/M.A.Holding | West Indies v England | Manchester | 1984 |

## BOWLING RECORDS
## SIX WICKETS IN AN INNINGS

| | | | | |
|---|---|---|---|---|
| 8-19 | W.P.U.C.J Vaas | Sri Lanka v Zimbabwe | Colombo (SSC) | 2001-02 |
| 7-15 | G.D.McGrath | Australia v Namibia | Potchefstroom | 2002-03 |
| 7-20 | A.J.Bichel | Australia v England | Port Elizabeth | 2002-03 |
| 7-30 | M.Muralitharan | Sri Lanka v India | Sharjah | 2000-01 |
| 7-36 | Waqar Younis | Pakistan v England | Leeds | 2001 |
| 7-37 | Aqib Javed | Pakistan v India | Sharjah | 1991-92 |
| 7-51 | W.W.Davis | West Indies v Australia | Leeds | 1983 |
| 6-12 | A.Kumble | India v West Indies | Calcutta | 1993-94 |
| 6-14 | G.J.Gilmour | Australia v England | Leeds | 1975 |
| 6-14 | Imran Khan | Pakistan v India | Sharjah | 1984-85 |
| 6-15 | C.E.H.Croft | West Indies v England | Kingstown | 1980-81 |
| 6-16 | Shoaib Akhtar | Pakistan v New Zealand | Karachi | 2001-02 |
| 6-18 | Azhar Mahmood | Pakistan v West Indies | Sharjah | 1999-00 |
| 6-19 | H.K.Olonga | Zimbabwe v England | Cape Town | 1999-00 |
| 6-20 | B.C.Strang | Zimbabwe v Bangladesh | Nairobi | 1997-98 |
| 6-23 | A.A.Donald | South Africa v Kenya | Nairobi | 1996-97 |
| 6-23 | A.Nehra | India v England | Durban | 2002-03 |
| 6-23 | S.E.Bond | New Zealand v Australia | Port Elizabeth | 2002-03 |

| 6-25 | S.B.Styris | New Zealand v West Indies | Port-of-Spain | 2002 |
|------|-----------|---------------------------|---------------|------|
| 6-25 | W.P.U.C.J Vaas | Sri Lanka v Bangladesh | Pietermaritzburg | 2002-03 |
| 6-26 | Waqar Younis | Pakistan v Sri Lanka | Sharjah | 1989-90 |
| 6-28 | H.K.Olonga | Zimbabwe v Kenya | Bulawayo | 2002-03 |
| 6-29 | B.P.Patterson | West Indies v India | Nagpur | 1987-88 |
| 6-29 | S.T.Jayasuriya | Sri Lanka v England | Moratuwa | 1992-93 |
| 6-30 | Waqar Younis | Pakistan v New Zealand | Auckland | 1993-94 |
| 6-35 | S.M.Pollock | South Africa v West Indies | East London | 1998-99 |
| 6-35 | Abdul Razzaq | Pakistan v Bangladesh | Dhaka | 2001-02 |
| 6-39 | K.H.MacLeay | Australia v India | Nottingham | 1983 |
| 6-41 | I.V.A.Richards | West Indies v India | Delhi | 1989-90 |
| 6-44 | Waqar Younis | Pakistan v New Zealand | Sharjah | 1996-97 |
| 6-49 | L.Klusener | South Africa v Sri Lanka | Lahore | 1997-98 |
| 6-50 | A.H.Gray | West Indies v Australia | Port-of-Spain | 1990-91 |
| 6-59 | Waqar Younis | Pakistan v Australia | Nottingham | 2001 |

The best for England is 5-15 by M.A.Ealham (v Z, Kimberley, 1999-00); for Bangladesh 4-36 by Saiful Islam (v SL, Sharjah, 1994-95); and for Kenya 5-24 by C.O.Obuya (v SL, Nairobi, 2002-03).

## 150 WICKETS IN A CAREER

| | | | LOI | O | R | W | Avge | Best | 4w | R/Over |
|------|---|----|-----|------|------|-----|-------|------|----|--------|
| Wasim Akram | P | | 356 | 3031 | 11812 | 502 | 23.52 | 5-15 | 23 | 3.89 |
| Waqar Younis | P | | 262 | 2116.2 | 9919 | 416 | 23.84 | 7-36 | 27 | 4.68 |
| M.Muralitharan | SL | | 213 | 1919.5 | 7341 | 321 | 22.86 | 7-30 | 15 | 3.82 |
| J.Srinath | I | | 229 | 1989.1 | 8847 | 315 | 28.08 | 5-23 | 10 | 4.44 |
| A.Kumble | I | | 241 | 2152.3 | 9129 | 308 | 29.63 | 6-12 | 10 | 4.24 |
| S.K.Warne | A | | 193 | 1766.4 | 7514 | 291 | 25.82 | 5-33 | 13 | 4.25 |
| Saqlain Mushtaq | P | | 168 | 1453.4 | 6223 | 288 | 21.60 | 5-20 | 17 | 4.28 |
| W.P.U.C.J.Vaas | SL | | 220 | 1791.3 | 7544 | 278 | 27.13 | 8-19 | 7 | 4.21 |
| G.D.McGrath | A | | 179 | 1579.4 | 6160 | 277 | 22.23 | 7-15 | 13 | 3.89 |
| A.A.Donald | SA | | 164 | 1426.5 | 5926 | 272 | 21.78 | 6-23 | 13 | 4.15 |
| S.M.Pollock | SA | | 186 | 1624.4 | 6121 | 268 | 22.83 | 6-35 | 13 | 3.76 |
| Kapil Dev | I | | 225 | 1867 | 6945 | 253 | 27.45 | 5-43 | 4 | 3.72 |
| S.T.Jayasuriya | SL | | 297 | 1807.4 | 8703 | 244 | 35.66 | 6-29 | 9 | 4.81 |
| C.A.Walsh | WI | | 205 | 1803.4 | 6915 | 227 | 30.46 | 5- 1 | 7 | 3.83 |
| C.E.L.Ambrose | WI | | 176 | 1558.5 | 5430 | 225 | 24.13 | 5-17 | 10 | 3.48 |
| C.J.McDermott | A | | 138 | 1243.5 | 5018 | 203 | 24.71 | 5-44 | 5 | 4.04 |
| B.K.V.Prasad | I | | 161 | 1354.5 | 6332 | 196 | 32.30 | 5-27 | 4 | 4.67 |
| S.R.Waugh | A | | 325 | 1480.3 | 6764 | 195 | 34.68 | 4-33 | 3 | 4.56 |
| C.Z.Harris | NZ | | 225 | 1658.4 | 7130 | 195 | 36.56 | 5-42 | 3 | 4.29 |
| C.L.Hooper | WI | | 227 | 1595.3 | 6957 | 193 | 36.04 | 4-34 | 3 | 4.36 |
| H.H.Streak | Z | | 157 | 1311.3 | 6002 | 190 | 31.58 | 5-32 | 6 | 4.57 |
| Aqib Javed | P | | 163 | 1335.3 | 5721 | 182 | 31.43 | 7-37 | 6 | 4.28 |
| Imran Khan | P | | 175 | 1243.3 | 4845 | 182 | 26.62 | 6-14 | 4 | 3.90 |
| L.Klusener | SA | | 154 | 1095.4 | 5140 | 175 | 29.37 | 6-49 | 7 | 4.69 |
| D.Gough | E | | 111 | 1015.1 | 4380 | 174 | 25.17 | 5-44 | 9 | 4.31 |
| J.H.Kallis | SA | | 174 | 1088.2 | 5070 | 167 | 30.35 | 5-30 | 4 | 4.65 |
| A.B.Agarkar | I | | 110 | 930.3 | 4769 | 166 | 28.72 | 4-25 | 7 | 5.12 |
| Mushtaq Ahmed | P | | 143 | 1247.1 | 5296 | 161 | 32.89 | 5-36 | 4 | 4.25 |
| R.J.Hadlee | NZ | | 115 | 1030.2 | 3407 | 158 | 21.56 | 5-25 | 6 | 3.31 |
| M.D.Marshall | WI | | 136 | 1195.5 | 4233 | 157 | 26.96 | 4-18 | 6 | 3.54 |
| M.Prabhakar | I | | 129 | 1060 | 4534 | 157 | 28.87 | 5-33 | 6 | 4.28 |
| C.L.Cairns | NZ | | 162 | 1054.2 | 4968 | 156 | 31.84 | 5-42 | 3 | 4.71 |
| Abdul Razzaq | P | | 124 | 915.4 | 4057 | 154 | 26.34 | 6-35 | 7 | 4.43 |

The most for Bangladesh is 37 (38 matches) by Khaled Mahmud, and for Kenya 54 (58) by T.M.Odoyo.

## HAT-TRICKS

| Jalaluddin | Pakistan v Australia | Hyderabad | 1982-83 |
|-----------|---------------------|-----------|---------|
| B.A.Reid | Australia v New Zealand | Sydney | 1985-86 |
| C.Sharma | India v New Zealand | Nagpur | 1987-88 |
| Wasim Akram | Pakistan v West Indies | Sharjah | 1989-90 |
| Wasim Akram | Pakistan v Australia | Sharjah | 1989-90 |
| Kapil Dev | India v Sri Lanka | Calcutta | 1990-91 |

| | | | | |
|---|---|---|---|---|
| Aqib Javed | Pakistan v India | Sharjah | 1991-92 |
| D.K.Morrison | New Zealand v India | Napier | 1993-94 |
| Waqar Younis | Pakistan v New Zealand | East London | 1994-95 |
| Saqlain Mushtaq | Pakistan v Zimbabwe | Peshawar | 1996-97 |
| E.A.Brandes | Zimbabwe v England | Harare | 1996-97 |
| A.M.Stuart | Australia v Pakistan | Melbourne | 1996-97 |
| Saqlain Mushtaq | Pakistan v Zimbabwe | The Oval | 1999 |
| W.P.U.C.J Vaas | Sri Lanka v Zimbabwe | Colombo (SSC) | 2001-02 |
| Mohammad Sami | Pakistan v West Indies | Sharjah | 2001-02 |
| W.P.U.C.J Vaas[1] | Sri Lanka v Bangladesh | Pietermaritzburg | 2002-03 |
| B.Lee | Australia v Kenya | Durban | 2002-03 |

[1] The first three balls of the match. Took four wickets in opening over (W W W 4 wide W 0).

## WICKET-KEEPING RECORDS
### SIX DISMISSALS IN AN INNINGS

| | | | | | |
|---|---|---|---|---|---|
| 6 | (6ct) | A.C.Gilchrist | Australia v South Africa | Cape Town | 1999-00 |
| 6 | (6ct) | A.J.Stewart | England v Zimbabwe | Manchester | 2000 |
| 6 | (5ct/1st) | R.D.Jacobs | West Indies v Sri Lanka | Colombo (RPS) | 2001-02 |
| 6 | (5ct/1st) | A.C.Gilchrist | Australia v England | Sydney | 2002-03 |
| 6 | (6ct) | A.C.Gilchrist | Australia v Namibia | Potchefstroom | 2002-03 |

## 100 DISMISSALS IN A CAREER
*(† Excluding catches taken in the field)*

| Total | | | LOI | Ct | St |
|---|---|---|---|---|---|
| 270 | A.C.Gilchrist | Australia | 157 | 233 | 37 |
| 257† | Moin Khan | Pakistan | 182 | 191 | 66 |
| 233 | I.A.Healy | Australia | 168 | 194 | 39 |
| 211 | M.V.Boucher | South Africa | 143 | 201 | 10 |
| 204 | P.J.L.Dujon | West Indies | 167 | 183 | 21 |
| 198 | R.S.Kaluwitharana | Sri Lanka | 177 | 127 | 71 |
| 191 | Rashid Latif | Pakistan | 147 | 156 | 35 |
| 165 | D.J.Richardson | South Africa | 122 | 148 | 17 |
| 165† | A.Flower | Zimbabwe | 185 | 133 | 32 |
| 163 | R.D.Jacobs | West Indies | 118 | 139 | 24 |
| 163† | A.J.Stewart | England | 138 | 148 | .15 |
| 154† | N.R.Mongia | India | 139 | 110 | 44 |
| 136† | A.C.Parore | New Zealand | 148 | 111 | .25 |
| 124 | R.W.Marsh | Australia | 92 | 120 | 4 |
| 103 | Salim Yousuf | Pakistan | 86 | 81 | 22 |

## FIELDING RECORDS
### FIVE CATCHES IN AN INNINGS

| | | | | |
|---|---|---|---|---|
| 5 | J.N.Rhodes | South Africa v West Indies | Bombay | 1993-94 |

## 100 CATCHES IN A CAREER
*(Excluding catches taken while keeping wicket)*

| Total | | | LOI |
|---|---|---|---|
| 156 | M.Azharuddin | India | 334 |
| 127 | A.R.Border | Australia | 273 |
| 120 | C.L.Hooper | West Indies | 227 |
| 111 | S.R.Waugh | Australia | 325 |
| 109 | R.S.Mahanama | Sri Lanka | 213 |
| 108 | M.E.Waugh | Australia | 244 |
| 105 | J.N.Rhodes | South Africa | 245 |
| 101 | I.V.A.Richards | West Indies | 187 |

The most for England is 64 in 120 matches by G.A.Hick; for New Zealand 98 (197) by S.P.Fleming; for Pakistan 90 (250) by Ijaz Ahmed; and for Zimbabwe 76 (199) by G.W.Flower.

# ALL-ROUND RECORDS

## 50 RUNS AND 5 WICKETS IN A MATCH

| | | | | | |
|---|---|---|---|---|---|
| I.V.A.Richards | 119 | 5-41 | West Indies v New Zealand | Dunedin | 1986-87 |
| K.Srikkanth | 70 | 5-27 | India v New Zealand | Vishakhapatnam | 1988-89 |
| M.E.Waugh | 57 | 5-24 | Australia v West Indies | Melbourne | 1992-93 |
| L.Klusener | 54 | 6-49 | South Africa v Sri Lanka | Lahore | 1997-98 |
| Abdul Razzaq | 70* | 5-48 | Pakistan v India | Hobart | 1999-00 |
| G.A.Hick | 80 | 5-33 | England v Zimbabwe | Harare | 1999-00 |
| Shahid Afridi | 61 | 5-40 | Pakistan v England | Lahore | 2000-01 |
| S.C.Ganguly | 71* | 5-34 | India v Zimbabwe | Kanpur | 2000-01 |
| S.B.Styris | 63* | 6-25 | New Zealand v West Indies | Port-of-Spain | 2002 |
| R.C.Irani | 53 | 5-26 | England v India | The Oval | 2002 |

## 1000 RUNS AND 100 WICKETS

| | |
|---|---|
| England | I.T.Botham (2113/145) |
| Australia | S.P.O'Donnell (1242/108); S.K.Warne (1016/291); S.R.Waugh (7569/195) |
| South Africa | W.J.Cronje (5565/114); J.H.Kallis (5965/167); L.Klusener (3381/175); S.M.Pollock (1893/268) |
| West Indies | C.L.Hooper (5761/193); I.V.A.Richards (6721/118) |
| New Zealand | C.L.Cairns (3886/156); R.J.Hadlee (1751/158); C.Z.Harris (4072/195) |
| India | Kapil Dev (3782/253); M.Prabhakar (1858/157); R.J.Shastri (3108/129); S.R.Tendulkar (12219/112) |
| Pakistan | Abdul Razzaq (2288/154); Azhar Mahmood (1309/112); Imran Khan (3709/182); Mudassar Nazar (2654/111); Shahid Afridi (3887/131); Wasim Akram 3717/502) |
| Sri Lanka | P.A.de Silva (9284/106); H.D.P.K.Dharmasena (1040/133); S.T.Jayasuriya (8966/244); W.P.U.C.J.Vaas (1447/278) |
| Zimbabwe | H.H.Streak (2132/190) |

## APPEARANCE RECORDS

### 250 MATCHES

| | | | | | | |
|---|---|---|---|---|---|---|
| 356 | Wasim Akram | Pakistan | | 290 | Inzamam-ul-Haq | Pakistan |
| 334 | M.Azharuddin | India | | 283 | Salim Malik | Pakistan |
| 325 | S.R.Waugh | Australia | | 273 | A.R.Border | Australia |
| 314 | S.R.Tendulkar | India | | 269 | A.Ranatunga | Sri Lanka |
| 308 | P.A.de Silva | Sri Lanka | | 262 | Waqar Younis | Pakistan |
| 297 | S.T.Jayasuriya | Sri Lanka | | 250 | Ijaz Ahmed | Pakistan |

The most for England is 170 by A.J.Stewart; for South Africa 245 by J.N.Rhodes; for West Indies 238 by D.L.Haynes; for New Zealand 225 by C.Z.Harris; and for Zimbabwe 213 by A.Flower.

### 100 MATCHES AS CAPTAIN

| LOI | | | W | L | T | NR | % Won (exc NR) |
|---|---|---|---|---|---|---|---|
| 193 | A.Ranatunga | Sri Lanka | 89 | 95 | 1 | 8 | 46.11 |
| 178 | A.R.Border | Australia | 107 | 67 | 1 | 3 | 60.11 |
| 174 | M.Azharuddin | India | 90 | 76 | 2 | 6 | 51.72 |
| 139 | Imran Khan | Pakistan | 75 | 59 | 1 | 4 | 53.96 |
| 138 | W.J.Cronje | South Africa | 99 | 35 | 1 | 3 | 71.74 |
| 137 | S.P.Fleming | New Zealand | 55 | 73 | 1 | 8 | 40.15 |
| 115 | S.T.Jayasuriya | Sri Lanka | 65 | 45 | 2 | 3 | 56.52 |
| 109 | Wasim Akram | Pakistan | 66 | 41 | 2 | – | 64.15 |
| 108 | I.V.A.Richards | West Indies | 68 | 36 | – | 4 | 64.15 |
| 106 | S.R.Waugh | Australia | 67 | 35 | 3 | 1 | 63.21 |
| 100 | S.C.Ganguly | India | 54 | 43 | – | 3 | 54.00 |

The most for England is 56 by N.Hussain and for Zimbabwe 86 by A.D.R.Campbell.

### 100 LOI UMPIRING APPEARANCES

| | | | | | |
|---|---|---|---|---|---|
| 127 | D.R.Shepherd | England | June 1983 | to | March 2003 |
| 111 | S.A.Bucknor | West Indies | March 1989 | to | March 2003 |
| 102 | D.L.Orchard | South Africa | December 1994 | to | February 2003 |
| 100 | R.S.Dunne | New Zealand | February 1989 | to | February 2002 |
| 100 | R.E.Koertzen | South Africa | December 1992 | to | March 2003 |

# WOMEN'S TEST CRICKET RECORDS

1934-35 to 1 May 2003

Compiled by Marion Collin

## RESULTS SUMMARY

| | Opponents | Tests | E | A | NZ | SA | WI | I | P | SL | Ire | Drawn |
|---|---|---|---|---|---|---|---|---|---|---|---|---|
| | | | | | | | *Won by* | | | | | *Drawn* |
| **England** | Australia | 40 | 6 | 10 | – | – | – | – | – | – | – | 24 |
| | New Zealand | 22 | 6 | – | 0 | – | – | – | – | – | – | 16 |
| | South Africa | 4 | 1 | – | – | 0 | – | – | – | – | – | 3 |
| | West Indies | 3 | 2 | – | – | – | 0 | – | – | – | – | 1 |
| | India | 9 | 1 | – | – | – | – | 0 | – | – | – | 8 |
| **Australia** | New Zealand | 13 | – | 4 | 1 | – | – | – | – | – | – | 8 |
| | West Indies | 2 | – | 0 | – | – | 0 | – | – | – | – | 2 |
| | India | 8 | – | 3 | – | – | – | 0 | – | – | – | 5 |
| **New Zealand** | South Africa | 3 | – | – | 1 | 0 | – | – | – | – | – | 2 |
| | India | 5 | – | – | 0 | – | – | 0 | – | – | – | 5 |
| **South Africa** | India | 1 | – | – | – | 0 | – | 1 | – | – | – | – |
| **West Indies** | India | 6 | – | – | – | – | 1 | 1 | – | – | – | 4 |
| **Pakistan** | Sri Lanka | 1 | – | – | – | – | – | – | 0 | 1 | – | – |
| | Ireland | 1 | – | – | – | – | – | – | 0 | – | 1 | – |
| | | 118 | 16 | 17 | 2 | 0 | 1 | 2 | 0 | 1 | 1 | 78 |

| | Tests | Won | Lost | Drawn | Toss Won |
|---|---|---|---|---|---|
| England | 78 | 16 | 10 | 52 | 48 |
| Australia | 63 | 17 | 7 | 39 | 20 |
| New Zealand | 43 | 2 | 10 | 31 | 21 |
| South Africa | 8 | – | 3 | 5 | 4 |
| West Indies | 11 | 1 | 3 | 7 | 5† |
| India | 29 | 2 | 5 | 22 | 13† |
| Pakistan | 2 | – | 2 | – | 1 |
| Sri Lanka | 1 | 1 | – | – | 1 |
| Ireland | 1 | 1 | – | – | – |

† *Results of tosses in five of the six India v West Indies Tests in 1976-77 are not known*

## TEAM RECORDS
### HIGHEST INNINGS TOTALS

| | | | |
|---|---|---|---|
| 569-6d | Australia v England | Guildford | 1998 |
| 525 | Australia v India | Ahmedabad | 1983-84 |
| 517-8 | New Zealand v England | Scarborough | 1996 |
| 503-5d | England v New Zealand | Christchurch | 1934-35 |
| 467 | India v England | Taunton | 2002 |
| 427-4d | Australia v England | Worcester | 1998 |
| 426-9d | India v England | Blackpool | 1986 |
| 414 | England v New Zealand | Scarborough | 1996 |
| 414 | England v Australia | Guildford | 1998 |
| 404-9d | India v South Africa | Paarl | 2001-02 |
| 403-8d | New Zealand v India | Nelson | 1994-95 |

*The highest totals for countries not included above are:*

| | | | |
|---|---|---|---|
| 282 | West Indies v Australia | Montego Bay | 1975-76 |
| 266-8d | South Africa v England | Cape Town | 1960-61 |
| 193-3d | Ireland v Pakistan | Dublin | 2000 |
| 171 | Pakistan v Sri Lanka | Colombo | 1997-98 |

## LOWEST INNINGS TOTALS

| | | | |
|---|---|---|---|
| 35 | England v Australia | Melbourne | 1957-58 |
| 38 | Australia v England | Melbourne | 1957-58 |
| 44 | New Zealand v England | Christchurch | 1934-35 |
| 47 | Australia v England | Brisbane | 1934-35 |
| 53 | Pakistan v Ireland | Dublin | 2000 |

*The lowest innings totals for countries not included above are:*

| | | | |
|---|---|---|---|
| 67 | West Indies v England | Canterbury | 1979 |
| 89 | South Africa v New Zealand | Durban | 1971-72 |
| 65 | India v West Indies | Jammu | 1976-77 |

## BATTING RECORDS
## 1000 RUNS IN TESTS

| | | | M | I | NO | HS | Avge | 100 | 50 |
|---|---|---|---|---|---|---|---|---|---|
| 1935 | J.A.Brittin | England | 27 | 44 | 5 | 167 | 49.61 | 5 | 11 |
| 1594 | R.Heyhoe-Flint | England | 22 | 38 | 3 | 179 | 45.54 | 3 | 10 |
| 1301 | D.A.Hockley | New Zealand | 19 | 29 | 4 | 126* | 52.04 | 4 | 7 |
| 1164 | C.A.Hodges | England | 18 | 31 | 2 | 158* | 40.13 | 2 | 6 |
| 1110 | S.Agarwal | India | 13 | 23 | 1 | 190 | 50.45 | 4 | 4 |
| 1078 | E.Bakewell | England | 12 | 22 | 4 | 124 | 59.88 | 4 | 7 |
| 1007 | M.E.Maclagan | England | 14 | 25 | 1 | 119 | 41.95 | 2 | 6 |

## HIGHEST INDIVIDUAL INNINGS

| | | | | |
|---|---|---|---|---|
| 214 | M.Raj | I v E | Taunton | 2002 |
| 209* | K.L.Rolton | A v E | Leeds | 2001 |
| 204 | K.E.Flavell | NZ v E | Scarborough | 1996 |
| 204‡ | M.A.J.Goszko | A v E | Shenley | 2001 |
| 200 | J.Broadbent | A v E | Guildford | 1998 |
| 193 | D.A.Annetts | A v E | Collingham | 1987 |
| 190 | S.Agarwal | I v E | Worcester | 1986 |
| 189 | E.A.Snowball | E v NZ | Christchurch | 1934-35 |
| 179 | R.Heyhoe-Flint | E v A | The Oval | 1976 |
| 176* | K.L.Rolton | A v E | Worcester | 1998 |
| 167 | J.A.Brittin | E v A | Harrogate | 1998 |
| 161* | E.C.Drumm | E v A | Christchurch | 1994-95 |
| 160 | B.A.Daniels | E v NZ | Scarborough | 1996 |
| 158* | C.A.Hodges | E v NZ | Canterbury | 1984 |
| 155* | P.F.McKelvey | NZ v E | Wellington | 1968-69 |

‡ *On debut*

## 5 HUNDREDS

| | | | | | | | | Opponents | | | | | |
|---|---|---|---|---|---|---|---|---|---|---|---|---|---|
| | | | M | I | E | A | NZ | SA | WI | IND | P | SL | IRE |
| 5 | J.A.Brittin (E) | | 27 | 44 | – | 3 | 1 | – | – | 1 | – | – | – |

## HIGHEST PARTNERSHIP FOR EACH WICKET

| | | | | | |
|---|---|---|---|---|---|
| 1st | 178 | B.J.Haggett/B.J.Clark | A v I | Sydney | 1990-91 |
| 2nd | 235 | E.A.Snowball/M.E.Hide | E v NZ | Christchurch | 1934-35 |
| 3rd | 309 | L.A.Reeler/D.A.Annetts | A v E | Collingham | 1987 |
| 4th | 253 | K.L.Rolton/L.C.Broadfoot | A v E | Leeds | 2001 |
| 5th | 136 | L.C.Sthalekar/A.J.Blackwell | A v E | Sydney | 2002-03 |
| 6th | 132 | B.A.Daniels/K.M.Leng | E v NZ | Scarborough | 1996 |
| 7th | 157 | M.Raj/J.Goswami | I v E | Taunton | 2002 |
| 8th | 181 | S.J.Griffiths/D.L.Wilson | A v NZ | Auckland | 1989-90 |
| 9th | 107 | B.Botha/M.Payne | SA v NZ | Cape Town | 1971-72 |
| 10th | 78 | E.Barker/H.Hegarty | E v A | Adelaide | 1957-58 |
| | 78 | S.Gupta/S.Chakraborty | I v A | Lucknow | 1983-84 |

## BOWLING RECORDS
## 50 WICKETS IN TESTS

| Wkts | | | M | Balls | Runs | Avge | Best | 5wI | 10wM |
|------|------|---|----|-------|------|-------|------|-----|------|
| 77 | M.B.Duggan | E | 17 | 3734 | 1039 | 13.49 | 7- 6 | 5 | – |
| 68 | E.R.Wilson | A | 11 | 2885 | 803 | 11.80 | 7- 7 | 4 | 2 |
| 63 | D.F.Edulji | I | 20 | 5098† | 1624 | 25.77 | 6- 64 | 1 | – |
| 60 | M.E.Maclagan | E | 14 | 3432 | 935 | 15.58 | 7- 10 | 3 | – |
| 57 | R.H.Thompson | A | 16 | 4304 | 1040 | 18.24 | 5- 33 | 1 | – |
| 56 | S.Kulkarni | I | 18 | 3320 | 1599 | 28.55 | 6- 99 | 5 | – |
| 55 | J.Lord | NZ | 15 | 3108 | 1049 | 19.07 | 6-119 | 4 | 1 |
| 50 | E.Bakewell | E | 12 | 2697 | 831 | 16.62 | 7- 61 | 3 | 1 |

*† Excludes balls bowled in Sixth Test v West Indies 1976-77*

## TEN WICKETS IN A TEST

| | | | | |
|------|------------|--------|------------|---------|
| 11-16 | E.R.Wilson | A v E | Melbourne | 1957-58 |
| 11-63 | J.Greenwood | E v WI | Canterbury | 1979 |
| 11-107 | L.C.Pearson | E v A | Sydney | 2002-03 |
| 10-65 | E.R.Wilson | A v NZ | Wellington | 1947-48 |
| 10-75 | E.Bakewell | E v WI | Birmingham | 1979 |
| 10-107 | K.Price | A v I | Lucknow | 1983-84 |
| 10-118 | D.A.Gordon | A v E | Melbourne | 1968-69 |
| 10-137 | J.Lord | NZ v A | Melbourne | 1978-79 |

## SEVEN WICKETS IN AN INNINGS

| | | | | |
|------|--------------|--------|------------|---------|
| 8-53 | N.David | I v E | Jamshedpur | 1995-96 |
| 7-6 | M.B.Duggan | E v A | Melbourne | 1957-58 |
| 7-7 | E.R.Wilson | A v E | Melbourne | 1957-58 |
| 7-10 | M.E.Maclagan | E v A | Brisbane | 1934-35 |
| 7-18 | A.Palmer | A v E | Brisbane | 1934-35 |
| 7-24 | L.Johnston | A v NZ | Melbourne | 1971-72 |
| 7-34 | G.E.McConway | E v I | Worcester | 1986 |
| 7-41 | J.Burley | NZ v E | The Oval | 1966 |
| 7-51 | L.C.Pearson | E v A | Sydney | 2002-03 |
| 7-61 | E.Bakewell | E v WI | Birmingham | 1979 |

## HAT-TRICK

| | | | |
|------------|----------------------|-----------|---------|
| E.R.Wilson | Australia v England | Melbourne | 1957-58 |

## WICKET-KEEPING AND FIELDING RECORDS
## 25 DISMISSALS IN TESTS

| Total | | | Tests | Ct | St |
|-------|-------------|-------------|-------|----|----|
| 58 | C.Matthews | Australia | 20 | 46 | 12 |
| 36 | S.A.Hodges | England | 11 | 19 | 17 |
| 28 | B.Brentnall | New Zealand | 10 | 16 | 12 |

## EIGHT DISMISSALS IN A TEST

| | | | | |
|------------|-----------|--------|-------------|---------|
| 9 (8ct, 1 st) | C.Matthews | A v I | Adelaide | 1990-91 |
| 8 (6ct, 2st) | L.Nye | E v NZ | New Plymouth | 1991-92 |

## SIX DISMISSALS IN AN INNINGS

| | | | | |
|------------|-------------|---------|-------------|---------|
| 8 (6ct, 2st) | L.Nye | E v NZ | New Plymouth | 1991-92 |
| 6 (2ct, 4st) | B.Brentnall | NZ v SA | Johannesburg | 1971-72 |

## 20 CATCHES IN THE FIELD IN TESTS

| Total | | | Tests |
|-------|-------------|-----------|-------|
| 25 | C.A.Hodges | England | 18 |
| 21 | S.Shah | India | 20 |
| 20 | L.A.Fullston | Australia | 12 |

## APPEARANCE RECORDS
## 25 TEST MATCH APPEARANCES

| | | | |
|----|-------------|---------|---------|
| 27 | J.A.Brittin | England | 1979-98 |

# TEST MATCHES RESULTS SUMMARY

Matches completed before 9 April 2003

| | Opponents | Tests | E | A | SA | WI | NZ | I | P | SL | Z | B | Tied | Drawn |
|---|---|---|---|---|---|---|---|---|---|---|---|---|---|---|
| England | Australia | 306 | 95 | 125 | – | – | – | – | – | – | – | – | – | 86 |
| | South Africa | 120 | 50 | – | 23 | – | – | – | – | – | – | – | – | 47 |
| | West Indies | 126 | 31 | – | – | 52 | – | – | – | – | – | – | – | 43 |
| | New Zealand | 85 | 38 | – | – | – | 7 | – | – | – | – | – | – | 40 |
| | India | 91 | 33 | – | – | – | – | 16 | – | – | – | – | – | 42 |
| | Pakistan | 60 | 16 | – | – | – | – | – | 10 | – | – | – | – | 34 |
| | Sri Lanka | 12 | 7 | – | – | – | – | – | – | 3 | – | – | – | 2 |
| | Zimbabwe | 4 | 1 | – | – | – | – | – | – | – | 0 | – | – | 3 |
| Australia | South Africa | 71 | – | 39 | 15 | – | – | – | – | – | – | – | – | 17 |
| | West Indies | 95 | – | 42 | – | 31 | – | – | – | – | – | – | 1 | 21 |
| | New Zealand | 41 | – | 18 | – | – | 7 | – | – | – | – | – | – | 16 |
| | India | 60 | – | 29 | – | – | – | 13 | – | – | – | – | 1 | 17 |
| | Pakistan | 49 | – | 21 | – | – | – | – | 11 | – | – | – | – | 17 |
| | Sri Lanka | 13 | – | 7 | – | – | – | – | – | 1 | – | – | – | 5 |
| | Zimbabwe | 1 | – | 1 | – | – | – | – | – | – | 0 | – | – | – |
| South Africa | West Indies | 11 | – | – | 7 | 2 | – | – | – | – | – | – | – | 2 |
| | New Zealand | 27 | – | – | 15 | – | 3 | – | – | – | – | – | – | 9 |
| | India | 14 | – | – | 7 | – | – | 2 | – | – | – | – | – | 5 |
| | Pakistan | 9 | – | – | 5 | – | – | – | 1 | – | – | – | – | 3 |
| | Sri Lanka | 13 | – | – | 8 | – | – | – | – | 1 | – | – | – | 4 |
| | Zimbabwe | 5 | – | – | 4 | – | – | – | – | – | 0 | – | – | 1 |
| | Bangladesh | 2 | – | – | 2 | – | – | – | – | – | – | 0 | – | – |
| West Indies | New Zealand | 32 | – | – | – | 10 | 7 | – | – | – | – | – | – | 15 |
| | India | 78 | – | – | – | 30 | – | 10 | – | – | – | – | – | 38 |
| | Pakistan | 39 | – | – | – | 13 | – | – | 12 | – | – | – | – | 14 |
| | Sri Lanka | 6 | – | – | – | 1 | – | – | – | 3 | – | – | – | 2 |
| | Zimbabwe | 4 | – | – | – | 3 | – | – | – | – | – | – | – | 1 |
| | Bangladesh | 2 | – | – | – | 2 | – | – | – | – | – | 0 | – | – |
| New Zealand | India | 42 | – | – | – | – | 9 | 14 | – | – | – | – | – | 19 |
| | Pakistan | 43 | – | – | – | – | 6 | – | 20 | – | – | – | – | 17 |
| | Sri Lanka | 18 | – | – | – | – | 7 | – | – | 4 | – | – | – | 7 |
| | Zimbabwe | 11 | – | – | – | – | 5 | – | – | – | 0 | – | – | 6 |
| | Bangladesh | 2 | – | – | – | – | 2 | – | – | – | – | 0 | – | – |
| India | Pakistan | 47 | – | – | – | – | – | 5 | 9 | – | – | – | – | 33 |
| | Sri Lanka | 23 | – | – | – | – | – | 8 | – | 3 | – | – | – | 12 |
| | Zimbabwe | 9 | – | – | – | – | – | 5 | – | – | 2 | – | – | 2 |
| | Bangladesh | 1 | – | – | – | – | – | 1 | – | – | – | 0 | – | – |
| Pakistan | Sri Lanka | 28 | – | – | – | – | – | – | 13 | 6 | – | – | – | 9 |
| | Zimbabwe | 14 | – | – | – | – | – | – | 8 | – | 2 | – | – | 4 |
| | Bangladesh | 3 | – | – | – | – | – | – | 3 | – | – | 0 | – | – |
| Sri Lanka | Zimbabwe | 13 | – | – | – | – | – | – | – | 8 | 0 | – | – | 5 |
| | Bangladesh | 3 | – | – | – | – | – | – | – | 3 | – | 0 | – | – |
| Zimbabwe | Bangladesh | 4 | – | – | – | – | – | – | – | – | 3 | 0 | – | 1 |
| | | 1637 | 271 | 282 | 86 | 144 | 53 | 74 | 87 | 32 | 7 | 0 | 2 | 599 |

| | Tests | Won | Lost | Drawn | Tied | Toss Won |
|---|---|---|---|---|---|---|
| England | 804 | 271 | 236 | 297 | – | 389 |
| Australia | 636 | 282 | 173 | 179 | 2 | 323 |
| South Africa | 272 | 86 | 98 | 88 | – | 124 |
| West Indies | 393 | 144 | 112 | 136 | 1 | 209 |
| New Zealand | 301 | 53 | 119 | 129 | – | 153 |
| India | 365 | 74 | 122 | 168 | 1 | 184 |
| Pakistan | 292 | 87 | 74 | 131 | – | 138 |
| Sri Lanka | 129 | 32 | 51 | 46 | – | 70 |
| Zimbabwe | 65 | 7 | 35 | 23 | – | 38 |
| Bangladesh | 17 | – | 16 | 1 | – | 9 |

# TEST CRICKET RECORDS

To 9 April 2003

## TEAM RECORDS

### HIGHEST INNINGS TOTALS

| | | | |
|---|---|---|---|
| 952-6d | Sri Lanka v India | Colombo (RPS) | 1997-98 |
| 903-7d | England v Australia | The Oval | 1938 |
| 849 | England v West Indies | Kingston | 1929-30 |
| 790-3d | West Indies v Pakistan | Kingston | 1957-58 |
| 758-8d | Australia v West Indies | Kingston | 1954-55 |
| 729-6d | Australia v England | Lord's | 1930 |
| 708 | Pakistan v England | The Oval | 1987 |
| 701 | Australia v England | The Oval | 1934 |
| 699-5 | Pakistan v India | Lahore | 1989-90 |
| 695 | Australia v England | The Oval | 1930 |
| 692-8d | West Indies v England | The Oval | 1995 |
| 687-8d | West Indies v England | The Oval | 1976 |
| 681-8d | West Indies v England | Port-of-Spain | 1953-54 |
| 676-7 | India v Sri Lanka | Kanpur | 1986-87 |
| 674-6 | Pakistan v India | Faisalabad | 1984-85 |
| 674 | Australia v India | Adelaide | 1947-48 |
| 671-4 | New Zealand v Sri Lanka | Wellington | 1990-91 |
| 668 | Australia v West Indies | Bridgetown | 1954-55 |
| 660-5d | West Indies v New Zealand | Wellington | 1994-95 |
| 659-8d | Australia v England | Sydney | 1946-47 |
| 658-8d | England v Australia | Nottingham | 1938 |
| 657-7d | India v Australia | Calcutta | 2000-01 |
| 657-8d | Pakistan v West Indies | Bridgetown | 1957-58 |
| 656-8d | Australia v England | Manchester | 1964 |
| 654-5 | England v South Africa | Durban | 1938-39 |
| 653-4d | England v India | Lord's | 1990 |
| 653-4d | Australia v England | Leeds | 1993 |
| 652-7d | England v India | Madras | 1984-85 |
| 652-7d | Australia v South Africa | Johannesburg | 2001-02 |
| 652-8d | West Indies v England | Lord's | 1973 |
| 652 | Pakistan v India | Faisalabad | 1982-83 |
| 650-6d | Australia v West Indies | Bridgetown | 1964-65 |

The highest for South Africa is 622-9d (v A, Durban, 1969-70), for Zimbabwe 563-9d (v WI, Harare, 2001), and for Bangladesh 400 (v I, Dhaka, 2000-01).

## LOWEST INNINGS TOTALS

| 26 | New Zealand v England | Auckland | 1954-55 |
|----|----------------------|----------|---------|
| 30 | South Africa v England | Port Elizabeth | 1895-96 |
| 30 | South Africa v England | Birmingham | 1924 |
| 35 | South Africa v England | Cape Town | 1898-99 |
| 36 | Australia v England | Birmingham | 1902 |
| 36 | South Africa v Australia | Melbourne | 1931-32 |
| 42 | Australia v England | Sydney | 1887-88 |
| 42 | New Zealand v Australia | Wellington | 1945-46 |
| 42 | India v England | Lord's | 1974 |
| 43 | South Africa v England | Cape Town | 1888-89 |
| 44 | Australia v England | The Oval | 1896 |
| 45 | England v Australia | Sydney | 1886-87 |
| 45 | South Africa v Australia | Melbourne | 1931-32 |
| 46 | England v West Indies | Port-of-Spain | 1993-94 |
| 47 | South Africa v England | Cape Town | 1888-89 |
| 47 | New Zealand v England | Lord's | 1958 |

The lowest for West Indies is 51 (v A, Port-of-Spain, 1998-99), for Pakistan 53 (v A, Sharjah, 2002-03), for Sri Lanka 71 (v P, Kandy, 1994-95), and for Zimbabwe 63 (v WI, Port-of-Spain, 1999-00), and for Bangladesh 87 (v WI, Dhaka, 2002-03).

## BATTING RECORDS
### 4000 RUNS IN A TEST CAREER

| Runs | | | M | I | NO | HS | Avge | 100 | 50 |
|------|---|---|---|---|----|----|------|-----|----|
| 11174 | A.R.Border | A | 156 | 265 | 44 | 205 | 50.56 | 27 | 63 |
| 10122 | S.M.Gavaskar | I | 125 | 214 | 16 | 236* | 51.12 | 34 | 45 |
| 10039 | S.R.Waugh | A | 156 | 245 | 42 | 200 | 49.45 | 29 | 46 |
| 8900 | G.A.Gooch | E | 118 | 215 | 6 | 333 | 42.58 | 20 | 46 |
| 8832 | Javed Miandad | P | 124 | 189 | 21 | 280* | 52.57 | 23 | 43 |
| 8811 | S.R.Tendulkar | I | 105 | 169 | 16 | 217 | 57.58 | 31 | 35 |
| 8540 | I.V.A.Richards | WI | 121 | 182 | 12 | 291 | 50.23 | 24 | 45 |
| 8231 | D.I.Gower | E | 117 | 204 | 18 | 215 | 44.25 | 18 | 39 |
| 8187 | A.J.Stewart | E | 126 | 225 | 21 | 190 | 40.13 | 15 | 43 |
| 8114 | G.Boycott | E | 108 | 193 | 23 | 246* | 47.72 | 22 | 42 |
| 8032 | G.St A.Sobers | WI | 93 | 160 | 21 | 365* | 57.78 | 26 | 30 |
| 8029 | M.E.Waugh | A | 128 | 209 | 17 | 153* | 41.81 | 20 | 47 |
| 7728 | M.A.Atherton | E | 115 | 212 | 7 | 185* | 37.70 | 16 | 46 |
| 7624 | M.C.Cowdrey | E | 114 | 188 | 15 | 182 | 44.06 | 22 | 38 |
| 7572 | B.C.Lara | WI | 90 | 157 | 4 | 375 | 49.49 | 18 | 37 |
| 7558 | C.G.Greenidge | WI | 108 | 185 | 16 | 226 | 44.72 | 19 | 34 |
| 7525 | M.A.Taylor | A | 104 | 186 | 13 | 334* | 43.49 | 19 | 40 |
| 7515 | C.H.Lloyd | WI | 110 | 175 | 14 | 242* | 46.67 | 19 | 39 |
| 7487 | D.L.Haynes | WI | 116 | 202 | 25 | 184 | 42.29 | 18 | 39 |
| 7422 | D.C.Boon | A | 107 | 190 | 20 | 200 | 43.65 | 21 | 32 |
| 7249 | W.R.Hammond | E | 85 | 140 | 16 | 336* | 58.45 | 22 | 24 |
| 7110 | G.S.Chappell | A | 87 | 151 | 19 | 247* | 53.86 | 24 | 31 |
| 6996 | D.G.Bradman | A | 52 | 80 | 10 | 334 | 99.94 | 29 | 13 |
| 6971 | L.Hutton | E | 79 | 138 | 15 | 364 | 56.67 | 19 | 33 |
| 6868 | D.B.Vengsarkar | I | 116 | 185 | 22 | 166 | 42.13 | 17 | 35 |
| 6806 | K.F.Barrington | E | 82 | 131 | 15 | 256 | 58.67 | 20 | 35 |
| 6361 | P.A.de Silva | SL | 93 | 159 | 11 | 267 | 42.97 | 20 | 22 |
| 6227 | R.B.Kanhai | WI | 79 | 137 | 6 | 256 | 47.53 | 15 | 28 |
| 6215 | M.Azharuddin | I | 99 | 147 | 9 | 199 | 45.03 | 22 | 21 |
| 6214 | Inzamam-ul-Haq | P | 85 | 140 | 13 | 329 | 48.92 | 17 | 32 |
| 6149 | R.N.Harvey | A | 79 | 137 | 10 | 205 | 48.41 | 21 | 24 |

| Runs | | | M | I | NO | HS | Avge | 100 | 50 |
|---|---|---|---|---|---|---|---|---|---|
| 6133 | G.Kirsten | SA | 89 | 155 | 12 | 275 | 42.88 | 16 | 29 |
| 6080 | G.R.Viswanath | I | 91 | 155 | 10 | 222 | 41.93 | 14 | 35 |
| 5949 | R.B.Richardson | WI | 86 | 146 | 12 | 194 | 44.39 | 16 | 27 |
| 5807 | D.C.S.Compton | E | 78 | 131 | 15 | 278 | 50.06 | 17 | 28 |
| 5768 | Salim Malik | P | 103 | 154 | 22 | 237 | 43.69 | 15 | 29 |
| 5762 | C.L.Hooper | WI | 102 | 173 | 15 | 233 | 36.46 | 13 | 27 |
| 5614 | R.Dravid | I | 69 | 118 | 13 | 217 | 53.46 | 14 | 28 |
| 5444 | M.D.Crowe | NZ | 77 | 131 | 11 | 299 | 45.36 | 17 | 18 |
| 5410 | J.B.Hobbs | E | 61 | 102 | 7 | 211 | 56.94 | 15 | 28 |
| 5357 | K.D.Walters | A | 74 | 125 | 14 | 250 | 48.26 | 15 | 33 |
| 5345 | I.M.Chappell | A | 75 | 136 | 10 | 196 | 42.42 | 14 | 26 |
| 5334 | J.G.Wright | NZ | 82 | 148 | 7 | 185 | 37.82 | 12 | 23 |
| 5312 | M.J.Slater | A | 74 | 131 | 7 | 219 | 42.84 | 14 | 21 |
| 5248 | Kapil Dev | I | 131 | 184 | 15 | 163 | 31.05 | 8 | 27 |
| 5234 | W.M.Lawry | A | 67 | 123 | 12 | 210 | 47.15 | 13 | 27 |
| 5200 | I.T.Botham | E | 102 | 161 | 6 | 208 | 33.54 | 14 | 22 |
| 5138 | J.H.Edrich | E | 77 | 127 | 9 | 310* | 43.54 | 12 | 24 |
| 5109 | G.P.Thorpe | E | 77 | 140 | 18 | 200* | 41.87 | 11 | 30 |
| 5105 | A.Ranatunga | SL | 93 | 155 | 12 | 135* | 35.69 | 4 | 38 |
| 5062 | Zaheer Abbas | P | 78 | 124 | 11 | 274 | 44.79 | 12 | 20 |
| 4882 | T.W.Graveney | E | 79 | 123 | 13 | 258 | 44.38 | 11 | 20 |
| 4869 | R.B.Simpson | A | 62 | 111 | 7 | 311 | 46.81 | 10 | 27 |
| 4866 | N.Hussain | E | 81 | 144 | 13 | 207 | 37.14 | 12 | 27 |
| 4794 | A.Flower | Z | 63 | 112 | 19 | 232* | 51.54 | 12 | 27 |
| 4789 | S.T.Jayasuriya | SL | 76 | 128 | 12 | 340 | 41.28 | 10 | 22 |
| 4737 | I.R.Redpath | A | 66 | 120 | 11 | 171 | 43.45 | 8 | 31 |
| 4656 | A.J.Lamb | E | 79 | 139 | 10 | 142 | 36.09 | 14 | 18 |
| 4555 | H.Sutcliffe | E | 54 | 84 | 9 | 194 | 60.73 | 16 | 23 |
| 4554 | D.J.Cullinan | SA | 70 | 115 | 12 | 275* | 44.21 | 14 | 20 |
| 4537 | P.B.H.May | E | 66 | 106 | 9 | 285* | 46.77 | 13 | 22 |
| 4502 | E.R.Dexter | E | 62 | 102 | 8 | 205 | 47.89 | 9 | 27 |
| 4486 | J.H.Kallis | SA | 66 | 107 | 18 | 189* | 50.40 | 11 | 25 |
| 4455 | E.de C.Weekes | WI | 48 | 81 | 5 | 207 | 58.61 | 15 | 19 |
| 4415 | K.J.Hughes | A | 70 | 124 | 6 | 213 | 37.41 | 9 | 22 |
| 4409 | M.W.Gatting | E | 79 | 138 | 14 | 207 | 35.55 | 10 | 21 |
| 4399 | A.I.Kallicharran | WI | 66 | 109 | 10 | 187 | 44.43 | 12 | 21 |
| 4389 | A.P.E.Knott | E | 95 | 149 | 15 | 135 | 32.75 | 5 | 30 |
| 4378 | M.Amarnath | I | 69 | 113 | 10 | 138 | 42.50 | 11 | 24 |
| 4356 | I.A.Healy | A | 119 | 182 | 23 | 161* | 27.39 | 4 | 22 |
| 4334 | R.C.Fredericks | WI | 59 | 109 | 7 | 169 | 42.49 | 8 | 26 |
| 4295 | S.P.Fleming | NZ | 73 | 126 | 7 | 174* | 36.09 | 4 | 33 |
| 4264 | R.T.Ponting | A | 64 | 101 | 12 | 197 | 47.91 | 14 | 17 |
| 4236 | R.A.Smith | E | 62 | 112 | 15 | 175 | 43.67 | 9 | 28 |
| 4114 | Mudassar Nazar | P | 76 | 116 | 8 | 231 | 38.09 | 10 | 17 |
| 4100 | S.C.Ganguly | I | 67 | 112 | 11 | 173 | 40.59 | 9 | 20 |
| 4077 | J.L.Langer | A | 59 | 97 | 5 | 250 | 44.31 | 13 | 16 |
| 4052 | Saeed Anwar | P | 55 | 91 | 2 | 188* | 45.52 | 11 | 25 |
| 4025 | S.T.Jayasuriya | SL | 73 | 115 | 24 | 204* | 44.23 | 10 | 18 |

The most for Bangladesh is 1039 by Habibul Bashar (34 innings).

## 750 RUNS IN A SERIES

| Runs | | Series | | M | I | NO | HS | Avge | 100 | 50 |
|---|---|---|---|---|---|---|---|---|---|---|
| 974 | D.G.Bradman | A v E | 1930 | 5 | 7 | – | 334 | 139.14 | 4 | – |
| 905 | W.R.Hammond | E v A | 1928-29 | 5 | 9 | 1 | 251 | 113.12 | 4 | – |
| 839 | M.A.Taylor | A v E | 1989 | 6 | 11 | 1 | 219 | 83.90 | 2 | 5 |

| Runs | | Series | | M | I | NO | HS | Avge | 100 | 50 |
|------|-----------|--------|---------|---|----|----|------|--------|-----|-----|
| 834 | R.N.Harvey | A v SA | 1952-53 | 5 | 9 | – | 205 | 92.66 | 4 | 3 |
| 829 | I.V.A.Richards | WI v E | 1976 | 4 | 7 | – | 291 | 118.42 | 3 | 2 |
| 827 | C.L.Walcott | WI v A | 1954-55 | 5 | 10 | – | 155 | 82.70 | 5 | 2 |
| 824· | G.St A.Sobers | WI v P | 1957-58 | 5 | 8 | 2 | 365* | 137.33 | 3 | 3 |
| 810 | D.G.Bradman | A v E | 1936-37 | 5 | 9 | – | 270 | 90.00 | 3 | 1 |
| 806 | D.G.Bradman | A v SA | 1931-32 | 5 | 5 | 1 | 299* | 201.50 | 4 | – |
| 798 | B.C.Lara | WI v E | 1993-94 | 5 | 8 | – | 375 | 99.75 | 2 | 2 |
| 779 | E.de C.Weekes | WI v I | 1948-49 | 5 | 7 | – | 194 | 111.28 | 4 | 2 |
| 774 | S.M.Gavaskar | I v WI | 1970-71 | 4 | 8 | 3 | 220 | 154.80 | 4 | 3 |
| 765 | B.C.Lara | WI v E | 1995 | 6 | 10 | 1 | 179 | 85.00 | 3 | 3 |
| 761 | Mudassar Nazar | P v I | 1982-83 | 6 | 8 | 2 | 231 | 126.83 | 4 | 1 |
| 758 | D.G.Bradman | A v E | 1934 | 5 | 8 | – | 304 | 94.75 | 2 | 1 |
| 753 | D.C.S.Compton | E v SA | 1947 | 5 | 8 | – | 208 | 94.12 | 4 | 2 |
| 752 | G.A.Gooch | E v I | 1990 | 3 | 6 | – | 333 | 125.33 | 3 | 2 |

## HIGHEST INDIVIDUAL INNINGS

| | | | | |
|------|-----------------|----------|----------------|---------|
| 375 | B.C.Lara | WI v E | St John's | 1993-94 |
| 365* | G.St A.Sobers | WI v P | Kingston | 1957-58 |
| 364 | L.Hutton | E v A | The Oval | 1938 |
| 340 | S.T.Jayasuriya | SL v I | Colombo (RPS) | 1997-98 |
| 337 | Hanif Mohammed | P v WI | Bridgetown | 1957-58 |
| 336* | W.R.Hammond | E v NZ | Auckland | 1932-33 |
| 334* | M.A.Taylor | A v P | Peshawar | 1998-99 |
| 334 | D.G.Bradman | A v E | Leeds | 1930 |
| 333 | G.A.Gooch | E v I | Lord's | 1990 |
| 329 | Inzamam-ul-Haq | P v NZ | Lahore | 2001-02 |
| 325 | A.Sandham | E v WI | Kingston | 1929-30 |
| 311 | R.B.Simpson | A v E | Manchester | 1964 |
| 310* | J.H.Edrich | E v NZ | Leeds | 1965 |
| 307 | R.M.Cowper | A v E | Melbourne | 1965-66 |
| 304 | D.G.Bradman | A v E | Leeds | 1934 |
| 302 | L.G.Rowe | WI v E | Bridgetown | 1973-74 |
| 299* | D.G.Bradman | A v SA | Adelaide | 1931-32 |
| 299 | M.D.Crowe | NZ v SL | Wellington | 1990-91 |
| 291 | I.V.A.Richards | WI v E | The Oval | 1976 |
| 287 | R.E.Foster | E v A | Sydney | 1903-04 |
| 285* | P.B.H.May | E v WI | Birmingham | 1957 |
| 281 | V.V.S.Laxman | I v A | Calcutta | 2000-01 |
| 280* | Javed Miandad | P v I | Hyderabad | 1982-83 |
| 278 | D.C.S.Compton | E v P | Nottingham | 1954 |
| 277 | B.C.Lara | WI v A | Sydney | 1992-93 |
| 275* | D.J.Cullinan | SA v NZ | Auckland | 1998-99 |
| 275 | G.Kirsten | SA v E | Durban | 1999-00 |
| 274 | R.G.Pollock | SA v A | Durban | 1969-70 |
| 274 | Zaheer Abbas | P·v E | Birmingham | 1971 |
| 271 | Javed Miandad | P v NZ | Auckland | 1988-89 |
| 270* | G.A.Headley | WI v E | Kingston | 1934-35 |
| 270 | D.G.Bradman | A v E | Melbourne | 1936-37 |
| 268 | G.N.Yallop | A v P | Melbourne | 1983-84 |
| 267* | B.A.Young | NZ v SL | Dunedin | 1996-97 |
| 267 | P.A.de Silva | SL v NZ | Wellington | 1990-91 |
| 266 | W.H.Ponsford | A v E | The Oval | 1934 |
| 266 | D.L.Houghton | Z v SL | Bulawayo | 1994-95 |
| 262* | D.L.Amiss | E v WI | Kingston | 1973-74 |
| 261 | F.M.M.Worrell | WI v E | Nottingham | 1950 |

| 260 | C.C.Hunte | WI v P | Kingston | 1957-58 |
|---|---|---|---|---|
| 260 | Javed Miandad | P v E | The Oval | 1987 |
| 259 | G.M.Turner | NZ v WI | Georgetown | 1971-72 |
| 258 | T.W.Graveney | E v WI | Nottingham | 1957 |
| 258 | S.M.Nurse | WI v NZ | Christchurch | 1968-69 |
| 257* | Wasim Akram | P v Z | Sheikhupura | 1996-97 |
| 256 | R.B.Kanhai | WI v I | Calcutta | 1958-59 |
| 256 | K.F.Barrington | E v A | Manchester | 1964 |
| 255* | D.J.McGlew | SA v NZ | Wellington | 1952-53 |
| 254 | D.G.Bradman | A v E | Lord's | 1930 |
| 251 | W.R.Hammond | E v A | Sydney | 1928-29 |
| 250 | K.D.Walters | A v NZ | Christchurch | 1976-77 |
| 250 | S.F.A.F.Bacchus | WI v I | Kanpur | 1978-79 |
| 250 | J.L.Langer | A v E | Melbourne | 2002-03 |

The highest for Bangladesh is 145 by Aminul Islam (v I, Dhaka, 2000-01).

## 18 HUNDREDS

| | | | | | | | Opponents | | | | | | |
|---|---|---|---|---|---|---|---|---|---|---|---|---|---|
| | | | 200 | I | E | A | SA | WI | NZ | I | P | SL | Z | B |
| 34 | S.M.Gavaskar | I | 4 | 214 | 4 | 8 | – | 13 | 2 | – | 5 | 2 | – | – |
| 31 | S.R.Tendulkar | I | 2 | 169 | 6 | 6 | 3 | 3 | 3 | – | 1 | 6 | 3 | – |
| 29 | D.G.Bradman | A | 12 | 80 | 19 | – | 4 | 2 | – | 4 | – | – | – | – |
| 29 | S.R.Waugh | A | 1 | 245 | 10 | – | 2 | 6 | 2 | 2 | 3 | 3 | 1 | – |
| 27 | A.R.Border | A | 2 | 265 | 8 | – | – | 3 | 5 | 4 | 6 | 1 | – | – |
| 26 | G.St A.Sobers | WI | 2 | 160 | 10 | 4 | *– | – | 1 | 8 | 3 | – | – | – |
| 24 | G.S.Chappell | A | 4 | 151 | 9 | – | – | 5 | 3 | 1 | 6 | – | – | – |
| 24 | I.V.A.Richards | WI | 3 | 182 | 8 | 5 | – | – | 1 | 8 | 2 | – | – | – |
| 23 | Javed Miandad | P | 6 | 189 | 2 | 6 | – | 2 | 7 | 5 | – | 1 | – | – |
| 22 | W.R.Hammond | E | 7 | 140 | – | 9 | 6 | 1 | 4 | 2 | – | – | – | – |
| 22 | M.Azharuddin | I | – | 147 | 6 | 2 | 4 | – | 2 | – | 3 | 5 | – | – |
| 22 | M.C.Cowdrey | E | – | 188 | – | 5 | 3 | 6 | 2 | 3 | 3 | – | – | – |
| 22 | G.Boycott | E | 1 | 193 | – | 7 | 1 | 5 | 2 | 4 | 3 | – | – | – |
| 21 | R.N.Harvey | A | 2 | 137 | 6 | – | 8 | 3 | – | 4 | – | – | – | – |
| 21 | D.C.Boon | A | 1 | 190 | 7 | – | – | 3 | 3 | 6 | 1 | 1 | – | – |
| 20 | K.F.Barrington | E | 1 | 131 | – | 5 | 2 | 3 | 3 | 3 | 4 | – | – | – |
| 20 | P.A.de Silva | SL | 2 | 159 | 2 | 1 | – | – | 2 | 5 | 8 | – | 1 | 1 |
| 20 | M.E.Waugh | A | – | 209 | 6 | – | 4 | 4 | 1 | 1 | 3 | 1 | – | – |
| 20 | G.A.Gooch | E | 2 | 215 | – | 4 | – | 5 | 4 | 5 | 1 | 1 | – | – |
| 19 | L.Hutton | E | 4 | 138 | – | 5 | 4 | 5 | 3 | 2 | – | – | – | – |
| 19 | C.H.Lloyd | WI | 1 | 175 | 5 | 6 | – | – | – | 5 | 7 | 1 | – | – |
| 19 | C.G.Greenidge | WI | 4 | 185 | 7 | 4 | – | – | 2 | 5 | 1 | – | – | – |
| 19 | M.A.Taylor | A | 2 | 186 | 6 | – | 2 | 1 | 2 | 2 | 4 | 2 | – | – |
| 18 | B.C.Lara | WI | 4 | 157 | 6 | 3 | – | – | 1 | 1 | – | 4 | – | – |
| 18 | D.L.Haynes | WI | 1 | 202 | 5 | 5 | – | – | 3 | 2 | 3 | – | – | – |
| 18 | D.I.Gower | E | 2 | 204 | – | 9 | – | 1 | 4 | 2 | 2 | – | – | – |

The most for South Africa is 16 by G.Kirsten (155 innings), for New Zealand 17 by M.D.Crowe (131), and for Zimbabwe 12 by A.Flower (112). The most double hundreds by batsmen not included above is 4 by Zaheer Abbas (12 hundreds for Pakistan) and 3 by R.B.Simpson (10 for Australia).

## HIGHEST PARTNERSHIP FOR EACH WICKET

| 1st | 413 | V.Mankad/Pankaj Roy | I v NZ | Madras | 1955-56 |
|---|---|---|---|---|---|
| 2nd | 576 | S.T.Jayasuriya/R.S.Mahanama | SL v I | Colombo (RPS) | 1997-98 |
| 3rd | 467 | A.H.Jones/M.D.Crowe | NZ v SL | Wellington | 1990-91 |
| 4th | 411 | P.B.H.May/M.C.Cowdrey | E v WI | Birmingham | 1957 |
| 5th | 405 | S.G.Barnes/D.G.Bradman | A v E | Sydney | 1946-47 |

| 6th | 346 | J.H.W.Fingleton/D.G.Bradman | A v E | Melbourne | 1936-37 |
| 7th | 347 | D.St E.Atkinson/C.C.Depeiza | WI v A | Bridgetown | 1954-55 |
| 8th | 313 | Wasim Akram/Saqlain Mushtaq | P v Z | Sheikhupura | 1996-97 |
| 9th | 195 | M.V.Boucher/P.L.Symcox | SA v P | Johannesburg | 1997-98 |
| 10th | 151 | B.F.Hastings/R.O.Collinge | NZ v P | Auckland | 1972-73 |
| | 151 | Azhar Mahmood/Mushtaq Ahmed | P v SA | Rawalpindi | 1997-98 |

## BOWLING RECORDS
### 200 WICKETS IN TESTS

| Wkts | | | M | Balls | Runs | Avge | 5 wI | 10 wM |
|------|---|---|---|-------|------|------|------|-------|
| 519 | C.A.Walsh | WI | 132 | 30019 | 12688 | 24.45 | 22 | 3 |
| 491 | S.K.Warne | A | 107 | 29876 | 12624 | 25.71 | 23 | 6 |
| 437 | M.Muralitharan | SL | 78 | 26147 | 10281 | 23.52 | 36 | 11 |
| 434 | Kapil Dev | I | 131 | 27740 | 12867 | 29.64 | 23 | 2 |
| 431 | R.J.Hadlee | NZ | 86 | 21918 | 9612 | 22.29 | 36 | 9 |
| 422 | G.D.McGrath | A | 91 | 21575 | 9056 | 21.45 | 23 | 3 |
| 414 | Wasim Akram | P | 104 | 22627 | 9779 | 23.62 | 25 | 5 |
| 405 | C.E.L.Ambrose | WI | 98 | 22104 | 8500 | 20.98 | 22 | 3 |
| 383 | I.T.Botham | E | 102 | 21815 | 10878 | 28.40 | 27 | 4 |
| 376 | M.D.Marshall | WI | 81 | 17584 | 7876 | 20.94 | 22 | 4 |
| 373 | Waqar Younis | P | 87 | 16224 | 8788 | 23.56 | 22 | 5 |
| 362 | Imran Khan | P | 88 | 19458 | 8258 | 22.81 | 23 | 6 |
| 355 | D.K.Lillee | A | 70 | 18467 | 8493 | 23.92 | 23 | 7 |
| 349 | A.Kumble | I | 76 | 23790 | 9768 | 27.98 | 20 | 4 |
| 330 | A.A.Donald | SA | 72 | 15519 | 7344 | 22.25 | 20 | 3 |
| 325 | R.G.D.Willis | E | 90 | 17357 | 8190 | 25.20 | 16 | – |
| 309 | L.R.Gibbs | WI | 79 | 27115 | 8989 | 29.09 | 18 | 2 |
| 307 | F.S.Trueman | E | 67 | 15178 | 6625 | 21.57 | 17 | 3 |
| 297 | D.L.Underwood | E | 86 | 21862 | 7674 | 25.83 | 17 | 6 |
| 291 | C.J.McDermott | A | 71 | 16586 | 8332 | 28.63 | 14 | 2 |
| 278 | S.M.Pollock | SA | 68 | 15108 | 5759 | 20.71 | 14 | 1 |
| 266 | B.S.Bedi | I | 67 | 21364 | 7637 | 28.71 | 14 | 1 |
| 259 | J.Garner | WI | 58 | 13169 | 5433 | 20.97 | 7 | – |
| 252 | J.B.Statham | E | 70 | 16056 | 6261 | 24.84 | 9 | 1 |
| 249 | M.A.Holding | WI | 60 | 12680 | 5898 | 23.68 | 13 | 2 |
| 248 | R.Benaud | A | 63 | 19108 | 6704 | 27.03 | 16 | 1 |
| 246 | G.D.McKenzie | A | 60 | 17681 | 7328 | 29.78 | 16 | 3 |
| 242 | B.S.Chandrasekhar | I | 58 | 15963 | 7199 | 29.74 | 16 | 2 |
| 236 | A.V.Bedser | E | 51 | 15918 | 5876 | 24.89 | 15 | 5 |
| 236 | Abdul Qadir | P | 67 | 17126 | 7742 | 32.80 | 15 | 5 |
| 236 | J.Srinath | I | 67 | 15104 | 7196 | 30.49 | 10 | 1 |
| 235 | G.St A.Sobers | WI | 93 | 21599 | 7999 | 34.03 | 6 | – |
| 234 | A.R.Caddick | E | 62 | 13558 | 6999 | 29.91 | 13 | 1 |
| 228 | D.Gough | E | 56 | 11503 | 6288 | 27.57 | 9 | – |
| 228 | R.R.Lindwall | A | 61 | 13650 | 5251 | 23.03 | 12 | – |
| 216 | C.V.Grimmett | A | 37 | 14513 | 5231 | 24.21 | 21 | 7 |
| 212 | M.G.Hughes | A | 53 | 12285 | 6017 | 28.38 | 7 | 1 |
| 206 | W.P.U.C.J.Vaas | SL | 64 | 14180 | 6244 | 30.31 | 7 | 2 |
| 205 | Saqlain Mushtaq | P | 47 | 13647 | 5932 | 28.93 | 13 | 3 |
| 202 | A.M.E.Roberts | WI | 47 | 11136 | 5174 | 25.61 | 11 | 2 |
| 202 | J.A.Snow | E | 49 | 12021 | 5601 | 26.66 | 8 | 1 |
| 200 | J.R.Thomson | A | 51 | 10535 | 5387 | 28.00 | 8 | 1 |

The most for Zimbabwe is 180 in 51 Tests by H.H.Streak and for Bangladesh 24 in 14 Tests by Manjural Islam.

## 35 WICKETS IN A SERIES

| Wkts | | | Series | M | Balls | Runs | Avge | 5 wI | 10 wM |
|------|---|---|--------|---|-------|------|------|------|-------|
| 49 | S.F.Barnes | E v SA | 1913-14 | 4 | 1356 | 536 | 10.93 | 7 | 3 |
| 46 | J.C.Laker | E v A | 1956 | 5 | 1703 | 442 | 9.60 | 4 | 2 |
| 44 | C.V.Grimmett | A v SA | 1935-36 | 5 | 2077 | 642 | 14.59 | 5 | 3 |
| 42 | T.M.Alderman | A v E | 1981 | 6 | 1950 | 893 | 21.26 | 4 | – |
| 41 | R.M.Hogg | A v E | 1978-79 | 6 | 1740 | 527 | 12.85 | 5 | 2 |
| 41 | T.M.Alderman | A v E | 1989 | 6 | 1616 | 712 | 17.36 | 6 | 1 |
| 40 | Imran Khan | P v I | 1982-83 | 6 | 1339 | 558 | 13.95 | 4 | 2 |
| 39 | A.V.Bedser | E v A | 1953 | 5 | 1591 | 682 | 17.48 | 5 | 1 |
| 39 | D.K.Lillee | A v E | 1981 | 6 | 1870 | 870 | 22.30 | 2 | 1 |
| 38 | M.W.Tate | E v A | 1924-25 | 5 | 2528 | 881 | 23.18 | 5 | 1 |
| 37 | W.J.Whitty | A v SA | 1910-11 | 5 | 1395 | 632 | 17.08 | 2 | – |
| 37 | H.J.Tayfield | SA v E | 1956-57 | 5 | 2280 | 636 | 17.18 | 4 | 1 |
| 36 | A.E.E.Vogler | SA v E | 1909-10 | 5 | 1349 | 783 | 21.75 | 4 | 1 |
| 36 | A.A.Mailey | A v E | 1920-21 | 5 | 1465 | 946 | 26.27 | 4 | 2 |
| 36 | G.D.McGrath | A v E | 1997 | 6 | 1499 | 701 | 19.47 | 2 | – |
| 35 | G.A.Lohmann | E v SA | 1895-96 | 3 | 520 | 203 | 5.80 | 4 | 2 |
| 35 | B.S.Chandrasekhar | I v E | 1972-73 | 5 | 1747 | 662 | 18.91 | 4 | 1 |
| 35 | M.D.Marshall | WI v E | 1988 | 5 | 1219 | 443 | 12.65 | 3 | 1 |

The most for New Zealand is 33 by R.J.Hadlee (3 Tests v A, 1985-86), for Sri Lanka 30 by M.Muralitharan (3 Tests v Z, 2001-02), and for Zimbabwe 22 by H.H.Streak (3 Tests v P, 1994-95).

## 15 WICKETS IN A TEST († *On debut*)

| 19- 90 | J.C.Laker | E v A | Manchester | 1956 |
|--------|-----------|-------|-----------|------|
| 17-159 | S.F.Barnes | E v SA | Johannesburg | 1913-14 |
| 16-136‡ | N.D.Hirwani | I v WI | Madras | 1987-88 |
| 16-137† | R.A.L.Massie | A v E | Lord's | 1972 |
| 16-220 | M.Muralitharan | SL v E | The Oval | 1998 |
| 15- 28 | J.Briggs | E v SA | Cape Town | 1888-89 |
| 15- 45 | G.A.Lohmann | E v SA | Port Elizabeth | 1895-96 |
| 15- 99 | C.Blythe | E v SA | Leeds | 1907 |
| 15-104 | H.Verity | E v A | Lord's | 1934 |
| 15-123 | R.J.Hadlee | NZ v A | Brisbane | 1985-86 |
| 15-124 | W.Rhodes | E v A | Melbourne | 1903-04 |
| 15-217 | Harbhajan Singh | I v A | Madras | 2000-01 |

The best analysis for South Africa is 13-165 by H.J.Tayfield (v A, Melbourne, 1952-53), for West Indies 14-149 by M.A.Holding (v E, The Oval, 1976), for Pakistan 14-116 by Imran Khan (v SL, Lahore, 1981-82), and for Zimbabwe 11-257 by A.G.Huckle (v NZ, Bulawayo, 1997-98).

## NINE WICKETS IN AN INNINGS

| 10-53 | J.C.Laker | E v A | Manchester | 1956 |
|-------|-----------|-------|-----------|------|
| 10-74 | A.Kumble | I v P | Delhi | 1998-99 |
| 9-28 | G.A.Lohmann | E v SA | Johannesburg | 1895-96 |
| 9-37 | J.C.Laker | E v A | Manchester | 1956 |
| 9-51 | M.Muralitharan | SL v Z | Kandy | 2001-02 |
| 9-52 | R.J.Hadlee | NZ v A | Brisbane | 1985-86 |
| 9-56 | Abdul Qadir | P v E | Lahore | 1987-88 |
| 9-57 | D.E.Malcolm | E v SA | The Oval | 1994 |
| 9-65 | M.Muralitharan | SL v E | The Oval | 1998 |
| 9-69 | J.M.Patel | I v A | Kanpur | 1959-60 |
| 9-83 | Kapil Dev | I v WI | Ahmedabad | 1983-84 |
| 9-86 | Sarfraz Nawaz | P v A | Melbourne | 1978-79 |
| 9-95 | J.M.Noreiga | WI v I | Port-of-Spain | 1970-71 |

| 9-102 | S.P.Gupte | I v WI | Kanpur | 1958-59 |
| 9-103 | S.F.Barnes | E v SA | Johannesburg | 1913-14 |
| 9-113 | H.J.Tayfield | SA v E | Johannesburg | 1956-57 |
| 9-121 | A.A.Mailey | A v E | Melbourne | 1920-21 |

The best analysis for Zimbabwe is 8-109 by P.A.Strang (v NZ, Bulawayo, 2000-01), and for Bangladesh 6-81 by Manjural Islam (v Z, Bulawayo, 2000-01 – on debut).

## HAT-TRICKS

| F.R.Spofforth | Australia v England | Melbourne | 1878-79 |
| W.Bates | England v Australia | Melbourne | 1882-83 |
| J.Briggs | England v Australia | Sydney | 1891-92 |
| G.A.Lohmann | England v South Africa | Port Elizabeth | 1895-96 |
| J.T.Hearne | England v Australia | Leeds | 1899 |
| H.Trumble | Australia v England | Melbourne | 1901-02 |
| H.Trumble | Australia v England | Melbourne | 1903-04 |
| T.J.Matthews (2)[2] | Australia v South Africa | Manchester | 1912 |
| M.J.C.Allom[1] | England v New Zealand | Christchurch | 1929-30 |
| T.W.J.Goddard | England v South Africa | Johannesburg | 1938-39 |
| P.J.Loader | England v West Indies | Leeds | 1957 |
| L.F.Kline | Australia v South Africa | Cape Town | 1957-58 |
| W.W.Hall | West Indies v Pakistan | Lahore | 1958-59 |
| G.M.Griffin | South Africa v England | Lord's | 1960 |
| L.R.Gibbs | West Indies v Australia | Adelaide | 1960-61 |
| P.J.Petherick[1] | New Zealand v Pakistan | Lahore | 1976-77 |
| C.A.Walsh[3] | West Indies v Australia | Brisbane | 1988-89 |
| M.G.Hughes[3] | Australia v West Indies | Perth | 1988-89 |
| D.W.Fleming[1] | Australia v Pakistan | Rawalpindi | 1994-95 |
| S.K.Warne | Australia v England | Melbourne | 1994-95 |
| D.G.Cork | England v West Indies | Manchester | 1995 |
| D.Gough | England v Australia | Sydney | 1998-99 |
| Wasim Akram[4] | Pakistan v Sri Lanka | Lahore | 1998-99 |
| Wasim Akram[4] | Pakistan v Sri Lanka | Dhaka | 1998-99 |
| D.N.T.Zoysa[5] | Sri Lanka v Zimbabwe | Harare | 1999-00 |
| Abdul Razzaq | Pakistan v Sri Lanka | Galle | 2000-01 |
| G.D.McGrath | Australia v West Indies | Perth | 2000-01 |
| Harbhajan Singh | India v Australia | Calcutta | 2000-01 |
| Mohammad Sami | Pakistan v Sri Lanka | Lahore | 2001-02 |

[1] On debut. [2] Hat-trick in each innings. [3] Involving both innings. [4] In successive Tests. [5] His first 3 balls (second over of the match).

## WICKET-KEEPING RECORDS

### 100 DISMISSALS IN TESTS†

| Total | | | Tests | Ct | St |
|---|---|---|---|---|---|
| 395 | I.A.Healy | Australia | 119 | 366 | 29 |
| 355 | R.W.Marsh | Australia | 96 | 343 | 12 |
| 270† | P.J.L.Dujon | West Indies | 79 | 265 | 5 |
| 269 | A.P.E.Knott | England | 95 | 250 | 19 |
| 228 | Wasim Bari | Pakistan | 81 | 201 | 27 |
| 227 | M.V.Boucher | South Africa | 58 | 221 | 6 |
| 224† | A.J.Stewart | England | 75 | 211 | 13 |
| 219 | T.G.Evans | England | 91 | 173 | 46 |
| 201† | A.C.Parore | New Zealand | 67 | 194 | 7 |
| 198 | S.M.H.Kirmani | India | 88 | 160 | 38 |
| 189 | D.L.Murray | West Indies | 62 | 181 | 8 |
| 187 | A.T.W.Grout | Australia | 51 | 163 | 24 |
| 176 | I.D.S.Smith | New Zealand | 63 | 168 | 8 |

| Total | | | Tests | Ct | St |
|---|---|---|---|---|---|
| 174 | R.W.Taylor | England | 57 | 167 | 7 |
| 168 | A.C.Gilchrist | Australia | 39 | 155 | 13 |
| 165 | R.D.Jacobs | West Indies | 47 | 157 | 8 |
| 165 | R.C.Russell | England | 54 | 153 | 12 |
| 152 | D.J.Richardson | South Africa | 42 | 150 | 2 |
| 151† | A.Flower | Zimbabwe | 55 | 142 | 9 |
| 141 | J.H.B.Waite | South Africa | 50 | 124 | 17 |
| 133† | Moin Khan | Pakistan | 60 | 113 | 20 |
| 130 | K.S.More | India | 49 | 110 | 20 |
| 130 | W.A.S.Oldfield | Australia | 54 | 78 | 52 |
| 112† | J.M.Parks | England | 43 | 101 | 11 |
| 112 | Rashid Latif | Pakistan | 34 | 102 | 10 |
| 107 | N.R.Mongia | India | 44 | 99 | 8 |
| 104 | Salim Yousuf | Pakistan | 32 | 91 | 13 |
| 101† | J.R.Murray | West Indies | 31 | 98 | 3 |

The most for Sri Lanka is 94 (74 ct, 20 st) by R.S.Kaluwitharana in 40 Tests.

† Excluding catches taken in the field

## 25 DISMISSALS IN A SERIES

| 28 | R.W.Marsh | Australia v England | 1982-83 |
|---|---|---|---|
| 27 (inc 2st) | R.C.Russell | England v South Africa | 1995-96 |
| 27 (inc 2st) | I.A.Healy | Australia v England (6 Tests) | 1997 |
| 26 (inc 3st) | J.H.B.Waite | South Africa v New Zealand | 1961-62 |
| 26 | R.W.Marsh | Australia v West Indies (6 Tests) | 1975-76 |
| 26 (inc 5st) | I.A.Healy | Australia v England (6 Tests) | 1993 |
| 26 (inc 1st) | M.V.Boucher | South Africa v England | 1998 |
| 26 (inc 2st) | A.C.Gilchrist | Australia v England | 2001 |
| 25 (inc 2st) | I.A.Healy | Australia v England | 1994-95 |
| 25 (inc 2st) | A.C.Gilchrist | Australia v England | 2002-03 |

## TEN DISMISSALS IN A TEST

| 11 | R.C.Russell | England v South Africa | Johannesburg | 1995-96 |
|---|---|---|---|---|
| 10 | R.W.Taylor | England v India | Bombay | 1979-80 |
| 10 | A.C.Gilchrist | Australia v New Zealand | Hamilton | 1999-00 |

## SEVEN DISMISSALS IN AN INNINGS

| 7 | Wasim Bari | Pakistan v New Zealand | Auckland | 1978-79 |
|---|---|---|---|---|
| 7 | R.W.Taylor | England v India | Bombay | 1979-80 |
| 7 | I.D.S.Smith | New Zealand v Sri Lanka | Hamilton | 1990-91 |
| 7 | R.D.Jacobs | West Indies v Australia | Melbourne | 2000-01 |

## FIVE STUMPINGS IN AN INNINGS

| 5 | K.S.More | India v West Indies | Madras | 1987-88 |
|---|---|---|---|---|

## FIELDING RECORDS
## 100 CATCHES IN TESTS

| Total | | | Tests | Total | | | Tests |
|---|---|---|---|---|---|---|---|
| 181 | M.E.Waugh | Australia | 128 | 120 | M.C.Cowdrey | England | 114 |
| 157 | M.A.Taylor | Australia | 104 | 116 | B.C.Lara | West Indies | 90 |
| 156 | A.R.Border | Australia | 156 | 115 | C.L.Hooper | West Indies | 102 |
| 122 | G.S.Chappell | Australia | 87 | 111 | S.P.Fleming | New Zealand | 73 |
| 122 | I.V.A.Richards | West Indies | 121 | 110 | R.B.Simpson | Australia | 62 |
| 120 | I.T.Botham | England | 102 | 110 | W.R.Hammond | England | 85 |

| Total | | | Tests | | Total | | | Tests |
|---|---|---|---|---|---|---|---|---|
| 109 | G.St A.Sobers | West Indies | 93 | | 105 | I.M.Chappell | Australia | 75 |
| 108 | S.M.Gavaskar | India | 125 | | 105 | M.Azharuddin | India | 99 |
| 108 | S.R.Waugh | Australia | 156 | | 103 | G.A.Gooch | England | 118 |

The most for South Africa is 78 by G.Kirsten (89 Tests), for Pakistan 93 by Javed Miandad (124), for Sri Lanka 79 by H.P.Tillekeratne (62), and for Zimbabwe 60 by A.D.R.Campbell (60).

## 15 CATCHES IN A SERIES

| 15 | J.M.Gregory | | Australia v England | | 1920-21 |
|---|---|---|---|---|---|

## SEVEN CATCHES IN A TEST

| 7 | G.S.Chappell | Australia v England | Perth | 1974-75 |
|---|---|---|---|---|
| 7 | Yajurvindra Singh | India v England | Bangalore | 1976-77 |
| 7 | H.P.Tillekeratne | Sri Lanka v New Zealand | Colombo (SSC) | 1992-93 |
| 7 | S.P.Fleming | New Zealand v Zimbabwe | Harare | 1997-98 |

## FIVE CATCHES IN AN INNINGS

| 5 | V.Y.Richardson | Australia v South Africa | Durban | 1935-36 |
|---|---|---|---|---|
| 5 | Yajurvindra Singh | India v England | Bangalore | 1976-77 |
| 5 | M.Azharuddin | India v Pakistan | Karachi | 1989-90 |
| 5 | K.Srikkanth | India v Australia | Perth | 1991-92 |
| 5 | S.P.Fleming | New Zealand v Zimbabwe | Harare | 1997-98 |

## APPEARANCE RECORDS
## 100 TEST MATCH APPEARANCES

| 156 | A.R.Border | Australia | | 115 | M.A.Atherton | England |
|---|---|---|---|---|---|---|
| 156 | S.R.Waugh | Australia | | 114 | M.C.Cowdrey | England |
| 132 | C.A.Walsh | West Indies | | 110 | C.H.Lloyd | West Indies |
| 131 | Kapil Dev | India | | 108 | G.Boycott | England |
| 128 | M.E.Waugh | Australia | | 108 | C.G.Greenidge | West Indies |
| 126 | A.J.Stewart | England | | 107 | D.C.Boon | Australia |
| 125 | S.M.Gavaskar | India | | 107 | S.K.Warne | Australia |
| 124 | Javed Miandad | Pakistan | | 105 | S.R.Tendulkar | India |
| 121 | I.V.A.Richards | West Indies | | 104 | M.A.Taylor | Australia |
| 119 | I.A.Healy | Australia | | 104 | Wasim Akram | Pakistan |
| 118 | G.A.Gooch | England | | 103 | Salim Malik | Pakistan |
| 117 | D.I.Gower | England | | 102 | I.T.Botham | England |
| 116 | D.L.Haynes | West Indies | | 102 | C.L.Hooper | West Indies |
| 116 | D.B.Vengsarkar | India | | | | |

The most for South Africa is 89 by G.Kirsten, for New Zealand 86 by R.J.Hadlee, for Sri Lanka 93 by P.A.de Silva and A.Ranatunga, for Zimbabwe 63 by A.Flower and G.W.Flower, and for Bangladesh 17 by Habibul Bashar.

## 100 CONSECUTIVE TEST APPEARANCES

| 153 | A.R.Border | Australia | March 1979 to March 1994 |
|---|---|---|---|
| 107 | M.E.Waugh | Australia | June 1993 to October 2002 |
| 106 | S.M.Gavaskar | India | January 1975 to February 1987 |

## 75 TESTS AS CAPTAIN

| 93 | A.R.Border | Australia | December 1984 to March 1994 |
|---|---|---|---|

## 50 TEST UMPIRING APPEARANCES

| 77 | S.A.Bucknor | (West Indies) | April 1989 to January 2003 |
|---|---|---|---|
| 69 | D.R.Shepherd | (England) | August 1985 to December 2002 |
| 66 | H.D.Bird | (England) | July 1973 to June 1996 |
| 64 | S.Venkataraghavan | (India) | January 1992 to January 2003 |

# TEST MATCH SCORES

# PAKISTAN v WEST INDIES (1st Test)

At Sharjah C.A. Stadium, UAE, on 31 January, 1, 2, 3, 4 February.
Toss: Pakistan. Result: **PAKISTAN** won by 170 runs.
Debuts: Pakistan – Naved Latif; West Indies – R.O.Hinds.

## PAKISTAN

| | | | | |
|---|---|---|---|---|
| Taufiq Umar | b Hooper | 24 | run out | 23 |
| Naved Latif | lbw b Dillon | 0 | c Jacobs b Dillon | 20 |
| Younis Khan | c Gayle b Hooper | 53 | c Jacobs b Cuffy | 32 |
| Inzamam-ul-Haq | c Jacobs b Dillon | 10 | c Hooper b Dillon | 48 |
| Yousuf Youhana | b Cuffy | 146 | c Dillon b Cuffy | 12 |
| Abdul Razzaq | c Jacobs b W.W.Hinds | 34 | c Ganga b Collins | 29 |
| †Rashid Latif | b Gayle | 150 | not out | 47 |
| Saqlain Mushtaq | c and b Dillon | 17 | | |
| *Waqar Younis | not out | 25 | | |
| Shoaib Akhtar | b Gayle | 20 | | |
| Danish Kaneria | c and b Gayle | 0 | | |
| Extras | (B 6, LB 7, W 1) | 14 | (NB 3) | 3 |
| **Total** | | **493** | (6 wickets declared) | **214** |

## WEST INDIES

| | | | | |
|---|---|---|---|---|
| D.Ganga | lbw b Saqlain | 20 | b Shoaib | 34 |
| C.H.Gayle | b Saqlain | 68 | b Shoaib | 66 |
| S.L.Campbell | lbw b Kaneria | 6 | run out | 20 |
| W.W.Hinds | st Rashid b Kaneria | 59 | c Rashid b Shoaib | 8 |
| *C.L.Hooper | lbw b Razzaq | 56 | lbw b Razzaq | 13 |
| S.Chanderpaul | b Waqar | 66 | c Rashid b Razzaq | 0 |
| R.O.Hinds | c Rashid b Waqar | 62 | not out | 9 |
| †R.D.Jacobs | c Kaneria b Waqar | 6 | lbw b Razzaq | 0 |
| M.Dillon | run out | 5 | b Shoaib | 0 |
| C.E.Cuffy | b Waqar | 0 | b Shoaib | 0 |
| P.T.Collins | not out | 1 | b Razzaq | 12 |
| Extras | (LB 4, W 1, NB 12) | 17 | (B 1, LB 1, NB 7) | 9 |
| **Total** | | **366** | | **171** |

| WEST INDIES | O | M | R | W | | O | M | R | W |
|---|---|---|---|---|---|---|---|---|---|
| Dillon | 42 | 10 | 140 | 3 | | 17 | 3 | 46 | 2 |
| Collins | 33 | 3 | 96 | 0 | (3) | 14.4 | 1 | 56 | 1 |
| Cuffy | 35 | 10 | 75 | 1 | (2) | 19 | 3 | 78 | 2 |
| Hooper | 32 | 7 | 85 | 2 | | 5 | 0 | 23 | 0 |
| R.O.Hinds | 4 | 0 | 31 | 0 | | | | | |
| W.W.Hinds | 8 | 1 | 26 | 1 | (5) | 2 | 0 | 11 | 0 |
| Gayle | 7.5 | 0 | 27 | 3 | | | | | |

| PAKISTAN | O | M | R | W | | O | M | R | W |
|---|---|---|---|---|---|---|---|---|---|
| Waqar Younis | 25.3 | 4 | 93 | 4 | | 9 | 2 | 35 | 2 |
| Shoaib Akhtar | 18 | 4 | 68 | 0 | (4) | 16 | 7 | 24 | 5 |
| Abdul Razzaq | 18 | 2 | 49 | 1 | (5) | 7.5 | 1 | 24 | 4 |
| Danish Kaneria | 26 | 4 | 75 | 2 | (3) | 19 | 7 | 56 | 0 |
| Saqlain Mushtaq | 36 | 12 | 71 | 2 | (2) | 11 | 5 | 30 | 0 |
| Taufiq Umar | 2 | 0 | 6 | 0 | | | | | |

### FALL OF WICKETS

| | P | WI | P | WI |
|---|---|---|---|---|
| Wkt | 1st | 1st | 2nd | 2nd |
| 1st | 3 | 88 | 35 | 76 |
| 2nd | 45 | 96 | 54 | 115 |
| 3rd | 80 | 126 | 101 | 125 |
| 4th | 94 | 180 | 134 | 146 |
| 5th | 178 | 231 | 146 | 149 |
| 6th | 382 | 352 | 214 | 150 |
| 7th | 438 | 353 | – | 150 |
| 8th | 457 | 362 | – | 155 |
| 9th | 493 | 363 | – | 155 |
| 10th | 493 | 366 | – | 171 |

Umpires: Riazuddin (12) and G.Sharp (*England*) (15).
Referee: M.H.Denness (*England*) (13).

Test No. 1587/38 (P282/WI380)

# PAKISTAN v WEST INDIES (2nd Test)

At Sharjah C.A. Stadium, UAE, on 7, 8, 9, 10 February.
Toss: West Indies. Result: **PAKISTAN** won by 244 runs.
Debuts: None.

## PAKISTAN

| Batsman | Dismissal 1 | R | | Dismissal 2 | R |
|---|---|---|---|---|---|
| Taufiq Umar | c Ganga b Dillon | 8 | (2) | lbw b Dillon | 69 |
| Shahid Afridi | b Cuffy | 107 | (1) | c Jacobs b Dillon | 0 |
| Younis Khan | c Ganga b Collins | 153 | | c Ganga b Dillon | 71 |
| Inzamam-ul-Haq | c Hooper b Ramnarine | 36 | | c sub (D.Brown) b Collins | 6 |
| Yousuf Youhana | b Dillon | 60 | | not out | 52 |
| Abdul Razzaq | not out | 64 | | run out | 16 |
| †Rashid Latif | c Hooper b Ramnarine | 16 | | not out | 2 |
| Saqlain Mushtaq | b Cuffy | 5 | | | |
| *Waqar Younis | lbw b Ramnarine | 2 | | | |
| Shoaib Akhtar | c and b Cuffy | 4 | | | |
| Danish Kaneria | c Gayle b Cuffy | 0 | | | |
| Extras | (B 12, LB 2, NB 3) | 17 | | (LB 6, W 1, NB 2) | 9 |
| **Total** | | **472** | | (5 wickets declared) | **225** |

## WEST INDIES

| Batsman | Dismissal 1 | R | | Dismissal 2 | R |
|---|---|---|---|---|---|
| D.Ganga | b Shahid | 65 | | lbw b Shoaib | 21 |
| C.H.Gayle | b Shoaib | 6 | | lbw b Waqar | 4 |
| W.W.Hinds | b Saqlain | 25 | | c Taufiq b Saqlain | 34 |
| *C.L.Hooper | not out | 84 | | lbw b Saqlain | 1 |
| S.Chanderpaul | c Youhana b Kaneria | 16 | | lbw b Razzaq | 19 |
| M.Dillon | c Taufiq b Shoaib | 0 | (8) | lbw b Razzaq | 0 |
| R.O.Hinds | lbw b Razzaq | 11 | (6) | lbw b Waqar | 46 |
| †R.D.Jacobs | b Saqlain | 31 | | not out | 35 |
| D.Ramnarine | b Shoaib | 0 | | b Razzaq | 0 |
| C.E.Cuffy | b Shoaib | 4 | | b Waqar | 15 |
| P.T.Collins | c Inzamam b Saqlain | 1 | | b Waqar | 0 |
| Extras | (B 7, LB 8, W 6) | 21 | | (B 2, LB 6, NB 6) | 14 |
| **Total** | | **264** | | | **189** |

| WEST INDIES | O | M | R | W | | O | M | R | W |
|---|---|---|---|---|---|---|---|---|---|
| Dillon | 27 | 6 | 63 | 2 | | 18 | 2 | 57 | 3 |
| Collins | 30 | 5 | 99 | 1 | (3) | 14 | 2 | 56 | 1 |
| Cuffy | 29 | 3 | 82 | 4 | (2) | 20 | 3 | 52 | 0 |
| Ramnarine | 36 | 5 | 137 | 3 | (5) | 12 | 1 | 39 | 0 |
| Hooper | 7 | 0 | 41 | 0 | | | | | |
| R.O.Hinds | 5 | 1 | 24 | 0 | (4) | 12 | 3 | 15 | 0 |
| Gayle | 1 | 0 | 12 | 0 | | | | | |

| PAKISTAN | O | M | R | W | | O | M | R | W |
|---|---|---|---|---|---|---|---|---|---|
| Waqar Younis | 9 | 1 | 24 | 0 | | 10 | 2 | 44 | 4 |
| Shoaib Akhtar | 18 | 3 | 63 | 4 | | 8 | 3 | 23 | 1 |
| Danish Kaneria | 13 | 2 | 34 | 1 | (6) | 11 | 2 | 25 | 0 |
| Saqlain Mushtaq | 21.5 | 4 | 75 | 3 | | 19 | 8 | 42 | 2 |
| Shahid Afridi | 15 | 0 | 34 | 1 | | 2 | 0 | 14 | 0 |
| Abdul Razzaq | 8 | 1 | 19 | 1 | (3) | 11 | 2 | 33 | 3 |

### FALL OF WICKETS

| Wkt | P 1st | WI 1st | P 2nd | WI 2nd |
|---|---|---|---|---|
| 1st | 12 | 19 | 0 | 19 |
| 2nd | 202 | 88 | 144 | 46 |
| 3rd | 272 | 116 | 145 | 47 |
| 4th | 364 | 159 | 175 | 84 |
| 5th | 393 | 170 | 216 | 114 |
| 6th | 416 | 189 | – | 161 |
| 7th | 447 | 236 | – | 162 |
| 8th | 454 | 237 | – | 162 |
| 9th | 463 | 247 | – | 189 |
| 10th | 472 | 264 | – | 189 |

Umpires: D.B.Hair (*Australia*) (43) and Shakil Khan (6).
Referee: M.H.Denness (*England*) (14).        **Test No. 1588/39 (P283/WI381)**

# INDIA v ZIMBABWE (1st Test)

At Vidarbha C.A. Ground, Nagpur, on 21, 22, 23, 24, 25 February.
Toss: Zimbabwe. Result: **INDIA** won by an innings and 101 runs.
Debuts: None.

## ZIMBABWE

| | | | | | |
|---|---|---|---|---|---|
| *S.V.Carlisle | run out | 77 | | lbw b Khan | 28 |
| T.R.Gripper | c Dasgupta b Khan | 5 | | c sub (V.Sehwag) b Harbhajan | 60 |
| A.D.R.Campbell | c Laxman b Kumble | 57 | | c Laxman b Kumble | 30 |
| A.Flower | b Khan | 3 | | c Dravid b Kumble | 8 |
| G.J.Rennie | c sub (V.Sehwag) b Srinath | 9 | | c sub (V.Sehwag) b Kumble | 25 |
| G.W.Flower | c Dravid b Kumble | 14 | (7) | lbw b Kumble | 1 |
| H.H.Streak | c Das b Khan | 24 | (8) | c Ganguly b Kumble | 8 |
| †T.Taibu | b Kumble | 1 | | c sub (V.Sehwag) b Harbhajan | 0 |
| T.J.Friend | not out | 60 | (10) | not out | 6 |
| R.W.Price | run out | 18 | (6) | c Dravid b Harbhajan | 4 |
| B.T.Watambwa | c Laxman b Kumble | 0 | | c Tendulkar b Harbhajan | 1 |
| Extras | (B 6, LB 11, NB 2) | 19 | | (B 1, LB 8, NB 2) | 11 |
| **Total** | | **287** | | | **182** |

## INDIA

| | | |
|---|---|---|
| S.S.Das | c Campbell b Price | 105 |
| †D.Dasgupta | b Price | 33 |
| R.Dravid | b Streak | 65 |
| S.R.Tendulkar | c A.Flower b Price | 176 |
| *S.C.Ganguly | c G.W.Flower b Price | 38 |
| V.V.S Laxman | c Rennie b Price | 13 |
| S.B.Bangar | not out | 100 |
| Z.Khan | b Watambwa | 0 |
| A.Kumble | not out | 13 |
| J.Srinath | | |
| Harbhajan Singh | | |
| Extras | (B 16, LB 2, W 3, NB 6) | 27 |
| **Total** | (7 wickets declared) | **570** |

| INDIA | O | M | R | W | | O | M | R | W |
|---|---|---|---|---|---|---|---|---|---|
| Srinath | 22 | 6 | 65 | 1 | | 6 | 3 | 20 | 0 |
| Khan | 14 | 2 | 45 | 3 | (3) | 8 | 1 | 33 | 1 |
| Bangar | 8 | 3 | 20 | 0 | | | | | |
| Kumble | 33.5 | 12 | 82 | 4 | (2) | 37 | 15 | 63 | 5 |
| Harbhajan Singh | 26 | 8 | 58 | 0 | (4) | 31.4 | 9 | 46 | 4 |
| Tendulkar | | | | | (5) | 6 | 2 | 11 | 0 |

| ZIMBABWE | O | M | R | W |
|---|---|---|---|---|
| Streak | 34 | 9 | 108 | 1 |
| Watambwa | 25.5 | 6 | 87 | 1 |
| Price | 68 | 18 | 182 | 5 |
| Friend | 22 | 3 | 61 | 0 |
| G.W.Flower | 30 | 8 | 96 | 0 |
| Gripper | 5 | 0 | 18 | 0 |

FALL OF WICKETS

| | Z | I | Z |
|---|---|---|---|
| Wkt | 1st | 1st | 2nd |
| 1st | 12 | 79 | 32 |
| 2nd | 118 | 209 | 80 |
| 3rd | 125 | 247 | 103 |
| 4th | 151 | 344 | 147 |
| 5th | 175 | 376 | 156 |
| 6th | 182 | 547 | 159 |
| 7th | 194 | 547 | 161 |
| 8th | 227 | – | 167 |
| 9th | 286 | – | 181 |
| 10th | 287 | – | 182 |

Umpires: D.R.Shepherd (60) (*England*) and S.Venkataraghavan (51).
Referee: J.R.Reid (*New Zealand*) (50).        **Test No. 1589/8 (I350/Z62)**

# INDIA v ZIMBABWE (2nd Test)

At Feroz Shah Kotla, Delhi, on 28 February, 1, 2, 3, 4 March.
Toss: Zimbabwe. Result: **INDIA** won by four wickets.
Debuts: None.

## ZIMBABWE

| | | | | | |
|---|---|---|---|---|---|
| *S.V.Carlisle | b Srinath | 0 | c and b Harbhajan | | 37 |
| T.R.Gripper | c Dravid b Khan | 8 | c Dravid b Harbhajan | | 10 |
| A.D.R.Campbell | c Dravid b Khan | 16 | c Dravid b Harbhajan | | 2 |
| A.Flower | c Das b Harbhajan | 92 | c Das b Harbhajan | | 0 |
| D.D.Ebrahim | lbw b Srinath | 94 | lbw b Kumble | | 22 |
| G.W.Flower | run out | 30 | c Harbhajan b Kumble | | 49 |
| H.H.Streak | b Kumble | 0 | lbw b Kumble | | 9 |
| T.J.Friend | c Tendulkar b Harbhajan | 43 | b Harbhajan | | 0 |
| †T.Taibu | lbw b Kumble | 13 | c Bangar b Kumble | | 10 |
| R.W.Price | b Kumble | 0 | c Das b Harbhajan | | 3 |
| B.T.Watambwa | not out | 3 | not out | | 1 |
| Extras | (B 5, LB 16, NB 9) | 30 | (B 2, NB 1) | | 3 |
| **Total** | | **329** | | | **146** |

## INDIA

| | | | | | |
|---|---|---|---|---|---|
| S.S.Das | c Taibu b Streak | 13 | lbw b Streak | | 31 |
| †D.Dasgupta | lbw b Friend | 19 | run out | | 1 |
| *S.C.Ganguly | c Gripper b Price | 136 | lbw b G.W.Flower | | 20 |
| S.R.Tendulkar | lbw b Price | 36 | (5) lbw b Price | | 42 |
| R.Dravid | run out | 1 | (6) c A.Flower b Price | | 6 |
| V.Sehwag | lbw b Streak | 74 | | | |
| S.B.Bangar | run out | 4 | not out | | 3 |
| A.Kumble | not out | 34 | (4) c Gripper b G.W.Flower | | 0 |
| J.Srinath | c Gripper b Price | 0 | | | |
| Harbhajan Singh | lbw b Streak | 9 | (8) not out | | 14 |
| Z.Khan | b Streak | 8 | | | |
| Extras | (B 9, LB 6, W 1, NB 4) | 20 | (LB 4, NB 5) | | 9 |
| **Total** | | **354** | (6 wickets) | | **126** |

| INDIA | O | M | R | W | | O | M | R | W | | FALL OF WICKETS | | | |
|---|---|---|---|---|---|---|---|---|---|---|---|---|---|---|
| Srinath | 18 | 4 | 37 | 2 | | 4 | 0 | 12 | 0 | | | Z | I | Z | I |
| Khan | 22 | 4 | 76 | 2 | | 3 | 0 | 12 | 0 | | Wkt | 1st | 1st | 2nd | 2nd |
| Bangar | 7 | 1 | 25 | 0 | | | | | | | 1st | 0 | 24 | 23 | 3 |
| Kumble | 34 | 13 | 88 | 3 | | 29.3 | 8 | 58 | 4 | | 2nd | 11 | 58 | 31 | 36 |
| Harbhajan Singh | 27.5 | 5 | 70 | 2 | (3) | 31 | 5 | 62 | 6 | | 3rd | 65 | 142 | 31 | 36 |
| Sehwag | 1 | 0 | 6 | 0 | | | | | | | 4th | 181 | 144 | 69 | 93 |
| Tendulkar | 1 | 0 | 6 | 0 | | | | | | | 5th | 246 | 264 | 95 | 103 |
| | | | | | | | | | | | 6th | 246 | 280 | 113 | 105 |
| ZIMBABWE | | | | | | | | | | | 7th | 289 | 321 | 114 | – |
| Streak | 37.2 | 11 | 92 | 4 | | 16.5 | 4 | 53 | 1 | | 8th | 310 | 331 | 129 | – |
| Watambwa | 18 | 5 | 47 | 0 | | | | | | | 9th | 310 | 340 | 142 | – |
| Friend | 19 | 2 | 75 | 1 | (2) | 3 | 0 | 17 | 0 | | 10th | 329 | 354 | 146 | – |
| Price | 50 | 16 | 108 | 3 | (3) | 19 | 9 | 24 | 2 | | | | | | |
| G.W.Flower | 5 | 0 | 17 | 0 | (4) | 6 | 3 | 22 | 2 | | | | | | |
| Gripper | | | | | (5) | 1 | 0 | 6 | 0 | | | | | | |

Umpires: E.A.R.de Silva (*Sri Lanka*) (11) and A.V.Jayaprakash (13).
Referee: J.R.Reid (*New Zealand*) (51).          **Test No. 1590/9 (1351/Z63)**

# SOUTH AFRICA v AUSTRALIA (1st Test)

At The Wanderers, Johannesburg, on 22, 23, 24 February.
Toss: Australia. Result: **AUSTRALIA** won by an innings and 360 runs.
Debuts: South Africa – A.G.Prince.

## AUSTRALIA

| | | |
|---|---|---|
| J.L.Langer | lbw b Donald | 28 |
| M.L.Hayden | c Boucher b Nel | 122 |
| R.T.Ponting | c Boucher b Nel | 39 |
| M.E.Waugh | c Boucher b Ntini | 53 |
| *S.R.Waugh | c Gibbs b Kallis | 32 |
| D.R.Martyn | c Kirsten b Kallis | 133 |
| †A.C.Gilchrist | not out | 204 |
| S.K.Warne | c McKenzie b Boje | 12 |
| B.Lee | not out | 4 |
| J.N.Gillespie | | |
| G.D.McGrath | | |
| Extras | (B 2, LB 14, W 4, NB 5) | 25 |
| **Total** | (7 wickets declared) | 652 |

## SOUTH AFRICA

| | | | | | |
|---|---|---|---|---|---|
| H.H.Gibbs | lbw b Warne | 34 | st Gilchrist b Warne | 47 |
| G.Kirsten | c Warne b McGrath | 1 | c Martyn b Gillespie | 12 |
| A.G.Prince | c Hayden b Gillespie | 49 | b Warne | 28 |
| J.H.Kallis | c Warne b Lee | 3 | c Gilchrist b McGrath | 8 |
| N.D.McKenzie | c Gillespie b McGrath | 16 | not out | 27 |
| H.H.Dippenaar | c Gilchrist b McGrath | 2 | lbw b Warne | 1 |
| *†M.V.Boucher | c Gilchrist b Lee | 23 | b Warne | 1 |
| N.Boje | c M.E.Waugh b Gillespie | 0 | c Ponting b McGrath | 5 |
| M.Ntini | c S.R.Waugh b Lee | 9 | b McGrath | 0 |
| A.Nel | lbw b Warne | 7 | c Langer b McGrath | 0 |
| A.A.Donald | not out | 3 | c Hayden b McGrath | 0 |
| Extras | (B 4, LB 3, NB 5) | 12 | (W 1, NB 3) | 4 |
| **Total** | | 159 | | 133 |

| SOUTH AFRICA | O | M | R | W | | O | M | R | W |
|---|---|---|---|---|---|---|---|---|---|
| Donald | 15.2 | 2 | 72 | 1 | | | | | |
| Ntini | 33 | 8 | 124 | 1 | | | | | |
| Kallis | 24 | 1 | 116 | 2 | | | | | |
| Nel | 30.4 | 6 | 121 | 2 | | | | | |
| Boje | 35 | 4 | 153 | 1 | | | | | |
| McKenzie | 8 | 0 | 50 | 0 | | | | | |

| AUSTRALIA | O | M | R | W | | O | M | R | W |
|---|---|---|---|---|---|---|---|---|---|
| McGrath | 14 | 6 | 28 | 3 | | 12.3 | 4 | 21 | 5 |
| Gillespie | 15 | 5 | 58 | 2 | (3) | 4 | 1 | 13 | 1 |
| Warne | 9 | 0 | 26 | 2 | (4) | 12 | 3 | 44 | 4 |
| Lee | 10 | 1 | 40 | 3 | (2) | 10 | 2 | 55 | 0 |

### FALL OF WICKETS

| | A | SA | SA |
|---|---|---|---|
| Wkt | 1st | 1st | 2nd |
| 1st | 46 | 11 | 20 |
| 2nd | 113 | 51 | 89 |
| 3rd | 224 | 55 | 98 |
| 4th | 272 | 108 | 98 |
| 5th | 293 | 113 | 107 |
| 6th | 610 | 113 | 109 |
| 7th | 643 | 116 | 122 |
| 8th | – | 146 | 122 |
| 9th | – | 155 | 122 |
| 10th | – | 159 | 133 |

Umpires: S.A.Bucknor (*West Indies*) (64) and R.E.Koertzen (28).
Referee: C.W.Smith (*West Indies*) (40).          Test No. 1591/69 (SA264/A626)

# SOUTH AFRICA v AUSTRALIA (2nd Test)

At Newlands, Cape Town, on 8, 9, 10, 11, 12 March.
Toss: South Africa. Result: **AUSTRALIA** won by four wickets.
Debuts: South Africa – G.C.Smith, A.J.Hall, D.Pretorius.

## SOUTH AFRICA

| | | | | | |
|---|---|---|---|---|---|
| H.H.Gibbs | c M.E.Waugh b Gillespie | 12 | c Ponting b Warne | 39 |
| G.Kirsten | c M.E.Waugh b Lee | 7 | lbw b Lee | 87 |
| G.C.Smith | c Ponting b McGrath | 3 | c Gilchrist b Warne | 68 |
| J.H.Kallis | c Gilchrist b McGrath | 23 | lbw b Warne | 73 |
| N.D.McKenzie | b Warne | 20 | run out | 99 |
| A.G.Prince | c Gilchrist b McGrath | 10 | c Ponting b Warne | 20 |
| *†M.V.Boucher | c Gilchrist b Lee | 26 | lbw b Gillespie | 37 |
| A.J.Hall | c Gilchrist b Gillespie | 70 | run out | 0 |
| P.R.Adams | c Warne b Gillespie | 35 | not out | 23 |
| M.Ntini | c M.E.Waugh b Warne | 14 | c Langer b Warne | 11 |
| D.Pretorius | not out | 5 | c M.E.Waugh b Warne | 0 |
| Extras | (B 4, LB 5, NB 5) | 14 | (B 8, LB 3, W 2, NB 3) | 16 |
| **Total** | | **239** | | **473** |

## AUSTRALIA

| | | | | | |
|---|---|---|---|---|---|
| J.L.Langer | b Ntini | 37 | b Pretorius | 58 |
| M.L.Hayden | c Hall b Kallis | 63 | c Boucher b Kallis | 96 |
| R.T.Ponting | c Boucher b Adams | 47 | not out | 100 |
| M.E.Waugh | c Gibbs b Ntini | 25 | c Boucher b Ntini | 16 |
| *S.R.Waugh | b Adams | 0 | b Adams | 14 |
| D.R.Martyn | c Boucher b Ntini | 2 | lbw b Adams | 0 |
| †A.C.Gilchrist | not out | 138 | c McKenzie b Kallis | 24 |
| S.K.Warne | c Kallis b Adams | 63 | not out | 15 |
| B.Lee | c Prince b Kallis | 0 | | |
| J.N.Gillespie | c Kallis b Adams | 0 | | |
| G.D.McGrath | lbw b Ntini | 2 | | |
| Extras | (B 2, LB 1, W 2) | 5 | (LB 6, NB 5) | 11 |
| **Total** | | **382** | (6 wickets) | **334** |

| AUSTRALIA | O | M | R | W | O | M | R | W |
|---|---|---|---|---|---|---|---|---|
| McGrath | 20 | 4 | 42 | 3 | 25 | 7 | 56 | 0 |
| Gillespie | 15 | 4 | 52 | 3 | 29 | 10 | 81 | 1 |
| Lee | 16 | 1 | 65 | 2 | (4) 22 | 3 | 99 | 1 |
| Warne | 28 | 10 | 70 | 2 | (3) 70 | 15 | 161 | 6 |
| M.E.Waugh | 1 | 0 | 1 | 0 | 9 | 3 | 34 | 0 |
| Martyn | | | | | 4 | 0 | 15 | 0 |
| S.R.Waugh | | | | | 3 | 0 | 16 | 0 |
| **SOUTH AFRICA** | | | | | | | | |
| Ntini | 22.5 | 5 | 93 | 4 | 24 | 4 | 90 | 1 |
| Pretorius | 11 | 1 | 72 | 0 | 14 | 5 | 60 | 1 |
| Kallis | 16 | 1 | 65 | 2 | (5) 17 | 2 | 68 | 2 |
| Hall | 11 | 1 | 47 | 0 | 3 | 0 | 6 | 0 |
| Adams | 20 | 1 | 102 | 4 | (3) 21.1 | 0 | 104 | 2 |

| | | FALL OF WICKETS | | | |
|---|---|---|---|---|---|
| | | SA | A | SA | A |
| Wkt | 1st | 1st | 2nd | 2nd |
| 1st | 15 | 67 | 84 | 102 |
| 2nd | 18 | 130 | 183 | 201 |
| 3rd | 25 | 162 | 254 | 251 |
| 4th | 70 | 168 | 284 | 268 |
| 5th | 73 | 176 | 350 | 268 |
| 6th | 92 | 185 | 431 | 305 |
| 7th | 147 | 317 | 433 | – |
| 8th | 216 | 338 | 440 | – |
| 9th | 229 | 343 | 464 | – |
| 10th | 239 | 382 | 473 | – |

Umpires: S.A.Bucknor (*West Indies*) (65) and R.E.Koertzen (29).
Referee: C.W.Smith (*West Indies*) (41).          Test No. 1592/70 (SA265/A627)

# SOUTH AFRICA v AUSTRALIA (3rd Test)

At Kingsmead, Durban, on 15, 16, 17, 18 March.
Toss: South Africa. Result: **SOUTH AFRICA** won by five wickets.
Debuts: None.

## AUSTRALIA

| | | | | | |
|---|---|---|---|---|---|
| J.L.Langer | c Kirsten b Terbrugge | 11 | | c Boucher b Terbrugge | 18 |
| M.L.Hayden | c McKenzie b Kallis | 28 | | c Prince b Terbrugge | 0 |
| R.T.Ponting | run out | 89 | | c Terbrugge b Ntini | 34 |
| M.E.Waugh | c Smith b Kallis | 45 | | b Kallis | 30 |
| *S.R.Waugh | c Boucher b Adams | 7 | | c Kallis b Ntini | 42 |
| D.R.Martyn | b Terbrugge | 11 | | c Boucher b Kallis | 0 |
| †A.C.Gilchrist | c Smith b Adams | 91 | | c Boucher b Kallis | 16 |
| S.K.Warne | c Boucher b Ntini | 26 | | c McKenzie b Adams | 13 |
| B.Lee | b Ntini | 0 | (10) | not out | 23 |
| J.N.Gillespie | c Boucher b Hall | 1 | (9) | c Kallis b Adams | 3 |
| G.D.McGrath | not out | 4 | | b Ntini | 0 |
| Extras | (W 2) | 2 | | (B 1, LB 3, W 1, NB 2) | 7 |
| **Total** | | **315** | | | **186** |

## SOUTH AFRICA

| | | | | | |
|---|---|---|---|---|---|
| G.Kirsten | c Gilchrist b Lee | 21 | (2) | run out | 64 |
| H.H.Gibbs | c Gilchrist b Gillespie | 51 | (1) | c Martyn b M.E.Waugh | 104 |
| P.R.Adams | c Hayden b Lee | 6 | | | |
| G.C.Smith | c Gilchrist b McGrath | 1 | (3) | c Gilchrist b M.E.Waugh | 42 |
| J.H.Kallis | c and b Warne | 16 | (4) | not out | 61 |
| N.D.McKenzie | c Martyn b Lee | 25 | (5) | c Hayden b Warne | 4 |
| A.G.Prince | c Lee b Warne | 0 | (6) | c M.E.Waugh b Warne | 48 |
| *†M.V.Boucher | c and b Warne | 0 | (7) | not out | 8 |
| A.J.Hall | not out | 27 | | | |
| M.Ntini | c McGrath b Warne | 14 | | | |
| D.J.Terbrugge | c Gilchrist b Lee | 0 | | | |
| Extras | (LB 1, W 1, NB 4) | 6 | | (LB 2, W 2, NB 5) | 9 |
| **Total** | | **167** | | (5 wickets) | **340** |

| SOUTH AFRICA | O | M | R | W | | O | M | R | W | | FALL OF WICKETS | | | |
|---|---|---|---|---|---|---|---|---|---|---|---|---|---|---|
| | | | | | | | | | | | A | SA | A | SA |
| Ntini | 20 | 3 | 87 | 2 | | 17 | 2 | 65 | 3 | *Wkt* | *1st* | *1st* | *2nd* | *2nd* |
| Terbrugge | 16 | 2 | 61 | 2 | | 4 | 1 | 21 | 2 | 1st | 11 | 48 | 4 | 142 |
| Kallis | 20 | 3 | 95 | 2 | (5) | 11 | 2 | 29 | 3 | 2nd | 61 | 74 | 19 | 216 |
| Hall | 9.1 | 2 | 35 | 1 | (3) | 4 | 1 | 20 | 0 | 3rd | 169 | 75 | 77 | 218 |
| Adams | 9 | 0 | 37 | 1 | (4) | 13 | 0 | 47 | 2 | 4th | 178 | 85 | 90 | 232 |
| | | | | | | | | | | 5th | 182 | 109 | 90 | 331 |
| **AUSTRALIA** | | | | | | | | | | 6th | 230 | 119 | 114 | – |
| McGrath | 11 | 4 | 26 | 1 | | 28 | 11 | 54 | 0 | 7th | 287 | 119 | 128 | – |
| Lee | 17.2 | 1 | 82 | 4 | | 20 | 2 | 75 | 0 | 8th | 289 | 148 | 150 | – |
| Gillespie | 14 | 6 | 25 | 1 | | 15 | 2 | 58 | 0 | 9th | 311 | 167 | 186 | – |
| Warne | 13 | 4 | 33 | 4 | | 30 | 6 | 108 | 2 | 10th | 315 | 167 | 186 | – |
| M.E.Waugh | | | | | | 11.5 | 1 | 43 | 2 | | | | | |

Umpires: D.L.Orchard (27) and S.Venkataraghavan (*India*) (52).
Referee: C.W.Smith (*West Indies*) (42).                Test No. 1593/71 (SA266/A628)

# SOUTH AFRICA v AUSTRALIA 2001-02

## SOUTH AFRICA – BATTING AND FIELDING

| | M | I | NO | HS | Runs | Avge | 100 | 50 | Ct/St |
|---|---|---|---|---|---|---|---|---|---|
| A.J.Hall | 2 | 3 | 1 | 70 | 97 | 48.50 | – | 1 | 1 |
| H.H.Gibbs | 3 | 6 | – | 104 | 287 | 47.83 | 1 | 1 | 2 |
| N.D.McKenzie | 3 | 6 | 1 | 99 | 191 | 38.20 | – | 1 | 4 |
| J.H.Kallis | 3 | 6 | 1 | 73 | 184 | 36.80 | – | 2 | 4 |
| G.Kirsten | 3 | 6 | – | 87 | 192 | 32.00 | – | 2 | 2 |
| P.R.Adams | 2 | 3 | 1 | 35 | 64 | 32.00 | – | – | – |
| G.C.Smith | 2 | 4 | – | 68 | 114 | 28.50 | – | 1 | 2 |
| A.G.Prince | 3 | 6 | – | 49 | 155 | 25.83 | – | – | 2 |
| M.V.Boucher | 3 | 6 | 1 | 37 | 95 | 19.00 | – | – | 13 |
| M.Ntini | 3 | 5 | – | 14 | 48 | 9.60 | – | – | – |

*Played in one Test:* N.Boje 0, 5; H.H.Dippenaar 2, 1; A.A.Donald 3*, 0; D.Pretorius 5*, 0; A.Nel 7, 0; D.J.Terbrugge 0 (1 ct).

## SOUTH AFRICA – BOWLING

| | O | M | R | W | Avge | Best | 5wI | 10wM |
|---|---|---|---|---|---|---|---|---|
| D.J.Terbrugge | 20 | 3 | 82 | 4 | 20.50 | 2- 21 | – | – |
| P.R.Adams | 63.1 | 1 | 290 | 10 | 29.00 | 4-102 | – | – |
| J.H.Kallis | 88 | 9 | 373 | 11 | 33.90 | 3- 29 | – | – |
| M.Ntini | 116.5 | 22 | 459 | 11 | 41.72 | 4- 93 | – | – |
| A.Nel | 30.4 | 6 | 121 | 2 | 60.50 | 2-121 | – | – |

*Also bowled:* N.Boje 35-4-153-1; A.A.Donald 15.2-2-72-1; A.J.Hall 27.1-4-108-1; N.D.McKenzie 8-0-50-0; D.Pretorius 25-6-132-1.

## AUSTRALIA – BATTING AND FIELDING

| | M | I | NO | HS | Runs | Avge | 100 | 50 | Ct/St |
|---|---|---|---|---|---|---|---|---|---|
| A.C.Gilchrist | 3 | 5 | 2 | 204* | 473 | 157.66 | 2 | 1 | 13/1 |
| R.T.Ponting | 3 | 5 | – | 100* | 309 | 77.25 | 1 | 1 | 4 |
| M.L.Hayden | 3 | 5 | – | 122 | 309 | 61.80 | 1 | 2 | 4 |
| M.E.Waugh | 3 | 5 | – | 53 | 169 | 33.80 | – | 1 | 6 |
| S.K.Warne | 3 | 5 | 1 | 63 | 129 | 32.25 | – | 1 | 5 |
| J.L.Langer | 3 | 5 | – | 58 | 152 | 30.40 | – | 1 | 2 |
| D.R.Martyn | 3 | 5 | – | 133 | 146 | 29.20 | 1 | – | 3 |
| S.R.Waugh | 3 | 5 | – | 42 | 95 | 19.00 | – | – | 1 |
| B.Lee | 3 | 4 | 2 | 23* | 27 | 13.50 | – | – | 1 |
| G.D.McGrath | 3 | 3 | 1 | 4* | 6 | 3.00 | – | – | 1 |
| J.N.Gillespie | 3 | 3 | – | 3 | 4 | 1.33 | – | – | 1 |

## AUSTRALIA – BOWLING

| | O | M | R | W | Avge | Best | 5wI | 10wM |
|---|---|---|---|---|---|---|---|---|
| G.D.McGrath | 110.3 | 36 | 227 | 12 | 18.91 | 5- 21 | 1 | – |
| S.K.Warne | 162 | 38 | 442 | 20 | 22.10 | 6-161 | 1 | – |
| J.N.Gillespie | 92 | 28 | 287 | 8 | 35.87 | 3- 52 | – | – |
| M.E.Waugh | 21.5 | 4 | 78 | 2 | 39.00 | 2- 43 | – | – |
| B.Lee | 95.2 | 10 | 416 | 10 | 41.60 | 4- 82 | – | – |

*Also bowled:* D.R.Martyn 4-0-15-0; S.R.Waugh 3-0-16-0.

# PAKISTAN v SRI LANKA
## (Asian Test Championship – Final)

At Gaddafi Stadium, Lahore, on 6, 7, 8, 9, 10 March.
Toss: Sri Lanka. Result: **SRI LANKA** won by eight wickets.
Debuts: None.

### PAKISTAN

| | | | | |
|---|---|--:|---|--:|
| Shahid Afridi | run out | 9 | st Sangakkara b Muralitharan | 70 |
| Taufiq Umar | c Samaraweera b Vaas | 6 | b Vaas | 19 |
| Younis Khan | b Muralitharan | 46 | c Samaraweera b Zoysa | 19 |
| Inzamam-ul-Haq | c Jayasuriya b Fernando | 29 | lbw b Vaas | 99 |
| Yousuf Youhana | c Sangakkara b Fernando | 6 | c Atapattu b Muralitharan | 7 |
| Abdul Razzaq | lbw b Vaas | 24 | lbw b Muralitharan | 5 |
| Shoaib Malik | c Sangakkara b Fernando | 13 | c Samaraweera b Zoysa | 21 |
| †Rashid Latif | c Sangakkara b Muralitharan | 36 | c Muralitharan b Vaas | 2 |
| *Waqar Younis | b Muralitharan | 19 | c Tillekeratne b Muralitharan | 25 |
| Shoaib Akhtar | lbw b Muralitharan | 15 | not out | 4 |
| Mohammad Sami | not out | 0 | c Sangakkara b Vaas | 0 |
| Extras | (LB 4, W 1, NB 26) | 31 | (B 12, LB 2, W 1, NB 39) | 54 |
| **Total** | | **234** | | **325** |

### SRI LANKA

| | | | | |
|---|---|--:|---|--:|
| M.S Atapattu | c Shoaib Akhtar b Waqar | 0 | c Rashid b Sami | 1 |
| *S.T.Jayasuriya | c Rashid b Razzaq | 88 | c Youhana b Shoaib Akhtar | 1 |
| †K.Sangakkara | b Younis Khan b Razzaq | 230 | not out | 14 |
| D.P.M.deS.Jayawardena | c Inzamam b Sami | 68 | not out | 12 |
| R.P.Arnold | b Shoaib Akhtar | 44 | | |
| W.P.U.J.C.Vaas | c Taufiq b Razzaq | 43 | | |
| H.P.Tillekeratne | not out | 19 | | |
| T.T.Samaraweera | c Rashid b Shoaib Akhtar | 8 | | |
| T.C.B.Fernando | lbw b Sami | 7 | | |
| D.N.T.Zoysa | lbw b Sami | 0 | | |
| M.Muralitharan | b Sami | 0 | | |
| Extras | (B 1, LB 7, W 5, NB 8) | 21 | (LB 1, W 2, NB 2) | 5 |
| **Total** | | **528** | (2 wickets) | **33** |

| SRI LANKA | O | M | R | W | O | M | R | W |
|---|--:|--:|--:|--:|--:|--:|--:|--:|
| Vaas | 17 | 2 | 62 | 2 | 22.5 | 3 | 85 | 4 |
| Zoysa | 9 | 2 | 29 | 0 | 21 | 3 | 54 | 2 |
| Fernando | 16 | 1 | 84 | 3 | 14 | 2 | 68 | 0 |
| Muralitharan | 25 | 9 | 55 | 4 | 34 | 8 | 72 | 4 |
| Jayasuriya | | | | | 1 | 0 | 7 | 0 |
| Samaraweera | | | | | 9 | 1 | 25 | 0 |

| PAKISTAN | O | M | R | W | | O | M | R | W |
|---|--:|--:|--:|--:|---|--:|--:|--:|--:|
| Waqar Younis | 30 | 4 | 123 | 1 | | | | | |
| Shoaib Akhtar | 27 | 4 | 114 | 2 | (1) | 3.2 | 0 | 17 | 1 |
| Mohammad Sami | 36.5 | 4 | 120 | 4 | (2) | 3 | 0 | 15 | 1 |
| Abdul Razzaq | 29 | 5 | 82 | 3 | | | | | |
| Shoaib Malik | 14 | 3 | 55 | 0 | | | | | |
| Shahid Afridi | 3 | 0 | 26 | 0 | | | | | |

**FALL OF WICKETS**

| | P | SL | P | SL |
|---|--:|--:|--:|--:|
| Wkt | 1st | 1st | 2nd | 2nd |
| 1st | 18 | 0 | 31 | 1 |
| 2nd | 18 | 203 | 66 | 14 |
| 3rd | 104 | 376 | 150 | – |
| 4th | 108 | 447 | 166 | – |
| 5th | 127 | 447 | 181 | – |
| 6th | 147 | 501 | 281 | – |
| 7th | 176 | 519 | 285 | – |
| 8th | 216 | 528 | 291 | – |
| 9th | 219 | 528 | 321 | – |
| 10th | 234 | 528 | 325 | – |

Umpires: Athar Zaidi (8) and D.J.Harper (*Australia*) (17).
Referee: A.M.Ebrahim (*Zimbabwe*) (4).      **Test No. 1594/28 (P284/SL122)**

# NEW ZEALAND v ENGLAND (1st Test)

At Lancaster Park, Christchurch, on 13, 14, 15, 16 March.
Toss: New Zealand. Result: **ENGLAND** won by 98 runs.
Debuts: New Zealand – I.G.Butler.

## ENGLAND

| | | | | | |
|---|---|---|---|---|---|
| M.E.Trescothick | c Parore b Cairns | 0 | c Vettori b Butler | | 33 |
| M.P.Vaughan | c Parore b Cairns | 27 | b Butler | | 0 |
| M.A.Butcher | c Butler b Cairns | 34 | hit wicket b Butler | | 34 |
| *N.Hussain | lbw b Drum | 106 | c Parore b Drum | | 11 |
| G.P.Thorpe | c Fleming b Drum | 17 | not out | | 200 |
| M.R.Ramprakash | c Parore b Astle | 31 | b Drum | | 11 |
| A.Flintoff | lbw b Astle | 0 | c sub (M.N.McKenzie) b Astle | | 137 |
| †J.S.Foster | lbw b Drum | 19 | not out | | 22 |
| A.F.Giles | c Drum b Butler | 8 | | | |
| A.R.Caddick | lbw b Butler | 0 | | | |
| M.J.Hoggard | not out | 0 | | | |
| Extras | (B 1, LB 10, NB 9) | 20 | (B 6, LB 4, NB 10) | | 20 |
| **Total** | | **228** | (6 wickets declared) | | **468** |

## NEW ZEALAND

| | | | | | |
|---|---|---|---|---|---|
| M.H.Richardson | lbw b Hoggard | 2 | c Foster b Caddick | | 76 |
| M.J.Horne | c Thorpe b Hoggard | 14 | c Foster b Caddick | | 4 |
| D.L.Vettori | c Foster b Hoggard | 42 | (8) c Flintoff b Giles | | 12 |
| L.Vincent | b Hoggard | 12 | (3) c Butcher b Caddick | | 0 |
| *S.P.Fleming | c Giles b Caddick | 12 | (4) c Foster b Flintoff | | 48 |
| N.J.Astle | lbw b Hoggard | 10 | (5) c Foster b Hoggard | | 222 |
| C.D.McMillan | c Vaughan b Hoggard | 40 | (6) c and b Caddick | | 24 |
| C.L.Cairns | c Flintoff b Caddick | 0 | (11) not out | | 23 |
| †A.C.Parore | lbw b Caddick | 7 | (7) b Caddick | | 1 |
| C.J.Drum | not out | 2 | (9) lbw b Flintoff | | 0 |
| I.G.Butler | c Hussain b Hoggard | 0 | (10) c Foster b Caddick | | 4 |
| Extras | (LB 5, NB 8) | 13 | (B 9, LB 11, W 1, NB 16) | | 37 |
| **Total** | | **147** | | | **451** |

| NEW ZEALAND | O | M | R | W | | O | M | R | W | FALL OF WICKETS | | | | |
|---|---|---|---|---|---|---|---|---|---|---|---|---|---|---|
| | | | | | | | | | | | E | NZ | E | NZ |
| Cairns | 15 | 4 | 58 | 3 | (3) | 4 | 0 | 8 | 0 | Wkt | 1st | 1st | 2nd | 2nd |
| Drum | 20.2 | 8 | 36 | 3 | (1) | 32 | 6 | 130 | 2 | 1st | 0 | 4 | 11 | 42 |
| Butler | 16 | 2 | 59 | 2 | (2) | 23 | 2 | 137 | 3 | 2nd | 0 | 50 | 53 | 53 |
| Astle | 18 | 10 | 32 | 2 | (5) | 5.4 | 0 | 20 | 1 | 3rd | 46 | 65 | 81 | 119 |
| Vettori | 9 | 1 | 26 | 0 | (6) | 22 | 3 | 97 | 0 | 4th | 83 | 79 | 85 | 189 |
| McMillan | 3 | 1 | 6 | 0 | (4) | 10 | 0 | 66 | 0 | 5th | 139 | 93 | 106 | 242 |
| | | | | | | | | | | 6th | 151 | 117 | 387 | 252 |
| ENGLAND | | | | | | | | | | 7th | 196 | 117 | – | 300 |
| Caddick | 18 | 8 | 50 | 4 | | 25 | 8 | 122 | 6 | 8th | 214 | 117 | – | 301 |
| Hoggard | 21.2 | 7 | 63 | 6 | | 24.3 | 5 | 142 | 1 | 9th | 226 | 146 | – | 333 |
| Flintoff | 12 | 2 | 29 | 0 | (4) | 16 | 1 | 94 | 2 | 10th | 228 | 147 | – | 451 |
| Giles | | | | | (3) | 28 | 6 | 73 | 1 | | | | | |

Umpires: B.F.Bowden (3) and E.A.R.de Silva (*Sri Lanka*) (12).
Referee: J.L.Hendriks (*West Indies*) (17).                    Test No. 1595/83 (NZ294/E790)

# NEW ZEALAND v ENGLAND (2nd Test)

At Basin Reserve, Wellington, on 21 (*no play*), 22, 23, 24, 25 March.
Toss: New Zealand. Result: **MATCH DRAWN**.
Debuts: None

## ENGLAND

| | | | | | |
|---|---|---|---|---|---|
| M.E.Trescothick | c Vincent b Vettori | 37 | | c Richardson b Vettori | 88 |
| M.P.Vaughan | c Fleming b Drum | 7 | | c Drum b Vettori | 34 |
| M.A.Butcher | c Astle b Drum | 47 | | c Martin b Drum | 60 |
| *N.Hussain | c Astle b Vettori | 66 | (5) | not out | 13 |
| G.P.Thorpe | c Fleming b Martin | 11 | (6) | not out | 1 |
| M.R.Ramprakash | b Butler | 24 | | | |
| A.Flintoff | c Drum b Butler | 2 | (4) | c and b Vettori | 75 |
| †J.S.Foster | not out | 25 | | | |
| A.F.Giles | c McMillan b Butler | 10 | | | |
| A.R.Caddick | c Richardson b Martin | 10 | | | |
| M.J.Hoggard | c Parore b Butler | 7 | | | |
| Extras | (B 4, LB 2, W 6, NB 22) | 34 | | (B 5, LB 13, NB 4) | 22 |
| **Total** | | **280** | | (4 wickets declared) | **293** |

## NEW ZEALAND

| | | | | | |
|---|---|---|---|---|---|
| M.H.Richardson | c Giles b Caddick | 60 | | c Thorpe b Giles | 4 |
| M.J.Horne | b Caddick | 8 | | c Foster b Flintoff | 38 |
| L.Vincent | c Thorpe b Giles | 57 | | lbw b Hoggard | 71 |
| *S.P.Fleming | c Thorpe b Caddick | 3 | | b Hoggard | 11 |
| N.J.Astle | c Hussain b Giles | 4 | | not out | 11 |
| C.D.McMillan | lbw b Caddick | 41 | | not out | 17 |
| †A.C.Parore | c Ramprakash b Giles | 0 | | | |
| D.L.Vettori | c Thorpe b Caddick | 11 | | | |
| C.J.Drum | c Trescothick b Giles | 2 | | | |
| I.G.Butler | c Foster b Caddick | 12 | | | |
| C.S.Martin | not out | 0 | | | |
| Extras | (B 2, LB 9, NB 9) | 20 | | (B 3, LB 1, NB 2) | 6 |
| **Total** | | **218** | | (4 wickets) | **158** |

| NEW ZEALAND | O | M | R | W | | O | M | R | W | | FALL OF WICKETS | | | | |
|---|---|---|---|---|---|---|---|---|---|---|---|---|---|---|---|
| Butler | 18.3 | 2 | 60 | 4 | | 6 | 0 | 32 | 0 | | | E | NZ | E | NZ |
| Drum | 24 | 6 | 85 | 2 | | 16 | 2 | 78 | 1 | | Wkt | 1st | 1st | 2nd | 2nd |
| Martin | 17 | 3 | 58 | 2 | (5) | 7 | 1 | 40 | 0 | | 1st | 26 | 16 | 79 | 28 |
| Vettori | 25 | 3 | 62 | 2 | (3) | 24 | 1 | 90 | 3 | | 2nd | 63 | 135 | 194 | 65 |
| Astle | 1 | 0 | 1 | 0 | (4) | 9 | 4 | 18 | 0 | | 3rd | 133 | 138 | 209 | 128 |
| McMillan | 3 | 0 | 8 | 0 | | 3 | 0 | 17 | 0 | | 4th | 163 | 143 | 291 | 131 |
| | | | | | | | | | | | 5th | 221 | 147 | – | – |
| **ENGLAND** | | | | | | | | | | | 6th | 221 | 149 | – | – |
| Caddick | 28.3 | 8 | 63 | 6 | | 17 | 6 | 31 | 0 | | 7th | 223 | 178 | – | – |
| Hoggard | 13 | 5 | 32 | 0 | | 13 | 4 | 31 | 2 | | 8th | 238 | 201 | – | – |
| Giles | 37 | 3 | 103 | 4 | | 33 | 11 | 53 | 1 | | 9th | 250 | 207 | – | – |
| Flintoff | 10 | 4 | 9 | 0 | | 16 | 6 | 24 | 1 | | 10th | 280 | 218 | – | – |
| Vaughan | | | | | | 5 | 1 | 15 | 0 | | | | | | |

Umpires: R.S.Dunne (39) and D.B.Hair (*Australia*) (44).
Referee: J.L.Hendriks (*West Indies*) (18).  **Test No. 1596/84 (NZ295/E791)**

# NEW ZEALAND v ENGLAND (3rd Test)

At Eden Park, Auckland, on 30, 31 (*no play*) March, 1, 2, 3 April.
Toss: New Zealand. Result: **NEW ZEALAND** won by 78 runs.
Debuts: New Zealand – A.R.Adams.

## NEW ZEALAND

| | | | | | | |
|---|---|---|---|---|---|---|
| M.H.Richardson | b Caddick | 5 | | c sub (U.Afzaal) b Butcher | 25 |
| L.Vincent | b Caddick | 10 | (9) | c Giles b Hoggard | 10 |
| *S.P.Fleming | c Ramprakash b Hoggard | 1 | | b Hoggard | 1 |
| C.Z.Harris | lbw b Flintoff | 71 | | lbw b Butcher | 43 |
| N.J.Astle | c Thorpe b Caddick | 2 | | c Butcher b Flintoff | 65 |
| C.D.McMillan | lbw b Caddick | 41 | | not out | 50 |
| †A.C.Parore | c sub (U.Afzaal) b Flintoff | 45 | (2) | c Thorpe b Hoggard | 36 |
| D.L.Vettori | lbw b Hoggard | 3 | | c Foster b Flintoff | 0 |
| A.R.Adams | c Giles b Flintoff | 7 | (7) | b Flintoff | 11 |
| D.R.Tuffey | c Butcher b Hoggard | 0 | | b Hoggard | 5 |
| C.J.Drum | not out | 2 | | | |
| Extras | (LB 10, NB 5) | 15 | | (B 3, LB 9, W 1, NB 10) | 23 |
| **Total** | | **202** | | **(9 wickets declared)** | **269** |

## ENGLAND

| | | | | | | |
|---|---|---|---|---|---|---|
| M.E.Trescothick | lbw b Tuffey | 0 | | b Drum | 14 |
| M.P.Vaughan | c Parore b Adams | 27 | | c Fleming b Drum | 36 |
| M.A.Butcher | c Richardson b Tuffey | 0 | | c sub (B.G.K.Walker) b Astle | 35 |
| *N.Hussain | c Fleming b Drum | 2 | | c and b Adams | 82 |
| G.P.Thorpe | b Tuffey | 42 | | c Parore b Tuffey | 3 |
| M.R.Ramprakash | c Parore b Tuffey | 9 | (7) | b Tuffey | 2 |
| A.Flintoff | c Parore b Adams | 29 | (6) | b Tuffey | 0 |
| †J.S.Foster | not out | 16 | | c Parore b Adams | 23 |
| A.F.Giles | lbw b Tuffey | 0 | | not out | 21 |
| A.R.Caddick | b Tuffey | 20 | | c Vettori b Drum | 4 |
| M.J.Hoggard | c Fleming b Adams | 0 | | c Astle b Adams | 2 |
| Extras | (B 1, LB 11, NB 3) | 15 | | (B 1, LB 8, NB 2) | 11 |
| **Total** | | **160** | | | **233** |

| ENGLAND | O | M | R | W | O | M | R | W |
|---|---|---|---|---|---|---|---|---|
| Caddick | 25 | 5 | 70 | 4 | 11 | 3 | 41 | 0 |
| Hoggard | 28.2 | 10 | 66 | 3 | 19.1 | 3 | 68 | 4 |
| Flintoff | 16 | 6 | 49 | 3 | 23 | 1 | 108 | 3 |
| Butcher | 5 | 3 | 6 | 0 | 9 | 2 | 34 | 2 |
| Giles | 1 | 0 | 1 | 0 | 2 | 0 | 6 | 0 |

| NEW ZEALAND | O | M | R | W | O | M | R | W |
|---|---|---|---|---|---|---|---|---|
| Tuffey | 19 | 6 | 54 | 6 | 16 | 3 | 62 | 3 |
| Drum | 10 | 3 | 45 | 1 | 10 | 0 | 52 | 3 |
| Adams | 15.4 | 2 | 44 | 3 | 16 | 3 | 61 | 3 |
| McMillan | 1 | 0 | 5 | 0 | | | | |
| Astle | | | | | (4) 19 | 6 | 44 | 1 |
| Vettori | | | | | (5) 2 | 0 | 5 | 0 |

### FALL OF WICKETS

| | NZ | E | NZ | E |
|---|---|---|---|---|
| Wkt | 1st | 1st | 2nd | 2nd |
| 1st | 12 | 0 | 53 | 23 |
| 2nd | 17 | 0 | 55 | 73 |
| 3rd | 17 | 11 | 91 | 122 |
| 4th | 19 | 60 | 166 | 125 |
| 5th | 86 | 75 | 217 | 125 |
| 6th | 172 | 118 | 232 | 155 |
| 7th | 191 | 122 | 235 | 204 |
| 8th | 198 | 124 | 262 | 207 |
| 9th | 200 | 159 | 269 | 230 |
| 10th | 202 | 160 | – | 233 |

Umpires: D.B.Cowie (22) and S.Venkataraghavan (*India*) (53).
Referee: J.L.Hendriks (*West Indies*) (19).   **Test No. 1597/85 (NZ296/E792)**

# NEW ZEALAND v ENGLAND 2001-02

### NEW ZEALAND – BATTING AND FIELDING

|                 | M | I | NO | HS  | Runs | Avge  | 100 | 50 | Ct/St |
|-----------------|---|---|----|-----|------|-------|-----|----|-------|
| N.J.Astle       | 3 | 6 | 1  | 222 | 314  | 62.80 | 1   | 1  | 3     |
| C.D.McMillan    | 3 | 6 | 2  | 50* | 213  | 53.25 | –   | 1  | 1     |
| M.H.Richardson  | 3 | 6 | –  | 76  | 172  | 28.66 | –   | 2  | 3     |
| L.Vincent       | 3 | 6 | –  | 71  | 160  | 26.66 | –   | 2  | 1     |
| A.C.Parore      | 3 | 5 | –  | 45  | 82   | 16.40 | –   | –  | 10    |
| M.J.Horne       | 2 | 4 | –  | 38  | 64   | 16.00 | –   | –  | –     |
| D.L.Vettori     | 3 | 5 | –  | 42  | 68   | 13.60 | –   | –  | 3     |
| S.P.Fleming     | 3 | 6 | –  | 48  | 76   | 12.66 | –   | –  | 6     |
| I.G.Butler      | 2 | 3 | –  | 12  | 16   | 5.33  | –   | –  | 1     |
| C.J.Drum        | 3 | 4 | 2  | 2*  | 6    | 3.00  | –   | –  | 3     |

*Played in one Test:* A.R.Adams 7, 11 (1 ct); C.L.Cairns 0, 23*; C.Z.Harris 71, 43; C.S.Martin 0* (1 ct); D.R.Tuffey 0, 5.

### NEW ZEALAND – BOWLING

|              | O     | M  | R   | W  | Avge  | Best | 5wI | 10wM |
|--------------|-------|----|-----|----|-------|------|-----|------|
| D.R.Tuffey   | 35    | 9  | 116 | 9  | 12.88 | 6-54 | 1   | –    |
| A.R.Adams    | 31.4  | 6  | 105 | 6  | 17.50 | 3-44 | –   | –    |
| C.L.Cairns   | 19    | 4  | 66  | 3  | 22.00 | 3-58 | –   | –    |
| N.J.Astle    | 52.4  | 20 | 115 | 4  | 28.75 | 2-32 | –   | –    |
| I.G.Butler   | 63.3  | 6  | 288 | 9  | 32.00 | 4-60 | –   | –    |
| C.J.Drum     | 112.2 | 25 | 426 | 12 | 35.50 | 3-36 | –   | –    |
| C.S.Martin   | 24    | 4  | 98  | 2  | 49.00 | 2-58 | –   | –    |
| D.L.Vettori  | 82    | 8  | 280 | 5  | 56.00 | 3-90 | –   | –    |

*Also bowled:* C.D.McMillan 20-1-102-0.

### ENGLAND – BATTING AND FIELDING

|                 | M | I | NO | HS   | Runs | Avge  | 100 | 50 | Ct/St |
|-----------------|---|---|----|------|------|-------|-----|----|-------|
| G.P.Thorpe      | 3 | 6 | 2  | 200* | 274  | 68.50 | 1   | –  | 7     |
| N.Hussain       | 3 | 6 | 1  | 106  | 280  | 56.00 | 1   | 2  | 2     |
| J.S.Foster      | 3 | 5 | 3  | 25*  | 105  | 52.50 | –   | –  | 9     |
| A.Flintoff      | 3 | 6 | –  | 137  | 243  | 40.50 | 1   | 1  | 3     |
| M.A.Butcher     | 3 | 6 | –  | 66   | 176  | 29.33 | –   | 1  | 2     |
| M.E.Trescothick | 3 | 6 | –  | 88   | 172  | 28.66 | –   | 1  | 1     |
| M.P.Vaughan     | 3 | 6 | –  | 36   | 131  | 21.83 | –   | –  | 1     |
| M.R.Ramprakash  | 3 | 5 | –  | 31   | 77   | 15.40 | –   | –  | 2     |
| A.F.Giles       | 3 | 4 | 1  | 21*  | 39   | 13.00 | –   | –  | 4     |
| A.R.Caddick     | 3 | 4 | –  | 20   | 34   | 8.50  | –   | –  | 1     |
| M.J.Hoggard     | 3 | 4 | 1  | 7    | 9    | 3.00  | –   | –  | –     |

### ENGLAND – BOWLING

|              | O     | M  | R   | W  | Avge  | Best  | 5wI | 10wM |
|--------------|-------|----|-----|----|-------|-------|-----|------|
| A.R.Caddick  | 124.3 | 37 | 377 | 19 | 19.84 | 6- 63 | 2   | –    |
| M.A.Butcher  | 14    | 5  | 40  | 2  | 20.00 | 2- 34 | –   | –    |
| M.J.Hoggard  | 119.2 | 34 | 402 | 17 | 23.65 | 7- 63 | 1   | –    |
| A.Flintoff   | 93    | 20 | 313 | 9  | 34.77 | 3- 49 | –   | –    |
| A.F.Giles    | 100   | 20 | 236 | 6  | 39.33 | 4-103 | –   | –    |

*Also bowled:* M.P.Vaughan 5-1-15-0.

# WEST INDIES v INDIA (1st Test)

At Bourda, Georgetown, Guyana, on 11, 12, 13, 14, 15 (*no play*) April.
Toss: West Indies. Result: **MATCH DRAWN**.
Debuts: West Indies – A.Sanford.

## WEST INDIES

| | | |
|---|---|---|
| C.H.Gayle | c Dasgupta b Srinath | 12 |
| S.C.Williams | lbw b Srinath | 13 |
| R.R.Sarwan | c Khan b Sarandeep | 53 |
| B.C.Lara | c Dasgupta b Srinath | 0 |
| *C.L.Hooper | c Saraندeep b Kumble | 233 |
| S.Chanderpaul | lbw b Khan | 140 |
| †J.R.Murray | lbw b Khan | 0 |
| M.V.Nagamootoo | not out | 15 |
| M.Dillon | lbw b Bangar | 0 |
| A.Sanford | lbw b Kumble | 1 |
| C.E.Cuffy | run out | 0 |
| Extras | (B 1, LB 4, W 3, NB 26) | 34 |
| **Total** | | **501** |

## INDIA

| | | |
|---|---|---|
| S.S.Das | b Sanford | 33 |
| †D.Dasgupta | lbw b Cuffy | 0 |
| *S.C.Ganguly | c Nagamootoo b Dillon | 5 |
| S.R.Tendulkar | lbw b Nagamootoo | 79 |
| R.Dravid | not out | 144 |
| V.V.S.Laxman | c Gayle b Cuffy | 69 |
| S.B.Bangar | lbw b Cuffy | 0 |
| A.Kumble | c Nagamootoo b Sanford | 3 |
| Sarandeep Singh | not out | 39 |
| J.Srinath | | |
| Z.Khan | | |
| Extras | (B 4, LB 12, W 2, NB 5) | 23 |
| **Total** | (7 wickets) | **395** |

| INDIA | O | M | R | W |
|---|---|---|---|---|
| Srinath | 33 | 8 | 91 | 3 |
| Khan | 32 | 9 | 97 | 2 |
| Bangar | 27 | 6 | 63 | 2 |
| Kumble | 45.1 | 7 | 145 | 2 |
| Ganguly | 2 | 1 | 2 | 0 |
| Sarandeep Singh | 21 | 5 | 80 | 1 |
| Tendulkar | 3 | 0 | 18 | 0 |

| WEST INDIES | O | M | R | W |
|---|---|---|---|---|
| Dillon | 32.3 | 5 | 115 | 1 |
| Cuffy | 27 | 6 | 57 | 3 |
| Sanford | 25 | 5 | 81 | 2 |
| Nagamootoo | 40 | 13 | 103 | 1 |
| Hooper | 12 | 4 | 16 | 0 |
| Gayle | 4 | 2 | 7 | 0 |

FALL OF WICKETS

| | WI | I |
|---|---|---|
| Wkt | 1st | 1st |
| 1st | 21 | 6 |
| 2nd | 37 | 21 |
| 3rd | 44 | 99 |
| 4th | 157 | 144 |
| 5th | 450 | 263 |
| 6th | 454 | 270 |
| 7th | 494 | 275 |
| 8th | 494 | – |
| 9th | 499 | – |
| 10th | 501 | – |

Umpires: E.A.R.de Silva (*Sri Lanka*) (13) and D.J.Harper (*Australia*) (18).
Referee: R.S.Madugalle (*Sri Lanka*) (39). **Test No. 1598/71 (WI382/1352)**

# WEST INDIES v INDIA (2nd Test)

At Queen's Park Oval, Port-of-Spain, Trinidad, on 19, 20, 21, 22, 23 April.
Toss: West Indies. Result: **INDIA** won by 37 runs.
Debuts: India – A.Ratra.

## INDIA

| | | | | | |
|---|---|--:|---|---|--:|
| S.S.Das | lbw b Dillon | 10 | | lbw b Dillon | 0 |
| S.B.Bangar | c Murray b Sanford | 9 | | c Hooper Sanford | 16 |
| R.Dravid | b Black | 67 | | c Murray b Cuffy | 36 |
| S.R.Tendulkar | lbw b Cuffy | 117 | | lbw b Sanford | 0 |
| *S.C.Ganguly | c Dillon b Hooper | 25 | | not out | 75 |
| V.V.S.Laxman | not out | 69 | | b Dillon | 74 |
| †A.Ratra | c Murray b Cuffy | 0 | | lbw b Cuffy | 2 |
| Harbhajan Singh | c Cuffy b Sanford | 0 | | c Gayle b Cuffy | 0 |
| Z.Khan | b Sanford | 5 | (10) | run out | 4 |
| J.Srinath | lbw b Black | 18 | (9) | c Williams b Dillon | 2 |
| A.Nehra | c Hooper b Black | 0 | | b Dillon | 0 |
| Extras | (B 4, LB 13, NB 2) | 19 | | (B 5, LB 2, NB 2) | 9 |
| **Total** | | **339** | | | **218** |

## WEST INDIES

| | | | | | |
|---|---|--:|---|---|--:|
| C.H.Gayle | c Das b Srinath | 13 | (2) | c Harbhajan b Khan | 52 |
| S.C.Williams | c Das b Harbhajan | 43 | (1) | c Dravid b Srinath | 13 |
| R.R.Sarwan | c Dravid b Nehra | 35 | | c Dravid b Harbhajan | 41 |
| B.C.Lara | c Ratra b Khan | 52 | | c Dravid b Nehra | 47 |
| *C.L.Hooper | c Ganguly b Khan | 50 | | c Das b Nehra | 22 |
| S.Chanderpaul | lbw b Srinath | 1 | | not out | 67 |
| †J.R.Murray | lbw b Srinath | 0 | | run out | 1 |
| M.Dillon | lbw b Nehra | 9 | | b Srinath | 0 |
| M.I.Black | run out | 6 | | c Das b Srinath | 3 |
| A.Sanford | c Tendulkar b Harbhajan | 12 | | b Nehra | 1 |
| C.E.Cuffy | not out | 1 | | c Bangar b Khan | 24 |
| Extras | (B 5, LB 8, W 3, NB 7) | 23 | | (B 2, LB 5, W 4, NB 13) | 24 |
| **Total** | | **245** | | | **275** |

| WEST INDIES | O | M | R | W | | O | M | R | W |
|---|--:|--:|--:|--:|---|--:|--:|--:|--:|
| Dillon | 28 | 7 | 82 | 1 | | 21.1 | 7 | 42 | 4 |
| Cuffy | 30 | 12 | 49 | 2 | | 20 | 6 | 53 | 3 |
| Sanford | 29 | 5 | 111 | 3 | (4) | 17 | 5 | 46 | 2 |
| Black | 17.5 | 7 | 53 | 3 | (3) | 14 | 3 | 36 | 0 |
| Hooper | 11 | 4 | 27 | 1 | | 17 | 4 | 28 | 0 |
| Sarwan | | | | | | 3 | 0 | 6 | 0 |

| INDIA | O | M | R | W | | O | M | R | W |
|---|--:|--:|--:|--:|---|--:|--:|--:|--:|
| Srinath | 22 | 4 | 71 | 3 | | 32 | 9 | 69 | 3 |
| Nehra | 20 | 4 | 52 | 2 | | 31 | 8 | 72 | 3 |
| Khan | 14 | 2 | 47 | 2 | (4) | 21.1 | 5 | 55 | 2 |
| Harbhajan Singh | 19.5 | 3 | 51 | 2 | (3) | 30 | 8 | 66 | 1 |
| Bangar | 2 | 0 | 11 | 0 | | | | | |
| Tendulkar | | | | | (5) | 1 | 0 | 6 | 0 |

### FALL OF WICKETS

| Wkt | I | WI | I | WI |
|---|--:|--:|--:|--:|
| | 1st | 1st | 2nd | 2nd |
| 1st | 18 | 50 | 6 | 27 |
| 2nd | 38 | 80 | 54 | 125 |
| 3rd | 162 | 136 | 54 | 157 |
| 4th | 218 | 179 | 56 | 164 |
| 5th | 276 | 180 | 205 | 237 |
| 6th | 282 | 180 | 210 | 238 |
| 7th | 287 | 210 | 210 | 238 |
| 8th | 298 | 217 | 213 | 254 |
| 9th | 339 | 232 | 218 | 263 |
| 10th | 339 | 245 | 218 | 275 |

Umpires: E.A.R.de Silva (*Sri Lanka*) (14) and D.J.Harper (*Australia*) (19).
Referee: R.S.Madugalle (*Sri Lanka*) (40). **Test No. 1599/72 (WI383/I353)**

# WEST INDIES v INDIA (3rd Test)

At Kensington Oval, Bridgetown, Barbados, on 2, 3, 4, 5 May.
Toss: West Indies. Result: **WEST INDIES** won by ten wickets.
Debuts: None.

## INDIA

| | | | | | |
|---|---|---|---|---|---|
| S.S.Das | b Dillon | 0 | c Sarwan b Dillon | | 35 |
| W.Jaffer | c Jacobs b Dillon | 12 | run out | | 51 |
| R.Dravid | run out | 17 | c Jacobs b Sanford | | 14 |
| S.R.Tendulkar | c Jacobs b Collins | 0 | lbw b Dillon | | 8 |
| *S.C.Ganguly | c Dillon b Sanford | 48 | not out | | 60 |
| V.V.S.Laxman | b Cuffy | 1 | c Hooper b Collins | | 43 |
| †A.Ratra | c Jacobs b Dillon | 1 | lbw b Dillon | | 13 |
| Harbhajan Singh | c Dillon b Sanford | 13 | b Cuffy | | 3 |
| Z.Khan | c Sarwan b Sanford | 4 | c Jacobs b Sarwan | | 46 |
| J.Srinath | lbw b Dillon | 0 | c Gayle b Sarwan | | 0 |
| A.Nehra | not out | 0 | c Collins b Dillon | | 3 |
| Extras | (W 2, NB 4) | 6 | (LB 6, NB 14) | | 20 |
| **Total** | | **102** | | | **296** |

## WEST INDIES

| | | | | | |
|---|---|---|---|---|---|
| S.C.Williams | c Jaffer b Khan | 18 | (2) not out | | 4 |
| C.H.Gayle | lbw b Khan | 14 | (1) not out | | 0 |
| R.R.Sarwan | c Jaffer b Nehra | 60 | | | |
| B.C.Lara | c and b Nehra | 55 | | | |
| *C.L.Hooper | c Tendulkar b Harbhajan | 115 | | | |
| S.Chanderpaul | not out | 101 | | | |
| †R.D.Jacobs | c Ratra b Nehra | 0 | | | |
| M.Dillon | c Das b Nehra | 6 | | | |
| P.T.Collins | b Harbhajan | 0 | | | |
| A.Sanford | lbw b Harbhajan | 0 | | | |
| C.E.Cuffy | run out | 1 | | | |
| Extras | (B 3, LB 8, NB 13) | 24 | (NB 1) | | 1 |
| **Total** | | **394** | (0 wickets) | | **5** |

| WEST INDIES | O | M | R | W | O | M | R | W |
|---|---|---|---|---|---|---|---|---|
| Dillon | 11 | 1 | 41 | 4 | 31.2 | 8 | 82 | 4 |
| Cuffy | 9 | 4 | 17 | 1 | 24 | 16 | 26 | 1 |
| Collins | 8 | 0 | 24 | 1 | 22 | 1 | 78 | 1 |
| Sanford | 5.4 | 0 | 20 | 3 | 15 | 3 | 78 | 1 |
| Hooper | | | | | 5 | 0 | 11 | 0 |
| Gayle | | | | | 3 | 0 | 14 | 0 |
| Sarwan | | | | | 1 | 0 | 1 | 2 |

| INDIA | O | M | R | W | | O | M | R | W |
|---|---|---|---|---|---|---|---|---|---|
| Srinath | 32 | 7 | 85 | 0 | | | | | |
| Nehra | 32 | 9 | 112 | 4 | | | | | |
| Khan | 29 | 8 | 83 | 2 | | | | | |
| Ganguly | 7 | 5 | 9 | 0 | | | | | |
| Harbhajan Singh | 34.5 | 7 | 87 | 3 | (2) | 0.2 | 0 | 4 | 0 |
| Tendulkar | 1 | 0 | 7 | 0 | (1) | 1 | 0 | 1 | 0 |

### FALL OF WICKETS

| | I | WI | I | WI |
|---|---|---|---|---|
| Wkt | 1st | 1st | 2nd | 2nd |
| 1st | 0 | 30 | 80 | — |
| 2nd | 26 | 35 | 101 | — |
| 3rd | 27 | 154 | 117 | — |
| 4th | 50 | 161 | 118 | — |
| 5th | 51 | 376 | 183 | — |
| 6th | 61 | 376 | 208 | — |
| 7th | 78 | 392 | 211 | — |
| 8th | 86 | 393 | 285 | — |
| 9th | 101 | 393 | 285 | — |
| 10th | 102 | 394 | 296 | — |

Umpires: E.A.R.de Silva (*Sri Lanka*) (15) and D.J.Harper (*Australia*) (20).
Referee: R.S.Madugalle (*Sri Lanka*) (41).           **Test No. 1600/73 (WI384/1354)**

# WEST INDIES v INDIA (4th Test)

At Recreation Ground, St John's, Antigua, on 10, 11, 12, 13, 14 May.
Toss: West Indies. Result: **MATCH DRAWN**.
Debuts: None.

## INDIA

| | | |
|---|---|---:|
| S.S.Das | b Collins | 3 |
| W.Jaffer | c Jacobs b Collins | 86 |
| R.Dravid | b Dillon | 91 |
| S.R.Tendulkar | c Jacobs b Collins | 0 |
| *S.C.Ganguly | c Hinds b Cuffy | 45 |
| V.V.S.Laxman | hit wicket b Dillon | 130 |
| A.Kumble | c Chanderpaul b Dillon | 6 |
| †A.Ratra | not out | 115 |
| Z.Khan | c Jacobs b Cuffy | 4 |
| J.Srinath | c Lara b Cuffy | 15 |
| A.Nehra | not out | 1 |
| Extras | (LB 6, W 1, NB 10) | 17 |
| **Total** | (9 wickets declared) | **513** |

## WEST INDIES

| | | |
|---|---|---:|
| C.H.Gayle | c Ratra b Khan | 32 |
| W.W.Hinds | b Tendulkar | 65 |
| R.R.Sarwan | lbw b Khan | 51 |
| B.C.Lara | lbw b Kumble | 4 |
| *C.L.Hooper | c Nehra b Tendulkar | 136 |
| S.Chanderpaul | not out | 136 |
| †R.D.Jacobs | c Laxman b Dravid | 118 |
| M.Dillon | b Jaffer | 43 |
| P.T.Collins | c sub (Harbhajan Singh) b Jaffer | 11 |
| A.Sanford | c Khan b Laxman | 2 |
| C.E.Cuffy | not out | 0 |
| Extras | (B 10, LB 9, W 6, NB 6) | 31 |
| **Total** | (9 wickets declared) | **629** |

| WEST INDIES | O | M | R | W |
|---|---|---|---|---|
| Dillon | 51 | 14 | 116 | 3 |
| Cuffy | 40 | 7 | 87 | 3 |
| Collins | 44 | 10 | 125 | 3 |
| Sanford | 32 | 6 | 113 | 0 |
| Hooper | 13 | 4 | 29 | 0 |
| Hinds | 2 | 0 | 9 | 0 |
| Sarwan | 9 | 3 | 23 | 0 |
| Gayle | 5 | 1 | 5 | 0 |

| INDIA | O | M | R | W |
|---|---|---|---|---|
| Srinath | 45 | 19 | 82 | 0 |
| Nehra | 49 | 16 | 122 | 0 |
| Khan | 48 | 14 | 129 | 2 |
| Ganguly | 12 | 0 | 44 | 0 |
| Tendulkar | 34 | 5 | 107 | 2 |
| Kumble | 14 | 5 | 39 | 1 |
| Laxman | 17 | 6 | 32 | 1 |
| Dravid | 9 | 3 | 18 | 1 |
| Jaffer | 11 | 3 | 18 | 2 |
| Das | 8 | 2 | 28 | 0 |
| Ratra | 1 | 0 | 1 | 0 |

## FALL OF WICKETS

| | I | WI |
|---|---|---|
| Wkt | 1st | 1st |
| 1st | 13 | 65 |
| 2nd | 168 | 121 |
| 3rd | 168 | 135 |
| 4th | 233 | 196 |
| 5th | 235 | 382 |
| 6th | 257 | 548 |
| 7th | 474 | 607 |
| 8th | 485 | 625 |
| 9th | 508 | 628 |
| 10th | – | – |

Umpires: D.R.Shepherd (*England*) (61) and R.B.Tiffin (*Zimbabwe*) (25).
Referee: R.S.Madugalle (*Sri Lanka*) (42). **Test No. 1601/74(WI385/I355)**

# WEST INDIES v INDIA (5th Test)

At Sabina Park, Kingston, Jamaica, on 18, 19, 20, 21, 22 May.
Toss: India. Result: **WEST INDIES** won by 155 runs.
Debuts: None.

## WEST INDIES

| | | | | | |
|---|---|---|---|---|---|
| C.H.Gayle | c Jaffer b Khan | 68 | c Ganguly b Srinath | 15 |
| W.W.Hinds | c Jaffer b Harbhajan | 113 | c Laxman b Srinath | 6 |
| R.R.Sarwan | c Das b Harbhajan | 65 | c Das b Khan | 12 |
| B.C.Lara | c Ratra b Nehra | 9 | b Khan | 35 |
| *C.L.Hooper | c Dravid b Srinath | 17 | c Ratra b Khan | 6 |
| S.Chanderpaul | c Ratra b Srinath | 58 | c and b Khan | 35 |
| †R.D.Jacobs | b Harbhajan | 59 | c sub (D.Mongia) b Harbhajan | 16 |
| M.Dillon | lbw b Harbhajan | 0 | b Nehra | 4 |
| P.T.Collins | c Laxman b Nehra | 12 | b Harbhajan | 24 |
| A.Sanford | c and b Harbhajan | 1 | c Ganguly b Harbhajan | 5 |
| C.E.Cuffy | not out | 0 | not out | 3 |
| Extras | (B 5, LB 6, W 5, NB 4) | 20 | (LB 4, NB 8) | 12 |
| **Total** | | **422** | | **197** |

## INDIA

| | | | | | |
|---|---|---|---|---|---|
| S.S.Das | lbw b Cuffy | 33 | lbw b Collins | 10 |
| W.Jaffer | c Jacobs b Dillon | 0 | c Hinds b Collins | 7 |
| R.Dravid | lbw b Dillon | 5 | lbw b Sanford | 30 |
| S.R.Tendulkar | b Sanford | 41 | b Collins | 86 |
| *S.C.Ganguly | c Jacobs b Dillon | 36 | c Sarwan b Sanford | 28 |
| V.V.S.Laxman | not out | 65 | c Dillon b Sanford | 23 |
| †A.Ratra | c Hinds b Dillon | 4 | lbw b Cuffy | 19 |
| Harbhajan Singh | c Hinds b Dillon | 4 | c Cuffy b Gayle | 17 |
| Z.Khan | c Lara b Cuffy | 6 | c Collins b Dillon | 12 |
| J.Srinath | c Gayle b Collins | 2 | b Cuffy | 4 |
| A.Nehra | run out | 0 | not out | 0 |
| Extras | (LB 6, NB 11) | 17 | (B 5, LB 1, W 1, NB 9) | 16 |
| **Total** | | **212** | | **252** |

| INDIA | O | M | R | W | | O | M | R | W |
|---|---|---|---|---|---|---|---|---|---|
| Srinath | 32 | 8 | 111 | 2 | | 16 | 3 | 49 | 2 |
| Nehra | 30 | 14 | 72 | 2 | | 9 | 2 | 23 | 1 |
| Khan | 24 | 4 | 78 | 1 | | 20 | 2 | 79 | 4 |
| Ganguly | 8 | 4 | 12 | 0 | | | | | |
| Harbhajan Singh | 38 | 3 | 138 | 5 | (4) | 17.2 | 2 | 42 | 3 |

| WEST INDIES | O | M | R | W | | O | M | R | W |
|---|---|---|---|---|---|---|---|---|---|
| Dillon | 24 | 4 | 71 | 5 | | 22.3 | 6 | 77 | 1 |
| Cuffy | 22 | 5 | 49 | 2 | | 18 | 6 | 34 | 2 |
| Collins | 19 | 2 | 54 | 1 | | 17 | 4 | 60 | 3 |
| Sanford | 9 | 1 | 27 | 1 | | 19 | 8 | 48 | 3 |
| Hooper | 1 | 0 | 5 | 0 | | 5 | 1 | 15 | 0 |
| Gayle | | | | | | 4 | 2 | 7 | 1 |
| Sarwan | | | | | | 3 | 0 | 5 | 0 |

### FALL OF WICKETS

| | WI | I | WI | I |
|---|---|---|---|---|
| Wkt | 1st | 1st | 2nd | 2nd |
| 1st | 111 | 5 | 17 | 19 |
| 2nd | 246 | 15 | 24 | 25 |
| 3rd | 264 | 84 | 38 | 77 |
| 4th | 264 | 86 | 60 | 170 |
| 5th | 292 | 168 | 81 | 176 |
| 6th | 401 | 178 | 117 | 209 |
| 7th | 409 | 184 | 122 | 228 |
| 8th | 411 | 194 | 170 | 242 |
| 9th | 422 | 197 | 187 | 252 |
| 10th | 422 | 212 | 197 | 252 |

Umpires: D.R.Shepherd (*England*) (62) and R.B.Tiffin (*Zimbabwe*) (26).
Referee: R.S.Madugalle (*Sri Lanka*) (43).          **Test No. 1602/75(WI386/I356)**

# WEST INDIES v INDIA 2001-02

## WEST INDIES – BATTING AND FIELDING

| | M | I | NO | HS | Runs | Avge | 100 | 50 | Ct/St |
|---|---|---|---|---|---|---|---|---|---|
| S.Chanderpaul | 5 | 7 | 3 | 140 | 562 | 140.50 | 3 | 3 | 1 |
| C.L.Hooper | 5 | 7 | – | 233 | 579 | 82.71 | 3 | 1 | 3 |
| W.W.Hinds | 2 | 3 | – | 113 | 184 | 61.33 | 1 | 1 | 4 |
| R.D.Jacobs | 3 | 4 | – | 118 | 193 | 48.25 | 1 | 1 | 10 |
| R.R.Sarwan | 5 | 7 | – | 65 | 317 | 45.28 | – | 4 | 3 |
| C.H.Gayle | 5 | 8 | 1 | 68 | 206 | 29.42 | – | 2 | 4 |
| B.C.Lara | 5 | 7 | – | 55 | 202 | 28.85 | – | 2 | 4 |
| S.C.Williams | 3 | 5 | 1 | 43 | 91 | 22.75 | – | – | 1 |
| P.T.Collins | 3 | 4 | – | 24 | 47 | 11.75 | – | – | 2 |
| M.Dillon | 5 | 7 | – | 43 | 62 | 8.85 | – | – | 4 |
| A.Sanford | 5 | 7 | – | 12 | 22 | 3.14 | – | – | – |
| C.E.Cuffy | 5 | 7 | 4 | 4 | 9 | 3.00 | – | – | 2 |
| J.R.Murray | 2 | 3 | – | 1 | 1 | 0.33 | – | – | 3 |

*Played in one Test:* M.I.Black 6, 3; M.V.Nagamootoo 15* (2 ct).

## WEST INDIES – BOWLING

| | O | M | R | W | Avge | Best | 5wI | 10wM |
|---|---|---|---|---|---|---|---|---|
| R.R.Sarwan | 16 | 3 | 35 | 2 | 17.50 | 2- 1 | – | – |
| C.E.Cuffy | 190 | 62 | 372 | 17 | 21.88 | 3-53 | – | – |
| M.Dillon | 221.3 | 52 | 626 | 23 | 27.21 | 5-71 | 1 | – |
| M.I.Black | 31.5 | 10 | 89 | 3 | 29.66 | 3-53 | – | – |
| A.Sanford | 151.4 | 33 | 524 | 15 | 34.93 | 3-20 | – | – |
| P.T.Collins | 110 | 17 | 341 | 9 | 37.88 | 3-60 | – | – |

*Also bowled:* C.H.Gayle 16-5-33-1; W.W.Hinds 2-0-9-0; C.L.Hooper 64-17-131-1; M.V.Nagamootoo 40-13-103-1.

## INDIA – BATTING AND FIELDING

| | M | I | NO | HS | Runs | Avge | 100 | 50 | Ct/St |
|---|---|---|---|---|---|---|---|---|---|
| V.V.S.Laxman | 5 | 8 | 2 | 130 | 474 | 79.00 | 1 | 4 | 3 |
| R.Dravid | 5 | 8 | 1 | 144* | 404 | 57.71 | 1 | 2 | 5 |
| S.C.Ganguly | 5 | 8 | 2 | 75* | 322 | 53.66 | – | 2 | 3 |
| S.R.Tendulkar | 5 | 8 | – | 117 | 331 | 41.37 | 1 | 2 | 2 |
| W.Jaffer | 3 | 5 | – | 86 | 156 | 31.20 | – | 2 | 4 |
| A.Ratra | 4 | 7 | 1 | 115* | 153 | 25.50 | 1 | – | 6 |
| S.S.Das | 5 | 8 | – | 35 | 124 | 15.50 | – | – | 1 |
| Z.Khan | 5 | 7 | – | 46 | 81 | 11.57 | – | – | 3 |
| S.B.Bangar | 2 | 3 | – | 16 | 25 | 8.33 | – | – | 1 |
| Harbhajan Singh | 3 | 6 | – | 17 | 37 | 6.16 | – | – | 2 |
| J.Srinath | 5 | 7 | – | 18 | 41 | 5.85 | – | – | – |
| A.Kumble | 2 | 2 | – | 6 | 9 | 4.50 | – | – | – |
| A.Nehra | 4 | 7 | 3 | 4 | 4 | 1.00 | – | – | – |

*Played in one Test:* D.Dasgupta 0 (2 ct); Sarandeep Singh 39* (1 ct).

## INDIA – BOWLING

| | O | M | R | W | Avge | Best | 5wI | 10wM |
|---|---|---|---|---|---|---|---|---|
| W.Jaffer | 11 | 3 | 18 | 2 | 9.00 | 2- 18 | – | – |
| Harbhajan Singh | 140.2 | 23 | 388 | 14 | 27.71 | 5-138 | 1 | – |
| A.Nehra | 171 | 53 | 453 | 12 | 37.75 | 4-112 | – | – |
| Z.Khan | 188.1 | 44 | 568 | 15 | 37.86 | 4- 79 | – | – |
| J.Srinath | 212 | 58 | 558 | 13 | 42.92 | 3- 69 | – | – |
| A.Kumble | 59.1 | 12 | 174 | 3 | 58.00 | 2-145 | – | – |
| S.R.Tendulkar | 40 | 5 | 139 | 2 | 69.50 | 2-107 | – | – |

*Also bowled:* S.B.Bangar 29-6-74-1; S.S.Das 8-2-28-0; R.Dravid 9-3-18-1; S.C.Ganguly 29-10-67-0; V.V.S.Laxman 17-6-32-1; A.Ratra 1-0-1-0; Sarandeep Singh 21-5-80-1.

# PAKISTAN v NEW ZEALAND (1st Test)

At Gaddafi Stadium, Lahore, on 1, 2, 3 May.
Toss: Pakistan. Result: **PAKISTAN** won by an innings and 324 runs.
Debuts: New Zealand – R.G.Hart.

## PAKISTAN

| | | |
|---|---|---|
| Imran Nazir | c Richardson b McMillan | 127 |
| Shahid Afridi | c Hart b Tuffey | 0 |
| Younis Khan | c Fleming b Vettori | 27 |
| Inzamam-ul-Haq | c Tuffey b Walker | 329 |
| Yousuf Youhana | c Fleming b Martin | 29 |
| Abdul Razzaq | lbw b Tuffey | 25 |
| †Rashid Latif | c and b Harris | 7 |
| Saqlain Mushtaq | b McMillan | 30 |
| *Waqar Younis | c and b McMillan | 10 |
| Shoaib Akhtar | st Hart b Walker | 37 |
| Danish Kaneria | not out | 4 |
| Extras | (B 1, LB 8, W 1, NB 8) | 18 |
| **Total** | | **643** |

## NEW ZEALAND

| | | | | | |
|---|---|---|---|---|---|
| M.H.Richardson | b Shoaib | 8 | c Rashid b Saqlain | 32 |
| M.J.Horne | b Shoaib | 4 | c Rashid b Waqar | 0 |
| L.Vincent | c Rashid b Kaneria | 21 | c Rashid b Kaneria | 57 |
| *S.P.Fleming | b Shoaib | 2 | c sub (Mohd Sami) b Kaneria | 66 |
| C.Z.Harris | b Shoaib | 2 | lbw b Razzaq | 43 |
| C.D.McMillan | c Shahid b Saqlain | 15 | lbw b Kaneria | 2 |
| †R.G.Hart | lbw b Waqar | 4 | b Kaneria | 0 |
| D.L.Vettori | c Waqar b Saqlain | 7 | c sub (Shoaib Malik) b Razzaq | 5 |
| B.G.K.Walker | lbw b Shoaib | 0 | not out | 15 |
| D.R.Tuffey | not out | 6 | c Younis Khan b Kaneria | 12 |
| C.S.Martin | b Shoaib | 0 | c sub (Shoaib Malik) b Saqlain | 0 |
| Extras | (B 1, NB 3) | 4 | (B 4, LB 6, NB 4) | 14 |
| **Total** | | **73** | | **246** |

| NEW ZEALAND | O | M | R | W | O | M | R | W |
|---|---|---|---|---|---|---|---|---|
| Tuffey | 25 | 7 | 94 | 2 | | | | |
| Martin | 31 | 12 | 108 | 1 | | | | |
| Vettori | 40 | 4 | 178 | 1 | | | | |
| Walker | 14.5 | 3 | 97 | 2 | | | | |
| Harris | 29 | 3 | 109 | 1 | | | | |
| McMillan | 18 | 1 | 48 | 3 | | | | |

| PAKISTAN | O | M | R | W | O | M | R | W |
|---|---|---|---|---|---|---|---|---|
| Waqar Younis | 10 | 6 | 21 | 1 | 9 | 1 | 38 | 1 |
| Shoaib Akhtar | 8.2 | 4 | 11 | 6 | | | | |
| Danish Kaneria | 6 | 1 | 19 | 1 | (3) 32 | 3 | 110 | 5 |
| Saqlain Mushtaq | 6 | 1 | 21 | 2 | 17.3 | 3 | 38 | 2 |
| Abdul Razzaq | | | | | (2) 14 | 2 | 47 | 2 |
| Shahid Afridi | | | | | (5) 4 | 1 | 3 | 0 |

### FALL OF WICKETS

| | P | NZ | NZ |
|---|---|---|---|
| Wkt | 1st | 1st | 2nd |
| 1st | 1 | 12 | 3 |
| 2nd | 57 | 17 | 69 |
| 3rd | 261 | 19 | 101 |
| 4th | 355 | 21 | 186 |
| 5th | 384 | 53 | 193 |
| 6th | 399 | 57 | 193 |
| 7th | 510 | 66 | 204 |
| 8th | 534 | 67 | 227 |
| 9th | 613 | 73 | 245 |
| 10th | 643 | 73 | 246 |

Umpires: S.A.Bucknor (*West Indies*) (66) and R.E.Koertzen (*South Africa*) (30).
Referee: M.J.Procter (*South Africa*) (1).          **Test No. 1603/43 (P285/NZ297)**
**The 2nd and 3rd Tests were cancelled following a suicide bomb explosion outside
the teams' Karachi hotel shortly before the start of the 2nd Test.**

# ENGLAND v SRI LANKA (1st Test)

At Lord's, London, on 16, 17, 18, 19, 20 May.
Toss: Sri Lanka. Result: **MATCH DRAWN**.
Debuts: None.

## SRI LANKA

| | | | | |
|---|---|---|---|---|
| M.S.Atapattu | c Trescothick b Cork | 185 | c Butcher b Caddick | 7 |
| *S.T.Jayasuriya | run out | 18 | | |
| †K.C.Sangakkara | c Flintoff b Hoggard | 10 | (2) not out | 6 |
| D.P.M.deS.Jayawardena | c Trescothick b Flintoff | 107 | (3) not out | 14 |
| P.A.de Silva | c Stewart b Cork | 88 | | |
| R.P.Arnold | c Trescothick b Hoggard | 50 | | |
| H.P.Tillekeratne | not out | 17 | | |
| W.P.U.C.J.Vaas | c Trescothick b Cork | 6 | | |
| D.N.T.Zoysa | c Stewart b Flintoff | 28 | | |
| T.C.B.Fernando | not out | 6 | | |
| P.D.R.L.Perera | | | | |
| Extras | (B 1, LB 13, W 1, NB 25) | 40 | (B 5, LB 2, NB 8) | 15 |
| **Total** | (8 wickets declared) | **555** | (1 wicket) | **42** |

## ENGLAND

| | | | | |
|---|---|---|---|---|
| M.E.Trescothick | c Jayasuriya b Zoysa | 13 | lbw b Zoysa | 76 |
| M.P.Vaughan | c Zoysa b Perera | 64 | c Sangakkara b Perera | 115 |
| M.A.Butcher | c Jayawardena b Fernando | 17 | run out | 105 |
| *N.Hussain | c Sangakkara b Zoysa | 57 | lbw b Perera | 68 |
| G.P.Thorpe | lbw b Perera | 27 | c Fernando b De Silva | 65 |
| J.P.Crawley | c Sangakkara b Vaas | 31 | not out | 41 |
| †A.J.Stewart | run out | 7 | not out | 26 |
| A.Flintoff | c Sangakkara b Fernando | 12 | | |
| D.G.Cork | c Sangakkara b Fernando | 0 | | |
| A.R.Caddick | c Sangakkara b Perera | 13 | | |
| M.J.Hoggard | not out | 0 | | |
| Extras | (B 4, LB 7, W 9, NB 14) | 34 | (B 1, LB 9, W 1, NB 22) | 33 |
| **Total** | | **275** | (5 wickets declared) | **529** |

| ENGLAND | O | M | R | W | | O | M | R | W |
|---|---|---|---|---|---|---|---|---|---|
| Caddick | 38.3 | 6 | 135 | 0 | | 7 | 2 | 10 | 1 |
| Hoggard | 39 | 4 | 160 | 2 | (3) | 1 | 0 | 7 | 0 |
| Cork | 35.3 | 11 | 93 | 3 | | | | | |
| Flintoff | 39 | 8 | 101 | 2 | (2) | 5 | 0 | 18 | 0 |
| Butcher | 3 | 0 | 17 | 0 | | | | | |
| Vaughan | 14 | 2 | 35 | 0 | | | | | |
| SRI LANKA | | | | | | | | | |
| Vaas | 21.1 | 4 | 51 | 1 | | 44 | 8 | 113 | 0 |
| Zoysa | 19 | 3 | 82 | 2 | | 34 | 6 | 84 | 1 |
| Fernando | 22 | 5 | 83 | 3 | (5) | 26 | 1 | 96 | 0 |
| Perera | 11 | 0 | 48 | 3 | (3) | 30 | 4 | 90 | 2 |
| De Silva | | | | | (4) | 27 | 7 | 63 | 1 |
| Jayasuriya | | | | | | 25 | 6 | 66 | 0 |
| Arnold | | | | | | 4 | 1 | 7 | 0 |
| Tillekeratne | | | | | | 1 | 1 | 0 | 0 |

| FALL OF WICKETS | | | | |
|---|---|---|---|---|
| | SL | E | E | SL |
| Wkt | 1st | 1st | 2nd | 2nd |
| 1st | 38 | 17 | 168 | 16 |
| 2nd | 55 | 43 | 213 | — |
| 3rd | 261 | 149 | 372 | — |
| 4th | 407 | 203 | 432 | — |
| 5th | 492 | 203 | 483 | — |
| 6th | 492 | 214 | | |
| 7th | 505 | 237 | | |
| 8th | 540 | 237 | | |
| 9th | — | 267 | | |
| 10th | — | 275 | | |

Umpires: D.J.Harper (*Australia*) (21) and S.Venkataraghavan (*India*) (54).
Referee: G.R.Viswanath (*India*) (3).          **Test No. 1604/10 (E793/SL123)**

# ENGLAND v SRI LANKA (2nd Test)

At Edgbaston, Birmingham, on 30, 31 May, 1, 2 June.
Toss: England. Result: **ENGLAND** won by an innings and 111 runs.
Debuts: None.

## SRI LANKA

| | | | | | |
|---|---|---|---|---|---|
| M.S.Atapattu | c Stewart b Hoggard | 13 | | b Hoggard | 56 |
| *S.T.Jayasuriya | c Stewart b Caddick | 8 | | b Hoggard | 12 |
| †K.C.Sangakkara | c Stewart b Flintoff | 16 | | lbw b Hoggard | 1 |
| D.P.M.deS.Jayawardena | c Flintoff b Caddick | 47 | | c Thorpe b Caddick | 59 |
| P.A.de Silva | c Trescothick b Hoggard | 10 | | c Thorpe b Caddick | 47 |
| H.P.Tillekeratne | lbw b Tudor | 20 | | b Caddick | 39 |
| R.P.Arnold | c Flintoff b Caddick | 1 | | c Giles b Hoggard | 4 |
| W.P.U.C.J.Vaas | b Flintoff | 23 | | st Stewart b Giles | 28 |
| D.N.T.Zoysa | c Hoggard b Tudor | 0 | (10) | not out | 1 |
| T.C.B.Fernando | run out | 13 | (9) | b Hoggard | 0 |
| M.Muralitharan | not out | 0 | | absent injured | – |
| Extras | (B 1 NB 10) | 11 | | (B 4, LB 4, NB 17) | 25 |
| **Total** | | **162** | | | **272** |

## ENGLAND

| | | |
|---|---|---|
| M.E.Trescothick | c Tillekeratne b Vaas | 161 |
| M.P.Vaughan | c Jayasuriya b Muralitharan | 46 |
| M.A.Butcher | b Muralitharan | 94 |
| *N.Hussain | b Muralitharan | 22 |
| G.P.Thorpe | c Vaas b Fernando | 123 |
| †A.J.Stewart | c Tillekeratne b Muralitharan | 7 |
| A.Flintoff | c Tillekeratne b Muralitharan | 29 |
| A.J.Tudor | c Tillekeratne b Zoysa | 3 |
| A.F.Giles | c Sangakkara b Zoysa | 0 |
| A.R.Caddick | c Sangakkara b Zoysa | 3 |
| M.J.Hoggard | not out | 17 |
| Extras | (LB 19, W 6, NB 15) | 40 |
| **Total** | | **545** |

| ENGLAND | O | M | R | W | O | M | R | W |
|---|---|---|---|---|---|---|---|---|
| Caddick | 17 | 4 | 47 | 3 | 25 | 4 | 67 | 3 |
| Hoggard | 17 | 4 | 55 | 2 | 23 | 2 | 92 | 5 |
| Giles | 4 | 1 | 7 | 0 | (4) 26.1 | 3 | 57 | 1 |
| Tudor | 9.5 | 3 | 25 | 2 | (5) 9 | 1 | 25 | 0 |
| Flintoff | 5 | 0 | 27 | 2 | (3) 6 | 0 | 23 | 0 |

| SRI LANKA | O | M | R | W |
|---|---|---|---|---|
| Vaas | 41 | 3 | 141 | 1 |
| Zoysa | 24 | 3 | 93 | 3 |
| Muralitharan | 64 | 12 | 143 | 5 |
| Fernando | 21.5 | 3 | 92 | 1 |
| Jayasuriya | 6 | 2 | 27 | 0 |
| De Silva | 7 | 0 | 30 | 0 |

### FALL OF WICKETS

| | SL | E | SL |
|---|---|---|---|
| Wkt | 1st | 1st | 2nd |
| 1st | 23 | 92 | 28 |
| 2nd | 23 | 294 | 30 |
| 3rd | 76 | 338 | 135 |
| 4th | 96 | 341 | 156 |
| 5th | 100 | 368 | 233 |
| 6th | 108 | 426 | 238 |
| 7th | 141 | 436 | 247 |
| 8th | 141 | 444 | 247 |
| 9th | 159 | 454 | 272 |
| 10th | 162 | 545 | – |

Umpires: D.J.Harper (*Australia*) (22) and S.Venkataraghavan (*India*) (55).
Referee: G.R.Viswanath (*India*) (4).                **Test No. 1605/11 (E794/SL124)**

# ENGLAND v SRI LANKA (3rd Test)

At Old Trafford, Manchester, on 13, 14, 15, 16, 17 June.
Toss: England. Result: **ENGLAND** won by ten wickets.
Debuts: None.

## ENGLAND

| | | | | |
|---|---|---|---|---|
| M.E.Trescothick | c Jayawardena b Muralitharan | 81 | not out | 23 |
| M.P.Vaughan | c Vaas b Fernando | 36 | not out | 24 |
| M.A.Butcher | lbw b Vaas | 123 | | |
| *N.Hussain | c Muralitharan b Fernando | 16 | | |
| G.P.Thorpe | c Sangakkara b Upashantha | 32 | | |
| †A.J.Stewart | c Tillekeratne b Muralitharan | 123 | | |
| A.Flintoff | run out | 1 | | |
| A.J.Tudor | c Arnold b Vaas | 19 | | |
| A.F.Giles | c Sangakkara b Muralitharan | 45 | | |
| A.R.Caddick | not out | 2 | | |
| M.J.Hoggard | lbw b Fernando | 7 | | |
| Extras | (B 5, LB 10, NB 12) | 27 | (LB 2, NB 1) | 3 |
| **Total** | | **512** | (0 wickets) | **50** |

## SRI LANKA

| | | | | | |
|---|---|---|---|---|---|
| M.S.Atapattu | retired hurt | 10 | (10) | lbw b Giles | 6 |
| R.P.Arnold | c Vaughan b Tudor | 62 | (1) | c Stewart b Tudor | 109 |
| †K.C.Sangakkara | c Thorpe b Hoggard | 40 | | lbw b Tudor | 32 |
| D.P.M.deS.Jayawardena | c and b Tudor | 17 | | c Hussain b Giles | 28 |
| P.A.de Silva | c Hussain b Flintoff | 18 | | c Vaughan b Tudor | 40 |
| *S.T.Jayasuriya | lbw b Hoggard | 35 | (2) | b Hoggard | 26 |
| H.P.Tillekeratne | c Flintoff b Giles | 20 | (6) | not out | 32 |
| W.P.U.C.J.Vaas | lbw b Hoggard | 14 | (7) | lbw b Hoggard | 1 |
| K.E.A.Upashantha | c Stewart b Tudor | 1 | (8) | c Stewart b Flintoff | 3 |
| C.R.D.Fernando | not out | 6 | (9) | lbw b Giles | 4 |
| M.Muralitharan | c Stewart b Tudor | 6 | | c sub (M.J.Powell) b Giles | 0 |
| Extras | (B 1, LB 3, NB 20) | 24 | | (B 9, LB 9, W 2, NB 7) | 27 |
| **Total** | | **253** | | | **308** |

| SRI LANKA | O | M | R | W | | O | M | R | W | FALL OF WICKETS | | | | |
|---|---|---|---|---|---|---|---|---|---|---|---|---|---|---|
| Vaas | 38 | 8 | 121 | 2 | | 1 | 0 | 8 | 0 | | E | SL | SL | E |
| Upashantha | 8 | 0 | 65 | 1 | | | | | | *Wkt* | *1st* | *1st* | *2nd* | *2nd* |
| Fernando | 29.2 | 2 | 154 | 3 | (2) | 2 | 0 | 23 | 0 | 1st | 66 | 107 | 44 | – |
| Muralitharan | 60 | 20 | 137 | 3 | (3) | 2 | 0 | 17 | 0 | 2nd | 192 | 142 | 110 | – |
| De Silva | 2 | 0 | 5 | 0 | | | | | | 3rd | 219 | 149 | 170 | – |
| Jayasuriya | 8 | 2 | 15 | 0 | | | | | | 4th | 262 | 171 | 233 | – |
| | | | | | | | | | | 5th | 354 | 219 | 263 | – |
| ENGLAND | | | | | | | | | | 6th | 361 | 227 | 264 | – |
| Caddick | 5.3 | 2 | 17 | 0 | | | | | | 7th | 400 | 228 | 270 | – |
| Hoggard | 16 | 4 | 38 | 3 | (1) | 37 | 8 | 97 | 2 | 8th | 502 | 240 | 285 | – |
| Flintoff | 23 | 5 | 65 | 1 | (2) | 29 | 7 | 78 | 1 | 9th | 503 | 253 | 308 | – |
| Tudor | 25 | 8 | 65 | 4 | | 21 | 6 | 44 | 3 | 10th | 512 | – | 308 | – |
| Giles | 23 | 3 | 64 | 1 | (3) | 24.2 | 6 | 42 | 4 | | | | | |
| Vaughan | | | | | (5) | 2 | 0 | 9 | 0 | | | | | |

Umpires: S.A.Bucknor (*West Indies*) (67) and D.L.Orchard (*South Africa*) (28).
Referee: G.R.Viswanath (*India*) (5).          **Test No. 1606/12 (E795/SL125)**

# ENGLAND v SRI LANKA 2002

## ENGLAND – BATTING AND FIELDING

|  | M | I | NO | HS | Runs | Avge | 100 | 50 | Ct/St |
|---|---|---|---|---|---|---|---|---|---|
| M.E.Trescothick | 3 | 5 | 1 | 161 | 354 | 88.50 | 1 | 2 | 5 |
| M.A.Butcher | 3 | 4 | – | 123 | 339 | 84.75 | 2 | 1 | 1 |
| M.P.Vaughan | 3 | 5 | 1 | 115 | 285 | 71.25 | 1 | 1 | 2 |
| G.P.Thorpe | 3 | 4 | – | 123 | 247 | 61.75 | 1 | 1 | 3 |
| A.J.Stewart | 3 | 4 | 1 | 123 | 163 | 54.33 | 1 | – | 8/2 |
| N.Hussain | 3 | 4 | – | 68 | 163 | 40.75 | – | 2 | 2 |
| M.J.Hoggard | 3 | 3 | 2 | 17* | 24 | 24.00 | – | – | 1 |
| A.F.Giles | 2 | 2 | – | 45 | 45 | 22.50 | – | – | 1 |
| A.Flintoff | 3 | 3 | – | 29 | 42 | 14.00 | – | – | 4 |
| A.J.Tudor | 2 | 2 | – | 19 | 22 | 11.00 | – | – | 1 |
| A.R.Caddick | 3 | 3 | 1 | 13 | 18 | 9.00 | – | – | – |

*Played in one Test:* D.G.Cork 0; J.P.Crawley 31, 41*.

## ENGLAND – BOWLING

|  | O | M | R | W | Avge | Best | 5wI | 10wM |
|---|---|---|---|---|---|---|---|---|
| A.J.Tudor | 64.5 | 18 | 159 | 9 | 17.66 | 4-65 | – | – |
| D.G.Cork | 35.3 | 11 | 93 | 3 | 31.00 | 3-93 | – | – |
| A.F.Giles | 77.3 | 11 | 190 | 6 | 31.66 | 4-62 | – | – |
| M.J.Hoggard | 133 | 22 | 449 | 14 | 32.07 | 5-92 | 1 | – |
| A.R.Caddick | 93 | 18 | 276 | 7 | 39.42 | 3-47 | – | – |
| A.Flintoff | 107 | 20 | 312 | 6 | 52.00 | 2-27 | – | – |

*Also bowled:* M.A.Butcher 3-0-17-0; M.P.Vaughan 16-2-44-0.

## SRI LANKA – BATTING AND FIELDING

|  | M | I | NO | HS | Runs | Avge | 100 | 50 | Ct/St |
|---|---|---|---|---|---|---|---|---|---|
| M.S.Atapattu | 3 | 6 | 1 | 185 | 277 | 55.40 | 1 | 1 | – |
| D.P.M.deS.Jayawardena | 3 | 6 | 1 | 107 | 272 | 54.40 | 1 | 1 | 3 |
| R.P.Arnold | 3 | 5 | – | 109 | 226 | 45.20 | 1 | 2 | 1 |
| H.P.Tillekeratne | 3 | 5 | 2 | 39 | 128 | 42.66 | – | – | 5 |
| P.A.de Silva | 3 | 5 | – | 88 | 203 | 40.60 | – | 1 | – |
| K.C.Sangakkara | 3 | 6 | 1 | 40 | 105 | 21.00 | – | – | 10 |
| S.T.Jayasuriya | 3 | 5 | – | 35 | 99 | 19.80 | – | – | 1 |
| D.N.T.Zoysa | 2 | 3 | 1 | 28 | 29 | 14.50 | – | – | 1 |
| W.P.U.C.J.Vaas | 3 | 5 | – | 28 | 72 | 14.40 | – | – | 2 |
| T.C.B.Fernando | 2 | 3 | 1 | 13 | 19 | 9.50 | – | – | 1 |
| M.Muralitharan | 2 | 3 | 1 | 6 | 6 | 3.00 | – | – | 1 |

*Played in one Test:* C.R.D.Fernando 6*, 4; P.D.R.L.Perera did not bat. K.E.A.Upashantha 1, 3.

## SRI LANKA – BOWLING

|  | O | M | R | W | Avge | Best | 5wI | 10wM |
|---|---|---|---|---|---|---|---|---|
| P.D.R.L.Perera | 41 | 4 | 138 | 5 | 27.60 | 3- 48 | – | – |
| M.Muralitharan | 126 | 32 | 297 | 8 | 37.12 | 5-143 | 1 | – |
| D.N.T.Zoysa | 77 | 12 | 259 | 6 | 43.16 | 3- 93 | – | – |
| C.R.D.Fernando | 31.2 | 2 | 177 | 3 | 59.00 | 3-154 | – | – |
| T.C.B.Fernando | 69.5 | 8 | 271 | 4 | 67.75 | 3- 83 | – | – |
| W.P.U.C.J.Vaas | 145.1 | 23 | 434 | 4 | 108.50 | 2-121 | – | – |

*Also bowled:* R.P.Arnold 4-1-7-0; P.A.de Silva 36-7-98-1; S.T.Jayasuriya 39-10-108-0; H.P.Tillekeratne 1-1-0-0; K.E.A.Upashantha 8-0-65-1.

# WEST INDIES v NEW ZEALAND (1st Test)

At Kensington Oval, Bridgetown, Barbados, on 21, 22, 23, 24 June.
Toss: West Indies. Result: **NEW ZEALAND** won by 204 runs.
Debuts: West Indies – D.B.Powell.

## NEW ZEALAND

| | | | | | |
|---|---|---|---|---|---|
| M.H.Richardson | b Sanford | 41 | | c Lara b Collins | 0 |
| L.Vincent | c Jacobs b Dillon | 14 | | lbw b Collins | 2 |
| *S.P.Fleming | c Gayle b Hooper | 130 | (7) | c Hinds b Sanford | 34 |
| C.Z.Harris | c Lara b Collins | 0 | | lbw b Powell | 19 |
| N.J.Astle | c Lara b Dillon | 2 | | c Lara b Collins | 77 |
| C.D.McMillan | lbw b Sanford | 6 | | c Hooper b Collins | 1 |
| †R.G.Hart | not out | 57 | (8) | c Hinds b Collins | 24 |
| D.L.Vettori | c Hinds b Collins | 39 | | b Sanford | 11 |
| D.R.Tuffey | lbw b Powell | 28 | (3) | c Gayle b Hooper | 31 |
| S.E.Bond | b Powell | 5 | | not out | 6 |
| I.G.Butler | run out | 3 | | c Jacobs b Collins | 26 |
| Extras | (LB 8, NB 4) | 12 | | (LB 8, W 1, NB 3) | 12 |
| **Total** | | **337** | | | **243** |

## WEST INDIES

| | | | | | |
|---|---|---|---|---|---|
| C.H.Gayle | c Vettori b Bond | 3 | | lbw b Bond | 73 |
| W.W.Hinds | c McMillan b Tuffey | 10 | | c Richardson b Vettori | 37 |
| R.R.Sarwan | c Butler b Bond | 0 | | c Vettori b Bond | 18 |
| B.C.Lara | b Vettori | 28 | | b Bond | 73 |
| *C.L.Hooper | c Tuffey b Butler | 4 | | c Fleming b Tuffey | 16 |
| S.Chanderpaul | not out | 35 | | c Fleming b Vettori | 17 |
| †R.D.Jacobs | c Astle b Vettori | 4 | | c Astle b Vettori | 6 |
| P.T.Collins | c Vincent b Butler | 8 | (9) | lbw b Bond | 8 |
| A.Sanford | c Hart b Butler | 1 | | not out | 0 |
| D.B.Powell | c Harris b Vettori | 0 | (8) | c Astle b Butler | 2 |
| M.Dillon | c Fleming b Vettori | 0 | | c Vincent b Bond | 0 |
| Extras | (LB 4, NB 8) | 12 | | (B 5, LB 11, W 2, NB 1) | 19 |
| **Total** | | **107** | | | **269** |

| WEST INDIES | O | M | R | W | | O | M | R | W | | FALL OF WICKETS | | | |
|---|---|---|---|---|---|---|---|---|---|---|---|---|---|---|
| | | | | | | | | | | | | NZ | WI | NZ | WI |
| Dillon | 28 | 5 | 73 | 2 | (3) | 6 | 3 | 11 | 0 | | Wkt | 1st | 1st | 2nd | 2nd |
| Collins | 24 | 5 | 80 | 2 | (1) | 30.4 | 8 | 76 | 6 | | 1st | 38 | 6 | 0 | 68 |
| Powell | 21 | 6 | 41 | 2 | (2) | 20 | 4 | 61 | 1 | | 2nd | 88 | 6 | 11 | 133 |
| Sanford | 28.4 | 7 | 101 | 2 | | 17 | 5 | 68 | 2 | | 3rd | 89 | 31 | 48 | 142 |
| Hooper | 13 | 5 | 21 | 1 | | 17 | 8 | 19 | 1 | | 4th | 106 | 47 | 69 | 179 |
| Gayle | 10 | 3 | 12 | 0 | | | | | | | 5th | 117 | 62 | 88 | 204 |
| Sarwan | 1 | 0 | 1 | 0 | | | | | | | 6th | 225 | 73 | 164 | 216 |
| | | | | | | | | | | | 7th | 278 | 90 | 181 | 222 |
| NEW ZEALAND | | | | | | | | | | | 8th | 323 | 93 | 205 | 252 |
| Bond | 12 | 1 | 34 | 2 | | 21 | 7 | 78 | 5 | | 9th | 333 | 103 | 213 | 269 |
| Tuffey | 7 | 3 | 16 | 1 | | 15 | 5 | 43 | 1 | | 10th | 337 | 107 | 243 | 269 |
| Butler | 11 | 2 | 26 | 3 | | 14 | 0 | 58 | 1 | | | | | | |
| Vettori | 12.1 | 2 | 27 | 4 | | 19 | 3 | 53 | 3 | | | | | | |
| Astle | | | | | | 5 | 4 | 4 | 0 | | | | | | |
| Harris | | | | | | 9 | 3 | 17 | 0 | | | | | | |

Umpires: R.E.Koertzen (*South Africa*) (31) and S.Venkataraghavan (*India*) (56).
Referee: Wasim Raja (*Pakistan*) (1).          Test No. 1607/31 (WI387/I298)

# WEST INDIES v NEW ZEALAND (2nd Test)

At Queen's Park, St George's, Grenada, on 28, 29, 30 June, 1, 2 July.
Toss: West Indies. Result: **MATCH DRAWN**.
Debuts: New Zealand – S.B.Styris.

## NEW ZEALAND

| | | | | | |
|---|---|---|---|---|---|
| M.H.Richardson | c Gayle b Collins | 95 | c Jacobs b Nagamootoo | | 71 |
| L.Vincent | b Cuffy | 24 | b Sarwan | | 54 |
| *S.P.Fleming | c Lara b Collins | 6 | c Lara b Hooper | | 5 |
| C.Z.Harris | c Jacobs b Hooper | 0 | c Sarwan b Nagamootoo | | 17 |
| N.J.Astle | lbw b Collins | 69 | c Hinds b Hooper | | 0 |
| D.L.Vettori | c Jacobs b Collins | 1 | | | |
| C.D.McMillan | c Lara b Cuffy | 14 | | | |
| S.B.Styris | b Sanford | 107 | (6) not out | | 69 |
| †R.G.Hart | c Hinds b Hooper | 20 | (7) not out | | 28 |
| S.E.Bond | lbw b Chanderpaul | 17 | | | |
| I.G.Butler | not out | 5 | | | |
| Extras | (LB 6, W 2, NB 7) | 15 | (LB 7, NB 5) | | 12 |
| **Total** | | **373** | (5 wickets) | | **256** |

## WEST INDIES

| | | |
|---|---|---|
| C.H.Gayle | c Hart b Bond | 204 |
| W.W.Hinds | b Bond | 10 |
| R.R.Sarwan | run out | 39 |
| B.C.Lara | c Hart b Styris | 48 |
| *C.L.Hooper | lbw b Bond | 17 |
| S.Chanderpaul | c Fleming b Bond | 51 |
| †R.D.Jacobs | c Styris b Butler | 17 |
| M.V.Nagamootoo | c Hart b Styris | 32 |
| P.T.Collins | lbw b Vettori | 14 |
| A.Sanford | c Butler b Bond | 12 |
| C.E.Cuffy | not out | 0 |
| Extras | (B 4, LB 2, W 5, NB 15) | 26 |
| **Total** | | **470** |

| WEST INDIES | O | M | R | W | | O | M | R | W |
|---|---|---|---|---|---|---|---|---|---|
| Collins | 30 | 9 | 68 | 4 | | 17 | 7 | 28 | 0 |
| Cuffy | 35 | 12 | 76 | 2 | | 10 | 3 | 20 | 0 |
| Sanford | 22.5 | 4 | 74 | 1 | (4) | 14 | 3 | 27 | 0 |
| Nagamootoo | 33 | 11 | 88 | 0 | (3) | 42 | 16 | 75 | 2 |
| Hooper | 25 | 3 | 44 | 2 | | 34 | 10 | 66 | 2 |
| Gayle | 3 | 1 | 5 | 0 | | 6 | 2 | 7 | 0 |
| Chanderpaul | 4 | 0 | 12 | 1 | (8) | 2 | 2 | 0 | 0 |
| Sarwan | | | | | (7) | 6 | 0 | 26 | 1 |

| NEW ZEALAND | O | M | R | W |
|---|---|---|---|---|
| Bond | 30.1 | 7 | 104 | 5 |
| Butler | 21 | 4 | 83 | 1 |
| Styris | 25 | 3 | 88 | 2 |
| Vettori | 41 | 9 | 134 | 1 |
| Astle | 12 | 2 | 15 | 0 |
| Harris | 15 | 4 | 40 | 0 |

### FALL OF WICKETS

| | NZ | WI | NZ |
|---|---|---|---|
| Wkt | 1st | 1st | 2nd |
| 1st | 61 | 28 | 117 |
| 2nd | 81 | 128 | 132 |
| 3rd | 82 | 204 | 148 |
| 4th | 205 | 242 | 149 |
| 5th | 206 | 385 | 157 |
| 6th | 208 | 394 | – |
| 7th | 256 | 441 | – |
| 8th | 312 | 448 | – |
| 9th | 361 | 470 | – |
| 10th | 373 | 470 | – |

Umpires: R.E.Koertzen (*South Africa*) (32) and S.Venkataraghavan (*India*) (57).
Referee: Wasim Raja (*Pakistan*) (2).

**Test No. 1608/32 (WI388/NZ299)**

# SRI LANKA v BANGLADESH (1st Test)

At P.Saravanamuttu Stadium, Colombo, on 21, 22, 23 July.
Toss: Sri Lanka. Result: **SRI LANKA** won by an innings and 196 runs.
Debuts: Sri Lanka – W.R.S.de Silva; Bangladesh – Alamgir Kabir, Ehsanul Haque, Hannan Sarkar, Talha Jubair.

## BANGLADESH

| | | | | |
|---|---|---|---|---|
| Hannan Sarkar | lbw b Jayasuriya | 55 | lbw b WRS de Silva | 1 |
| Al Sahariar | lbw b WRS de Silva | 13 | c Sangakkara b Muralitharan | 67 |
| Ehsanul Haque | b CRD Fernando | 2 | c TCB Fernando b CRD Fernando | 5 |
| Habibul Bashar | lbw b Muralitharan | 24 | b Muralitharan | 34 |
| Akram Khan | c HAPW Jayawardena b TCB Fernando | 20 | c Sangakkara b Muralitharan | 5 |
| Aminul Islam | c Arnold b Muralitharan | 0 | c Sangakkara b Muralitharan | 0 |
| *†Khaled Masud | c Jayasuriya b Muralitharan | 23 | c TCB Fernando b PA de Silva | 26 |
| Enamul Haque | st HAPW Jayawardena b Muralitharan | 1 | b CRD Fernando | 22 |
| Manjural Islam | b TCB Fernando | 0 | c Sangakkara b Muralitharan | 2 |
| Alamgir Kabir | b Muralitharan | 0 | b WRS de Silva | 0 |
| Talha Kabir | not out | 0 | not out | 5 |
| Extras | (B 8, LB 4, W 1, NB 10) | 23 | (LB 5, W 1, NB 11) | 17 |
| **Total** | | **161** | | **184** |

## SRI LANKA

| | | |
|---|---|---|
| M.S.Atapattu | b Talha | 20 |
| R.P.Arnold | c sub (Fahim Muntasir) b Manjural | 25 |
| K.C.Sangakkara | run out | 75 |
| D.P.M.deS.Jayawardena | b Talha | 0 |
| P.A.de Silva | lbw b Enamul | 206 |
| *S.T.Jayasuriya | c sub (Mohd Ashraful) b Enamul | 145 |
| †H.A.P.W.Jayawardena | c Al Sahariar b Manjural | 5 |
| T.C.B.Fernando | not out | 31 |
| M.Muralitharan | c Al Sahariar b Enamul | 0 |
| C.R.D.Fernando | c Habibul b Enamul | 15 |
| W.R.S.de Silva | not out | 5 |
| Extras | (LB 6, W 2, NB 6) | 14 |
| **Total** | (9 wickets declared) | **541** |

| SRI LANKA | O | M | R | W | | O | M | R | W |
|---|---|---|---|---|---|---|---|---|---|
| T.C.B.Fernando | 10 | 3 | 38 | 2 | (3) | 7 | 2 | 34 | 0 |
| W.R.S.de Silva | 13 | 3 | 31 | 2 | | 11 | 1 | 35 | 2 |
| C.R.D.Fernando | 10 | 3 | 40 | 1 | (1) | 11 | 4 | 24 | 2 |
| Muralitharan | 19.4 | 6 | 39 | 5 | | 25 | 6 | 59 | 5 |
| Jayasuriya | 1 | 0 | 1 | 1 | | 10 | 2 | 20 | 0 |
| P.A.de Silva | | | | | | 2.3 | 1 | 7 | 1 |

| BANGLADESH | O | M | R | W |
|---|---|---|---|---|
| Manjural Islam | 25 | 1 | 128 | 2 |
| Talha Jubair | 21 | 0 | 120 | 2 |
| Alamgir Kabir | 15 | 1 | 82 | 0 |
| Enamul Haque | 38 | 6 | 144 | 4 |
| Habibul Bashar | 9 | 0 | 43 | 0 |
| Ehsanul Haque | 3 | 0 | 18 | 0 |

| | | FALL OF WICKETS | | |
|---|---|---|---|---|
| | | | B | SL | B |
| | | Wkt | 1st | 1st | 2nd |
| | | 1st | 32 | 35 | 2 |
| | | 2nd | 50 | 49 | 14 |
| | | 3rd | 107 | 56 | 91 |
| | | 4th | 111 | 206 | 113 |
| | | 5th | 116 | 440 | 113 |
| | | 6th | 148 | 447 | 124 |
| | | 7th | 151 | 491 | 158 |
| | | 8th | 156 | 491 | 161 |
| | | 9th | 161 | 524 | 166 |
| | | 10th | 161 | – | 184 |

Umpires: S.A.Bucknor (*West Indies*) (68) and D.R.Shepherd (*England*) (63).
Referee: Wasim Raja (*Pakistan*) (3).                    **Test No. 1609/2 (SL126/B12)**

# SRI LANKA v BANGLADESH (2nd Test)

At Sinhalese Sports Club, Colombo, on 28, 29, 30, 31 July.
Toss: Bangladesh. Result: **SRI LANKA** won by 288 runs.
Debuts: Sri Lanka – M.K.G.C.P.Lakshitha, J.Mubarak, M.N.Nawaz; Bangladesh – Alok
Kapali, Tapash Baisya, Tushar Imran.

## SRI LANKA

| | | | | |
|---|---|---|---|---|
| M.G.Vandort | lbw b Alok | 61 | b Talha | 140 |
| J.Mubarak | lbw b Tapash | 24 | run out | 31 |
| M.N.Nawaz | c Masud b Fahim | 21 | not out | 78 |
| H.P.Tillekeratne | c and b Fahim | 18 | not out | 5 |
| *S.T.Jayasuriya | c Masud b Manjural | 85 | | |
| T.T.Samaraweera | c Habibul b Manjural | 58 | | |
| †H.A.P.W.Jayawardena | c Masud b Manjural | 0 | | |
| U.D.U.Chandana | c Habibul b Alok | 20 | | |
| T.C.B.Fernando | not out | 29 | | |
| W.R.S.de Silva | c Masud b Talha | 5 | | |
| M.K.G.C.P.Lakshitha | c Alok b Talha | 40 | | |
| Extras | (B 1, LB 5, NB 6) | 12 | (B 4, LB 1, W 1, NB 3) | 9 |
| **Total** | | **373** | (2 wickets declared) | **263** |

## BANGLADESH

| | | | | |
|---|---|---|---|---|
| Hannan Sarkar | lbw b Fernando | 5 | c Jayawardena b De Silva | 30 |
| Al Sahariar | c Jayawardena b Jayasuriya | 12 | b De Silva | 6 |
| Habibul Bashar | lbw b Fernando | 11 | c Jayawardena b Lakshitha | 3 |
| Mohammed Ashraful | b Lakshitha | 4 | c Mubarak b Samaraweera | 75 |
| Tushar Imran | lbw b Lakshitha | 8 | st Jayawardena b Chandana | 28 |
| *†Khaled Masud | c Tillekeratne b Samaraweera | 15 | (7) not out | 13 |
| Alok Kapali | lbw b Jayasuriya | 39 | (6) c Mubarak b Samaraweera | 23 |
| Fahim Muntasir | c and b Samaraweera | 7 | (9) lbw b De Silva | 1 |
| Tapash Baisya | not out | 52 | (8) c Chandana b De Silva | 3 |
| Manjural Islam | c Jayawardena b Jayasuriya | 0 | c Tillekeratne b Samaraweera | 0 |
| Talha Jubair | c Jayasuriya b Chandana | 0 | c Mubarak b Samaraweera | 0 |
| Extras | (LB 4, NB 10) | 14 | (LB 1, NB 1) | 2 |
| **Total** | | **164** | | **184** |

| BANGLADESH | O | M | R | W | | O | M | R | W |
|---|---|---|---|---|---|---|---|---|---|
| Manjural Islam | 23 | 4 | 46 | 3 | | 9 | 0 | 28 | 0 |
| Talha Jubair | 21.4 | 3 | 74 | 2 | | 14 | 1 | 52 | 1 |
| Tapash Baisya | 12 | 1 | 69 | 1 | (4) | 8 | 0 | 40 | 0 |
| Fahim Muntasir | 18 | 3 | 46 | 2 | (5) | 19 | 3 | 56 | 0 |
| Alok Kapali | 29 | 2 | 122 | 2 | (3) | 11 | 0 | 54 | 0 |
| Habibul Bashar | 3 | 1 | 10 | 0 | | 5 | 0 | 28 | 0 |

| SRI LANKA | O | M | R | W | | O | M | R | W |
|---|---|---|---|---|---|---|---|---|---|
| Fernando | 15 | 3 | 36 | 2 | | 5 | 2 | 12 | 0 |
| De Silva | 11 | 2 | 45 | 0 | | 13 | 5 | 35 | 4 |
| Jayasuriya | 7 | 2 | 17 | 3 | (4) | 9 | 4 | 14 | 0 |
| Lakshitha | 12 | 5 | 33 | 2 | (3) | 12 | 2 | 48 | 1 |
| Samaraweera | 12 | 3 | 18 | 2 | | 11.4 | 1 | 49 | 4 |
| Chandana | 5 | 1 | 11 | 1 | | 10 | 3 | 25 | 1 |

### FALL OF WICKETS

| | SL | B | SL | B |
|---|---|---|---|---|
| Wkt | 1st | 1st | 2nd | 2nd |
| 1st | 60 | 20 | 80 | 27 |
| 2nd | 90 | 28 | 252 | 36 |
| 3rd | 131 | 31 | – | 40 |
| 4th | 133 | 43 | – | 99 |
| 5th | 260 | 51 | – | 167 |
| 6th | 260 | 72 | – | 168 |
| 7th | 298 | 86 | – | 171 |
| 8th | 298 | 123 | – | 175 |
| 9th | 309 | 163 | – | 184 |
| 10th | 373 | 164 | – | 184 |

Umpires: S.A.Bucknor (*West Indies*) (69) and D.R.Shepherd (*England*) (64).
Referee: Wasim Raja (*Pakistan*) (4).                    Test No. 1610/3 (SL127/B13)

# ENGLAND v INDIA (1st Test)

At Lord's, London, on 25, 26, 27, 28, 29 July.
Toss: England. Result: **ENGLAND** won by 170 runs.
Debuts: England – S.P.Jones.

## ENGLAND

| | | | | | |
|---|---|---|---|---|---|
| M.A.Butcher | c Jaffer b Kumble | 29 | | lbw b Kumble | 18 |
| M.P.Vaughan | lbw b Khan | 0 | | c Jaffer b Nehra | 100 |
| *N.Hussain | c Ratra b Agarkar | 155 | | c Ratra b Agarkar | 12 |
| G.P.Thorpe | b Khan | 4 | | c Ganguly b Kumble | 1 |
| J.P.Crawley | c Dravid b Sehwag | 64 | | not out | 100 |
| †A.J.Stewart | lbw b Kumble | 19 | (7) | st Ratra b Kumble | 33 |
| A.Flintoff | c Ratra b Agarkar | 59 | (6) | c Tendulkar b Nehra | 7 |
| C.White | st Ratra b Kumble | 53 | | not out | 6 |
| A.F.Giles | b Nehra | 19 | | | |
| S.P.Jones | c Dravid b Kumble | 44 | | | |
| M.J.Hoggard | not out | 10 | | | |
| Extras | (B 11, LB 11, W 2, NB 7) | 31 | | (B 5, LB 14, NB 5) | 24 |
| **Total** | | **487** | | (6 wickets declared) | **301** |

## INDIA

| | | | | | |
|---|---|---|---|---|---|
| W.Jaffer | b Hoggard | 1 | | c Hussain b Vaughan | 53 |
| V.Sehwag | b Giles | 84 | | b Jones | 27 |
| R.Dravid | c Vaughan b Hoggard | 46 | | b Giles | 63 |
| A.Nehra | lbw b Flintoff | 0 | (11) | c Thorpe b White | 19 |
| S.R.Tendulkar | c Stewart b White | 16 | (4) | b Hoggard | 12 |
| *S.C.Ganguly | c Vaughan b Flintoff | 2 | (5) | lbw b Hoggard | 0 |
| V.V.S.Laxman | not out | 43 | | c Vaughan b Jones | 74 |
| †A.Ratra | c Stewart b Jones | 1 | (7) | c Butcher b Hoggard | 1 |
| A.B.Agarkar | c Flintoff b Jones | 2 | (8) | not out | 109 |
| A.Kumble | b White | 4 | (9) | c and b Hoggard | 15 |
| Z.Khan | c Thorpe b Hoggard | 3 | (10) | c Stewart b White | 7 |
| Extras | (B 4, LB 8, NB 8) | 20 | | (B 4, LB 3, W 2, NB 8) | 17 |
| **Total** | | **221** | | | **397** |

| INDIA | O | M | R | W | | O | M | R | W | | FALL OF WICKETS | | | |
|---|---|---|---|---|---|---|---|---|---|---|---|---|---|---|
| | | | | | | | | | | | | E | I | E | I |
| Nehra | 30 | 4 | 101 | 1 | | 14 | 1 | 80 | 2 | | Wkt | 1st | 1st | 2nd | 2nd |
| Khan | 36 | 13 | 90 | 3 | | 11 | 1 | 41 | 0 | | 1st | 0 | 2 | 32 | 61 |
| Agarkar | 21 | 3 | 98 | 2 | (4) | 11.4 | 1 | 53 | 1 | | 2nd | 71 | 128 | 65 | 110 |
| Kumble | 42.2 | 9 | 128 | 3 | (3) | 24 | 1 | 84 | 3 | | 3rd | 78 | 130 | 76 | 140 |
| Ganguly | 3 | 1 | 16 | 0 | | | | | | | 4th | 223 | 162 | 213 | 140 |
| Sehwag | 10 | 0 | 32 | 1 | | 2 | 0 | 10 | 0 | | 5th | 263 | 168 | 228 | 165 |
| Tendulkar | | | | | (5) | 2 | 0 | 14 | 0 | | 6th | 356 | 177 | 287 | 170 |
| ENGLAND | | | | | | | | | | | 7th | 357 | 191 | – | 296 |
| Hoggard | 16.5 | 4 | 33 | 3 | | 24 | 7 | 87 | 4 | | 8th | 390 | 196 | – | 320 |
| Flintoff | 19 | 9 | 22 | 2 | | 17 | 2 | 87 | 0 | | 9th | 452 | 209 | – | 334 |
| Giles | 9 | 1 | 47 | 1 | (5) | 29 | 7 | 75 | 1 | | 10th | 487 | 221 | – | 397 |
| Jones | 21 | 2 | 61 | 2 | | 17 | 1 | 68 | 2 | | | | | | |
| White | 16 | 3 | 46 | 2 | (3) | 16.4 | 2 | 61 | 2 | | | | | | |
| Vaughan | | | | | | 6 | 2 | 12 | 1 | | | | | | |

Umpires: R.E.Koertzen (*South Africa*) (33) and R.B.Tiffin (*Zimbabwe*) (27).
Referee: M.J.Procter (*South Africa*)(2).     **Test No. 1611/88 (E796/1357)**

# ENGLAND v INDIA (2nd Test)

At Trent Bridge, Nottingham, on 8, 9, 10, 11, 12 August.
Toss: India. Result: **MATCH DRAWN**.
Debuts: England – S.J.Harmison, R.W.T.Key; India – P.A.Patel.

## INDIA

| | | | | | |
|---|---|---|---|---|---|
| W.Jaffer | b Hoggard | 0 | (2) lbw b Flintoff | | 5 |
| V.Sehwag | b White | 106 | (1) lbw b Hoggard | | 0 |
| R.Dravid | c Key b Hoggard | 13 | lbw b Cork | | 115 |
| S.R.Tendulkar | b Cork | 34 | b Vaughan | | 92 |
| *S.C.Ganguly | c Stewart b Hoggard | 68 | b Harmison | | 99 |
| V.V.S.Laxman | c Key b Flintoff | 22 | c White b Cork | | 14 |
| A.B.Agarkar | c Butcher b Harmison | 34 | lbw b Vaughan | | 32 |
| †P.A.Patel | c Flintoff b Harmison | 0 | not out | | 19 |
| Harbhajan Singh | c Hussain b Harmison | 54 | b Harmison | | 1 |
| Z.Khan | not out | 14 | not out | | 14 |
| A.Nehra | c Stewart b Hoggard | 0 | | | |
| Extras | (B 1, LB 8, W 2, NB 1) | 12 | (B 5, LB 12, W 4, NB 12) | | 33 |
| **Total** | | **357** | (8 wickets declared) | | **424** |

## ENGLAND

| | | |
|---|---|---|
| R.W.T.Key | b Nehra | 17 |
| M.P.Vaughan | c Patel b Agarkar | 197 |
| M.A.Butcher | c Dravid b Harbhajan | 53 |
| *N.Hussain | c Patel b Harbhajan | 3 |
| J.P.Crawley | c Jaffer b Khan | 22 |
| †A.J.Stewart | b Khan | 87 |
| A.Flintoff | b Khan | 33 |
| C.White | not out | 94 |
| D.G.Cork | c Jaffer b Harbhajan | 31 |
| M.J.Hoggard | c Dravid b Nehra | 32 |
| S.J.Harmison | c Jaffer b Agarkar | 3 |
| Extras | (B 9, LB 17, W 4, NB 15) | 45 |
| **Total** | | **617** |

| ENGLAND | O | M | R | W | | O | M | R | W |
|---|---|---|---|---|---|---|---|---|---|
| Hoggard | 35.1 | 10 | 105 | 4 | | 23 | 0 | 109 | 1 |
| Cork | 11 | 3 | 45 | 1 | (4) | 12 | 1 | 54 | 2 |
| Harmison | 20 | 7 | 57 | 3 | | 29 | 5 | 63 | 2 |
| Flintoff | 27 | 6 | 85 | 1 | (2) | 22 | 2 | 95 | 1 |
| White | 8 | 0 | 56 | 1 | (6) | 8 | 2 | 15 | 0 |
| Vaughan | | | | | (5) | 21 | 5 | 71 | 2 |

| INDIA | O | M | R | W |
|---|---|---|---|---|
| Nehra | 32 | 3 | 138 | 2 |
| Khan | 26 | 4 | 110 | 3 |
| Agarkar | 24.5 | 3 | 93 | 2 |
| Harbhajan Singh | 45 | 3 | 175 | 3 |
| Ganguly | 5 | 0 | 42 | 0 |
| Tendulkar | 6 | 0 | 15 | 0 |
| Sehwag | 6 | 1 | 18 | 0 |

## FALL OF WICKETS

| | I | E | I |
|---|---|---|---|
| Wkt | 1st | 1st | 2nd |
| 1st | 6 | 56 | 0 |
| 2nd | 34 | 221 | 11 |
| 3rd | 108 | 228 | 174 |
| 4th | 179 | 272 | 309 |
| 5th | 218 | 335 | 339 |
| 6th | 285 | 432 | 378 |
| 7th | 287 | 433 | 395 |
| 8th | 295 | 493 | 396 |
| 9th | 356 | 596 | – |
| 10th | 357 | 617 | – |

Umpires: R.E.Koertzen (*South Africa*) (34) and R.B.Tiffin (*Zimbabwe*) (28).
Referee: C H.Lloyd (*West Indies*) (12).                    **Test No. 1612/89 (E797/1358)**

# ENGLAND v INDIA (3rd Test)

At Headingley, Leeds, on 22, 23, 24, 25, 26 August.
Toss: India. Result: **INDIA** won by an innings and 46 runs.
Debuts: None.

## INDIA

| | | |
|---|---|---|
| S.B.Bangar | c Stewart b Flintoff | 68 |
| V.Sehwag | c Flintoff b Hoggard | 8 |
| R.Dravid | st Stewart b Giles | 148 |
| S.R.Tendulkar | lbw b Caddick | 193 |
| *S.C.Ganguly | b Tudor | 128 |
| V.V.S.Laxman | c Hussain b Tudor | 6 |
| A.B.Agarkar | b Caddick | 2 |
| †P.A.Patel | not out | 7 |
| Harbhajan Singh | c Hoggard b Caddick | 18 |
| A.Kumble | | |
| Z.Khan | | |
| Extras | (B 14, LB 13, W 5, NB 18) | 50 |
| **Total** | (8 wickets declared) | **628** |

## ENGLAND

| | | | | | |
|---|---|---|---|---|---|
| R.W.T.Key | c Laxman b Khan | 30 | lbw b Kumble | 34 | |
| M.P.Vaughan | c Sehwag b Agarkar | 61 | lbw b Agarkar | 15 | |
| M.A.Butcher | lbw b Kumble | 16 | c Dravid b Bangar | 42 | |
| *N.Hussain | lbw b Khan | 25 | c Sehwag b Kumble | 110 | |
| J.P.Crawley | c Laxman b Harbhajan | 13 | c Sehwag b Bangar | 12 | |
| †A.J.Stewart | not out | 78 | c Dravid b Kumble | 47 | |
| A.Flintoff | lbw b Harbhajan | 0 | c Dravid b Khan | 0 | |
| A.J.Tudor | c Sehwag b Agarkar | 1 | c Sehwag b Harbhajan | 21 | |
| A.F.Giles | lbw b Kumble | 25 | run out | 10 | |
| A.R.Caddick | b Harbhajan | 1 | c Ganguly b Kumble | 3 | |
| M.J.Hoggard | c Sehwag b Kumble | 0 | not out | 1 | |
| Extras | (B 1, LB 12, NB 10) | 23 | (B 3, LB 5, NB 6) | 14 | |
| **Total** | | **273** | | **309** | |

| ENGLAND | O | M | R | W | O | M | R | W | FALL OF WICKETS | | | |
|---|---|---|---|---|---|---|---|---|---|---|---|---|
| | | | | | | | | | | I | E | E |
| Hoggard | 36 | 12 | 102 | 1 | | | | | Wkt | 1st | 1st | 2nd |
| Caddick | 40.1 | 5 | 150 | 3 | | | | | 1st | 15 | 67 | 28 |
| Tudor | 36 | 10 | 146 | 2 | | | | | 2nd | 185 | 109 | 76 |
| Flintoff | 27 | 6 | 68 | 1 | | | | | 3rd | 335 | 130 | 116 |
| Giles | 39 | 3 | 134 | 1 | | | | | 4th | 584 | 140 | 148 |
| Butcher | 1 | 1 | 0 | 0 | | | | | 5th | 596 | 164 | 267 |
| Vaughan | 1 | 0 | 1 | 0 | | | | | 6th | 602 | 164 | 267 |
| | | | | | | | | | 7th | 604 | 185 | 267 |
| INDIA | | | | | | | | | 8th | 628 | 255 | 299 |
| Khan | 19 | 3 | 59 | 2 | 22 | 7 | 63 | 1 | 9th | – | 258 | 307 |
| Agarkar | 15 | 4 | 59 | 2 | 18 | 5 | 59 | 1 | 10th | – | 273 | 307 |
| Bangar | 4 | 1 | 9 | 0 | 13 | 2 | 54 | 2 | | | | |
| Kumble | 33 | 7 | 93 | 3 | 29.5 | 12 | 66 | 4 | | | | |
| Harbhajan Singh | 18 | 6 | 40 | 3 | 27 | 7 | 56 | 1 | | | | |
| Sehwag | | | | | 1 | 0 | 3 | 0 | | | | |

Umpires: E.A.R.de Silva (*Sri Lanka*) (16) and D.L.Orchard (*South Africa*) (29).
Referee: C H.Lloyd (*West Indies*) (13).        **Test No. 1613/90 (E798/1359)**

# ENGLAND v INDIA (4th Test)

At Kennington Oval, London, on 5, 6, 7, 8, 9 (*no play*) September.
Toss: England. Result: **MATCH DRAWN**.
Debuts: None.

## ENGLAND

| | | | | | |
|---|---|---|---|---|---|
| M.E.Trescothick | c Bangar b Khan | 57 | not out | | 58 |
| M.P.Vaughan | c Ratra b Khan | 195 | not out | | 47 |
| M.A.Butcher | c Dravid b Harbhajan | 54 | | | |
| J.P.Crawley | lbw b Bangar | 26 | | | |
| *N.Hussain | c Laxman b Bangar | 10 | | | |
| †A.J.Stewart | c Ratra b Harbhajan | 23 | | | |
| D.G.Cork | lbw b Harbhajan | 52 | | | |
| A.J.Tudor | c Dravid b Harbhajan | 2 | | | |
| A.F.Giles | c Dravid b Kumble | 31 | | | |
| A.R.Caddick | not out | 14 | | | |
| M.J.Hoggard | lbw b Harbhajan | 0 | | | |
| Extras | (B 12, LB 31, W 1, NB 7) | 51 | (B 4, NB 5) | | 9 |
| **Total** | | **515** | (0 wickets) | | **114** |

## INDIA

| | | |
|---|---|---|
| S.B.Bangar | c Butcher b Hoggard | 21 |
| V.Sehwag | c Cork b Caddick | 12 |
| R.Dravid | run out | 217 |
| S.R.Tendulkar | lbw b Caddick | 54 |
| *S.C.Ganguly | c Stewart b Cork | 51 |
| V.V.S.Laxman | c Giles b Caddick | 40 |
| A.B.Agarkar | b Vaughan | 31 |
| †A.Ratra | c Butcher b Caddick | 8 |
| A.Kumble | c Hussain b Giles | 7 |
| Harbhajan Singh | b Giles | 17 |
| Z.Khan | not out | 6 |
| Extras | (B 10, LB 6, NB 28) | 44 |
| **Total** | | **508** |

| INDIA | O | M | R | W | | O | M | R | W |
|---|---|---|---|---|---|---|---|---|---|
| Khan | 28 | 4 | 83 | 2 | | 5 | 0 | 37 | 0 |
| Agarkar | 24 | 4 | 111 | 0 | (5) | 4 | 0 | 15 | 0 |
| Bangar | 24 | 8 | 48 | 2 | (2) | 2 | 0 | 6 | 0 |
| Harbhajan Singh | 38.4 | 6 | 115 | 5 | | 7 | 1 | 24 | 0 |
| Kumble | 35 | 11 | 105 | 1 | (3) | 10 | 2 | 28 | 0 |
| Ganguly | 4 | 1 | 6 | 0 | | | | | |
| Tendulkar | 2 | 0 | 4 | 0 | | | | | |

| ENGLAND | O | M | R | W |
|---|---|---|---|---|
| Hoggard | 25 | 2 | 97 | 1 |
| Caddick | 43 | 11 | 114 | 4 |
| Giles | 49 | 12 | 98 | 2 |
| Tudor | 19 | 2 | 80 | 0 |
| Cork | 22 | 5 | 67 | 1 |
| Vaughan | 12 | 1 | 36 | 1 |

| FALL OF WICKETS | | | |
|---|---|---|---|
| | E | I | E |
| Wkt | 1st | 1st | 2nd |
| 1st | 98 | 18 | — |
| 2nd | 272 | 87 | — |
| 3rd | 349 | 178 | — |
| 4th | 367 | 283 | — |
| 5th | 372 | 396 | — |
| 6th | 434 | 465 | — |
| 7th | 446 | 473 | — |
| 8th | 477 | 477 | — |
| 9th | 514 | 493 | — |
| 10th | 515 | 508 | — |

Umpires: E.A.R.de Silva (*Sri Lanka*) (17) and D.L.Orchard (*South Africa*) (30).
Referee: C H.Lloyd (*West Indies*) (14).          **Test No. 1614/91 (E799/I360)**

# ENGLAND v INDIA 2002

## ENGLAND – BATTING AND FIELDING

|  | M | I | NO | HS | Runs | Avge | 100 | 50 | Ct/St |
|---|---|---|---|---|---|---|---|---|---|
| C.White | 2 | 3 | 2 | 94* | 153 | 153.00 | – | 2 | 1 |
| M.P.Vaughan | 4 | 7 | 1 | 197 | 615 | 102.50 | 3 | 1 | 3 |
| A.J.Stewart | 4 | 6 | 1 | 87 | 287 | 57.40 | – | 2 | 7/1 |
| N.Hussain | 4 | 6 | – | 155 | 315 | 52.50 | 2 | – | 4 |
| J.P.Crawley | 4 | 6 | 1 | 100* | 237 | 47.40 | 1 | 1 | – |
| D.G.Cork | 2 | 2 | – | 52 | 83 | 41.50 | – | 1 | 1 |
| M.A.Butcher | 4 | 6 | – | 54 | 212 | 35.33 | – | 2 | 4 |
| R.W.T.Key | 2 | 3 | – | 34 | 81 | 27.00 | – | – | 2 |
| A.F.Giles | 3 | 4 | – | 31 | 85 | 21.25 | – | – | 1 |
| A.Flintoff | 3 | 5 | – | 59 | 99 | 19.80 | – | 1 | 3 |
| M.J.Hoggard | 4 | 5 | 2 | 32 | 43 | 14.33 | – | – | 2 |
| A.R.Caddick | 2 | 3 | 1 | 14* | 18 | 9.00 | – | – | – |
| A.J.Tudor | 2 | 3 | – | 21 | 24 | 8.00 | – | – | – |

*Played in one Test:* S.J.Harmison 3; S.P.Jones 44; G.P.Thorpe 4, 1 (2 ct); M.E.Trescothick 57, 58*.

## ENGLAND – BOWLING

|  | O | M | R | W | Avge | Best | 5wI | 10wM |
|---|---|---|---|---|---|---|---|---|
| S.J.Harmison | 49 | 12 | 120 | 5 | 24.00 | 3- 57 | – | – |
| M.P.Vaughan | 40 | 8 | 120 | 4 | 30.00 | 2- 71 | – | – |
| S.P.Jones | 38 | 3 | 129 | 4 | 32.25 | 2- 61 | – | – |
| C.White | 48.4 | 7 | 178 | 5 | 35.60 | 2- 46 | – | – |
| A.R.Caddick | 83.1 | 16 | 264 | 7 | 37.71 | 4-114 | – | – |
| M.J.Hoggard | 160 | 35 | 533 | 14 | 38.07 | 4- 87 | – | – |
| D.G.Cork | 45 | 9 | 166 | 4 | 41.50 | 2- 54 | – | – |
| A.F.Giles | 126 | 23 | 354 | 5 | 70.80 | 2- 98 | – | – |
| A.Flintoff | 112 | 25 | 357 | 5 | 71.40 | 2- 22 | – | – |
| A.J.Tudor | 55 | 12 | 226 | 2 | 113.00 | 2-146 | – | – |

*Also bowled:* M.A.Butcher 1-1-0-0.

## INDIA – BATTING AND FIELDING

|  | M | I | NO | HS | Runs | Avge | 100 | 50 | Ct/St |
|---|---|---|---|---|---|---|---|---|---|
| R.Dravid | 4 | 6 | – | 217 | 602 | 100.33 | 3 | 1 | 10 |
| S.R.Tendulkar | 4 | 6 | – | 193 | 401 | 66.83 | 1 | 2 | 1 |
| S.C.Ganguly | 4 | 6 | – | 128 | 351 | 58.50 | 1 | 3 | 2 |
| S.B.Bangar | 2 | 2 | – | 68 | 89 | 44.50 | – | 1 | 1 |
| A.B.Agarkar | 4 | 6 | 1 | 109* | 210 | 42.00 | 1 | – | 1 |
| V.V.S.Laxman | 4 | 6 | 1 | 74 | 199 | 39.80 | – | 1 | 3 |
| V.Sehwag | 4 | 6 | – | 106 | 237 | 39.50 | 1 | 1 | 6 |
| P.A.Patel | 2 | 3 | 2 | 19* | 26 | 26.00 | – | – | 1 |
| Harbhajan Singh | 3 | 4 | – | 54 | 90 | 22.50 | – | 1 | – |
| Z.Khan | 4 | 5 | 3 | 14* | 44 | 22.00 | – | – | – |
| W.Jaffer | 4 | 4 | – | 53 | 59 | 14.75 | – | 1 | 5 |
| A.Kumble | 3 | 3 | – | 15 | 22 | 7.33 | – | – | – |
| A.Nehra | 2 | 3 | – | 19 | 19 | 6.33 | – | – | – |
| A.Ratra | 2 | 3 | – | 8 | 10 | 3.33 | – | – | 5/2 |

## INDIA – BOWLING

|  | O | M | R | W | Avge | Best | 5wI | 10wM |
|---|---|---|---|---|---|---|---|---|
| S.B.Bangar | 43 | 11 | 117 | 4 | 29.25 | 2- 48 | – | – |
| Harbhajan Singh | 135.4 | 23 | 410 | 12 | 34.16 | 5-115 | 1 | – |
| A.Kumble | 174.1 | 42 | 504 | 14 | 36.00 | 4- 66 | – | – |
| Z.Khan | 147 | 32 | 483 | 11 | 43.90 | 3- 90 | – | – |
| A.B.Agarkar | 118.3 | 20 | 488 | 8 | 61.00 | 2- 59 | – | – |
| A.Nehra | 76 | 8 | 319 | 5 | 63.80 | 2- 80 | – | – |

*Also bowled:* S.C.Ganguly 12-2-64-0; V.Sehwag 19-1-63-1; S.R.Tendulkar 10-0-33-0.

# PAKISTAN v AUSTRALIA (1st Test)

At P.Saravanamuttu Stadium, Colombo, on 3, 4, 5, 6, 7 October.
Toss: Australia. Result: **AUSTRALIA** won by 41 runs.
Debuts: None.

## AUSTRALIA

| | | | | | |
|---|---|---|---|---|---|
| J.L.Langer | c Rashid b Razzaq | 72 | c Taufiq b Saqlain | | 25 |
| M.L.Hayden | c Imran b Waqar | 4 | c Taufiq b Saqlain | | 34 |
| R.T.Ponting | c Younis Khan b Waqar | 141 | b Shoaib | | 7 |
| M.E.Waugh | c and b Saqlain | 55 | b Shoaib | | 0 |
| *S.R.Waugh | c Younis Khan b Saqlain | 31 | lbw b Shoaib | | 0 |
| D.R.Martyn | c Younis Khan b Saqlain | 67 | c Imran b Saqlain | | 20 |
| †A.C.Gilchrist | not out | 66 | b Shoaib | | 5 |
| S.K.Warne | c Faisal b Shoaib | 0 | lbw b Shoaib | | 5 |
| B.Lee | b Shoaib | 2 | c Misbah b Saqlain | | 12 |
| J.N.Gillespie | lbw b Shoaib | 0 | lbw b Sami | | 1 |
| G.D.McGrath | lbw b Saqlain | 4 | not out | | 5 |
| Extras | (B 4, LB 16, NB 5) | 25 | (B 4, LB 12, NB 2) | | 18 |
| **Total** | | **467** | | | **127** |

## PAKISTAN

| | | | | | |
|---|---|---|---|---|---|
| Imran Nazir | lbw b McGrath | 0 | c McGrath b Warne | | 40 |
| Taufiq Umar | c Ponting b Gillespie | 0 | c M.E.Waugh b Lee | | 88 |
| Abdul Razzaq | c Gilchrist b Warne | 11 | lbw b Warne | | 4 |
| Younis Khan | c Langer b Lee | 58 | lbw b Warne | | 51 |
| Misbah-ul-Haq | c M.E.Waugh b Warne | 17 | c S.R.Waugh b Warne | | 10 |
| Faisal Iqbal | c M.E.Waugh b Warne | 83 | c Ponting b McGrath | | 39 |
| †Rashid Latif | c Martyn b Warne | 66 | c Gilchrist b Gillespie | | 11 |
| Saqlain Mushtaq | lbw b Warne | 1 | c S.R.Waugh b McGrath | | 1 |
| *Waqar Younis | lbw b Warne | 14 | c Gilchrist b Gillespie | | 1 |
| Shoaib Akhtar | c McGrath b Warne | 5 | lbw b McGrath | | 6 |
| Mohammad Sami | not out | 0 | not out | | 6 |
| Extras | (B 7, LB 14, NB 3) | 24 | (B 3, LB 6, NB 8) | | 17 |
| **Total** | | **279** | | | **274** |

| PAKISTAN | O | M | R | W | | O | M | R | W |
|---|---|---|---|---|---|---|---|---|---|
| Waqar Younis | 16 | 2 | 86 | 2 | | 8 | 1 | 23 | 0 |
| Shoaib Akhtar | 21 | 5 | 51 | 3 | | 8 | 2 | 21 | 5 |
| Mohammad Sami | 20 | 3 | 93 | 0 | (5) | 6 | 0 | 13 | 0 |
| Abdul Razzaq | 17 | 1 | 78 | 1 | | | | | |
| Saqlain Mushtaq | 40.5 | 6 | 136 | 4 | (3) | 15.5 | 0 | 46 | 4 |
| Taufiq Umar | 2 | 1 | 3 | 0 | (4) | 2 | 0 | 8 | 0 |
| AUSTRALIA | | | | | | | | | |
| McGrath | 15 | 3 | 40 | 1 | | 24.2 | 12 | 38 | 3 |
| Gillespie | 12 | 2 | 55 | 1 | | 23.3 | 8 | 62 | 2 |
| Lee | 11 | 3 | 49 | 1 | | 14 | 1 | 63 | 1 |
| Warne | 24.3 | 7 | 94 | 7 | | 30.3 | 3 | 94 | 4 |
| M.E.Waugh | | | | | | 5 | 1 | 10 | 0 |

### FALL OF WICKETS

| Wkt | A 1st | P 1st | A 2nd | P 2nd |
|---|---|---|---|---|
| 1st | 5 | 2 | 61 | 91 |
| 2nd | 188 | 4 | 74 | 117 |
| 3rd | 272 | 45 | 74 | 173 |
| 4th | 302 | 75 | 74 | 187 |
| 5th | 329 | 116 | 74 | 230 |
| 6th | 457 | 219 | 85 | 248 |
| 7th | 458 | 239 | 89 | 251 |
| 8th | 462 | 267 | 107 | 252 |
| 9th | 462 | 274 | 112 | 259 |
| 10th | 467 | 279 | 127 | 274 |

Umpires: S.A.Bucknor (*West Indies*) (70) and S.Venkataraghavan (*India*) (58).
Referee: C.H.Lloyd (*West Indies*) (15).           **Test No. 1615/47 (P286/A629)**

# PAKISTAN v AUSTRALIA (2nd Test)

At Sharjah C.A. Stadium, UAE, on 11, 12 October.
Toss: Pakistan. Result: **AUSTRALIA** won by an innings and 198 runs.
Debuts: None.

## PAKISTAN

| | | | | |
|---|---|---|---|---|
| Imran Nazir | c Warne b McGrath | 0 | c Gilchrist b Warne | 16 |
| Taufiq Umar | b Lee | 0 | run out | 0 |
| Abdul Razzaq | c Martyn b Warne | 21 | retired hurt | 4 |
| Younis Khan | c Bichel b McGrath | 5 | lbw b McGrath | 0 |
| Misbah-ul-Haq | c M.E.Waugh b Bichel | 2 | c S.R.Waugh b Bichel | 12 |
| Faisal Iqbal | lbw b Warne | 4 | c M.E.Waugh b Warne | 7 |
| †Rashid Latif | not out | 4 | c M.E.Waugh b Bichel | 0 |
| Saqlain Mushtaq | lbw b Warne | 0 | c Warne b Lee | 9 |
| Shoaib Akhtar | c Gilchrist b Bichel | 1 | c S.R.Waugh b Warne | 2 |
| *Waqar Younis | lbw b Warne | 0 | lbw b Warne | 0 |
| Danish Kaneria | b Lee | 8 | not out | 1 |
| Extras | (B 8, LB 2, NB 4) | 14 | (NB 2) | 2 |
| Total | | **59** | | **53** |

## AUSTRALIA

| | | |
|---|---|---|
| J.L.Langer | run out | 37 |
| M.L.Hayden | c Imran b Saqlain | 119 |
| R.T.Ponting | lbw b Kaneria | 44 |
| M.E.Waugh | lbw b Saqlain | 2 |
| *S.R.Waugh | c sub (Imran Farhat) b Saqlain | 0 |
| D.R.Martyn | c Taufiq b Razzaq | 34 |
| †A.C.Gilchrist | c Taufiq b Shoaib | 17 |
| S.K.Warne | c Younis Khan b Saqlain | 19 |
| B.Lee | lbw b Razzaq | 12 |
| A.J.Bichel | not out | 2 |
| G.D.McGrath | lbw b Razzaq | 0 |
| Extras | (B 15, LB 7, NB 2) | 24 |
| Total | | **310** |

| AUSTRALIA | O | M | R | W | O | M | R | W |
|---|---|---|---|---|---|---|---|---|
| McGrath | 7 | 4 | 10 | 2 | 6 | 2 | 5 | 1 |
| Lee | 7.5 | 1 | 15 | 2 | 5 | 2 | 16 | 1 |
| Bichel | 6 | 2 | 13 | 2 | 7 | 1 | 19 | 2 |
| Warne | 11 | 4 | 11 | 4 | 6.5 | 2 | 13 | 4 |

| PAKISTAN | O | M | R | W |
|---|---|---|---|---|
| Waqar Younis | 8 | 2 | 25 | 0 |
| Shoaib Akhtar | 14 | 3 | 42 | 1 |
| Danish Kaneria | 26 | 2 | 116 | 1 |
| Abdul Razzaq | 10.1 | 3 | 22 | 3 |
| Saqlain Mushtaq | 34 | 2 | 83 | 4 |

| | FALL OF WICKETS | | |
|---|---|---|---|
| | P | A | P |
| Wkt | 1st | 1st | 2nd |
| 1st | 0 | 55 | 0 |
| 2nd | 1 | 145 | 13 |
| 3rd | 8 | 148 | 32 |
| 4th | 23 | 148 | 34 |
| 5th | 41 | 224 | 36 |
| 6th | 46 | 252 | 50 |
| 7th | 46 | 285 | 52 |
| 8th | 49 | 304 | 52 |
| 9th | 50 | 310 | 53 |
| 10th | 59 | 310 | – |

Umpires: S.A.Bucknor (*West Indies*) (71) and S.Venkataraghavan (*India*) (59).
Referee: C.H.Lloyd (*West Indies*) (16).  **Test No. 1616/48 (P287/A630)**

# PAKISTAN v AUSTRALIA (3rd Test)

At Sharjah C.A. Stadium, UAE, on 19, 20, 21, 22 October.
Toss: Australia. Result: **AUSTRALIA** won by an innings and 20 runs.
Debuts: None.

## AUSTRALIA

| | | |
|---|---|---|
| J.L.Langer | b Waqar | 4 |
| M.L.Hayden | c Faisal b Saqlain | 89 |
| R.T.Ponting | b Waqar | 150 |
| M.E.Waugh | c Rashid b Saqlain | 23 |
| *S.R.Waugh | not out | 103 |
| D.R.Martin | lbw b Waqar | 0 |
| †A.C.Gilchrist | c Rashid b Kaneria | 34 |
| S.K.Warne | lbw b Kaneria | 11 |
| B.Lee | run out | 1 |
| A.J.Bichel | c Taufiq b Kaneria | 9 |
| G.D.McGrath | c Rashid b Waqar | 3 |
| Extras | (B 4, LB 10, NB 3) | 17 |
| **Total** | | **444** |

## PAKISTAN

| | | | | | |
|---|---|---|---|---|---|
| Taufiq Umar | lbw b McGrath | 5 | c Gilchrist b McGrath | 1 |
| Imran Farhat | lbw b Warne | 29 | c Gilchrist b Bichel | 18 |
| Younis Khan | c Gilchrist b McGrath | 5 | lbw b McGrath | 4 |
| Faisal Iqbal | c Gilchrist b Warne | 9 | run out | 2 |
| Misbah-ul-Haq | lbw b Bichel | 11 | lbw b Warne | 17 |
| Hasan Raza | not out | 54 | c Gilchrist b Bichel | 68 |
| †Rashid Latif | c M.E.Waugh b Warne | 17 | lbw b Warne | 17 |
| Saqlain Mushtaq | b McGrath | 44 | lbw b Warne | 10 |
| *Waqar Younis | lbw b McGrath | 6 | c M.E.Waugh b McGrath | 24 |
| Mohammad Sami | lbw b Warne | 0 | c Martyn b Bichel | 22 |
| Danish Kaneria | st Gilchrist b Warne | 15 | not out | 2 |
| Extras | (B 3, LB 10, W 2, NB 11) | 26 | (LB 9, NB 9) | 18 |
| **Total** | | **221** | | **203** |

| PAKISTAN | O | M | R | W | O | M | R | W |
|---|---|---|---|---|---|---|---|---|
| Waqar Younis | 17.3 | 5 | 55 | 4 | | | | |
| Mohammad Sami | 28 | 6 | 81 | 0 | | | | |
| Saqlain Mushtaq | 45 | 5 | 159 | 2 | | | | |
| Danish Kaneria | 36 | 8 | 128 | 3 | | | | |
| Taufiq Umar | 2 | 0 | 7 | 0 | | | | |

| AUSTRALIA | O | M | R | W | O | M | R | W |
|---|---|---|---|---|---|---|---|---|
| McGrath | 16 | 4 | 41 | 4 | 7 | 2 | 18 | 3 |
| Lee | 11 | 1 | 47 | 0 | 18 | 5 | 44 | 0 |
| Warne | 30.1 | 10 | 74 | 5 | (4) 21 | 3 | 56 | 3 |
| Bichel | 9 | 0 | 31 | 1 | (3) 11.2 | 1 | 43 | 3 |
| M.E.Waugh | 4 | 0 | 10 | 0 | 10 | 3 | 33 | 0 |
| Ponting | 1 | 0 | 5 | 0 | | | | |

### FALL OF WICKETS

| | A | P | P |
|---|---|---|---|
| Wkt | 1st | 1st | 2nd |
| 1st | 4 | 22 | 6 |
| 2nd | 188 | 50 | 12 |
| 3rd | 233 | 50 | 18 |
| 4th | 308 | 70 | 30 |
| 5th | 308 | 76 | 58 |
| 6th | 363 | 100 | 86 |
| 7th | 403 | 191 | 102 |
| 8th | 404 | 198 | 157 |
| 9th | 418 | 199 | 197 |
| 10th | 444 | 221 | 203 |

Umpires: S.A.Bucknor (*West Indies*) (72) and S.Venkataraghavan (*India*) (60).
Referee: C.H.Lloyd (*West Indies*) (17).          **Test No. 1617/49 (P288/A631)**

# PAKISTAN v AUSTRALIA 2002-03

## PAKISTAN – BATTING AND FIELDING

| | M | I | NO | HS | Runs | Avge | 100 | 50 | Ct/St |
|---|---|---|---|---|---|---|---|---|---|
| Faisal Iqbal | 3 | 6 | – | 83 | 144 | 24.00 | – | 1 | 2 |
| Rashid Latif | 3 | 6 | 1 | 66 | 115 | 23.00 | – | 1 | 4 |
| Younis Khan | 3 | 6 | – | 58 | 123 | 20.50 | – | 2 | 4 |
| Taufiq Umar | 3 | 6 | – | 88 | 94 | 15.66 | – | 1 | 5 |
| Imran Nazir | 2 | 4 | – | 40 | 56 | 14.00 | – | – | 3 |
| Mohammad Sami | 2 | 4 | 2 | 22 | 28 | 14.00 | – | – | – |
| Abdul Razzaq | 2 | 4 | 1 | 21 | 40 | 13.33 | – | – | – |
| Danish Kaneria | 2 | 4 | 2 | 15 | 26 | 13.00 | – | – | – |
| Misbah-ul-Haq | 3 | 6 | – | 17 | 69 | 11.50 | – | – | 1 |
| Saqlain Mushtaq | 3 | 6 | – | 44 | 65 | 10.83 | – | – | 1 |
| Waqar Younis | 3 | 6 | – | 24 | 45 | 7.50 | – | – | – |
| Shoaib Akhtar | 2 | 4 | – | 6 | 14 | 3.50 | – | – | – |

*Played in one Test:* Hasan Raza 54*, 68; Imran Farhat 29, 18.

## PAKISTAN – BOWLING

| | O | M | R | W | Avge | Best | 5wI | 10wM |
|---|---|---|---|---|---|---|---|---|
| Shoaib Akhtar | 43 | 10 | 114 | 9 | 12.66 | 5- 21 | 1 | – |
| Abdul Razzaq | 27.1 | 4 | 100 | 4 | 25.00 | 3- 22 | – | – |
| Saqlain Mushtaq | 135.4 | 13 | 424 | 14 | 30.28 | 4- 46 | – | – |
| Waqar Younis | 49.3 | 10 | 189 | 6 | 31.50 | 4- 55 | – | – |
| Danish Kaneria | 62 | 10 | 244 | 4 | 61.00 | 3-128 | – | – |
| Mohammad Sami | 54 | 9 | 187 | 1 | 187.00 | 1- 13 | – | – |

*Also bowled:* Taufiq Umar 6-1-18-0.

## AUSTRALIA – BATTING AND FIELDING

| | M | I | NO | HS | Runs | Avge | 100 | 50 | Ct/St |
|---|---|---|---|---|---|---|---|---|---|
| R.T.Ponting | 3 | 4 | – | 150 | 342 | 85.50 | 2 | – | 2 |
| M.L.Hayden | 3 | 4 | – | 119 | 246 | 61.50 | 1 | 1 | – |
| S.R.Waugh | 3 | 4 | 1 | 103* | 134 | 44.66 | 1 | – | 4 |
| A.C.Gilchrist | 3 | 4 | 1 | 66* | 122 | 40.66 | – | 1 | 10/1 |
| J.L.Langer | 3 | 4 | – | 72 | 138 | 34.50 | – | 1 | 1 |
| D.R.Martyn | 3 | 4 | – | 67 | 121 | 30.25 | – | 1 | 3 |
| M.E.Waugh | 3 | 4 | – | 55 | 80 | 20.00 | – | 1 | 8 |
| A.J.Bichel | 2 | 2 | 1 | 9 | 11 | 11.00 | – | – | 1 |
| S.K.Warne | 3 | 4 | – | 19 | 30 | 7.50 | – | – | 2 |
| B.Lee | 3 | 4 | – | 12 | 27 | 6.75 | – | – | – |
| G.D.McGrath | 3 | 4 | 1 | 5* | 12 | 4.00 | – | – | 2 |

*Played in one Test:* J.N.Gillespie 0, 1.

## AUSTRALIA – BOWLING

| | O | M | R | W | Avge | Best | 5wI | 10wM |
|---|---|---|---|---|---|---|---|---|
| G.D.McGrath | 75.2 | 27 | 152 | 14 | 10.85 | 4-41 | – | – |
| S.K.Warne | 124 | 29 | 342 | 27 | 12.66 | 7-94 | 2 | 1 |
| A.J.Bichel | 33.2 | 4 | 106 | 8 | 13.25 | 3-43 | – | – |
| J.N.Gillespie | 35.3 | 10 | 117 | 3 | 39.00 | 2-62 | – | – |
| B.Lee | 66.5 | 13 | 234 | 5 | 46.80 | 2-15 | – | – |

*Also bowled:* R.T.Ponting 1-0-5-0; M.E.Waugh 19-4-71-0.

# INDIA v WEST INDIES (1st Test)

At Wankhede Stadium, Bombay, on 9, 10, 11, 12 October.
Toss: India. Result: **INDIA** won by an innings and 112 runs.
Debuts: None.

## INDIA

| | | |
|---|---|---|
| S.B.Bangar | c Sarwan b Dillon | 55 |
| V.Sehwag | c Jacobs b Dillon | 147 |
| R.Dravid | retired hurt | 100 |
| S.R.Tendulkar | c Jacobs b Dillon | 35 |
| *S.C.Ganguly | lbw b Cuffy | 4 |
| V.V.S.Laxman | st Jacobs b Nagamootoo | 45 |
| †P.A.Patel | not out | 21 |
| Harbhajan Singh | c Jacobs b Cuffy | 0 |
| A.Kumble | c Hooper b Nagamootoo | 0 |
| Z.Khan | lbw b Nagamootoo | 0 |
| J.Srinath | c Jacobs b Hooper | 31 |
| Extras | (LB 7, W 3, NB 9) | 19 |
| **Total** | | **457** |

## WEST INDIES

| | | | | | |
|---|---|---|---|---|---|
| C.H.Gayle | lbw b Khan | 7 | | c Ganguly b Harbhajan | 42 |
| W.W.Hinds | c sub (S.S.Das) b Harbhajan | 1 | | b Harbhajan | 40 |
| R.R.Sarwan | lbw b Kumble | 22 | | c Tendulkar b Kumble | 17 |
| M.Dillon | b Srinath | 21 | (9) | c Dravid b Harbhajan | 0 |
| S.Chanderpaul | c and b Kumble | 54 | (4) | not out | 36 |
| *C.L.Hooper | c Bangar b Khan | 23 | (5) | c and b Harbhajan | 1 |
| R.O.Hinds | lbw b Khan | 9 | (6) | c Sehwag b Kumble | 2 |
| †R.D.Jacobs | c Ganguly b Khan | 0 | (7) | c Ganguly b Kumble | 0 |
| M.V.Nagamootoo | c Harbhajan b Kumble | 9 | (8) | c Ganguly b Harbhajan | 18 |
| P.T.Collins | lbw b Kumble | 0 | | c Dravid b Harbhajan | 8 |
| C.E.Cuffy | not out | 4 | | c and b Harbhajan | 0 |
| Extras | (LB 5, NB 2) | 7 | | (B 8, LB 15, NB 1) | 24 |
| **Total** | | **157** | | | **188** |

| WEST INDIES | O | M | R | W | | O | M | R | W |
|---|---|---|---|---|---|---|---|---|---|
| Dillon | 31.2 | 9 | 54 | 3 | | | | | |
| Collins | 28 | 7 | 76 | 0 | | | | | |
| Cuffy | 28.4 | 6 | 88 | 2 | | | | | |
| Nagamootoo | 47 | 12 | 132 | 3 | | | | | |
| Hooper | 11.5 | 3 | 40 | 1 | | | | | |
| W.W.Hinds | 4 | 0 | 11 | 0 | | | | | |
| R.O.Hinds | 10 | 0 | 40 | 0 | | | | | |
| Gayle | 2 | 1 | 3 | 0 | | | | | |
| Sarwan | 1 | 0 | 6 | 0 | | | | | |
| **INDIA** | | | | | | | | | |
| Srinath | 11 | 5 | 16 | 1 | | 4 | 2 | 19 | 0 |
| Khan | 16 | 4 | 41 | 4 | | 4 | 0 | 26 | 0 |
| Harbhajan Singh | 21 | 8 | 37 | 1 | (4) | 28.3 | 12 | 48 | 7 |
| Kumble | 24.5 | 5 | 51 | 4 | (5) | 25 | 8 | 50 | 3 |
| Sehwag | 2 | 0 | 7 | 0 | | | | | |
| Bangar | | | | | (3) | 6 | 1 | 20 | 0 |
| Tendulkar | | | | | (6) | 1 | 0 | 2 | 0 |

FALL OF WICKETS

| | I | WI | WI |
|---|---|---|---|
| Wkt | 1st | 1st | 2nd |
| 1st | 201 | 7 | 60 |
| 2nd | 213 | 27 | 105 |
| 3rd | 281 | 43 | 107 |
| 4th | 296 | 59 | 110 |
| 5th | 401 | 103 | 117 |
| 6th | 407 | 119 | 117 |
| 7th | 408 | 123 | 158 |
| 8th | 408 | 145 | 158 |
| 9th | 457 | 146 | 184 |
| 10th | – | 157 | 188 |

Umpires: E.A.R.de Silva (*Sri Lanka*) (18) and D.R.Shepherd (*England*) (65).
Referee: M.J.Procter (*South Africa*) (3).     **Test No. 1618/76 (1361/WI389)**

# INDIA v WEST INDIES (2nd Test)

At M.A.Chidambaram Stadium, Chepauk, Madras, on 17, 18, 19, 20 October.
Toss: West Indies. Result: **INDIA** won by eight wickets.
Debuts: West Indies – G.R.Breese, J.J.C.Lawson.

## WEST INDIES

| | | | | | |
|---|---|---|---|---|---|
| C.H.Gayle | c Tendulkar b Harbhajan | 23 | c Kumble b Srinath | | 0 |
| W.W.Hinds | lbw b Kumble | 18 | c Ganguly b Harbhajan | | 61 |
| R.R.Sarwan | b Srinath | 19 | lbw b Khan | | 78 |
| S.Chanderpaul | c Patel b Kumble | 27 | c Harbhajan b Srinath | | 3 |
| *C.L.Hooper | c Ganguly b Khan | 35 | c Patel b Kumble | | 46 |
| R.O.Hinds | lbw b Kumble | 16 | c Kumble b Harbhajan | | 7 |
| †R.D.Jacobs | c Sehwag b Harbhajan | 9 | c Patel b Khan | | 3 |
| G.R.Breese | c Sehwag b Harbhajan | 5 | c Ganguly b Harbhajan | | 0 |
| M.Dillon | b Kumble | 4 | lbw b Harbhajan | | 4 |
| P.T.Collins | not out | 1 | not out | | 6 |
| J.J.C.Lawson | c Ganguly b Kumble | 0 | b Khan | | 2 |
| Extras | (B 8, LB 1, NB 1) | 10 | (B 12, LB 3, W 1, NB 3) | | 19 |
| **Total** | | **167** | | | **229** |

## INDIA

| | | | | | |
|---|---|---|---|---|---|
| S.B.Bangar | c Hooper b Dillon | 40 | c Gayle b Hooper | | 20 |
| V.Sehwag | b Collins | 61 | st Jacobs b Hooper | | 33 |
| R.Dravid | b Lawson | 11 | not out | | 6 |
| S.R.Tendulkar | b Lawson | 43 | not out | | 16 |
| *S.C.Ganguly | lbw b Dillon | 0 | | | |
| V.V.S.Laxman | c and b Breese | 24 | | | |
| †P.A.Patel | st Jacobs b Breese | 23 | | | |
| Harbhajan Singh | b Dillon | 37 | | | |
| J.Srinath | run out | 39 | | | |
| A.Kumble | not out | 12 | | | |
| Z.Khan | run out | 4 | | | |
| Extras | (B 4, LB 10, W 1, NB 7) | 22 | (LB 3, NB 3) | | 6 |
| **Total** | | **316** | (2 wickets) | | **81** |

| INDIA | O | M | R | W | | O | M | R | W | | FALL OF WICKETS | | | |
|---|---|---|---|---|---|---|---|---|---|---|---|---|---|---|
| Srinath | 10 | 5 | 14 | 1 | | 9 | 4 | 16 | 2 | | | WI | I | WI | I |
| Khan | 10 | 3 | 21 | 1 | | 12.4 | 5 | 23 | 3 | | *Wkt* | *1st* | *1st* | *2nd* | *2nd* |
| Bangar | 6 | 3 | 29 | 0 | | | | | | | 1st | 40 | 93 | 0 | 50 |
| Harbhajan Singh | 29 | 13 | 56 | 3 | (3) | 30 | 6 | 79 | 4 | | 2nd | 46 | 109 | 96 | 61 |
| Kumble | 23.3 | 10 | 30 | 5 | (4) | 26 | 3 | 87 | 1 | | 3rd | 62 | 155 | 107 | – |
| Sehwag | 1 | 0 | 8 | 0 | (5) | 2 | 0 | 9 | 0 | | 4th | 117 | 155 | 179 | – |
| **WEST INDIES** | | | | | | | | | | | 5th | 135 | 180 | 208 | – |
| Dillon | 26 | 11 | 44 | 3 | | 5 | 1 | 10 | 0 | | 6th | 142 | 204 | 210 | – |
| Collins | 23 | 5 | 59 | 1 | | 2 | 0 | 7 | 0 | | 7th | 161 | 255 | 210 | – |
| Lawson | 20 | 4 | 63 | 2 | | 2 | 0 | 2 | 0 | | 8th | 166 | 281 | 214 | – |
| Breese | 26.1 | 3 | 108 | 2 | | 5.1 | 0 | 27 | 0 | | 9th | 166 | 305 | 222 | – |
| Hooper | 6 | 2 | 19 | 0 | | 7 | 1 | 32 | 2 | | 10th | 167 | 316 | 229 | – |
| R.O.Hinds | 5 | 1 | 9 | 0 | | | | | | | | | | | |

Umpires: E.A.R.de Silva (*Sri Lanka*) (19) and D.R.Shepherd (*England*) (66).
Referee: M.J.Procter (*South Africa*) (4). **Test No. 1619/77 (I362/WI390)**

# INDIA v WEST INDIES (3rd Test)

At Eden Gardens, Calcutta, on 30, 31 October, 1, 2, 3 November.
Toss: India. Result: **MATCH DRAWN**.
Debuts: None.

## INDIA

| | | | | | |
|---|---|---|---|---|---|
| S.B.Bangar | c Hinds b Cuffy | 77 | c Chanderpaul b Dillon | 0 |
| V.Sehwag | lbw b Dillon | 35 | c Chanderpaul b Dillon | 10 |
| R.Dravid | lbw b Powell | 14 | lbw b Powell | 17 |
| S.R.Tendulkar | c Gayle b Lawson | 36 | c Gayle b Cuffy | 176 |
| *S.C.Ganguly | c Jacobs b Hooper | 29 | lbw b Cuffy | 16 |
| V.V.S.Laxman | c Gayle b Dillon | 48 | not out | 154 |
| †P.A.Patel | c Chanderpaul b Lawson | 47 | run out | 27 |
| Harbhajan Singh | b Cuffy | 6 | c Hooper b Samuels | 26 |
| J.Srinath | c Hooper b Dillon | 46 | c Hooper b Chanderpaul | 21 |
| A.Kumble | lbw b Powell | 4 | not out | 8 |
| A.Nehra | not out | 0 | | |
| Extras | (LB 7, W 1, NB 8) | 16 | (B 8, LB 7, W 1) | 16 |
| **Total** | | **358** | (8 wickets declared) | **471** |

## WEST INDIES

| | | |
|---|---|---|
| C.H.Gayle | c Sehwag b Kumble | 88 |
| W.W.Hinds | c Ganguly b Harbhajan | 100 |
| R.R.Sarwan | st Patel b Harbhajan | 2 |
| M.Dillon | b Harbhajan | 0 |
| S.Chanderpaul | c Harbhajan b Sehwag | 140 |
| *C.L.Hooper | c Patel b Nehra | 19 |
| M.N.Samuels | c Sehwag b Harbhajan | 104 |
| †R.D.Jacobs | not out | 22 |
| D.B.Powell | lbw b Kumble | 0 |
| J.J.C Lawson | lbw b Kumble | 5 |
| C.E.Cuffy | c Laxman b Harbhajan | 0 |
| Extras | (B 4, LB 7, NB 6) | 17 |
| **Total** | | **497** |

| WEST INDIES | O | M | R | W | O | M | R | W |
|---|---|---|---|---|---|---|---|---|
| Dillon | 22 | 3 | 82 | 3 | 25 | 6 | 85 | 2 |
| Cuffy | 25 | 4 | 84 | 2 | 17 | 3 | 52 | 2 |
| Lawson | 20 | 3 | 76 | 2 | 22 | 3 | 65 | 0 |
| Powell | 16.2 | 4 | 62 | 2 | 25 | 4 | 53 | 1 |
| Hooper | 15 | 5 | 36 | 1 | 20 | 1 | 63 | 0 |
| Gayle | 2 | 0 | 6 | 0 | 23 | 5 | 70 | 0 |
| Sarwan | 1 | 0 | 5 | 0 | 8 | 1 | 38 | 0 |
| Samuels | | | | | 16 | 3 | 21 | 1 |
| Chanderpaul | | | | | 3 | 0 | 9 | 1 |

| INDIA | O | M | R | W | FALL OF WICKETS | | | |
|---|---|---|---|---|---|---|---|---|
| | | | | | | I | WI | I |
| Srinath | 19 | 3 | 62 | 0 | *Wkt* | *1st* | *1st* | *2nd* |
| Nehra | 23 | 9 | 66 | 1 | 1st | 49 | 172 | 0 |
| Harbhajan Singh | 57.3 | 15 | 115 | 5 | 2nd | 72 | 186 | 11 |
| Kumble | 54 | 9 | 169 | 3 | 3rd | 116 | 186 | 49 |
| Bangar | 6 | 3 | 14 | 0 | 4th | 165 | 213 | 87 |
| Tendulkar | 7 | 0 | 33 | 0 | 5th | 242 | 255 | 301 |
| Sehwag | 5 | 0 | 27 | 1 | 6th | 271 | 450 | 373 |
| | | | | | 7th | 280 | 469 | 407 |
| | | | | | 8th | 353 | 470 | 458 |
| | | | | | 9th | 358 | 496 | – |
| | | | | | 10th | 358 | 497 | – |

Umpires: E.A.R.de Silva (*Sri Lanka*) (20) and D.R.Shepherd (*England*) (67).
Referee: M.J.Procter (*South Africa*) (5). **Test No. 1620/78 (1363/WI391)**

# INDIA v WEST INDIES 2002-03

## INDIA – BATTING AND FIELDING

|                | M | I | NO | HS   | Runs | Avge  | 100 | 50 | Ct/St |
|----------------|---|---|----|------|------|-------|-----|----|-------|
| V.V.S.Laxman   | 3 | 4 | 1  | 154* | 271  | 90.33 | 1   | –  | 1     |
| S.R.Tendulkar  | 3 | 5 | 1  | 176  | 306  | 76.50 | 1   | –  | 2     |
| V.Sehwag       | 3 | 5 | –  | 147  | 286  | 57.20 | 1   | 1  | 5     |
| R.Dravid       | 3 | 5 | 2  | 100* | 148  | 49.33 | 1   | –  | 2     |
| P.A.Patel      | 3 | 4 | 1  | 47   | 118  | 39.33 | –   | –  | 4/1   |
| S.B.Bangar     | 3 | 4 | –  | 77   | 192  | 38.40 | –   | 2  | 1     |
| J.Srinath      | 3 | 4 | –  | 46   | 137  | 34.25 | –   | –  | –     |
| Harbhajan Singh| 3 | 4 | –  | 37   | 69   | 17.25 | –   | –  | 5     |
| S.C.Ganguly    | 3 | 4 | –  | 29   | 49   | 12.25 | –   | –  | 9     |
| A.Kumble       | 3 | 4 | 2  | 12*  | 24   | 12.00 | –   | –  | 3     |
| Z.Khan         | 2 | 2 | –  | 4    | 4    | 2.00  | –   | –  | –     |

*Played in one Test:* A.Nehra 0*.

## INDIA – BOWLING

|                | O     | M  | R   | W  | Avge  | Best | 5wI | 10wM |
|----------------|-------|----|-----|----|-------|------|-----|------|
| Z.Khan         | 42.4  | 12 | 111 | 8  | 13.87 | 4-41 | –   | –    |
| Harbhajan Singh| 166   | 54 | 335 | 20 | 16.75 | 7-48 | 2   | –    |
| A.Kumble       | 153.2 | 35 | 387 | 16 | 24.18 | 5-30 | 1   | –    |
| J.Srinath      | 53    | 19 | 127 | 4  | 31.75 | 2-16 | –   | –    |

*Also bowled:* S.B.Bangar 18-7-63-0; A.Nehra 23-9-66-1; V.Sehwag 10-0-51-1; S.R.Tendulkar 8-0-35-0.

## WEST INDIES – BATTING AND FIELDING

|                | M | I | NO | HS  | Runs | Avge  | 100 | 50 | Ct/St |
|----------------|---|---|----|-----|------|-------|-----|----|-------|
| S.Chanderpaul  | 3 | 5 | 1  | 140 | 260  | 65.00 | 1   | 1  | 3     |
| W.W.Hinds      | 3 | 5 | –  | 100 | 220  | 44.00 | 1   | 1  | 1     |
| C.H.Gayle      | 3 | 5 | –  | 88  | 160  | 32.00 | –   | 1  | 4     |
| R.R.Sarwan     | 3 | 5 | –  | 78  | 138  | 27.60 | –   | 1  | 1     |
| C.L.Hooper     | 3 | 5 | –  | 46  | 124  | 24.80 | –   | –  | 6     |
| R.D.Jacobs     | 3 | 5 | 1  | 22* | 34   | 8.50  | –   | –  | 5/3   |
| R.O.Hinds      | 2 | 4 | –  | 16  | 34   | 8.50  | –   | –  | –     |
| P.T.Collins    | 2 | 4 | 2  | 8   | 15   | 7.50  | –   | –  | –     |
| M.Dillon       | 3 | 5 | –  | 21  | 29   | 5.80  | –   | –  | –     |
| J.J.C.Lawson   | 2 | 3 | –  | 5   | 7    | 2.33  | –   | –  | –     |
| C.E.Cuffy      | 2 | 3 | 1  | 4*  | 4    | 2.00  | –   | –  | –     |

*Played in one Test:* G.R.Breese 5, 0 (1 ct); M.V.Nagamootoo 9, 18; D.B.Powell 0; M.N.Samuels 104.

## WEST INDIES – BOWLING

|                | O     | M  | R   | W | Avge  | Best  | 5wI | 10wM |
|----------------|-------|----|-----|---|-------|-------|-----|------|
| M.Dillon       | 109.2 | 30 | 275 | 11| 25.00 | 3- 44 | –   | –    |
| C.E.Cuffy      | 70.4  | 13 | 224 | 6 | 37.33 | 2- 52 | –   | –    |
| D.B.Powell     | 41.2  | 8  | 115 | 3 | 38.33 | 2- 62 | –   | –    |
| M.V.Nagamootoo | 47    | 12 | 132 | 3 | 44.00 | 3-132 | –   | –    |
| C.L.Hooper     | 59.5  | 20 | 190 | 4 | 47.50 | 2- 32 | –   | –    |
| J.J.C.Lawson   | 64    | 10 | 206 | 4 | 51.50 | 2- 63 | –   | –    |
| G.R.Breese     | 31.2  | 3  | 135 | 2 | 67.50 | 2-108 | –   | –    |

*Also bowled:* S.Chanderpaul 3-0-9-1; P.T.Collins 53-12-142-1; C.H.Gayle 27-6-79-0; R.O.Hinds 15-1-49-0; W.W.Hinds 4-0-11-0; M.N.Samuels 16-3-21-1; R.R.Sarwan 10-1-49-0.

# SOUTH AFRICA v BANGLADESH (1st Test)

At Buffalo Park, East London, on 18, 19, 20, 21 October.
Toss: Bangladesh. Result: **SOUTH AFRICA** won by an innings and 107 runs.
Debuts: South Africa – M.van Jaarsveld.

## SOUTH AFRICA

| | | |
|---|---|---|
| G.C.Smith | c Manjural b Sanwar | 200 |
| H.H.Gibbs | c Tushar b Tapash | 41 |
| G.Kirsten | c Alok b Talha | 150 |
| J.H.Kallis | not out | 75 |
| A.G.Prince | c Alok b Talha | 2 |
| M.van Jaarsveld | not out | 39 |
| *†M.V.Boucher | | |
| D.J.Terbrugge | | |
| C.W.Henderson | | |
| M.Ntini | | |
| M.Hayward | | |
| Extras | (B 2, LB 1, W 4, NB 15) | 22 |
| **Total** | (4 wickets declared) | **529** |

## BANGLADESH

| | | | | | |
|---|---|---|---|---|---|
| Javed Omar | lbw b Terbrugge | 7 | c Gibbs b Hayward | | 10 |
| Al Sahariar | b Hayward | 18 | b Ntini | | 71 |
| Habibul Bashar | c Boucher b Ntini | 38 | c Terbrugge b Hayward | | 21 |
| Sanwar Hossain | c Boucher b Ntini | 31 | lbw b Terbrugge | | 49 |
| Tushar Imran | b Ntini | 0 | (6) c Van Jaarsveld b Henderson | | 8 |
| Alok Kapali | c Kallis b Henderson | 35 | (7) lbw b Terbrugge | | 10 |
| *†Khaled Masud | c Van Jaarsveld b Hayward | 4 | (5) lbw b Terbrugge | | 33 |
| Mohammed Rafique | not out | 17 | b Terbrugge | | 19 |
| Tapash Baisya | c Boucher b Ntini | 2 | c Kirsten b Terbrugge | | 10 |
| Manjural Islam | b Ntini | 4 | c sub (A.C.Thomas) b Ntini | | 8 |
| Talha Jubair | c Boucher b Terbrugge | 3 | not out | | 4 |
| Extras | (LB 9, W 1, NB 1) | 11 | (B 3, LB 3, NB 3) | | 9 |
| **Total** | | **170** | | | **252** |

| BANGLADESH | O | M | R | W | | O | M | R | W |
|---|---|---|---|---|---|---|---|---|---|
| Manjural Islam | 29 | 3 | 104 | 0 | | | | | |
| Tapash Baisya | 30 | 3 | 148 | 1 | | | | | |
| Talha Jubair | 26 | 5 | 108 | 2 | | | | | |
| Mohammed Rafique | 23 | 2 | 85 | 0 | | | | | |
| Alok Kapali | 18 | 0 | 72 | 0 | | | | | |
| Sanwar Hossain | 3 | 0 | 9 | 1 | | | | | |
| **SOUTH AFRICA** | | | | | | | | | |
| Hayward | 15 | 3 | 50 | 2 | (3) | 16 | 2 | 65 | 2 |
| Terbrugge | 11.4 | 3 | 43 | 2 | | 15 | 1 | 46 | 5 |
| Henderson | 9 | 2 | 23 | 1 | (5) | 28 | 8 | 58 | 1 |
| Ntini | 15 | 9 | 19 | 5 | (1) | 18.5 | 6 | 55 | 2 |
| Kallis | 8 | 2 | 26 | 0 | (4) | 10 | 3 | 22 | 0 |

FALL OF WICKETS

| | SA | B | B |
|---|---|---|---|
| Wkt | 1st | 1st | 2nd |
| 1st | 87 | 21 | 22 |
| 2nd | 359 | 25 | 78 |
| 3rd | 440 | 91 | 121 |
| 4th | 448 | 97 | 158 |
| 5th | – | 100 | 176 |
| 6th | – | 130 | 211 |
| 7th | – | 149 | 212 |
| 8th | – | 155 | 231 |
| 9th | – | 161 | 244 |
| 10th | – | 170 | 252 |

Umpires: D.J.Harper (*Australia*) (23) and R.B.Tiffin (*Zimbabwe*) (29).
Referee: R.S.Madugalle (*Sri Lanka*) (44).          **Test No. 1621/1 (SA267/B14)**

# SOUTH AFRICA v BANGLADESH (2nd Test)

At North West Cricket Stadium, Potchefstroom, on 25, 26, 27 October.
Toss: Bangladesh. Result: **SOUTH AFRICA** won by an innings and 160 runs.
Debuts: Bangladesh – Rafiqul Islam.

## BANGLADESH

| | | | | | |
|---|---|---|---|---|---|
| Hannan Sarkar | c Kallis b Ntini | 65 | | b Ntini | 17 |
| Al Sahariar | c Smith b Hayward | 30 | | c Kallis b Hayward | 27 |
| Habibul Bashar | c Boucher b Pollock | 40 | | c Boucher b Ntini | 7 |
| Sanwar Hossain | lbw b Ntini | 0 | | c Kallis b Ntini | 6 |
| *†Khaled Masud | c Van Jaarsveld b Kallis | 20 | (6) | c Boucher b Kallis | 9 |
| Rafiqul Islam | c Gibbs b Kallis | 6 | (8) | c Kirsten b Kallis | 1 |
| Tushar Imran | c Boucher b Pollock | 8 | (5) | c Prince b Hayward | 0 |
| Alok Kapali | not out | 38 | (7) | c Boucher b Kallis | 23 |
| Tapash Baisya | c Van Jaarsveld b Hayward | 2 | | c Gibbs b Kallis | 0 |
| Manjural Islam | c Smith b Henderson | 0 | | c Gibbs b Kallis | 5 |
| Talha Jubair | run out | 0 | | not out | 1 |
| Extras | (B 4, NB 2) | 6 | | (LB 8, NB 3) | 11 |
| **Total** | | **215** | | | **107** |

## SOUTH AFRICA

| | | |
|---|---|---|
| G.C.Smith | c Masud b Sanwar | 24 |
| H.H.Gibbs | run out | 114 |
| G.Kirsten | c Masud b Talha | 160 |
| J.H.Kallis | not out | 139 |
| A.G.Prince | c Masud b Talha | 0 |
| M.van Jaarsveld | lbw b Tapash | 11 |
| †M.V.Boucher | not out | 14 |
| *S.M.Pollock | | |
| C.W.Henderson | | |
| M.Ntini | | |
| M.Hayward | | |
| Extras | (B 13, LB 2, NB 5) | 20 |
| **Total** | (5 wickets declared) | **482** |

| SOUTH AFRICA | O | M | R | W | O | M | R | W | FALL OF WICKETS | | | |
|---|---|---|---|---|---|---|---|---|---|---|---|---|
| | | | | | | | | | | B | SA | B |
| Pollock | 16 | 6 | 38 | 2 | 6 | 0 | 25 | 0 | *Wkt* | *1st* | *1st* | *2nd* |
| Ntini | 21 | 4 | 69 | 2 | 12 | 1 | 37 | 3 | 1st | 52 | 61 | 33 |
| Hayward | 14 | 3 | 64 | 2 | 8 | 3 | 16 | 2 | 2nd | 136 | 202 | 43 |
| Kallis | 13 | 4 | 26 | 2 | 4.3 | 1 | 21 | 5 | 3rd | 136 | 436 | 52 |
| Henderson | 5.5 | 2 | 14 | 1 | | | | | 4th | 140 | 436 | 60 |
| | | | | | | | | | 5th | 162 | 452 | 61 |
| **BANGLADESH** | | | | | | | | | 6th | 169 | – | 95 |
| Manjural Islam | 26 | 7 | 80 | 0 | | | | | 7th | 184 | – | 101 |
| Tapash Baisya | 28 | 3 | 103 | 1 | | | | | 8th | 197 | – | 101 |
| Talha Jubair | 26 | 3 | 109 | 2 | | | | | 9th | 202 | – | 104 |
| Alok Kapali | 20 | 2 | 75 | 0 | | | | | 10th | 215 | – | 107 |
| Sanwar Hossain | 20 | 1 | 98 | 1 | | | | | | | | |
| Habibul Bashar | 1 | 0 | 2 | 0 | | | | | | | | |

Umpires: D.J.Harper (*Australia*) (24) and R.B.Tiffin (*Zimbabwe*) (30).
Referee: R.S.Madugalle (*Sri Lanka*) (45).          **Test No. 1622/2 (SA268/B15)**

# AUSTRALIA v ENGLAND (1st Test)

At Woolloongabba, Brisbane, on 7, 8, 9, 10 November.
Toss: England. Result: **AUSTRALIA** won by 384 runs.
Debuts: None.

## AUSTRALIA

| | | | | | |
|---|---|---|---|---|---|
| J.L.Langer | c Stewart b Jones | 32 | c Stewart b Caddick | | 22 |
| M.L.Hayden | c Stewart b Caddick | 197 | c and b Giles | | 103 |
| R.T.Ponting | b Giles | 123 | c Trescothick b Caddick | | 3 |
| D.R.Martyn | c Trescothick b White | 26 | c Hussain b Giles | | 64 |
| *S.R.Waugh | c Crawley b Caddick | 7 | (6) c Trescothick b Caddick | | 12 |
| D.S.Lehmann | c Butcher b Giles | 30 | (7) not out | | 20 |
| †A.C.Gilchrist | c Giles b White | 0 | (5) not out | | 60 |
| S.K.Warne | c Butcher b Caddick | 57 | | | |
| A.J.Bichel | lbw b Giles | 0 | | | |
| J.N.Gillespie | not out | 0 | | | |
| G.D.McGrath | lbw b Giles | 0 | | | |
| Extras | (B 1, LB 11, W 1, NB 7) | 20 | (B 3, LB 5, NB 4) | | 12 |
| Total | | 492 | (5 wickets declared) | | 296 |

## ENGLAND

| | | | | | |
|---|---|---|---|---|---|
| M.E.Trescothick | c Ponting b McGrath | 72 | c Gilchrist b Gillespie | | 1 |
| M.P.Vaughan | c Gilchrist b McGrath | 33 | lbw b McGrath | | 0 |
| M.A.Butcher | c Hayden b McGrath | 54 | c Ponting b Warne | | 40 |
| *N.Hussain | c Gilchrist b Gillespie | 51 | c Ponting b McGrath | | 11 |
| J.P.Crawley | not out | 69 | run out | | 0 |
| †A.J.Stewart | b Gillespie | 0 | c Hayden b Warne | | 0 |
| C.White | b McGrath | 12 | c Hayden b McGrath | | 13 |
| A.F.Giles | c Gilchrist b Bichel | 13 | c Gilchrist b McGrath | | 4 |
| A.R.Caddick | c Ponting b Bichel | 7 | c Lehmann b Warne | | 4 |
| M.J.Hoggard | c Hayden b Warne | 4 | not out | | 1 |
| S.P.Jones | absent hurt | – | absent hurt | | – |
| Extras | (B 2, LB 8, NB 7) | 17 | (LB 1, NB 4) | | 5 |
| Total | | 325 | | | 79 |

| ENGLAND | O | M | R | W | O | M | R | W |
|---|---|---|---|---|---|---|---|---|
| Caddick | 35 | 9 | 108 | 3 | 23 | 2 | 95 | 3 |
| Hoggard | 30 | 4 | 122 | 0 | 13 | 2 | 42 | 0 |
| Jones | 7 | 0 | 32 | 1 | | | | |
| White | 27 | 4 | 105 | 2 | (3) 11 | 0 | 61 | 0 |
| Giles | 29.2 | 3 | 101 | 4 | (4) 24 | 2 | 90 | 2 |
| Butcher | 2 | 0 | 12 | 0 | | | | |
| **AUSTRALIA** | | | | | | | | |
| McGrath | 30 | 9 | 87 | 4 | 12 | 3 | 36 | 4 |
| Gillespie | 18 | 4 | 51 | 2 | 6 | 1 | 13 | 1 |
| Bichel | 23 | 4 | 74 | 2 | | | | |
| Warne | 26.5 | 4 | 87 | 1 | (3) 10.2 | 3 | 29 | 3 |
| Waugh | 4 | 2 | 5 | 0 | | | | |
| Lehmann | 5 | 0 | 11 | 0 | | | | |

### FALL OF WICKETS

| | A | E | A | E |
|---|---|---|---|---|
| Wkt | 1st | 1st | 2nd | 2nd |
| 1st | 67 | 49 | 30 | 1 |
| 2nd | 339 | 170 | 39 | 3 |
| 3rd | 378 | 171 | 192 | 33 |
| 4th | 399 | 268 | 213 | 34 |
| 5th | 408 | 270 | 242 | 35 |
| 6th | 415 | 283 | – | 66 |
| 7th | 478 | 308 | – | 74 |
| 8th | 478 | 308 | – | 74 |
| 9th | 492 | 325 | – | 79 |
| 10th | 492 | – | – | – |

Umpires: S.A.Bucknor (*West Indies*) (73) and R.E.Koertzen (*South Africa*) (35).
Referee: Wasim Raja (*Pakistan*) (5).

**Test No. 1623/302 (A632/E800)**

# AUSTRALIA v ENGLAND (2nd Test)

At Adelaide Oval on 21, 22, 23, 24 November.
Toss: England. Result: **AUSTRALIA** won by an innings and 51 runs.
Debuts: None.

## ENGLAND

| | | | | | |
|---|---|---|---|---|---|
| M.E.Trescothick | b McGrath | 35 | | lbw b Gillespie | 0 |
| M.P.Vaughan | c Warne b Bichel | 177 | | c McGrath b Warne | 41 |
| R.W.T.Key | c Ponting b Warne | 1 | (5) | c Lehmann b Bichel | 1 |
| *N.Hussain | c Gilchrist b Warne | 47 | | b Bichel | 10 |
| M.A.Butcher | c Gilchrist b Gillespie | 22 | (3) | lbw b McGrath | 4 |
| †A.J.Stewart | lbw b Gillespie | 29 | | lbw b Warne | 57 |
| C.White | c Bichel b Gillespie | 1 | | c sub (B.Lee) b McGrath | 5 |
| R.K.J.Dawson | lbw b Warne | 6 | | c Gilchrist b McGrath | 19 |
| A.R.Caddick | b Warne | 0 | (11) | not out | 6 |
| M.J.Hoggard | c Gilchrist b Gillespie | 6 | (9) | b McGrath | 1 |
| S.J.Harmison | not out | 3 | (10) | lbw b Warne | 0 |
| Extras | (LB 7, NB 8) | 15 | | (B 3, LB 4, NB 8) | 15 |
| **Total** | | **342** | | | **159** |

## AUSTRALIA

| | | |
|---|---|---|
| J.L.Langer | c Stewart b Dawson | 48 |
| M.L.Hayden | c Caddick b White | 46 |
| R.T.Ponting | c Dawson b White | 154 |
| D.R.Martyn | c Hussain b Harmison | 95 |
| *S.R.Waugh | c Butcher b White | 34 |
| D.S.Lehmann | c sub (A.Flintoff) b White | 5 |
| †A.C.Gilchrist | c Stewart b Harmison | 54 |
| S.K.Warne | c and b Dawson | 25 |
| A.J.Bichel | b Hoggard | 48 |
| J.N.Gillespie | not out | 0 |
| G.D.McGrath | | |
| Extras | (B 1, LB 17, W 7, NB 18) | 43 |
| **Total** | (9 wickets declared) | **552** |

| AUSTRALIA | O | M | R | W | | O | M | R | W | | FALL OF WICKETS | | | |
|---|---|---|---|---|---|---|---|---|---|---|---|---|---|---|
| McGrath | 30 | 11 | 77 | 1 | | 17.2 | 6 | 41 | 4 | | | E | A | E |
| Gillespie | 26.5 | 8 | 78 | 4 | | 12 | 1 | 44 | 1 | | Wkt | 1st | 1st | 2nd |
| Bichel | 20 | 2 | 78 | 1 | (4) | 5 | 0 | 31 | 2 | | 1st | 88 | 101 | 5 |
| Warne | 34 | 10 | 93 | 4 | (3) | 25 | 7 | 36 | 3 | | 2nd | 106 | 114 | 17 |
| Waugh | 5 | 1 | 9 | 0 | | | | | | | 3rd | 246 | 356 | 36 |
| | | | | | | | | | | | 4th | 295 | 397 | 40 |
| **ENGLAND** | | | | | | | | | | | 5th | 295 | 414 | 114 |
| Caddick | 20 | 2 | 95 | 0 | | | | | | | 6th | 308 | 423 | 130 |
| Hoggard | 26 | 4 | 84 | 1 | | | | | | | 7th | 325 | 471 | 130 |
| Harmison | 28.2 | 8 | 106 | 2 | | | | | | | 8th | 325 | 548 | 132 |
| White | 28 | 2 | 106 | 4 | | | | | | | 9th | 337 | 552 | 134 |
| Dawson | 37 | 2 | 143 | 2 | | | | | | | 10th | 342 | – | 159 |

Umpires: S.A.Bucknor (*West Indies*) (74) and R.E.Koertzen (*South Africa*) (36).
Referee: Wasim Raja (*Pakistan*) (6).           **Test No. 1624/303 (A633/E801)**

# AUSTRALIA v ENGLAND (3rd Test)

At W.A.C.A. Ground, Perth, on 29, 30 November, 1 December.
Toss: England. Result: **AUSTRALIA** won by an innings and 48 runs.
Debuts: None.

## ENGLAND

| | | | | | |
|---|---|---|---|---|---|
| M.E.Trescothick | c Gilchrist b Lee | 34 | | c Gilchrist b Lee | 4 |
| M.P.Vaughan | c Gilchrist b McGrath | 34 | | run out | 9 |
| M.A.Butcher | run out | 9 | (4) | lbw b McGrath | 0 |
| *N.Hussain | c Gilchrist b Lee | 8 | (5) | c Gilchrist b Warne | 61 |
| R.W.T.Key | b Martyn | 47 | (6) | lbw b McGrath | 23 |
| †A.J.Stewart | c Gilchrist b McGrath | 7 | (7) | not out | 66 |
| C.White | c Martyn b Lee | 2 | (8) | st Gilchrist b Warne | 15 |
| A.J.Tudor | c Martyn b Warne | 0 | (9) | retired hurt | 3 |
| R.K.J.Dawson | not out | 19 | (3) | c Waugh b Gillespie | 8 |
| C.E.W.Silverwood | c Hayden b Gillespie | 10 | | absent hurt | – |
| S.J.Harmison | b Gillespie | 6 | (10) | b Lee | 5 |
| Extras | (LB 2, NB 7) | 9 | | (B 8, LB 5, W 1, NB 15) | 29 |
| **Total** | | **185** | | | **223** |

## AUSTRALIA

| | | |
|---|---|---|
| J.L.Langer | run out | 19 |
| M.L.Hayden | c Tudor b Harmison | 30 |
| R.T.Ponting | b White | 68 |
| D.R.Martyn | c Stewart b Tudor | 71 |
| D.S.Lehmann | c Harmison b White | 42 |
| *S.R.Waugh | b Tudor | 53 |
| †A.C.Gilchrist | c Tudor b White | 38 |
| S.K.Warne | run out | 35 |
| B.Lee | c Key b White | 41 |
| J.N.Gillespie | b White | 27 |
| G.D.McGrath | not out | 8 |
| Extras | (B 4, LB 5, NB 15) | 24 |
| **Total** | | **456** |

| AUSTRALIA | O | M | R | W | O | M | R | W |
|---|---|---|---|---|---|---|---|---|
| McGrath | 17 | 5 | 30 | 2 | (2) 21 | 9 | 24 | 2 |
| Gillespie | 17.2 | 8 | 43 | 2 | (3) 15 | 4 | 35 | 1 |
| Lee | 20 | 1 | 78 | 3 | (1) 18.1 | 3 | 72 | 2 |
| Warne | 9 | 0 | 32 | 1 | 26 | 5 | 70 | 2 |
| Martyn | 1 | 1 | 0 | 1 | 2 | 0 | 9 | 0 |

| ENGLAND | O | M | R | W |
|---|---|---|---|---|
| Silverwood | 4 | 0 | 29 | 0 |
| Tudor | 29 | 2 | 144 | 2 |
| Harmison | 28 | 7 | 86 | 1 |
| White | 23.1 | 3 | 127 | 5 |
| Butcher | 10 | 1 | 40 | 0 |
| Dawson | 1 | 0 | 21 | 0 |

## FALL OF WICKETS

| Wkt | E 1st | A 1st | E 2nd |
|---|---|---|---|
| 1st | 47 | 31 | 13 |
| 2nd | 69 | 85 | 33 |
| 3rd | 83 | 159 | 34 |
| 4th | 101 | 226 | 34 |
| 5th | 111 | 264 | 102 |
| 6th | 121 | 316 | 169 |
| 7th | 135 | 348 | 208 |
| 8th | 156 | 416 | 223 |
| 9th | 173 | 423 | – |
| 10th | 185 | 456 | – |

Umpires: S.A.Bucknor (*West Indies*) (75) and R.E.Koertzen (*South Africa*) (37).
Referee: Wasim Raja (*Pakistan*) (7).     **Test No. 1625/304 (A634/E802)**

# AUSTRALIA v ENGLAND (4th Test)

At Melbourne Cricket Ground on 26, 27, 28, 29, 30 December.
Toss: Australia. Result: **AUSTRALIA** won by five wickets.
Debuts: Australia – M.L.Love.

## AUSTRALIA

| | | | | | |
|---|---|---|---|---|---|
| J.L.Langer | c Caddick b Dawson | 250 | lbw b Caddick | | 24 |
| M.L.Hayden | c Crawley b Caddick | 102 | c sub (A.J.Tudor) b Caddick | | 1 |
| R.T.Ponting | b White | 21 | c Foster b Harmison | | 30 |
| D.R.Martyn | c Trescothick b White | 17 | c Foster b Harmison | | 0 |
| *S.R.Waugh | c Foster b White | 77 | c Butcher b Caddick | | 14 |
| M.L.Love | not out | 62 | not out | | 6 |
| †A.C.Gilchrist | b Dawson | 1 | not out | | 10 |
| B.Lee | | | | | |
| J.N.Gillespie | | | | | |
| S.C.G.MacGill | | | | | |
| G.D.McGrath | | | | | |
| Extras | (LB 11, W 5, NB 5) | 21 | (B 8, LB 5, NB 9) | | 22 |
| **Total** | (6 wickets declared) | **551** | (5 wickets) | | **107** |

## ENGLAND

| | | | | | |
|---|---|---|---|---|---|
| M.E.Trescothick | c Gilchrist b Lee | 37 | lbw b MacGill | | 37 |
| M.P.Vaughan | b McGrath | 11 | c Love b MacGill | | 145 |
| M.A.Butcher | lbw b Gillespie | 25 | c Love b Gillespie | | 6 |
| *N.Hussain | c Hayden b MacGill | 24 | c and b McGrath | | 23 |
| R.K.J.Dawson | c Love b MacGill | 6 | (9) not out | | 15 |
| R.W.T.Key | lbw b Lee | 0 | (5) c Ponting b Gillespie | | 52 |
| J.P.Crawley | c Langer b Gillespie | 17 | (6) b Lee | | 33 |
| C.White | not out | 85 | (7) c Gilchrist b MacGill | | 21 |
| †J.S.Foster | lbw b Waugh | 19 | (8) c Love b MacGill | | 6 |
| A.R.Caddick | b Gillespie | 17 | c Waugh b MacGill | | 10 |
| S.J.Harmison | c Gilchrist b Gillespie | 2 | b Gillespie | | 7 |
| Extras | (B 3, LB 10, NB 14) | 27 | (B 3, LB 21, W 2, NB 6) | | 32 |
| **Total** | | **270** | | | **387** |

| ENGLAND | O | M | R | W | O | M | R | W |
|---|---|---|---|---|---|---|---|---|
| Caddick | 36 | 6 | 126 | 1 | 12 | 1 | 51 | 3 |
| Harmison | 36 | 7 | 108 | 0 | 11.1 | 1 | 43 | 2 |
| White | 33 | 5 | 133 | 3 | | | | |
| Dawson | 28 | 1 | 121 | 2 | | | | |
| Butcher | 13 | 2 | 52 | 0 | | | | |

| AUSTRALIA | O | M | R | W | O | M | R | W |
|---|---|---|---|---|---|---|---|---|
| McGrath | 16 | 5 | 41 | 1 | 19 | 5 | 44 | 1 |
| Gillespie | 16.3 | 7 | 25 | 4 | 24.4 | 6 | 71 | 3 |
| MacGill | 36 | 10 | 108 | 2 | 48 | 10 | 152 | 5 |
| Lee | 17 | 4 | 70 | 2 | 27 | 4 | 87 | 1 |
| Waugh | 4 | 0 | 13 | 1 | 2 | 0 | 9 | 0 |

FALL OF WICKETS

| | A | E | E | A |
|---|---|---|---|---|
| Wkt | 1st | 1st | 2nd | 2nd |
| 1st | 195 | 13 | 67 | 8 |
| 2nd | 235 | 73 | 89 | 58 |
| 3rd | 265 | 94 | 169 | 58 |
| 4th | 394 | 111 | 236 | 83 |
| 5th | 545 | 113 | 287 | 90 |
| 6th | 551 | 118 | 342 | – |
| 7th | – | 172 | 342 | – |
| 8th | – | 227 | 356 | – |
| 9th | – | 264 | 378 | – |
| 10th | – | 270 | 387 | – |

Umpires: D.L.Orchard (*South Africa*) (35) and R.B.Tiffin (*Zimbabwe*) (33).
Referee: Wasim Raja (*Pakistan*) (8).          **Test No. 1626/305 (A635/E803)**

# AUSTRALIA v ENGLAND (5th Test)

At Sydney Cricket Ground on 2, 3, 4, 5, 6 January.
Toss: England. Result: **ENGLAND** won by 225 runs.
Debuts: None.

## ENGLAND

| | | | | | |
|---|---|---:|---|---|---:|
| M.E.Trescothick | c Gilchrist b Bichel | 19 | b Lee | | 22 |
| M.P.Vaughan | c Gilchrist b Lee | 0 | lbw b Bichel | | 183 |
| M.A.Butcher | b Lee | 124 | c Hayden b MacGill | | 34 |
| *N.Hussain | c Gilchrist b Gillespie | 75 | c Gilchrist b Lee | | 72 |
| R.W.T.Key | lbw b Waugh | 3 | c Hayden b Lee | | 14 |
| J.P.Crawley | not out | 35 | lbw b Gillespie | | 8 |
| †A.J.Stewart | b Bichel | 71 | not out | | 38 |
| R.K.J.Dawson | c Gilchrist b Bichel | 2 | c and b Bichel | | 12 |
| A.R.Caddick | b MacGill | 7 | c Langer b MacGill | | 8 |
| M.J.Hoggard | st Gilchrist b MacGill | 0 | b MacGill | | 0 |
| S.J.Harmison | run out | 4 | not out | | 20 |
| Extras | (B 6, LB 3, NB 13) | 22 | (B 9, LB 20, W 2, NB 10) | | 41 |
| **Total** | | **362** | (9 wickets declared) | | **452** |

## AUSTRALIA

| | | | | | |
|---|---|---:|---|---|---:|
| J.L.Langer | c Hoggard b Caddick | 25 | lbw b Caddick | | 3 |
| M.L.Hayden | lbw b Caddick | 15 | lbw b Hoggard | | 2 |
| R.T.Ponting | c Stewart b Caddick | 7 | (4) lbw b Caddick | | 11 |
| D.R.Martyn | c Caddick b Harmison | 26 | (5) c Stewart b Dawson | | 21 |
| *S.R.Waugh | c Butcher b Hoggard | 102 | (6) b Caddick | | 6 |
| M.L.Love | c Trescothick b Harmison | 0 | (7) b Harmison | | 27 |
| †A.C.Gilchrist | c Stewart b Harmison | 133 | (8) c Butcher b Caddick | | 37 |
| A.J.Bichel | c Crawley b Hoggard | 4 | (3) lbw b Caddick | | 49 |
| B.Lee | c Stewart b Hoggard | 0 | c Stewart b Caddick | | 46 |
| J.N.Gillespie | not out | 31 | not out | | 3 |
| S.C.G.MacGill | c Hussain b Hoggard | 1 | b Caddick | | 1 |
| Extras | (B 2, LB 6, W 2, NB 9) | 19 | (B 6, LB 8, W 3, NB 3) | | 20 |
| **Total** | | **363** | | | **226** |

| AUSTRALIA | O | M | R | W | | O | M | R | W | FALL OF WICKETS | | | | |
|---|---|---|---|---|---|---|---|---|---|---|---|---|---|---|
| | | | | | | | | | | | E | A | E | A |
| Gillespie | 27 | 10 | 62 | 1 | | 18.3 | 4 | 70 | 1 | | | | | |
| Lee | 31 | 9 | 97 | 2 | | 31.3 | 5 | 132 | 3 | *Wkt* | *1st* | *1st* | *2nd* | *2nd* |
| Bichel | 21 | 5 | 86 | 3 | (4) | 25.3 | 5 | 82 | 2 | 1st | 4 | 36 | 37 | 5 |
| MacGill | 44 | 8 | 106 | 2 | (3) | 41 | 8 | 120 | 3 | 2nd | 32 | 45 | 124 | 5 |
| Waugh | 4 | 3 | 2 | 1 | (6) | 6 | 2 | 5 | 0 | 3rd | 198 | 56 | 313 | 25 |
| Martyn | | | | | (5) | 3 | 1 | 14 | 0 | 4th | 210 | 146 | 344 | 93 |
| | | | | | | | | | | 5th | 240 | 150 | 345 | 99 |
| **ENGLAND** | | | | | | | | | | 6th | 332 | 241 | 356 | 109 |
| Hoggard | 21.3 | 4 | 92 | 4 | | 13 | 3 | 35 | 1 | 7th | 337 | 267 | 378 | 139 |
| Caddick | 23 | 3 | 121 | 3 | | 22 | 5 | 94 | 7 | 8th | 348 | 267 | 407 | 181 |
| Harmison | 20 | 4 | 70 | 3 | | 9 | 1 | 42 | 1 | 9th | 350 | 349 | 409 | 224 |
| Dawson | 16 | 0 | 72 | 0 | | 10 | 2 | 41 | 1 | 10th | 362 | 363 | – | 226 |

Umpires: D.L.Orchard (*South Africa*) (36) and R.B.Tiffin (*Zimbabwe*) (34).
Referee: Wasim Raja (*Pakistan*) (9).          **Test No. 1627/306 (A636/E804)**

# AUSTRALIA v ENGLAND 2002-03

## AUSTRALIA – BATTING AND FIELDING

|  | M | I | NO | HS | Runs | Avge | 100 | 50 | Ct/St |
|---|---|---|---|---|---|---|---|---|---|
| M.L.Hayden | 5 | 8 | – | 197 | 496 | 62.00 | 3 | – | 8 |
| J.N.Gillespie | 5 | 5 | 4 | 31* | 61 | 61.00 | – | – | – |
| A.C.Gilchrist | 5 | 8 | 2 | 133 | 333 | 55.50 | 1 | 2 | 23/2 |
| J.L.Langer | 5 | 8 | – | 250 | 423 | 52.87 | 1 | – | 2 |
| R.T.Ponting | 5 | 8 | – | 154 | 417 | 52.12 | 2 | 1 | 6 |
| M.L.Love | 2 | 4 | 2 | 62* | 95 | 47.50 | – | 1 | 4 |
| D.R.Martyn | 5 | 8 | – | 95 | 320 | 40.00 | – | 3 | 2 |
| S.K.Warne | 3 | 3 | – | 57 | 117 | 39.00 | – | 1 | 1 |
| S.R.Waugh | 5 | 8 | – | 102 | 305 | 38.12 | 1 | 2 | 2 |
| D.S.Lehmann | 3 | 4 | 1 | 42 | 97 | 32.33 | – | – | – |
| B.Lee | 3 | 3 | – | 46 | 87 | 29.00 | – | – | 2 |
| A.J.Bichel | 3 | 4 | – | 49 | 101 | 25.25 | – | – | 2 |
| G.D.McGrath | 4 | 2 | 1 | 8* | 8 | 8.00 | – | – | 2 |
| S.C.G.MacGill | 2 | 2 | – | 1 | 2 | 1.00 | – | – | – |

## AUSTRALIA – BOWLING

|  | O | M | R | W | Avge | Best | 5wI | 10wM |
|---|---|---|---|---|---|---|---|---|
| G.D.McGrath | 162.2 | 53 | 380 | 19 | 20.00 | 4- 36 | – | – |
| J.N.Gillespie | 181.5 | 53 | 492 | 20 | 24.60 | 4- 25 | – | – |
| S.K.Warne | 131.1 | 29 | 347 | 14 | 24.78 | 4- 93 | – | – |
| A.J.Bichel | 94.3 | 14 | 351 | 10 | 35.10 | 3- 86 | – | – |
| S.C.G.MacGill | 169 | 36 | 486 | 12 | 40.50 | 5-152 | 1 | – |
| B.Lee | 144.4 | 26 | 536 | 13 | 41.23 | 3- 78 | – | – |

*Also bowled:* D.S.Lehmann 5-0-11-0; D.R.Martyn 6-2-23-1; S.R.Waugh 25-8-43-2.

## ENGLAND – BATTING AND FIELDING

|  | M | I | NO | HS | Runs | Avge | 100 | 50 | Ct/St |
|---|---|---|---|---|---|---|---|---|---|
| M.P.Vaughan | 5 | 10 | – | 183 | 633 | 63.30 | 3 | – | – |
| A.J.Stewart | 4 | 8 | 2 | 71 | 268 | 44.66 | – | 3 | 11 |
| J.P.Crawley | 3 | 6 | 2 | 69* | 162 | 40.50 | – | 1 | 3 |
| N.Hussain | 5 | 10 | – | 75 | 382 | 38.20 | – | 4 | 3 |
| M.A.Butcher | 5 | 10 | – | 124 | 318 | 31.80 | 1 | 1 | 6 |
| M.E.Trescothick | 5 | 10 | – | 72 | 261 | 26.10 | – | 1 | 5 |
| C.White | 4 | 8 | 1 | 85* | 154 | 22.00 | – | 1 | – |
| R.W.T.Key | 4 | 8 | – | 52 | 141 | 17.62 | – | 1 | 1 |
| R.K.J.Dawson | 4 | 8 | 2 | 19* | 87 | 14.50 | – | – | 2 |
| S.J.Harmison | 4 | 8 | 2 | 20* | 47 | 7.83 | – | – | 1 |
| A.R.Caddick | 4 | 8 | 1 | 17 | 52 | 7.42 | – | – | 1 |
| M.J.Hoggard | 3 | 6 | 1 | 6 | 12 | 2.40 | – | – | 1 |

*Played in one Test:* J.S.Foster 19, 6 (3 ct); A.F.Giles 13, 4 (2 ct); S.P.Jones did not bat; C.E.W.Silverwood 10; A.J.Tudor 0, 3* (2 ct).

## ENGLAND – BOWLING

|  | O | M | R | W | Avge | Best | 5wI | 10wM |
|---|---|---|---|---|---|---|---|---|
| A.F.Giles | 53.2 | 5 | 191 | 6 | 31.83 | 4-101 | – | – |
| A.R.Caddick | 171 | 28 | 690 | 20 | 34.50 | 7- 94 | 1 | 1 |
| C.White | 122.1 | 14 | 532 | 14 | 38.00 | 5-127 | 1 | – |
| S.J.Harmison | 132.3 | 28 | 455 | 9 | 50.55 | 3- 70 | – | – |
| M.J.Hoggard | 103.3 | 17 | 375 | 6 | 62.50 | 4- 92 | – | – |
| R.K.J.Dawson | 96 | 5 | 398 | 5 | 79.60 | 2-121 | – | – |

*Also bowled:* M.A.Butcher 25-3-104-0; S.P.Jones 7-0-32-1; C.E.W.Silverwood 4-0-29-0; A.J.Tudor 29-2-144-2.

# SOUTH AFRICA v SRI LANKA (1st Test)

At The Wanderers, Johannesburg, on 8, 9, 10 November.
Toss: Sri Lanka. Result: **SOUTH AFRICA** won by an innings and 64 runs.
Debuts: Sri Lanka – K.H.R.K.Fernando.

## SRI LANKA

| | | | | | |
|---|---|---|---|---|---|
| M.S.Atapattu | b Pollock | 34 | c Smith b Elworthy | | 43 |
| R.P.Arnold | c Smith b Ntini | 0 | c Kallis b Ntini | | 0 |
| †K.C.Sangakkara | c Smith b Elworthy | 26 | c Boucher b Ntini | | 7 |
| D.P.M.deS.Jayawardena | c Boucher b Kallis | 39 | c Kirsten b Pollock | | 1 |
| *S.T.Jayasuriya | c Smith b Kallis | 32 | b Pollock | | 0 |
| H.P.Tillekeratne | run out | 24 | c Elworthy b Hall | | 27 |
| K.H.R.K.Fernando | c Kirsten b Kallis | 0 | lbw b Elworthy | | 0 |
| W.P.U.C.J.Vaas | c Kallis b Hall | 1 | c Kirsten b Ntini | | 32 |
| C.R.D.Fernando | b Pollock | 7 | not out | | 4 |
| M.Muralitharan | c Ntini b Hall | 10 | b Hall | | 0 |
| P.D.R.L.Perera | not out | 11 | b Hall | | 4 |
| Extras | (B 4, LB 2, W 1, NB 1) | 8 | (B 4, LB 7, W 1) | | 12 |
| **Total** | | **192** | | | **130** |

## SOUTH AFRICA

| | | |
|---|---|---|
| G.C.Smith | c Tillekeratne b KHRK Fernando | 73 |
| G.Kirsten | c Muralitharan b KHRK Fernando | 55 |
| M.van Jaarsveld | b KHRK Fernando | 5 |
| J.H.Kallis | c Sangakkara b Vaas | 75 |
| A.G.Prince | c Perera b Vaas | 3 |
| N.D.McKenzie | lbw b Vaas | 0 |
| †M.V.Boucher | c Sangakkara b Muralitharan | 38 |
| *S.M.Pollock | c Sangakkara b CRD Fernando | 38 |
| A.J.Hall | lbw b Muralitharan | 31 |
| S.Elworthy | lbw b Muralitharan | 6 |
| M.Ntini | not out | 2 |
| Extras | (B 16, LB 10, W 5, NB 31) | 62 |
| **Total** | | **386** |

| **SOUTH AFRICA** | O | M | R | W | | O | M | R | W |
|---|---|---|---|---|---|---|---|---|---|
| Pollock | 18 | 8 | 45 | 2 | | 8 | 3 | 17 | 2 |
| Ntini | 14 | 5 | 45 | 1 | | 10 | 4 | 22 | 3 |
| Elworthy | 15.3 | 3 | 42 | 1 | (4) | 10 | 3 | 39 | 2 |
| Kallis | 17 | 8 | 35 | 3 | (3) | 11 | 3 | 40 | 0 |
| Hall | 11 | 6 | 19 | 2 | | 11 | 3 | 10 | 3 |
| **SRI LANKA** | | | | | | | | | |
| Vaas | 22 | 2 | 79 | 4 | | | | | |
| Perera | 10.2 | 2 | 40 | 0 | | | | | |
| C.R.D.Fernando | 20 | 2 | 95 | 1 | | | | | |
| Muralitharan | 31.2 | 8 | 83 | 3 | | | | | |
| K.H.R.K.Fernando | 21 | 2 | 63 | 3 | | | | | |

### FALL OF WICKETS

| Wkt | SL 1st | SA 1st | SL 2nd |
|---|---|---|---|
| 1st | 2 | 133 | 2 |
| 2nd | 46 | 148 | 16 |
| 3rd | 86 | 175 | 21 |
| 4th | 137 | 179 | 25 |
| 5th | 140 | 180 | 77 |
| 6th | 140 | 249 | 81 |
| 7th | 141 | 329 | 122 |
| 8th | 152 | 378 | 122 |
| 9th | 165 | 378 | 122 |
| 10th | 192 | 386 | 130 |

Umpires: D.J.Harper (*Australia*) (25) and R.B.Tiffin (*Zimbabwe*) (31).
Referee: G.R.Viswanath (*Sri Lanka*) (6). **Test No. 1628/12 (SA269/SL128)**

# SOUTH AFRICA v SRI LANKA (2nd Test)

At Centurion Park, (Verwoerdburg), Pretoria, on 15, 16, 17, 18, 19 November.
Toss: South Africa. Result: **SOUTH AFRICA** won by three wickets.
Debuts: None.

## SRI LANKA

| | | | | | |
|---|---|---|---|---|---|
| M.S.Atapattu | c Kirsten b Kallis | 17 | c Boucher b Kallis | | 22 |
| J.Mubarak | c Smith b Pollock | 48 | c Boucher b Ntini | | 15 |
| †K.Sangakkara | c Pollock b Hall | 35 | c Boucher b Ntini | | 89 |
| D.P.M.deS.Jayawardena | b Pollock | 44 | lbw b Ntini | | 40 |
| H.P.Tillekeratne | not out | 104 | c Boucher b Kallis | | 6 |
| R.P.Arnold | c Boucher b Kallis | 2 | lbw b Pollock | | 4 |
| K.H.R.K.Fernando | c Kallis b Ntini | 24 | c Hall b Ntini | | 14 |
| W.P.U.C.J.Vaas | c Boucher b Ntini | 7 | lbw b Kallis | | 17 |
| M.K.G.C.P.Lakshitha | c Kirsten b Ntini | 2 | c Pollock b Kallis | | 0 |
| C.R.D.Fernando | c Boucher b Ntini | 0 | c Boucher b Elworthy | | 14 |
| M.Muralitharan | b Kallis | 27 | not out | | 0 |
| Extras | (LB 10, W 1, NB 2) | 13 | (B 13, LB 1, W 7, NB 3) | | 24 |
| **Total** | | **323** | | | **245** |

## SOUTH AFRICA

| | | | | | |
|---|---|---|---|---|---|
| G.C.Smith | lbw b CRD Fernando | 15 | lbw b Vaas | | 0 |
| H.H.Gibbs | run out | 92 | c Sangakkara b CRD Fernando | | 7 |
| G.Kirsten | c KHRK Fernando b CRD Fernando | 11 | c Mubarak b CRD Fernando | | 11 |
| J.H.Kallis | b KHRK Fernando | 84 | b CRD Fernando | | 6 |
| A.G.Prince | c Sangakkara b Vaas | 20 | c Sangakkara b CRD Fernando | | 5 |
| N.D.McKenzie | lbw b Lakshitha | 28 | (7) b Muralitharan | | 39 |
| †M.V.Boucher | c and b Lakshitha | 63 | (8) not out | | 22 |
| *S.M.Pollock | not out | 99 | (9) not out | | 6 |
| A.J.Hall | lbw b Muralitharan | 0 | (6) c Arnold b Muralitharan | | 16 |
| S.Elworthy | c Tillekeratne b Muralitharan | 5 | | | |
| M.Ntini | c Arnold b Vaas | 8 | | | |
| Extras | (B 4, LB 10, W 4, NB 5) | 23 | (B 5, LB 1, NB 6) | | 12 |
| **Total** | | **448** | (7 wickets) | | **124** |

| SOUTH AFRICA | O | M | R | W | O | M | R | W | | FALL OF WICKETS | | | |
|---|---|---|---|---|---|---|---|---|---|---|---|---|---|
| Pollock | 29 | 11 | 51 | 2 | 17 | 7 | 45 | 1 | | | SL | SA | SL | SA |
| Ntini | 29 | 6 | 86 | 4 | 22 | 5 | 52 | 4 | | *Wkt* | *1st* | *1st* | *2nd* | *2nd* |
| Elworthy | 21 | 4 | 71 | 0 | 12 | 1 | 54 | 1 | | 1st | 34 | 45 | 23 | 0 |
| Kallis | 15.5 | 2 | 71 | 3 | (5) 14.2 | 5 | 39 | 4 | | 2nd | 90 | 71 | 60 | 13 |
| Hall | 14 | 3 | 34 | 1 | (4) 8 | 0 | 29 | 0 | | 3rd | 108 | 211 | 179 | 23 |
| Smith | | | | | 4 | 2 | 12 | 0 | | 4th | 189 | 219 | 180 | 31 |
| | | | | | | | | | | 5th | 207 | 258 | 185 | 44 |
| SRI LANKA | | | | | | | | | | 6th | 263 | 264 | 205 | 73 |
| Vaas | 33.3 | 7 | 81 | 2 | 8 | 2 | 28 | 1 | | 7th | 277 | 396 | 209 | 112 |
| Lakshitha | 22 | 2 | 71 | 2 | (4) 2 | 1 | 6 | 0 | | 8th | 281 | 400 | 209 | – |
| C.R.D.Fernando | 27 | 0 | 91 | 2 | (2) 12 | 0 | 49 | 4 | | 9th | 281 | 408 | 245 | – |
| Muralitharan | 57 | 10 | 133 | 2 | (3) 13.3 | 1 | 35 | 2 | | 10th | 323 | 448 | 245 | – |
| K.H.R.K.Fernando | 18 | 5 | 45 | 1 | | | | | | | | | | |
| Mubarak | 2 | 0 | 6 | 0 | | | | | | | | | | |
| Jayawardena | 2 | 1 | 2 | 0 | | | | | | | | | | |
| Arnold | 5 | 2 | 5 | 0 | | | | | | | | | | |

Umpires: D.J.Harper (*Australia*) (26) and R.B.Tiffin (*Zimbabwe*) (32).
Referee: G.R.Viswanath (India) (7). **Test No. 1629/13 (SA270/SL129)**

# ZIMBABWE v PAKISTAN (1st Test)

At Harare Sports Club on 9, 10, 11, 12 November.
Toss: Zimbabwe. Result: **PAKISTAN** won by 119 runs.
Debuts: Zimbabwe – N.B.Mahwire; Pakistan – Kamran Akmal.

## PAKISTAN

| | | | | | |
|---|---|--:|---|---|--:|
| Taufiq Umar | c A.Flower b Blignaut | 75 | c Taibu b Blignaut | | 111 |
| Salim Elahi | c Campbell b Blignaut | 2 | c Campbell b Olonga | | 0 |
| Younis Khan | c Ebrahim b Blignaut | 40 | c Campbell b Olonga | | 8 |
| Inzamam-ul-Haq | c sub (M.A.Vermeulen) b Olonga | 39 | c G.W.Flower b Olonga | | 112 |
| Yousuf Youhana | lbw b Price | 63 | c Taibu b Blignaut | | 0 |
| Hasan Raza | c Campbell b Mahwire | 46 | c Blignaut b Price | | 11 |
| †Kamran Akmal | b Price | 0 | b Price | | 38 |
| Saqlain Mushtaq | c A.Flower b Whittall | 2 | not out | | 29 |
| *Waqar Younis | lbw b Blignaut | 2 | b Blignaut | | 0 |
| Shoaib Akhtar | c G.W.Flower b Blignaut | 1 | c Taibu b Olonga | | 16 |
| Mohammad Sami | not out | 0 | c G.W.Flower b Olonga | | 17 |
| Extras | (LB 2, W 4, NB 9) | 15 | (B 4, LB 3, W 11, NB 9) | | 27 |
| **Total** | | **285** | | | **369** |

## ZIMBABWE

| | | | | | |
|---|---|--:|---|---|--:|
| D.D.Ebrahim | c Inzamam b Sami | 31 | b Shoaib | | 69 |
| H.Masakadza | c Kamran b Sami | 9 | c Salim b Shoaib | | 0 |
| *A.D.R.Campbell | b Shoaib | 2 | c Kamran b Sami | | 30 |
| G.W.Flower | lbw b Waqar | 31 | c Kamran b Saqlain | | 69 |
| A.Flower | c Kamran b Sami | 29 | c and b Shoaib | | 67 |
| G.J.Whittall | b Shoaib | 7 | c Younis Khan b Saqlain | | 2 |
| †T.Taibu | not out | 51 | lbw b Waqar | | 28 |
| A.M.Blignaut | c Raza b Sami | 50 | c Younis Khan b Saqlain | | 12 |
| N.B.Mahwire | c Younis Khan b Saqlain | 4 | lbw b Waqar | | 3 |
| R.W.Price | c Younis Khan b Saqlain | 2 | not out | | 5 |
| H.K.Olonga | b Shoaib | 3 | b Shoaib | | 5 |
| Extras | (LB 1, W 2, NB 3) | 6 | (B 8, LB 6, W 1, NB 5) | | 20 |
| **Total** | | **225** | | | **310** |

| ZIMBABWE | O | M | R | W | | O | M | R | W |
|---|--:|--:|--:|--:|---|--:|--:|--:|--:|
| Blignaut | 21 | 4 | 79 | 5 | | 20 | 1 | 81 | 3 |
| Olonga | 16 | 2 | 46 | 1 | | 17.5 | 1 | 93 | 5 |
| Mahwire | 14.5 | 1 | 58 | 1 | | 14 | 4 | 60 | 0 |
| Price | 16 | 4 | 56 | 2 | (5) | 24 | 5 | 66 | 2 |
| Whittall | 22 | 10 | 44 | 1 | (4) | 14 | 5 | 62 | 0 |
| **PAKISTAN** | | | | | | | | | |
| Waqar Younis | 14 | 3 | 58 | 1 | | 16 | 1 | 73 | 2 |
| Shoaib Akhtar | 14.5 | 1 | 43 | 3 | | 18.3 | 4 | 75 | 4 |
| Mohammad Sami | 19 | 3 | 53 | 4 | | 15 | 3 | 50 | 1 |
| Saqlain Mushtaq | 19 | 5 | 70 | 2 | | 31 | 5 | 98 | 3 |
| Taufiq Umar | | | | | | 1 | 1 | 0 | 0 |

| FALL OF WICKETS | | | | |
|---|--:|--:|--:|--:|
| | P | Z | P | Z |
| Wkt | 1st | 1st | 2nd | 2nd |
| 1st | 7 | 36 | 10 | 4 |
| 2nd | 122 | 41 | 25 | 10 |
| 3rd | 125 | 43 | 205 | 162 |
| 4th | 217 | 76 | 207 | 201 |
| 5th | 246 | 93 | 238 | 203 |
| 6th | 251 | 136 | 292 | 256 |
| 7th | 262 | 199 | 318 | 280 |
| 8th | 271 | 203 | 318 | 291 |
| 9th | 274 | 209 | 339 | 301 |
| 10th | 285 | 225 | 369 | 310 |

Umpires: D.L.Orchard (*South Africa*) (31) and S.Venkataraghavan (*India*) (61).
Referee: C.H.Lloyd (*West Indies*) (18).          **Test No. 1630/13 (Z64/P289)**

# ZIMBABWE v PAKISTAN (2nd Test)

At Queens Sports Club, Bulawayo, on 16, 17, 18, 19 November.
Toss: Zimbabwe. Result: **PAKISTAN** won by ten wickets.
Debuts: Zimbabwe – M.A.Vermeulen.

## ZIMBABWE

| | | | | | |
|---|---|---|---|---|---|
| D.D.Ebrahim | lbw b Waqar | 5 | lbw b Waqar | 7 |
| M.A.Vermeulen | lbw b Shoaib | 2 | lbw b Waqar | 26 |
| *A.D.R.Campbell | c Kamran b Saqlain | 46 | b Sami | 62 |
| G.W.Flower | lbw b Saqlain | 54 | b Shoaib | 43 |
| A.Flower | c Inzamam b Shoaib | 30 | lbw b Waqar | 13 |
| H.Masakadza | c Kamran b Saqlain | 0 | c Yousuf b Saqlain | 16 |
| †T.Taibu | c Kamran b Saqlain | 15 | c Yousuf b Waqar | 37 |
| A.M.Blignaut | c Taufiq b Saqlain | 4 | st Kamran b Saqlain | 41 |
| M.L.Nkala | not out | 10 | c Kamran b Saqlain | 14 |
| R.W.Price | b Saqlain | 1 | b Sami | 12 |
| H.K.Olonga | b Saqlain | 8 | not out | 3 |
| Extras | (LB 3, W 1, NB 3) | 7 | (LB 5, NB 2) | 7 |
| **Total** | | **178** | | **281** |

## PAKISTAN

| | | | | |
|---|---|---|---|---|
| Taufiq Umar | c Taibu b Olonga | 34 | not out | 21 |
| Salim Elahi | b Olonga | 27 | not out | 30 |
| Younis Khan | b Blignaut | 52 | | |
| Inzamam-ul-Haq | b Price | 11 | | |
| Yousuf Youhana | b Price | 159 | | |
| Hasan Raza | b Olonga | 4 | | |
| †Kamran Akmal | lbw b Nkala | 56 | | |
| Saqlain Mushtaq | c sub (C.K.Coventry) b Price | 14 | | |
| Mohammad Sami | c Campbell b Blignaut | 1 | | |
| *Waqar Younis | c Ebrahim b Price | 6 | | |
| Shoaib Akhtar | not out | 9 | | |
| Extras | (B 10, LB 5, W 2, NB 8, pen 5) | 30 | (B 1, W 1, NB 4) | 6 |
| **Total** | | **403** | (0 wickets) | **57** |

| PAKISTAN | O | M | R | W | | O | M | R | W |
|---|---|---|---|---|---|---|---|---|---|
| Waqar Younis | 13 | 6 | 20 | 1 | | 21.2 | 4 | 78 | 4 |
| Shoaib Akhtar | 16 | 3 | 39 | 2 | (3) | 12 | 4 | 61 | 1 |
| Mohammad Sami | 15 | 3 | 38 | 0 | (4) | 19 | 6 | 47 | 2 |
| Saqlain Mushtaq | 25.5 | 2 | 66 | 7 | (2) | 38 | 9 | 89 | 3 |
| Taufiq Umar | 2 | 0 | 12 | 0 | | | | | |
| Hasan Raza | | | | | (5) | 1 | 0 | 1 | 0 |
| **ZIMBABWE** | | | | | | | | | |
| Blignaut | 22.4 | 5 | 75 | 2 | | | | | |
| Olonga | 20 | 4 | 69 | 3 | (1) | 4.3 | 0 | 35 | 0 |
| Price | 51.3 | 14 | 116 | 4 | (2) | 4 | 1 | 21 | 0 |
| Nkala | 25 | 5 | 93 | 1 | | | | | |
| G.W.Flower | 12 | 4 | 26 | 0 | | | | | |
| A.Flower | 0.2 | 0 | 4 | 0 | | | | | |

### FALL OF WICKETS

| | SL | Z | SL | Z |
|---|---|---|---|---|
| Wkt | 1st | 1st | 2nd | 2nd |
| 1st | 4 | 63 | 28 | – |
| 2nd | 8 | 64 | 37 | – |
| 3rd | 94 | 82 | 125 | – |
| 4th | 119 | 209 | 146 | – |
| 5th | 119 | 225 | 171 | – |
| 6th | 155 | 346 | 171 | – |
| 7th | 159 | 374 | 226 | – |
| 8th | 161 | 387 | 248 | – |
| 9th | 170 | 387 | 265 | – |
| 10th | 178 | 403 | 281 | – |

Umpires: D.L.Orchard (*South Africa*) (32) and S.Venkataraghavan (*India*) (62).
Referee: C.H.Lloyd (*West Indies*) (19).   **Test No. 1631/14 (Z65/P290)**

# BANGLADESH v WEST INDIES (1st Test)

At Bangabandhu National Stadium, Dhaka, on 8, 9, 10 December.
Toss: West Indies. Result: **WEST INDIES** won by an innings and 310 runs.
Debuts: Bangladesh – Anwar ('Piju') Hossain; West Indies – V.C.Drakes.

## BANGLADESH

| | | | | | |
|---|---|---|---|---|---|
| Hannan Sarkar | b Collins | 0 | c Ganga b Drakes | | 25 |
| Anwar Hossain | c Jacobs b Drakes | 2 | b Drakes | | 12 |
| Mohammad Ashraful | c Jacobs b Collins | 6 | b Drakes | | 0 |
| Habibul Bashar | c Ganga b Collins | 24 | lbw b Collins | | 22 |
| Aminul Islam | lbw b Lawson | 5 | lbw b Lawson | | 12 |
| Alok Kapali | lbw b Drakes | 52 | lbw b Lawson | | 0 |
| *†Khaled Masud | b Drakes | 22 | lbw b Lawson | | 0 |
| Naimur Rahman | c Gayle b Collins | 1 | not out | | 5 |
| Enamul Haque | b Collins | 6 | c Jacobs b Lawson | | 0 |
| Tapash Baisya | c Jacobs b Drakes | 7 | b Lawson | | 0 |
| Talha Jubair | not out | 4 | b Lawson | | 0 |
| Extras | (LB 6, W 1, NB 3) | 10 | (B 4, LB 3, NB 4) | | 11 |
| **Total** | | **139** | | | **87** |

## WEST INDIES

| | | |
|---|---|---|
| C.H.Gayle | c Masud b Tapash | 51 |
| W.W.Hinds | c Naimur b Tapash | 75 |
| R.R.Sarwan | c Naimur b Talha | 119 |
| S.Chanderpaul | c Masud b Enamul | 4 |
| M.N.Samuels | lbw b Talha | 91 |
| D.Ganga | run out | 40 |
| *†R.D.Jacobs | not out | 91 |
| V.C.Drakes | c sub (Al Sahariar) b Naimur | 15 |
| D.B.Powell | st Masud b Ashraful | 16 |
| P.T.Collins | c Habibul b Ashraful | 13 |
| J.J.C.Lawson | lbw b Talha | 1 |
| Extras | (LB 8, W 3, NB 9) | 20 |
| **Total** | | **536** |

| WEST INDIES | O | M | R | W | | O | M | R | W |
|---|---|---|---|---|---|---|---|---|---|
| Collins | 17.1 | 7 | 26 | 5 | | 9 | 2 | 30 | 1 |
| Drakes | 18 | 2 | 61 | 4 | | 9 | 3 | 19 | 3 |
| Lawson | 19 | 2 | 24 | 1 | (4) | 6.5 | 4 | 3 | 6 |
| Powell | 10 | 2 | 22 | 0 | (3) | 7 | 1 | 28 | 0 |

| BANGLADESH | O | M | R | W |
|---|---|---|---|---|
| Tapash Baisya | 34 | 3 | 117 | 2 |
| Talha Jubair | 31 | 3 | 135 | 3 |
| Naimur Rahman | 36 | 5 | 118 | 1 |
| Enamul Haque | 46 | 13 | 101 | 1 |
| Mohammad Ashraful | 13 | 0 | 57 | 2 |

| FALL OF WICKETS | | | |
|---|---|---|---|
| | B | WI | B |
| Wkt | 1st | 1st | 2nd |
| 1st | 0 | 131 | 30 |
| 2nd | 4 | 132 | 30 |
| 3rd | 25 | 150 | 44 |
| 4th | 40 | 326 | 80 |
| 5th | 44 | 377 | 80 |
| 6th | 117 | 417 | 80 |
| 7th | 118 | 453 | 81 |
| 8th | 124 | 493 | 83 |
| 9th | 135 | 527 | 87 |
| 10th | 139 | 536 | 87 |

Umpires: D.L.Orchard (*South Africa*) (33) and D.R.Shepherd (*England*) (68).
Referee: R.S.Madugalle (*Sri Lanka*) (46).              Test No. 1632/1 (B16/WI392)

# BANGLADESH v WEST INDIES (2nd Test)

At M.A.Aziz Stadium, Chittagong, on 16, 17, 18 December.
Toss: Bangladesh. Result: **WEST INDIES** won by seven wickets.
Debuts: None.

## BANGLADESH

| | | | | | |
|---|---|---|---|---|---|
| Hannan Sarkar | c Gayle b Powell | 15 | b Drakes | | 13 |
| Al Sahariar | lbw b Drakes | 25 | lbw b Powell | | 34 |
| Habibul Bashar | c Jacobs b Powell | 3 | c Jacobs b Collins | | 0 |
| Sanwar Hossain | c Jacobs b Lawson | 36 | c Gayle b Lawson | | 24 |
| Mohammad Ashraful | c Powell b Collins | 28 | c Sarwan b Lawson | | 15 |
| Alok Kapali | c Gayle b Collins | 2 | c Jacobs b Powell | | 85 |
| *†Khaled Masud | c Sarwan b Drakes | 32 | lbw b Drakes | | 5 |
| Enamul Haque | c Samuels b Lawson | 8 | not out | | 11 |
| Tapash Baisya | hit wicket b Powell | 5 | c Chanderpaul b Powell | | 0 |
| Manjural Islam | b Collins | 21 | b Collins | | 0 |
| Talha Jubair | not out | 4 | c Jacobs b Collins | | 0 |
| Extras | (LB 5, NB 10) | 15 | (B 1, LB 12, W 3, NB 9) | | 25 |
| **Total** | | **194** | | | **212** |

## WEST INDIES

| | | | | | |
|---|---|---|---|---|---|
| C.H.Gayle | b Talha | 38 | b Tapash | | 37 |
| W.W.Hinds | c Masud b Tapash | 14 | lbw b Tapash | | 26 |
| R.R.Sarwan | c Masud b Manjural | 17 | c Enamul b Manjural | | 13 |
| S.Chanderpaul | c Masud b Enamul | 16 | not out | | 19 |
| M.N.Samuels | c Sahariar b Talha | 31 | not out | | 15 |
| D.Ganga | c Tapash b Sanwar | 63 | | | |
| *†R.D.Jacobs | c Masud b Tapash | 59 | | | |
| V.C.Drakes | run out | 26 | | | |
| D.B.Powell | b Tapash | 1 | | | |
| P.T.Collins | not out | 12 | | | |
| J.J.C.Lawson | c Habibul b Tapash | 6 | | | |
| Extras | (B 8, LB 4, NB 1) | 13 | (LB 1) | | 1 |
| **Total** | | **296** | (3 wickets) | | **111** |

| WEST INDIES | O | M | R | W | | O | M | R | W |
|---|---|---|---|---|---|---|---|---|---|
| Collins | 16.1 | 3 | 60 | 3 | | 23 | 8 | 58 | 3 |
| Drakes | 9 | 3 | 23 | 2 | | 18 | 6 | 52 | 2 |
| Powell | 16 | 4 | 51 | 3 | (4) | 13 | 2 | 36 | 3 |
| Lawson | 22 | 9 | 55 | 2 | (3) | 18 | 5 | 53 | 2 |
| **BANGLADESH** | | | | | | | | | |
| Manjural Islam | 21 | 11 | 34 | 1 | | 8 | 2 | 38 | 1 |
| Tapash Baisya | 21.3 | 2 | 72 | 4 | | 9 | 0 | 45 | 2 |
| Talha Jubair | 20 | 5 | 58 | 2 | | 3 | 0 | 20 | 0 |
| Enamul Haque | 19 | 3 | 62 | 1 | | | | | |
| Mohammad Ashraful | 5 | 0 | 29 | 0 | (4) | 1 | 0 | 3 | 0 |
| Sanwar Hossain | 7 | 1 | 29 | 1 | | | | | |
| Alok Kapali | | | | | (5) | 0.3 | 0 | 4 | 0 |

### FALL OF WICKETS

| | B | WI | B | WI |
|---|---|---|---|---|
| Wkt | 1st | 1st | 2nd | 2nd |
| 1st | 43 | 16 | 44 | 52 |
| 2nd | 43 | 53 | 45 | 77 |
| 3rd | 48 | 74 | 76 | 81 |
| 4th | 112 | 99 | 100 | – |
| 5th | 116 | 127 | 126 | – |
| 6th | 125 | 226 | 137 | – |
| 7th | 144 | 264 | 210 | – |
| 8th | 153 | 278 | 210 | – |
| 9th | 189 | 279 | 210 | – |
| 10th | 194 | 296 | 212 | – |

Umpires: D.L.Orchard (*South Africa*) (34) and D.R.Shepherd (*England*) (69).
Referee: R.S.Madugalle (*Sri Lanka*) (47). **Test No. 1633/2 (B17/WI393)**

# NEW ZEALAND v INDIA (1st Test)

At Basin Reserve, Wellington, on 12, 13, 14 December.
Toss: New Zealand. Result: **NEW ZEALAND** won by ten wickets.
Debuts: New Zealand – J.D.P.Oram.

## INDIA

| | | | | | |
|---|---|---|---|---|---|
| S.B.Bangar | c Styris b Tuffey | 1 | lbw b Oram | | 12 |
| V.Sehwag | b Tuffey | 2 | lbw b Bond | | 12 |
| R.Dravid | b Styris | 76 | b Bond | | 7 |
| S.R.Tendulkar | lbw b Oram | 8 | b Bond | | 51 |
| *S.C.Ganguly | c Vincent b Bond | 17 | c Hart b Bond | | 2 |
| V.V.S.Laxman | c Hart b Bond | 0 | c Fleming b Oram | | 0 |
| †P.A.Patel | c Vincent b Oram | 8 | c Fleming b Tuffey | | 10 |
| A.B.Agarkar | c Astle b Styris | 12 | c McMillan b Tuffey | | 9 |
| Harbhajan Singh | c McMillan b Styris | 0 | c Styris b Tuffey | | 1 |
| Z.Khan | c Oram b Bond | 19 | c Styris b Oram | | 9 |
| A.Nehra | not out | 10 | not out | | 0 |
| Extras | (LB 1, W 1, NB 6) | 8 | (LB 1, NB 7) | | 8 |
| **Total** | | **161** | | | **121** |

## NEW ZEALAND

| | | | | | |
|---|---|---|---|---|---|
| M.H.Richardson | lbw b Khan | 89 | not out | | 14 |
| L.Vincent | c Patel b Bangar | 12 | not out | | 21 |
| *S.P.Fleming | b Khan | 25 | | | |
| C.D.McMillan | lbw b Bangar | 9 | | | |
| N.J.Astle | c Harbhajan b Khan | 41 | | | |
| S.B.Styris | st Patel b Harbhajan | 0 | | | |
| J.D.P.Oram | lbw b Harbhajan | 0 | | | |
| †R.G.Hart | lbw b Khan | 6 | | | |
| D.L.Vettori | c Patel b Khan | 21 | | | |
| D.R.Tuffey | not out | 9 | | | |
| S.E.Bond | b Agarkar | 2 | | | |
| Extras | (B 6, LB 12, W 2, NB 8, pen 5) | 33 | (W 1) | | 1 |
| **Total** | | **247** | (0 wickets) | | **36** |

| NEW ZEALAND | O | M | R | W | O | M | R | W |
|---|---|---|---|---|---|---|---|---|
| Bond | 18.4 | 4 | 66 | 3 | 13.1 | 5 | 33 | 4 |
| Tuffey | 16 | 7 | 25 | 2 | 9 | 3 | 35 | 3 |
| Oram | 15 | 4 | 31 | 2 | 11 | 3 | 28 | 3 |
| Styris | 6 | 0 | 28 | 3 | 5 | 0 | 24 | 0 |
| Astle | 3 | 1 | 10 | 0 | | | | |
| **INDIA** | | | | | | | | |
| Khan | 25 | 8 | 53 | 5 | 3 | 0 | 13 | 0 |
| Nehra | 19 | 4 | 50 | 0 | 4.3 | 0 | 21 | 0 |
| Agarkar | 13.1 | 1 | 54 | 1 | | | | |
| Bangar | 15 | 4 | 23 | 2 | | | | |
| Harbhajan Singh | 17 | 4 | 33 | 2 | (3) 2 | 1 | 2 | 0 |
| Ganguly | 2 | 0 | 11 | 0 | | | | |

| FALL OF WICKETS | | | | |
|---|---|---|---|---|
| | I | NZ | I | NZ |
| Wkt | 1st | 1st | 2nd | 2nd |
| 1st | 2 | 30 | 23 | – |
| 2nd | 9 | 96 | 31 | – |
| 3rd | 29 | 111 | 31 | – |
| 4th | 51 | 181 | 33 | – |
| 5th | 55 | 182 | 36 | – |
| 6th | 92 | 186 | 76 | – |
| 7th | 118 | 201 | 88 | – |
| 8th | 118 | 228 | 96 | – |
| 9th | 147 | 237 | 121 | – |
| 10th | 161 | 247 | 121 | – |

Umpires: E.A.R.de Silva (*Sri Lanka*) (21) and D.J.Harper (*Australia*) (27).
Referee: M.J.Procter (*South Africa*) (6). **Test No. 1634/41 (NZ300/I364)**

# NEW ZEALAND v INDIA (2nd Test)

At Seddon Park, Hamilton, on 19 (no play), 20, 21, 22 December.
Toss: New Zealand. Result: **NEW ZEALAND** won by four wickets.
Debuts: None.

## INDIA

| | | | | | |
|---|---|---|---|---|---|
| S.B.Bangar | c Oram b Tuffey | 1 | | c and b Tuffey | 7 |
| V.Sehwag | c Richardson b Bond | 1 | (7) | c Tuffey b Bond | 25 |
| R.Dravid | c Hart b Tuffey | 9 | | c sub (M.J.Mason) b Oram | 39 |
| S.R.Tendulkar | c Styris b Tuffey | 9 | | b Tuffey | 32 |
| *S.C.Ganguly | c Fleming b Tuffey | 5 | | c Hart b Oram | 5 |
| V.V.S.Laxman | b Bond | 23 | | b Astle | 4 |
| †P.A.Patel | c Hart b Oram | 8 | (2) | b Tuffey | 0 |
| Harbhajan Singh | b Bond | 20 | | c Hart b Tuffey | 18 |
| Z.Khan | b Oram | 0 | | c Astle b Oram | 0 |
| A.Nehra | c Fleming b Bond | 7 | | c Hart b Oram | 10 |
| T.Yohannan | not out | 0 | | not out | 8 |
| Extras | (LB 12, NB 4) | 16 | | (LB 1, W 2, NB 3) | 6 |
| **Total** | | **99** | | | **154** |

## NEW ZEALAND

| | | | | |
|---|---|---|---|---|
| M.H.Richardson | lbw b Khan | 13 | c Patel b Nehra | 28 |
| L.Vincent | c Dravid b Khan | 3 | c Patel b Yohannan | 9 |
| *S.P.Fleming | c and b Khan | 21 | c Khan b Nehra | 32 |
| C.D.McMillan | c Dravid b Nehra | 4 | lbw b Nehra | 18 |
| N.J.Astle | c Harbhajan b Nehra | 0 | c Patel b Khan | 14 |
| S.B.Styris | lbw b Harbhajan | 13 | c Patel b Harbhajan | 17 |
| J.D.P.Oram | c Tendulkar b Harbhajan | 3 | not out | 26 |
| †R.G.Hart | lbw b Khan | 3 | not out | 11 |
| D.L.Vettori | c Laxman b Khan | 6 | | |
| D.R.Tuffey | run out | 13 | | |
| S.E.Bond | not out | 0 | | |
| Extras | (B 1, LB 4, NB 10) | 15 | (LB 4, NB 1) | 5 |
| **Total** | | **94** | (6 wickets) | **160** |

| NEW ZEALAND | O | M | R | W | | O | M | R | W |
|---|---|---|---|---|---|---|---|---|---|
| Bond | 14.2 | 7 | 39 | 4 | | 10 | 0 | 58 | 1 |
| Tuffey | 9 | 6 | 12 | 4 | | 16 | 3 | 41 | 4 |
| Oram | 10 | 1 | 22 | 2 | | 12.5 | 2 | 41 | 4 |
| Styris | 2 | 0 | 10 | 0 | | | | | |
| Astle | 3 | 2 | 4 | 0 | (4) | 5 | 1 | 13 | 1 |
| INDIA | | | | | | | | | |
| Khan | 13.2 | 4 | 29 | 5 | | 13 | 0 | 56 | 1 |
| Yohannan | 9 | 4 | 16 | 0 | | 16 | 5 | 27 | 1 |
| Nehra | 8 | 3 | 20 | 2 | | 16.2 | 4 | 34 | 3 |
| Bangar | 2 | 1 | 4 | 0 | | | | | |
| Harbhajan Singh | 6 | 0 | 20 | 2 | (4) | 11 | 0 | 39 | 1 |

### FALL OF WICKETS

| | I NZ | I NZ |
|---|---|---|
| Wkt | 1st 1st | 2nd 2nd |
| 1st | 1 7 | 2 30 |
| 2nd | 11 39 | 8 52 |
| 3rd | 26 47 | 57 89 |
| 4th | 34 48 | 64 90 |
| 5th | 40 60 | 85 105 |
| 6th | 70 64 | 110 136 |
| 7th | 91 69 | 130 – |
| 8th | 92 79 | 131 – |
| 9th | 93 93 | 137 – |
| 10th | 99 94 | 154 – |

Umpires: E.A.R.de Silva (*Sri Lanka*) (22) and D.J.Harper (*Australia*) (28).
Referee: M.J.Procter (*South Africa*) (7).  **Test No. 1635/42 (NZ301/I365)**

# SOUTH AFRICA v PAKISTAN (1st Test)

At Kingsmead, Durban, on 26, 27, 28, 29 December.
Toss: Pakistan. Result: **SOUTH AFRICA** won by ten wickets.
Debuts: None.

## SOUTH AFRICA

| | | | | |
|---|---|---|---|---|
| G.C.Smith | c Kamran b Sami | 16 | not out | 13 |
| H.H.Gibbs | c Faisal b Waqar | 11 | not out | 25 |
| G.Kirsten | c Younis Khan b Saqlain | 56 | | |
| J.H.Kallis | b Sami | 105 | | |
| H.H.Dippenaar | c Kamran b Saqlain | 1 | | |
| N.D.McKenzie | b Waqar | 24 | | |
| †M.V.Boucher | c Faisal b Saqlain | 55 | | |
| *S.M.Pollock | c Kamran b Waqar | 21 | | |
| N.Boje | not out | 37 | | |
| M.Ntini | c Taufiq b Saqlain | 0 | | |
| M.Hayward | b Sami | 10 | | |
| Extras | (B 4, LB 5, NB 23) | 32 | (LB 1, NB 6) | 7 |
| **Total** | | **368** | (0 wickets) | **45** |

## PAKISTAN

| | | | | |
|---|---|---|---|---|
| Taufiq Umar | c Smith b Hayward | 39 | lbw b Boje | 39 |
| Salim Elahi | c McKenzie b Ntini | 39 | c Smith b Ntini | 18 |
| Younis Khan | lbw b Pollock | 1 | c Boucher b Kallis | 30 |
| Inzamam-ul-Haq | c and b Ntini | 18 | c Gibbs b Boje | 13 |
| Yousuf Youhana | c Smith b Ntini | 12 | c McKenzie b Hayward | 42 |
| Faisal Iqbal | run out | 6 | b Kallis | 17 |
| Abdul Razzaq | c McKenzie b Hayward | 1 | c Boucher b Hayward | 22 |
| †Kamran Akmal | c Pollock b Hayward | 12 | c Boucher b Ntini | 29 |
| Saqlain Mushtaq | b Hayward | 0 | c Boucher b Pollock | 4 |
| *Waqar Younis | b Hayward | 28 | c Kirsten b Pollock | 15 |
| Mohammad Sami | not out | 0 | not out | 11 |
| Extras | (LB 1, W 1, NB 3) | 5 | (LB 2, W 1, NB 7) | 10 |
| **Total** | | **161** | | **250** |

| PAKISTAN | O | M | R | W | | O | M | R | W |
|---|---|---|---|---|---|---|---|---|---|
| Waqar Younis | 25 | 3 | 91 | 3 | | | | | |
| Mohammad Sami | 26 | 5 | 92 | 3 | (1) | 5 | 0 | 36 | 0 |
| Abdul Razzaq | 19 | 3 | 57 | 0 | | | | | |
| Saqlain Mushtaq | 37 | 4 | 119 | 4 | (2) | 4 | 2 | 8 | 0 |
| **SOUTH AFRICA** | | | | | | | | | |
| Pollock | 14 | 5 | 23 | 1 | (2) | 17.3 | 4 | 29 | 2 |
| Ntini | 18 | 4 | 59 | 3 | (1) | 21 | 2 | 73 | 2 |
| Hayward | 10.4 | 1 | 56 | 5 | (4) | 13 | 1 | 63 | 2 |
| Kallis | 6 | 0 | 22 | 0 | (3) | 17 | 5 | 30 | 2 |
| Boje | | | | | | 19 | 2 | 53 | 2 |

| FALL OF WICKETS | | | | |
|---|---|---|---|---|
| | SA | P | P | SA |
| Wkt | 1st | 1st | 2nd | 2nd |
| 1st | 27 | 77 | 50 | – |
| 2nd | 33 | 83 | 64 | – |
| 3rd | 155 | 83 | 88 | – |
| 4th | 159 | 107 | 132 | – |
| 5th | 214 | 119 | 156 | – |
| 6th | 252 | 120 | 184 | – |
| 7th | 286 | 120 | 199 | – |
| 8th | 344 | 120 | 216 | – |
| 9th | 344 | 145 | 226 | – |
| 10th | 368 | 161 | 250 | – |

Umpires: S.A.Bucknor (*West Indies*) (76) and S.Venkataraghavan (*India*) (63).
Referee: G.R.Viswanath (*India*) (8).                Test No. 1636/8 (SA271/P291)

# SOUTH AFRICA v PAKISTAN (2nd Test)

At Newlands, Cape Town, on 2, 3, 4, 5 January.
Toss: South Africa. Result: **SOUTH AFRICA won** by an innings and 142 runs.
Debuts: None.

## SOUTH AFRICA

| | | |
|---|---|---|
| G.C.Smith | b Zahid | 151 |
| H.H.Gibbs | c Younis Khan b Saqlain | 228 |
| G.Kirsten | c Younis Khan b Waqar | 19 |
| J.H.Kallis | lbw b Sami | 31 |
| H.H.Dippenaar | c Kamran b Saqlain | 62 |
| N.D.McKenzie | c Kamran b Zahid | 51 |
| †M.V.Boucher | b Saqlain | 7 |
| *S.M.Pollock | not out | 36 |
| N.Boje | not out | 7 |
| M.Ntini | | |
| M.Hayward | | |
| Extras | (B 1, LB 5, W 1, NB 21) | 28 |
| **Total** | (7 wickets declared) | **620** |

## PAKISTAN

| | | | | |
|---|---|---|---|---|
| Taufiq Umar | c Kallis b Ntini | 135 | c Boucher b Pollock | 67 |
| Salim Elahi | c Smith b Pollock | 10 | c Dippenaar b Ntini | 0 |
| Younis Khan | lbw b Pollock | 46 | c McKenzie b Kallis | 2 |
| Inzamam-ul-Haq | c Dippenaar b Hayward | 32 | st Boucher b Boje | 60 |
| Yousuf Youhana | c Boucher b Hayward | 0 | c Kallis b Boje | 50 |
| Faisal Iqbal | b Ntini | 24 | c Pollock b Ntini | 11 |
| †Kamran Akmal | lbw b Pollock | 0 | lbw b Ntini | 4 |
| Saqlain Mushtaq | c Boucher b Ntini | 1 | run out | 9 |
| *Waqar Younis | c Kallis b Pollock | 0 | lbw b Hayward | 9 |
| Mohammad Sami | not out | 0 | not out | 9 |
| Mohammad Zahid | c Smith b Ntini | 0 | c Pollock b Ntini | 0 |
| Extras | (LB 1, NB 3) | 4 | (LB 1, W 1, NB 3) | 5 |
| **Total** | | **252** | | **226** |

| PAKISTAN | O | M | R | W | O | M | R | W | | FALL OF WICKETS | | |
|---|---|---|---|---|---|---|---|---|---|---|---|---|
| | | | | | | | | | | SA | P | P |
| Waqar Younis | 28 | 4 | 121 | 1 | | | | | Wkt | 1st | 1st | 2nd |
| Mohammad Sami | 28 | 2 | 124 | 1 | | | | | 1st | 368 | 36 | 0 |
| Mohammad Zahid | 25 | 3 | 108 | 2 | | | | | 2nd | 413 | 152 | 9 |
| Saqlain Mushtaq | 50 | 3 | 237 | 3 | | | | | 3rd | 414 | 208 | 130 |
| Younis Khan | 4 | 0 | 24 | 0 | | | | | 4th | 463 | 208 | 130 |
| | | | | | | | | | 5th | 548 | 240 | 184 |
| SOUTH AFRICA | | | | | | | | | 6th | 557 | 247 | 190 |
| Pollock | 23 | 6 | 45 | 4 | 12 | 5 | 32 | 1 | 7th | 594 | 251 | 203 |
| Ntini | 20.4 | 7 | 62 | 4 | 15.1 | 2 | 33 | 4 | 8th | – | 252 | 216 |
| Kallis | 12 | 2 | 35 | 0 | 6 | 1 | 34 | 1 | 9th | – | 252 | 221 |
| Hayward | 15 | 2 | 56 | 2 | 11 | 3 | 44 | 1 | 10th | – | 252 | 226 |
| Boje | 17 | 2 | 53 | 0 | 15 | 0 | 82 | 2 | | | | |

Umpires: S.A.Bucknor (*West Indies*) (77) and S.Venkataraghavan (*India*) (64).
Referee: G.R.Viswanath (*India*) (9). **Test No. 1637/9 (SA272/P292)**

# SECOND XI FIXTURES 2003

| | | |
|---|---|---|
| No symbol | Second XI Championship | 3 days |
| * | Second XI Championship | 4 days |
| † | Second XI Trophy | 1 day |

## APRIL

| | | |
|---|---|---|
| 28–May 1 | Manchester (OT) | *Lancs v Derbys |
| 30–May 2 | Gowerton CC | Glam v Middx |
| | Moseley CC | Warwks v Northants |

## MAY

| | | |
|---|---|---|
| 6-8 | Basingstoke | Hants v Surrey |
| 13-15 | Sully Centurions | Glam v Glos |
| 13-16 | Stamford Bridge | *Yorks v Durham |
| 14-16 | Hinckley | Leics v Lancs |
| | Shenley | Middx v Kent |
| | Cheam | Surrey v Sussex |
| | Ombersley | Worcs v Derbys |
| 16 | Newport | †Glam v Glos |
| 19-21 | Derby | Derbys v Northants |
| 20-23 | Nottingham (TB) | *Notts v Leics |
| 21-23 | Beckenham | Kent v Warwks |
| | Southgate | Middx v Essex |
| | Taunton | Somerset v Hants |
| 26-29 | Blackpool | *Lancs v Durham |
| 27-29 | Southampton | Hants v Sussex |
| | Milton Keynes | Northants v Surrey |
| | Bradford & Bingley | Yorks v Notts |
| 27-30 | Coventry/N Wwk | *Warwks v Glam |
| 28-30 | Denby CC | Derbys v Leics |
| | Bristol | Glos v Somerset |

## JUNE

| | | |
|---|---|---|
| 2 | Southampton | †Hants v Glam |
| 3-5 | Maidstone | Kent v Glos |
| | Leicester | Leics v Notts |
| 3-6 | Chelmsford | *Essex v Middx |
| 4-6 | Taunton | Somerset v Surrey |
| | Stratford-u-Avon | Warwks v Lancs |
| | Kidderminster | Worcs v Northants |
| 9 | Neath | †Glam v Somerset |
| | Purley | †Surrey v MCC YC |
| 9-12 | Stockton | *Durham v Yorks |
| 10-12 | Bournemouth SC | Hants v Glos |
| 10-13 | Knowle & Dorridge | *Warwks v Notts |
| 11-13 | Billericay | Essex v Sussex |
| | Crosby | Lancs v Surrey |
| | Hinckley | Leics v Derbys |
| 12 | Ealing | †Middx v Minor C |
| 13 | Luton CC | †Minor C v Northants |
| 16 | Maidstone | †Kent v Surrey |
| | Uxbridge (Vine L) | †MCC YC v Essex |
| | North Perrott | †Somerset v Worcs |

## JUNE

| | | |
|---|---|---|
| 16-19 | Hartlepool | *Durham v Lancs |
| 17 | Nottingham (Boots) | †Notts v Derbys |
| 17-19 | Todmorden | Yorks v Glam |
| 18 | Sandiacre CC | †Derbys v Notts |
| | Tonbridge School | †Kent v Sussex |
| 18-20 | Esher (Imber Ct) | Surrey v Hants |
| 19 | Milton Keynes | †Minor C v Warwks |
| 20 | Beckenham | †Kent v MCC YC |
| | Milton Keynes | †Minor C v Middx |
| 23 | Chester-le-St | †Durham v Yorks |
| | Old Brentwoods | †Essex v Sussex |
| | Bristol | †Glos v Worcs |
| | Southampton | †Hants v Somerset |
| | Widnes | †Lancs v Notts |
| | Harborne | †Warwks v Leics |
| 24 | Chester-le-St | †Durham v Notts |
| | Sutton | †Surrey v Sussex |
| 25 | Colchester | †Essex v Surrey |
| | Usk | †Glam v Worcs |
| | Finchley | †Middx v Leics |
| | Uxbridge (Vine L) | †MCC YC v Kent |
| | Leeds | †Yorks v Lancs |
| | Taunton | †Somerset v Glos |
| 26 | Chesterfield | †Derbys v Yorks |
| | Southport | †Lancs v Durham |
| | Milton Keynes | †Northants v Warwks |
| | Banstead | †Surrey v Kent |
| | Kidderminster | †Worcs v Hants |
| 27 | Chesterfield | †Derbys v Durham |
| | Bishop's Stortford | †Essex v MCC YC |
| | Newport | †Glam v Hants |
| | Hinckley | †Leics v Northants |
| | Birmingham | †Warwks v Minor C |
| 30 | Bristol U (tbc) | †Glos v Glam |
| | Farnsfield CC | †Notts v Lancs |
| | Studley | †Warwks v Middx |
| | York | †Yorks v Durham |

## JULY

| | | |
|---|---|---|
| 1 | Canterbury | †Kent v Essex |
| | Wormsley | †MCC YC v Surrey |
| | Milton Keynes | †Northants v Leics |
| | Notts Unity | †Notts v Durham |
| | Old Hill | †Worcs v Somerset |
| 2 | Southampton | †Hants v Glos |
| | Nelson CC | †Lancs v Yorks |

## JULY

| | | |
|---|---|---|
| | Hinckley | †Leics v Warwks |
| | Hove | †Sussex v MCC YC |
| | Old Hill | † Worcs v Glam |
| 3 | Sunderland | †Durham v Derbys |
| | Banstead | †Surrey v Essex |
| | Hove | †Sussex v Kent |
| | W Brom Dartmouth | †Warwks v Northants |
| 4 | Darlington | †Durham v Lancs |
| | Southampton | †Hants v Worcs |
| | Hinckley | †Leics v Middx |
| | O Northamptonians | †Northants v Minor C |
| | Horsham | †Sussex v Surrey |
| | Castleford | †Yorks v Derbys |
| 7 | Uxbridge (Vine L) | †MCC YC v Sussex |
| | Winchmore Hill | †Middx v Northants |
| | Welbeck | †Notts v Yorks |
| | Taunton | †Somerset v Hants |
| | Ombersley | †Worcs v Glos |
| 8-10 | Coggleshall | Essex v Kent |
| 8-11 | Nottingham (TB) | *Notts v Surrey |
| 9-11 | Oakham S | Leics v Durham |
| | North Perrott | Somerset v Glam |
| 10 | Middleton CC | †Lancs v Derbys |
| | Northampton | †Northants v Middx |
| 11 | Glossop | †Derbys v Lancs |
| | Coggleshall | †Essex v Kent |
| | Bristol | †Glos v Hants |
| 14 | Bristol | †Glos v Somerset |
| | Richmond | †Middx v Warwks |
| | Eastbourne | †Sussex v Essex |
| 14-17 | Denby CC | *Derbys v Notts |
| 15-18 | Canterbury | *Kent v Worcs |
| | Hove | *Sussex v Hants |
| | Stamford Bridge | *Yorks v Lancs |
| 16-18 | Bristol | Glos v Glam |
| | Northampton | Northants v Middx |
| 21 | Millfield S | †Somerset v Glam |
| | New Rover CC | †Yorks v Notts |
| 22-24 | Darlington | Durham v Notts |
| | Southampton | Hants v Northants |
| 22-25 | The Oval | *Surrey v Essex |
| 23-25 | Chesterfield | Derbys v Yorks |
| | Taunton | Somerset v Glos |
| | Worthing | Sussex v Middx |
| 24 | Luton CC | †Minor C v Leics |
| 25 | Oakham S | †Leics v Minor C |
| 28-30 | S Northumberland | Durham v Surrey |
| | Cardiff | Glam v Lancs |

| | | |
|---|---|---|
| 29-Aug 1 | Chelmsford | *Essex v Warwks |
| 30-Aug 1 | Northampton | Northants v Worcs |
| | Worksop C | Notts v Kent |
| | Taunton | Somerset v Sussex |

## AUGUST

| | | |
|---|---|---|
| 4-6 | Merchant Taylors' S | Middx v Durham |
| 5-7 | Cheltenham C | Glos v Sussex |
| | Milton Keynes | Northants v Essex |
| | Nottingham (Boots) | Notts v Derbys |
| | Walmley | Warwks v Yorks |
| 6-8 | Panteg | Glam v Lancs |
| | Wimbledon | Surrey v Kent |
| | Kidderminster | Worcs v Somerset |
| 11 (12) | (tbc) | †Trophy Semi-Finals |
| 13-15 | Seaton Carew | Durham v Warwks |
| | Bristol | Glos v Northants |
| | Beckenham | Kent v Middx |
| | The Oval | Surrey v Derbys |
| | Horsham | Sussex v Yorks |
| 19-21 | Abergavenny | Glam v Worcs |
| | Hatherley & Reddings | Glos v Leics |
| | Stowe S | Northants v Warwks |
| 19-22 | Canterbury | *Kent v Essex |
| | Liverpool | *Lancs v Somerset |
| | Hove | *Sussex v Surrey |
| 20-22 | Dunstall CC | Derbys v Durham |
| | Uxbridge (Vine L) | Middx v Hants |
| 25-27 | Northampton | Northants v Durham |
| 26-28 | Southampton | Hants v Glam |
| | Pudsey Congs CC | Yorks v Essex |
| 26-29 | Notts Unity | *Notts v Lancs |
| | Barnt Green | *Worcs v Warwks |
| 27-29 | Hinckley | Leics v Somerset |
| | Uxbridge | Middx v Surrey |
| | Eastbourne | Sussex v Kent |

## SEPTEMBER

| | | |
|---|---|---|
| 2-4 | Worcester | Worcs v Glos |
| 2-5 | Manchester (OT) | *Lancs v Yorks |
| 3-5 | Halstead | Essex v Leics |
| | Cardiff | Glam v Somerset |
| | Nottingham (Boots) | Notts v Hants |
| | Hastings | Sussex v Warwks |
| 8 (9) | (tbc) | †Trophy Final |
| 10-12 | Lytham | Lancs v Sussex |
| | Northampton | Northants v Leics |
| | Kenilworth Wardens | Warwks v Worcs |
| 16-18 | Manchester (OT) | Lancs v Worcs |

3-day matches. † Noon start (1st day)

| Venue | Div | Match | Venue | Div | Match |
|---|---|---|---|---|---|
| **MAY** | | | †South Wilts | W | Wilts v Oxon |
| 25-27 Falkland CC | W | Berks v Oxon | 14-16 St Austell | W | Cornwall v Cheshire |
| Marlow | E | Bucks v Herts | 23-25 Manor Park | E | Norfolk v Herts |
| **JUNE** | | | 27-29 †Bedford Town | E | Beds v Northumb |
| 1-3 Dunstable | E | Beds v Cumb | Reading CC | W | Berks v Salop |
| March | E | Cambs v Suffolk | Beaconsfield | E | Bucks v Lincs |
| Oxton | W | Cheshire v Dorset | †Chester (B Hall) | W | Cheshire v Herefords |
| †Truro | W | Cornwall v Devon | Camborne | W | Cornwall v Wilts |
| †Luctonians | W | Herefords v Salop | Carlisle | E | Cumb v Herts |
| Grantham | E | Lincs v Norfolk | Manor Park | E | Norfolk v Cambs |
| Jesmond | E | Northumb v Staffs | Thame | W | Oxon v Dorset |
| †Pontypridd | W | Wales MC v Wilts | Walsall | E | Staffs v Suffolk |
| 22-24 Alderley Edge | W | Cheshire v Berks | | | |
| Barrow | E | Cumb v Lincs | **AUGUST** | | |
| †Bovey Tracey | W | Devon v Wales MC | 3-5 †Fenners | E | Cambs v Bucks |
| Dean Park | W | Dorset v Salop | Exmouth | W | Devon v Dorset |
| †Challow & Childrey | W | Oxon v Cornwall | Bishop's Stortford | E | Herts v Suffolk |
| Longton | E | Staffs v Cambs | Manor Park | E | Norfolk v Staffs |
| Ransomes, Ipswich | E | Suffolk v Beds | †Jesmond | E | Northumb v Cumb |
| Corsham | W | Wilts v Herefords | †Abergavenny | W | Wales MC v Cheshire |
| 29-1 Jul Colwall | W | Herefords v Oxon | Westbury | W | Wilts v Berks |
| Hertford | E | Herts v Beds | 17-19 Finchampstead | W | Berks v Devon |
| †Jesmond | E | Northumb v Bucks | Wing (Ascott Park) | E | Bucks v Beds |
| Shrewsbury | W | Salop v Devon | †Netherfield | E | Cumb v Staffs |
| Bury St Edmunds | E | Suffolk v Lincs | †Dean Park | W | Dorset v Wilts |
| †Swansea | W | Wales MC v Cornwall | †Luctonians | W | Herefords v Cornwall |
| | | | †Long Marston | E | Herts v Northumb |
| **JULY** | | | Grantham | E | Lincs v Cambs |
| 13-15 Luton | E | Beds v Norfolk | †Banbury | W | Oxon v Wales MC |
| March | E | Cambs v Cumb | †Whitchurch | W | Salop v Cheshire |
| Torquay | W | Devon v Herefords | Mildenhall | E | Suffolk v Norfolk |
| Dean Park | W | Dorset v Berks | | | |
| Grantham | E | Lincs v Northumb | **SEPTEMBER** | | |
| †Bridgnorth | W | Salop v Wales MC | 7-9 (tba – E Div) | | **CHAMPIONSHIP FINAL** |
| **JULY** | | | | | |
| Stone | E | Staffs v Bucks | | | |

# MCCA KNOCK-OUT TROPHY FIXTURES 2003

† Noon start ‡ 11.30am start

**FIRST ROUND – MAY 18**

| | | |
|---|---|---|
| 1 | †Manor Park | Norfolk v Cornwall |
| 2 | Torquay | Devon v Salop |
| 3 | ‡Harpenden | Herts v Wales MC |
| 4 | Jesmond | Northumb v Lincs |

**SECOND ROUND – JUNE 8**

| | | |
|---|---|---|
| 5 | †Chippenham | Wilts v Bucks |
| 6 | Manor Park/(tba) | Winner # 1 v Cambs |
| 7 | Thatcham | Berks v Winner # 3 |
| 8 | Bovey T/Wroxeter | Winner # 2 v Cumb |
| 9 | †Copdock | Suffolk v Beds |
| 10 | Porthill Park | Staffs v Herefords |
| 11 | Challow & Childrey | Oxon v Dorset |

**SECOND ROUND – JUNE 11**

| | | |
|---|---|---|
| 12 | Cheadle Hulme | Cheshire v Winner # 4 |

**QUARTER-FINALS – JULY 6**

| | | |
|---|---|---|
| 13 | Porthill Pk/(tba) | Winner # 10 v Winner # 6 |
| 14 | (tba) | Winner # 5 v Winner # 8 |
| 15 | Finch'd/Welwyn | Winner # 7 v Winner # 12 |
| 16 | (tba) | Winner # 11 v Winner # 9 |

**SEMI-FINALS – AUGUST 10** (Reserve Aug 11)

| | | |
|---|---|---|
| 17 | Neston/(tba) | Winner # 15 v Winner # 13 |
| 18 | Dunstable/(tba) | Winner # 16 v Winner # 14 |

**FINAL – SEPTEMBER 2** (Reserve Sep 3)

| | |
|---|---|
| 19 | Lord's |

# PRINCIPAL FIXTURES 2003

CC1  Frizzell County Championship (1st Div)
CC2  Frizzell County Championship (2nd Div)
CGT  Cheltenham & Gloucester Trophy
FCF  First-Class Friendly
LOI  NatWest Limited-Overs International
NL1  National League (1st Division)
NL2  National League (2nd Division)

TM   npower Test Match
T20  Twenty/20 Cup
UCCE Univ Centre of Cricketing Excellence

F    Floodlit
S    Live on Sky Sports TV
4    Live on Channel 4 TV

---

**Sat 12 – Mon 14 April**
FCF  Cambridge   Cambridge UCCE v Essex
     Cardiff     Glamorgan v Cardiff UCCE
     Bristol     Glos v Brad/Leeds UCCE
FCF  Nottingham  Notts v Durham UCCE
FCF  Oxford      Oxford UCCE v Middx
FCF  Taunton     Somerset v Loughboro' UCCE

**Fri 18 – Sun 21 April**
CC2  Derby       Derbyshire v Glamorgan
CC1  Chelmsford  Essex v Middlesex
CC2  Bristol     Glos v Somerset
CC1  Nottingham  Notts v Warwicks
CC1  The Oval    Surrey v Lancashire
CC2  Worcester   Worcs v Hampshire
CC2  Leeds       Yorkshire v Northants

**Fri 18 – Mon 20 April**
FCF  Cambridge   Cambridge UCCE v Kent
     Hove        Sussex v Cardiff UCCE

**Wed 23 – Sat 26 April**
CC2  Cardiff     Glamorgan v Hampshire
CC1  Canterbury  Kent v Leics
CC1  Manchester  Lancashire v Notts
CC1  Lord's      Middlesex v Sussex
CC2  Northampton Northants v Glos
CC2  Taunton     Somerset v Durham
CC1  Birmingham  Warwicks v Essex

**Wed 23 – Fri 25 April**
     Derby       Derbys v Brad/Leeds UCCE
FCF  Oxford      Oxford UCCE v Worcs
FCF  The Oval    Surrey v Loughboro' UCCE

**Sun 27 April**
NL1  Chelmsford  Essex v Surrey
NL1  Bristol     Glos v Worcs
NL1  Canterbury  Kent v Leics
NL2  Manchester  Lancashire v Northants
NL2  Lord's      Middlesex v Derbyshire
NL2  Taunton     Somerset v Durham
NL1  Birmingham  Warwicks v Yorkshire

**Wed 30 April – Sat 3 May**
CC2  Derby       Derbyshire v Somerset
CC2  Chester-le-St Durham v Glos

CC2  Southampton Hampshire v Yorkshire
CC1  Leicester   Leics v Essex
CC1  The Oval    Surrey v Warwicks
CC1  Hove        Sussex v Kent
CC2  Worcester   Worcs v Northants

**Sat 3 – Tue 6 May**
FCF  Birmingham  British U v Zimbabweans

**Sun 4 May**
NL2  Derby       Derbyshire v Somerset
NL2  Chester-le-St Durham v Scotland
NL1  SLeicester  Leics v Glamorgan
NL2  Southampton Hampshire v Sussex
NL2  Northampton Northants v Notts
NL1  The Oval    Surrey v Warwicks

**Mon 5 May**
NL2  Chester-le-St Durham v Lancashire
NL1  Cardiff     Glamorgan v Kent
NL1  Bristol     Glos v Leics
NL2  Southampton Hampshire v Middlesex
NL2  Nottingham  Notts v Derbyshire
NL2  Hove        Sussex v Northants
NL1  SWorcester  Worcs v Surrey
NL1  Leeds       Yorkshire v Essex

**Wed 7 May** *(Reserve 8 May)*
CGT  (SNorthampton) Round 3 *(see p 302)*

**Fri 9 – Mon 12 May**
CC2  Cardiff     Glamorgan v Glos
CC1  Lord's      Middlesex v Lancashire
CC1  Nottingham  Notts v Surrey
CC1  Birmingham  Warwicks v Sussex
FCF  Worcester   Worcs v Zimbabweans
CC2  Leeds       Yorkshire v Derbyshire

**Fri 9 – Sun 11 May**
FCF  Cambridge   Camb UCCE v Northants
FCF  Chester-le-St Durham v Durham UCCE
FCF  Leicester   Leics v Loughboro' UCCE
FCF  Oxford      Oxford UCCE v Hampshire

**Fri 9 May**
NL2  Edinburgh   Scotland v Somerset

**Sat 10 May**
NL1   <sup>S</sup>Chelmsford   Essex v Kent

**Wed 14 – Sat 17 May**
CC2   Chester-le-St   Durham v Worcs
CC2   Bristol   Glos v Hampshire
CC1   Canterbury   Kent v Middlesex
CC1   Manchester   Lancashire v Essex
CC2   Northampton   Northants v Yorkshire
CC2   Taunton   Somerset v Glamorgan
CC1   The Oval   Surrey v Leics

**Wed 14 – Fri 16 May**
  Abergavenny   Cardiff UCCE v Warwicks

**Thur 15 – Sun 18 May**
FCF   Hove   Sussex v Zimbabweans

**Sun 18 May**
NL1   Cardiff   Glamorgan v Glos
NL2   <sup>S</sup>Manchester   Lancashire v Hampshire
NL1   Leicester   Leics v Yorkshire
NL2   Northampton   Northants v Derbyshire
NL2   Taunton   Somerset v Notts
NL1   The Oval   Surrey v Kent
NL1   Birmingham   Warwicks v Essex

**Mon 19 May**
NL2   Edinburgh   Scotland v Middlesex

**Tue 20 May**
NL2   Edinburgh   Scotland v Derbyshire

**Wed 21 – Sat 24 May**
CC2   Chester-le-St   Durham v Derbyshire
CC1   Chelmsford   Essex v Surrey
CC1   Southampton   Hampshire v Somerset
CC1   Leicester   Leics v Middlesex
CC2   Horsham   Sussex v Notts
CC1   Birmingham   Warwicks v Kent
CC2   Worcester   Worcs v Glos
CC2   Leeds   Yorkshire v Glamorgan

**Wed 21 – Fri 23 May**
FCF   Durham   Durham UCCE v Lancashire

**Thur 22 – Mon 26 May**
TM1   <sup>4</sup>Lord's   England v Zimbabwe

**Sun 25 May**
NL2   Chester-le-St   Durham v Derbyshire
NL1   Bristol   Glos v Surrey
NL2   Southampton   Hampshire v Somerset
NL2   Manchester   Lancashire v Scotland
NL2   Shenley   Middlesex v Northants
NL2   Horsham   Sussex v Notts
NL1   Worcester   Worcs v Kent
NL1   Leeds   Yorkshire v Glamorgan

**Wed 28 May** *(Reserve 29 May)*
CGT   (<sup>S</sup>*tbc*)   Round 4 (*see p 302*)

**Fri 30 – Mon 2 June**
CC2   Derby   Derbyshire v Worcs
CC1   Canterbury   Kent v Lancashire
FCF   Shenley   Middlesex v Zimbabweans
CC2   Northampton   Northants v Glamorgan
CC1   Nottingham   Notts v Essex
CC1   The Oval   Surrey v Sussex
CC2   Leeds   Yorkshire v Durham

**Sun 1 June**
NL2   <sup>S</sup>Edinburgh   Scotland v Hampshire
NL1   Leicester   Leics v Glos

**Wed 4 – Sat 7 June**
CC2   Swansea   Glamorgan v Derbyshire
CC2   Gloucester   Glos v Northants
CC2   Southampton   Hampshire v Durham
CC1   Tunbridge W   Kent v Sussex
CC1   Liverpool   Lancashire v Leics
CC1   Lord's   Middlesex v Essex
CC2   Bath   Somerset v Worcs
CC1   Birmingham   Warwicks v Notts

**Wed 4 – Fri 6 June**
  Bradford   Brad/Leeds UCCE v Yorks

**Thur 5 – Mon 9 June**
TM2   <sup>S</sup>Chester-le-St   England v Zimbabwe

**Sat 7 June**
  Glasgow   Scotland v Pakistan

**Sun 8 June**
NL1   Swansea   Glamorgan v Worcs
NL1   Gloucester   Glos v Warwicks
NL2   Southampton   Hampshire v Durham
NL1   Tunbridge W   Kent v Yorkshire
NL2   Manchester   Lancashire v Notts
NL2   Lord's   Middlesex v Sussex
NL2   Bath   Somerset v Northants
NL1   The Oval   Surrey v Essex

**Mon 9 June**
  <sup>F</sup>Chelmsford   Essex v Pakistanis

**Tue 10/Wed 11 June** *(Reserve 11/12 June)*
CGT   (<sup>S</sup>*tbc*)   Quarter-Finals

**Wed 11 June**
  N'ton/S'ton/   Northants/Hants/Sussex v
  Hove   Pakistanis

**Fri 13 June**
  Belfast   Ireland v Zimbabwe
T20   Chester-le-St   Durham v Notts
T20   <sup>S</sup>Southampton   Hampshire v Sussex
T20   Taunton   Somerset v Warwicks

**Fri 13 June**

| | | |
|---|---|---|
| T20 | The Oval | Surrey v Middlesex |
| T20 | Worcester | Worcs v Northants |

**Sat 14 June**

| | | |
|---|---|---|
| | Cardiff | Wales v England |
| | Leicester | Leics v Pakistanis |
| T20 | SEsher (Imber Ct) | Surrey v Essex |
| T20 | 4Leeds | Yorkshire v Derbyshire |

**Sun 15 June**

| | | |
|---|---|---|
| | Eglinton | Ireland v Zimbabwe |
| NL2 | Derby | Derbyshire v Lancashire |
| NL1 | Chelmsford | Essex v Warwicks |
| NL1 | Beckenham | Kent v Glos |
| NL2 | Northampton | Northants v Sussex |
| NL2 | SNottingham | Notts v Durham |
| NL2 | Taunton | Somerset v Scotland |
| NL1 | Worcester | Worcs v Leics |

**Mon 16 June**

| | | |
|---|---|---|
| T20 | SCardiff | Glamorgan v Northants |
| T20 | Bristol | Glos v Worcs |
| T20 | Beckenham | Kent v Hampshire |
| T20 | Leicester | Leics v Yorkshire |
| T20 | Nottingham | Notts v Lancashire |
| T20 | Esher (Imber Ct) | Surrey v Sussex |

**Tue 17 June**

| | | |
|---|---|---|
| LOI | FSManchester | England v Pakistan |
| NL2 | Richmond | Middlesex v Scotland |
| | Taunton | Somerset v Zimbabweans |

**Wed 18 June**

| | | |
|---|---|---|
| | Clontarf | Ireland v South Africa |
| T20 | Chester-le-St | Durham v Leics |
| T20 | Cardiff | Glamorgan v Somerset |
| T20 | Southampton | Hampshire v Essex |
| T20 | FHove | Sussex v Middlesex |
| T20 | SWorcester | Worcs v Warwicks |

**Thur 19 June**

| | | |
|---|---|---|
| T20 | Derby | Derbyshire v Notts |
| T20 | Bristol | Glos v Northants |
| | Southampton | Hants v Zimbabweans |
| T20 | SManchester | Lancs v Yorkshire |
| T20 | Richmond | Middlesex v Kent |

**Fri 20 June**

| | | |
|---|---|---|
| LOI | SThe Oval | England v Pakistan |
| T20 | FChelmsford | Essex v Kent |
| T20 | Leicester | Leics v Lancashire |
| T20 | Northampton | Northants v Somerset |
| | FHove | Sussex v S Africans |
| T20 | Birmingham | Warwicks v Glamorgan |
| T20 | Leeds | Yorkshire v Durham |

**Sat 21 June**

| | | |
|---|---|---|
| T20 | Manchester | Lancashire v Derbyshire |

| | | |
|---|---|---|
| T20 | Nottingham | Notts v Leics |
| T20 | STaunton | Somerset v Glos |
| T20 | Hove | Sussex v Essex |

**Sun 22 June**

| | | |
|---|---|---|
| LOI | SLord's | England v Pakistan |
| | Chelmsford | Essex v Zimbabweans |
| NL2 | Manchester | Lancashire v Durham |
| | Northampton | Northants v S Africans |
| NL2 | Nottingham | Notts v Middlesex |
| NL1 | Birmingham | Warwicks v Glamorgan |
| NL1 | Leeds | Yorkshire v Leics |

**Mon 23 June**

| | | |
|---|---|---|
| T20 | Derby | Derbyshire v Durham |
| T20 | Cardiff | Glamorgan v Worcs |
| T20 | SCanterbury | Kent v Surrey |
| T20 | Uxbridge | Middlesex v Hampshire |
| T20 | Birmingham | Warwicks v Glos |

**Tue 24 June**

| | | |
|---|---|---|
| T20 | Bristol | Glos v Glamorgan |
| T20 | FChelmsford | Essex v Middlesex |
| T20 | Southampton | Hampshire v Surrey |
| T20 | Manchester | Lancashire v Durham |
| T20 | Leicester | Leics v Derbyshire |
| T20 | Northampton | Northants v Warwicks |
| T20 | FHove | Sussex v Kent |
| T20 | Worcester | Worcs v Somerset |
| T20 | SLeeds | Yorkshire v Notts |

**Wed 25 June**

| | | |
|---|---|---|
| | Durham | British U v India A |
| | Worcester | Worcs v S Africans |

**Thur 26 – 29 June**

| | | |
|---|---|---|
| FCF | Cambridge | Cambridge U v Oxford U |

**Thur 26 June**

| | | |
|---|---|---|
| LOI | SNottingham | England v Zimbabwe |

**Fri 27 – 30 June**

| | | |
|---|---|---|
| | Chester-le-St | Durham v India A |
| CC1 | Chelmsford | Essex v Kent |
| CC2 | Cardiff | Glamorgan v Worcs |
| CC2 | Southampton | Hampshire v Glos |
| CC1 | Leicester | Leics v Notts |
| CC1 | Lord's | Middlesex v Surrey |
| CC2 | Northampton | Northants v Derbyshire |
| CC2 | Taunton | Somerset v Yorkshire |
| CC1 | Hove | Sussex v Warwicks |

**Sat 28 June**

| | | |
|---|---|---|
| LOI | SThe Oval | England v South Africa |

**Sun 29 June**

| | | |
|---|---|---|
| LOI | SCanterbury | Zimbabwe v South Africa |

**Mon 30 June**

| | | |
|---|---|---|
| | Nottingham | UCCE Challenge Final |

**Tue 1 July**
LOI   <sup>S</sup>Leeds      England v Zimbabwe

**Wed 2 – Sat 5 July**
CC2    Derby      Derbyshire v Yorkshire
CC1    Chelmsford      Essex v Lancashire
CC1    Leicester      Leics v Warwicks
CC2    Northampton      Northants v Hampshire
CC2    Taunton      Somerset v Glos
CC1    The Oval      Surrey v Kent
CC2    Worcester      Worcs v Durham

**Wed 2 – Fri 4 July**
FCF    Nottingham      Notts v India A

**Wed 2 July**
     Lord's      Cambridge U v Oxford U

**Wed 3 July**
LOI   <sup>FS</sup>Manchester      England v South Africa

**Sat 5 July**
LOI   <sup>S</sup>Cardiff      South Africa v Zimbabwe

**Sun 6 July**
LOI   <sup>S</sup>Bristol      England v Zimbabwe
NL1    Maidstone      Kent v Glamorgan
     Leicester      Leics v India A
NL2    Lord's      Middlesex v Lancashire
NL2    Northampton      Northants v Hampshire
NL2    Edinburgh      Scotland v Notts
NL2    Taunton      Somerset v Sussex
NL1    The Oval      Surrey v Yorkshire
NL1    Worcester      Worcs v Warwicks

**Mon 7 July**
NL2    Edinburgh      Scotland v Durham

**Tue 8 July**
LOI   <sup>FS</sup>Birmingham England v South Africa

**Wed 9 – Sat 12 July**
CC2    Derby      Derbyshire v Glos
CC2    Chester-le-St      Durham v Northants
CC2    Cardiff      Glamorgan v Somerset
CC1    Maidstone      Kent v Notts
CC1    Southgate      Middlesex v Leics
CC1    Arundel      Sussex v Essex
CC1    Birmingham      Warwicks v Surrey

**Wed 9 – Fri 11 July**
FCF    Leeds      Yorkshire v India A

**Wed 9 July**
NL2    Edinburgh      Scotland v Lancashire

**Thur 10 July**
LOI   <sup>S</sup>Southampton      South Africa v Zimbabwe

**Sat 12 July**
LOI   <sup>S</sup>Lord's      NWT FINAL (*Reserve 14 July*)

**Sun 13 July**
NL2    Chester-le-St      Durham v Northants
NL1    Cardiff      Glamorgan v Essex
NL2    Southampton      Hampshire v Notts
     Blackpool      Lancashire v India A
NL1    Oakham S      Leics v Warwicks
NL2    Southgate      Middlesex v Somerset
NL2    Arundel      Sussex v Derbyshire
NL1    Birmingham      Warwicks v Surrey

**Tue 15 – Fri 18 July**
CC2    Chester-le-St      Durham v Yorkshire
CC2    Southampton      Hampshire v Glamorgan
CC1    Leicester      Leics v Sussex
CC1    Blackpool      Lancashire v Kent
CC1    Southgate      Middlesex v Warwicks
CC2    Worcester      Worcs v Derbyshire

**Tue 15 – Thur 17 July**
FCF    Taunton      Somerset v S Africans
FCF    The Oval      Surrey v India A

**Thur 17 July**
NL1   <sup>F</sup>Chelmsford      Essex v Glos

**Sat 19 – Mon 21 July**
FCF    Arundel      South Africa v India A

**Sat 19 July**
T20   <sup>S</sup>(tba)      Semi-Finals/<sup>F</sup>Final

**Mon 21 July**
NL2   <sup>FS</sup>Nottingham      Notts v Hampshire

**Tue 22 July**
NL2   <sup>FS</sup>Hove      Sussex v Durham

**Wed 23 – Sat 26 July**
CC1    Southend      Essex v Leics
CC2    Cheltenham      Glos v Worcs
CC1    Manchester      Lancashire v Warwicks
CC2    Northampton      Northants v Somerset
CC1    Guildford      Surrey v Middlesex
CC2    Scarborough      Yorkshire v Hampshire

**Wed 23 July**
NL2   <sup>FS</sup>Derby      Derbyshire v Notts

**Thur 24 – Mon 28 July**
TM1   <sup>4</sup>Birmingham      England v South Africa

**Thur 24 – Sun 27 July**
CC2    Derby      Derbyshire v Durham

**Thur 24 – Sat 26 July**
FCF    Swansea      Glamorgan v India A

**Fri 25 – Mon 28 July**
CC1    Nottingham      Notts v Sussex

## Sun 27 July

| | | |
|---|---|---|
| NL1 | Southend | Essex v Leics |
| NL1 | Cheltenham | Glos v Glamorgan |
| NL2 | Northampton | Northants v Middlesex |
| NL1 | Guildford | Surrey v Worcs |
| NL1 | Scarborough | Yorkshire v Kent |

## Mon 28 July

| | | |
|---|---|---|
| | Cheltenham | Glos v India A |
| NL2 | FManchester | Lancashire v Somerset |

## Tue 29 July

| | | |
|---|---|---|
| NL1 | FSWorcester | Worcs v Glamorgan |

## Wed 30 July – Sat 2 August

| | | |
|---|---|---|
| CC2 | Chester-le-St | Durham v Somerset |
| CC2 | Cheltenham | Glos v Yorkshire |
| CC1 | Canterbury | Kent v Essex |
| CC1 | Leicester | Leics v Lancashire |
| CC1 | Nottingham | Notts v Middlesex |
| CC1 | Hove | Sussex v Surrey |
| FCF | Birmingham | Warwicks v India A |

## Wed 30 July

| | | |
|---|---|---|
| NL2 | FSSouthampton | Hampshire v Northants |

## Thur 31 July – Mon 4 August

| | | |
|---|---|---|
| TM2 | 4Lord's | England v South Africa |

## Thur 31 July – Sun 3 August

| | | |
|---|---|---|
| CC2 | Southampton | Hampshire v Northants |
| CC2 | Worcester | Worcs v Glamorgan |

## Sun 3 August

| | | |
|---|---|---|
| NL2 | Derby | Derbyshire v Middlesex |
| NL2 | Chester-le-St | Durham v Somerset |
| NL1 | Cheltenham | Glos v Yorkshire |
| NL1 | Canterbury | Kent v Essex |
| NL1 | Leicester | Leics v Warwicks |
| NL2 | Cleethorpes | Notts v Lancashire |
| NL2 | Hove | Sussex v Scotland |

## Mon 4 August

| | | |
|---|---|---|
| NL2 | Southampton | Hampshire v Scotland |
| NL2 | FManchester | Lancashire v Derbyshire |

## Tue 5 August

| | | |
|---|---|---|
| NL2 | Chester-le-St | Durham v Notts |
| NL1 | FChelmsford | Essex v Glamorgan |
| NL2 | Taunton | Somerset v Middlesex |
| NL1 | FSThe Oval | Surrey v Glos |
| NL2 | FHove | Sussex v Hampshire |

## Wed 6 August

| | | |
|---|---|---|
| NL2 | Northampton | Northants v Scotland |
| NL1 | FSLeeds | Yorkshire v Warwicks |
| | Shenley | PCA Masters v S Africans |

## Thur 7 – Sat 9 August

| | | |
|---|---|---|
| FCF | Cant'y/Bristol | Kent/Glos v S Africans |

## Thur 7/Sat 9 August (*Reserve 8/10 August*)

| | | |
|---|---|---|
| CGT | 4(both) | Semi-Final |

## Sun 10 August

| | | |
|---|---|---|
| NL2 | Derby | Derbyshire v Sussex |
| NL1 | Cardiff | Glamorgan v Warwickshire |
| NL1 | Leicester | Leics v Essex |
| NL2 | SLord's | Middlesex v Durham |
| NL2 | Taunton | Somerset v Hampshire |

## Mon 11 August

| | | |
|---|---|---|
| NL1 | FSCanterbury | Kent v Worcs |

## Tue 12 August

| | | |
|---|---|---|
| NL2 | FSNorthampton | Northants v Somerset |

## Wed 13 – Sat 16 August

| | | |
|---|---|---|
| CC2 | Cardiff | Glamorgan v Durham |
| CC2 | Southampton | Hampshire v Derbyshire |
| CC1 | Lord's | Middlesex v Kent |
| CC1 | Whitgift S | Surrey v Notts |
| CC2 | Scarborough | Yorkshire v Worcs |

## Wed 13 August

| | | |
|---|---|---|
| NL2 | FHove | Sussex v Lancashire |
| NL1 | FSBirmingham | Warwicks v Leics |

## Thur 14 – Mon 18 August

| | | |
|---|---|---|
| TM3 | 4Nottingham | England v South Africa |

## Thur 14 – Sun 17 August

| | | |
|---|---|---|
| CC2 | Taunton | Somerset v Northants |
| CC1 | Hove | Sussex v Lancashire |
| CC1 | Birmingham | Warwicks v Leics |

## Sun 17 August

| | | |
|---|---|---|
| NL2 | Southampton | Hampshire v Derbyshire |
| NL2 | Lord's | Middlesex v Notts |
| NL1 | Whitgift S | Surrey v Glamorgan |
| NL1 | Scarborough | Yorkshire v Worcs |

## Tue 19 – Fri 22 August

| | | |
|---|---|---|
| CC2 | Bristol | Glos v Glamorgan |

## Tue 19 August

| | | |
|---|---|---|
| NL2 | FSManchester | Lancashire v Middlesex |

## Wed 20 – Sat 23 August

| | | |
|---|---|---|
| CC2 | Derby | Derbyshire v Northants |
| CC2 | Chester-le-St | Durham v Hampshire |
| CC1 | Colchester | Essex v Sussex |
| CC1 | Nottingham | Notts v Kent |
| CC2 | Worcester | Worcs v Somerset |

## Wed 20 August

| | | |
|---|---|---|
| NL1 | FSLeicester | Leics v Surrey |

## Thur 21 – Mon 25 August

| | | |
|---|---|---|
| TM4 | 4Leeds | England v South Africa |

## Thur 21 – Sun 24 August

| | | |
|---|---|---|
| CC1 | Manchester | Lancashire v Middlesex |

| CC1 | Leicester | Leics v Surrey |
|---|---|---|

**Sun 24 August**

| NL2 | Derby | Derbyshire v Northants |
|---|---|---|
| NL2 | Chester-le-St | Durham v Hampshire |
| NL1 | Colwyn Bay | Glamorgan v Yorkshire |
| NL2 | Nottingham | Notts v Sussex |
| NL1 | Birmingham | Warwks v Kent |
| NL1 | Worcester | Worcs v Glos |

**Mon 25 – Thur 28 August**

| CC2 | Colwyn Bay | Glamorgan v Yorkshire |
|---|---|---|

**Tue 26 – Fri 29 August**

| CC1 | Manchester | Lancashire v Surrey |
|---|---|---|
| CC1 | Nottingham | Notts v Leics |
| CC2 | Taunton | Somerset v Hampshire |
| CC1 | Birmingham | Warwks v Middlesex |

**Tue 26 August**

| NL2 | FS Chester-le-St | Durham v Sussex |
|---|---|---|
| NL2 | Edinburgh | Scotland v Northants |

**Wed 27 August**

| NL1 | FS Bristol | Glos v Kent |
|---|---|---|

**Thur 28 – Sat 30 August**

| FCF | Derby | Derbyshire v S Africans |
|---|---|---|

**Thur 28 August**

| NL1 | F Colchester | Essex v Worcs |
|---|---|---|
| NL2 | Edinburgh | Scotland v Sussex |

**Sat 30 August** *(Reserve 31 August)*

| CGT | ⁴Lord's | Final |
|---|---|---|

**Sun 31 August**

| NL2 | S Derby | Derbyshire v Durham |
|---|---|---|
| NL2 | Nottingham | Notts v Northants |
| NL1 | Birmingham | Warwks v Glos |
| NL1 | Leeds | Yorkshire v Surrey |

**Mon 1 September**

| NL2 | FS Taunton | Somerset v Lancashire |
|---|---|---|

**Tue 2 September**

| NL1 | FS Cardiff | Glamorgan v Leics |
|---|---|---|

**Wed 3 – Sat 6 September**

| CC1 | Chelmsford | Essex v Notts |
|---|---|---|
| CC2 | Bristol | Glos v Derbyshire |
| CC2 | Southampton | Hampshire v Worcs |
| CC2 | Northampton | Northants v Durham |
| CC1 | Birmingham | Warwks v Lancashire |
| CC2 | Leeds | Yorkshire v Somerset |

**Wed 3 September**

| NL1 | FS Canterbury | Kent v Surrey |
|---|---|---|
| NL2 | F Hove | Sussex v Middlesex |

**Thur 4 – Mon 8 September**

| TM5 | ⁴The Oval | England v South Africa |
|---|---|---|

**Thur 4 – Sun 7 September**

| CC1 | Canterbury | Kent v Surrey |
|---|---|---|

**Fri 5 – Mon 8 September**

| CC1 | Hove | Sussex v Middlesex |
|---|---|---|

**Sun 7 September**

| NL2 | Derby | Derbyshire v Scotland |
|---|---|---|
| NL1 | Bristol | Glos v Essex |
| NL2 | Southampton | Hampshire v Lancashire |
| NL2 | Northampton | Northants v Durham |
| NL2 | Nottingham | Notts v Somerset |
| NL1 | Worcester | Worcs v Yorkshire |

**Tue 9 September**

| NL1 | Birmingham | Warwks v Worcs |
|---|---|---|

**Wed 10 – Sat 13 September**

| CC2 | Cardiff | Glamorgan v Northants |
|---|---|---|
| CC2 | Bristol | Glos v Durham |
| CC1 | Manchester | Lancashire v Sussex |
| CC1 | Leicester | Leics v Kent |
| CC1 | Lord's | Middlesex v Notts |
| CC2 | Taunton | Somerset v Derbyshire |

**Wed 10 September**

| NL1 | FS Chelmsford | Essex v Yorkshire |
|---|---|---|

**Thur 11 – Sun 14 September**

| CC1 | Chelmsford | Essex v Warwicks |
|---|---|---|

**Fri 12 – Mon 15 September**

| CC2 | Worcester | Worcs v Yorkshire |
|---|---|---|

**Sun 14 September**

| NL1 | Cardiff | Glamorgan v Surrey |
|---|---|---|
| NL2 | Manchester | Lancashire v Sussex |
| NL1 | Leicester | Leics v Kent |
| NL2 | Lord's | Middlesex v Hampshire |
| NL2 | Nottingham | Notts v Scotland |
| NL2 | Taunton | Somerset v Derbyshire |

**Wed 17 – Sat 20 September**

| CC2 | Derby | Derbyshire v Hampshire |
|---|---|---|
| CC2 | Chester-le-St | Durham v Glamorgan |
| CC1 | Canterbury | Kent v Warwicks |
| CC2 | Northampton | Northants v Worcs |
| CC1 | Nottingham | Notts v Lancashire |
| CC1 | The Oval | Surrey v Essex |
| CC1 | Hove | Sussex v Leics |
| CC2 | Leeds | Yorkshire v Glos |

**Sun 21 September**

| NL2 | Derby | Derbyshire v Hampshire |
|---|---|---|
| NL2 | Chester-le-St | Durham v Middlesex |
| NL1 | Canterbury | Kent v Warwicks |
| NL2 | Northampton | Northants v Lancashire |
| NL1 | The Oval | Surrey v Leics |
| NL2 | Hove | Sussex v Somerset |
| NL1 | Worcester | Worcs v Essex |
| NL1 | Leeds | Yorkshire v Glos |

**Round 3 – Weds 7 May** (*Reserve 8 May*)

| | | |
|---|---|---|
| 29 | Luton | Beds v Warwickshire |
| 36 | Reading | Berkshire v Durham |
| 31 | Wing | Bucks v Glos |
| 32 | March | Cambs v Yorkshire |
| 38 | Truro | Cornwall v Kent |
| 41 | Exmouth | Devon v Lancashire |
| 30 | Darlington | Durham CB v Glamorgan |
| 33 | Chelmsford | Essex CB v Essex |
| 44 | Southampton | Hampshire v Sussex |
| 34 | Canterbury | Kent CB v Derbyshire |
| 37 | Lincoln | Lincs v Notts |
| 43 | Northampton | Northants v Middlesex |
| 42 | Jesmond | Northumb v Leics |
| 40 | Edinburgh | Scotland v Somerset |
| 39 | Stone | Staffs v Surrey |
| 35 | Worcester | Worcs CB v Worcs |

**Round 4 – Weds 28 May** (*Res 29 May*)

| | | | |
|---|---|---|---|
| 45 | *Winner # 43* | v | *Winner # 44* |
| 46 | *Winner # 42* | v | *Winner # 37* |
| 47 | *Winner # 36* | v | *Winner # 41* |
| 48 | *Winner # 40* | v | *Winner # 39* |
| 49 | *Winner # 38* | v | *Winner # 31* |
| 50 | *Winner # 35* | v | *Winner # 32* |
| 51 | *Winner # 29* | v | *Winner # 33* |
| 52 | *Winner # 30* | v | *Winner # 34* |

**Quarter-Finals** 10/11 (11/12) June
**Semi-Finals** 7/9 (8/9/10) August
**Final** 30 August

## C & G TROPHY QUALIFICATION FOR 2004

**Round 1 – Thur 28 Aug 2003** (*Res 29 Aug*)

| | | |
|---|---|---|
| 3 | Luton | Bedfordshire v Cheshire |
| 4 | Exmouth | Devon v Suffolk |
| 2 | Bournemouth | Dorset v Buckinghamshire |
| 10 | Bishop's Stortford | Hertfordshire v Ireland |
| 6 | Amstelveen (*tbc*) | Holland v Cornwall |
| 7 | Horsford, Norwich | Norfolk v Lincolnshire |
| 5 | Oswestry | Shropshire v Northumberland |
| 8 | Abergavenny | Wales v Denmark |

**Sun 31 Aug 2003** (*Reserve 1 Sep*)

| | | |
|---|---|---|
| 9 | Banbury | Oxfordshire v Herefordshire |
| 1 | Edinburgh | Scotland v Cumberland |

FIRST ROUND BYES: Berkshire, Cambridgeshire, Staffordshire and Wiltshire.
First-class counties enter in Round 3.
CB Cricket Board 'recreational team'.

## ENGLAND U-19 v SOUTH AFRICA

| | | |
|---|---|---|
| TM1 | Leeds | Fri 1 – Mon 4 August |
| TM2 | Worcester | Mon 11 – Thu 14 August |
| TM3 | Chelmsford | Sat 16 – Tue 19 August |
| LOI1 | Arundel | Tue 26 August |
| LOI2 | Hove | Thu 28 August |
| LOI3 | Hove | Fri 29 August |

## WOMEN'S TEST MATCH SERIES

**England v South Africa**

| | | |
|---|---|---|
| TM1 | Shenley | Thur 7 – Sun 10 August |
| TM2 | Taunton | Wed 20 – Sat 23 August |

## WOMEN'S LIMITED-OVERS
**England v South Africa**

| | | |
|---|---|---|
| LOI | Chelmsford | Wed 13 August |
| LOI | Bristol | Sat 16 August |
| LOI | Cardiff | Sun 17 August |

## WOMEN'S COUNTY CHAMPIONSHIP

Sat 26 – Wed 30 July (5 rounds)
Cambridge – various College grounds

## WOMEN'S SUPER 4s

| | |
|---|---|
| Sat 17 May | Oxford – Marston/The Parks |
| Sun 25 May | Taunton – King's College |
| Mon 26 May | Taunton – King's College |
| Sun 1 Jun | Reading CC |
| Sun 15 Jun | Worksop College |
| Sat 21 Jun | Oxford – The Parks/(*tbc*) |

# FIELDING CHART

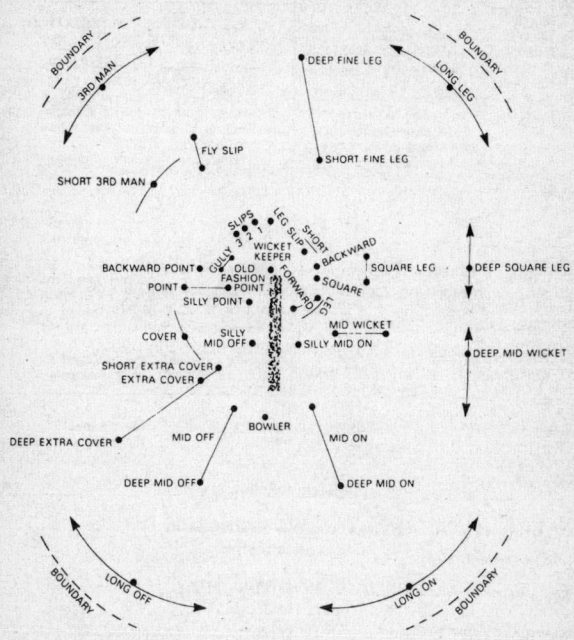

First published in 2003 by
HEADLINE BOOK PUBLISHING

Cover photographs: (*Front*) Andrew Flintoff
(Lancashire and England) © Patrick Eagar;
(*back*) Mark Butcher (Surrey and England)
© Patrick Eagar.

10 9 8 7 6 5 4 3 2 1

ISBN 0 7553 1040 3

Typeset by
Letterpart Limited, Reigate, Surrey

Printed and bound in Great Britain by
Clays Ltd, St Ives plc.

HEADLINE BOOK PUBLISHING
A division of Hodder Headline
338 Euston Road
London NW1 3BH

www.headline.co.uk
www.hodderheadline.com